A

REFERENCE GUIDE

TO

MINIATURE MAKERS MARKS

Dedicated
to
the world of miniaturists
and
miniature enthusiasts,
our children
and
grandchildren

A
REFERENCE GUIDE
TO
MINIATURE MAKERS MARKS

Published by
Lee S. Frank
Alice Hanaw Frank
Minneapolis, Minnesota

Alice and Lee Frank
P. O. Box 16023
Minneapolis, MN 55416-0023

Library of Congress Catalog Card Number: 95-90359
ISBN: 0-9644481-0-6

Publisher's Cataloging in Publication
(Prepared by Quality Books Inc.)

Frank, Lee S.
A reference guide to miniature makers marks / Lee S. Frank, Alice Hanaw Frank.
p. cm.
Includes bibliographical references and index,
Preassigned LCCN: 95-90359.
ISBN 0-9644481-0-6

1. Miniature objects--Trademarks. I. Title.

NK8470.F73 1996 688'.1
QB195-20523

Printed in the United States of America
by Thomson-Shore, Inc.
First printing: May 1996

CONTENTS

ACKNOWLEDGMENTS

There are numerous people without whose help this book could never have been written. Their cooperation, kindness, and valuable time have all contributed to its completion. We are most grateful to Marge Adams, Jackie Andrews, Dougless Strickland Bitler, Ellen and John Blauer, Moise Bloch, Mary Eccher, Wilfred M. Kullman, Jr., Peggy Norris, Sarah Salisbury, and Phyllis Tucker, all of whom went beyond the call of duty, making themselves available to our needs when there were questions to be answered or queries to be clarified.

We would also like to express our appreciation to the International Guild of Miniature Artisans (IGMA), National Association of Miniature Enthusiasts (NAME), Cottage Industry Miniature Trade Association (CIMTA), the Miniature Industry Association of America (MIAA), *Nutshell News*, and *Miniature Collector* for their information and assistance in contacting miniature artisans worldwide. We are especially appreciative of the artisans themselves who took of their precious time to provide accurate data together with expressions of goodwill and encouragement towards our efforts. We wish to thank all those individuals who have not been mentioned specifically by name, of which there were many, but who were also extremely instrumental in supplying contacts for our research.

We are most indebted to Barbara Marshall and Bill Robertson for time and effort freely given at the Toy & Miniature Museum of Kansas City. Barbara was most gracious, allowing us open and uninterrupted access to the entire museum and its archives. Bill's assistance was invaluable to our research in checking the marks on the many miniatures within the museum. Their continuous help and support has been an enormous contribution to the development of this project.

We would like to give a special tribute to Barbara J. Raheb for her unending support and generosity. Barbara graciously and unselfishly opened her home to us, putting aside her own priorities and personal miniature publishing business. Her knowledge was instrumental in providing us with the tools necessary to publish our own book in the most professional manner possible. Without Barbara's support and sisterly love this book may never have become a reality.

We owe a debt of appreciation to our children and their families: Kenneth L. Frank, Debra L. McGovern, and Lisa K. Frank, for giving unselfishly in words of support, boosting our morale when the task at hand seemed monumentally enormous, and for giving their understanding when our time with them was limited.

Finally, we wish to thank Sybil Harp and Jeanne Delgado of *Nutshell News* for volunteering to undertake the most thankless job of all–proof-reading our entire book. Theirs was the crucial, tedious and time-consuming effort that lent the final professional touch to the entire compilation.

To everyone, our profound gratitude and heartfelt thanks.

INTRODUCTION

When we began to inventory our miniature collection a few years ago, we realized one of the most important parts of that record was to know who made the miniature pieces we purchased. As time went on and we talked to other collectors, it became evident they had the same need for this information. We decided to write a "booklet" that would benefit all of those who had a love for miniatures. As we began our research, the list of artisan names mushroomed until our original concept became a full-scale book.

We realized at this point our first effort would not be a comprehensive compilation due to the kind of information, or lack of it, our investigative efforts uncovered. This is due in part to a number of reasons: a lack of response from many individuals we contacted who failed to respond to our application, persons who are unknown to us at the time of this writing, crafts-persons who are now deceased, persons retired from the hobby who have no access to the avenues we used to contact them, or whom we have no way of contacting, and individuals who did not fully understand the purpose or thrust of our planned book and therefore failed to respond.

It is our hope that with this initial publication there will be a better understanding of our intent. It is primarily to provide a reference guide collectors can use to identify pieces in their collections as time goes by and memory dims. It will also provide invaluable help to museums or beneficiaries to identify pieces in a collection, and to gain some insight into the craftspeople through their autobiographies and biographies and other information, as well as the time frame in which they worked.

All of the textual information contained herein has been supplied by one or more of the following sources: the individual artisan, a second party from personal knowledge or contact, NAME AOH profiles, *Nutshell News* and *Miniature Collector* articles. We have made every attempt to decipher all information obtained in a clear, concise manner to assure its accuracy, even to the extent of direct communication for clarification where question or doubt was raised. Despite such meticulous precautions and care, errors can still unavoidably occur.

Some artisans referred us to articles from magazines, newspapers, or other forms of published material requesting we extract their biographical background from the publication involved. Unfortunately, the copywrite law, lack of time and personal knowledge of the individual made it impossible for us to assume responsibility for the composition of a proper biography on this basis.

We have explored every known source possible to obtain information. However, if the reader has any knowledge of a miniatures artisan (*whether living, deceased, or retired*) who has sold miniature creations to the public at any time and who is not referenced in this book, please complete a copy of the sample questionnaire, *in its entirety*, which is found at the back of the book. Return this form to the address indicated on the questionnaire for consideration and possible future inclusion.

If any discrepancies have been noted in the content of this book which would affect the informational value of the artisan involved, you are invited to so advise the publisher, *in writing*, to that effect.

Our ultimate goal is to produce a reference guide that is as comprehensive as possible for posterity. It is our intent that this reference guide book not only add value to miniatures, but aid in recognizing a popular hobby as the **art form** it so richly deserves.

ABBREVIATIONS

AOH	Academy of Honor
ASMA	Australian Societies of Miniature Art
CIMTA	Cottage Industry Miniature Trade Association
DAG	Doll Artisan Guild
EGA	Embroidery Guild of America
GNOME	Greater Niagara Original Miniatures Enthusiasts
HIA	Hobby Industry of America
IDMA	International Doll Makers Association
IGMA	International Guild of Miniature Artisans
IMA	International Miniature Artists
IPAT	International Porcelain Artists & Teachers
MAA	Miniature Artists of America
MASF	Miniature Art Society of Florida
MBS	Miniature Book Society
MIAA	Miniature Industry Association of America
MJSA	Manufacturing Jewelers and Silversmiths of America
MPSG	Miniature Painters, Sculptors and Gravers Society
NALED	National Association of Limited Edition Dealers
NAME	National Association of Miniature Enthusiasts
NIADA	National Institute of American Doll Artists
ODACA	Original Doll Artist Council of America
SAM	Society of American Miniaturists
TAMS	Top Artisans' Miniature Show
UFDC	United Federation of Dolls Clubs

FOUNDING YEARS OF ORGANIZATIONS AND AWARDS

NATIONAL ASSOCIATION OF MINIATURE ENTHUSIASTS......1972

International Miniature Artists 1975

Academy of Honor......1984

Mell Prescott......1986

INTERNATIONAL GUILD OF MINIATURE ARTISANS 1979

Fellow......1979

Artisan......1980

Crystal......1988

MINIATURE INDUSTRY ASSOCIATION OF AMERICA......1979

COTTAGE INDUSTRY MINIATURE TRADE ASSOCIATION......1980

HOW TO USE THIS GUIDE

Part of the research in preparing this reference guide was to determine an easy way to find the miniature maker's mark. All the information on each artisan is presented under the following headings:

Artisan, Business Name, Identification Marks, Category,
Honors, Recognition, Autobiography

Some listings may not have all these headings for only one reason: the information supplied to us by the artisans were left blank. If no information for a certain heading was furnished, that heading was omitted.

The last section of this reference guide is a comprehensive index . All entries are listed alphabetically by last name, business name, category and sub-category, with page numbers. You can find the artisan you are seeking in four possible ways. The chapters are divided into alphabetical sections. Turning to the pages listed you should find the marking similar to the one on the miniature piece you are researching.

A

ARTISAN: **ABRAMS, JIM & CHRIS**

BUSINESS NAME: Real Good Toys

IDENTIFICATION MARKS:

1991 to present

Real Good Toys
BARRE, VERMONT 05641

Real Good Toys
BARRE, VERMONT 05641

Logo burned into wood foundation of dollhouses

CATEGORY:

Dollhouse; Structures

HONORS:

Exhibits: Under President Carter's Christmas Tree in the Blue Room of the White House, Washington DC 1980; Smithsonian Institution 1981; The American Crafts Council National Show, Rhinebeck, New York 1976; The National Crafts Fair, Frederick, Maryland 1976

BIOGRAPHY:

In 1972, John Javna and Joanne McCracken wanted a dollhouse for their daughter. When none could be found, they began creating dollhouse kits that could be manufactured and sold for a reasonable price. By 1973, "Real Good Toys" was on its way!

They introduced many innovative designs and in 1976 earned the acceptance into two of the nation's most prestigious juried craft events, *The American Crafts Council National Show* and *The National Crafts Fair,* where they met Jim Abrams. Jim joined Real Good Toys as production manager and in January, 1980, became a full partner with John.

National attention focused on Real Good Toys when their Victorian dollhouse was featured under President Carter's Christmas tree in the Blue Room of the White House in December, 1980. In 1981, the Smithsonian Institution recognized their high standards of quality and craftsmanship when they asked the company to redesign and produce an edition of an antique house in its collection.

In 1981, Jim and his wife, Chris, became the principal owners of the company and shortly thereafter, The Children's Choice line of kits was introduced. That same year, they purchased Batrie Dollhouse Company who featured all the finishing materials required to finish the dollhouse included in one box. This appealed to many stores as they could now depend on a sales force with only a general knowledge of the hobby and it also created the "one-stop" sale.

In October, 1987, they purchased a local granite shed. Factory renovation and a move were completed by May 1988, resulting in increased efficiency, greater production capabilities, and a higher standard of working conditions. Shortly thereafter, they introduced a Model Assembly Program of building finished models for in-store display.

Simplicity Pattern Company wanted a dollhouse to complement their new line of miniature furnishings, and patterns and production on this house began in 1989. It was an immediate success with its unique interlocking parts and slot and groove construction. As Christmas, 1990, came to a close, Playscale Fashion Dollhouse prototypes were being designed. Real Good Toys has been aggressively and continually designing new products, and is looking forward to a changing and challenging marketplace in the 1990's.

Jim was elected to the Board of Directors of the Miniatures Industry Association of America in 1986, and re-elected in 1989. He served as trade show chairman.

ARTISAN: **ACQUISTO, JEANNETTE VINES**

BUSINESS NAME: Detail in Scale

IDENTIFICATION MARKS:

CATEGORY:

Furniture: contemporary, upholstered

RECOGNITION:

Nutshell News

AUTOBIOGRAPHY:

My first experience with making miniature furniture was early in my childhood when my Barbie dolls were in need of a place to live. I remember going to the garage and fitting together small blocks of wood to make a chair. I padded and covered the wood with cloth, then as an afterthought I nailed in three flat head nails to serve as a built in telephone stand, how innovative I felt, and how convenient for Barbie. My dollhouse or rooms grew from dresser top onto the floor with walls made of books.

I grew up, married and raised two children, occasionally seeing a dollhouse display and being captivated, but not pursuing it seriously until about 1979. At that time I had purchased a real highboy dresser for my bedroom, and when a friend admired it and wished for one herself, I took on the challenge and made my first miniature reproduction piece. Unfortunately after weeks of work, I could not part with it and still display it in my home.

I left the miniature business in 1987 to return to college. I have since acquired a BA and an MA and am presently working on my Ph.D. in counseling Psychology. I currently have a private practice as a psychotherapist, attend the University of New Mexico full-time and still have my two children in my home with the oldest in college herself.

I have never lost my love for miniatures or my desire to become involved with them, but I have had to put my creative side on hold for many years now. On occasion, my brother, Pete Acquisto and his wife Dee, grace me with a piece of their silver as a gift, and my delight is rekindled! I fully intend to reenter the miniature world as a collector and builder, but not in a business capacity. In my moves and life changes, I have carefully packed and carted all my treasured miniature possessions with me. They are an expression of who I am and a part of my life.

ARTISAN: **ACQUISTO, PETE**

BUSINESS NAME: Acquisto Silver Company

IDENTIFICATION MARKS:

 Prior to 1982  1982 to present

CATEGORY:

Silversmith; Silverware; Silver: reproductions

HONORS:

IGMA Fellow 1984; NAME AOH 1985; Exhibit: Toy & Miniature Museum of Kansas City

ACQUISTO, PETE, continued

RECOGNITION:

Nutshell News; Nutshell News Calendar; Miniature Collector; Washington Post; Boca Raton Magazine; Gift Reporter; Masters in Miniature, 12 Artisans At Work, Volume 1, Anne Day Smith, Kalmbach Publishing, 1987

BIOGRAPHY:

Pete was born near Santa Fe, New Mexico, moved to California for ten years, and returned to New Mexico with his family. He has lived in Albuquerque ever since. His mother is a native New Mexican and his father a Sicilian from Baffalo, NY. His father was a wonderful carver of furniture. Pete attended the University of New Mexico and became interested in jewelry making. He and Dee were married in 1970 and they have a son, Michael. Pete was a jeweler for ten years before he became interested in miniatures. In 1980 he made one of his first pieces and the transition began from jewelry to miniature reproductions in sterling silver. He works in one-inch and ½-inch scales. He has done several limited edition pieces in 18K gold. These pieces are all numbered and trademarked. The collection of silver reproductions has grown to over 50 pieces, mostly of English and American silversmiths from the 16th to the 18th century. Pete became an IGMA Fellow in 1984 and NAME AOH in 1985. His work is in many miniature museums across the United States and overseas. Pete enjoys golf, racquet ball, and swimming.

ARTISAN: ADAMS, ALAN REGINALD

IDENTIFICATION MARKS:

A

1/8th-inch high, cut into left shoulder blade

CATEGORY:

Dolls: babies

The dolls I make are used as models for my wife's needlework. (see Christine Adams)

ARTISAN: ADAMS, CHERYL D.

BUSINESS NAME: Cheryl Adams Creations in Miniature
"Second Childhood"

IDENTIFICATION MARKS:

CDA '92

CATEGORY:

Accessories; Fimo; Paintings; Sculptures

HONORS:

Best in Show, Bright Star Queen City Miniature Show, 1985

ARTISAN: **ADAMS, CHRISTINE**

BUSINESS NAME: Christine Adams Miniature Designs

IDENTIFICATION MARKS:

All pieces sold with a label & logo attached

CATEGORY:

Knitting; Needlework

HONORS:

IGMA Artisan 1994; Member of British Toymakers Guild

RECOGNITION:

Dolls House World, No. 2, 1989; No. 21, 1992; *International Dolls House News*, Winter 1992

AUTOBIOGRAPHY:

I first began knitting miniatures in 1989, although I had knitted full-sized garments for many years. Being a trained Nursery Nurse it seemed natural that I concentrated my designs on baby wear. My designs are exclusive and are for periods from the early eighteen hundreds to the present day. They are knitted in fine crochet cottons, lace threads and silk threads. The tiny garments are finished with buttons and silk ribbon bows. I also knit adult garments as special orders.

Having first attended a local fair in April 1989 I was asked to exhibit my work at The London Dolls House Festival in May 1989, and have been fortunate to be included many times. I also exhibit at Miniatura, at the National Exhibition Center and have attended the International Artisans Fair, in London.

see "Alan Reginald Adams"

ARTISAN: **ADAMS, JOAN**

BUSINESS NAME: Miniature Rugs by Adams

IDENTIFICATION MARKS:

Joan Adams Original
Name of Rug Date

Ribbon label glued on rugs

Logo on graphs

CATEGORY:

Needlework: graphs; Rugs

RECOGNITION:

Nutshell News, Jan. 1986, pg. 74-77, "Joan Adams' Plush Persians," Sheila DeTurk

AUTOBIOGRAPHY:

Two years before retiring in 1980 I discovered miniatures. The Altrusa Club of Sarasota, Florida was decorating a Christmas house and I was asked to supervise the project. That seemed to be a good excuse to make a dollhouse. I worked every evening and every weekend until we opened the first week of December. From that experience came a fascination with rugs and rug designs. The graphs I used for those first rugs were too simple for my taste so I tried designing my own. I've never stopped since then, although because of family duties I've slowed down the last few years.

As to professional background, I taught elementary school for 11 years and was an elementary school principal for 13. I retired early to care for an ill parent who since passed away. I'm just now, in 1994, beginning to get back to designing seriously.

ARTISAN: **ADAMS, KATE**

BUSINESS NAME: Kate Adams Designs

IDENTIFICATION MARKS:

CATEGORY:

Beds: coverings; Quilts; Textiles

HONORS:

IGMA Fellow 1988; 1st Place, Best of Class & Peoples Choice, Marin Needlework & Quilt Show, San Rafael, CA 1988; 1st Place, Best of Class, Marin Needlework & Quilt Show, San Rafael, CA 1989; Exhibits: Ames Gallery of American Folk Art, Walnut Creek, CA 1986; Smoky Mountain Quilt Competition & Show, Museum of Science and Energy, Oak Ridge, TN 1989; Birmingham Bloomfield Art Association, Birmingham, Michigan, 1989 & 1992; The Art of the Quilt, 13 replicas from the Esprit Collection, Amish, Archbishops Mansion, San Francisco, 1990; Ferrin Gallery at Pinch Pottery, Northampton, MA 1990; Maine Women in the Arts, Brickstore Museum, Kennebunk, Maine 1990; Lincoln Gallery, MWA, Kennebunkport, ME 1991

RECOGNITION:

Nutshell News, Vol. 14, No. 9, Sept. 1984, pg. 62-64; Vol. 16, No. 2, Feb. 1986, pg. 42-43; *Nutshell News Calendar*, Feb. 1986; *Miniatures Showcase,* Fall 1984; Vol. 1, 1986, pg. 20, 26, 52; Vol. 4, No. 4, 1989, pg. 18-20, 22, 24; Vol. 5, No. 1, 1990, pg. 41-43, 56-57; Colonial Homes, Vol. 17, No. 5, 1991, pg. 68-71, 133; Ladies Circle Patchwork Quilt, No. 81, May/Jun. 1992, pg. 31

AUTOBIOGRAPHY:

Coming from five generations of Oklahoma quilters, I grew up with a great appreciation of quilts and textile arts. My work is a medium of personal expression and documents an important aspect of American womens' cultural heritage. I have been a member of the International Guild of Miniature Artisans from 1983 to present, receiving my Fellowship Award in 1988. Since 1987 I have been an instructor at the Guild school in Castine, Maine.

Among my experiences, from 1973 to 1976 I did costume design & management for Palace Players, Point Reyes, California. From 1976 to 1978 I was involved with the Renaissance Pleasure Faire and Dickens Christmas Fair in San Francisco. I did freelance clothing and costume design in the San Francisco Bay area from 1978 to 1981. Since 1974 I have been curator of seven community quilt shows in Point Reyes, CA, and since 1981 I have been involved in design, production and sales of miniature quilts. I was on the Board of Directors, 1990-1994, of the American Quilt Study Group, in which I have been a continuing participant since 1985.

My objectives are to continue research and reproduction of traditional quilt patterns with antique fabrics in miniature scale. Through teaching workshops I hope to promote the craft of quilting and heritage knowledge. I would also like to expand sales of miniature quilts to the folk art collector.

ARTISAN: **ADAMS, MARJORIE**

BUSINESS NAME: Adams Distinctive Miniatures

IDENTIFICATION MARKS:

CATEGORY:

Accessories; Fans; Furniture; Paintings: oil, watercolor

ADAMS, MARJORIE, continued

HONORS:

IGMA Fellow 1985; NAME AOH 1990; President of IGMA 1990 & 1991; Exhibits: National Geographic, "Small Wonders—The Delightful World of Miniatures," Explorers Hall, Washington, DC, 1987; Toy & Miniature Museum of Kansas City

RECOGNITION:

Masters in Miniature, 12 Artisans At Work, Volume 1, Anne Day Smith, Kalmbach Publishing, 1987, chapter 2; *Miniature Collector,* No. 45, Sept/Oct. 1984, pg. 12-15, "Picture Perfect," Louise Fecher; *Record Herald,* Washington CH, Ohio, Jan. 25, 1985; Oct. 16, 1987; *Weekly Advertiser,* Washington CH, Ohio Jul. 12, 1992, pg. 1-2

AUTOBIOGRAPHY:

I graduated from Ohio Wesleyan University with a major in Fine Arts. In 1977, I painted my first miniature painting and in 1979, I put paintings and fans in Priscilla's Dolls House for sale. Seven years in my own business of Adams Gifts, six years experience in a frame store and three years as office manager at Delaware Speech and Hearing Center, Ohio rounded out my background for starting a full-time business, "Adams Distinctive Miniatures," in 1981. In 1987, by request, a group of 18 paintings and one fan were on display in the National Geographic Exhibit "Small Wonders—The Delightful World of Miniatures," at Express Hall in Washington, DC. Giving numerous talks on miniatures and since 1987, teaching at the International Guild of Miniature Artisans School, Castine, Maine have added to my experience in miniatures.

ARTISAN: ALBERT, FERENC J.

BUSINESS NAME: Albert Custom Glassblowing
Ferenc J. Albert

IDENTIFICATION MARKS:

Unmarked

Identified by Antique reproductions; Old English Hobnail, Diamond Thumbprint, Rib-patterns

CATEGORY:

Glass: handblown

HONORS:

IGMA Fellow 1981; NAME AOH 1994; Exhibit, Toy & Miniature Museum of Kansas City

RECOGNITION:

Nutshell News, Jul. 1980, pg. 73; Oct. 1982, pg. 65; Dec. 1987, pg. 67; Dec. 1989, pg. 78; Dec. 1990, pg. 64; Dec. 1992, pg. 75; Feb. 1993, pg. 68; *Miniature Collector*, No. 20, pg. 24; No. 29, pg. 29; No. 49. pg. 41

AUTOBIOGRAPHY:

I was born in Budapest, Hungary, and emigrated to the United States in 1956. My wife, M.M., and I have been married for 30 years, 1963, and have two daughters. I received my training in scientific glassblowing at the Budapest Institute of Technology, and off-hand (art) pipe glass blowing at Southern Connecticut State College. My experience comes from years in the department of scientific research at the University of Budapest, five years in Cleveland, Ohio, working at Euclid Glass Engineering Laboratory and 25 years with IBM in New York.

In days past, I have enjoyed the sport and hobby of the kayak. I held the National Championship in Hungary in 1952 and 1953, and was National Champion in 1963, 1964 and 1969, in the United States.

I have always been interested in miniatures! In a glass lab in Budapest, many years ago, I started making tiny apparatus for a miniature still! But it was here in the United States in 1975 that my career in miniatures started seriously.

Helene Norris, who had a large collection of full-size Sandwich Glass, asked me to make miniature reproductions of her Diamond Thumbprint pieces. She provided me with reference books, anthologies, and lots of help and encouragement. The result was my Diamond Thumbprint line of glass miniatures, and later the old English Hobnail and, more recently, the Rib pattern.

What was originally a hobby, became a full-time obsession! In 1987, I elected to take early retirement from IBM to become a full-time miniaturist.

Through the years, I've found the best part of being in miniatures is the people you meet. I've had the good fortune to collaborate on projects with many fine artists such as Nic Nichols, Phyllis Tucker, Chet Spacher, David Krupick, Pete Acquisto, Bruce Phillips, Ernie Levy, and Monique Jouvenel to name only a few.

ARTISAN: **ALLEN, HOLLY**

BUSINESS NAME: Pride and Precious Originals

IDENTIFICATION MARKS:

H. Allen "93"   H. ALLEN "93"

CATEGORY:

Toys: antique reproductions, nursery, sculpture

HONORS:

IGMA Artisan 1988

RECOGNITION:

Nutshell News, Jan. 1989, pg. 46-48, "A Novel Approach," Anne Day Smith

AUTOBIOGRAPHY:

I have been sculpting figures and toys since 1987. My sister Melissa Wyatt, a doll maker, and I began attending shows that same year. We attended mainly Washington and Philadelphia area shows, sometimes Chicago and Wilmington. Now, however, I sell mainly through five dealers scattered across the US.

I work in Super Sculpey and wood. My work has included carrousels, figurines, dogs, cats, ½-inch scale dolls, wreaths, painted screens, miniature dioramas, and mainly, dollhouse toys. I also work full-time as a wall covering designer for York Wallcoverings, since 1988. I am becoming very interested in ½-inch scale. I was born in York, Pennsylvania in May 1966.

ARTISAN: **ALLIN, WENDY**

BUSINESS NAME: Wendy Allin Miniatures

IDENTIFICATION MARKS:

Smaller pieces unmarked

Wendy

Mark included year, preceding 1985

CATEGORY:

Accessories; Bears; Cakes; Christmas; Confectionery; Flowers & Plants; Food; Holiday Items; Kits; Photographs; Shellwork; Stationery; Toys

HONORS:

Save The Children Fund Miniaturist Competitions, Highly Commended 1984; Prize Winner 1987

RECOGNITION:

Nutshell News, Vol. 21, No. 9, Sept. 1991, pg. 48-51; *International Dolls' House News,* Vol. 14, No. 4, Winter 1985, pg. 20; Vol. 19, No. 2, Summer 1990, Cover; *Home Miniaturist,* Jul. 1988, pg. 7-8

ALLIN, WENDY, continued

AUTOBIOGRAPHY:

I have been collecting for many years and began to make items which were not easily available in the earlier years, and have also traded for some time.

ARTISAN: **AMOROSO, ANN MARIE J.**

BUSINESS NAME: Amoroso Originals

IDENTIFICATION MARKS:

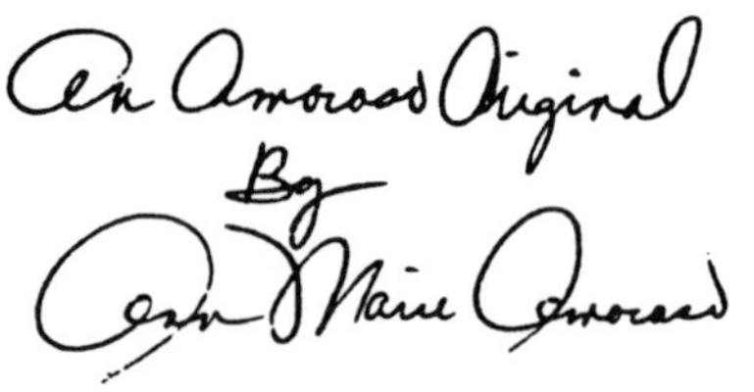

CATEGORY:

Beds: dressed; Furniture; Tables: dressing

BIOGRAPHY:

Ann-Marie was introduced to miniatures by an Aunt Millie living and collecting in Massachusetts. Millie gave Ann-Marie's daughters some miniature roomboxes in 1969 and thus the bug bit!

Dorothy Everett from Fantasy Dollhouses in Costa Mesa, California, requested to see items Ann-Marie made and she ordered frequently. Dorothy would challenge items, asking if Ann-Marie could make them, and thus, a business was born. Her first miniature show was in March 1979, so much fun, not much money!

Ann-Marie's apprenticeship was actually making Barbie doll clothes for her daughters, and Dorothy Everett decided miniatures wouldn't be too difficult.

ARTISAN: **ANDERSON, PIA TROELL**

IDENTIFICATION MARKS:

Unmarked

CATEGORY:

Carpets; Needlework

HONORS:

IGMA Artisan 1991, Fellow 1994; 1st Place, Woodlawn International Exhibition, twice with a miniature carpet

RECOGNITION:

Nutshell News, Mar. 1992, pg. 72; Mar. 1994, pg. 44, Show Scene; Jun. 1994, pg. 58, Show Scene

BIOGRAPHY:

Pia Troell Anderson was born in Sweden and became a US citizen in 1957. She served in Poland, Berlin, and at the United Nations in New York as a member of the Swedish Foreign Service, as well as in Iran, Spain, France, and Great Britain as the wife of an American Diplomat.

Pia Anderson's interest in handicrafts blossomed during a sojourn of several years in Paris, when she took up both weaving and embroidery, petit point. She embroidered several antique chairs, including two from the era of Louis XVI, and large tapestries. In the United States, she turned more and more to miniature Oriental carpets, reproducing the traditional designs from Persia, other Middle Eastern countries, and China.

Her work has won international recognition. She took 1st place in the Woodlawn International Exhibition two times with a miniature carpet. Mrs. Anderson works in both DMC and silk, principally meshes 22 and 40. Among the designs she has mastered are Bokhara, Isfahan, Kurdistan, et. al. and Chinese dragon designs.

She also does miniature pillows for dollhouses, and has executed orders for several custom carpets for specific dollhouse rooms.

ARTISAN: **ANDERSON, WILMA**

IDENTIFICATION MARKS:

Unmarked

CATEGORY:

Crocheting; Needlework

ARTISAN: **ANDREWS, ELISABETT B.**

IDENTIFICATION MARKS:

Used on painted furniture
1975 to present

Incised in porcelain
Occasionally painted
Also on small pieces

CATEGORY:

Furniture: hand painted; Porcelain

RECOGNITION:

Miniature Collector, No. 34, Dec. 1982, Pg. 48; Spring 1988, Pg. 26, Show Stopper; Winter 1991, pg. 22, Show Stopper; *Nutshell News*; Mar. 1983, pg. 84; Dec. 1987, pg. 68, Show Scene; Vol. 22, No. 2, Feb. 1992

ARTISAN: **ANDREWS, JACQUELINE** (Deceased)

BUSINESS NAME: Andrews Miniatures

IDENTIFICATION MARKS:

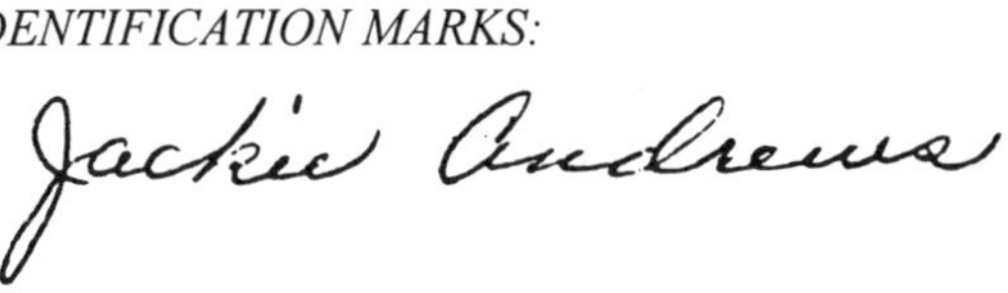

CATEGORY:

Dolls: Handbags; Roomboxes; Shadow Boxes

HONORS:

NAME AOH; Mell Prescott Award 1993; IGMA Crystal Award 1989; Honorary Chairman 1989, "Wedding of the Year," Gulf South Miniature & Dollhouse Event, New Orleans, Louisiana; Outstanding Citizen 1960 Ashland, Virginia

RECOGNITION:

TV coverage interview for National News, Charles Osgood, 1978; *Miniature Gazette; Miniatures Showcase; Nutshell News; Miniature Collector*, Nov/Dec. 1995, pg. 32-37, Celebrating a Ledgend: Jackie Andrews, Mary Kaliski; *The Andrews Collection*, Personal Treasures, Anne Day Smith, Dee's Delights, Inc. 1988

ANDREWS, JACQUELINE, continued

AUTOBIOGRAPHY:

I played dollhouse with orange crates as a child and built furniture out of "sticks and straws." I got my first dollhouse as an adult in 1963 and everything grew from there. A friend in town, Bill Hewlett, gave me, as a surprise, a dollhouse. It was an exact copy of Lake View, the home where I was raised.

Joe and I were married in 1939. There was little time for personal endeavors as I raised five children and was constantly involved with Cub Scouts, Brownies, and being room mother for 17 years.

I learned that Margaret Whitton was selling her miniatures business, and that was the birth of Andrews Miniatures. When I found some time for myself, I joined a miniatures club. Returning home from a meeting one day, I told my husband that some friends wanted to sell "Wilton." Joe didn't know what I was talking about until I explained it was a dollhouse. We mutually decided to make a trip to Williamsburg so he could see for himself, whereupon he said he liked it but didn't feel we could afford it. With some thought he added that he had a shipment of miniatures coming in from overseas and after payment, he wouldn't have enough money for Wilton, "But you have my permission to do what you can."

The next morning I went to the bank and spoke with the President. I explained I needed money to buy a house in Williamsburg. When he was told the price, he asked with alarm, "You can buy a house in Williamsburg for that amount of money?" I hastened to explain the house in question was a dollhouse and that if the bank did decide to loan me the money for the purchase, it could not interfere with any business my husband may have with them. He told me he would have to go before the bank board and get their approval before he could make such a loan. When he appeared before the board of directors, he compared the purchase of my dollhouse to a farmer in the country requesting a loan on a litter of unborn pigs. I got the loan! And, I got the house!

I had seen Carter's Grove when it was being built at about four different stages. I jokingly told Betty Marvin, who was having the house built, that if anything happened and Williamsburg Foundation did not accept the house, I would take it. Later I received a telephone call saying the house was mine and I owned it for 11 years. Some of the furnishings came with it: it contained 35 rooms. I also have an antique doll collection which was started in a rather unusual way back in 1963. I was helping a friend pack after her mother had passed away. My son, John, was playing with the discarded items in the back yard when I went in search of him, and among the objects he was playing with were seven antique dolls. I brought them home and that was the beginning of my collection.

I have been the nighttime supervisor for the Randolph Macon College infirmary, in Ashland, Virginia, since 1968. I served as Secretary of NAME from 1978 to 1980, and Junior Vice President from 1980 to 1982 continuing on the Board of Directors to 1986.

Editor's Note: Jackie more than lived up to her sharing in her contributions and love for miniatures, and the people involved with them. She was truly the epitome of what this hobby is really all about.

ARTISAN: **ANDREWS, JOE** (Deceased)

BUSINESS NAME: Andrews Miniatures

IDENTIFICATION MARKS:

CATEGORY:

Furniture

HONORS:

Founding member IMA; NAME AOH; Bicentennial Seal of Approval, US Bicentennial Society Board of Trustees 1976; Honorary Chairman 1989, Wedding of the Year, Gulf South Miniature & Dollhouse Event, New Orleans, Louisiana; Plaque award, Contribution to Miniatures, Bull Run Miniature Club, Manassas, Virginia

ANDREWS, JOE, continued

RECOGNITION:

Miniatures Showcase; Miniature Gazette; Nutshell News; The Andrews Collection, Personal Treasures, Anne Day Smith, Dee's Delights, Inc. 1988

BIOGRAPHY:

Born and raised in Pennsylvania, Joe began cabinet work while in grade school. He learned the use of basic tools, and then trained with power tools so that when he entered high school he could do more advanced cabinet-making. The encouragement from his mother made these activities even more enjoyable.

However, in order to prepare for college, Joe had to give up cabinet work in high school after his freshman year. He went on to Randolph Macon College in Ashland, Virginia where he met his wife, Jackie, whom he married in 1939. Jackie's father's hobby was fine cabinet-making, specializing in Queen Anne, Sheraton, Chippendale and Hepplewhite. Joe worked with him gaining extensive knowledge, especially that of finishing hard woods such as mahogany and walnut.

When Jackie decided to make purses shaped like houses, she asked Joe to help. The "house purse" started both Joe and Jackie in the miniatures business. The couple attended a UFDC Regional Convention in Washington, DC, 1972, and Joe was fascinated by the miniature furniture he saw, especially the replicas of what he had been making in full-scale. He tried his hand at one-inch scale focusing on classic pieces, later concentrating on the Queen Anne pieces, namely the highboy, lowboy, and bachelor chest. After improving those three pieces, they were submitted to the US Bicentennial Society Board of Trustees in 1975, and Joe was awarded the Bicentennial Seal of Approval. This allowed him to use the seal on the three pieces manufactured in the future and the pieces that were placed on sale for the Bicentennial Year in 1976.

Joe and Jackie's business began to grow. At first, Joe had his own furniture designs made in Taiwan and imported them to sell in the United States. He attended doll shows selling his miniature furniture in the early seventies. Participation in many shows resulted in phenomenal growth. He loved to travel and meet new friends. Working so many shows gave him great pleasure.

(AOH profile, by Ferbie Claudon, authorized reprint by NAME)

ARTISAN: **ANDRIELLA, JO ANN HOBBS**

BUSINESS NAME: Jo Ann's Originals

IDENTIFICATION MARKS:

Jo Ann H. Andriella

CATEGORY:

Dolls: original, porcelain

HONORS:

IGMA Fellow

RECOGNITION:

Nutshell News, Oct. 1989, pg. 77; Sept. 1986, pg. 84; Sept. 1985, pg. 69; Jul. 1986, pg. 64; Mar. 1984, pg. 54; Feb. 1993 pg. 74-75; *Miniatures Showcase,* Spring 1990 pg. 67; *Doll Artistry,* Jul. 1991 pg. 21; *St. Petersburg Times*, 1990

AUTOBIOGRAPHY:

I got my artistic and creative talent from both of my parents. I started drawing at an early age, designing clothes for my paper dolls, and years later for my two daughters. I took art in high school and oil painting lessons from a prominent artist in my home state. I started out working in a stained glass studio, and this led eventually to miniatures. My first miniatures were small sculpted dolls and toys made with Sculpy. I then used my talents doing oil painting and decorating furniture. My favorite work now is creating original hand-sculpted fashion ladies in one-inch and ½-inch scales.

ARTISAN: **ANSLINGER, HERMANIA**

BUSINESS NAME: Hermania Anslinger

IDENTIFICATION MARKS:

 On smallest pieces

CATEGORY:

Furniture

HONORS:

IMA Achievement Award; NAME AOH; Exhibit: Toy & Miniature Museum of Kansas City

RECOGNITION:

Hobbies Magazine, Sept. 1961, pg. 122; *The Collector's Guide to Dollhouse and Dollhouse Miniatures*, Marian O'Brien 1974, pg. 113, 155; *Inside The World of Miniatures and Dollhouses,* Bernard Rosner & Jay Beckerman, Mckay Press, 1976, pg. 38-41, 90-91, 227; *This Side of Yesterday in Miniatures,* Catherine B. MacLaren, 1975, pg. 47-48, 117; *Miniature Reflections,* Patricia Diedrick, Vol. 1, No. 1, pg. 23; Vol. 1, No. 2, pg. 11-16; *Great Fall Tribune*, 1941; *Spokesman Review*, Feb. 1964; Aug. 5, 1968; Jun. 27, 1992; *Spokane Daily Chronicle,* Jun. 29, 1972; Jul. 26, 1979

AUTOBIOGRAPHY:

I am self-taught. When I was three years old my mom made a wooden doll bed from scraps of pine kindling wood. I remember sitting on the kitchen table watching. It was about 14 inches long, she painted it white and trimmed it with round head brass tacks. Every time I see a piece of pine, the odor of it reminds me of that bed. No doubt, that had some reason for my interest in making things of wood! She never made anything else of wood. She was a dressmaker and seamstress.

Most all my miniatures have been signed Hermania Anslinger for years. I have made animals in action, circus performers, and figures of all kinds made of wood, ivory and semi-precious stones. The furniture has been of mahogany, walnut, and a few pieces of ebony. The first pieces were basswood, in the 1940's.

ARTISAN: **AOKI, MINORU**

IDENTIFICATION MARKS:

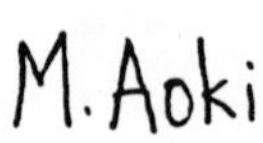

1983

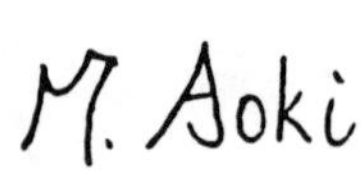

1985

1986

present

CATEGORY:

Furniture: American, European, Japanese

HONORS:

IGMA Artisan 1989

RECOGNITION:

Nutshell News, Jan. 1988, pg. 8, 56-57; Jun. 1988, pg. 60, 62; Oct. 1989, pg. 76; *Miniature Gazette,* Fall 1987, pg. 44-46; *Miniature Collector,* Fall 1989, pg. 23

AOKI, MINORU, continued

AUTOBIOGRAPHY:

My family has been in woodworking for four generations. I was born in 1954 and was brought up with wood dust and scraps. I attended the Meiji University in Tokyo and, in 1976, I started making miniature furniture.

I participated in the IGMA show in 1989 and the TAMS show in 1988 and 1989. I have many friends in the United States. I was awarded IGMA Artisan in 1989 the first Japanese man to have this honor.

Marquetry, inlay and carving are my favorites. In a few years I will finish making a new series of Japanese and American furniture and room settings.

ARTISAN: APPLEBAUM, JUDY HERMAN

BUSINESS NAME: Judy Herman Applebaum

IDENTIFICATION MARKS:

CATEGORY:

Accessories; Finishes: faux; Furniture: faux

HONORS:

IGMA Artisan

AUTOBIOGRAPHY:

As a little girl, I always wanted trains, but Mother said trains were for boys and that dolls and dollhouses were for girls. As an adult, I went into a train store fully intending to buy a train set, but in the back of the store the proprietor was building dollhouses, and I walked out with a house instead.

My background in art started in the program for gifted children at the Dayton Art Institute. I have taken many classes in painting, gilding, and faux finishes at many schools and museums all over the country. I teach a weekly arts & crafts class for blind students in New York City.

ARTISAN: ARCHER, ROBERT H., JR.

BUSINESS NAME: Robert Archer Designs

IDENTIFICATION MARKS:

CATEGORY:

Costuming; Figures

HONORS:

IGMA Artisan 1991

RECOGNITION:

Dolls in Miniature; Doll Crafter; Nutshell News

ARCHER, ROBERT H., JR., continued

BIOGRAPHY:

This costume designer and pattern maker acquired skills at the University of Richmond, in Virginia, the Traphagen School of Fashion, New York City, and is a graduate of Ringling School of Art, Sarasota, Florida, majoring in Fashion Design and Illustration.

Mr. Archer has designed fabrics, served as both designer and costume master for ballet and theatrical productions, designed and constructed couture clothing and wedding gowns, and designed ballroom dance competition costumes.

Active in pattern making and clothing design from the age of three (his grandfather was a tailor) at his grandmother's side, he has been involved in doll making and costuming. In 1976, he created his first fashion doll going on to win local, state, national and international awards in competition. He has also won numerous awards for his original paper dolls.

Mr. Archer received Artisan status in the International Guild of Miniature Artisans in March 1991. His individualized figures for the consummate collector have been featured in *Dolls in Miniature, Doll Crafter*, and *Nutshell News*.

He has served on the Board of Directors, First vice-president, and President for two terms of the International Doll Makers Association. He is a charter member of the Tidewater Doll Club of Virginia and is a founder of the Doll Study Club of Tidewater serving as President of both clubs. He is a former member of the Blue Bonnet Bebes of Houston, Texas. All clubs are a part of the United Federation of Doll Clubs. He is a member of the Creative Doll Artists of Virginia, and served as chairman of the 1996 Regional Conference in Norfolk.

Mr. Archer has conducted workshops nationally, adult seminars on the college level and has been an instructor at the Meredith Doll Symposium in Raleigh, North Carolina in 1981, 1983 and 1985. He brings the world of haute couture to the miniature field in both one-inch and ½-inch scale. His work is highlighted in authentic period costumes, ethnic, fantasy, and modern adaptations. Exquisite fabrics, trims, beadwork, and accessories are the trade mark of this talented artist.

ARTISAN: ARMSTRONG, FRANCES

BUSINESS NAME: Toys in Miniature

IDENTIFICATION MARKS:

Very tiny pieces and stuffed animals unmarked

FEA — On wooden pieces large enough

F. E. Armstrong — On dollhouses, roomboxes 1/144 scale

CATEGORY:

Animals: stuffed; Toys

RECOGNITION:

Nutshell News; Teddy Bear & Friends

AUTOBIOGRAPHY:

I have been making miniatures since I was very small, and professionally, since 1979. I try to combine this with an academic career. I have a Ph.D. in English, and am at the moment a post-doctoral fellow at the University of Toronto, doing research on the theory of, what else, "littleness!"

ARTISAN: **ARMSTRONG, RUTH** (also see listing on page 500)

BUSINESS NAME: Ruth Armstrong

IDENTIFICATION MARKS:

  Engraved on bottom of metal object; glued on metal tag; wired on hang tag, metal or paper; pieces prior to 1983 may be signed in India ink on bottom

 Signed in India ink on bottom of small painted pieces, or engraved on plain metal

CATEGORY:

Metal: tin; Pattern Maker; Tinsmith

AUTOBIOGRAPHY:

When the miniature explosion got underway about 1980, I was already making 3-D dioramic ghost town buildings with the interiors they remembered in distorted perspective. I had been a freelance hobby writer, in print somewhere all the time, for about 15 years. Going into scale furnishings just came naturally, and I was soon making items for a shop near St. Louis, where we then lived. Most of the things available were the sparkling new and luxurious stuff of little dreams. It seemed odd to ignore the "short and simple annals" of the westward pioneers I came from, so it was those I began to make. I went right on writing and putting the patterns in print, but now for miniature publications, though I also wrote about full-sized hobbies as I went along.

My engineer husband helped me with the technical end of using the real wood, metal, and glass proper to the era. My mother did the photography and taught me how.

I have a college degree in interior design, with a minor in English from the University of Colorado. I am a fair artist with pen and ink, doing machinery and landscape. I am at home in a wood shop and enjoy making things so they seem to work. I stick with the original materials used, which is a challenge I enjoy. Most of my work is in one-inch scale, but there are about two housefuls and several extra Colonial dining sets and little accessories out there in ½-inch scale. All these items are signed and logged.

My memory is pictorial, and goes back in detail to a time when I was less than two, so I have not only the suburbia furnishings of the twenties and thirties imprinted, I also have the turn of the century rooms that the depression froze in time in the homes of my aunts and uncles out in Texas, Kansas and Oklahoma. I enjoy recording a little world that will tell whoever inherits it that we were not all royalty. My best reward is the recognition of someone who once used that item full-sized as a child and meets my miniature as an old friend.

ARTISAN: **ARNOLD, JENNY & JEFF**

BUSINESS NAME: Warwick Miniatures, Ltd.

IDENTIFICATION MARKS:

Unmarked

CATEGORY:

Accessories; Animals

HONORS:

British Toymakers Guild

ARTISAN: **ASKEW, LUCY**

IDENTIFICATION MARKS:
Unmarked

CATEGORY:
Fireplaces; Mirrors

HONORS:
Highly Commended Award, British Toymakers Guild

RECOGNITION:
Making Dolls Houses in 1/12 Scale, Brian Nicholls, David & Charles, 1992 pg. 43, 55, 67, 71, 79

AUTOBIOGRAPHY:
I started making models and miniatures, being completely self-taught, and I made three models of buildings, their gardens and their interiors for major exhibitions at the Victoria and Albert Museum in London, England. I then attended a two year course in architectural model making at Medway College of Design, Rochester, England, and was awarded a diploma with distinction. I worked for five years as an architectural model maker, specializing in museum work, before giving up my job to raise a family. I now combine looking after my children and making miniatures at home.

ARTISAN: **ATHERTON, ELIZABETH**

BUSINESS NAME: Apple Tree Dolls

IDENTIFICATION MARKS:

On my molds only

CATEGORY:
Dolls

RECOGNITION:
Home Miniaturist, Nov. 1989

AUTOBIOGRAPHY:
I have been making miniature dolls since approximately 1982, and use mostly Janna Joseph and Parker-Levi molds and also a few of my own molds.

ARTISAN: **ATKINSON, SUE**

BUSINESS NAME: Sunday Dolls

IDENTIFICATION MARKS:

Sunday Dolls England, with year
inside skirt or coat

CATEGORY:
Dolls; Publications; Writer

ATKINSON, SUE, continued

RECOGNITION:

Making & Dressing Dolls' House Dolls in 1/12 Scale, Sue Atkinson, David & Charles Press, England, 1992; *Dolls In Miniature,* Spring 1992; *Dolls Magazine*, Winter 1992; *Home Miniaturist*, Issue 63; *Dolls House World*, Issue 22, Nov/Dec. 1992, pg. 38-39, 42-45, "Dressed to Thrill;" *International Dolls House News*, Winter 1992

BIOGRAPHY:

Sue Atkinson started making cloth dolls, then tried resin casting, before adapting to dollhouse scale in 1979. Under the name Sunday Dolls, she became the United Kingdom and European agent for Joy Parker's Swallowhill kits. Although dressing these originally as samples, demand for dressed dolls could only be met by a team of talented needle women, and the need for small scale trims and fabrics led to a thriving haberdashery business which is now separate under the name, The Dollshouse Draper.

Sunday Dolls specialize in Victorian and Edwardian families, but undertake any commissions, their dolls going all over the world. They can be seen at the London Dollshouse Festival and other major British shows. Sue has taken them to several NAME National Houseparties and the IGMA Show. Her new book *Making and Dressing Dolls' House Dolls in 1/12 Scale* was published by David & Charles Press in September 1992.

ARTISAN: **AUDETTE, DARRYL**

BUSINESS NAME: Darryl Audette

IDENTIFICATION MARKS:

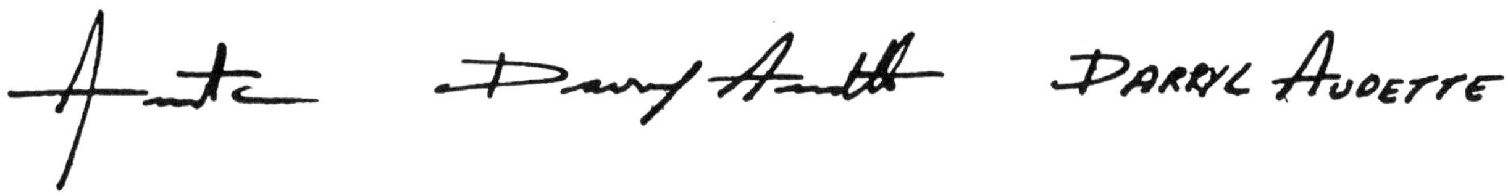

CATEGORY:

Animals: horses; Dioramas; Figures

HONORS:

Best in Show, Canada Juried Show 1992; Best in Show, M.M.S.S. (Manitoba) 1990

RECOGNITION:

Nutshell News; Winnipeg Free Press, Oct. 1980; Nov. 12, 1992; CKND Television, Marjorie Stevens Show, Feb. 1992; *Winnipeg Lance*, 1991 & 1992

ARTISAN: **AUGER, MARIAN**

BUSINESS NAME: M. A. Miniature of Fine Art

IDENTIFICATION MARKS:

CATEGORY:

Art: fine; Paintings

HONORS:

Exhibited with The Royal Society of Miniature Painters, Sculptors and Gravers

RECOGNITION:

East Anglia TV; Great Yarmouth Mercury, Jan. 10, 1992 (Great Britain)

B

ARTISAN: **BABCOCK, KATHIE**

BUSINESS NAME: Kathie Babcock

IDENTIFICATION MARKS:

KB '93

CATEGORY:

Baskets; Flowers & Plants

HONORS:

IGMA Artisan 1993

AUTOBIOGRAPHY:

My first introduction to miniatures came through my mother, Mary McGrath. Although I had admired her work for years I never went to a miniature show until 1988. After being totally overwhelmed, I left having fallen in love with all the tiny pots of flowers.

I went home determined to try making some myself. My first few attempts were tulips made of Sculpey. I quickly decided that there had to be a better way! After trying a few different methods I settled on paper as being the most realistic and most workable for me. I have been experimenting and adding new flowers ever since.

The first few shows I exhibited at my mother let me put a display at the end of her table. Things went well so I ventured out on my own. In 1990 I took a few basket weaving classes and decided that there must be a way to weave in miniature. After much trial and error I developed a method that was manageable and enjoyable. Since then I have continued working in both areas.

ARTISAN: **BACKSTROM, MARCIA**

BUSINESS NAME: Marcia Backstrom's Dolls

IDENTIFICATION MARKS:

MB93 MB

CATEGORY:

Dolls: original; Kits: doll

HONORS:

IGMA Artisan

RECOGNITION:

Contemporary Doll Magazine, 1992, 1st Issue; *Dolls In Miniature*, Vol. 1, No. 3, Fall 1991, Cover, pg. 5-8, "A Gift of Talent"

AUTOBIOGRAPHY:

I never dreamed I would ever be a doll artist. I've always been interested in a two dimensional art form such as painting, portrait & portrait work. In college I did take one sculpting class, however it was an abstract art course. The human figure studies were very exciting to me. I went on to receive my Bachelor of Arts Degree, and I taught school for four years.

BACKSTROM, MARTCIA, continued

After having my two boys, I decided to find a career from home. My aunt bought me a dollhouse kit and soon I was hooked on miniatures. I made several dolls and began to take them to shows, where they were very enthusiastically received.

I like dollmaking because I enjoy people, especially the ones with lots of character in their faces, which tell the stories of their lives. It gives me a lot of pleasure to watch the expressions on their faces when they look at my dolls and begin to build whole scenes around them. The dolls always remind them of someone they knew or know now. Doll making gives me a lot of enjoyment.

ARTISAN: **BACON, VICKI**

BUSINESS NAME: Victoria's Smallwares

IDENTIFICATION MARKS:

CATEGORY:
Furniture: bamboo, upholstered

RECOGNITION:
Miniatures Showcase, Vol. 5, No. 3, Summer 1990, pg. 18, 46; Vol. 5, No. 4, Fall 1990, pg. 31

ARTISAN: **BAHL, THERESE**

BUSINESS NAME: Therese Bahl

IDENTIFICATION MARKS:

on earlier pieces

CATEGORY:
Folk Art

HONORS:
IGMA Artisan 1984; IGMA Fellow 1987; Exhibits: Toy & Miniature Museum of Kansas City; Abby Aldrich Rockefeller Folk Art Center, Williamsburg, VA

RECOGNITION:
Nutshell News, Nov. 1983, pg. 52-54; Oct. 1985, pg. 80, Show Scene; May 1986, pg. 61-62; Jul. 1986, pg. 20; Aug. 1986, pg. 68, 73; Sept. 1986, pg. 72-73; Feb. 1987, pg. 67; Jun. 1987, pg. 61; Sept. 1987, pg. 108; Oct. 1987 pg. 78; Apr. 1988, pg. 71; Dec. 1988, Cover, pg. 48, 75; Mar. 1989, Cover; Sept. 1991, pg. 79; Mar. 1992, pg. 72; Jun. 1992, pg. 63-64; *Miniatures Showcase*, Fall 1986, pg. 18, 22; Fall 1989; *Miniature Collector*, Winter 1985, pg. 26; Dec. 1986, pg. 11; *Miniature Gazette*, Winter 1986, pg. 26-27; Spring 1991, pg. 22-23; Fall 1989, pg. 14; *Nutshell News Calendar*, Jan. 1992

BAHL, THERESE, continued

BIOGRAPHY:

Therese Bahl has a fine arts background from Carnegie Mellon, and has extensive training in Early American Decoration from master teachers of the Esther Stevens School, at Fletcher Farm in Vermont. She has taught full size and miniature painting for more than twenty years.

Therese has done portrait work, newspaper illustration, and American Folk Art. She has been an instructor at the IGMA Castine, Maine school for many years. She specializes in wall murals in roomboxes, both one inch and ½-scale, and in reproducing American Folk Art in miniature. She does several shows a year.

Therese is a member of NAME and IGMA. She served on the IGMA board for six years, holding the positions of Artisan Selection Chairman, and of President of the International Guild of Miniature Artisans.

ARTISAN: **BAILEY, JANET D.**

BUSINESS NAME: Elfin Heirlooms

IDENTIFICATION MARKS:

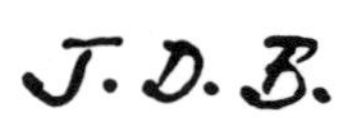

Small pieces

CATEGORY:

Furniture: handpainted

RECOGNITION:

Nutshell News, Dec. 1987, pg. 69; Sept. 1988, pg. 67; Dec. 1988, pg. 84; Jan. 1989, pg. 25; Oct. 1990, pg. 73; Nov. 1990, pg. 78; Sept. 1991, pg. 78; Feb. 1992, pg. 67; *Country Crafts & Collectibles*, Winter 1991, pg. 57; *Miniature Collector*, Fall 1992, pg. 23; *Miniature Gazette*, Summer 1989, pg. 57

BIOGRAPHY:

Janet Bailey studied four years under two members of H.S.E.A.D. (Historical Society of Early American Decorators). She painted and decorated early American furniture for 16 years. She began painting miniature furniture in 1980, and has been showing her work at miniature shows ever since. She is a member of NAME and the Cape Cod Miniature Society.

ARTISAN: **BALESTRIERI, FRANK & BECKI**

BUSINESS NAME: Balestrieri Miniature Decoys
Balestrieri Miniatures

IDENTIFICATION MARKS:

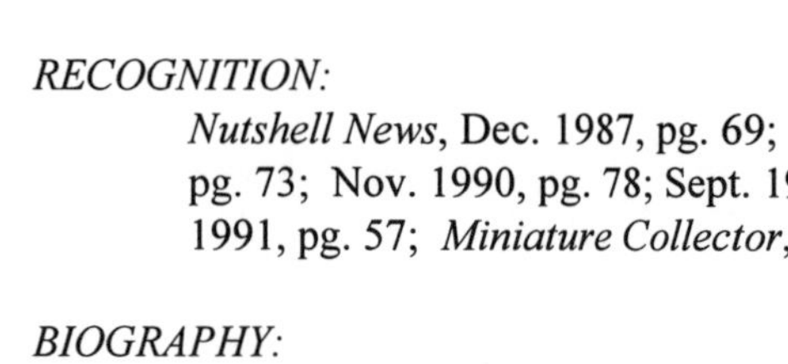

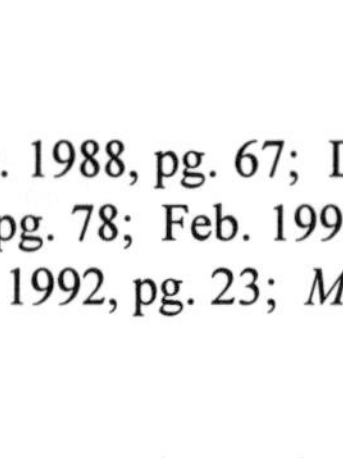

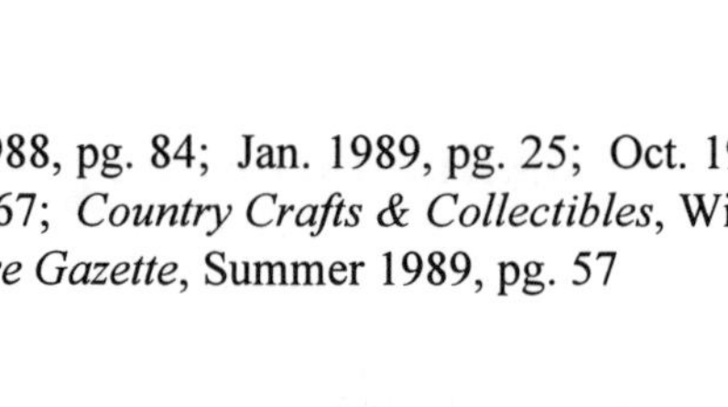

BALESTRIERI, FRANK & BECKI, continued

CATEGORY:

Carvings; Decoys; Sculptures

HONORS:

IGMA Artisan, Fellow; NAME AOH 1991; 3rd Place, Pacific Flyway Decoy Carver's Show & Exhibit, Miniature Division 1977; Exhibit: Toy & Miniature Museum of Kansas City

RECOGNITION:

Nutshell News, Jun. 1984; *Miniature Collector; Miniatures Showcase; Country Living*, Mar. 1991

AUTOBIOGRAPHY:

I was born in Martinez, California on March 9, 1950 as the oldest of three children to Mario and Jennie Balestrieri. My father was in the retail and wholesale produce business, and was an avid hunter and fisherman. As a member of a local duck club, he often had the task of repairing and repainting wood duck decoys. Growing up for the first five years of my life in my grandmother's home, the first thing I can recall was seeing old decoys in my grandmother's basement and outside in her backyard being prepared for the hunting season. Since that time, I have always had an affinity for ducks, geese, and all matter of birds and wildlife.

At ten, I carved my first "miniature" decoy, a mallard of approximately five inch length. I also helped my father paint and repair decoys. Relatives and friends saw my miniature decoy carvings, and began to request them. I gave them away as gifts and sold a few for very modest amounts.

In college, a friend of mine suggested I take some of my miniature waterfowl carvings to a local art gallery. They were taken on consignment and sold very well. I continued to carve both life-size and miniature decoys throughout my college years for spending money.

In 1973, I was hired as a speech pathologist in a farming community south of San Jose, California called Morgan Hill. I have been employed for numerous positions within the school district and county of Santa Clara, for the past 21 years.

Up until 1976, I pretty much made decoys without any formal training or art courses, outside of art classes taken in high school, which were part of the curriculum. I also worked in a vacuum, as I did not confer with others. In 1976, I discovered a waterfowl decoy show, the Pacific Flyway Decoy Carver's Show & Exhibit, and found others like me! The following year, my father and I entered miniature decoy pieces into the show, and won third place in the miniature division. In subsequent years, I entered my miniature pieces, approximately 1/5-scale, into various decoy shows and won numerous awards, including 1st place and best of show.

In 1980, a woman came to the Pacific Flyway Decoy Show and bought several of my pieces. While purchasing them, she asked if I would like to do a miniature show. She said my decoys were "big" (by this time most of them were approximately two-inch scale) but she thought customers would appreciate the little decoys. I was a bit hesitant at her offer, so she offered to pay for my table fee if I would come to the show, and I agreed. That show was my first miniature show. My two-inch scale decoys sold very well, but people kept asking for one-inch scale decoys. I didn't think it was possible for me to carve such a tiny decoy, but after the show on Saturday, I went home and attempted to carve a scale mallard. With great care, I carved and painted my first miniature mallard. The next day, I went back to the show and proudly displayed my first scale model mallard. From that one mallard, I took over 25 orders! I've been doing miniature decoys and other birds since.

My wife, Becki, is also involved in miniatures. For a period of three years, she made one-inch scale weathervanes of wood. She is an excellent painter and craftswoman. As the decoy business continued to expand, I taught her how to paint the decoys, and today, she is an active partner in the creation of our scale model birds.

ARTISAN: BALLANTYNE, MAUREEN

BUSINESS NAME: Maureen Ballantyne

IDENTIFICATION MARKS:

Unmarked

CATEGORY:

Animals; Birds

BALLANTYNE, MAUREEN, continued

RECOGNITION:

Miniature Collector, Summer 1992, pg. 18; *London Times* 1992; *Dolls House World,* 1991, pg. 13; *Good Housekeeping,* 1992

ARTISAN: BANGHART, BRENDA D.

BUSINESS NAME: ¼" to 1' Scale Miniatures by Brenda D. Banghart

IDENTIFICATION MARKS:

Smaller pieces unmarked

B.D.B.

CATEGORY:

Accessories; Dolls; Furniture; Holiday Items

RECOGNITION:

Nutshell News, Vol. 12, No. 3, Mar. 1982, pg. 39; Vol. 15, No. 4, Apr. 1985, pg. 22, 25; *Miniature Gazette*, Vol. 18, No. 1, Fall 1989, pg. 56; Vol. 18, No. 4, Summer 1990, pg. 28

ARTISAN: BANTLE, BRUCE C.

BUSINESS NAME: The Miniature Makers

IDENTIFICATION MARKS:

1976 to present

B Bantle with year

CATEGORY:

Furniture: Colonial, Shaker

AUTOBIOGRAPHY:

The Miniature Maker was started in 1976, when my wife, Nancy, was building a dollhouse for our daughter. My background was in manufacturing and woodworking.

ARTISAN: **BARNETT, JOHN T. MCSD**

BUSINESS NAME: Lilliput Designs
Lilliput Enterprises

IDENTIFICATION MARKS:

Copyright © 199
Lilliput Designs
NORTHAMPTON

John Barnett MCSD
Chartered Designer

John Barnett

JT Barnett

Lilliput Enterprises

John Barnett FTC
Cabinet Maker

JTB

CATEGORY:

Furniture: designs; Tools: miniature making

HONORS:

MCSD, MBIM, MBIAT, LCG, FTC (Furniture Industry)

RECOGNITION:

Entry in *Baron's Who's Who in Interior Design* 1990-1991, International Edition, pg. 16

AUTOBIOGRAPHY:

I had an interest in models and small scale replicas since I was a boy. I made model aircraft, boats and cars in my youth and have used scale models of buildings and furniture professionally for the whole of my working life as a Designer and Architectural Technician.

I first became interested in one-inch scale furniture and houses after visiting *Miniatura*, International Fair for the Dollhouse Enthusiasts, in the early 1980's. These visits coincided with a job in High Wycombe where there is a collection of one-inch scale Windsor chairs in the local museum.

After leaving my job as Design Manager for the Northampton based Anglia Building Society in 1988 I joined a well known miniaturist and worked with him on the production of one-inch scale metal miniatures for sale at fairs and by mail order. While visiting these fairs it became clear that there was a gap in the market for a supplier of specialist tools for miniature work. To meet this need, I helped my wife Cynthia, form a small specialist company, Lilliput Enterprises. Lilliput Designs (Northampton) followed shortly after to provide design services associated with scale buildings, furniture and interiors.

In July 1987 Margaret Downing gathered together a small group of like-minded individuals and Northant's Miniaturists Association was born. I became a founding member and served as Honorary Treasurer and Fair Organizer. The event has proven international clientele, regularly attracting over 1000 visitors, some from as far away as Australia and Croatia. I am also a member of Midlands Miniaturists Association and the International Guild of Miniature Artisans. I am listed in Baron's International *Who's Who in Interior Design.*

One of my more interesting duties as an official of the NMA was to commission the artwork for the Society's current logo which is based on the Rod Forss "Shoe House." This involved negotiations with the American Museum of Childhood Angels Attic of Santa Monica, California, the owners of the shoe. The logo has particular significance to Northant's Miniaturists Association as Northampton was once a shoemaking town and the group of course has an interest in dolls houses.

ARTISAN: **BARROWS, R. V.**

BUSINESS NAME: R. V. Barrows

IDENTIFICATION MARKS:
Unmarked

CATEGORY:
Finishes: exterior, interior

ARTISAN: **BARTLETT, LORRAINE L.**

BUSINESS NAME: Miniature Ambitions

IDENTIFICATION MARKS:
Unmarked, Fall 1984 - April 1985
Handle change on baskets Sept. 1987; First nesting set, beginning 1989

A BARTLETT BASKET ORIGINAL	BARTLETT BASKET
April 1985 to present, string tags or glued tags, graduated sizes	½-inch scale, glued tags

CATEGORY:
Baskets

HONORS:
IGMA Artisan 1990; Northeast Basketmaker's Guild 1993

RECOGNITION:
Nutshell News, Feb. 1990, pg. 56, Show Scene; *Miniatures Showcase*, Fall 1989, pg. 22-24, 28-29; Winter 1990, pg. 36, 42, 45

AUTOBIOGRAPHY:
I have been interested in miniatures since I was a young girl. I took a course in miniature furniture making in 1980. After making numerous pieces of miniature furniture, I started making miniature accessories for my tables. This led first to foods and then flowers, which I felt needed baskets to make them look extra special. I found some very basic instructions in an out-dated craft magazine and some materials at a now long-vacant craft store. I was now ready to make my first miniature basket. The first basket was made in the fall of 1984 and I have been making and collecting baskets ever since. My goal is to make authentic-looking replicas in miniature, of full-sized working baskets of both historical and contemporary nature.

ARTISAN: **BASKET, NANCY**

BUSINESS NAME: Kudzu Kabin Designs

IDENTIFICATION MARKS:
Unmarked, 1981-1989

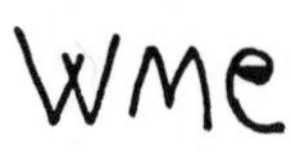

1990 - 1993 birch bark baskets marked *Basket* in Cherokee; mark on small handmade Kudzu paper

1993 to present, lightening design

BASKET, NANCY, continued

CATEGORY:
Baskets

HONORS:
IGMA Artisan

RECOGNITION:
Natural Baskets, 1992, pg. 94; *Pine Needle Basketry,* Judy Mulford, 1987; *News Basket* Shereen LaPlantz, "Nancy Oh," 1986; *Miniature Gazette*, 1986, "It's A Small Basket, But Do You Make Miniatures?"

AUTOBIOGRAPHY:
Following tradition, I have chosen my last name as a reflection of the work I do as my Cherokee great-great-great grandmother, Margaret Basket, must have done. I feel as the Tima Weaver, "Creating baskets is something more than what I do for money. I feel the old ones guiding my fingers and I am proud to be making something beautiful."

In Seattle, Washington in 1981 I helped found the first basketry guild in the United States. Since that time I have worked to bring miniaturists and makers of full-scale basketry together. I have researched Native American miniature baskets by reading books, collecting stories, visiting museums, reservations and talking with Native American people still making miniature baskets. I work with universities, anthropologists and archeologists in collecting information on baskets in miniature. I specialize in coiled basketry using the same materials and techniques used by many tribes in the US. Some of the materials I use are corn husks, horse hair, sweet grass, birch bark, porcupine quills and pine needles.

My baskets, as of 1993, are signed with my family design, that of lightening.

ARTISAN: **BATESON, NEIL**

BUSINESS NAME: N.P. Bateson - Miniature Cabinet Maker

IDENTIFICATION MARKS:

Neil Bateson
HORNSEA
ENGLAND
1993.

N° 1

CATEGORY:
Furniture: inlaid, period, veneered

HONORS:
LCGI, Outstanding achievement in education training & industry for Furniture

RECOGNITION:
International Dolls House News, Vol. 22, No. 2, Summer 1993, pg. 7; *Dolls House World*, Issue 26, Jul/Aug. 1993, pg. 12-13

AUTOBIOGRAPHY:
At the age of 16 I began an apprenticeship with one of the top full-sized furniture makers in Great Britain, John L. Corlyon, making exclusive reproductions for stately homes and embassies in London. We also made furniture for Middle East palaces and private jet aircraft, specializing in veneering and carving of the furniture. I then moved on to specialize in antiques and antique restoration with a well known local craftsman, J. R.Gelesthrope, where I learned about the different periods of English furniture and the construction methods used.

I also studied the construction and history of furniture at Hull College England, where I won awards for top student and best exam results in my city and Guilds London Institute exams where I gained distinctions at ordinary and advanced level, this helped me to receive my L.C.G.I. from the city and Guilds in full-sized furniture.

While working with full-sized furniture I won three gold medals at the London Woodworker Exhibitions twice as a junior and as a senior in 1992 for a satinwood and ebony carved and veneered Vienna wall clock. Being very interested in furniture I traveled around the country to various woodwork and furniture exhibitions. One of these was the London Dolls House Festival. This was the first time I had seen miniature furniture and I thought it would be a challenge to make something in one-inch scale. The first piece of miniature furniture I sold was a one-inch scale George I chest of drawers and over the next few months I received more orders for my miniature furniture until it reached the point where I decided to start my own business in March 1993. As I am under the age of 25, I was invited to exhibit my work at the Prince of Wales exhibition for young business people. This gave me the opportunity to show my work to the Prince of Wales in July 1993!

ARTISAN: **BATT, TOM**

BUSINESS NAME: Tom Batt

IDENTIFICATION MARKS:

Old masters, signed reverse side

Original paintings

CATEGORY:
Paintings: oil

HONORS:
IGMA Artisan

RECOGNITION:
Miniature Gazette, Vol. 9, No. 1, Fall 1980, pg. 8; *Dolls House World*, Issue No. 5 1989/90, pg. 3, 9-12; Issue No. 15, 1991, pg. 54

AUTOBIOGRAPHY:
I started miniature oil painting as a hobby in 1976. I do not have any formal training in Art. My lifetime occupation, until my early retirement, was as a Stereo and Electrotyper.

ARTISAN: **BAZYLKO, GALIA**

BUSINESS NAME: Galia Bazylko Miniatures & Dolls

IDENTIFICATION MARKS:

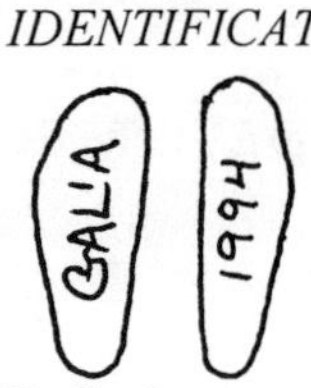

Dolls, bottom of feet, year made

Other pieces marked with full name and year made

CATEGORY:
Accessories; Dolls: original; Figures: historical

HONORS:
IGMA Fellow 1980; Exhibit: Rosalie Whyel Museum of Doll Art, Bellevue, Washington

BAZYLKO, GALIA, continued

RECOGNITION:

Nutshell News, Jan. 1986; Feb. 1986; Mar. 1986; Apr. 1986; May 1986; Jun. 1986; Jul. 1986; Aug. 1986; Sept. 1986; Oct. 1986; Nov. 1986; Nov. 1988; Nov. 1989; Mar. 1991; May 1991; Jul. 1991; Oct. 1991; Nov. 1991; Jan. 1992; Apr. 1992; Jun. 1992; Jan. 1993; Apr. 1993; Jun. 1993; Sept. 1993; Jul. 1993; Nov. 1993; Jan. 1994; *Small Talk*, Nov. 1978; *Miniature Gazette*, Spring 1980; *Miniature Collector*, Jan. 1980; Jan. 1987; *Doll Reader*, Nov. 1993, pg. 151

BIOGRAPHY:

Over the course of 20 years, Galia Bazylko's exquisitely detailed one-inch scale figures have become legendary for their historically accurate costuming and the breathtaking realism of the figures themselves. Beginning her career in miniatures while still a teenager, and through her five-year course of study at the University of Washington, majoring in Costume Studies and Textile Science, Galia's focus has always been to create dolls of precise proportion and refinement. All of her figures are one-of-a-kind and costumed in the finest antique laces and silks. No molds of any kind are used.

Galia has received much recognition through her articles for miniature publications, including several extensive series of articles on: the First Ladies of the United States; Legends of Stage and Screen; and most recently, Royal Portraits; all of which feature photographs of portrait figures created by Galia. Her work has been exhibited internationally and may be seen in the collections of several museums, including the Rosalie Whyel Museum of Doll Art in Bellevue, Washington, which owns Galia's one-inch Russian Orthodox Wedding. She has recently begun creating large scale dolls including several 31-inch portrait figures for the Whyel Museum.

ARTISAN: **BEALS, JUDY**

BUSINESS NAME: The J. Beals Studio

IDENTIFICATION MARKS:

CATEGORY:

Accessories; Furniture

HONORS:

IGMA Artisan 1988; Craftsmanship Award, It's A Small World 1979

RECOGNITION:

Nutshell News, Vol. 16, No. 7, Jul. 1986, pg. 48-50, "A New Perspective," Emily Kendall; *Miniatures Showcase*, Summer 1990, Cover, pg. 11, 26-27; *How To Build Miniature Furniture and Room Settings*, Judy Beals, Kalmbach Publishing Co., 1983

AUTOBIOGRAPHY:

It was 1976, I was almost ready to give birth to my daughter, Amanda, and found myself confined to quarters by the doctor. That summer was long and hot. I needed to think of ways to keep busy and decided to make Christmas presents. My niece was going to get a dollhouse that her father had built for her that year. I decided to furnish it as my gift to her. So with balsa wood and a razor blade, I blazed my trail into miniatures. To me, the process of design and construction was so fascinating that after the Christmas gift was done, I wanted to start all over again. My mission was to create the perfect miniature no matter how long it took. So I began to invest in tools and equipment, making some upholstered pieces which a local hobby shop was interested in selling. It was then that I realized what my new career would be and The J. Beals Studio began. I was able to do what I loved and share it with others. It's been 17 years, including artisan membership in IGMA, a book in its second printing, and thousands of miniature components, but I still enjoy the mental challenge of miniature design and the happiness that my pieces bring to others.

ARTISAN: **BECKER, GEORGE** (Submitted by Pat Arnell)

IDENTIFICATION MARKS:

Becker

Block script last name only, with year
Letter code in block letters (1981 - AT)

Some pieces may have date and © only

Larger pieces, Metal Plate engraved in block letters **Made by George Becker**

CATEGORY:
Bathroom: period; Bars; Fireplaces: settings; Furniture: period

ARTISAN: **BECKWITH, JAMES W.**

BUSINESS NAME: Beckwith Miniatures

IDENTIFICATION MARKS:

JB

CATEGORY:
Brasswork; Lathe Work: hand turned

HONORS:
IGMA Artisan; Exhibit: Toy & Miniature Museum of Kansas City

RECOGNITION:
Nutshell News, Jun. 1983, Cover; *Miniatures Catalog*, 5th Edition, pg. 354

AUTOBIOGRAPHY:
see Judy Beckwith

ARTISAN: **BECKWITH, JUDY**

BUSINESS NAME: Beckwith Miniatures

IDENTIFICATION MARKS:

J. BECKWITH

printed with year

CATEGORY:
Paintings: watercolor

HONORS:
IGMA Fellow; Exhibits, Children's Museum of New York; Toy & Miniature Museum of Kansas City

RECOGNITION:
Nutshell News, Jun. 1983; *Miniature Collector*, No. 31, pg. 30-31; *Miniatures Catalog*, 5th Edition, pg. 327

BECKWITH, JUDY, continued

AUTOBIOGRAPHY:

Our miniature careers began when a friend saw one of Judy's miniature paintings (4 x 5 inches). She said can't you paint any smaller, and we asked why? She indicated that there were many miniature enthusiasts that collected one-inch scale creations. So, Judy started painting real miniatures and Jim helped by doing the matting and the framing. We received valued advice on this new venture from Paul Runyon, a top cabinetmaker, superb miniaturist and family friend.

Judy continued to paint her watercolor paintings while Jim found that just doing frames was very tedious and exacting work. So he purchased a miniature lathe to make turned easels for Judy's paintings. Soon he was making fine accessories such as candle sticks, bowls, and plates out of brass and wood. Judy became a Fellow in IGMA and Jim also became an Artisan. Judy served on the board of directors during the early years of the guild.

ARTISAN: BEERS, BRIAN & SUZANNE

BUSINESS NAME: Bearly Big Enough

IDENTIFICATION MARKS:

BBE
with year

CATEGORY:

Furniture: handpainted

RECOGNITION:

Nutshell News, Nov. 1992, Show Scene

AUTOBIOGRAPHY:

Bearly Big Enough was created after Brian and I designed and built a large saltbox house for our teddy bears to live in. We began to furnish it using kits, then made changes to the kits and finally, built our own furniture. After attending a few miniature shows we decided to sell our own furniture which was the beginning of Bearly Big Enough in 1989. All our furniture is hand-crafted, painted and antiqued to a warm finish. Many of the designs are taken from full-size pieces. Our scale is one-inch equals one-foot. The paintings are all done free hand and give a uniqueness and individuality to our work. Though our teddies are now homeless (we sold the saltbox) it is because Bearly Big Enough is busy selling its furniture to people and shops all over the United States.

ARTISAN: BEGLAN, MARIE-FRANCE

IDENTIFICATION MARKS:

Unmarked

CATEGORY:

Accessories; Dolls: dolls' dolls; Toys

HONORS:

British Toy Guild

RECOGNITION:

Dolls House World; Home Miniaturist; Nutshell News; Dolls in Miniature

BEGLAN, MARIE-FRANCE, continued

AUTOBIOGRAPHY:

I bought a dolls house for my daughter in 1980, it all started there and then. I did my first fair in 1983, and I have been making dolls and accessories since then, non-stop, even during holidays! I do two fairs in England and two fairs in France each year.

ARTISAN: **BELL, JEANNE**

BUSINESS NAME: Wee Three

IDENTIFICATION MARKS:

Some pieces unmarked

Three dimensional Gold Tone bell, ¼" H x ¼" W

CATEGORY:

Needlework

HONORS:

IGMA Fellow; Exhibit: Toy & Miniature Museum of Kansas City

RECOGNITION:

Miniature Collector; No. 52, Spring 1986, pg. 20; No. 54, Fall 1986, pg. 38; *Antiques & Collecting*, Dec. 1987, pg. 42; *Dollmaking*, Vol. 8, No. 3, Fall 1992, pg. 25

AUTOBIOGRAPHY:

I graduated from college in 1943 with a Bachelor of Arts degree in Music, and have also studied a number of other Fine Arts. I was born in 1922 and can remember doing needlework from the time I was five years old. Over the years I have done knitting, crocheting, needlepoint, cross stitch, sewing, tatting and have also drawn work. In 1982, I started doing miniature scale needlework in all the above needlework categories.

ARTISAN: **BELL-SPANN, DEIDRA**

BUSINESS NAME: Ayanna Doll Sculptures

IDENTIFICATION MARKS:

ayanna doll sculptures

d.b.s. '92
d.b. SPANN '92 — Used when space is limited

d. BELL-SPANN '92 — 1991 to present

CATEGORY:

Dolls; Kits: doll; Molds; Publications, How-to; Writer

HONORS:

IGMA Fellow

BELL-SPANN, DEIDRA, continued

RECOGNITION:

Nutshell News, Mar. 1984, pg. 72-75; *Miniature Collector,* Fall 1985, pg. 26-28; *Baltimore Business Journal,* Feb. 1988, Vol. 5, No. 37, pg. 1, 25

AUTOBIOGRAPHY:

I am a Designer, Artist by profession turned Doll Maker in 1973 when my mother literally dragged me off kicking and screaming to a doll making class. Doll Making in miniatures and full-scale was self-taught as was the sculpting of human forms.

I received my Master of Fine Arts from Howard University. One year after leaving college, much to my surprise, I became fascinated with miniatures and even turned down a head designer job at a major textile company in New York, to pursue miniature doll design. I travel extensively over the country teaching and doing shows.

ARTISAN: BELLINGER, ARLENE

IDENTIFICATION MARKS:

Arlene Printed cloth label

CATEGORY:

Flowers & Plants; Millinery; Quilts

ARTISAN: BELLOUS, GINA C.

BUSINESS NAME: Gina C. Bellous Creations

IDENTIFICATION MARKS:

CATEGORY:

Dolls: porcelain

HONORS:

IGMA Artisan 1994; Exhibit: The Carole & Barry Kaye Museum of Miniatures, Los Angeles, California

RECOGNITION:

Nutshell News, Feb. 1994, pg. 36-40, "Portraits in Porcelain," Jeanne Delgado; Oct. 1994, pg. 53; *Miniatures Showcase*, Fall 1991, pg. 29; Summer 1991, pg. 21, 22, 35, 37; Fall 1991, pg. 29, 41; Winter 1992, pg. 39; *Dolls In Miniature*, Summer 1991, pg. 67

AUTOBIOGRAPHY:

I have been making miniature porcelain dolls since 1987. I started specializing in custom portrait dolls within the last two years, and have done many interesting dolls for clients. The Phantom of the Opera – L.A. Company asked me to do a set of Phantom & Christine dolls for their charity auction to help fight Aids, November 15, 1992.

A set of these dolls will also be on display at The Carole & Barry Kaye Museum of Miniatures, Los Angeles, California. I have been commissioned to do Michael Jackson and stars from other Broadway plays to be featured at the museum. I have also donated dolls to various organizations for raffles.

ARTISAN: **BENFORD, JAMES**

IDENTIFICATION MARKS: (Submitted by William R. Robertson)

ARTISAN: **BENNETT, BONNIE H.**

BUSINESS NAME: Bonnie Bennett Handcrafted Miniatures

IDENTIFICATION MARKS:

BB

CATEGORY:

Accessories; Furniture; Toys

RECOGNITION:

Nutshell News, May 1981, pg. 32-34; *Miniatures Showcase*, Fall 1986, pg. 44; Spring 1987, pg. 56; Summer 1987, pg. 35; *Through The Looking Glass*, Ann Ruble, Boynton and Associates, Inc., 1984, pg. 18

AUTOBIOGRAPHY:

For years my father, Marshall Harrison, was employed by Newport News Shipbuilding to build models of all the ships constructed at the shipyard. His exceptional talent overflowed into his home life and, as a child, I had wooden boats to float in the bathtub, dollhouse furniture and a wonderfully crafted miniature circus.

Although I had always been fascinated by tiny things, it wasn't until I had children of my own and began building my daughter a dollhouse that I discovered not only great enjoyment in designing and building miniatures but also some obviously inherited ability in art, carpentry and working in small-scale.

With the help of my Dad, my new "hobby" developed into a business specializing in nursery furniture and toys, which were sold through shops, mail order and miniature shows. It was at a show that I met Ann Ruble Molpus, at that time the editor of *Nutshell News*. Following that meeting, an article featuring my work was written for the magazine. Shortly there after, while living in Northern Virginia not far from the *Nutshell News* offices, I was offered the position of Special Projects Editor. For 13 years I test built and edited how-to articles, designed and built rooms for cover photos, assembled kits, wrote reviews and covered shows. A terrific job, I was blessed to have had the opportunity to do what I enjoy so much and at the same time work with and meet many wonderful and talented people in the miniatures field.

ARTISAN: **BENNETT, JANICE L.**

BUSINESS NAME: Janice L. Bennett

IDENTIFICATION MARKS:

Unmarked

CATEGORY:

Accessories; Floral Arrangements; Flowers & Plants

HONORS:

IGMA Fellow

BENNETT, JANICE L., continued

RECOGNITION:

Nutshell News Calendar, Apr. 1986, *Miniatures Showcase*, Fall 1987, pg. 11, 24, 30-31, 42, 48; Spring 1988, pg. 8, 13, 22; Summer 1988, pg. 58; Fall 1988, Cover, pg. 9, 19, Winter 1988, Cover, pg. 9, 44-45; Spring 1989, pg. 56; Summer 1989, pg. 30; Winter 1989, pg. 31, 35; Spring 1990, pg. 41-42; Summer 1990, pg. 21-22, 41; Fall 1990, pg. 35, 82; Winter 1990, pg. 18, 44; Winter 1991, pg. 24, 62; Spring 1992, pg. 30-33; Winter 1992, pg. 61

ARTISAN: BENNETT, JENNIFER & HERBERT

BUSINESS NAME: The Bennetts
Hand & Heart

IDENTIFICATION MARKS:

H+H	JBH
1972 - 1977	1977 to present

CATEGORY:

Accessories: period, wooden; Dishes: porcelain; Furniture; Porcelain: handpainted

RECOGNITION:

Nutshell News; Miniatures Showcase, Vol. 1, Fall 1986, pg. 12; Vol. 4, No. 1, Winter 1989 pg. 43; Vol. 4, No. 2, Spring 1989, pg. 35; Vol. 5, No. 1, Winter 1990, pg. 36; Vol. 8, No. 5, Sept. 1993, pg. 34-35, 38-39; *St. Louis Post Dispatch*, Dec. 19, 1973, Everyday Magazine, Cover Story, pg. 1E; Sept. 20, 1978, Everyday Magazine, Cover Story, pg. 1F

AUTOBIOGRAPHY:

We started in miniatures in 1973, when we both retired. The first project was building dollhouses and country stores. We made ten dollhouses, sold six and still have four; made three stores and kept two of those. We soon switched to accessories and in the past 20 years have made and discontinued several hundred items. We presently make about 200 different items. Herbert makes furniture and wood accessories of what Wallace Nutting called "the Pilgrim Century." Jennifer makes porcelain dishes and accessories. We both collaborate in items of wood with petit point, such as footstools, pole screens, boxes, etc.

We started out by doing retail shows, and did them for about 10 years. We were charter members of CIMTA and did their shows for about five years. For the past five years we have worked strictly mail order, both wholesale and retail. We are both in our 80's now and slowing down some. Down but not out!

ARTISAN: BENNETT, JILL

BUSINESS NAME: J Designs

IDENTIFICATION MARKS:

Individual pieces unmarked

J
Designs

Company logo

BENNETT, JILL, continued

CATEGORY:
Dolls: dolls' dolls

HONORS:
Toymaker of the Year, British Toymakers' Guild

RECOGNITION:
Nutshell News; Contemporary Dolls Magazine; Dolls House World; Dolls in Miniature

ARTISAN: **BENSON, RON** (Deceased)

BUSINESS NAME: Ron Benson

IDENTIFICATION MARKS:

1980 to present

CATEGORY:
Porcelain; Reproductions: porcelain

HONORS:
Exhibit: Toy & Miniature Museum of Kansas City

RECOGNITION:
Nutshell News; Miniature Collector, No. 47, pg. 29; *Miniatures Showcase*

AUTOBIOGRAPHY:
I have been working with miniatures since the second grade. My teacher gave me an orange crate to use as I liked, and my friend's sister gave me a ½-inch scale mantle. I made a Walt Disney house using books for walls. I worked in a visual ½-inch scale.

My training was in History and Theatre. I graduated from the University of Texas at El Paso, in 1967, and was in the antiques and museum field before starting miniatures. My specialty in full-size antiques is furniture!

ARTISAN: **BENZELL, JOAN**

BUSINESS NAME: Joan's Bisque Be'Be's
Petite Porcelain Ltd.

IDENTIFICATION MARKS:

1980 to present

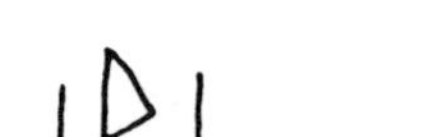

1978 to present

1978 to 1982

BENZELL, JOAN, continued

CATEGORY:

Costuming; Dolls: antique reproductions, babies, children, molds, original, porcelain; Kits: dolls

HONORS:

IGMA Fellow 1984; NAME AOH 1994; Honorary Chairman 1993, "Pirates, Buccaneers, & Privateers," Gulf South Miniature & Dollhouse Event, New Orleans, Louisiana; Original Doll Artist Council of America, 1994

RECOGNITION:

Nutshell News, Vol. 12, No. 7, Jul. 1982; *Miniature Collector*, No. 39, Oct. 1983; No. 88, Mar/Apr. 1995, pg. 30-35, "Doll Artist Joan Benzell," Dougless Strickland Bitler; *Doll Crafter*, Oct. 1990; *The Doll Artisan*, Vol. 2, No. 4, Apr/May 1979; Vol. 3, No. 4, Apr/May 1980; Vol. 5, No. 5, Jun/Jul. 1982; Vol. 6, No. 2, Dec. 1982/Jan. 1983; Vol. 7, No. 1, Oct/Nov. 1983; *Small Dolls,* Vol. 1, 1992

BIOGRAPHY:

Joan Benzell is a native of New Jersey, having lived in New York state for 18 years and returning to New Jersey in 1983. She always enjoyed sewing, painting and dolls. A graduate of The Berkeley School of Business, she was an Executive Secretary in an engineering office for several years.

Joan and her husband Lou were high school sweethearts. They have four children, Lauri, Lisa, Louis and Lance, and many grandchildren, all of whom love and appreciate the dolls created in the Benzell household.

In 1976, after eight years of teaching in her own ceramic studio, "Joan's Kiln Korner," Joan decided to close the door and combine her love of dolls with her knowledge of porcelain and china painting. Adding her creative ability in dressmaking she began to produce collectible dolls ranging in size from 10" to 18". In February of 1977, she successfully began to make dollhouse doll reproductions. In 1983, she created her own originals in one-inch scale. Both her reproductions and originals have won 1st place ribbons and other special awards.

Joan gets much support from her husband. While she was learning about making dolls, Lou learned about mold making. Together their venture makes a successful team. Joan's dolls are sold under the name of Joan's Bisque Be'Be's.

In 1989, a new family of dolls was created for the wholesale market. These dolls are sold under the name of Petite Porcelain Ltd. In 1986, in a joint effort with Susan Sirkis, a one-inch scale half doll was created and called a "Footloose" doll.

Joan has written numerous articles relating to all phases of miniature doll making. She lectures and presents slide programs and has exhibited her dolls in museums and special exhibits in the Northeast.

She has been a member of the Doll Artisan Guild since its formation and is an instructor of miniature dolls as well as a senior judge for their competitions since 1978. In addition she teaches seminars and workshops in all phases of miniature dollmaking throughout the United States.

In 1976 Joan became a member of United Federation of Doll Clubs. She has held the office of President for two terms in the Jersey Cape Doll and Toy Club and was Chairman of a Regional Conference held in Ocean City, New Jersey in 1994.

Joan has been a member of NAME since 1977. She has served as Regional Coordinator for M-1. In 1990 she was Chairman of M-1's Regional Houseparty in Atlantic City. In 1992 she Co-Chaired the National Houseparty in Philadelphia. In 1984 she was elected to status of Fellow in the International Guild of Miniature Artisans. In 1993 she was Honorary Chairman for the Annual Miniature & Dollhouse Event sponsored by the National Kidney Foundation of Louisiana in New Orleans.

ARTISAN: **BERGMAN, BETH**

BUSINESS NAME: In A Miniature Manor

IDENTIFICATION MARKS:

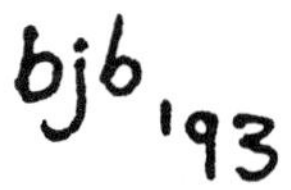

All lower case

BERGMAN, BETH, continued

CATEGORY:

Furniture: handpainted

RECOGNITION:

The Concord Tribune, North Carolina, Sunday, Jul. 28, 1991

BIOGRAPHY:

Beth began her formal art training in the fourth grade, attending a children's art school held after regular class for three years. She continued to study art in high school and college. A trip to Ireland in 1984 inspired her to change from oils to pastels and her work won many awards in area art shows, including a purchase award in a national drawing competition. Meanwhile, she earned a living in the field of graphic design.

Beth's interest in miniatures dates back to childhood, as she and her sister had a wonderful huge, old wooden dollhouse given to them by an aunt. Beth recalls trying to make furniture for it. She had the good sense to hang onto the house when it was no longer a plaything.

Living in Charlotte, North Carolina for many years, Beth visited the Southern Christmas Show's Enchanted Village exhibit of miniatures, which introduced her to today's miniature world. One year she decided to bring out the old dollhouse and fix it up. Before that project was finished she had bought a kit for another house, and was thoroughly hooked on miniatures.

Being creative by nature, Beth has always enjoyed building her miniatures and making much of the contents. The idea for making miniature furniture to sell came at a show where she saw some import furniture that had been painted over. Thinking "I can paint better than that, plus I can make the furniture better," launched what is now In A Miniature Manor, Beth's business that specializes in handmade furniture with a stained finish over which she paints various designs or scenes. Most of the work has been in one-inch scale, but ½-inch is being added and ¼-inch being considered.

ARTISAN: **BERMAN, JUDY** (Deceased)
(Submitted by Phyllis S. Tucker)

BUSINESS NAME: Chrysnbon, Inc.

IDENTIFICATION MARKS:

Unmarked

Heritage in Miniatures

CHRYSNBON

Logo

CATEGORY:

Accessories; Kits: furniture

HONORS:

NAME AOH 1985; Mell Prescott Award 1989; IGMA Crystal Award 1994

RECOGNITION:

Enterprise Publications, 1967; *The Citizen,* 1972; *Homestyle,* 1974; *Suburban Life*, 1976; *Miniatures Dealer*, Nov. 1981, Cover Story

AUTOBIOGRAPHY:

About 1967 my son John gave me a magnificent replica of a theatre console electric organ. It needed a special home and we built a four-room doll house in an old fashion door in my home. Then I began to make little things. I started to make dreams come true, first for myself and then for others on a small scale. Nostalgia played a large part in what we began. It became a "cause" to preserve a part of America's heritage and to find a way to bring quality miniature furniture to a large number of people. It was never my intention to offend artisans turning out quality pieces or belittle the use of fine wood. I wanted to create a product in a medium available to the average individual.

I designed the pieces and my son John engineered them for production. We created them in high impact polystyrene for the flexibility and detail. We chose to offer the pieces in kit form both for shipping ease and effective cost. This also allowed even a beginner to create a "master piece" at the lowest price. The more people involved in miniatures on any level, the more the demand for fine miniature work would eventually evolve.

I probably helped to standardize the one-inch scale as it was simple and easy for me to understand. Although my little organ John made was in 1½-inch scale, I had trouble with that math, so we created our kits in what is now the industry standard. Although I am no longer directly involved in the production, I still feel a part of the sharing. Filling a need for my own self expression and giving that same opportunity to others through my kits has been one of the joys of my life.

ARTISAN: **BERNIER, JANE, DDS**

BUSINESS NAME: Borrower's Press

IDENTIFICATION MARKS:

All books signed Jane Bernier, in script, and numbered

CATEGORY:

Author; Books: binder, miniature; Designer; Printer; Publications; Publisher; Writer

HONORS:

IGMA Fellow; Exhibit: Toy & Miniature Museum of Kansas City

AUTOBIOGRAPHY:

I am a miniature book artist, designer, printer, binder, and publisher, doing this for about 11 years from 1974 to 1985. I have not published since 1985, when I graduated from Case Western Reserve University, Dental school.

ARTISAN: **BERSE, SHIRLEY**

BUSINESS NAME: Be Original

IDENTIFICATION MARKS:

 1987 to present

 1987 to present

CATEGORY:

Beds; Dolls: Dresden, porcelain; Furniture: wicker; Kits

HONORS:

Honorary Chairman 1991, "Flappers and Fast Living," Gulf South Miniature & Dollhouse Event, New Orleans, Louisiana

RECOGNITION:

Nutshell News, Sept. 1992, pg. 73-74

AUTOBIOGRAPHY:

I attended Washington Irving School, and The Art Institute, in New York, majoring in Textile Design. Since 1972 I have been teaching silversmithing at Chastain Art Center for the city of Atlanta. I have always been a hobbyist with a passion for HO, Z, and N scale trains. I have been building my own towns on my model railroad layout never realizing it would lead me to miniatures.

I now specialize in the construction and design of ½-inch and ¼-inch scale wicker furniture, ¾-inch high Dresden type porcelain dolls and ½-inch gold plated brass beds.

ARTISAN: **BESHENKOVSKY, NATASHA**

BUSINESS NAME: Natasha Fine Handpainted Miniatures

IDENTIFICATION MARKS:

CATEGORY:

Art: objects; Furniture: handpainted

HONORS:

IGMA Artisan; Club de la Miniature Française, The Pen and Brush, Inc.; Exhibit: Toy & Miniature Museum of Kansas City

RECOGNITION:

Nutshell News; Miniature Collector; Antiques & Collectors Hobbies; Town and Country; Le Figaro; Antiques & the Arts Weekly

BIOGRAPHY:

Natasha was born in Moscow, USSR. She studied painting at the Moscow Art School of the Academy of Fine Arts, from 1956 to 1963. She graduated from the Institute of Cinema, in 1968 as a Film Director, specializing in Animation, and worked at the Central Studio of Animated Films, in Moscow as a Director of Animation, set designer and screenwriter from 1968 through 1977.

She moved to the United States in 1978. Working as a miniature painter and designer of miniature art objects, decorates furniture in period styles from Renaissance to Art Nouveau, shadow boxes, music boxes, fans and jewelry. Her work is included in most major private collections and museums of miniature art in the USA, Canada, Latin America and Europe. Natasha also works as a painter in watercolor.

ARTISAN: **BIGGERS, JULIAN**

BUSINESS NAME: JLB Miniatures

IDENTIFICATION MARKS:

Monogram/Brand

number in series

in gold

CATEGORY:

Furniture

HONORS:

IGMA Artisan 1984, Fellow 1987

BIGGERS, JULIAN, continued

RECOGNITION:

Nutshell News, Vol. 21, No. 12, Dec. 1991, pg. 60-63; Vol. 17, No. 9, Sept. 1987, pg. 92-94

AUTOBIOGRAPHY:

I began 50 years ago with model airplanes, at a time when you had to cut all the pieces out of a sheet of balsa. Eventually I moved on to model ships after a short five year detour making military figures. I discovered miniatures on a trip to England and seeing Queen Mary's doll house. I made my first piece, a desk in 1981, just as a change of pace from model ships. It sold at a local store and I have not made a ship since. I became a Guild Artisan in 1984, and attended the "Master's" class taught by Dennis Hillman at the Guild School. I became a Guild Fellow in 1987, and have been teaching at the Guild school in Castine, Maine since 1988. I graduated from the University of Texas, Austin, with a Ph.D. in Educational Psychology, and am a Professor of Educational Psychology at Texas Tech University.

ARTISAN: BILLEN, RUTH V. & HAROLD J.

BUSINESS NAME: Ruth V. Billen

IDENTIFICATION MARKS:

CATEGORY:

Frames; Mirrors; Paintings

AUTOBIOGRAPHY:

I am an artist who, by chance, "went small." I bought a dollhouse at a garage sale for our two granddaughters, about 1980. Finishing the work on the furnishings, windows, etc. I knew the rooms needed paintings, no artist can abide empty walls! Harold always helped me frame my larger pieces, so I asked him to make the frames for a few tiny pieces I painted.

I painted small from that time on, giving it a rest for a few years, then returning to it when I retired from my office job a few years ago. On the second time around, I decided to mat my paintings, so all the pictures are matted in ovals or circles and framed with Harold's frames. We travel a lot and sell to shops across the US. A couple of years ago we also started making mirrors, which we decorate with wallpaper inserts.

ARTISAN: BINDER, SUZETTE LOEFFELL

BUSINESS NAME: Suzette Loeffell Originals

IDENTIFICATION MARKS:

Brass butterfly

CATEGORY:

Accessories; Chandeliers; Lighting

HONORS:

Exhibits: San Angelo Art Museum, San Angelo, Texas; The Palace of the Governors, Sante Fe, New Mexico

BINDER, SUZETTE LOEFFELL, continued

RECOGNITION:

Nutshell News, Sept. 1984, pg. 52-56; Oct. 1984; Sept. 1991, pg. 44-47

AUTOBIOGRAPHY:

I've always loved small things though dollhouse miniatures never occurred to me until 1976, when I saw an ad for a $30.00 Greenleaf kit in our newspaper, and thought that my husband and I might have fun making it. Before that time, I had been involved in theatre both on and off stage; also I had been an interior decorator and a dress designer of beaded appliquéed clothes; in other words, a craft minded bead lady. The four room San Francisco Victorian taught my husband, Dick, and me many possibilities, and we were hooked! Dick expressed his engineering ability in constructing and wiring that first house and all of the others since, as well as solving many interior problems for me.

We have been making historical, and in many cases, half timbered houses ever since, among which are a 1590 Tudor Manor house, a 1650 Nuremberg baby house, a 1775 French Chateau, and a 1900 Institute of Art. Currently we are working on an 1850 Russian peasant house, a 12th century Romanesque church, a 1870 Parisian Bakery and an 1850 English Georgian house. Each of our 20 houses and roomboxes has appropriate dolls in it and that collection numbers 150. The thrill of research and accuracy, and finding ways of creating miniatures which no one else makes is forever challenging and satisfying.

We sell my crystal chandeliers, French clocks, paintings and other accessories at English, French, and German shows. We've also done shows in New Mexico.

In gratitude for this exciting hobby and the resultant expertise, and for all the valuable associations we have given six dollhouses to children's hospital wards, to a 4H group for the children to furnish, and to children in need. We have helped 35 children with special problems to begin a roombox or house with a "magic shoe box" of goodies and ideas. I am now working with a 12 year old, talented, focused apprentice.

French miniaturist Denyse Denisselle said that she would like to live to be 200 years old because she had so much to do. Isn't that the truth? I feel the same way.

ARTISAN: **BIRD, COLIN**

BUSINESS NAME: Colin Bird

IDENTIFICATION MARKS:

CATEGORY:

Furniture

AUTOBIOGRAPHY:

I became interested in miniatures when visiting a fair, here in England, where my father Kenneth Bird was exhibiting his miniature water color paintings. I have been making furniture since 1990 and selling it mainly at fairs for the last two years. I specialize in Windsor chairs but also make tables and dressers. I am entirely self-taught. My full-time job is a telephone engineer.

ARTISAN: **BIRD, KENNETH J. F.**

BUSINESS NAME: Kenneth J. F. Bird

IDENTIFICATION MARKS:

K.J. F. Bird 1992 — Signature only in corner of painting
Signature & Year on back of framed picture

With year made

CATEGORY:
Paintings: watercolor

RECOGNITION:
Dolls House World, No. 14, 1991, pg. 37-39, "Focus On A Craftsman"

AUTOBIOGRAPHY:
Having always been attracted by the work of the Victorian water-colorists I have tried to recapture in my miniatures the charm and character of this period. I do not make precise copies of other artists' work; each painting is a genuine original work of art, and therefore very collectable.

My higher education started with a scholarship to Ipswich School of Art, Suffolk, England from 1937 through 1939. After the war I spent eight years as a free-lance commercial artist. From 1957 to 1986 I was first Head of Art & Publicity Studio, Reprographic Services, and the Printing Department at Pfizer Ltd., a worldwide Pharmaceutical Company. I have been creating miniature paintings since 1983.

ARTISAN: **BIRKEMEIER, WILLIAM & PEGGY**

BUSINESS NAME: Studio B Miniatures

IDENTIFICATION MARKS:

B — 1976 to 1988

CATEGORY:
Brasswork; Furniture; Lighting Devices; Tinware

RECOGNITION:
Nutshell News; The Scale Cabinetmaker; American Period Interiors in Miniature, Kate Doordan Klavan, 1984; *This Side of Yesterday*, Catherine B. MacLaren, 1975

ARTISAN: **BISHOP, TOM**

BUSINESS NAME: Miniland Inc.

IDENTIFICATION MARKS:

JB — Known as Tom Bishop, uses initial of proper first name, "John," in his mark

CATEGORY:
Furniture; Toys

ARTISAN: **BLACK, BARBARA**

BUSINESS NAME: Barbara's Miniatures

IDENTIFICATION MARKS:

Unmarked

CATEGORY:

Accessories; Clothing; Figures; Flowers and Plants; Food; Furniture: Southwestern; Holiday Items; Linens; Roomboxes; Tinware

RECOGNITION:

Miniatures Showcase, Fall 1987, pg. 14, 18, 24, 32, 43-44; Winter 1988, Cover, pg. 9-10; *Nutshell News*, Mar. 1989, Cover, pg. 65; Sept. 1992, pg. 72, Show Scene

BIOGRAPHY:

After her children were grown to high school age, Barbara decided to fulfill a long-held desire to build and furnish her own dollhouse. The result was a large, two story seven room adobe style house that was reminiscent of many in her native Santa Fe, New Mexico. This project took several months and, even now, years later, is still being added to.

While working on the house, Barbara discovered an interest and talent for creating unique and unusual items in miniature. Among her best recognized products are her various food items, particularly foods of the Spanish and Mexican Southwestern United States. Her choices of colors makes her food items particularly realistic.

Having won first place ribbons in every show in which it was entered, her dollhouse has not been exhibited for several years, but is still an on-going project. Her foods and some of the over 200 items Barbara creates have been shown on the pages of *Nutshell News, Miniatures Showcase* and other miniature hobby publications.

ARTISAN: **BLACKFORD, JAN**

BUSINESS NAME: Jan's Mini Magic

IDENTIFICATION MARKS:

CATEGORY:

Wicker

ARTISAN: **BLACKHAM, JACK**

BUSINESS NAME: Blackham's Studio

IDENTIFICATION MARKS:

CATEGORY:

Furniture; Marble

BLACKHAM, JACK, continued

HONORS:

IGMA Artisan 1981, Fellow 1984; Exhibit: Toy & Miniature Museum of Kansas City

RECOGNITION:

The Scale Cabinetmaker, Aug. 1979, pg. 44-45; *Miniature Collector*, Nov/Dec. 1986, pg. 18; Winter 1993, pg. 33; Spring 1994, pg. 24; Winter 1994, pg. 46-51; *Maison de Poupee*, Autumn 1992, pg. 7

BIOGRAPHY:

Jack Blackham was a mechanical engineer for General Electric and Martin Marietta, specializing in glass and glass machining. Jack, and his wife and partner, Mittsy, specialize in Marble in one-inch and ½-inch scale. Jack has been an instructor at the International Guild of Miniature Artisans Guild School in Castine, Maine since 1986. He is a member of IGMA and served on its Board of Trustees for six years, holding the position of President for two years. He also served an additional term of two years as Chairperson of the Guild Council for Fellow Selection.

ARTISAN: BLACKHAM, MITTSY

BUSINESS NAME: Blackham's Studio

CATEGORY:

Bears; Flowers & Plants; Furniture; Marble

HONORS:

IGMA Artisan 1989; Exhibit, Toy & Miniature Museum of Kansas City

RECOGNITION:

The Scale Cabinetmaker, Aug. 1979, pg. 44-45; *Miniature Collector*, Nov/Dec. 1986, pg. 18; Winter 1993, pg. 33; Spring 1994, pg. 24; Winter 1994, pg. 46-51; *Maison de Poupee*, Autumn 1992, pg. 7

BIOGRAPHY:

Mittsy Blackham started Blackham's Studio in 1974. She and her husband Jack specialize in marble and marble products in one-inch and ½-inch scale. She is a member of IGMA and has been the Administrative Assistant for the Guild since 1986. She has served on the Guilds Artisan Selection Committee and the Guild School Committee. Mittsy is a former Director of CIMTA.

ARTISAN: BLACKLOCK, WILLIAM GORDON

BUSINESS NAME: Gordon Blacklock

IDENTIFICATION MARKS:

Mark appears alongside the hallmark of the London Assay Office and is registered

CATEGORY:

Silver; Silversmith

BLACKLOCK, WILLIAM GORDON, continued

HONORS:

IGMA Artisan; Exhibit: Toy & Miniature Museum of Kansas City

RECOGNITION:

Nutshell News, Mar. 1988; *Antiques & Collecting Hobbies*, Feb. 1990, pg. 56-58; *International Dolls House News,* Summer 1986, Cover; 1991 Back Cover; *Home Miniaturist,* 1989

AUTOBIOGRAPHY:

I was trained through an apprenticeship to be an engineering fitter and turner. Over a period of 37 years I worked in a variety of jobs, as a coal mine, Merchant Navy, and finally in the Imperial Chemical Industries. During that time my interest kept going in Areo modeling and oil painting.

In 1977 I took a course in making jewelry working mainly with silver and gold. By 1981 I left my native industry to concentrate on making jewelry. By chance I met a man, through a mutual acquaintance, who made copper and brass miniatures. After further investigation into the hobby I decided to make them. I now concentrate solely on miniatures which I sell to 10 countries worldwide.

ARTISAN: BLACKWOOD, JOAN C.

BUSINESS NAME: Wee Beauties

IDENTIFICATION MARKS:

On foot

CATEGORY:

Dolls

RECOGNITION:

Nutshell News, Oct. 1983, pg. 50-52; Dec. 1984, Cover; *Concord Monitor,* newspaper 1984

BIOGRAPHY:

Joan was born in Newark, NJ on January 17, 1943. She has an older twin sister, Jane, who was actually responsible for introducing Joan to the world of miniatures. Neither Jane or Joan had any special training to prepare them for doll making. They both have natural talent and are quick to give God the credit for it. Joan graduated from Nyack College with a BS Degree in 1964. In addition to her doll making activities, she has also been busy teaching junior high school, specializing in Science and History.

The mark that Joan uses is the sign of the fish, which was used by early Christians, to indicate their faith. The two vertical lines in her mark indicate that she is the second in her family to make dolls.

ARTISAN: BLAKE, CAROL

BUSINESS NAME: Juno Originals

IDENTIFICATION MARKS:

JUNO

CATEGORY:

Glass: hand blown; Millinery; Pottery: Egyptian, Indian

RECOGNITION:

Miniature Gazette, Summer 1985, pg. 19; *Nutshell News,* Nov. 1987, pg. 88-90; *Miniatures Showcase,* Winter 1991, pg. 29

ARTISAN: **BLANKENFELD, BETTY**

BUSINESS NAME: Betty Blankenfeld
Victorian Miniatures

IDENTIFICATION MARKS:

Numbered month/year

CATEGORY:
Bathroom; Furniture: period; Kitchen

HONORS:
IGMA Artisan 1990

RECOGNITION:
Hobbies, Vol. 86, No. 12, 1982, pg. 52-53; Vol. 87, No. 2, 1982, pg. 58-59; *Rocky Mountain Miniature Journal*, Vol. 3, No. 2, 1983, pg. 7-9; *Nutshell News*, Jul. 1988, pg. 48-50

AUTOBIOGRAPHY:
At the time I started making miniatures in 1977, I had never seen any really good pieces, only children's dollhouse toy furniture. But I knew what it should look like, real furniture, but tiny, and it should have the character that antiques always seem to have.

I had helped refinish late Victorian furniture since my grade school days, so had an understanding of the way it was constructed. Between that and experience doing many kinds of crafts, drawing, painting, and a love of making things, I had the perfect background when the miniature bug hit!

After producing the first dozen pieces, I started to get requests for special pieces, mostly copies of furniture that people had inherited or remembered from childhood. The excitement and challenge of making a new and different piece has kept me from concentrating on certain types or styles of pieces, but I do try to stay roughly within the period 1850 to 1935.

ARTISAN: **BLAUER, ELLEN KRUCKER**

BUSINESS NAME: The Peddler's Shop ®

IDENTIFICATION MARKS:

E K (Ellen Krucker) back of dinnerware 1967 to present
stamped on metal piece and on Chandeliers, 1974 to 1982

Made especially for you
by
Ellen K. Blauer

Woven label on carpets or signed in black ink
Ellen K. Blauer, with year

CATEGORY:
Carpets; Chandeliers; Dinnerware; Lighting; Rugs

HONORS:
IGMA Artisan; Exhibit: Toy & Miniature Museum of Kansas City

BLAUER, ELLEN KRUCKER, continued

RECOGNITION:

Nutshell News, Jan. 1996, pg. 38-43, "Maynard Manor Revisited," Sybil Harp; *Miniature Collector; Stars & Stripes; National Enquirer; Netherlands Magazine; San Francisco Examiner; Appearances on 5 TV Channels*

BIOGRAPHY:

Ellen Gaines Krucker studied as a pianist for the concert stage and gave it up to become a housewife and mother. After the death of her husband, with two young children to support she became a church organist and textile weaver. She won several national awards for her weaving and decided to start a mail order business selling weaving materials. Her business, The Peddler's Shop, also carried imported beads and metal jewelry findings.

Through correspondence and phone conversations, a great enthusiasm developed with John Blauer. Ellen, who had created some miniatures for her own collection, started to create commercially for The Miniature Mart. The secret of her success was a painstaking attention to detail, countless hours of research, jeweler-like craftsmanship, and a natural artistic talent, which has made her one of the world's leading miniature craftswomen. There are many firsts to her credit in the world of miniatures. She was the first to offer miniature wallpaper, which she researched and designed. The first to do a series of authentic Collector's Plates representing some of the most famous patterns from the world's leading china factories. She was the first to do a series of Christmas plates. The first to do reproductions in miniature of antique Coca-Cola trays, and was the only person granted permission by the Coca-Cola Company to recreate these items in miniature at that time. Over the years, John and Ellen's mutual interest blossomed into romance and love. On February 3, 1973, they were married at the Victoria and Albert Wedding Chapel in Carson City, Nevada.

ARTISAN: **BLAUER, JOHN MAYNARD**

BUSINESS NAME: The Miniature Mart ®

IDENTIFICATION MARKS:

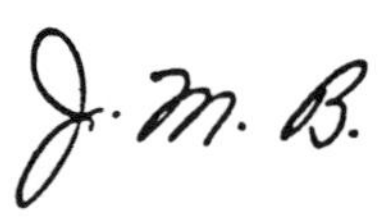

1956 to present, furniture pieces with accessories attached

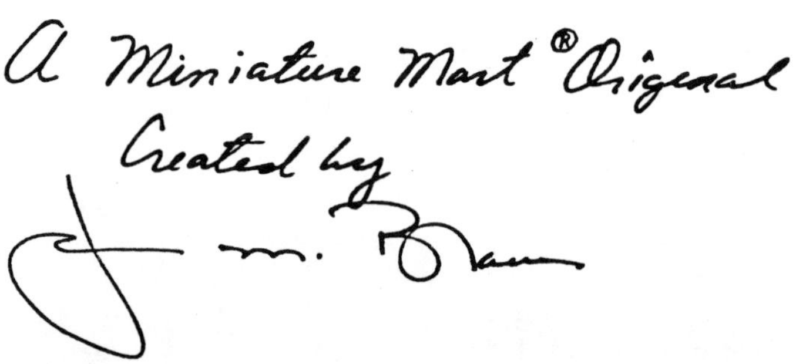

1956 to present, settings

used on Rogers Groups (a reproduction of styles like John Rogers) 1968 - 1985

CATEGORY:

Accessories; Chandeliers; Furniture; Lighting; Rogers Groups

HONORS:

IGMA Artisan; Exhibit: Toy & Miniature Museum of Kansas City

BLAUER, JOHN MAYNARD, continued

RECOGNITION:

Nutshell News, Jan. 1996, pg. 38-43, Maynard Manor Revisited, Sybil Harp; Mar. 1996, pg. 30-34, Maynard Manor, continued; *Miniature Collector; Hobbies Magazine; Stars & Stripes; National Enquirer; Netherlands Magazine; San Francisco Examiner;* Appearances on five TV Channels

BIOGRAPHY:

Born in San Francisco, December 31, 1926, John M. Blauer has been a collector and creator of miniatures since his early childhood. At the age of 14, he went to work for a theatrical costume house that supplied wardrobe for grand opera, stage plays and motion pictures. He continued working during summer vacations and weekends while he attended San Francisco State College, where he earned the Alpha Omega Best Actor Award in 1951, and returned to work full-time completing college.

His interest in miniatures and his fascination and appreciation of superior craftsmanship and microscopic detail come, he says, from his late father, Walter M. Blauer, a watchmaker for 50 years and foreman of the watch department of San Francisco's Shreve and Company. He also attributed his early interest in miniature furniture and household accessories to his mother, Etoile Millar Blauer, who often spoke of her extensive collection that was destroyed in the 1906 earthquake and fire. John started collecting in early childhood, always creating a background to exhibit his tiny belongings. Barnyards, jungles and circus settings were created to exhibit animals; battle fields and castles for lead soldiers and knights.

Through the years his tastes became more sophisticated and demanding until now he has the world's largest collection of perfectly scaled authentically accurate, one-inch to the foot miniatures. Over 8,000 of these Lilliputian treasures are housed in a 32 room structure called *Maynard Manor.* The structure which bears his grandmother's maiden name represents an English Manor house of the 1800s.

John had the opportunity to acquire several collections. The largest collection he purchased was from the widow of Jack Norworth, famous songwriter, whose "Shine On Harvest Moon" and "Take Me Out To The Ball Game" are now classics. There were over 10,000 pieces in Norworth's collection when he died in 1959. Norworth's father started the collection, while traveling throughout the world as treasurer with Buffalo Bill Cody's Wild West Show.

Several newspaper and magazine articles were published on John's collection, and such interest resulted from these publications that he decided to start a mail order business, the now famous Miniature Mart. The business was started principally to support his collecting habit, for once miniature collecting gets into the blood one is hooked for life!

In 1966 John started to correspond with a young widow, Ellen Gaines Krucker, and over the years their mutual interest blossomed into love and romance. They were married in 1973 in Carson City, Nevada. Many artists throughout the world create for them and their customers. Their studio is still in their home, a 22 room San Francisco Victorian built in 1876. Every room is dominated by a miniature setting or display case containing their vast collection. Blauer said recently that he and his wife had both been nonconformists at an early age. The 20th century has produced gigantic achievements, devastating wars, nuclear weapons, men on the moon, from early childhood everyone is told to "think big." John says "Ellen and I never could do this, we think small, and I guess we always will, principally because we really do appreciate the little things in life." John Blauer was one of the founders of NAME.

ARTISAN: **BLINKHORN, BRIAN**

BUSINESS NAME: Brian Blinkhorn

IDENTIFICATION MARKS:

Unmarked

If requested, signed  with date and name of purchaser

CATEGORY:

Chairs: Mediaeval Throne, Windsor; Furniture

BLINKHORN, BRIAN, continued

RECOGNITION:

International Dolls House News, Vol. 22, No. 2, Summer 1993, pg. 7; *Dolls House and Miniature Scene,* No. 4, Jun/Jul. 1993, pg. 38-39

AUTOBIOGRAPHY:

I started to make miniature furniture after accidentally entering a shop dedicated to doll house and one-inch scale miniatures, during 1990. I was immediately captivated! Having been a data processing professional for about 10 years, I had enough and was looking for a way out. At this time my wife's father had developed an interest in Windsor chairs, and showed me a number of catalogs of various traditional designs. Almost immediately I decided to make a one-inch scale smokers bow chair. Having limited woodwork experience and no wood turning experience I borrowed the relevant books from the local library, bought a lathe and spent many cold winter's evening in the garden shed. After three months of trial and error on the lathe I achieved what I considered to be an acceptable miniature chair. I spent the next few months developing my new skills and researching Windsor chairs. I became a full-time professional miniaturist late in 1991 and have an ever expanding range of Windsor chairs as standard products.

ARTISAN: BLODGETT, ANDREA GASTON

BUSINESS NAME: Cheź Andreé

IDENTIFICATION MARKS:

1980 to present

CATEGORY:

Dolls: Furniture, wicker

AUTOBIOGRAPHY:

At the age of 12 I began collecting antique dolls. By 1980 I found the cost of antique dolls was getting out of hand and discovered at the same time there were people making reproduction dolls. I took classes at that time and began with dollhouse dolls much to the surprise of my teacher. I have been working with one-inch scale miniatures since 1975. Although I still make the occasional doll I concentrate mostly in the design and creation of wicker furniture. My best friend saw my wicker, liked it and saw a market for it in Holland, if I would allow her to translate the instructions into Dutch. I have been selling, through her, in The Netherlands since 1986 and in the USA, through shops and at shows since 1989. I enjoy teaching classes in shops and for Miniature Clubs as requested. My wicker has been exhibited in both Belgium and the Netherlands.

ARTISAN: BOEKHOFF, TERRI A.

BUSINESS NAME: Quilts & Textile Arts in Miniature

IDENTIFICATION MARKS:

Some pieces unmarked

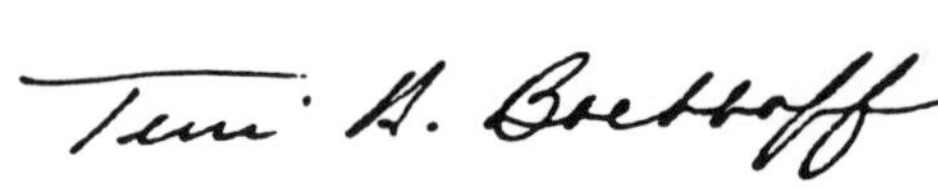

CATEGORY:

Quilts; Textiles

BOEKHOFF, TERRI A., continued

RECOGNITION:

Miniatures Showcase, Vol. 1, Fall 1986, Cover, pg. 14, 20; Vol. 3, No. 4, Fall 1988, pg. 34; Vol. 4, No. 1, Winter 1989, pg. 44; *Nutshell News*, Vol. 17, No. 1, Jan. 1987, pg. 22; Vol. 17, No. 8, Aug. 1987, pg. 22

AUTOBIOGRAPHY:

I graduated from the University of Iowa in 1981, with a BA in Art History. My areas of emphasis were Oriental Art, African Art and Textiles. I'm a lifelong seamstress, by trade, specializing in the making of full-size quilts. I am the owner and founder of Quilts & Textile Arts in Miniature, which I started in Iowa City, Iowa, in 1985. The business was sold in 1990 and I am currently the owner of Rod's Publishing in Iowa City. I am on the Board of Directors for Terrace Hill Society for Iowa's Governor's Mansion.

ARTISAN: **BOHLINGER, ARTHUR L.**

IDENTIFICATION MARKS:

1986 to present

CATEGORY:

Furniture: period

HONORS:

IGMA Artisan

AUTOBIOGRAPHY:

I am a retired mechanical engineer, and I started making miniature furniture as a hobby. Until now, I have only given pieces to friends and relatives as gifts. Attendance at the IGMA shows stimulated my desire to improve my work, and to concentrate primarily on miniature reproductions of period furniture, particularly those in the Queen Anne style.

ARTISAN: **BONNICE, SHERRY LYNN**

BUSINESS NAME: Mini Treasures

IDENTIFICATION MARKS:

JLM

Block letters, etched in porcelain back of body or shoulder plate

CATEGORY:

Dolls: porcelain; Kits: doll

RECOGNITION:

Dolls In Miniature, Vol. 3, No. 2, Summer 1993, pg. 79, 81, 84

AUTOBIOGRAPHY:

I have been doing miniature dolls since 1980. My dolls have been sold nationally by East Coast and West Coast sales reps, and have also sold Internationally through mail order. My mark JLM stands for Jesus loves me. I sell mostly miniature dolls ready-to-dress, but also do some dressed dolls.

ARTISAN: **BOORUM, PAM & PETE**

BUSINESS NAME: Smaller Than Life

IDENTIFICATION MARKS:

CATEGORY:

Accessories; Display Cases; Furniture; Tools

BIOGRAPHY:

Pam Boorum began making Colonial miniatures in 1979 after she and Pete took an evening course from Doug Howie at the High School in Peterborough, New Hampshire. Pete had been making full-scale period reproductions for several years and soon began designing and crafting furniture quality display cases.

A friend, John Nelson, who is an author and drafting teacher, became interested in helping Pam reduce many of the full-scale plans from his books to miniature. Pam has collected original drawings of several dozen pieces in this way. Pete started scaling and making his own miniature furniture in 1989. Smaller Than Life products can be seen through a few shows in the Northeast.

ARTISAN: **BOOTH, DAVID**

BUSINESS NAME: David Booth

IDENTIFICATION MARKS:

CATEGORY:

Chair: Windsor; Furniture

HONORS:

Three Gold Metals, *London Woodworker Show,* Miniature Section

RECOGNITION:

Miniature Collector, Winter 1987; *Dolls House World; Doll & Dolls House,* No. 1, Nov. 1988; *Nutshell News*

ARTISAN: **BORWICK, PATRICIA**

BUSINESS NAME: Patricia Borwick

IDENTIFICATION MARKS:

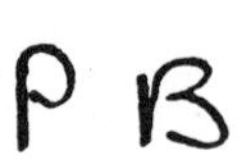

P B with date sewn into design

BORWICK, PATRICIA, continued

CATEGORY:

Carpets; Needlepoint; Needlework

HONORS:

Mulberry Bush Award, United Kingdom; Toronto Juried Show

AUTOBIOGRAPHY:

My training in interior decoration and design was in London. I never remember learning how to sew, however, I always did tapestry with my mother. The United Kingdom International press has mentioned me many times. I sewed carpets for Britannica House, which toured the world representing the best of British craftsmanship, and I have a carpet in the Oban collection, the best British Miniaturist of every decade. All the carpets and chair seats for Hever Castle collection are with John Hodgson. I am a member of the Embroiderers Guild.

ARTISAN: BOTKIN, MIKE & CHERREL

BUSINESS NAME: Miniature Cottage Shop

IDENTIFICATION MARKS:

CATEGORY:

Accessories; Shelves; Shops

AUTOBIOGRAPHY:

We have been making and selling miniatures since approximately 1982.

ARTISAN: BOWEN, RENÉE

BUSINESS NAME: Renée Bowen, Miniaturist
The Tin Feather

IDENTIFICATION MARKS:

CATEGORY:

Accessories; Furniture: Country, Shaker; Games; Kits: rug; Quilts

RECOGNITION:

Nutshell News, Jun. 1983; Dec. 1991, pg. 27; Jun. 1992, pg. 63-64; Aug. 1992, pg. 62; *Biddeford-Saco Journal*, Jun. 18, 1992; *Masters in Miniature, 12 Artisans At Work, Volume 1*, Anne Day Smith, Kalmbach Publishing, 1987, pg. 64-77

AUTOBIOGRAPHY:

I began making miniatures in 1975. My profession as an antiques dealer afforded me opportunity to use actual pieces as my models. My early pieces were mostly copies of antique toys, Shaker Furniture and accessories. The Shakers at Sabbathday Lake, Maine were most generous in letting me measure any of their pieces, so many of my Shaker pieces are native to Maine. My line has expanded through the years and now, in addition to Shaker Furniture, it includes American Country furniture, accessories, boxed games, quilts, rug kits for French knot rugs, and kits for needlepoint rugs.

My sales have been mostly through my own retail shop or mail order. I started doing shows only occasionally in 1981. My business locations through the years have been Kennebunk, Alfred, Paris Hill, and back to Kennebunk; all in Maine. I did business under the name of The Tin Feather for many years but dropped that name at the end of 1990 and am presently doing business under my name, in my shop, Antiques & Fine Miniatures, and I enjoy doing two or three shows a year.

ARTISAN: **BOYD, CAROL**

IDENTIFICATION MARKS:

CAROL BOYD 1993 C BOYD 1993

CATEGORY:

Dolls; Roomboxes: furnished; Vignettes: furnished

HONORS:

First Prize, United Federation of Doll Clubs 1972, 1976, 1980; First Place, Global Doll Society, Limburg, Germany 1984

RECOGNITION:

Nutshell News, Oct. 1988; Jan. 1990; *Miniatures Showcase*, Winter 1991; *Miniature Collector*, No. 20; *Miniature Gazette*, Winter 1984, Cover; Fall 1988; Summer 1992; *Petite Portraits*, Carol-Lynn Rossel Waugh

AUTOBIOGRAPHY:

I began building a dollhouse during our stay in Copenhagen, Denmark, in the late 1960's, where I met a Danish dollhouse museum owner who encouraged me. On return from Copenhagen in 1972, I began studying porcelain doll making seriously, originally by making full-sized reproductions of antique dolls. From there, I progressed to reproduction dollhouses and original porcelain dolls.

In 1976, during a posting in Italy, where my husband Bill was a diplomat, an Italian doll making friend and I made many reproductions from dolls in her collection. To help me, Bill learned the elements of mold making from an Italian artisan. Throughout the period, I continued to make miniature dolls for sale through the Washington Doll House and Toy Museum.

The diplomatic life, with its many representational responsibilities, made continuity in my doll making difficult. Although in 1972 and 1976, I won first prizes for costuming at the United Federation of Doll Clubs' national conventions and my reproduction of an antique Jumeau took first prize nationally in 1980. In 1984, three of my dolls took first place ribbons at the Global Doll Society meeting in Limburg, Germany. Portents of things to come, one of the prizes was for a scene featuring a doll collector.

When we returned to the States in 1985, I began seriously to work in miniatures, with a number of my scenes shown in local and national magazines. One effort, a "diet box," shows before-and-after views of a woman on a diet. Another, "Wet Cement," shows a mason whose work has just been trampled upon by a band of children. I've also done a "repose" series, which includes a woman in her garden, Repose Among the Posies, and a child in a laundry basket reading a story to her teddy bear, Repose in the Clothes. The latter won first prize at a teddy bear convention. My miniature needlework shop won first prizes at the prestigious Woodlawn Needlework Exhibition for best in category, best in show, and most popular. Two recent scenes dwelt on Americana. For the Philadelphia NAME Houseparty, Welcome Friends, I made a scene of newly arrived Vietnamese preparing for their first 4th of July, Friends We Have Welcomed; for Orlando, a mini Miss America pageant.

Although fascinated by and loving miniatures, dolls remain a strong interest for me. In constructing my scenes, I create the concept and do the interior decorating, but rely on my husband to be the carpenter and electrician. I continue to make all the dolls, make much of the furniture and, in outdoor scenes, do the landscaping.

ARTISAN: **BOYD, CECIL**

BUSINESS NAME: Cecil Boyd's Miniatures
Masterpiece Museum Miniatures
Tree House Studio

IDENTIFICATION MARKS:

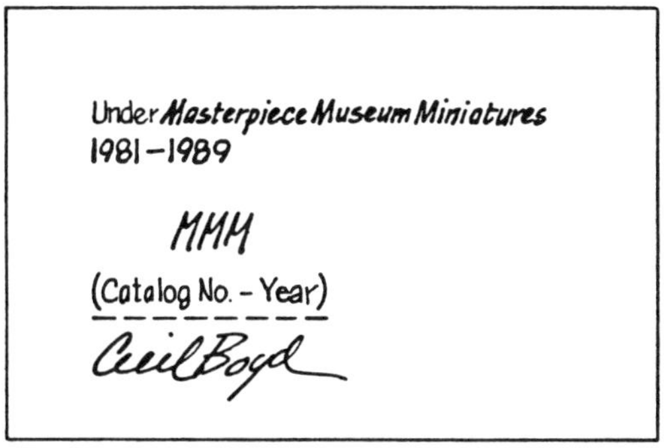

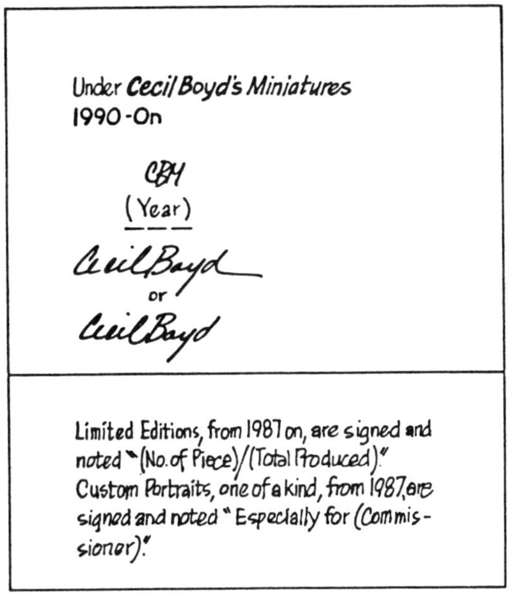

All pieces signed, identified and dated on the bottom

CATEGORY:
Dolls; Figures

HONORS:
IGMA Artisan 1987, Fellow 1990

RECOGNITION:
Commissioned by *National Handcraft Institute,* an affiliate of CBS, Inc., NY, to create an entire 1860 family to be marketed nationwide in kit form, 1978; *Creative and Collectible Miniatures*, Lillian Baker, Collector Books, 1984, Cover, plates, 11-14, 83, Color plates 1, 3-5, 9, 11-14, 17, Text, pg. 21-24; *Dollhouses and Dioramas*, Robert Schleicher, Chilton Book Co. 1980, pg. 88, 90, 119, 122-123; *Decorating & Crafts Ideas*, Oct. 1977, pg. 20-23; *Miniature Collector*, Winter 1988 pg. 16-18; *Nutshell News*, Mar. 1991, pg. 52-54

AUTOBIOGRAPHY:
I was born in 1926, growing up in Austin, Texas, where I graduated from Austin High School in 1944. My first job was with a department store display division. In 1949, I graduated from the University of Texas with a BFA in studio arts and art education. Alvin Boyd and I married in 1947. After graduating from college I took a position as a fashion illustrator in a Galveston, Texas department store, after which I worked as a medical illustrator for the University of Texas Medical Branch, Galveston in 1950. Our son Timothy was born in 1955.

After hurricane Carla in 1960, our family returned to Austin and I worked as a fine art painter at home. In 1965, I was as an illustrator in literature and graphic production for the Texas Parks & Wildlife Department. In 1970, I became an exhibit designer specializing in miniature settings and dioramas for the Visitor Center and park museum.

In 1977, I launched a studio business under the name of Masterpiece Museum Miniatures to provide a source of realistically precision-scaled, historically accurate human figures with an opening line of nine Victorian figures. I was commissioned in 1978 by the National Handcraft Institute, an affiliate of CBS, Inc. in New York, to create an entire 1860 family to be marketed nationwide in kit form.

By 1980, my line grew in numbers to include Roaring Twenties figures, nudes and contemporary figures. All work is still done by hand. I was appointed to the Board of Trustees to organize a Museum of Miniatures in the Southwest. The goal was reached in 1988 with the opening of the Southwest Miniature Collection in Dallas. I am honored as one of the founders.

My organization affiliations are: NAME 1978, Lone Star Miniaturists 1978, Society of American Miniaturists 1979, and the International Guild of Miniature Artisans 1986. The first NAME Houseparty I attended was in 1979. Since moving to Buda, Texas I established Tree House Studio, later changing the name of the business to Cecil Boyd's Miniatures. In 1992, I began offering portrait and customized figures as a popular specialty. I now offer over 50 different pieces.

ARTISAN: BOYTIM, THOMAS E.

BUSINESS NAME: Windsor Miniatures

IDENTIFICATION MARKS:

1977 to present

TB

CATEGORY:

Decoys; Furniture

HONORS:

IGMA Artisan

AUTOBIOGRAPHY:

I have been interested in miniatures since 1977. I am a 1970 graduate of West Point, University of Pennsylvania School of Dental Medicine, DMD, 1979 with a Residency in Periodontics, 1989. I am now a full-time US Air Force Periodontist.

ARTISAN: BRADLEY, CAROLINE K.

BUSINESS NAME: R C Miniatures

IDENTIFICATION MARKS:

CKB

CATEGORY:

Flowers and Plants; Food; Furniture

AUTOBIOGRAPHY:

I have no special miniature background, and am self-taught. I have attended workshops, and am now retired.

ARTISAN: **BRADLEY, RICHARD A.**

BUSINESS NAME: R C Miniatures

IDENTIFICATION MARKS:

RAB

CATEGORY:

Buildings; Dollhouse; Furniture; Structures

AUTOBIOGRAPHY:

I do not have any special miniature background. I have attended workshops, and am self-taught. I am now retired.

ARTISAN: **BRADSHAW, ROBERT W.**

BUSINESS NAME: Robert W. Bradshaw

IDENTIFICATION MARKS:

BOB BRADSHAW with date

R.W.B. RB smaller pieces

CATEGORY:

Dollhouse; Needlework; Paintings; Samplers; Tools

RECOGNITION:

British Newspapers

BIOGRAPHY:

Bob was born on the Fylde coast of Lancashire and studied at Manchester Regional College of Art. He worked in the display and exhibition industry in London and was, for several years responsible for the design of Blackpool Illuminations before becoming a full-time lecturer in display, ceramics and painting at Cassio College, Watford. Bob has always been very interested in models and miniatures both as a hobby and as a professional modelmaker.

Now having taken early retirement, he is able to devote time to producing dollhouses and miniatures, including furniture, fittings, tools, paintings and equipment. Not forgetting, the tiny embroideries and samplers by his wife Audrey all to the internationally recognized one-inch scale. "I try to capture the atmosphere and feel of the original as much as simply producing scale models."

ARTISAN: **BREHM, PAT**

BUSINESS NAME: Pat's Bloomers
Northwest Miniatures & Crafts

IDENTIFICATION MARKS:

Some unmarked

 1987 to present

BREHM, PAT, continued

CATEGORY:
Flowers and Plants

HONORS:
IGMA Artisan

RECOGNITION:
Miniatures Showcase, Summer 1991, pg. 57; *Miniature Gazette*, Fall 1992, pg. 60; *Nutshell News*, Feb. 1993, pg. 83

ARTISAN: BRENT, KAREN

BUSINESS NAME: BRENT

IDENTIFICATION MARKS:

Unmarked or  1980 to 1985 edition number incised

 1986 to 1988

 1988 to 1990 edition number and date

 1990 to present edition number and date

CATEGORY:
Animals: domestic, wildlife; Figures

HONORS:
IGMA Artisan

RECOGNITION:
Nutshell News, Feb. 1989, pg. 42-46; *A Book of Days, Then & Now*, Starr Ockenga, Houghton Mifflin Co. 1990

ARTISAN: BRIGGS, PAUL MICHAEL

IDENTIFICATION MARKS:

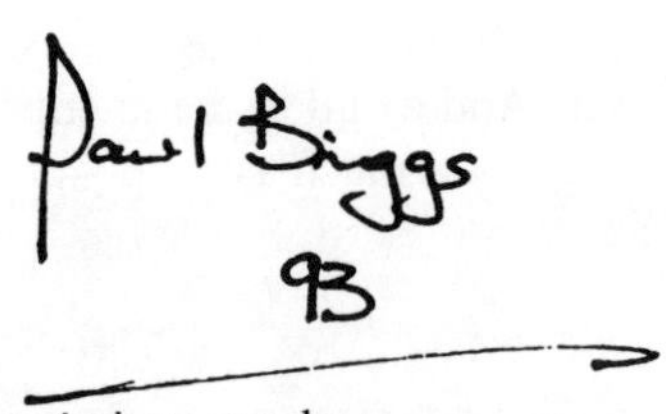

Initials on smaller pieces; All earlier pieces may have month and piece number

CATEGORY:
Marine

AUTOBIOGRAPHY:
I was born in Stockton-on-Tees, England in May 1947. I spent my early years in West Africa, but when I became school age lived in the United Kingdom. I studied Furniture & Industrial Design in the 1960's. My present position is as Senior Lecturer in Furniture & Product Design at the Trast Nottingham University. I spent one year as exchange professor at Kansas, USA, 1979-80 when I first got interested in miniatures.

BRIGGS, PAUL MICHAEL, continued

As a hobby I made model aircraft since the age of seven, specializing in scale rubber power. I have won many awards at International and National levels. In the miniature world I specialize in marine subjects, and much of my work being limited editions is done on a part time basis. I hope to take early retirement and then do my miniatures full-time.

ARTISAN: **BRIKE, BETTI**

BUSINESS NAME: Betti's Mini Mine

IDENTIFICATION MARKS:

Some unmarked

BB + date 1987 to present, small pieces

Betti Bee 1979 to 1987, on dolls

Address label on accessories

CATEGORY:

Accessories; Dolls: character; Figures; Sculptures

RECOGNITION:

Mississippi Press Plus, Dec. 9, 1982; Feb. 9, 1983; Aug. 13, 1991

AUTOBIOGRAPHY:

My work in miniatures started in 1978 after I viewed the Cornelia Vanderbilt Whitney touring dollhouse at the Jacksonville, Florida Children's Museum. I fell in love with the whole concept of miniaturing. Trial and error and stubborn determination have been my main source of education, but did gain some expertise from having worked at a costume and evening wear shop for some time. Also, arts and crafts of every kind have always been a part of my life.

A homemaker and craftsperson, I am relatively unknown as fame goes, but I have contributed several pieces of my work to charitable organizations, The National Kidney Foundation of Louisiana, and have donated an item for the NAME silent auction at the Gulf South Miniature & Dollhouse Event, in New Orleans. From 1979 to 1987 I sold my miniature foods and accessories through mail order as Betti's Mini Mine. I try to exhibit parts of my collection regularly, in local libraries. At present, I have begun figure sculpturing and want to concentrate on creating character dolls using Fimo and Sculpy.

ARTISAN: **BROWN, GAYE**

BUSINESS NAME: Gaye Brown

IDENTIFICATION MARKS:

CATEGORY:

Kits; Toys

RECOGNITION:

Nutshell News

BROWN, GAYE, continued

AUTOBIOGRAPHY:

I started collecting miniatures 17 years ago, in 1976. My first project was a dollhouse for my granddaughter. I was very active in the Miniature World of The Central Florida Club, where I served as Workshop Chairman, President, and Show Chairman. I served on the Board of Directors of NAME for six years. I have been making and selling smaller scale toys since 1986, doing shows across the country.

ARTISAN: **BROWN, LYNNE J.**

BUSINESS NAME: The Small Doll Company

IDENTIFICATION MARKS:

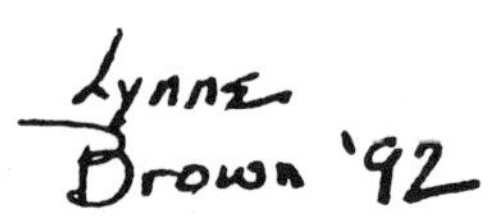

CATEGORY:

Dolls: porcelain

HONORS:

Two 1st Place Blue Ribbons, Iowa State Fair, 1991, 1993; One 2nd Place Red & Three 3rd Place White Ribbons, Iowa State Fair 1992; Golden Key Award, Jewelry Design 1972; Scholastic Arts Award, Sculpting 1972

RECOGNITION:

Miniatures Showcase, Fall 1989, pg. 44; Fall 1990, pg. 18, 34, 45; *Nutshell News*, Oct. 1991, Show Scene; Jan. 1992, Show Scene; *Urbandale News*, Sept. 20, 1990; TV, Ch 13, Sept. 1992, Urbandale, Iowa

AUTOBIOGRAPHY:

In 1972, I was presented with the Golden Key Award for outstanding design in jewelry, a Scholastic Arts Award and national exhibits, relating to doll sculpting and design. In 1973 to 1975, I was a theatrical seamstress and from 1976 to 1978, I was a tailor seamstress, both of which helped in my doll costuming and sewing. In 1978, I worked as a hairdresser and cosmetologist at Robinson's Beauty School and learned many techniques that I have applied to my miniature doll hairstyles. In 1982, I earned the BAAS, Bachelor of Applied Arts and Science degree, specializing in graphic arts design, photography, and video production. All relate to my current business which is photographic aids in catalog design. Graphic arts relates to doll design, sculpting, and costume coordination. From 1985 to 1987, I was Media Producer for Area Education Agency, developing skills for product promotion/art. I took up miniatures in 1978 and started making dolls for sale in 1988 with encouragement by a local shop owner. In 1994, I judged the miniatures category at the Iowa State Fair. NAME has asked me to contribute dolls for the National Houseparty in 1995.

I have done a great deal of personal study in costume design since 1988, specializing in Victorian period clothing and furniture. I now employ six people that each contribute to the final doll. All details, painting and hairstyles are done me personally. Limited edition dolls are done entirely by me from start to finish.

I am a member of IGMA, UFDC, CIMTA, and NAME.

ARTISAN: **BROWNHILL, JANET**

BUSINESS NAME: Country Treasures

IDENTIFICATION MARKS:

Food Handmade by
Janet Brownhill

With year

CATEGORY:

Food

RECOGNITION:

Nutshell News, Dec. 1989, pg. 83; May 1990, pg. 60; Jan. 1993, pg. 82; *Dolls House World; Decorative Dolls' House*, Caroline Hamilton, Ebury Press, London, 1990

AUTOBIOGRAPHY:

My background lies in Art and Design. I studied at Art school and then Art College. I spent many years making mice, setting them in scenes under Victorian type domes. More and more I was urged to make the food my mice ate for dollhouses, so eventually the mice were phased out and I concentrated on the food.

This developed from single items to my real love of making one-inch scale laden tables and board settings which I like to think of as three dimensional still life paintings. My inspiration comes from the changing seasons. The color and texture of an item, a piece of country furniture, or even an old toadstool picked up out of the woods.

ARTISAN: **BROWNHILL, PAUL**

BUSINESS NAME: Country Treasures

IDENTIFICATION MARKS:

CT

Stamped on smaller pieces

COUNTRY TREASURES MADE IN ENGLAND

Stamped on larger pieces

CATEGORY:

Brasswork; Coppersmith; Dinnerware; Dishes; Kitchen; Tinsmith; Tinware

RECOGNITION:

Dolls House World; Dolls & Dolls Houses, May 1989; *Making Miniatures,* Venus Dodge; *Decorative Dolls' Houses*, Caroline Hamilton, Ebury Press, London, 1990

BIOGRAPHY:

Paul spent many years as a toolmaker in the Engineering industry. He became involved in miniatures around 1982 after his wife Janet persuaded him to produce metal plates to use in her mouse settings. Although he was reluctant to do this at first, fate took a hand and he became a victim of Britain's industrial decline. He was then free to develop many miniature items, concentrating on kitchen ware and shop tins. His inspiration came from studying original pieces which were found around the home in museums and antique fairs.

ARTISAN: **BUCK, NORMA A.**

BUSINESS NAME: Roscana Miniatures

IDENTIFICATION MARKS:

CATEGORY:

Artifacts: native American, Holiday items

RECOGNITION:

Miniatures Showcase, Southwestern Issues

AUTOBIOGRAPHY:

Roscana was my Cherokee Great Grandmother. I feel that each time someone new learns about Native Americans through my miniatures, it honors her memory. I discovered miniatures in 1988, and wanted Kachinas so I got library books and went to work. Not knowing about X-acto knives, I used single edge razor blades for the first few. Learning is ongoing, and mostly everything I make I see in books. I also make a lot of accessories which appeal to the general public. My tiny clothespin dolls are a favorite. After high school I married Bill, and we raised five sons.

ARTISAN: **BUCKLEY, DON**

BUSINESS NAME: Don Buckley

IDENTIFICATION MARKS:

Small pieces

Brass plate, 1980 to present

CATEGORY:

Furniture: Country, period

HONORS:

IGMA Fellow; Honor, Master Model Railroader #199, National Model Railroad Association, Aug. 1993; Commission & Exhibit, Pennsbury Manor Museum, Pennsylvania

RECOGNITION:

Nutshell News, May/Jun. 1979, pg. 54-57, “Don Buckley's Nine Lives,” Ann Ruble; Jul/Aug. 1979; Jun. 1980 pg. 39, “Scale: The Large and Small Of It,” Ann Ruble, Catherine B. MacLaren; Oct. 1980, pg. 25-26, “Flights of Fancy - For Fun and Profit,” Ann Ruble; Jan. 1982, pg. 76, Show Scene, Ann Ruble; Apr. 1982; Jan. 1983, pg. 28-29, “The Class of '82,” Jane Mitchell; Jun. 1983, pg. 32-38, “A 'Country' State of Mind,” Jane Mitchell; Jul. 1985, pg. 56, Show Scene; *Miniature Collector*, Winter 1987, pg. 23, “Celebrating Ten Years of Miniature Collector,” AB; *Reproducing Period Furniture and Accessories in Miniature,* Virginia Merrill & Susan Merrill. Richardson, 1981; *Through The Looking Glass*, Boynton and Associates, Inc., Ann Ruble, 1984; *Engagement Calendar* 1979, Terry & Fred Rogal

BIOGRAPHY:

Don Buckley, born in 1924, has been an avid model builder since the age of six. He built planes, boats, trains, dioramas and for about 10 years, 18th Century American Country Furniture. His first love was jazz and he played briefly with the big bands before serving his country as a US Navy Lt. j.g. in WWII, Pacific. He then spent

spent 25 years on Madison Avenue as Creative Director of some of the top 10 advertising agencies. In 1970, he walked away from all of it, and started an environmental research foundation and an organic farm.

He remarried and he and Gloria founded Buckley & Buckley, a partnership dealing in 18th Century American Country Antiques. Don began making miniatures of pieces from life for the same reason Wallace Nutting once copied them in full-scale. It was a form of homework. Studying a piece to the point of being able to reproduce it enforced a level of concentration and retention that might not otherwise have been practical.

He loved early chairs, bannisterbacks, ladderbacks, Queen Anne's and Windsor's, also tables such as gatelegs, tavern tables, hutch tables, and tea tables. He also was interested in cupboards, blanket chests, ball-foot chests, and geometric chests. All of them were painted in the exact manner of their full-size prototypes. Don was the first Guild Fellow to wear and age his pieces like the heirlooms he was copying.

He became active in the Guild, serving as a trustee and Public Relations Director. He coined the phrase "in the pursuit of excellence," and "the annual gathering of the Guild," in the first several advertising campaigns he created pro bono for the organization. He taught at the Guild School in Castine in 1982, 1983 and 1984. He tried, unsuccessfully to create an interest and demand in two-inch scale, as a more challenging medium to the artisan. He became concerned that the popularity explosion of miniature collecting was impairing the quality and authenticity of miniature craftsmanship and leading to a commercial, political mass. As a result, he limited his work to commissions from knowledgeable collectors until 1986. His outlook for miniatures appears in the 10th Anniversary Issue of Miniature Collector, Winter 1987.

Don returned to his most beloved form of modeling, trains, and has been active in the National Model Railroad Association, which awarded him, in August 1993, the highest honor it bestows, Master Model Railroader (#199).

ARTISAN: **BUFTON, RON & KARLA**

BUSINESS NAME: Bufton's Collectable Miniatures

IDENTIFICATION MARKS:

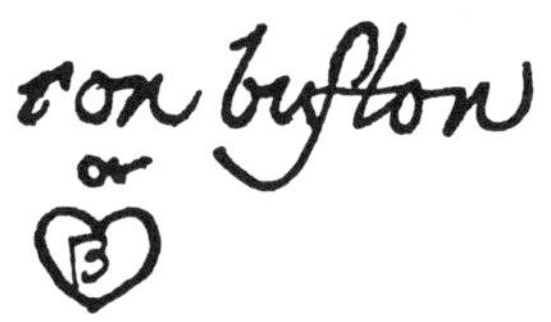

CATEGORY:

Accessories; Bears: teddy; Toys

HONORS:

Exhibits: Miniature Museum of the Southwest; Washington Dolls' House & Toy Museum; The Carole & Barry Kaye Museum of Miniatures; Angel's Attic Miniature Museum

AUTOBIOGRAPHY:

In September of 1968, I was working for the telephone company. I had purchased a small welding outfit and began to make some simple metal sculptures. To my surprise they found a ready market, and I soon had more orders than I could handle. I quit Ma Bell and became a sculptor. Within several months a local gallery offered me a one man show. My art career was launched!

In 1975, I was approached by the owner of a miniature store to fabricate some 2" x 1" hinges and latches for a miniature toy shop she had. Answering that call, I slowly made a transition from metal sculptor to miniaturist. Along the way Karla, my wife, began to try her hand at making miniature teddy bears. It didn't take her very long to gather her own following. She has expanded her line to include tiny doll's houses and vignettes which include her bears. Occasionally she gets ideas which involve some props or mechanisms from me. In addition to our being husband and wife, we also have a terrific working relationship together. Our line of miniatures focus on toys, teddies and accessories. We always hope that the things we make will bring a chuckle or a sigh of nostalgia from those who see them.

ARTISAN: **BURES, MARY**

BUSINESS NAME: A Grand Scale

IDENTIFICATION MARKS:

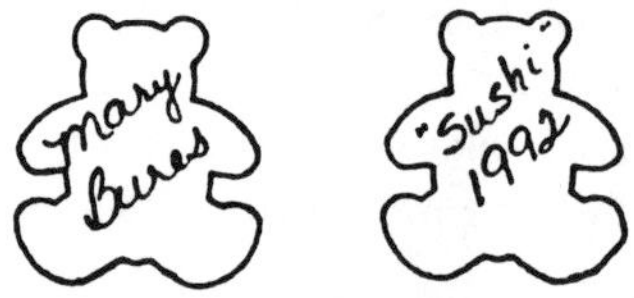

Tag with artisan's name, Bear's name and date

Jewelry tag signed as above

CATEGORY:

Animals: stuffed; Toys

HONORS:

IGMA Artisan, Fellow

RECOGNITION:

Nutshell News, Jul. 1989, pg. 39; *Miniature Showcase*, Fall 1991, pg. 53

AUTOBIOGRAPHY:

My husband, Steve, and I first became interested in miniatures in 1978. My brand new baby daughter and I were out and about one day when we happened onto a miniature shop. Oh, what a world that opened up for us! We started our dollhouse right away, and since Steve is an architect, we wanted to design and build it from scratch. We learned very quickly what expensive a hobby we had undertaken. I started applying all my previous craft experience to making miniatures myself. A shop started taking some items in trade for doors and windows and other things we needed for our house. My needlepoint items is where my business really began. Our first NAME Houseparty, as a dealer, was Oklahoma City in 1985, we were so pleased with the response we continued for about two years. In early 1987, after making "Holly Bearies" for Christmas presents in large scale, I sat looking at the pattern one day and thought, "why couldn't I make these for the dollhouse too?" Well, that was about 3200 miniature bears ago!

My bears started with a very simple pattern made into various calico, gingham and pin-dot cotton fabrics. I kept looking for and trying new materials, and soon, the velour, dressed bears were born. I spent a few years expanding my line and having a great time creating new characters. A friend showed me some new miniature bear fabric which I thought was very interesting, but I didn't do anything with it for over a year. It didn't work with the patterns and techniques I was using at the time. In the fall of 1990, I finally pulled out that small piece of fabric and started playing with it. I was thrilled with the "New Bear" born that day. I continue to play and create new patterns for all kinds of creatures. My line now includes not only bears, but also bunnies, giraffes, elephants, hippos, and kitties. All of my animals range in size from 5/8 inch to two inches tall, except the giraffes. Some of the first bears were not jointed and were usually in a sitting position. Their ears were higher on their head than their newer counterparts. They were not marked or tagged in any way. I started jointing their arms and legs in 1988. Some of the velour bears were displayed on matching calico-covered foam core bases which I signed and dated. Now, all of my bears have jointed arms and legs. Many of the new bears also have jointed heads. I used a snap in their neck for about six months before discovering that I could use very small washers and cotter pins instead.

ARTISAN: **BURGIN, KIM**

BUSINESS NAME: Kim's Miniatures, Inc.

IDENTIFICATION MARKS:

Unmarked

CATEGORY:

Food

ARTISAN: **BURKE, MARY SCHELLING**

IDENTIFICATION MARKS:

Mary Schelling Burke
Embroidery

MARY SCHELLING BURKE

CATEGORY:

Rugs; Wall: coverings, hangings

HONORS:

2nd place, Woman's Day Magazine, contest 1985; 7 Ribbon Awards, local art shows

RECOGNITION:

Miniatures Showcase, Nov. 1992, pg. 30; Winter Issue, 1992, pg. 28

AUTOBIOGRAPHY:

Though I have been an embroiderer for over 20 years, only recently have I explored the field of miniatures. After buying an antique dollhouse for my daughter a few years ago, I decided to embroider a rug for each of its six rooms. The designs I use are inspired by works of rug makers from the early twentieth century.

ARTISAN: **BURKEY, BILL**

BUSINESS NAME: Bill Burkey Animated Toys

IDENTIFICATION MARKS:

BURKEY

CATEGORY:

Furniture: golden oak; Toys: animated

HONORS:

IGMA Fellow

RECOGNITION:

Nutshell News, Oct. 1981, pg. 67-68; Oct. 1982, pg. 47; Jun. 1983, pg. 35; Aug. 1984, pg. 52; Sept. 1984, pg. 72; *Miniature Collector*, No. 29, pg. 14

AUTOBIOGRAPHY:

At this time I am not making miniatures, however, since I'm unable to pass on the completed projects that I have made I can, at least, pass on the process and instructions for the creation of animated toys.

ARTISAN: **BUTTFIELD, DONALD**

BUSINESS NAME: Miniatures Ltd.

IDENTIFICATION MARKS:

Don Buttfield
1977 #3

CATEGORY:
Furniture

HONORS:
Charter member IGMA; IGMA Fellow; IGMA Crystal Award 1993; Exhibit: Toy & Miniature Museum of Kansas City

RECOGNITION:
Nutshell News; The Complete Book of Making Miniatures, Thelma Newman and Virginia Merrill, 1975

AUTOBIOGRAPHY:

I was involved in the heavy construction business until 1973 when my wife persuaded me to change my vocation and suggested that I start making miniature furniture. I had always been interested in models, ships, trains, cars etc., and had even made a few pieces of furniture in 1½-inch scale. My cousin is a good friend of Paul Runyon and was kind enough to arrange a meeting. Paul was of invaluable help to me and not only showed me some of his tools, jigs, fixtures, equipment and techniques, but also gave me the names of a few of his customers, one of whom is Virginia Merrill. She was, at the time, in the process of getting together her first book, *The Complete Book of Making Miniatures*, and included some of my work within its covers. She also became one of my best customers and a very dear friend.

As a general rule I limited my production to five of any one piece but changed this rule twice, once to my chagrin. I told Paul that I intended to make some dining room tables. He suggested that I refrain because whoever bought a table would want at least six chairs, and six times five is thirty, and that's a lot of chairs! I prevailed with my folly and his prediction proved correct. I never had any desire to make chairs again. The other time I strayed was with the Chinese fish bowl on a stand. Debbie McKnight made the bowls for me and the pieces became very popular. However, since I could get only a few bowls at a time, making the stands never became a chore and I must have made 25 or so over the years.

As of now I have discontinued making miniatures due to slightly diminished eyesight and my interest in other things, such as one-inch scale furniture, house rehabilitation, grandchildren, etc. I feel, however, that I owe a great deal to the world of miniatures and its gift of friendships with so many collectors and crafts people, and the satisfaction of working with the Guild to establish their school.

ARTISAN: **BYER, JOAN**

BUSINESS NAME: CJ's Miniatures

IDENTIFICATION MARKS:

CJ'S
1992

CATEGORY:
Furniture

BYER, JOAN, continued

RECOGNITION:

Miniatures Showcase, Fall 1986, pg. 36; Winter 1989, pg. 28-29; Jan. 1993, pg. 45; *Miniature Collector*, Jan. 1993

BIOGRAPHY:

Until 1980, Carolyn Wilson and Joan Byer thought that their expertise lie in homemaking, husbands, and child rearing. When their nests became empty, the same year, these old friends looked at one another and said, "What do we do now?"

Their first adventure was a search to find Joan's childhood dollhouse. Her mother, unable to locate it, did find a builder of dollhouses, so they traveled to Joan's native state, New York, and returned home to Indiana with two houses. It was a wonderful learning experience. As they completed their dollhouses, they found other hobbyists as smitten. What fun traveling distances to miniature shops and shows, and discovering the wonders of handcrafted miniatures!

A friend with an antique business invited them to share space, if they were interested in making the selling of miniatures and dollhouses a business venture. After trying two locations in an area of Indiana without enough population to support such a specialty, they were on the verge of giving up, when a Board Member of a living history museum at Fort Wayne, Indiana asked if they would be interested in creating the simple, authentic, furnishings of the Fort, an 1816 Fort recreation, in miniature to be sold in the museum gift shop. Armed with camera and tape measure, they miniaturized the beds, tables, cupboards, etc. into one-inch scale miniature reproductions. They left shopkeeping and became makers of antiques in miniature, evolving and changing as their techniques improved. And so CJ's in its present form came to be.

Always willing to learn from constructive criticism and to try, try again, they listened when it was suggested they join CIMTA, Cottage Industry Miniature Trade Assoc., and found the shop keepers appreciated their efforts. With that acceptance in 1983, they became full time handcrafters. Their workshop is located in Carolyn's home in Columbia City, Indiana where they work five days a week, designing and marketing furniture, which can be found in retail shops and at shows throughout the country. The line includes one-inch and ½-inch scale Early American and Victorian Country pieces. They specialize in the aged look, finishing chairs, cupboards, pie safes etc. in appropriate colors and walnut, so they appear to be time worn. Their memberships include CIMTA, NAME, and Metro Minis of Fort Wayne, Indiana.

C

ARTISAN: **CAESAR, ANNE**

BUSINESS NAME: The Kitchen Captive

IDENTIFICATION MARKS:

Logo

CATEGORY:

Accessories: food; Beverage; Food

HONORS:

IGMA Artisan

RECOGNITION:

Nutshell News, Sept. 1992, pg. 51; *Miniatures Showcase*, Spring 1988, pg. 42; Fall 1988, pg. 24-27, 36-37; Spring 1989, pg. 38; Summer 1989, pg. 27; Fall 1989, pg. 35; Winter 1989, pg. 28, 39, 40-41; Spring 1990, pg. 47; Summer 1990, pg. 18-19; Winter 1990, pg. 32, 36; Spring 1991, pg. 27, 29, 37; Summer 1991, pg. 28, 69; Fall 1991, pg. 16, 37; Winter 1992, pg. 27; *Miniature Collector*, Winter 1988, pg. 89; Winter 1992, pg. 27; *Miniature Catalog*, 15th Edition 1992, pg. 244

AUTOBIOGRAPHY:

In 1959, I graduated from The Philadelphia College of Art, now called The University of Performing Arts, where I had majored in Illustration. From 1976 through 1985, I was a partner in "Dollhouse Goodies," crafting miniature food reproductions and selling them through shops and at miniatures shows.

Since 1986, I have worked alone under the business name "The Kitchen Captive." Until 1992 my foods were available in miniature shops in the US and Europe, but now I sell them at shows or by mail.

ARTISAN: **CAMERON, HOPE ELLIOTT**

BUSINESS NAME: Hope Elliott Miniatures

IDENTIFICATION MARKS:

CATEGORY:

Christmas; Flowers and Plants; Food; Holiday Items

HONORS:

IGMA Fellow; Blue Ribbon Award, Miniature Makers Society, New Jersey; Museum Recognition Award

RECOGNITION:

Life Magazine, Oct. 1979; *Seventeen Magazine*, Jan. 1981; *Miniature Collector*; *The Miniature Magazine*; *Miniature & Dollhouse Crafts*; *House Beautiful*; *Family Circle*; Today Show; Good Morning America; AM New York; Saturday Night Live

BIOGRAPHY:

Hope Elliott is a true originator in the world of miniatures, and has been creating magnificent, realistic items since childhood. The inventor of the "Perfect Pumpkin," won acclaim at the age of 12 when her original

original Hope's Harvest Shack won first prize at an important New Jersey miniatures competition. Hearing of this young lady and her incredible talent, Jean Schramm of the Enchanted Dollhouse sought out Hope and her beautifully realistic fruits, vegetables, flowers, Christmas trees and a host of other miniature delights. Hope's fame reached far and wide, as shops and museums throughout the world began to seek out and carry her creations.

When she was 13, she designed and handcrafted The Tomb of Tutankhamun, sculpting each piece by hand, and delicately painting and gold leafing the precious artifacts. The Tutankhamun project was featured in Life Magazine. Hope's work can be seen throughout the world in museums. Collectors will often visit a particular show only to see Hope and her work, and all comment on her incredible talent. Her work has been widely recognized and featured in many important publications as *Life Magazine, Seventeen Magazine, The Miniature Magazine, Nutshell News, Miniature Collector, Family Circle, House Beautiful* and more, plus on the Today Show, Good Morning America, AM New York and others throughout the world. Though many have attempted to copy Hope's work, few have ever succeeded in capturing her total realism and lifelike quality, reflecting her love of nature.

ARTISAN: **CAMPBELL, CAROLYN**

BUSINESS NAME: Carolyn's Cuties

IDENTIFICATION MARKS:

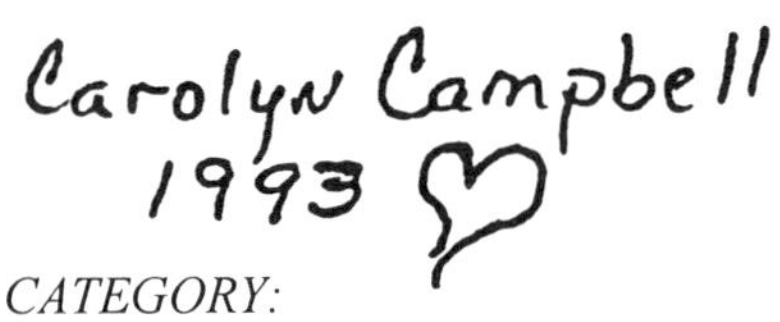

CATEGORY:
Dolls

HONORS:
IGMA Artisan

RECOGNITION:
Nutshell News

ARTISAN: **CAMPBELL, FERN**

BUSINESS NAME: Fernwood Miniatures

IDENTIFICATION MARKS:
Unmarked

CATEGORY:
Kits: furniture

RECOGNITION:
Miniature Gazette, Vol. 21, No. 1, Fall 1992, pg. 23

AUTOBIOGRAPHY:

I received my BFA Degree in 1945 from the Art Institute of Chicago. My husband and I built several houses during which I learned how to use power tools, producing furniture for our own home. Using plans from Furniture Designs, Evanston, Illinois, we learned how to build quality full-sized furniture. We made most of the furniture in our home.

I lead a girls club that developed into a miniature club after some of the girls desired to make dollhouses and dollhouse furniture. My friend and I began to display at miniature shows and tried several aspects in the miniatures field. I hit it with miniature furniture kits, and have been perfecting my expertise ever since using precision machinery and constantly working for perfection. My furniture kits are made just like the "real" furniture with mortises, tenons, dados, dovetails, etc. I began selling by mail and now have customers in every state of the Union and also in some foreign countries.

ARTISAN: **CAMPBELL, IRENE**

BUSINESS NAME: Irene Campbell

IDENTIFICATION MARKS:

CATEGORY:
China; Pottery: wheel thrown; Stoneware; Terra Cotta

HONORS:
National Diploma in Design NDD; Somerset Guild of Craftsmen

RECOGNITION:
Making Doll's Houses in 1/12 Scale, Brian Nicholls, David & Charles, 1992; *International Doll's House News; Home Miniaturist*

AUTOBIOGRAPHY:
I produce miniature pottery in 1/12-inch, 1/16-inch and 1/24inch scales in bone china, porcelain, terracotta and stoneware. I have a National Diploma in Design from Bath Academy of Art, and an Art Teachers Diploma from London University. I have been Head of the Art Department, and taught at Friends School Saffran Walden, Essex. I left teaching to develop my interest in pottery, becoming assistant thrower at Lakes Pottery Truso, Cornwall. It was there I made my first miniature, to win a bet. I then made them all the time for the tourists.

I am married with four daughters and returned to teaching part time, while making miniatures for friends dollhouses. My business has grown from there and I now have a studio and have been concentrating on miniatures since about 1977. I enjoy working on special individual pieces on a commission basis most of all, but I make everything needed for the dollhouse as long as it can be thrown.

ARTISAN: **CANNELLA, KAY**

BUSINESS NAME: Fine Art in Miniature

IDENTIFICATION MARKS:

CATEGORY:
Accessories; Folk Art; Painting

HONORS:
IGMA Artisan 1994

CANNELLA, KAY, continued

RECOGNITION:

Nutshell News, Mar. 1986, pg. 56; Jun. 1986, pg. 88; Sept. 1986, pg. 86; Mar. 1987, pg. 24; May 1988, pg. 20; Mar. 1990, pg. 45; Mar. 1992, pg. 69; *Miniature Collector*, Spring 1986, pg. 31; *Miniatures Showcase*, Vol. 1, Fall 1986, pg. 36; Fall 1988, Cover, pg. 4-8; Spring 1989, pg. 28, 34, 40

AUTOBIOGRAPHY:

Having been creative since I was a child, I went to school for costume design. After working in the garment industry for many years, it was time for a change. I went into the beauty business and owned a shop for awhile. During those years I was accumulating small antique picture frames, tin types and boxes.

In 1981, through a friend I learned of a miniatures club. I began to design many miniature accessories and sold them at the club. After I made friends with Chickie Fogel, she asked me to join Fine Art in Miniature. At that time, I was doing shows and selling my work. I also taught workshops at NAME Regionals and Nationals. I did a souvenir workshop for 300 people at Back to College weekend in Ashland, Virginia.

In 1990, I was commissioned to do a painting for a Colonial roombox. That painting started me in a new direction toward Folk Art and doing more miniature paintings. Although I have been painting for 35 years, I had to become accustomed to painting tiny. Most of my miniature paintings are done in acrylics. I also paint in oils, watercolors, and do Japanese brush painting.

I love all types of painting but I have a fascination for Folk Art. I think it is the primitiveness of it, and it almost always includes animals that I love. I make many types of accessories for dollhouses, Victorian, Country, Christmas and Folk Art.

In November 1993, I inherited Fine Art in Miniature from Chickie Fogel. I was awarded IGMA Artisan in May 1994 in the category of Folk Art Painting.

ARTISAN: **CARDINAL, CAROL**

BUSINESS NAME: Miniatures by C.C.

IDENTIFICATION MARKS:

Unmarked, some hair covered dogs

Accessories and Animals 1980 to present
Furniture 1977 to 1982

CATEGORY:

Accessories; Animals; Furniture

RECOGNITION:

Miniatures Showcase; Miniature Gazette; Nutshell News; Miniature Dealer; National Geographic Explorer; Miniature Collector

AUTOBIOGRAPHY:

I started making dogs in 1980 and am self-taught. I sell at shows, by mail order, and through other dealers. I love miniatures and the very nice people I have met in this hobby. Once in a while I also make a few accessories to go along with my dogs.

ARTISAN: **CARIOU, GERMAIN**

BUSINESS NAME: Cariou

IDENTIFICATION MARKS:

CATEGORY:

Accessories; Boxes; Clocks; Furniture; Musical Instruments

RECOGNITION:

Nutshell News, Vol. 23, No. 1, Jan. 1993, pg. 79, Show Scene; *Miniature Collector*, No. 67, Winter 1989, pg. 16; *Vogue*, Apr. 1993, pg. 40; *enfant Magazine; Dolls House,* London Festival, pg. 15

AUTOBIOGRAPHY:

My love for miniatures goes back about twelve years, to 1981, when I first had the desire to make a dollhouse for my daughter. This creation took me about four years to complete, during which time I became aware of and developed a fine taste for all miniature things; which was reinforced by the collector, Mrs. Denise Deniselle, who noticed my work at the time of the 1985 Dollhouse Exposition in Paris, where I was officially recognized with a diploma which was, for me, one of the highest awards in miniatures.

My first order goes back several years now when this collector first asked me to make several objects, many of which were suitable for exhibition and with my permission and knowledge, she began to sell my work through her miniature shops in Paris. She also commissioned me to do many scenes for different competitions and having won numerous prizes, I still remain as passionately eager as in the beginning, to create new rooms each year and to show them in different countries such as France, Holland, Belgium, Switzerland, Great Britain, and Spain.

I have also had the good fortune to be represented in several museums throughout the world, such as the United States, Spain and France. There have been many press articles and photos reporting on my collection which have had positive effects on my efforts and which have permitted me to continue the many new creative ideas I have for the future.

ARTISAN: **CARLISLE, MARY**

IDENTIFICATION MARKS:

Logo, labels, printed material

CATEGORY:

Furniture: period; Knitting; Patterns

AUTOBIOGRAPHY:

After teaching egg craft for eight years, I looked around for a new hobby which would make use of all the crafts I had followed over the years, and discovered that miniatures gave me the perfect answer. From sewing to carpentry the range was wide and as a result I have sustained my interest. After several years of working I began to teach and now cover a wide range of skills. One pupil has just built a copy of her grandfather's shop with only a photograph and her childhood memories for information. My next project is to build a scale copy of my father's old home, once a priory before the dissolution of the monasteries in Henry VIII time.

I spend my spare time inventing knitting patterns to scale. I like a challenge or problem but don't enjoy making endless copies of the same thing. My customers usually ask for special items such as a wedding buffet complete with cake. Having said this, we do have a catalogue with a permanent list of items such as food, furniture based on museum pieces at the Welsh National Folk Museum, knitting patterns, and kits of furniture and plants.

I continue working on new knitting patterns, plans for shop fittings, counters etc. for a retail shop. I have filmed my own teaching videos in both egg craft and miniatures. The videos came about because disabled and house bound people could not attend a course. I attend several shows, demonstrate, and answer questions at "The Welsh Doll House."

ARTISAN: **CARLISLE, ROBERT L. "BOB"**

BUSINESS NAME: Carlisle Miniatures

IDENTIFICATION MARKS:

1974 to 1976, sold only to Wee Littles and Wee C

September 1974 to present

R. L. Carlisle
Creston, Iowa

Rubber stamp, discontinued Sept. 1974

CATEGORY:

Furniture: period; Toys: wheeled

RECOGNITION:

Nutshell News, Jun. 1980, pg. 84; *Miniature Gazette*, Spring 1979, pg. 52; *This Side of Yesterday in Miniature,* Catherine B. MacLaren, 1975, pg. 46; *The Dollhouse & Miniature News,* Cover, pg. 1-2; *Inside The World of Miniatures and Dollhouses*, Rosner & Beckerman, McKay Press, 1976, pg. 45; In 1980 Hallmark used a setting of furniture on a Thanksgiving card, 50th 778-4

AUTOBIOGRAPHY:

In 1974, I was machine shop foreman in an aerospace foundry but I wanted to go into business for myself. I tried a few things, but shortage of shop space and cost of materials kept them from succeeding. Then someone gave me a miniatures catalog. I liked working small and was accustomed to precision. My first miniature was made in February of 1974. In March I rented a booth at a flea market in Omaha, and began selling my wares. I was lucky, people on vacation bought my miniatures and took them home and showed them to their favorite shop. Soon I was getting wholesale orders from all over. By July of 1974 I was able to quit my job to devote full-time to miniature making. My experience as a machinist allowed me to make special machines and tools for the production of miniatures. My photography hobby came in handy for catalog and advertising photos. I put out a mail-order catalog and eventually eliminated most wholesale accounts. As for my feeling about miniature making after twenty years; this is the kind of work I would rather do!

ARTISAN: **CARLSON, CAROLE STEPHENS**

BUSINESS NAME: B C Miniatures

IDENTIFICATION MARKS:

Unmarked before 1993

1993 to present

CARLSON, CAROLE STEPHENS, continued

CATEGORY:

Furniture; Room Settings

BIOGRAPHY:

Carole became interested in miniatures while attending a doll show that had a few tables of miniatures. One look and she was hooked! Having now taken several Brooke Tucker classes, Carole turned to furniture, making it look exactly the way she wanted for her roomboxes. She also enjoys finishing other peoples projects, when they don't have the time themselves. Carole sometimes helps her husband, Bill, with the finishing of his roomboxes. She does all the marketing and attends shows for their new business, B C Miniatures. She has a number of new projects in the works for their business, including needlepoint chair seats and crocheted work. Her major problem is that she has many more ideas than time.

ARTISAN: CARLSON, WILLIAM M.

BUSINESS NAME: B C Miniatures

IDENTIFICATION MARKS:

Unmarked before 1993

1993 to present

CATEGORY:

Roomboxes

AUTOBIOGRAPHY

I am a carpenter by trade, and became involved with miniatures at the instigation of my wife, Carole, who has been a miniaturist for several years. She needed a box for a Brooke Tucker class, which I made for her, as well as most of the class and her club members. Since then we have sold at shows and through the Tiny Dwelling in Alexandria, Virginia. I am most interested in the challenge of working out new designs for custom orders, and am thinking of branching out into dollhouses.

ARTISAN: CARON, JACKIE

BUSINESS NAME: House of Caron

IDENTIFICATION MARKS:

REPRO BY JACKIE CARON

CATEGORY:

Dolls: porcelain

HONORS:

2 Best of Class, 1 Best of Show, Awards and Trophies in doll competition

ARTISAN: **CARRADUS FAMILY** (see separate family member listings, below)

BUSINESS NAME: Carradus Gifts

IDENTIFICATION MARKS:

Carradus
Originals

CATEGORY:
Accessories: wooden; Aquariums; Birds; Christmas; Crocheting; Flowers and Plants; Food; Furniture; Holiday Items; Metal: handpainted; Needlework; Thimbles

RECOGNITION:
Miniatures Showcase, Summer 1989, pg. 16; Fall 1990, pg. 30, 45; Fall 1991, pg. 39; *Dubuque Telegraph-Herald*, Sept. 21, 1986; KWWL, Channel 7, Nov. 1986

BIOGRAPHY: (see biographical information listed under Mary Ann Carradus)

ARTISAN: **CARRADUS, DONNA**

BUSINESS NAME: Carradus Gifts

IDENTIFICATION MARKS:

CATEGORY:
Aquariums; Flowers and Plants

RECOGNITION:
Miniatures Showcase, Summer 1989, pg. 33, 36, 38; Fall 1989, pg. 44; Spring 1990, pg. 32; Fall 1990, pg. 46; Winter 1990, pg. 46, 48

BIOGRAPHY: (see biographical information listed under Mary Ann Carradus)

ARTISAN: **CARRADUS, GRACE**

BUSINESS NAME: Carradus Gifts

IDENTIFICATION MARKS:

Hand-crocheted
by Grace

CATEGORY:
Christmas; Crocheting; Holiday Items; Needlework

RECOGNITION:
Miniatures Showcase, Fall 1990, pg. 37, 46; Winter 1990, pg. 38, 41; Fall 1991, pg. 23, 25; Winter 1992, pg. 30, 32; *Miniature Dealer*, Cover, Oct. 1989

BIOGRAPHY: (see biographical information listed under Mary Ann Carradus)

ARTISAN: **CARRADUS, LeROY, (JOHN LeROY)**

BUSINESS NAME: Carradus Gifts

IDENTIFICATION MARKS:

CATEGORY:

Accessories: wooden; Furniture; Thimbles

RECOGNITION:

Miniatures Showcase, Summer 1989, pg. 27, 28; Fall 1989, pg. 44; Spring 1990, pg. 11; Fall 1990, pg. 45; Winter 1990, pg. 34, 49; Fall 1991, pg. 29; Summer 1991, pg. 35; Nov. 1992, pg. 37, 67

BIOGRAPHY: (see biographical information listed under Mary Ann Carradus)

ARTISAN: **CARRADUS, MARY ANN**

BUSINESS NAME: Carradus Gifts

IDENTIFICATION MARKS:

CATEGORY:

Accessories: handpainted metal; Birds; Food; Metal: handpainted

RECOGNITION:

Miniatures Showcase, Fall 1989, pg. 30, 42-44; Spring, 1990, pg. 32, 64; Fall 1990, pg. 41, 45-46; Winter 1990, pg. 46; Fall 1991, pg. 13, 23, 70; Nov. 1992, pg. 39; *Miniature Dealer*, Cover, Jan. 1991

BIOGRAPHY:

Carradus Gifts is a small family business composed of LeRoy, Grace, Mary Ann and Donna. While attending craft shows about 23 years ago, they began making a few miniature items to sell with their paintings, needlework and woodworking. They soon received requests for more miniatures.

Donna makes straw kitchen brooms, flowers and plants which include a single rose in a vase, boxed dozen roses, tulips, calla lilies, Easter lilies, bonsai, ferns, and a variety of cactus and flower arrangements.

Grace hand-crochets in fine threads of various colors; rugs, tablecloths, doilies, hats and drawstring purses that actually open and close. Tablecloths are made in three original patterns. Rugs are crocheted in ovals, rounds, with and without fringe, and runners with fringe to scale for thickness.

LeRoy makes miniature furniture and accessory pieces such as workable butter prints, copper-banded churns, tiny toothpick holders with toothpicks, covered boxes and blanket chests using hardwoods such as walnut, cherry, butternut, and cedar. He also uses ebony, rosewoods and tagua nut.

Mary Ann hand-sculpts hamburgers, a Williamsburg hog head platter, traditional turkey and ham platters, raw and cooked meats, frosted cakes, pies and other foods. She also sculpts a variety of birds, caged and wild such as parakeets, cockatiels, macaws, cockatoos, parrots, blue jays and cardinals.

Mary Ann & Donna also make aquariums, filled and spilled drinks, Easter eggs being dyed, and jack o' lanterns being carved.

They sell to stores around the US and have a retail business in northeast Iowa. It features miniatures, a variety of gift items and collector thimbles which the family also manufactures.

ARTISAN: **CASSON, VALERIE ANNE**

BUSINESS NAME: A Touch of England
The Brown Bag Kit Company

IDENTIFICATION MARKS:

Valerie Anne Casson

V. Casson   V. CASSON

V.A.C.

A Touch of England

THE BROWN BAG KIT COMPANY

Logo

CATEGORY:

Ceramics; Dolls; Figures; Furniture: handpainted

RECOGNITION:

Nutshell News, Jul. 1991; Feb. 1992, pg. 31; Sept. 1992, pg. 26; Apr. 1993, pg. 25; Jul. 1993 Center Page; *A World in Miniature Catalogue*, Oban, Scotland; *Fine Art in Miniature Catalogue*, Vol. 2, Fall 1989, pg. 70-71; *My Sisters Shoppe Catalogue*, 1992 Collection, Cover; 1993 Collection, Cover, back; Summer 1993, Center, Back Cover

AUTOBIOGRAPHY:

Originally from London, England, I've made the USA my home since approximately 1985. I started in the miniatures business in 1977 having a miniature shop and tearoom. I'm sure many of you who come to England on tours must have stopped for cream tea at Valerie Anne's at Hungerford!

I've always loved painting and modeling mostly self-taught by reading, trial, and error. Within the last year I've concentrated mostly on ceramics which I find totally fascinating. I have a range of twenty four teapots, Staffordshire dog, plates and tureens, which I will expand every six months. Most of these items are based on English designs from 1850 on.

I still do a lot of painted furniture and fire screens, mostly for the few shows I do and of course the catalogs.

ARTISAN: **CAVANAUGH, GLENDA**

BUSINESS NAME: The Miniature Cottage

IDENTIFICATION MARKS:

Cottage #—
Glenda Cavanaugh
month/year

Cottage #1 1985

CATEGORY:

Bird Feeders; Cottages: thatched; Structures

HONORS:

IGMA Artisan; Grand Prize Miniature Division Northwest Flower & Garden Show, Seattle, Washington

RECOGNITION:

The Home Miniaturist, May 1991, pg. 27; *Nutshell News*, Mar. 1992, pg. 70, Show Scene; *The Blaine Banner*, Apr. 2, 1992, Front Page

CAVANAUGH, GLENDA, continued

AUTOBIOGRAPHY:

I have been building authentically detailed English cottages with thatched roofs since 1985, in all three miniature scales. I have researched vernacular architecture both on site, in Britain and Europe, and in my extensive library on this subject. I have been taking miniaturists on tours, POSH Specialtours, in Britain, Europe and the USA since 1984 and make a point of visiting thatched cottages at every opportunity. I have degrees in Nursing, Travel, and Massage Therapy. I am an IGMA Artisan and I also belong to NAME and SAM, as well as a local miniatures club.

ARTISAN: CHAMBERS, G. A.

BUSINESS NAME: G A Chambers

IDENTIFICATION MARKS:

GAC

CATEGORY:

Boxes: jewelry, silver; Jewelry

HONORS:

IGMA Artisan 1992

AUTOBIOGRAPHY:

I served a five year apprenticeship with Garrards, the crown jeweler in diamond mounting; then became a freeman of the mystery of Goldsmiths of the city of London by service in 1978. I worked with Garrards for 17 years and have since moved on to another London workshop. I started making miniatures in 1988 and have exhibited at the London Dollhouse Festival. I became an IGMA Artisan in 1992.

ARTISAN: CHANDRONNAIT, AL

BUSINESS NAME: Al Chandronnait

IDENTIFICATION MARKS:

Ac

CATEGORY:

Accessories

HONORS:

IGMA Artisan

ARTISAN: **CHAPMAN, CAROL**

BUSINESS NAME: Gentle Memories

IDENTIFICATION MARKS:

CATEGORY:

Accessories; Christmas; Dolls: paper; Furniture: handpainted; Holiday Items

AUTOBIOGRAPHY:

My college degree is in elementary education. I'm part owner of a small local trucking company and work there full-time. Previously I owned a miniature shop and had a mail order catalog along with the store. I go to a few miniature shows a year and do some mail order.

ARTISAN: **CHAUVIN, ANNE**

BUSINESS NAME: Anne Chauvin Needlework

IDENTIFICATION MARKS:

 Initials stitched into work

 Smaller pieces

 Back of larger pieces

CATEGORY:

Needlework

HONORS:

IGMA Artisan

RECOGNITION:

Nutshell News, Vol. 22, No. 2, Feb. 1992, pg. 67; Vol. 22, No. 11, Nov. 1992, pg. 73; *Miniature Collector*, No. 77, Fall 1992, pg. 23; *Miniatures Showcase*, Vol. 7, No. 1, Winter 1992, pg. 31-33, 40-41; Vol. 7, No. 2, Spring 1992, pg. 30-31; Jan. 1993, pg. 32-34

ARTISAN: **CHEYNEY, Mr. W. H. & Mrs. J. M.**

BUSINESS NAME: Meadowcroft Miniatures

IDENTIFICATION MARKS:

Unmarked

CATEGORY:

Brasswork; Silversmith

AUTOBIOGRAPHY:

I am by trade an instrument maker, and have spent thirty-odd years manufacturing weights and measures equipment. I was, at the same time, a model engineer. A relative who made porcelain dolls asked if I could make some small brass shank buttons. I was able to make them for her and this developed into a small business making these buttons in brass and nickel silver. I have been at this enterprise since 1987.

ARTISAN: **CHITSON, DAVID SYDNEY**

BUSINESS NAME: Stillmore Homes

IDENTIFICATION MARKS:

Logo

CATEGORY:

Building Components; Dollhouse; Glass: stained; Kits: dollhouse; Shops; Wrought Iron

RECOGNITION:

Dolls House World, No. 15, 1991; *The Home Miniaturist*, No. 62, 1992

AUTOBIOGRAPHY:

I have been making and selling miniatures since 1984 in Great Britain. Houses form the largest part of my work, which is mainly one of a kind. I only use real materials, such as glass in the windows. This has been a trade mark of the houses I have built over the years. I write articles for *The Home Miniaturist* and *The Dolls House and Miniature Scene*, a newer magazine with a national distribution. In the last year I have been taught miniature wrought iron work by John Watkins and have added that to my list of accomplishments in the miniature field. I have to date exported to eight countries. Although I have a logo, this only appears on my letterhead, business cards, and advertisements.

ARTISAN: **CHRISTENSEN, NADA**

BUSINESS NAME: Nada Christensen, Ltd.

IDENTIFICATION MARKS:

Earliest dolls unmarked

Mark incised on back or under left ear

CATEGORY:

Accessories; Dolls: original, reproductions; Kits, doll

HONORS:

1st Place Ribbons, Doll Show Competitions; Stella Award, Lelia Award, International Dollmakers Association

AUTOBIOGRAPHY:

I have been working as a miniature porcelain doll maker since 1980 when a "big doll" making friend sold me her miniature doll molds because they were too hard to pour. I was born and raised in New Orleans and really became interested in miniatures when I was in music school at the University of Southern Louisiana, under the piano instruction of Frank Hanley of Lafayette, Louisiana, an old friend of mine. We would often sit and talk about antiques and dolls instead of having a piano lesson.

I graduated from USL in 1982, and started doing the Deep South Miniature and Dollhouse Show, now known as the Gulf South Miniature and Dollhouse Event in New Orleans, and a few other shows a year. I also collect antique to modern dolls of other sizes and have about four dollhouses. I am a member of the International Dollmakers Association, NAME and IGMA.

I now do about four to six shows a year and graduated from the University of Houston, in Pharmacy in 1993. My husband, Mark, and I have a son, Ben. I plan to continue my part-time mail order and show business. I do all of my own work, and try to keep my kit prices reasonable so that everyone can afford to make their own dolls. My china painting is fine quality because of my eyesight and love for detail. I now have over 200 commercial mini doll and accessory molds and have begun to produce my own original dolls.

ARTISAN: **CHUCKA, ROBERT A.**

BUSINESS NAME: The Olde Cabinetmaker

IDENTIFICATION MARKS: (Submitted by Barbara Marshall and Louise Hedrick)

Handmade by
Robert A Chucka
--
The Olde Cabinetmaker
Milwaukee, Wisconsin

Label

With year

Signed in pen

Signature **Robert A. Chucka,** also used, in script using pen, with date

CATEGORY:
Furniture

RECOGNITION:
Nutshell News, Feb. 1983, pg. 32-34, "The (Not Very) Olde Cabinetmaker," Jeanne Delgado

ARTISAN: **CHURCHILL, ILEAN M.**

BUSINESS NAME: A Wee Company

IDENTIFICATION MARKS:

CATEGORY:
Costuming; Furniture; Needlework

AUTOBIOGRAPHY:
I have been interested in miniatures since childhood. When I retired in 1981, I began by buying a dollhouse kit. Since then I have learned much about miniatures by reading and from other miniaturists. I have done many kinds of needlework since I was a child, and have taken several art courses over the years, including college night classes.

ARTISAN: **CINI, GUGLIELMO** (Deceased)

IDENTIFICATION MARKS:

CATEGORY:

Goldsmith; Silver; Silversmith

RECOGNITION:

Nutshell News, Feb. 1983, pg. 28-31, "The Essence of Tiffany's," Catherine B. MacLaren

BIOGRAPHY:

Born in Florence, Italy, Guglielmo worked originally as a craftsman in heirloom jewelry. He emigrated to Boston where he worked until 1957, when he relocated in Laguna Beach, California. He was commissioned by Colleen Moore to create a gold toilet set with diamonds and platinum, a ½-inch New Testament bound in gold and a jewel box ¼-inch high, with lock and key, and platinum wedding ring inside. After his work with Ms. Moore, he made many miniature pieces of gold and silver in one-inch scale.

(AOH profile, by Ferbie Claudon, authorized reprint by NAME)

ARTISAN: **CLANTON, RON**

BUSINESS NAME: Victorian Times Miniature Co.

IDENTIFICATION MARKS:

Name or model of House
Builders signature
Date built

CATEGORY:

Dollhouse: custom; Structures

RECOGNITION:

Nutshell News, Aug. 1988; *Miniature Catalog,* 4th Edition, Cover; *Nutshell News* Calendar, inside cover; KTUX Channel 4

AUTOBIOGRAPHY:

My work was represented on the Miniature Catalog #4 Cover. I have built houses for celebrities and miniature stores, and my work has been used as displays at Miniature Estates, Beverly Hills, CA and Mini Mouse in Anchorage, Alaska. I teach classes around the country. I am doing a custom house for a client in Boston. The house comes with its own landscaped table 6' x 9', with the house covering most of the tabletop area.

ARTISAN: **CLARK, JAMES C.**

BUSINESS NAME: Your Local Potter

IDENTIFICATION MARKS:

J. Clark
1975

1974 to 1976, Medium; Stoneware
Scratched into bottom of piece

CLARK, JAMES C., continued

1977 to 1990, Medium; Porcelain
Usually scratched; some written in blue slip

1977 to Present, Medium; Porcelain
As many as one piece in a 100 could have a *secret message* ranging from *Hi!*, inside jars; *Not made in Japan, This side down*, on bottom; *Sorry-no secret message, Hello up there*, inside lids. Many other variations including rare self-portraits may be found.

1990 to Present, Medium; Porcelain
Almost always written in blue slip, very rarely scratched

CATEGORY:
Ceramics; Porcelain: wheel thrown

HONORS:
President of A2 Potters Guild, 1991 - 1994

RECOGNITION:
Cartoonist for *Miniature Gazette*, 1990 to present; *Nutshell News*, Apr. 1980; *Miniature Collector*, Apr. 1980; Spring 1993

AUTOBIOGRAPHY:
In 1971, I got a teaching job in Zoology with minimal success. After taking a series of classes at the Potters Guild, in Ann Arbor, Michigan, I joined in 1973, while doing part time teaching at local colleges. In 1974, experimenting with smaller pots resulted in making thrown handles for stoneware casseroles. I actually made huge cumbersome miniatures in 1975 and was able to refine them the next year. In 1976, I decided to become a good potter working full-time and starting my own business. I registered Your Local Potter as my official business name, still teaching occasionally part time. In 1977, while roaming the Street Art Fair in Ann Arbor, I came across a person who sold miniature pots. I was blown away! I then found out through conversation that there were such things as miniatures shows and in 1978 I did my first show in Sandusky. That was where I was discovered and started attending miniatures shows throughout the Midwest, and occasionally beyond. I started selling by mail order in 1980 as a result of biography articles in *Nutshell News* and *Miniature Collector* and was too busy to teach anymore!

ARTISAN: CLARKE, SYLVIA

BUSINESS NAME: Fine Food in Miniature

IDENTIFICATION MARKS:

All marks used from 1983 to present, depending on space available

CATEGORY:
Fimo; Food

HONORS:
IGMA Artisan 1990

RECOGNITION:
Nutshell News, Aug. 1984, pg. 48-50

CLARKE, SYLVIA, continued

AUTOBIOGRAPHY:

I enjoy working with many mediums: wood, fabrics, and modeling compounds; though I am better known for my work with Fimo and foods. I have been making miniature table-ready foods, medieval to present, since 1982. More recently I have added garden fresh foods and fresh fowl to my repertoire. My foods are primarily made from Fimo.

I am mostly self-taught, using an experimental trial and error system that has brought results, though in later years I have picked up a few hints from others who are talented in working with Fimo. One of my joys of being involved in miniatures is the sharing of my hobby through the giving and taking of workshops since my first involvement in 1977. I am one of the founding members of the Miniature Enthusiasts of Ottawa, Canada, 1978, a member of NAME since 1978, a member of IGMA since 1984, and an IGMA Artisan since 1990.

ARTISAN: CLAUDON, CHARLES

BUSINESS NAME: The Butterfly Cat Studio

IDENTIFICATION MARKS:

CLAUDON

CATEGORY:

Animals: cats, dressed; Room settings; Vignettes

HONORS:

IGMA Artisan; NAME AOH 1985; Exhibit: Toy & Miniature Museum of Kansas City

RECOGNITION:

Articles written about Charles Claudon

Small Talk, Feb. 1977, pg. 10-11; *This Side of Yesterday in Miniatures*, Catherine B. MacLaren 1975; *The Dollhouse and Miniature News*, Oct. 1976, pg. 1-2; *Making Dollhouses & Dioramas*, Robert Schleicher, Chilton Book Co. 1980, pg. 112-117, 119, 123; *Tri-State Trader*, Sept. 18, 1982, pg. 51; *Through the Looking Glass*, Boynton and Associates, Inc., Ann Ruble 1984; *Masters in Miniature, 12 Artisans At Work, Volume 1*, Anne Day Smith, Kalmbach Publishing 1987; *Miniature Gazette*, Spring 1990, pg. 43

Articles written by Charles Claudon

Crafts Magazine, Jul. 1978, pg. 26-31; Mar. 1979, pg. 38-41; Feb. 1980, pg. 56-58; *Easter Ideals*, Mar. 1989, pg. 72-73; *Miniature Gazette*, Dec. 1976, pg. 39; Sept. 1977, pg. 59-60; Winter 1984, pg. 7-9; Summer 1986, pg. 56-57; *Nutshell News,* Fall, 1972, pg. 4-8; Winter 1977, pg. 25-28; Jan/Feb. 1979, pg. 28-29; Apr. 1980, pg. 39-41; Dec. 1980, pg. 24-26; Jan. 1981, pg. 24-28; Mar. 1982, pg. 28-30; Aug. 1982, pg. 64-67; *The Scale Cabinetmaker*, Summer 1981, pg. 10-15; Winter 1981, pg. 4-8

AUTOBIOGRAPHY:

I was born in Bloomington, Illinois, on October 23, 1943, and raised in Lexington, Illinois. I have a BS degree in Drama, from the Illinois State University, 1966, and an MA degree received in 1971 from the same university. On October 13, 1969, I married Ferbie Dazey Fox.

I am currently, and have been since 1969, teaching English at Rich East High School in Park Forest, Illinois. From 1969 to 1986, I was head of the drama program. Prior to that (1966-1969), I taught drama and English at Mac Arthur High School in Decatur, Illinois.

I've always had an interest in miniatures, having worked with models, settings, and figures. One of my favorite college courses was scene design for which I made my first real miniature setting: a model for *Desire Under The Elms,* which was constructed of illustration board and lighted with Italian Christmas tree lights. The set included a four-room New England salt-box house. During the next few weeks I made a total of eight ½-inch scale models. In 1969, I made my first dollhouse: Braymore-at-Carnavan, in one-inch scale. During the 1970's, I also taught some adult courses in miniatures.

In 1980, I started my own business, The Butterfly Cat Studio. I have concentrated on realistic cats and currently have over 21 different one-inch scale cat poses, five ½-inch scale poses and ¼-inch scale pose. The cats which I do are modeled on our three cats: Phyllis Marie (Button), China Silk, and Katie Scarlet. Together Ferbie and I produce a line of dressed cats called Kitty Kitsch. I sculpt and paint the cats and Ferbie dresses them.

I have been a member of NAME since 1973. From 1979-1982, I served as Regional Coordinator for Region A-1. Ferbie and I were honored to be elected to the Academy of Honor in 1985. The following year, I acted as hosting chairperson and Ferbie was co-host chairperson for the Chicago NAME National Houseparty. I have been on the NAME board since 1986. Ferbie and I are also artisans in the International Guild of Miniature Artisans. In July, 1992, I became President of NAME.

I have written for *Nutshell News, Miniature Gazette, Dollhouse and Miniature News, Small Talk, Crafts,* and *The Scale Cabinetmaker*. Ferbie and I were also written up in Anne Day Smith's *Masters in Miniatures, Volume 1*. From 1975 through 1987, I have completed several room settings and vignettes, several of which have been featured in miniature publications.

ARTISAN: CLAUDON, FERBIE

BUSINESS NAME: Ferbie Claudon

IDENTIFICATION MARKS:

CATEGORY:

Animal: cats, dressed; Costuming; Dolls: epoxy, original; Figures; Room settings; Vignettes

HONORS:

IGMA Artisan; NAME AOH, 1985; Exhibit: Toy & Miniature Museum of Kansas City

RECOGNITION:

Nutshell News, Dec. 1980, pg. 66-68; Jun. 1982, pg. 38-40; Sept. 1986; *Miniature Gazette*, Winter 1981, Cover; Spring 1984, pg. 30-32; *Park Forest Star*, 1979; *Masters in Miniature, 12 Artisans At Work, Volume 1*, Anne Day Smith, Kalmbach Publishing, 1987

AUTOBIOGRAPHY:

I was born in Madisonville, Kentucky, in 1942. After graduating from Murray State University in Kentucky with a BA degree in English and Business, I taught one year in junior high school in Madisonville and five years in high school in Decatur, Illinois.

In 1969, Chuck Claudon and I married and moved to Park Forest, Illinois. I decided to do substitute teaching for the next 12 years which gave me a chance to go back to a long-neglected hobby, dolls.

When I was very small, my parents began a collection of storybook dolls for me which I continued. I began sewing for and making rag dolls when I was in high school. In 1970, as the price of dolls went up and my personal income didn't, I decided to begin making my own costume dolls. An article about my work with the larger scaled costume dolls appeared in the Park Forest Star in 1979.

As Chuck's interest in one-inch scale increased and my room to store the larger dolls decreased, I too became interested in one-inch scale. My first attempts were five ½-inch soft sculpture costume dolls made with nylon hosiery. I had become interested in costume after making period costumes for the high school plays Chuck directed (such as Shakespeare's *Taming of the Shrew* with over 15 Elizabethan costumes).

After I discovered Super Sculpy, it became my sculpting medium. I did my first one-inch scale sculpted figures in 1980. The result was a Salvation Army scene of 1897, called "Banners and Bonnets." There are five figures playing for the Christmas kettle collection. I displayed this scene at the 1980 NAME Houseparty in Washington, DC. It appeared on the cover of the 1981 winter issue of *Miniature Gazette* and an article appeared in *Nutshell News*. Later I did a ½-inch scale version of the same scene. The one-inch scale vignette is in the collection of Canadian Mildred Mahoney.

Subsequent projects have included an elderly man on a park bench feeding the birds Thanksgiving Dinner; an 1860 bride-to-be receiving a letter saying her fiancé has been killed in the battle of Bull Run; five 1910-1913 suffragettes in a birdcage, "As Ye Sow, So Shall Ye Reap," exhibited at the St. Louis NAME

Houseparty in 1981 and featured in *Nutshell News*; and a novice ballerina and her professional counterpart placed in point shoes "On Toe," 1982, now in the collection of Dorothy Midgett.

In 1981, Chuck and I began a series of dressed cats called Kitty Kitsch. They are one-inch scaled cats dressed in a variety of periods, from a showgirl in feathered plumes to King Henry VIII and his six wives.

I began a line of ½-inch scale ladies in 1983. The originals are done in Super Sculpy and I have these cast in epoxy. They too are dressed in a variety of period styles. Since then I have added a ½-inch scale child, male figure, and baby to the line, along with a one-inch scale baby.

In 1985, I created Baby's Levee, 1874, a ½-inch scale hatbox vignette of five Victorian women visiting a new baby. The vignette was based on costume drawing in Peterson's Ladies National Magazine. The following year I did two hatbox vignettes, each called "Shopping Spree," one of a woman and child trying on hats shown by a sales clerk and one of three cats dressed the same way.

In 1985, I become a member of Name Academy of Honor. I am also an artisan in the International Guild of Miniature Artisans.

In 1986, I was hosting co-chairwoman for the Chicago NAME National Houseparty. Our Steering Committee formed the 993 Club, a NAME club devoted to ½-inch scale. I created a ½-inch scale room called Grandma's Bridge Party, complete with four elderly women and two children, and was featured in the September 1986 *Nutshell News*. I was AOH chairwoman for four years.

ARTISAN: CLEMENT, SHARON R.

BUSINESS NAME: Clement Collectibles

IDENTIFICATION MARKS:

SHARON © 1987 — 1987 to present; Ribbon sewn on back seam

SHARON'S JAMBEAREE — 1985 to 1987; Sewn in back seam

1989 to present; Plastic tag placed around neck with ribbon

CATEGORY:

Bears

RECOGNITION:

Miniatures Showcase, Vol. 4, No. 4, Fall 1989, pg. 42; Vol. 6, No. 2, Spring 1991, pg. 60; *Nutshell News*, Vol. 22, No. 1, Jan. 1992, pg. 68; *National Doll & Teddy Bear Collector*, Vol. 6, No. 3, Mar. 1990, pg. 1, 16; *Teddy Bear and Friends*, Vol. 9, No. 2, Mar. 1990, pg. 56

ARTISAN: CLIFT, DEREK JOHN

BUSINESS NAME: Bishopstoke Miniatures

IDENTIFICATION MARKS:

1987 to present

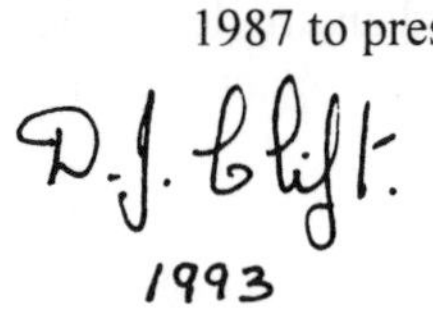

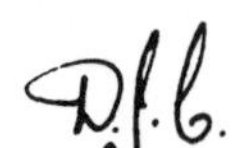

With or without date, used when space limited

CLIFT, DEREK JOHN, continued

CATEGORY:
Furniture

RECOGNITION:
Nutshell News, Jan. 1991, pg. 72; Jun. 1991, pg. 61; *International Dolls House News*, Vol. 18, No. 3, Autumn 1989, pg. 27; Vol. 21, No. 1, Spring 1992, pg. 21; *Dolls House World*, No. 26, 1993, pg. 13-14; *The Home Miniaturist*, No. 64, Dec. 1992/Jan. 1993, pg. 30; *Decorative Dolls' Houses*, Caroline Hamilton, Ebury Press, London, 1990, pg. 58

ARTISAN: CLINGER, WILLIAM S.

BUSINESS NAME: W. Spencer Clinger, Miniaturewright

IDENTIFICATION MARKS:

CATEGORY:
Benches; Chairs: rockers, Windsor; Furniture; Sleighs

RECOGNITION:
Nutshell News, Jul. 1989, pg. 62; Sept. 1989, pg. 67; Dec. 1990, pg. 71; Jan. 1992, pg. 68; Jun. 1992, pg. 65; *Miniature Gazette*, Spring 1987, pg. 37

AUTOBIOGRAPHY:
I earned my BS in 1958 at Virginia Commonwealth University, and my M.P.H. in 1963 at the University of North Carolina. My entire career was spent in the field of public health. In 1983, I retired from the US Public Health Service as a Captain, in the Commissioned Corps.

My second career in miniatures was basically unplanned, having only limited experience which I got making models as a teenager. In 1984, I made some one-inch scale wooden sleds and went to a locally sponsored miniatures show. Encouraged by my success, I started making one-inch scale Windsor style chairs in 1985. I have progressively added new chairs over the years and now make 37 different types of one-inch and ½-inch scale chairs, rockers and benches. As of the end of 1992, I have made and sold 9,002 chairs, rockers and benches.

ARTISAN: CLOUGH, ANNE

BUSINESS NAME: Mouse Couture

IDENTIFICATION MARKS:

CATEGORY:
Animals: dressed

HONORS:
IGMA Artisan

ARTISAN: **CNOSSEN, DONALD E.**

BUSINESS NAME: Don Cnossen

IDENTIFICATION MARKS:

DC Used when space is limited

1976 to present

CATEGORY:

Furniture

RECOGNITION:

Nutshell News, May/Jun. 1979; Feb. 1984, pg. 56; *Miniature Gazette*, Fall 1984; *St. Petersburg Times*, Tues., Oct. 18, 1977

ARTISAN: **COAD, ARLYN P.**

IDENTIFICATION MARKS:

CATEGORY:

Carvings: wood; Dolls: wax

HONORS:

IGMA Fellow; National Institute of America Doll Artists; Exhibit: Toy & Miniature Museum of Kansas City

RECOGNITION:

Nutshell News, Feb. 1982, pg. 68-70, "Minikins: Madame Coad's Medium;" Oct. 1982, pg. 64

BIOGRAPHY:

Co-founder and Artist Director of Coad Canada Puppets, Arlyn Coad began creating miniatures as a pastime while touring puppet productions with her husband. Originally her medium was wood carvings but a fascination with wax dolls led her into that medium in 1980. Eleven years later she retired as an Artist member of the National Institute of American Doll Artists and a Fellow of the International Guild of Miniature Artisans, although she still occasionally creates one of her exquisite miniature wax dolls.

ARTISAN: **COBBS, FRED**

BUSINESS NAME: Fred Cobbs Miniature Craftsman

IDENTIFICATION MARKS:

1980 to present

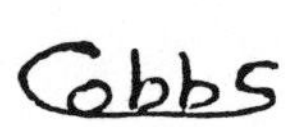

CATEGORY:

Accessories; Buildings; Machines; Nautical; Structures; Tools

COBBS, FRED, continued

HONORS:

IGMA Artisan

RECOGNITION:

Nutshell News, Dec. 1982, pg. 56-58, "Home for the Holidays," Sybil Harp; *Miniature Gazette*, Vol. 12, No. 3, Spring 1984, pg. 41-42, "Fred Cobbs, Georgia Miniaturist," Braxton Payne

AUTOBIOGRAPHY:

I have no background either in college, special education or occupation that would relate to miniatures. I just always have enjoyed models and ships.

ARTISAN: COLE, CHRISTOPHER, DR.

BUSINESS NAME: Longbarn Enterprise

IDENTIFICATION MARKS:

DESIGNED & MADE BY Christopher Cole — Sticker on back, lower right hand corner

CKC 15/92 — Serial number stamped below sticker, number in series/year

Logo

CATEGORY:

Dollhouse; Structures

RECOGNITION:

Build Your own Dolls House, Christopher Cole, Shepheard-Walwyn, London, England

AUTOBIOGRAPHY:

I spent most of my working life as a family doctor, General Practitioner, in England, but I had always made toys, furniture etc. for my own family. Anticipating retirement, I built up the dolls house business, and when I was 62, I left medicine and started building dollshouses full-time. We moved to North Yorkshire where I purchased an old corn water mill. We have now fully restored the mill and it is large enough to provide workshops and show rooms as well as living accommodations for myself and my wife, Doren, who is fully involved in the business. I learned these skills from other craftsmen and designing skills from my father, who was an architect.

ARTISAN: COLLINS, LYNNE L.

BUSINESS NAME: Lynne L. Collins

IDENTIFICATION MARKS:

LC

COLLINS, LYNNE L., continued

CATEGORY:

Accessories; China; Dinnerware

HONORS:

IGMA Artisan; Exhibits: Toy & Miniature Museum of Kansas City; Jefferson State Reception Room, Palm Springs Desert Museum, Palm Springs, California

RECOGNITION:

Nutshell News, Feb. 1983, pg. 57, Show Scene; Sept. 1985, pg. 64; Aug. 1986, pg. 68, Show Scene; Sept. 1988, pg. 68, Show Scene; Dec. 1988, pg. 72-73; Apr. 1989, pg. 73, Show Scene; Jun. 1990, pg. 67, Show Scene; Oct. 1990, pg. 66; Sept. 1991, Cover, pg. 67; *Miniature Collector*, No. 37, Jun. 1983, pg. 30-33, "The Many Facets of Lynne Collins," Mary Durland Fields; No. 38, Aug. 1983, pg. 38, Show Stopper; *Trouvailles*, Jan/Feb. 1985, pg. 33; *Nutshell News Calendar* 1989, Apr., Oct.

BIOGRAPHY:

Lynne Lee Collins is a lifetime resident of the state of Georgia. She has a Bachelor of Fine Arts Degree from the University of Georgia and is a homemaker, mother of two sons, Chris and Lee, and a former high school art teacher.

After becoming interested in miniatures in 1979, Lynne created her first 18th century china pieces using her Williamsburg Craft House catalog for reference and inspiration. She had been frustrated in trying to find authentic pieces to complete her miniature rooms. To obtain the specific shapes to scale, she makes her own models and molds. Some pieces must be kiln fired five or six times depending on the pattern.

Lynne participated in her first miniatures show in 1982 and although she has limited the number of shows each year, her work has been shown throughout the US and in Paris and London. An IGMA Artisan, Lynne has attended the Guild School in Castine, Maine.

A number of outstanding collections contain examples of Lynne's work including Ingeborg Reisser's rooms, Esther and Bill Robertson's, "Twin Manor" exhibit at the Toy & Miniature Museum of Kansas City, and the Jefferson State Reception Room in the Walter Annenberg Palm Springs Desert Museum, California.

Lynne's interest continues to be reproducing in accurate scale as nearly as possible, the shapes and pattern of antique pieces.

ARTISAN: COMSTOCK, ROBERT & PAULA

BUSINESS NAME: Hollow Habitats

IDENTIFICATION MARKS:

CATEGORY:

Accessories; Cabins: log; Houses: log

HONORS:

IGMA Artisan 1994 (Paula); Emmy Award 1974 (Paula); State Department & Community Civic Awards 1992 (Rob)

RECOGNITION:

Miniature Gazette, Fall 1992, "Roses," John Tucker; *Nutshell News*, May 1991; *S.A.M. Passport,* Apr. 1990

COMSTOCK, ROBERT & PAULA, continued

BIOGRAPHY:

Paula graduated from the University of Arkansas and went to work as a television news production secretary on NASA's Apollo 11 for BBC Television News in the US and then moved to New York City and worked at CBS News/Special Events and Foreign News as a Field Producer for 13 years. She received an Emmy Award in 1974.

Rob graduated from Stephen F. Austin State University with Forestry and Sociology Degrees. He worked for the state of Texas as a Park Ranger for eight years at Galveston Island State Park, and currently is Park Superintendent at Sheldon Lake State Park, Houston. State Department and Community Civic Awards 1992, President Optimist Club and Sheldon EMS, Board Channel Industry Advisory Council, Houston. Paula and Rob are happily married and have a son, Fletcher.

Paula started selling miniature crocheted items under the name Petite Crochet in 1988. Hollow Habitats debuted at Tom Bishop's Houston Texas show, in 1990. They have exhibited their personal miniature collection each summer at Harris County Library and have taught two semesters of miniatures in HISD's gifted and talented program at Vanguard-Pleasantville Elementary School. They teach and do Hollow Habitat workshops at the Houston Guild and various shows they attend. The summer of 1993, Paula taught miniatures to 8 to 14 year olds at San Jacinto Jr. College in their *Kids Kollege* program.

ARTISAN: **CONLON, SHIRLEY**

BUSINESS NAME: Shirley Conlon

IDENTIFICATION MARKS:

SJC

SC

CATEGORY:

Needlework; Samplers

RECOGNITION:

Miniatures Showcase, Fall 1989; Spring 1990; Summer 1990; Fall 1990; Winter 1990; Spring 1991; Fall 1991; Winter 1991; *Nutshell News*, May 1990, Cover; *Miniature Dealer*, Aug. 1990

ARTISAN: **CONNEEN, JANE W.**

BUSINESS NAME: The Little Farm Press

IDENTIFICATION MARKS:

4/75 Conneen ©'93 Edition number left side name on right

CATEGORY:

Art; Etchings: handpainted

HONORS:

IGMA Fellow; Best in Show, First in Graphics, American National Miniature Show, Laramie, Wyoming; First in Graphics, Miniature Art Society of New Jersey; Miniature Painters, Sculptors & Engravers Society, Washington, DC; Miniature Art Society, Florida; 2nd. Prize in Graphics, National.

National. Miniature Show, La Luz, New Mexico; 2nd Prize 6-inch and under, Miniature Art Society, Montana; Merit Awards, The Festival of the Masters, Disney World, Florida; Beaux Arts Festival of Art, Coral Gables, Florida; Distinguished Book Award, Miniature Book Society; eight one-person Exhibitions; 23 group Exhibitions; Participating in numerous Art Festivals.

RECOGNITION:

North Light Magazine, "Etching Through the Ages;" *Nutshell News; Miniature Books,* Louis Bondy, Sheppard Press, London; *Miniature Collector; Miniature Book Society Newsletter,* "Profile: Jane Conneen," Ann Bahar

BIOGRAPHY:

Jane Conneen is an artist whose Miniature Hand Colored Etchings evolved from her larger pen-and-ink and water-color botanical drawings. Though her first subjects were flowers, she soon developed an interest in architectural subjects and landscapes and her work became smaller and smaller. The first one-inch scale etchings were minuscule versions of her larger Herbs and Wildflowers. From there she went on to do a series of small vegetables, fruit, seashells, butterflies, birds and landscapes.

These miniature hand painted etchings are unique in their concept and technique. The embossment produced by the cut-out plates, along with the triple Museum Board mats, gives a remarkable feeling of depth and the clear, vivid, watercolors provide a visibility that is surprising in such very small works. In her present work, the average copper plates run 1½-inch to two-inch and most of the subjects reflect the artist's travels in Europe and throughout the United States. These also have inspired two miniature books (about two-inch, readable size) the first one, *The Winding Roads of Ireland* printed by Etching Press, and the second Staithes: *The Story of a Yorkshire Fishing Village*, printed by Letterpress. Each one has 10 hand-colored illustrations. Two more miniature books, *The Language of Herbs* and *The Language of Herbs II*, were printed by Gocco, also with 10 illustrations each.

Jane's studio is situated on a 5½ acre hillside in the foothills of the Poconos. Trees, herbs and wildflowers line the paths through the fields up to the top of the hill where there is a panoramic view of Blue Mountain and several Gaps, including Delaware Water Gap.

Her botanical drawings are in the collection of the Hunt Institute for Botanical Documentation. She is a fellow of the International Guild of Miniature Artisans, a member of the Miniature Painters, Sculptors and Gravers Society of Washington, DC, and numerous other print and miniature organizations. She is listed in *Who's Who in American Art.*

ARTISAN: **COOK, DOREEN M.**

BUSINESS NAME: Fantasie

IDENTIFICATION MARKS:

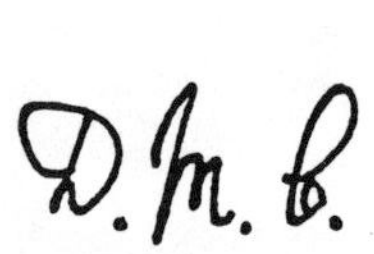

CATEGORY:

Furniture: wicker

RECOGNITION:

Dolls House World, Issue 21, 1992, pg. 34

ARTISAN: **COOK, MADELYN W.**

BUSINESS NAME: Lagniappe Enterprises

IDENTIFICATION MARKS:

Some unmarked

 with year

CATEGORY:

Accessories; Buildings; Furniture; Rooms

HONORS:

NAME AOH 1989; Exhibits: National Geographic Society Museum, Washington, DC, 1987/88; Fullerton Museum Center, Fullerton, CA, Jul. 1988

RECOGNITION:

Nutshell News, Apr. 1980, pg. 24-25; Oct. 1981, pg. 32-35; Oct. 1982, pg. 80-81; Oct. 1988, pg. 38-42; Apr. 1990, pg. 36-40; Mar. 1992, pg. 76-79; May 1992, pg. 82-85; *Miniature Collector*, Oct. 1979, pg. 32-37; Dec. 1979, pg. 35-37; Oct. 1982, pg. 42; *The Scale Cabinetmaker*, Vol. 4, No. 2, pg. 23; Vol. 4, No. 3, pg. 29, 40; Vol. 4, No. 4, pg. 39; Vol. 5, No. 1, pg. 30, 35; Vol. 5, No. 2, pg. 40; Vol. 5, No. 4, pg. 35, 37; Vol. 6, No. 1, pg. 10, 21; Vol. 6, No. 2, pg. 21, 33; Vol. 6, No. 3, pg. 22; Vol. 6, No. 4, pg. 19; Vol. 7, No. 1, pg. 16; Vol. 7, No. 3, pg. 19; Vol. 7, No. 4, pg. 29; Vol. 10, No. 1, pg. 14; *Small Talk*, Aug. 1977, Cover story; Nov. 1977, Cover story; *Nutshell News Plan Service*, No. 105, 1981, "Wicker Wizardry;" No. 123, 1983, "An Accent on Wicker;" *Through The Looking Glass*, Boynton and Associates, Inc., Ann Ruble, 1984; *American Period Interiors in Miniature*, Kate Doordan Klavan, 1984

BIOGRAPHY:

Madelyn was born and raised in the Wilmette, Illinois area, attending New Trier High School and Purdue University, Lafayette, Indiana. She feels like she was born into miniatures as her earliest memories were of her grandparents' centuries-old German tradition of a Christmas garden built and displayed under the Yule tree. Madelyn and her family have continued their own version featuring 900 figures and a dozen working mechanical features.

Her interest in period furnishings and history along with hobby pursuits in woodworking, sculpture, jewelry making, and needle crafts all culminated in her final vocation and avocation of miniatures. She ventured into the design and construction of roomboxes, buildings, furniture and accessories joining NAME in 1976. Her best known buildings are the one-inch scale "Lagniappe" and her ¼-inch scale "Hilltop" and "La Petite Lagniappe" (Tiny), all of which have been displayed at NAME National and Regional Houseparties and as fund raisers for various charities.

She sold miniatures for several years, but came to the conclusion that she could best share her hobby through writing and teaching. She wrote as "Master of Disguise" as well as designing plans for *The Scale Cabinetmaker*. She has designed wicker for the Nutshell News Plan Service. A continuing series of designs in ¼-inch scale started in *Nutshell News* in April 1990 and continues today. Her work has been featured throughout the country in museums, books, television, newspapers and magazines. She taught for many years at the College of Miniature Knowledge, a Mini/Cruise in 1992 and many NAME Regional and National Houseparties. She was elected to the NAME Academy of Honor in 1989. Her husband, Jim, shares in the hobby by photographing miniatures.

Although building miniatures has turned into her life's work, her biggest passion is skiing and racing where she has competed in National Championships.

ARTISAN: **COOK, TOOTIE**

BUSINESS NAME: Mini-Blessings

IDENTIFICATION MARKS:

COOK, TOOTIE, continued

CATEGORY:

Furniture; Houses

HONORS:

IGMA Artisan 1992

RECOGNITION:

Nutshell News, Jan. 1991, pg. 27

AUTOBIOGRAPHY:

My first introduction to miniatures was in Fall, 1989. That was a visit my son and I made to a local miniature shop. I could not believe what I was seeing. Needless to say, I was hooked!. My love for Louisiana came together with my found love of miniatures, which resulted in my first piece of scaled furniture, a Louisiana pie safe constructed in 1990. My life has not been the same since. Because I felt it was one of God's *many* blessings, I named my miniature business *Mini-Blessings.*

The same year I was accepted into the Gulf South Miniature and Dollhouse Event in New Orleans. The response was overwhelming. From that show I was commissioned to create a Louisiana home with all its furnishings and an article was written by Sarah Salisbury in Nutshell News. In 1992, I was recognized as an IGMA Artisan for my furniture. I was also commissioned by the New Orleans Museum of Art to replicate museum pieces in one-inch scale.

ARTISAN: COOKE, GILLIAN

BUSINESS NAME: Sid Cooke Dolls' Houses

IDENTIFICATION MARKS:

1984 to 1988, Printed in blue at base of all shops and houses

1989 to present, Printed in blue at base on assembled shops and houses

MADE BY SID & GILLIAN COOKE

1990 to present, Printed in red at base of kit pack shops and houses

CATEGORY:

Dollhouse: manufacturer; Structures

BIOGRAPHY:

Gillian Cooke trained in Textile Design at Birmingham Polytechnic. She joined Sid in miniatures in 1981. Since then her work has moved completely over to the manufacture of dolls' houses. As well as taking part in the production side, she handles the record-keeping side of the business. She has a BA Honors and an MA.

ARTISAN: **COOKE, SID**

BUSINESS NAME: Sid Cooke Dolls' Houses

IDENTIFICATION MARKS:

SID COOKE DOLLS' HOUSES

MADE BY SID & GILLIAN COOKE

With Compliments

SID COOKE DOLLS' HOUSES

CATEGORY:
Dollhouse: manufacturer; Structures

RECOGNITION:
Decorative Dolls' Houses, Caroline Hamilton, Ebury Press, London, 1990; *Dolls & Dolls' Houses*, No. 1, Guild of Master Craftsman

BIOGRAPHY:
Sid is a self-taught miniaturist. He has been manufacturing dolls' houses and shops for over 12 years, specializing in items for the collector. As well as producing larger shops and houses, Sid pioneered the introduction to the British market of small shops for miniatures, especially the single unit to fit on a bookshelf. In 1990, kit packs were introduced to the ever-changing range of products. Sid has appeared on British TV, and BBC radio, as well as being featured in local and national newspapers.
see "Gillian Cooke"

ARTISAN: **COOKE, HARRY** (Deceased)

IDENTIFICATION MARKS: (Submitted by William R. Robertson)

 month and year

Signed with vibrator engraver *made by Harry Cooke*

CATEGORY:
Furniture: period

HONORS:
NAME AOH; Exhibits: Philadelphia Museum of Art; Toy & Miniature Museum of Kansas City

RECOGNITION:
Nutshell News, Jun. 1984, pg. 49-54, "Way Down South in Dixie," Ann Ruble; *Miniature Gazette*, Vol. 4, No. 3, Mar. 1976, pg. 23, "Tiny Treasures Society's Third Annual Luncheon, The Boston Show," Jim Cunningham; Vol. 7, No. 3, Spring 1979, pg. 77, "1978 Saratoga Festival of Miniatures," Natalie Buckman; Vol. 10, No. 2, Winter 1981, pg. 25, "A 'Not So Small' Collection of Miniatures," Florence Lambert

BIOGRAPHY:
Harry Cooke's name was legendary to miniaturists, representing as it did the highest standards in the art of producing miniature 18th century furniture. As one of the members of Name Academy of Honor, he was part

of a select group of NAME members whose craftsmanship and support of miniaturing have earned them this recognition. Even though he used to create scale model ships and airplanes as a boy, and even though he was an active model railroader for 18 years, it was his wife, Thelma, who gave Harry a push in the direction of creating miniature furniture. Upon his retirement from Eastman Kodak Company, where he worked for 35 years as a chemical engineer and an executive, Harry was hunting around for a hobby which would keep him busy and productive. His wife, who was an expert needleworker, wanted him to get involved in something they could do together. With miniatures in mind, Thelma thought if they were to construct a model room, she could contribute needlework items such as petitpoint rugs, Bargello upholstery, crewel fire screen panels, draperies, etc., while he would build the room itself and its furniture.

Harry immersed himself in reading books about furniture, especially 18th century styles, visiting museums and antique shops or auctions in order to view original, full-sized prototypes. The first piece of miniature furniture he attempted was a 17th century blanket chest. His next pieces were increasingly elaborate and complex. The room Harry and Thelma finally chose to work on jointly was a reproduction of the second floor drawing room of the 18th century Samuel Powel house in Philadelphia. This fine example of early American Georgian architecture has been put on display at the Philadelphia Museum of Art. They estimate that they spent more than 2,000 hours in researching and recreating this room. Thelma even took a course in silversmithing so that she could make some tiny silver bowls they needed to complete the room. Between them, they made everything in the room except a porcelain cup and saucer and a silver teapot.

Inspired by an article and photos in the magazine *Antiques*, Harry began duplicating many of the pieces from the Pendleton Collection of the Rhode Island School of Design's Museum of Art. Three years of effort produced 10 pieces which were then accorded a special exhibit at the museum, a singular honor. He duplicated everything in exacting detail, even to the correct number of dovetails in a drawer. All the brasswork was made by Harry, and the tiny locks actually worked with a key. Carving was done with gravers, and files might have been used for the final finishing. Dovetails were cut with gravers, jeweler's saw, and final-fitted with files.

Once his craftsmanship became known to collectors of fine miniatures, almost everything he built was on a commission basis. Harry's assessment of his own work was that he probably contributed the most in the area of the carving he did on his miniatures. He may have been the first person to succeed in reproducing undercut talons on the ball and claw foot which is so characteristic of the Townsend-Goddard workshop. This little noticed aspect of his work can be found on a Newport Chippendale card table, originally attributed to John Goddard, which was Harry's contribution to the AOH display collection.

(from *Meet the members of AOH*, by Sarah Salisbury, authorized reprint by NAME)

ARTISAN: **COOLEY, HAROLD**

BUSINESS NAME: Hearth & Home Miniatures

IDENTIFICATION MARKS:

Most unmarked

CATEGORY:

Cookware; Fireplace: accessories; Reproductions: Colonial

HONORS:

IGMA Artisan

RECOGNITION:

Cleveland P.M. Magazine; Cleveland Plain Dealer; *Nutshell News*; *Miniatures Showcase*

AUTOBIOGRAPHY:

I worked as a welder and iron worker for 35 years.

ARTISAN: **CORKIN, NELL**

BUSINESS NAME: Miniature Miniatures

IDENTIFICATION MARKS:

NELL CORKIN 1993

CATEGORY:

Dollhouse: doll's dollhouse

HONORS:

IGMA Artisan

RECOGNITION:

Nutshell News, Sept. 1991, Show Scene; May 1993, pg. 32-35, "Houses to Have and to Hold," Anne Day Smith; *Miniature Gazette*, Spring 1993, pg. 46, "Ultramininut Spotlight on Nell Corkin," Jane Winston Kilkenny

AUTOBIOGRAPHY:

I began making miniatures as a child. My sister and I spent countless hours remodeling a dollhouse that my grandfather made for my mother. Inspired by the books my mother had showing the Thorne rooms at the Art Institute of Chicago, I was attempting roomboxes and scratch built furniture by the time I was a teenager, and collecting what pieces I could by mail from Chestnut Hill Studio. If there had been such a discipline, I would have majored in miniatures in college; since there wasn't, I settled for Art History. The knowledge I gained has been invaluable to me in designing the miniature buildings I am making now; it is very important to me that they be historically and aesthetically correct.

As I suspect was the case with many others in the sixties, I knew of very few people who collected or made miniatures. It was not until I moved to California in the late 70's and attended my first miniatures show that I realized, to my great delight, how many other people shared this interest.

In California, I discovered that I could actually make a living with miniatures as a special effects modelmaker, an occupation I have pursued since 1983. My work in special effects has allowed me to meet, work with and learn from, a great number of incredibly talented people, and to acquire new skills such as mold making and simple machining which would have been difficult to learn on my own. It has helped to give me a solid understanding of scale, since models for movies are done in every scale imaginable.

I first showed my 1/144-inch scale houses, which were partially scratch built, in 1991. Since 1992, the houses have been completely scratch built, from my own original designs. These include castles, cottages, Victorian mansions, and replicas of cabinet style dollhouses, as well as a special line of houses made from real walnuts. All are open at the back and can be used as dollhouses in a one-inch scale dollhouse, and are available furnished or unfurnished, with or without electric lights.

ARTISAN: **CORSO, JAMES**

BUSINESS NAME: Rebecca House Miniatures

IDENTIFICATION MARKS:

1961 to present

CATEGORY:

Dollhouse; Furniture

CORSO, JAMES, continued

BIOGRAPHY:

Jim has been handcrafting miniatures since 1979. He has built several houses from scratch, including a replication of the Maxwell mansion in Rockville, Connecticut. Jim has made furniture of all types in limited editions, and is an accomplished miniaturist. He is a member of MIAA.

ARTISAN: CORSO, THOMAS

BUSINESS NAME: Rebecca House Miniatures

IDENTIFICATION MARKS:

, 1988 to present

CATEGORY:

Accessories; Dollhouse; Furniture

ARTISAN: COSTANTINI, ALICE MARIE

BUSINESS NAME: Alice Marie Costantini

IDENTIFICATION MARKS:

1989 to present

CATEGORY:

Art: fine, Nouveau; Dolls; Furniture; Paintings; Sculptures; Structures; Wall: coverings, hangings

RECOGNITION:

Miniature Collector, Summer 1992, pg. 22, Show Stopper

AUTOBIOGRAPHY:

I was a professional, full-sized artwork creator, exhibitor and teacher since 1942, working in a variety of media. My BA degree is from Hunter College of the City University of New York, Art Major, English Minor, Phi Beta Kappa 1943. I continued art studies at Philips Collection Art School and American University in Washington, DC. I have taught painting, done graphic art, and studied at Montclair State University, NJ School of Visual Arts and Fashion Institute of Technology, where I studied Interior Design. I've also studied in the home study program of the New York School of Interior Design, and worked at interior design, jewelry making and ceramics.

While raising three sons in the suburbs, I taught art in my home studio located in Bergen County, NJ. My students were children, adults and seniors who came to me from all over the county. I designed and built my studio with my husband, an engineer. At that same time I exhibited my works extensively in Bergen County and New York City. With my children grown and on their own I moved back to New York City and returned to City College School of Architecture, at the age of 58, and worked in the Architecture field. Suddenly, after seeing my first miniature show in 1989, I shrank! That is, my work shrank, and I was hopelessly and blissfully addicted to crafting miniatures. Now all my talents and skills have a new purpose, and benefit my new business.

ARTISAN: **COTTRELL, T. C., JR.**

BUSINESS NAME: Cottrell Limited Editions

IDENTIFICATION MARKS: (Submitted by William R. Robertson)

Editions limited to between five and 15, pieces signed numbered and dated

CATEGORY:

Furniture

HONORS:

Exhibit: Toy & Miniature Museum of Kansas City

RECOGNITION:

Nutshell News, Oct. 1982, pg. 46-48, "Making Aviation History," Priscilla Serling; *Miniature Collector*, No. 13, Jun. 1979, pg. 41, Show Stoppers; *Miniature Gazette*, Vol. 7, No. 1, Fall 1978, pg. 81-82, "Collectors' Cornucopia Show," Faith B. Rogers; Vol. 7, No. 3, Spring 1979, pg. 8-10, "The Miniature Magazine House Tour," Faith Rogers

ARTISAN: **COULON, LAUREL L.**

BUSINESS NAME: 3 L and Friends

IDENTIFICATION MARKS:

1973 to present

CATEGORY:

Porcelain; Sculptures

HONORS:

NAME AOH

RECOGNITION:

Miniature Gazette; Nutshell News; The News Journal of Daytona Beach; Orlando Sentinel

AUTOBIOGRAPHY:

Tiny things have always fascinated me. When I was young, my father set up an "HO" railroad in the basement and I loved trying to make the towns look more realistic. I remember the jail the best, using tissue to cover the cot in the cell. My father was a mail carrier and took many other jobs on the side so that many of the tasks around the house fell to my brother Carl, and me, such as cutting down unwanted trees and tending the apiaries and selling the honey. I quickly learned "there wasn't anything you couldn't do if you set your mind to it," and that there was no such word as can't.

When I married and had a daughter, I purchased a dollhouse for her. After trying to find accessories to fill the house, and meeting with little success, I decided to make them myself. My daughter had little interest in the house, as it turns out, but I had developed quite an interest in creating tiny objects made of porcelain. My mark relates to my maiden name, Laurel Lanette Liberts.

ARTISAN: **COWLES, ARTHUR & MARY-DUDLEY** (Submitted by Roger L. & Nancy Gutheil)

BUSINESS NAME: Chestnut Hill Studio, Ltd.

IDENTIFICATION MARKS:

Most pieces rubber stamped with black ink: **Chestnut Hill Studio**
Paintings signed: **F. Potter**

CATEGORY:
Accessories; Ceramics; Drapes; Furniture; Paintings; Roomboxes; Wall: murals

ARTISAN: **CRAIG, JANET**

BUSINESS NAME: Janet Craig

IDENTIFICATION MARKS:

JC

CATEGORY:
Handwork; Quilts

ARTISAN: **CRANDALL, DAVID C.**

BUSINESS NAME: Moravia Pottery Co.

IDENTIFICATION MARKS:

1989 1990 1991 1992 1993

½" scale pieces | 1 in every 100 pieces | 1 in every 1500 pieces | 1 in every 5000 pieces

CATEGORY:
Pottery

RECOGNITION:
Nutshell News; Miniatures Showcase; Hobby; Merchandiser; Craft & Needlework Age; The Citizen, Auburn, NY, Wednesday, Sept. 30, 1992, Section C, Today

ARTISAN: **CRAVER, ELIZABETH "BETH"**

BUSINESS NAME: A Beth Of Spring

IDENTIFICATION MARKS:

CATEGORY:

Flowers and Plants: paper; Figures: Egyptian; Kits

RECOGNITION:

Miniature Collector, Summer 1990

AUTOBIOGRAPHY:

My handmade paper flowers are in vases, around birdbaths, birdhouses, mailboxes, ponds, trellises, etc. Individual flowers or garden plants are ready for pots or gardens. Supplies like fine wire, cloth covered wire, one-inch floral tape, dirt, lichen, greens, vases, birds, butterflies, kits for birdhouses and mailboxes, flower pots, window boxes, baskets, and more are available. My most popular items are the supplies to put ivy on walls or in pots, and the makings for impatiens. *Miniature Collector* pictured my birdhouse in their Summer 1990 issue. Recently I have begun to carry Egyptian figures and papyrus paintings. These are handmade in Egypt.

ARTISAN: **CRAWFORD, GERALD & LINDA**

BUSINESS NAME: Gerald Crawford

IDENTIFICATION MARKS:

Each piece accompanied by card with its history

CATEGORY:

Furniture: period, reproduction

HONORS:

Exhibits: Toy & Miniature Museum of Kansas City; Henry Francis DuPont Winterthur Museum, Winterthur, Delaware

RECOGNITION:

Nutshell News, May 1983, pg. 36-41, 49, "Arizona Artisans–The Pioneering Spirit Prevails," Marie Simington; Mar. 1984, pg. 56, Show Scene; Apr. 1984, pg. 40-43, 57; May 1984, pg. 50; Aug. 1984, pg. 65; Sept. 1984, pg. 94; *Miniature Collector*, No. 38, Aug. 1983, pg. 9, "Arizona Craftsman to Create Furniture for Winterthur Museum;" No. 49, Summer 1985, pg. 23, "The Art of the Cabinetmaker," Mary Durland Fields; No. 52, Spring 1986, "Celebrating the Art of Miniatures in South Carolina," Mary Durland Fields; *Miniatures Showcase*, Vol. 2, Winter 1987, pg. 18-22, "The Classics," Anne Day Smith; *Antiques & Collecting Hobbies*, Vol. 90, No. 4, June 1985, "Gerald Crawford's Winterthur Miniatures," Ann Bahar; *Fine Woodworking*, No. 88, Jun. 1991, pg. 116, "A Little $8,000 Note," Charley Robinson; *The Andrews Collection*, Personal Treasures, Anne Day Smith, 1988; *Fine Woodworking*, Biennial Design Book 4

CRAWFORD, GERALD & LINDA, continued

BIOGRAPHY:

When Gerald was nine, in 1962, he was fascinated by the Thorne Rooms on exhibit at the Phoenix Art Museum in Phoenix Arizona. Four years later, with one visit to master miniature maker Warren Dick's home and workshop, Gerald started making miniatures in a Western theme.

In 1967, encouraged by Warren Dick and inspired by his enthusiasm in his work, Gerald became interested in the furniture of Early American craftsman. After one year of studying and building miniatures of Early American furniture, he made his first recorded sale of miniature items. From 1972 to 1978, he worked with a local artist building hand weaving looms and equipment. He then started making custom furniture and period pieces.

In 1979, Warren Dick encouraged Linda and Gerald to begin making miniatures again. They chose to create authentic Early American furniture for discriminating collectors.

Nineteen hundred eighty-three was the year Gerald was selected and licensed by the Henry Francis DuPont Winterthur Museum and Gardens in Winterthur, Delaware to create authentic miniature reproductions of pieces chosen from their outstanding collections of American decorative arts. Working with one of the finest museums in the world, challenges them to create work that reflects our heritage. Each piece is signed and bears the Winterthur Museum trademark and is accompanied by a card telling about the piece in Queen Anne, Chippendale and Federal styles.

In 1988 and 1993, Gerald signed his second and third five-year licensing agreements with Winterthur Museum.

In 1990, a selection of their furniture traveled with other miniatures from Angels Attic of Santa Monica, California, for an eight month tour to several cities in Japan.

ARTISAN: CRAWLEY, JANICE

BUSINESS NAME: Janice Crawley

IDENTIFICATION MARKS:

Some pieces and dolls unmarked

 used when space is limited

Both 1981 to present

CATEGORY:

Dishes: ceramic; Dolls: porcelain

HONORS:

IGMA Artisan

RECOGNITION:

Nutshell News, Sept. 1987; *Doll Reader,* Sept. 1987; *Western Report*, Canada, Mar. 10, 1986; *Dolls House World*, No. 6, 1990; *The Home Miniaturist*, May 1991

AUTOBIOGRAPHY:

I trained as an Occupational Therapist, graduating from McGill University in 1959. I have always been interested in crafts especially ceramics and doll making. I discovered miniatures in 1980 at a show in Toronto, Ontario. It seemed to me a wonderful way to carry on with my ceramics, and have narrowed my interest to the dishes and the one-inch and 1½-inch dolls. I model a prototype from Sculpey and make my own plaster molds to slip cast the dishes and dolls. I have three kilns of varying size. I attend miniatures shows in Canada, England and the United States. I have taken classes in sculpting, oil painting and design.

ARTISAN: **CREED, TOBE**

BUSINESS NAME: Farrow Industries Inc.
Tobe Tailored by Farrow
To Be Tiny Inc.

IDENTIFICATION MARKS:
Most pieces unmarked

© TOBE Stamped in black on back

CATEGORY:
Accessories: brass, pewter; Reproductions: name brand

RECOGNITION:
Miniatures Dealer, Jun. 1992

AUTOBIOGRAPHY:

I am a New York native, and was strongly influenced by my mother who was well known in the field of interior design. In addition to my mothers creativity, I was fortunate to have a father who was a talented artist. While working in my parents' gallery I became knowledgeable of antiques. As my expertise developed I began to collect antique dolls. From this my interest turned to antique miniatures, which led to an interest in contemporary miniatures.

I soon realized there was a need for a wider range of miniature accessories. In 1975, I began to design and produce brass and pewter items which were distributed through an independent wholesaler. Some of these items have my trademark stamped on the back. During these years I was attending both retail and wholesale miniatures shows and in 1978 I became a supporting member of NAME.

In 1980, I purchased inventory which was the start of To Be Tiny Inc., specializing in American made miniature accessories. These items became available at retail shows throughout the United States. As the miniatures industry blossomed, I designed more items for my wholesale business which was incorporated under the name of Tobe Tailored. In 1985, Barbara Scholfield joined Tobe Tailored Inc. as a partner. In 1986, we joined CIMTA and introduced our brass and pewter wholesale line. In 1987, we became members of MIAA. In 1988, we purchased Farrow Industries Inc. By 1990, Tobe Tailored became a division of Farrow Industries. In the same year I was elected to the board of directors of MIAA, and served as Trade Show Chairman.

ARTISAN: **CREMINS, JOAN**

BUSINESS NAME: Petite People Plus

IDENTIFICATION MARKS:

P.P.P.

CATEGORY:
Dolls; Millinery

RECOGNITION:
Miniatures Showcase, 1988

AUTOBIOGRAPHY:

I was born in England 73 years ago, 1921, and my favorite toy was the dollhouse my father made for me out of packing cases. By todays' standards it was very crude, but I loved it. I used to spend hours cutting up bits of fabric making all kinds of things for the dollhouse. My husband, son and myself came to America in 1955, and we have loved every minute of it.

I met my partner, Elaine Kothe, when I was president of our local miniatures club, and she was treasurer. Elaine loves ceramics and I love fabrics, so from that, our business was born. I am still cutting up bits of fabric and dressing dolls. I always wanted to be a dress designer, but never had the opportunity to train for it. I am self-taught, and I am always learning.

I recently gave a talk on doll making and miniatures to my granddaughter's school class. It was received very well, and now my grandsons class wants me to talk to them!

see "Elaine Kothe"

ARTISAN: **CROPPER, KIT**

BUSINESS NAME: Kit Cropper Miniatures

IDENTIFICATION MARKS:

KitCropper with date

CATEGORY:

Dollhouse; Figures; Landscaping; Scenes; Structures

HONORS:

NAME AOH 1995

RECOGNITION:

Nutshell News, Jul. 1983, pg. 40-42; *Miniatures Showcase*, Spring 1989, Cover; Fall, 1991, Cover; *Miniature Gazette,* Fall 1991, pg. 61

AUTOBIOGRAPHY:

My educational background is in elementary education and counseling. I am a self-taught miniaturist.

ARTISAN: **CUDWORTH, HAROLD**

BUSINESS NAME: Harold Cudworth

IDENTIFICATION MARKS:

H.C. 19 HC 92

CATEGORY:

Furniture

RECOGNITION:

Home Miniaturist; Dolls House World; Yorkshire Evening Post

ARTISAN: **CUNNINGHAM, ANN T.**

BUSINESS NAME: Aunt Annie's

IDENTIFICATION MARKS:

Some pieces unmarked

A.T.C. 1975 to 1992

(A) 1992 to present

CUNNINGHAM, ANN T., continued

CATEGORY:

Breakaway boxes; Dollhouse

HONORS:

NAME Founders Award 1992; AOH 1995

RECOGNITION:

Nutshell News, Vol. 23, No. 2, Feb. 1993, pg. 60-62, 78-82

BIOGRAPHY:

Ann graduated with a BS from the University of Rhode Island in 1956. She taught Home Economics from 1956 to 1957. She has been married since 1956 to Richard A. Cunningham, and has three sons, Richard, Jr., Alexander, and John. Ann has been a miniature dealer since 1976, a member of NAME since 1975, club president 1975-1988, a NAME Regional Coordinator, 1988-1992, and a State Representative.

ARTISAN: CURDIE, JODY

BUSINESS NAME: Little Things by Jody

IDENTIFICATION MARKS:

CATEGORY:

Floor Coverings; Rugs: braided

RECOGNITION:

Miniature Gazette, Spring 1990, pg. 40; *Miniatures Showcase*, Spring, 1989, Summer, 1989, Fall, 1989, Winter, 1989; Summer, 1990, Winter, 1990; *Dollhouse Miniatures* Calendar 1993, Front Cover

ARTISAN: CURDIE, SCOTT

BUSINESS NAME: Wooden Wonders by Scott

IDENTIFICATION MARKS:

CATEGORY:

Furniture

ARTISAN: **CURRAN, CAROLYN NYGREN**

BUSINESS NAME: CNC Pottery

IDENTIFICATION MARKS

CNC POTTERY 1985 to present, Logo on printed material

CNC 1976 to present, vertical mark, incised or painted in dark slip on base of pot

CNC 1976 to present, slanted mark, incised or painted in dark slip on base of pot

"CNC" is the basic mark with variations due to brushwork or incising tool on a particular clay. The year may be found under the **CNC** mark in the case of Connoisseur Editions. The year, plus number, such as #3, from about 1980 to 1990, indicating third in a possible edition of 50 maximum; or number/number, such as #2/25, indicating second in a limited edition of a possible 25: 1990 to present.

1977 to 1979, CNC's decorated stoneware pieces were wheelthrown by CNC and decorated by Ann Murphy in the first two or three years. These pieces have **CNC/AM** incised at base of each pot.

CATEGORY:

Ceramics; Porcelain; Pottery

HONORS:

IGMA Fellow; 2nd Place, ceramics, glass & enamels category, 6th Annual Exhibition of Miniature Art, Del Bello Gallery, Toronto, Canada

RECOGNITION:

Nutshell News; Miniatures Showcase

BIOGRAPHY:

Carolyn Curran earned her BA in Art, Magna Cum Laude in 1960 at Brown University, Providence, RI. Primarily an art history major in college, her formal education in the arts was limited to a few basic art courses at Rhode Island School of Design as a Brown undergraduate. She is a self-taught potter and would have to point to books as her principal tutors. Under the business name of CNC Pottery, she created wheel thrown utilitarian wares for several years until 1976 when encouraged to create small scale work for a local shop. Since that time she has become well known both in the USA and abroad for her work in one-inch scale. Her reproductions of 19th century decorated stoneware in particular have found their way into many collections, and the Museum of Arts and Antiques in Saratoga Springs, New York houses an extensive collection of her work on permanent display. More recently she has been researching ancient Egyptian and other traditional cultures and has added miniatures of their pottery to her repertory.

Ms. Curran's background in art history has aided her in her miniature reproduction work, and she has done a great deal of research to assure authenticity. Her work in clay is not limited to reproductions, however, and she enjoys creating pots of her own inspiration whenever possible. She is an elected fellow of the International Guild of Miniature Artisans and has been an instructor at the guild's annual school in Castine, Maine for two years. A recent piece of hers, "Archeologist's Nightmare" won a 2nd place in the ceramics, glass and enamels category in the 6th Annual Exhibition of Miniature Art sponsored by Del Bello Gallery of Toronto, Canada. More recently she has been researching a small collection of ancient Cypriot pottery in the Hyde Collection, Glens Falls, New York, where she was guest curator for an exhibition of these artifacts in early 1993.

ARTISAN: **CURRAN, TERRY**

BUSINESS NAME: Terry Curran

IDENTIFICATION MARKS:
Unmarked

CATEGORY:
Builders Items: ceramic; Ceramics: household; Tiles: floor, wall

BIOGRAPHY;
Terry Curran studied Fine Arts at Stafford and Leeds Colleges of Art, England, earning a N.D.D. and A.T.D. Terry taught art for 20, leaving teaching in 1982 to concentrates full-time on making ceramic miniatures.

ARTISAN: **CURRIER, SCOTT**

BUSINESS NAME: Currier & Ives Foundation
CC & S Studios

IDENTIFICATION MARKS:

CATEGORY:
Art; Lithographs; Pictures

BIOGRAPHY:
The Currier & Ives Foundation is comprised of a number of small companies devoted to preserving and distributing the works of "Currier & Ives, Printmakers to the American People."

Scott Currier, a Senior officer of the Currier & Ives Foundation, and Great-Grand Nephew of Nathaniel Currier, produces miniatures of authentic Currier & Ives prints using the same techniques employed by the original firm. Mr. Currier started producing the hand painted miniature lithographs over 10 years ago for collectors of Original Currier & Ives prints. Each miniature print is issued as a limited edition, and is accompanied by a signed letter of authenticity. The prints are produced in one-inch scale.

Mr. Currier spends his days and nights navigating the field of marketing and advertising from his CC & S Studios outside of Denver, Colorado. The CC & S Studios produce and develop the PR and ad campaigns for a number of high-tech companies in the Front Range area. Mr. Currier produces his miniatures through CC & S Studios in conjunction with the Currier & Ives foundations. He describes his miniatures as a hobby and as a source of stress relief.

ARTISAN: **DAHL, BEVERLY**

BUSINESS NAME: Dahl House of Miniatures

IDENTIFICATION MARKS:

Certificate Of Original Beverly Dahl Design

This certificate is your guarantee that this extraordinarily fine miniature doll is a design created by Beverly Dahl. Each doll is to an exact scale of 1 inch equals 1 foot and is made entirely by hand. It represents many hours of intricate and highly skilled labor.

Beverly selects the finest silks and cottons. Each hair style and costume has been painstakingly researched so that you will have an authentic replica of an historic period to be treasured for many years to come and handed down as a family heirloom.

Beverly J Dahl
Beverly J. Dahl

Belle #4 — Doll's Name
11/92 — Date Created
1840-1870 — Period and Year

Hang tag:

cover		inside
Dahl House of Miniatures	Made with loving care by Beverly Dahl on 11/92	Period: 1840-70 Name: Bell Number in Series: #4 LH Porcelain

CATEGORY:

Dolls: porcelain; Kits; Millinery; Pattern Books

RECOGNITION:

Nutshell News, Jan. 1987; *Miniature Collector*, Aug. 1983; *Miniatures Showcase*

AUTOBIOGRAPHY:

In December 1979, Jim bought a 13 room dollhouse kit for his granddaughter. We both work in real-estate, and in 1980 the market was at a standstill. We devoted all our time trying to finish it for a May show at the Swedish Institute. Daily trips were made to our local miniature shop, and I took all the classes offered.

Our next attempts were two large roomboxes, one showing the Fashion House at Worth which needed quite a few dolls. I have a background in art and fashion design and worked with Barbie doll clothing. I also taught dancing for 29 years and designed the costumes, drafted patterns and wrote teaching manuals for the National dance conventions. After buying all the dressing books I could find, I realized the assembly instructions were quite sketchy, so I wrote a book on dressing and thus I was plunged into the world of doll dressing.

I now travel to approximately twenty miniature shows a year. My dolls are completely dressed underneath Swiss Batiste. Many are constructed with French hand sewing. Much of the lace is antique and the particular dress can never be repeated. I take pride in my wigging which is very elaborate. All costumes are researched and copied in miniature as close as possible. Victorian designs are my favorite because of their elaborate construction. Now I concentrate on working in fabric; dressing dolls, making hats and dressing beds. I also have kits and have written four pattern books.

ARTISAN: **DAHN, DAWN J.**

BUSINESS NAME: Dawn's Artistic Treasures

IDENTIFICATION MARKS:

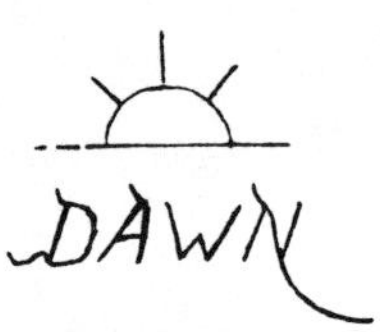

1985 to present

CATEGORY:

Furniture; Musical Instruments

DAHN, DAWN J., continued

HONORS:

IGMA Artisan; 1st Prize, Minnesota State Fair, 1981

RECOGNITION:

Nutshell News, Jul. 1992, New Products, pg. 28; *Miniature Collector,* Vol. 42 Mar/Apr. 1984, Cover, pg. 29

AUTOBIOGRAPHY:

I have no special education or background related to making miniatures. My interest was piqued by Thelma R. Newman and Virginia Merrill's publication, *The Complete Book of Making Miniatures for Room Settings and Dollhouses.* After making a few trial pieces, I wanted to do more realistic looking furniture. At that time, around 1980, I could not find patterns for detailed pieces, although there may have been some around. That's when I started drafting my own patterns, and still do. My miniature work, therefore, would probably be classified as self-taught.

ARTISAN: DAMPER, MATTHEW

BUSINESS NAME: Matthew Damper

IDENTIFICATION MARKS:

Unmarked

Certificate accompanies each piece, has name of purchaser, details of piece, date purchased and signature

CATEGORY:

Furniture

RECOGNITION:

The Home Miniaturist, Dec. 1992

AUTOBIOGRAPHY:

I started making one-inch scale miniatures in 1991, prior to which I had made a few smaller scale pieces using match sticks which were carved and jointed. I have been interested in model making since I was young. I started by buying cardboard kit models and building them. Soon I decided that using a kit was cheating, so I started designing my own. Printing costs were too high for me to be able to market them, so I turned to modeling furniture in wood, and haven't looked back.

I was born in June 1970, and have received no formal training in either carpentry or model making. I just work out my own ways of overcoming problems and achieving the desired result, which is to produce a miniature indistinguishable from the real thing in all respects other than size.

ARTISAN: DAVENPORT, JOHN

BUSINESS NAME: John Davenport

IDENTIFICATION MARKS:

with date

DAVENPORT, JOHN, continued

CATEGORY:

Furniture: period

HONORS:

IGMA Fellow; Exhibit: Toy & Miniature Museum of Kansas City

RECOGNITION:

Nutshell News, Sept. 1982, pg. 60; Mar. 1984, pg. 53; Mar. 1994, pg. 45, 47, 50, Show Scene; Jul. 1994, pg. 44; *Dolls House World*, No. 32, Jul/Aug. 1994, pg. 47; *Making Miniature Furniture,* John Davenport, 1990

AUTOBIOGRAPHY:

All the miniature furniture I make are one-of-a-kind pieces, signed and dated. For example I have made four Georgian secretaries and each one has its own distinguishing features within that period. My qualifications include apprenticeship cabinet maker for seven years, master cabinet maker for 18 years, nine of these spent on antique restoration work. I have been making miniatures since 1977 on a professional basis. About one third of my work is taken as commissions.

ARTISAN: **DAVIES, JANE**

BUSINESS NAME: Jane Davies

IDENTIFICATION MARKS:

CATEGORY:

Dolls: porcelain

HONORS:

British Doll Artisan Association, Artist member of NIADA

ARTISAN: **DAVIS, CHRISTINE P.**

BUSINESS NAME: Counterpane

IDENTIFICATION MARKS:

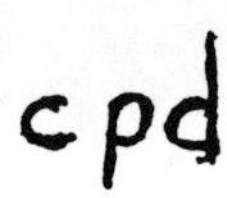 1992 to present

 1993 to present

CATEGORY:

Flowers and Plants; Kits: room

RECOGNITION:

Nutshell News, Summer 1991, Show Scene

DAVIS, CHRISTINE P., continued

AUTOBIOGRAPHY:

I had a tin dollhouse and a cardboard dollhouse in the mid forties, and have always been fascinated with little things. My grandfather built me a rather large 1½-inch scale dollhouse from wallboard, when I was about nine years old. From that I dreamed one day of having my very own special dollhouse. In 1986, I started planning my dollhouse, and call it "Nantucket 1830." From that I developed plans for a roombox one-inch or ½-inch scale and copyrighted these plans. A very proud moment! At that point, I was forever after hooked. I do not have a green thumb for full-size flowers and plants, but the idea came to me to miniaturize them. I researched all the methods until I came across directions for artificial flowers made from wire and silk. After several months of experimenting I developed my method and decided to sell. I do shows here in Connecticut and will soon expand to Massachusetts.

I joined NAME in 1986 and have attended two Regional and two National Houseparties. I had a table in the Mini Mart at the Phoenix and Philadelphia Nationals. I have been able to take three POSH tours to Europe, 1989 to Germany, 1990 to Belgium, Holland, Copenhagen, and 1991 to the North of France. Because of miniatures, my dreams of travel have materialized. I've met so many wonderful people and have friends who can finally share my interest.

ARTISAN: **DAVIS, HOWARD HAGAN & BARBARA BURTON**

BUSINESS NAME: Photography, Etc.

IDENTIFICATION MARKS:

(h) 1951 to present — Howard

BB-D with date — Barbara

CATEGORY:

Exotic Pieces; Furniture; Paintings; Roomboxes; Wall: murals (Howard)
Furniture; Houses; Roomboxes (Barbara)

HONORS:

4th Place, Photo Contest, Miniatures Showcase; Exhibit: Victorian Attic Train Roombox, Museum, Houston, Texas

RECOGNITION:

Nutshell News; Miniature Gazette

ARTISAN: **DAVIS, RAY C.**

BUSINESS NAME: Ray C. Davis

IDENTIFICATION MARKS:

RAY DAVIS 1992
1 OF 3
year made and limited edition number

CATEGORY:

Furniture, period

DAVIS, RAY C., continued

HONORS:

IGMA Artisan; Two Awards at the Richmond Art Assoc. "Hands of Man," 1982 - 1983

RECOGNITION:

Publication: *Pride* (Personnel Report & Instructional Developments in Education), Winter 1992, Richmond Community Schools, Richmond, Indiana; Radio Station WECI, Earlham College, Richmond, Indiana, 1982

AUTOBIOGRAPHY:

I became interested in miniature houses and furniture one-inch scale, in 1978 when my wife suggested I build a dollhouse for our daughter. After building a large Queen Ann Victorian dollhouse, I began concentrating on authentic pieces of early American and Victorian furniture. I later became enthused about French, English and Spanish museum quality pieces. When I became aware of the Thorne Rooms and the outstanding artisans of the Guild School, I began attending that School in Castine, Maine.

I was awarded Artisan Status following my second year of attendance. I have also studied with Jim Dorsett of the Scale Cabinetmaker. Most of the knowledge of miniatures has been self-taught, but certainly augmented by books, magazines, and mostly impacted by Harry Smith, and Jim & Helen Dorsett. I've always had an interest in arts and crafts but miniatures have given me the opportunity to go a step beyond. At this time I usually make only one or two of any one piece and sell only under pressure from collectors. Presently I am considering elevating an active hobby to a limited business. My formal education involves a BA in English and Social Studies, and an MA in Guidance and Counseling. I am retired after two wars and 37 years in the education field.

ARTISAN: DAVISON, CHRISTY L.

BUSINESS NAME: A. J. S. Productions

IDENTIFICATION MARKS:

Some unmarked, usually accompanied by certificate of authenticity

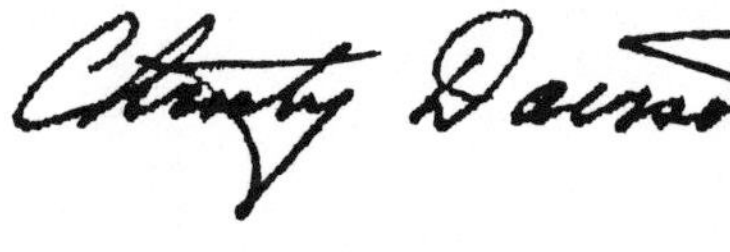
year made

year made

Both 1990 to present

CATEGORY:

Accessories; Bridal Items; Christmas; Confectionery; Costuming: Halloween; Dolls: fairies; Fimo; Flowers & Plants; Food; Halloween Items; Holiday Items; Masks: Mardi Gras; Mermaids; Metal: handpainted; Porcelain: fairies; Rugs; Toys

AUTOBIOGRAPHY:

I have been a tom boy, avid doll collector and lover of miniatures all my life. Growing up in Seattle, I would go to the museum and spend as long as I could staring at and studying the lighted dollhouse. I always wanted a dollhouse, but due to our financial situation, as a child, it was never possible to have my own. I got my first dollhouse when I was in my thirties, and now own quite a few, including a giant roombox, Wilson's Pond. In 1991, luck came my way and I won the special drawing at the Good Sam show. I was so excited, I think I broke my mother's ear drums! Anyway, my doll collection, dollhouse and roombox collection have overtaken our living room and are spilling out into the rest of the house! In 1990, I started making my own miniatures for sale. In my twenties I had become a cake designer, not just a decorator, they were sculpted cakes, self-taught other than the basic Wilton course. I was in demand, particularly by caterers, those that catered to the high and mighty, and the rich and famous of the San Francisco Bay area. This continued until 1987, when I became very ill. I have Spina

Bifida, Hydrocephalus and have recently been diagnosed with Systemic Lupus, and have been in a wheelchair since 1987. After I recovered enough to function again, I tried making the Fairmont Hotel and Mount Everest, in full-size cakes, for clients in San Francisco. The cakes turned out beautifully, but my mom had to run her legs off getting things for me. I never realized how much I stood while doing these cakes. It became obvious, at that time, I could no longer make full-size cakes without putting stress on my mother. Consequently, we came up with the idea of doing them in miniature with all the detail, just like the full-size cakes. I can now duplicate anyone's real wedding cake in miniature from a picture, any scale desired, even large enough to fill a large dome. A great gift for a keepsake!

From there it grew, with so many ideas, our line continues to expand. It has been a great outlet for both of us; my mother is a very talented artisan as well. I could not do the miniatures shows alone, and my mother has been wonderful enough to follow me in my endeavors. It's great to have her working along side me. We also live together, along with my grandmother who is 83. Besides our miniatures, we also do other crafts and collect donations for abused children, the homeless, and any others in need. We collect it and give it to the people in need, free.

We use my mom's initials for the name of the business, A.J.S. Productions. Not many people have seen us in the past year or so, but we are looking forward to changing that! I think my greatest accomplishment is never stopping, no matter what happens. Keeping a positive attitude, a hearty laugh and keeping a smile on my face, I take all the enjoyment out of life that I can get. My greatest strength is my mother's constant encouragement and belief in me, and always being there to give a helping hand.

I'm also well known for speeding in my wheelchair at shows, but so far I haven't had any victims!

see "Althea J. Smith"

ARTISAN: **DAWSON, ROBERT**

BUSINESS NAME: The Modelroom

IDENTIFICATION MARKS:

CATEGORY:

Furniture: gilt; Houses; Roomboxes

HONORS:

Exhibit: The Carol and Barry Kaye Museum of Miniatures, Los Angeles, California

RECOGNITION:

International Dolls' House News, Vol. 21, No. 3, Autumn 1992, pg. 27; *Dolls House World*, Winter 1993

AUTOBIOGRAPHY:

I traveled as a theatre designer and then began a business as architectural and theatre dollmaker. In 1992, I started working in the miniatures field. I exhibited at the London Dollshouse Festival for the first time in May 1993, with a room model of No. 26 Hatton Gardens, London, an early Georgian Room. I am responsible for much of the furniture for the "Palace of Fountainebleau" exhibited at The Carol & Barry Kaye Museum of Miniatures, Los Angeles, California. I work with my wife and partner, Nina Eklund.

ARTISAN: **DENNIS, NANCY**

BUSINESS NAME: Heirloom Creations
Miniatures... by Beth

IDENTIFICATION MARKS:
Unmarked pieces accompanied with Marked card

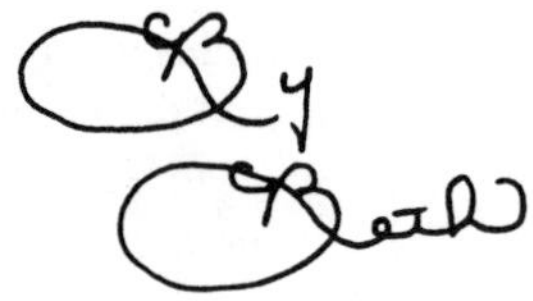

CATEGORY:
Dolls: original; Figures

AUTOBIOGRAPHY:

I've had various jobs over the years, and some education, but none that directly relates to my miniature and doll making.

I have made miniatures since 1983 and have slowly evolved to my present activity of making artist dolls to a scale of one-inch to one-foot, out of polymer clay. All of my dolls are one of a kind originals. I still do make some miscellaneous miniatures and have a miniatures shoppe, Heirloom Creations. In the past I have made blown glass miniatures and a lot of foods and porcelain. My marks depend on the size of the piece. If they are not marked then a card with my mark accompanies each piece.

ARTISAN: **DePRIEST, CHARLES**

IDENTIFICATION MARKS: (Submitted by William R. Robertson)

CATEGORY:
Brasswork; Trains: brass

HONORS:
Exhibit: Toy & Miniature Museum of Kansas City

RECOGNITION:
Nutshell News, Vol. 13, No. 8, Aug. 1983, pg. 48, Show Scene

ARTISAN: **DEVEREUX, THOMAS F.**

BUSINESS NAME: Sparkle Studio

IDENTIFICATION MARKS:
Most unmarked

TD printed, scratched into some Chinese pieces

CATEGORY:
Beds; Candlesticks; Chandeliers; Designer: exterior, interior; Drapes; Furniture: Chinese: period; Lamps; Lighting; Needlework; Roomboxes; Room Settings; Rugs; Sconces

DEVEREUX, THOMAS F., continued

HONORS:

Honorary Founder IMA 1976; Exhibit: Historical Museum, Blairsville, Georgia

RECOGNITION:

Miniature Gazette, Vol. 1, No. 1, Sept. 1972, pg. 10, “Chicago's Devereux Shares a Country Kitchen,” Tom Devereux; Vol. 5, No. 2, Dec. 1976, pg. 7, “Louis XV Dining Room;” Vol. 5, No. 3, Mar. 1977, pg. 47, “Plantation Parlor,” Tom Devereux; Vol. 5, No. 4, Jun. 1977, pg. 18-19, “Federal Period Bedroom,” Tom Devereux; Vol. 6, No. 1, Sept. 1977, pg. 51, “Early American Dining Room,” Tom Devereux; Vol. 11, No. 1, Fall 1982, pg. 26, “The Enchanted Palace,” Rita DeMarco

AUTOBIOGRAPHY:

I studied interior decoration and design, for a time, at the Art Institute of Chicago, where I lived all my life until 1975 when my sister and I retired and moved to Dixon, Illinois. How I started in miniatures was about 1962 when I bought a copy of *Hobbies Magazine* and wrote to John Blauer, Miniature Mart, San Francisco. We became, and still are, good friends, and I made many things for the Mart. In 1962, I started collecting scale pieces, putting them into room settings which I designed and made. I have many many pieces made for me, from my designs, by the best craftspersons of the 1960's, 70's and 80's. I bought oodles of miniatures from Joe Grey, then the only dealer in Chicago, who had every kind of beautifully crafted furniture, ceramics, china et al, from the early artists of miniatures.

About 1965 I began to design and make Austrian crystal chandeliers, wall sconces, candlesticks, candelabras and student lamps. I have 34 room settings from all periods and have always lent them for benefits. I have been mentioned in *Hobbies Magazine, Miniature Gazette, Nutshell News*, Marion O'Brien and Flora Gill Jacob's books and a few other books and publications. I have written a few articles for *Creative Crafts* and a few other minor publications.

I was an Honorary Founder of NAME, Secretary and President of IMA the forerunner of AOH. I still love miniatures and do what I can to help others get started. I did so many Chinese pieces of furniture for other collectors and have recently been honored by the Historical museum in Blairsville, Georgia for the Chinese room in the collection of Margarita Morgan, who donated her collection to the museum.

I have always been a collector of art objects, and have many Chinese pieces, figurines and also oodles of Franklin Mint collections; Faberge eggs, vases, chess sets, figurines, small dishes, music boxes, and about 65 of their large portrait dolls plus many smaller miniature dolls made by some of the finest artists, who still remain my friends.

ARTISAN: **DICK, WARREN** (Deceased)

IDENTIFICATION MARKS:

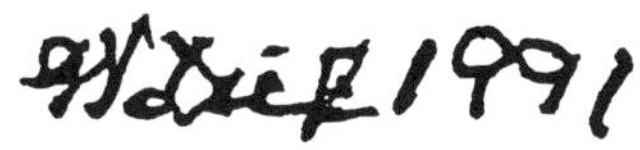

CATEGORY:

Chairs: rockers; Furniture: period, spinning wheels

HONORS:

NAME AOH 1978; Mell Prescott Award 1990

RECOGNITION:

Nutshell News, Nov. 1982, pg. 52; May 1983, pg. 36-37, “Arizona Artisans – The Pioneering Spirit Prevails,” Maire Simington; Jun. 1983, pg. 40-43; Jan. 1984, pg. 72; Apr. 1984, pg. 43, 76; Aug. 1984, pg. 71; *Miniature Collector*, No. 8, Aug. 1978, pg. 31, Show Stoppers

BIOGRAPHY:

Warren was considered one the early pioneers of miniature making. In the 1940's he worked in miniatures as a form of relaxation, after spending six years in the Air Force while working as a maintenance supervisor for a small freight airline.

DICK, WARREN, continued

In 1958, Warren and his wife, Margie, sought a less complicated life in Sedona, Arizona. They decided to combine their hobbies into a money making venture—a hobby, gift and art supply store which they created from the shell of an old barn. Customers became enthralled with Warren's small wagons and furniture which then had no particular scale. He became so busy supplying customers with these miniatures, they eventually had to close the store so he could devote all his time to miniature making.

Warren was a self-taught artist. He set up tools, jigs, etc., to make complete runs of his items. He worked in two-inch, 1½-inch, and ¼-inch scales, but when the popularity of miniatures increased, shop owners wanted one-inch scale, which is what he then worked in primarily. The number of his shop machines had continued to grow and he added many tools he made himself.

Warren had always researched the pieces he made. Earlier he was best known for his Boston rockers, cupboards, and spinning wheels, which included 27 different turnings plus many carving, fitting, and finishing steps. He studied the Sears and Roebuck Catalog and various Colonial Furniture books. At one time he did extensive work with furniture dating from 1680 to 1720. Occasionally his research led to a room setting which he viewed as a pleasant break from working on individual pieces.

(AOH profile, by Ferbie Claudon, authorized reprint by NAME)

ARTISAN: **DIDIER, DEBORAH**

BUSINESS NAME: DeBearahs

IDENTIFICATION MARKS:

Fold tag

CATEGORY:

Bears: teddy

RECOGNITION:

Teddy Bear and Friends Magazine, Vol. 12, No. 3, May/Jun. 1994, pg. 35, "Tribute to Tiny Teddies;" *Contemporary Teddy Bear Price Guide*, 1992, pg. 29

AUTOBIOGRAPHY:

My mother taught me to embroider when I was about six years old. I have loved hand sewing ever since. I have also been fascinated by miniatures for as long as I can remember. About 10 years ago, 1984, I saw a tiny Teddy Bear in a miniature shop. When I returned to the shop to buy it as a gift for my sister, it was gone! I decided to make one for her. It was such fun making that little bear that I have been making them ever since. I now make teddy bears 3/8-inch to two-inches tall. I sell them to individuals and shops all over the world.

ARTISAN: **Di DONATO, BARBARA A.**

BUSINESS NAME: Maria Nicole Miniatures

IDENTIFICATION MARKS:

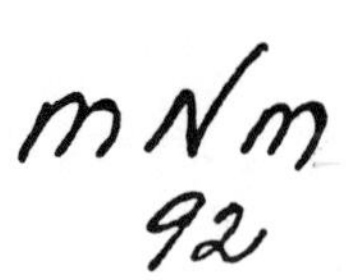

Year piece was made

Di DONATO, BARBARA A., continued

CATEGORY:

Beds; Rooms; Upholstery

AUTOBIOGRAPHY:

My business evolved out of the love I have for doll houses. I am an experienced seamstress in all phases of home decor and bridal evening wear. With some encouragement from my husband, I made a few pieces for my own use. They were customized to fit my house and because I am detail oriented I could not find what I wanted, in a shop. I was hooked! I started up my business in May of 1990 and have been successful at shows and in showing my work in some local shops. I also do custom orders in window treatments to match any decor.

ARTISAN: **di GIOIA, FIAMMA**

BUSINESS NAME: Fiamma di Gioia Miniature Art

IDENTIFICATION MARKS:

CATEGORY:

Paintings: watercolor

HONORS:

IGMA Artisan

AUTOBIOGRAPHY:

As a little kid I loved the smell of new crayons. Daddy always brought us lots of different kinds of paper for our art projects. We loved to show off our drawings to each other. We dug in clay in the woods and made all sorts of things, or rode our bikes to the creek with lunch and went wading in the water. Lots of my dreams are now coming true. I'm living in the house I dreamed of and built as a roombox, now the colors and collections are real.

ARTISAN: **DiMEO, LAURA**

BUSINESS NAME: Little Discoveries

IDENTIFICATION MARKS:

1989 to present

LD copyright, 1976

Company name sometimes used prior to 1992

DiMEO, LAURA, continued

Little Discoveries — Cases sometimes marked with company graphic

CATEGORY:

Accessories: food; Food

RECOGNITION:

Nutshell News, Vol. 22, No. 2, 1992, pg. 65; Vol. 22, Issue 4, 1992, pg. 71

BIOGRAPHY:

Little Discoveries is made up of three family members - Laura, her twin Annette and their mother Claire. Both Annette and her mother have theatrical backgrounds: Claire ran her own children's theatre for 25 years (called Discovery Workshop) and is now working as a traveling puppeteer as Claire DiMeo's Discovery Puppetts.

Annette studied acting in New York after college and settled there for six years working as a cabaret lighting and sound technician. Now back in New England, she recently changed careers and is working at Lotus Software Corporation.

Laura has been working in the film and television industry as a lighting technician (grip). Laura started making miniatures as a hobby to pass the time between freelance grip assignments. Annette and she made some miniature produce for their mother as a Christmas gift in 1989. Claire then introduced them to the world of handcrafted miniatures.

Little Discoveries began as a mail order and retail business in response to Claire's friends requesting some of Laura and Annette's fruits and vegetables. As of this date, we participate in regional miniatures shows, sell our products through our mail order catalogue and teach workshops to clubs, at shows and at NAME functions. All of us have attended the Guild School as pupils. We are members of NAME and IGMA.

ARTISAN: DIPPOLD, MARY ANN

BUSINESS NAME: Handwovens by Mary Ann

IDENTIFICATION MARKS:

Handwoven by Mary Ann — Printed on hem of coverlets

CATEGORY:

Linens; Needlework

HONORS:

Best of Show, Wisconsin Handweavers Show, 1990, 1991; 1st & 2nd Place, Miniature Category, Wisconsin Handweavers Show, 1992

AUTOBIOGRAPHY:

My weaving has taken awards at various Handweaving Shows and at the Wisconsin State Fair. The majority of my hand-woven miniatures are Coverlets for both single and double beds. They are miniaturized versions of patterns woven as early as the 1800's. Traditional pattern names are printed on the hem of each coverlet, as well as my logo.

ARTISAN: **DISNEY, GLENDA**

BUSINESS NAME: Dizzie's Minnies

IDENTIFICATION MARKS:

Dizzie's Minnies

CATEGORY:

Furniture: wicker

RECOGNITION:

Nutshell News, May 1989, pg. 69; *Miniatures Showcase*, Winter 1992, pg. 28

AUTOBIOGRAPHY:

Some years ago, I started a business called, Seat Yourself. Primarily, I replaced cane and other types of seats in antique chairs. I also offer wicker repair. After taking a class in miniature Victorian wicker, that Bobbie Walls offered, I began to make miniature versions of some of the wicker that I own. I now copy from pictures, and I love the challenge of making a picture come to life in three dimension.

ARTISAN: **DORMAN, MICHAEL WAYNE**

BUSINESS NAME: Atelier Lilliput Studio

IDENTIFICATION MARKS:

Used when space is limited

1992

DORMAN (1989-1992)
M. DORMAN (1989-1992)

On front of paintings if original or on back if reproduction of original work

CATEGORY:

Art: objects, supplies; Kits: picture frame; Paintings

HONORS:

IGMA Artisan; 1st, 2nd, 3rd Place & Honorable Mention in Juried Shows in St. Catherine's, Ontario (GNOME Show) & M.E.T. Toronto, Ontario, Canada

RECOGNITION:

Nutshell News, 1992; Magazine of *Le Club de la Miniature Française*, Paris, France, No. 21, Summer 1992

AUTOBIOGRAPHY:

I have always dabbled in art since my childhood, but only in 1972 did I attempt to do some serious work and have it shown in art galleries in my home town. In those days I did full-size art comprised of sepia pen and ink drawings of birds and small mammals. Although I had one year of art in high school and took one or two courses at the Dundas Valley School of Art, near Hamilton, Ontario, I am basically self-taught. In 1989 my friend, Karl Blindheim, an IGMA animal sculptor from Toronto, encouraged me to do paintings in miniature and

I have never looked back, since then. I work for the Canadian Post Office as a lettercarrier, but have a university degree in Anthropology, and a Certificate of Proficiency in the French language.

I have a 17 year old son who thinks miniaturists are from another planet! My near future plans in miniaturization are to create specialty items and objects d' art.

ARTISAN: DORSETT, JAMES H. & B. HELEN

BUSINESS NAME: Dorsett Publications, Inc.
Dorsett Miniatures

IDENTIFICATION MARKS:

Helen Dorsett Cabinetmaker Guide Vol 9 - 1984 | Helen Dorsett 1981 G7 | J.H. DORSETT TSC 8:2 11/83

Signature sometimes included name and year. When model signed was a design model, a prototype, for a published pattern/article or book the piece is signed with name and either full name of publication and date, such as "Cabinetmaker's Guide," Vol. 9, 1984, or shorthand for the publication, such as G7 or Guide Vol. 7, 1981

CATEGORY:

Author; Designer; Publications; Publications, How-to; Publisher; Writer

HONORS:

IGMA Crystal Award (both) 1992; NAME AOH (both); Exhibits: Peabody Historical Museum, Peabody, Kansas; American Museum, Bath, England

RECOGNITION:

Nutshell News, Vol. 24, No. 11, Nov. 1994, pg. 32-34, "A Classic Turns Thirty," Meghan Dorsett

AUTOBIOGRAPHY: Biographical data for:

B. Helen (Bennett) Dorsett
b. 12/28/27; d. 8/31/90
B.F.A. - University of Wichita, Kansas 1950
Graduate studies - The School of the Chicago Art Institute, 1952 - 1953

James H. Dorsett
b. 9/24/29
B.A. - University of Wichita, Kansas, 1951
B.D. - McCormick Theological Seminary, 1954
M.S. (Rural Sociology) - University of Missouri, Columbia, 1964
Ph.D... (High Plains Regionalism, Western American History)
University of Missouri, 1969

From 1954 to 1976, I was employed as an ordained minister, teaching assistant, research associate and assistant professor in Sociology. From 1976, to the present I have operated Dorsett Publications, Inc. which is the successor of Dorsett Miniatures, established as a business entity in 1964 in Columbia, Missouri. Helen and I established Dorsett Miniatures as a business entity in 1963, designing and producing two large commissions, plus a number of smaller projects for Emma Rankin Praether Poe of Peabody, Kansas. A dioramic setting for a collection of 18th century crèche dolls, and a large 1½-inch scale Victorian dollhouse and furnishings which are now on permanent display in the Peabody Historical Museum, Peabody, Kansas. In 1964, we began the publication of a Cabinetmaker's Guide for Doll House Furniture, a series of nine volumes of one-inch and ½-inch scale period furniture patterns, which we continued until 1984.

During 1965 and 1966, we produced miniature furniture (26 designs in all) in wholesale quantities for Peniston Miniatures, Los Gatos, California. They were designated by Peniston as HD-1 through HD-26. This is the only period in the past 33 years when we produced and sold multiple copies of single designs; with few exceptions, all other miniatures we've produced have been either discrete items, custom designed for a particular collector client, or design models for a published pattern, i.e., artists proofs. Between 1967 and 1989, Helen did individual commission work for an array of collector clients. During 1976, we established Dorsett Publications, Inc. and the first issue of *The Scale Cabinetmaker* was ready for distribution in October of that year.

Our other publications include *A Cabinetmaker's Guide For Dollhouse Furniture,* Vol. 1, 19th Century Furniture; Vol. 2, Victorian 1850-1880; Vol. 3, Jacobean, William & Mary 1650-1750; Vol. 4, Queen Anne 1720-1755; Vol. 5, Turn Of The Century Oak 1890-1915; Vol. 6, French 1715-1870; Vol. 7, Overstuffed Furniture 1875-1950; Vol. 8, Half Inch Furniture; Vol. 9, Federal Furniture 1788-1825; *An English Country Kitchen, Lamps Made Easy, Design Book One* (Shenandoah Designs), and *Small Scale Cabinetmaking.* The majority of our published articles have appeared in The Scale Cabinetmaker from 1976 to the present. Its 16 volume years included several hundred designs for furniture and structures, plus a pot full of workbench technique articles. Only to a limited degree have Helen and I been "commercial craftsmen" in miniatures. We have been teachers of the craft rather than purveyors of miniatures.

ARTISAN: **DOUCETTE, AMY BONEY**

BUSINESS NAME: Handworks

IDENTIFICATION MARKS:

Signature and year on tag sewn into inside seam of larger pieces
Secured to plastic box of smaller pieces, as of mid 1990.
Tags are shaped: bear, cloud, house etc.

CATEGORY:
Handwork; Knitting; Needlework

HONORS:
IGMA Artisan; Fellow

RECOGNITION:
Nutshell News, Jul. 1992, pg. 42-46

AUTOBIOGRAPHY:
I have been involved in miniatures since 1980, and owned a miniature store for several years during the 1980's. I closed the store for health reasons, and to spend more time with my husband and daughter. I have been doing local miniature shows for years and started traveling to other area shows in 1988. My knitting has evolved and improved over the years as I have explored new threads and yarns, color combinations, textures, patterns and scales. It is a continuing process. I have been publishing *Handworks Miniature Network* a bimonthly subscription newsletter since 1986. I have a degree in English & Elementary Education from the University of Washington. My grandmother Boney taught me to knit and crochet when I was a little girl and I have been at it ever since.

ARTISAN: **DOWD, HAZEL**

BUSINESS NAME: Little People

IDENTIFICATION MARKS:
All marks 1983 to present

DOWD, HAZEL, continued

CATEGORY:

Accessories; Clothing; Dolls; Millinery; Roomboxes; Shops

HONORS:

1st Place, CCCS (Cheshire County Craft Show) 1991; Highly Commended, CCCS 1993

RECOGNITION:

Guild of Major Craftsman Modelling and Miniature Crafts, No. 4, 1986, pg. 47-55; *Dolls House World,* No. 6, 1990, pg. 12, 53; No. 22, 1992, pg. 62

AUTOBIOGRAPHY:

I was born in Barrow-in-Furness, England on February 6, 1940. In 1985, I became interested in miniatures after visiting a Dolls House Fair, by accident. Until then I had always had an interest in crafts, such as dressmaking, embroidery, egg decorating, and painting flowers.

I bought my first doll kit and proceeded from there. I started to make my own dolls but I became allergic to the powder from the greenware, so I now buy from friends. I attend, as a dealer, Miniaturia NEC Birmingham, Leeds, Altrincham, Leighton Hall, all in England. I am most known for my hats, and love to demonstrate, teach workshops and visit clubs.

I have three 6 foot tall sons, two daughters-in-law, two grandsons and a very new granddaughter and of course my husband, John, without whom I could not manage as he drives me to all the venues and is my best critic.

I am a member of the newly formed MinTA (Miniatures Trade Association).

ARTISAN: **DRELLING, RUTH C.**

BUSINESS NAME: R C Miniatures

IDENTIFICATION MARKS:

RcD

CATEGORY:

Flowers and Plants; Food; Furniture

AUTOBIOGRAPHY:

I have no special miniatures background. I am self-taught as a miniature maker, and have attended many workshops. My employment is in the electronics field, and I do microscopic soldering.

ARTISAN: **DRINKWATER, H. F. & J.**

BUSINESS NAME: Tetbury Miniatures

IDENTIFICATION MARKS:

CATEGORY:

Beds; Furniture: upholstered

RECOGNITION:

The Home Miniaturist, Mar. 1989, pg. 29, 31; Mar. 1991, pg. 5, 37; No. 21, Sept/Oct. 1992, pg. 55; *Dolls and Dolls Houses*, May 1989, pg. 21; *Dolls House World*, No. 4, Nov/Dec. 1989, pg. 18; No. 5, Jan/Feb. 1990, pg. 30; No. 7, May/Jun. 1990, pg. 12-13; No. 17, Jan/Feb. 1992, pg. 54; No. 18, Mar/Apr. 1992, pg. 58; *Build a Dolls House*, Michael Morse

AUTOBIOGRAPHY:

H. Drinkwater - Danny; I am a graduate of West of England College of Art with an A.T.D., Art Teachers Diploma. I was Head of Art with ceramics and all crafts in Senior Schools, and am now retired.

J. Drinkwater - Josie: I am a graduate of West of England College of Art with a City & Guilds First Class certificate in Fashion drawing and design. I also attended Newton Park College, receiving a B.Ed. 2nd Class Honors; Bristol University with art/craft and ceramic sculpture. I worked as a Junior School teacher with responsibility for art, craft and ceramics, and am now retired. I am experienced in full-size furniture, upholstery, making of loose covers, and all home furnishings.

ARTISAN: DRUCKENMILLER, ESTHER S.

BUSINESS NAME: Oak Ridge Miniatures

IDENTIFICATION MARKS:

DRUCK

CATEGORY:

Furniture: handpainted; Paintings: oil, original, pets, slate, wildlife; Portraits

RECOGNITION:

Nutshell News, Nov. 1992

AUTOBIOGRAPHY:

As a child I painted and sketched. I remember distinctly my teacher in the fifth grade suggesting my mother had helped me with a detailed Egyptian painting for class. My grandmother had been an exceptional artist, but the gift had skipped my mother who exclaimed to the teacher "I could not do that in 100 years!"

During high school a local haberdasher sold my handpainted neck ties. This medium was a success and a 5th Avenue store in New York City gave me special orders to paint on ties. Fish lures, favorite pets, hobby features, etc. kept me busy, but the most challenging order was to paint the Philadelphia Phillies "1950" team players each in the position played.

Cutting silhouettes has always afforded me satisfaction and those whose profiles I have cut in minutes for visitors and requests at parties. Painting has always been a rewarding pleasure whether done on silk, canvass, walls, wood or slate.

My art career was interrupted by devoting time to a family of six, but in 1971 an inspiration led to painting animals on framed Vermont slate for private collectors, fine art galleries and boutiques. Awards were obtained in the few shows that I attended.

Last year a neighbor interested me in her wonderful dollhouse with detailed furniture and decorations. After painting specific pieces for her, it was obvious to me there was a widespread market for especially designed painted pieces to be sold to serious collectors at shows.

The discerning buyer now looks for the lifelike details of Oak Ridge Miniatures whether in furniture for the nursery or a gold framed miniature masterpiece of a customers home.

ARTISAN: **DUDLEY-COURSIEN, TERESA**

BUSINESS NAME: Northern Lites Miniatures

IDENTIFICATION MARKS:

T. Dudley 1974 to 1986

T. DUDLEY-Coursien 1986 to present

CATEGORY:

Accessories: African, Alaskan, American Indian, medieval, Western; Dolls: porcelain, soft body; Figures: African, Alaskan, American Indian, medieval, Western

RECOGNITION:

Los Angeles Times Magazine, Nov. 15, 1992, pg. 40-41; *Miniatures Showcase*, Summer 1988, pg. 20, 24-25; Mar. 1993, pg. 38-39

AUTOBIOGRAPHY:

My career in the miniatures industry stems from a deep interest in history and a sincere appreciation of the development of all cultures throughout the world. I have created miniature items for my own pleasure and, I hope, the pleasure of others since 1969.

My company, Northern Lites Miniatures, was born in 1981 while visiting Alaska, "The beautiful land of the midnight sun." I feel that true joy of creating comes from sharing that creation with others.

ARTISAN: **DUNGER, JUDITH**

BUSINESS NAME: Judith Dunger, Lacquer Dolls' House Furniture

IDENTIFICATION MARKS:

Judith Dunger

J
D Screens, some unmarked

CATEGORY:

Furniture: japanned

RECOGNITION:

International Dolls' House News, Vol. 20, No. 3, Autumn 1991, pg. 17; *Home Miniaturist,* No. 62, pg. 56; *The Miniatures Catalogue* of Great Britain

AUTOBIOGRAPHY:

I was born in 1953. I graduated from Leicester University in 1974 with a BA (honors) in English, having also studied the History of Art. I joined forces with my father, an antique restorer, and began to specialize in the restoration an antique Lacquer. Japanning some pieces for my little daughter's dolls' house gave me the idea of applying my expertise to miniatures and my new work was launched at the London Dolls' House Festival in May 1990. Since then the miniatures have proved so popular that they have completely taken over my other work. My father makes all my furniture, and I apply the finish. My miniature lacquer work seeks mostly to emulate the work of the English lacquerists of the 18th century. Many of the designs are taken from actual pieces, all are in accordance with the style of the period.

I am married and have a son and daughter.

ARTISAN: **DUNHAM, BETSY**

BUSINESS NAME: Dunham's Miniatures

IDENTIFICATION MARKS:

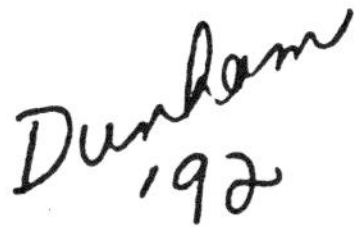

CATEGORY:

Accessories: country; Furniture

ARTISAN: **DUNNIWAY, DAVE & JEANNIE**

BUSINESS NAME: The Miniature Corner

IDENTIFICATION MARKS:

On ceramic pieces

Gold address sticker used on breakaway boxes and other pieces

CATEGORY:

Breakaway Boxes; Ceramics: container with scenes; Containers: scenes; Holiday Items; Metal; Pewter: handpainted, unpainted; Scenes: containers

RECOGNITION:

Tazewell News, “Itsy Bitsy Little Pieces,” Melissa Somogyl

ARTISAN: **DURIGG, JOAN**

BUSINESS NAME: Joan Durigg

IDENTIFICATION MARKS:

Label on slip or clothing

Scratched into porcelain on dolls back

CATEGORY:

Costuming; Dolls: original, porcelain

RECOGNITION:

Miniatures Showcase, Summer 1988; Vol. 5, No. 2, Spring 1990, pg. 74, “Fairy Godmother;” Vol. 6, No. 3, Summer 1991, pg. 33, “It's the Brides Day;” *Nutshell News*, Vol. 16, No. 6, Jun. 1986, pg. 88

ARTISAN: **DURSTENFELD, LIGIA**

BUSINESS NAME: Ligia's Miniatures

IDENTIFICATION MARKS:

DURSTENFELD, LIGIA, continued

CATEGORY:

Accessories; Boxes: silver; Enameling: glass on metal; Fabergé; Kaleidoscopes; Oriental Finishings; Paintings: silk; Silver

HONORS:

IGMA Artisan; NAME AOH 1995

RECOGNITION:

Nutshell News, Mar. 1979; Mar. 1980; Apr. 1982; Nov. 1982; May 1983; Oct. 1985; Oct. 1986; Aug. 1986; Nov. 1986; Jan. 1987; Apr. 1987; Jan. 1988; May 1988; Dec. 1988; Apr. 1989; Jan. 1990; Feb. 1991; Mar. 1992; *Miniature Collector*, Winter 1985; Fall 1986; Winter 1987; Winter 1988; Fall 1989; Spring 1990; Spring 1992, Cover; *Miniatures Showcase*, Summer 1991; *Democrat & Chronicle of Rochester, NY*, Jul. 29, 1983

AUTOBIOGRAPHY:

I have always liked miniatures! As a child, in Columbia, South America, I had a few porcelain pieces, quite beautiful. In the 6th or 7th grade my brother and I entered a fair and won first place. Using a cardboard house I had, we made a pharmacy or an apothecary store, with every detail, tiny bottles, boxes and labels, etc. How I wish I still had it! About 21 years ago, 1972, when my boys were getting into high school and college, I was helping to design miniature accessories for an importer. Pretty soon all my family got involved. We had some wonderful summers playing together. We helped at a couple of hospital fairs in California and put together a great exhibit at Christmas. My husband discovered he could turn beautiful ivory pieces and I did the Scrimshaw. Also he did vases and plates out of wood, and I painted them like porcelain. They were great, particularly since there were very few porcelains available then. Later on I took classes at UCLA in Enameling, glass on metal, an art form which I had always admired. With this media I have been able to create miniature replicas of Medieval and Oriental art which I always liked.

I hope I can continue creating new pieces for everyone to enjoy, and for my own satisfaction. How many of us can work very hard, enjoying every minute of it!

ARTISAN: DYKE, ROSEMARY JOHNSON

BUSINESS NAME: PlumPretty, Inc.

IDENTIFICATION MARKS:

Unmarked

CATEGORY:

Flowers and Plants

HONORS:

IGMA Fellow; Exhibit: Toy & Miniature Museum of Kansas City

RECOGNITION:

Nutshell News, Aug. 1980, pg. 50, 55; Sept. 1980, pg. 54; Apr. 1982, pg. 64-65; *Miniature Collector*, No. 20, pg. 34; No. 31, pg. 23; No. 33, pg. 28-29

AUTOBIOGRAPHY:

I have a Bachelor of Arts degree from the University of Arkansas. My interest in miniatures began in 1975 when my whole family participated in building a Barbie dollhouse for my daughter. I took some classes in miniature room building. One was a plant shop, and I showed it in Ashland, Virginia and the National NAME Houseparty in San Diego. After that I began making and selling plants at shows to pay for my collecting of miniatures. The Tracy's represented me at various shows which I couldn't attend. I am a Fellow of IGMA and past National Secretary of NAME.

E

ARTISAN: **EARLY, FRANK** (Submitted by William R. Robertson)

IDENTIFICATION MARKS:

Unmarked or printed label

MADE IN ENGLAND

CATEGORY:

Furniture: English, period

HONORS:

Pieces in: Thorne Rooms, Queen Mary's Doll House, Titania's Palace; Exhibits: Toy & Miniature Museum of Kansas City

RECOGNITION:

Nutshell News, Apr. 1985, pg. 38-39; *Fine Woodworking*, No. 99, Apr. 1993, pg. 84-85; *Miniature Collector*, No. 5, Feb. 1978, Cover, pg. 9; *International Dolls' House News*, Summer 1983, pg. 17-18; *Miniature Rooms*, The Thorne Rooms at The Art Institute of Chicago, 1983, pg. 100-101; *This Side of Yesterday in Miniatures*, Catherine B. MacLaren, 1975

BIOGRAPHY:

Mr. Early has been referred to as Fred, Frank, George and Percy. It is believed these are all the same man, specializing in Queen Ann furniture, working in Worthing, England from the 1920's to the 1940's. His name was probably Frank Percy Early. Dealers in both New York and England have sold his work.

During the late 1920's some of his work made its way into Queen Mary's Dolls' House designed by and the compulsion of the famous English architect Sir Edwin Lutyens. He was also working on some miniatures for Neville Wilkinson's "Titania's Palace" now on public display at Legoland in Denmark. A collector named Mrs. Carlisle saw his work in Queen Mary's collection and summoned him to her home where she commissioned a secretary identical to the one she had seen. From 1933 onward she acquired a number of Mr. Early's miniatures but also of interest are the insights into Mr. Early's life left by her family. Anthony, the oldest son remembers him as a large man with a drooping mustache, precise in his actions-such as when endorsing a receipt he pulled from his pocket a corked ink bottle, a relief pen-nib, blotting paper and stamp all in neat order. Mr. Early was a loner who preferred to keep to himself, and it is said, rather than risk an encounter on the pavement, he chose to walk in the middle of the road. He liked to work alone and did not appreciate visitors. In a letter Early wrote of his new shop in Shoreham "Not at all bad, quiet and free from other workers."

His miniature furniture was sold by various dealers over the years. Mrs. Thorne who created the Thorne Rooms, now at the Art Institute of Chicago, bought a clock and secretary desk almost identical from Arthur Punt, a London dealer. These are displayed in the Massachusetts Drawing Room, 1768. Early's work was also sold by the jewelry firm of James Robinson, in New York. The number of pieces he made is unknown but there are at least seven known secretaries.

(Part of article originally published in Fine Woodworking, April 1993)

ARTISAN: **EASTMAN-ROAN, CYNTHIA**

BUSINESS NAME: Cynthia Eastman-Roan Miniature Art Studios

IDENTIFICATION MARKS:

CATEGORY:

Art: fine; Painting: watercolor

EASTMAN-ROAN, CYNTHIA, continued

HONORS:

IGMA Fellow 1993; 1st Place 1992, Oils, Seascape, Miniature Painters, Sculptors & Gravers Society, Washington, DC, 69th International; 1st Place 1988, Best in Six Square Inch 1991, Montana 10th Annual International Miniature Art Exhibit; 3rd Place 1988, Georgia Miniature Art Society 3rd International Art Show; Best of Show 1989, 6th National Award of Excellence 1991, 7th National Award of Honor 1992, 2nd in Oils 1992, National League of American Pen Women 4th National Exhibit; 1st Place 1989, Seascape, Allegheny International Miniature Art Exhibit West Virginia; 3rd Place 1990, 21st International 1991, 1st Place, Acrylic Seascape, Miniature Art Society of New Jersey, 20th International Miniature Art Show; 3rd Place & American Frame Award 1990, Maryland National Bank Award 1991, Art Gallery of Fells Point, Baltimore MD; 3rd Place 1991, International Miniature Art Exhibit, Long Beach Island Art Studios & Gallery 7th Annual; Cash Award, Judges Chairman's Choice 1992, Laramie Wyoming; 1st Place 1988, 1989, Best In Per Square Inch 1991 Castle Gallery, Billings, Montana; First National Bank, Bluefield, West Virginia; 3rd Place 1990, Nutley Savings & Loan 20th Annual Miniature Art Show, Nutley, NJ; 4th, 5th, 6th National Exhibit, Best of Show, 1989, National League of American Pen Women; Award of Excellence 1991, Award of Honor, 1992; Miniature Art Society of Florida, 17th International., First Place in Marine, 1993; Miniature Art Society of New Jersey, 20th International Miniature Art Show, Third Place 1990, 21st International, First Place Acrylic seascape, 1991; Exhibits: Nevada Artist Association Gallery, Carson City, Nevada 1990; Arts Center of Grande Prairie, Stuttgart, Arkansas 1990; Frame Hut Gallery, 12th Annual International Miniature Art Show 1990; Eldorado Gallery, Colorado 9th Annual 1990; Miniature Painters, Sculptors & Gravers Society of Washington, DC, 55th, 56th, 57th Annual International Exhibits; Del Bello Gallery, Toronto, Ontario, Canada, 4th International Exhibition in Miniature Art 1990; Hyperian Gallery International Exhibition, Ottawa, Ontario, Canada 1990; Paper Mill Playhouse Art Gallery, Miniature Art Exhibition, Invitational 1990 & 1991; Le Petite Gallerie 3rd and 4th Annual Postage Stamp Miniature Show

RECOGNITION:

Miniatures Showcase, Vol. 4, No. 4, Fall 1989, pg. 41; Vol. 5, No. 2, Spring 1990, pg. 42; Vol. 5, No. 1, Winter 1990, pg. 5; Vol. 5, No. 4, Fall 1990, Cover, pg. 22; Vol. 6, No. 4, Fall 1991, pg. 45; *Dolls House World*, Issue 9, pg. 19; *California Art Review; Seafood Leader Magazine*, Oct. 1993; Society of Western Artists, Awards Signature Membership, 1988; East Bay Watercolor Society, Signature Membership 1993; National League of American Pen Women; Miniature Artists of America; Miniature Art Society of New Jersey, Invitational Membership; Miniature Art Societies of Florida, Georgia, and Montana; Miniature Painters, Sculptors & Gravers Society of Washington, DC Invitational Member

BIOGRAPHY:

Cynthia Eastman-Roan is originally from Toronto, Canada, and has made California her home for many years. Traveling and living around the world have given her many experiences that have enhanced her creative expression. An awards winning watercolorist, as well as miniaturist (Acrylics), Cynthia has created limited edition hand embossed watercolors. She is a versatile artist who loves new challenges, and continues to strive for excellence, which is essential for growth, as an artist.

A full member of East Bay Watercolor Society, and a signature member of Society of Western Artists, and a Fellow of International Guild of Miniature Artisans keep her quite busy. Cynthia's work has been included in numerous National and International shows and are in collections in the US, Canada and England. Her watercolors are noted for their luminous qualities, and have also won awards. Nature (in watercolors) and seascapes (in acrylic miniatures) are her favorite subjects, and paintings large and small add a good variety in her work. Cynthia has conducted many demonstrations for Bay Area art associations, and maintains a studio in California.

ARTISAN: **EATON, ROBIN**

IDENTIFICATION MARKS:

ROBIN RINEY 1991	ROBIN EATON 1992 ROBIN EATON 1992
1990 to 1991	1991 to present

CATEGORY:

Accessories; Furniture

RECOGNITION:

Miniatures Showcase, Winter 1992, Cover, pg. 50

AUTOBIOGRAPHY:

From 1990 to mid 1991, I was using my married name of Riney. My signature went on a few pieces of furniture, when I was mostly making Colonial hanging cradles. Since 1991, I have been using my maiden name, Eaton. I have stopped making furniture except for my own projects, and am concentrating on accessories, such as the breakfast tray on the winter 1992 *Miniatures Showcase* cover. I majored in Drama in college and received my BA in 1983. I worked for eleven years in the Graphic Arts & Printing industry and continued doing various theatre projects until late 1989 when I decided to pursue miniatures as a hobby again. I had a dollhouse as a child and collected furnishings on vacations through my teens. I hauled out the boxes filled with my childhood miniatures, began reading miniature magazines, visiting shops, and joined three clubs. This is how one gets addicted!

ARTISAN: **ECCHER, MARY**

BUSINESS NAME: "Pannikins" by M. E.
Miniatures by M. E.

IDENTIFICATION MARKS:

M. E.	AN ORIGINAL M.E. Pannikin By M.E.
1981 to present, on bottom with date	1982 to present, label on bottom of box with date

CATEGORY:

Beverages; Food

HONORS:

IGMA Artisan; NAME AOH 1991

RECOGNITION:

Creative Crafts and Miniatures Magazine, Apr. 1983; Oct. 1983; "Mary's Menus" monthly articles, *Nutshell News,* Feb. 1984, pg. 64-65, 91, "Beverages Galore;" Mar. 1984, pg. 86-87, "Gourmet Gaffs;" Apr. 1984, pg. 85, "Idaho's Pride;" May 1984, pg. 72-73, "The Great American Bake-Off;" Jun. 1984, pg. 93, 107, "Soup's On;" Jul. 1984, pg. 64-65, "Simmering Stews;" Aug. 1984, pg. 92-93, "Summer's Bounty;" Oct. 1984, pg. 101, 116, "A Spicy Halloween;" Nov. 1984, Cover, 106-107, "A Shaker Legacy;" Jan. 1985, pg. 100-102, "Mixology in Miniature;" Feb. 1985, pg. 87, 110, "Be My Valentine;" Mar. 1985, pg. 70-72, "Feast From the Emerald Isle;" Apr. 1985, pg. 72-73, 100, "Hard Boiled or Over Easy;" May 1985, pg. 94-95, 102, "Tex-Mex Fare;" Jun. 1985, pg. 78-81, "Fixin Up the Vittles;" Jul. 1985, pg. 76-77, 97, "Holiday Temptations;" Aug. 1985, pg. 78-80, "Creole-Acadian: A Happy Marriage;" Sept. 1985, pg. 90-91, 111, "I Scream, You Scream, We All Scream for Ice Cream;" Oct.

1985, pg. 102-103, 122, "Favorites From the Pulpy Ol' Pumpkin;" Nov. 1985, pg. 100-101, 128, "A Traditional Meal from America's Beginning;" Dec. 1985, pg. 94-95, 114, 116, "Elegant Entertaining for the Holidays;" Jan. 1986, pg. 92-93 "A New Year's Celebration;" Feb. 1986, pg. 92-93, 112, "Stout Hearted Fare;" Mar. 1986, pg. 84-85, "Ode to the Strawberry;" Apr. 1986, pg. 86-87, 95-96, "Foods With A Heritage;" May 1986, pg. 74-75, "America's Favorite One-Stop Meal;" Jun. 1986, pg. 94-95, 114, "Wedding Wishes;" Jul. 1986, pg. 84-85, "Traditional Holiday Favorites;" Aug. 1986, pg. 96-97, "Delectable Seafood Specialties;" Sept. 1986, pg. 104-105, "Time to Make the Doughnuts;" Oct. 1986, pg. 94-96, "Ghostly Treats and Phantom Floats;" Nov. 1986, pg. 100-101, "Thankful Desserts;" *Nutshell News,* Feb. 1983, pg. 57, Show Scene; Feb. 1984, pg. 53, Show Scene; Apr. 1987, pg. 58, "Time for Tea;" Mar. 1989, pg. 80-88, "The Flavors of America;" May, 1990, pg. 24-26, "Workshops - A Place to Learn and Share;" Oct. 1990, pg. 86-90, "Foods of the 30's and 40's;" Dec. 1990, Cover, pg. 34, "Private Eye" Sarah Salisbury; Oct. 1991, pg. 100-102, "Foods of the 50's and 60's;" Jul. 1992, Cover, pg. 76-78, "All-American Backyard Barbecue;" Jul. 1993, Cover, pg. 68-70, "Seashore Dining;" Oct. 1993, Cover, pg. 82-85, "Foods of Our Heritage;" *Miniature Gazette*, Fall 1985, pg. 25, "Egg Nog with Gingerbread Heart Cookies;" Summer 1990, pg. 29-30, "Tracking Down a Mystery;" Fall 1990, pg. 20-21, "A Matter of Taste," pg. 32, "Making Tacos;" Spring 1991, pg. 26-27, "The Ultimate Cookout;" Spring 1992, pg. 22-23, "The Flavors of Philadelphia;" *Miniatures Showcase*, Spring 1991

AUTOBIOGRAPHY:

My occupational background is in Corporate Public Relations and Business; and my recreational background is crafts and cooking, with a collection of cookbooks well exceeding 500. My love of miniatures was inbred during childhood, as I remember my mother's collection from Germany which she displayed at Christmas time, but my interest seriously surfaced about 1981. I am an avid collector of miniatures and dolls including houses and roomboxes. I have three sons, Andy, married to Susan, Jason, David, and a grandchild, Jessica.

I started my business of handcrafted foods and beverages as Miniatures by M.E. in 1981, changing the name to "Pannikins" by M.E. in 1982. I have authored the Mary's Menus articles and others for *Nutshell News* for several years. I love teaching workshops on the use of modeling compounds and resins in miniature cookery, all across the country. I am a member of CIMTA, IGMA, MIAA, NAME, and SAM. I served as 1st Vice President and membership chairman of IGMA, and on the Membership Committee for NAME. I have an Artisan Status in IGMA and was awarded NAME's Academy of Honor in 1991.

ARTISAN: EDMONDSON, SARA "SALLY" K.

BUSINESS NAME: STE's Mini Rugs Plus

IDENTIFICATION MARKS:

Unmarked

CATEGORY:

Kits: rug; Rugs; Wall: coverings, hangings

RECOGNITION:

Nutshell News, Aug. 1992, pg. 62; *Miniatures Showcase*, Fall 1986, pg. 14, 32, 36; Spring 1989, pg. 35; Summer 1989, pg. 28;

AUTOBIOGRAPHY:

My husband, Tom, did miniature weaving. After his death, in 1986, a local dealer said I should start to weave. In April of 1987, I went to Craft Industries in Houston, Texas and took their eight week course. Since that time, I have sold over 3500 rugs. I weave in one-inch, ½-inch, and ¼-inch scale. I have also donated more than 160 rugs to museums and charities including 100 to NAME for their Philadelphia show. My business is a pleasure rather than a job. I enjoy the creativity and sharing of talents. I am a graduate of Newark State College, now known as Kean College, Union, New Jersey, with a major in Elementary Education and a minor in Library Science. I have worked 20 years as an elementary school librarian.

ARTISAN: **EDWARDS, DAVID**

BUSINESS NAME: David Edwards Miniatures

IDENTIFICATION MARKS:

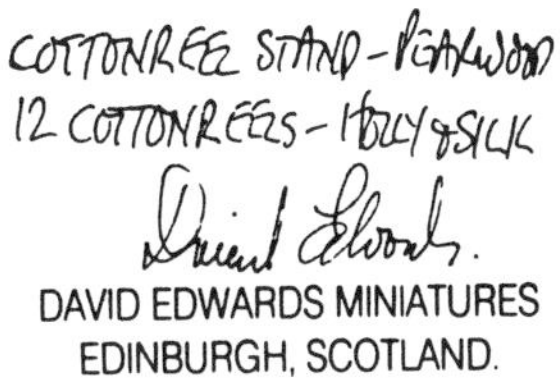

CATEGORY:

Accessories: kitchen; Bridal Items; Goldsmith; Silversmith

HONORS:

Exhibit: Toy & Miniature Museum of Kansas City

RECOGNITION:

Nutshell News; *International Dolls' House News*, Vol. 12, No. 3, Autumn 1983, pg. 16, "Scottish Craftsman"

BIOGRAPHY:

David Edwards is a lone craftsman specializing in one-inch scale dolls' house accessories in the finest woods, silver and gold. He has been a full-time miniaturist since 1983 and supplies wholesale only to a limited number of shops worldwide. His extensive range of parlour pieces, toilet articles and kitchen accessories include such rarities as gold thimbles, spectacles and wedding rings; boxwood recorders and spoons; hairbrushes and combs.

ARTISAN: **EGGLESTON, MARY ELLEN & DUAINE**

BUSINESS NAME: T. L. C. Dolls and Miniatures

IDENTIFICATION MARKS:

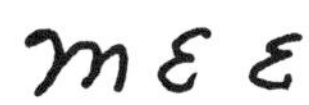

On small pieces

Marks incised in porcelain

CATEGORY:

Dolls: porcelain; Figures

BIOGRAPHY:

Mary Ellen (Condon) has a BS in Education with majors in Speech, English and Drama. She has an extensive background in stage set and costume design and taught high school Drama. She and Duaine have been making scale porcelain miniatures since 1978. She paints all the faces and costumes, while Duaine pours, makes molds, assembles and paints.

Duaine has a BS in Education and an MS in Education with a major in Industrial Education, and an Art minor. He is retired after teaching 40 years in secondary schools. He taught primarily Arts and Crafts. He still teaches Lapidary and Jewelry in the Adult School program. He also has a background in stage design and scale drawings. They went to college together and have been married since 1949. Their work is completely intertwined, they both clean porcelain and sculpt dolls.

They are both members of IGMA and NAME.

ARTISAN: **EGNER, DOT**

BUSINESS NAME: D'Egg Miniatures

IDENTIFICATION MARKS:

1985 to present

Back of piece

CATEGORY:

Accessories; Cross Stitch; Needlework

RECOGNITION:

Miniatures Showcase

AUTOBIOGRAPHY:

I have a BA in Chemistry and worked for awhile at the University of Pennsylvania. I have concentrated on my business since 1985, to help pay for my growing hobby! I also teach art in my parish school, kindergarten to 8th grade. Everything I do full-size I try to reduce. Right now I work in one-inch scale exclusively. All original needlework designs carry my mark on the back of the piece. The mark is my business name: D in an Egg. No, I don't do eggs, the egg comes from my surname, Egner.

ARTISAN: **EHRENS, ANN**

BUSINESS NAME: Small Wonders Handcrafted Miniatures, Inc.

IDENTIFICATION MARKS:

CATEGORY:

Accessories; Food

RECOGNITION:

Today Show, Feb. 16, 1983

ARTISAN: **EISMAN, MARIE**

BUSINESS NAME: Marie Eisman Miniatures

IDENTIFICATION MARKS:

mle 1092 Initials from outside of work looks like elm

month and year

CATEGORY:

Christmas; Glass: stained; Holiday Items; Lamps; Lighting

EISMAN, MARIE, continued

RECOGNITION:

Nutshell News, Nov. 1992, pg. 74, Show Scene

AUTOBIOGRAPHY:

As a child, I had a fiber board dollhouse which went the way of my youth. As an adult, I started collecting miniatures at a mall show and got hooked. After kitbashing a Greenleaf house into an antique shop for my mother, I decided it needed stained glass windows and lights. They became a do it yourself project for me, and I was quite pleased with the results. I am self-taught through trial and error, and have been selling since 1981.

ARTISAN: ELBERFELD, NANCY A.

BUSINESS NAME: Elberfeld House Miniatures

IDENTIFICATION MARKS:

Nancy A. Elberfeld N. ELBERFELD N.A.E. N.E.

All 1982 to present

CATEGORY:

Accessories; Dolls

RECOGNITION:

The Andrews Collection, Personal Treasures, Anne Day Smith, 1988, pg. 35, 76; *Miniatures Showcase*, Vol. 7, No. 4, Nov. 1992, pg. 46

AUTOBIOGRAPHY:

I began collecting miniatures in 1980 and selling my handcrafted miniatures at shows in 1982. I am a retired computer programmer, with an Associate Degree in Computer Science. I have taken numerous courses in oil painting, clay sculpture, woodcarving and quilting. I work in several mediums in miniature including wood, porcelain and cloth.

ARTISAN: ELLIOTT, HOPE (Submitted by William R. Robertson)

IDENTIFICATION MARKS:

Hope Elliott with year

Hand printed on paper label

CATEGORY:

Food

HONORS:

Exhibit: Toy & Miniature Museum of Kansas City

RECOGNITION:

Miniature Collector, No. 14, Aug. 1979, pg. 31-33, "Hope's Harvest," Bryce Webster

ARTISAN: **ELLIS, MARY M.**

BUSINESS NAME: Floral Fantasies By Mary

IDENTIFICATION MARKS:

1988 to present

Floral Fantasies
By Mary

FF
by
MARY

Floral Fantasies
By Mary
St. Louis, MO.

Floral
Fantasies
By Mary

FLORAL FANTASIES
BY MARY
ST. LOUIS, MO.

Attached to bottom of piece

CATEGORY:

Floral Arrangements; Flowers and Plants

HONORS:

IGMA Artisan 1989

RECOGNITION:

Nutshell News, Vol. 17, No. 10, Oct. 1987, pg. 44; *The Independent News*, Vol. 1, No. 5, Nov. 12, 1987, pg. 1

AUTOBIOGRAPHY:

In July of 1982, I started into the miniature field by decorating a cardboard dollhouse for my two granddaughters. I finished it in time to give it to them for Christmas of that year.

During the summer of 1982, I took a workshop class at The Doll House Galerie on making shell flowers. This led to my being invited to join a miniature club. At one of the club sessions we made baskets from needlepoint canvas. Later I tried filling the baskets with dried flowers although I wasn't satisfied with the results.

That same summer I took a class on making wicker beds from macrame cord. At the end of the class the teacher showed us how to make a small wicker basket. This type of basket appealed to me more than the canvas baskets, so I started making them exclusively. It was then that I became really interested in making flowers to fill them instead of using the dried variety.

I tried using Fimo and Barbara Meyer's first book on bread dough flowers was my guide. Using this book as a starting point I soon discovered the enjoyment of devising my own way of making different blossoms. I found that I really loved sculpting the flowers from Fimo and I have never been tempted to branch off into other mediums such as silk and paper. Sculpting is my first love. I do make fern from floral tape simply because I need them for my arrangements and I have never been able to figure out a way to make them from Fimo.

In 1983, The Dollhouse Galerie took some of my arrangements on consignment and later that same year I made my first sale to a miniature shop. It was then I decided that I needed a name for my fledgling business, however I did not have a signature or logo at that time. In 1984, Nicole Minnick contacted me about filling some of her beautiful vases. I agreed to try and we worked together for a couple of years, strictly by mail. I have never had the pleasure of meeting Nicole.

I started using a butterfly as my signature. This was unplanned and just evolved slowly. The first butterflies were made from Fimo, but I was not satisfied with them. Eventually I learned to make them out of treated paper which gives them a translucent look. Each hand-colored butterfly is individually made by me. I put one on each plant, flower arrangement or tree.

In 1987, I formed an ongoing business relationship with Jo Old, of Kansas, which has turned into a friendship. She sells my flowers at various shows she attends every year. That same year it was my good fortune to have an article written about my work and published in *Nutshell News*. Barbara Warner did the interview, and my husband did the photographs. Around the same time, a local paper, *The Independent News*, published an article about the flower arrangements.

I have no formal education in art or sculpting and also no formal training in flower arranging. I am most fortunate to have an excellent library of reference books giving me needed information on flowers, plants, baskets and butterflies.

ARTISAN: ELMER, GARY W. & CARROLL H.

BUSINESS NAME: GWE-CHE Collectibles

IDENTIFICATION MARKS:

GWE-CHE Collectibles	Burned into wood 1992 to present
GWE-CHE	Printed on wood prior to 1992

CATEGORY:

Furniture

HONORS:

IGMA Artisan 1990, Fellow (Gary)

RECOGNITION:

Nutshell News, Vol. 20, No. 11, Nov. 1990, pg. 62-65

BIOGRAPHY:

Gary W. Elmer graduated from Purdue University in 1956 with a degree in Chemical Engineering. He married Carroll in 1957 and worked for Amoco Oil Company for 36 years, retiring in 1992. He has been in miniatures since 1980. A turning point in his miniature career was attending the Guild School in Castine, Maine for four years. After the first year 1989, he applied and was accepted as a Guild Artisan in March 1990. In 1993, he was an instructor at the two day preschool at Castine. He especially enjoys designing and cutting out miniature furniture.

Carroll H. Elmer graduated from Purdue University in 1957. She has attended the Guild School in Castine, Maine since 1988. She enjoys collecting as well as making miniatures. She normally assembles and finishes the furniture they sell. GWE-CHE represents both Gary and Carroll's initials.

ARTISAN: ENTZMINGER, GLORIA

BUSINESS NAME: Miniatures By Gloria

IDENTIFICATION MARKS:

CATEGORY:

Metal: handpainted

RECOGNITION:

Nutshell News, Miniatures Showcase

ARTISAN: **EVANS, SARAH ANNE "SALLIE"**

BUSINESS NAME: Strawberry Creek

IDENTIFICATION MARKS:

CATEGORY:

Carpets; Kits: needlework; Needlepoint; Needlework; Rugs; Samplers; Upholstery

HONORS:

IGMA Artisan, Fellow

RECOGNITION:

Small Talk, Vol. 6, No. 1 Sept. 1981, pg. 22-23; *Needlepoint News,* May/Jun. 1986

BIOGRAPHY:

Sallie majored in Art at the University of Kentucky at Lexington, Kentucky, attended the University of Cincinnati Art School and the Academy of Art College in San Francisco. She is a Fellow member of the International Guild of Miniature Artisans, member-at-large of the Embroiders' Guild of America, member-at-large of the American Needlepointers Guild and a member of NAME.

Besides designing and creating miniature needlework kits for Strawberry Creek Designs, Sallie designs and handcrafts special commissions for collectors, in one-inch, ½-inch and ¼-inch scale. She also reproduces in miniature those favorite "real life" needlework items. The silk materials she uses are the finest possible, and she is ever on the alert for new fabrics and threads for use in making quality miniatures.

Historic reproduction in miniature is her specialty. Sallie enjoys teaching her techniques as well as using those techniques in her work. The challenge to create in miniature something of historic nature, something that has a museum quality excites her imagination and dares her to make it as perfect and as close to the real thing as possible, *A perfect illusion.* Part of that tendency for historic perfection is reflected in her ability to create miniature braided rugs with the exact techniques used in making real life braided rugs. She hand dyes most of the yarn she uses because the color range is not available for her use. She has developed her designs for over a period of 20 years, to help you appreciate and create your own fine needlework in miniature, as an art form. All the braided rugs Sallie makes are unique, one-of-a-kind, they are all different, never repeated.

F

ARTISAN: **FÁBREGA, ANDREA M.**

BUSINESS NAME: Andrea Fábrega
Fábrega Porcelain

IDENTIFICATION MARKS:

CATEGORY:

Ceramics: wheel thrown; Porcelain: wheel thrown; Pottery: wheel thrown

HONORS:

IGMA Artisan 1991; Award of Excellence, Eggshell Porcelain, California State Fair 1992; Juried member, Association of California Ceramicists, Sept. 1991

RECOGNITION:

Miniatures Showcase, Vol. 8, No. 2, Mar. 1993, pg. 19, 54; *Nutshell News*, Vol. 23, No. 2, Feb. 1993, pg. 77, Show Scene (red, green & purple vases credited in error to Nancy Warner); *Miniature Collector*, Vol. 16, No. 1, Spring 1993, pg. 57; Vol. 16, No. 2, Summer 1993, pg. 22-25, "Big Pots, Little Pots;" *Ceramics Monthly*, May 1994, Cover, "Miniature Porcelain"

AUTOBIOGRAPHY:

I graduated from Carnegie-Mellon University with a BS in economics in 1984 and immediately went into the workforce as a research analyst. I became increasingly dissatisfied with the string of careers I tried, although I have always appreciated the arts, I never actually gave a thought to do them seriously.

My first exposure to pottery was a beginning pottery class at Massachusetts of Technology (MIT) Student Art Association in 1989. While throwing big pots for two semesters, I attempted to create miniature pots because of my childhood interest in miniatures and the feeling that clay had the potential to show fantastic detail and precision. I found no literature on creating scale pottery so I began developing tools and techniques which enabled me to produce in clay the visions in my head. I chose porcelain because its translucency and fineness captured the jewel-like results I was after.

Each piece I create is hand-crafted individually. Using a full-sized potters' wheel I turn a teaspoon of well-aged English porcelain into a well-thrown vessel with good design and function and walls of even thickness, elements big potters strive for. Removable lids, pourable spouts, and a well-turned foot all contribute to the detailing which further emphasizes the feel of a big pot. I choose the method of glazing and firing depending on the form.

I stayed on at MIT to teach three semesters of miniature pottery and beginning pottery and to use their 24 hour-access studio. I became increasingly dissatisfied with electric kiln results. Test tiles out of a reduction kiln persuaded me to join Radcliffe Studio to take pottery classes. I started getting some very exciting results plus I was around serious potters. I sold a few pots while I kept my day job. After three semesters, I moved to Menlo Park, California in June 1991 where I started using the San Jose State University's fantastic facilities. I took a glaze chemistry class at San Francisco State and continue to take independent studies at SJSU.

I became an IGMA Artisan in March 1991. I was juried into the Association of California Ceramicists as an exhibiting member in September 1991. I started entering shows and selling my work in January 1992. I received an Award of Excellence and cash prize at the 1992 California State Fair in the small works division. I have finished my first year supporting myself as a full-time potter. My next goal is to be taken seriously by mainstream ceramists/collectors - that is, to show that a vessel an inch or two high can create the same impact that a wonderful full-size vessel can have on a viewer.

ARTISAN: **FALSTEIN, REBECCA**

BUSINESS NAME: Becky Saxe~Falstein

IDENTIFICATION MARKS:

BECKY SAXE~FALSTEIN

CATEGORY:

Books; Glass: stained; Paintings: watercolor; Signs: store front

RECOGNITION:

International Dolls House News, Vol. 21, No. 2, Summer 1992, pg. 7; Vol. 22, No. 3, Autumn 1993, pg. 10-11; *The Home Miniaturist*, Jan/Feb. 1992, Cover, pg. 7-8; *Dolls House World,* No. 18, 1992, pg. 11; No. 25, May/Jun. 1993, pg. 39, 56

AUTOBIOGRAPHY:

I am a qualified Graphic Designer running my own design consulting business since 1990. I am a member of a local miniature club which encouraged me to go into business in 1991, painting miniature watercolor pictures. These are painted on ivorine framed and mounted behind real glass. From there I have gone on and diversified.

I also make stained glass windows, doors and panels in any period by using a technique I learned many years ago at evening class and miniaturized it. My graphic design training has helped me to produce the hand lettered shop and pub signs. These are all hand illustrated or lettered onto wood.

At college during my four year course I was fortunate to be taught how to make leather bound books, full-size of course. This enabled me to miniaturize the techniques I learned and make one-inch scale books with end papers and separate leaves. Working from home producing graphics and making miniatures is most satisfying.

ARTISAN: **FARMER, EMILY P.**

BUSINESS NAME: Emily's

IDENTIFICATION MARKS:

Hang tag from back of neck with year typed or hand written inside

CATEGORY:

Bears: teddy; Kits; Toys

ARTISAN: **FARNSWORTH, MARTHA**

IDENTIFICATION MARKS;

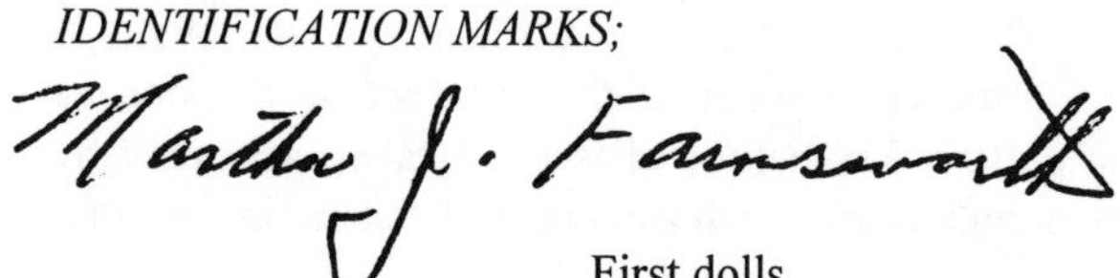

First dolls

On Petite Petit Point mark is incorporated into the design

FARNSWORTH, MARTHA, continued

CATEGORY:

Clothing; Costuming; Dolls: costuming, original; Needlepoint; Needlework

HONORS:

NAME Honorary Founder 1972; Founding member IMA now known as AOH; Mell Prescott Award 1988

RECOGNITION:

Nutshell News, Winter 1972, pg. 28-31, "Farnsworth's Folly," Susan Ohanian; Summer 1974, pg. 36-40, "A 'Little' About Martha Farnsworth," P. R. Lakcram; *Miniature Collector*, No. 3, Aug. 1977, pg. 35; No. 6, Mar. 1978, pg. 24; *Child Magazine*, Issue No. 10, Dec/Jan. 1993; *Miniature Gazette*, Vol. 1, No. 2, Dec. 1972, pg. 15, 27, 29, "Farnsworth's Folly," Susan Ohanian; Vol. 1, No. 4, Jun. 1973, pg. 24, "Miniature Needle Work," Carolyn Robbins; Vol. 6, No. 2, Winter 1977, pg. 82, "A Tribute to a Great Artist," Jerry Floor; Vol. 7, No. 1, Fall 1978, pg. 13-15, "A Visit to a Small Town," Howard P. Rubenstein

AUTOBIOGRAPHY:

I was born September 17, 1913 in Tulsa, Oklahoma. In 1934, I graduated from the Queen of Angels University of Nursing as an RN. My first introduction to miniatures was when a patient gave me a tiny porcelain miniature vase, although I didn't actually begin to collect until the 1940's. I started collecting dolls at that time and did the costuming. When dolls became too expensive to purchase, I made them myself and though my first attempts were not that good, I was so proud of my efforts, I signed all of them! I taught Ceramics, adult education classes, at Lincoln High School from 1957 to 1959, averaging about 50 students to the class. I also taught glove making and doll dressing for $2.00 an hour. The demand for my classes became so great I had to quit as it was beginning to take too much time from my family and our Emergency Ambulance Service.

Money was tight at that time and my husband had given me enough to buy a pair of shoes which I really needed. I used it instead for a down-payment on a miniature Traveler's Sample stove which I fell in love with. I had a jeweler do some repair work on it which led to his hand making many special items for a kitchen roombox of 1915.

One year on a trip to a local auction, I saw an Antique purse done in petite petit-point and my love affair in this area began. At that time, it was almost a lost art and supplies were very difficult to find. In the meantime, I continued to pursue my dollmaking activities, establishing the Monday Sewing Group whereby members received a doll made from an antique mold copy which I named "Miss Fancy." Members were given the doll and patterns to complete a wardrobe for her. I had been taught French sewing and French ruffling by my grandmother. Membership grew rapidly.

I attended a UFDC Convention in Universal City, California, in 1972 where Allegra Mott was present. We had an impromptu meeting in one of our hotel rooms, and it was at that time Allegra proposed a national organization for miniaturists which would eventually evolve into NAME. I was one of the founding members and designated Chairperson for the international miniature artists which was the beginning of AOH. Dorothy Carter of England was our first international member.

I developed my own techniques for doing petite petit-point, having coined the name to distinguish it from petit point and the term has stuck. I've given lessons in Canada, England and France as well as the U.S. My work is represented in several museums, both public and private on both sides of the Atlantic, as well as in many private collections, including that of Julie Eisenhower. I've done special projects to raise money for worthy causes such as the Lincoln Public Library and Lincoln Arts and have done many things to benefit disadvantaged children.

I've had a long and wonderful affiliation with the many people in the miniature collecting world, from the notables to the many people who are just discovering this little world and have always believed "knowledge is for sharing" which I've tried hard to do.

Editor's Note: Martha has been an inspiration to the miniature hobby in her sharing and giving of herself to all involved, through her love of miniatures.

ARTISAN: **FATZER, MALCOLM GHRAME**

BUSINESS NAME: Malcolmania
Malcolm Ghrame Fatzer

IDENTIFICATION MARKS:

CATEGORY:
Glass: handblown

RECOGNITION:
Nutshell News, Vol. 13, No. 12, Dec. 1983, pg. 71, Show Scene; Vol. 14, No. 11, Nov. 1984, pg. 73, Show Scene

BIOGRAPHY:
Malcolm Fatzer has had a love affair with miniatures. His contributions to the artglass world, coupled with his research into the history and processes of the 16th, 17th, and 18th century glass, has given him the skill and impetus to reproduce the shapes and styles of old collectors items in miniature.

The initial idea was to produce a line of prototypes that includes simple table glass ware of the late 1800's. Since then, new styles and designs have been created such as sets of intricate Venetian swirl tableware and mini-millefiore vases. Production is limited, since all the pieces are hand blown by Mr. Fatzer in a small studio in Santa Cruz, California to one-inch and ¼-inch scale.

Mr. Fatzer uses colored glass rather than soda glass for his creations, as well as techniques of his own invention to achieve the iridescence or pattern proper to the style of the piece. He blows Pyrex which is incredibly durable and equally as beautiful. His work is one of a kind. Malcolm's work shows the influence of time spent in the Academia DiBelle Arti and blowing glass in Murano, Italy. After the initial two to 12 months of research the pieces take anywhere from 15 minutes to three hours to complete.

ARTISAN: **FAUROT, JEANNE & WES**

BUSINESS NAME: Willoughby's Eighteenth Century

IDENTIFICATION MARKS:

 Gold leafed

CATEGORY:
Furniture: period

RECOGNITION:
The Collector's Guide to Dollhouses and Dollhouse Miniatures, Marian Maeve O'Brien, 1974, pg. 13-15, 108-111, 114-116, 140, 162-164, 169, 176-177, 185, 203; *The Christian Science Monitor*, Apr. 26, 1971, pg. 4; *The San Jose Mercury News,* California Today Magazine, Jun. 13, 1971, pg. 26-27; *Los Altos Town Crier*, Dec. 15, 1971, pg. 6-7; *Acquire Magazine*, Jul. 1975, pg. 23-24

FAUROT, JEANNE & WES, continued

AUTOBIOGRAPHY:

During our years in Washington DC, we became quite aware of our tremendously movable society. Also, we had some years working with retired crafts people and found that miniatures were such a delightful answer to the accomplishment of one's dreams. People who moved often gathered less and less furniture and yet their taste for lovely things continued. People who were retired moved into smaller quarters but their love of beauty still needed an outlet. So the making of eighteenth century miniature furniture came into being. It could be packed and moved at will, and you could have one room's worth or 20 room's worth. One's dreams need fulfilling.

We studied at Stanford University libraries, particularly in their rare book section, and read diaries until we had a feel for the period. It was a fantastic era where everything seemed possible. We were particularly interested in George Washington as we had lived near his home and had traveled often to his mother's township. Somehow one gets a fantasized view of people in great prominence. So when we read a message from George Washington's mother to him on a certain date, after he was a well-known figure, we smiled. It read, "George, I want you to come home today." It seems he had visited Williamsburg without dropping by her home in Fredericksburg. Needless to say, George came home. This put such a different light on the man who was someone's son.

As we build our eighteenth century pieces we see the state of thought and energy that allowed it to come into being in that earlier period and have through our historical catalog shared some of it. As they said in that day, "A good morrow morning to you."

ARTISAN: FELTROPE, CLIFF

BUSINESS NAME: Small Accomplishments

IDENTIFICATION MARKS:

Very small pieces unsigned

All marks current

CATEGORY:

Weapons

RECOGNITION:

Nutshell News, Jul/Aug. 1979, pg. 96; Jun. 1984, pg. 72; *The Miniature Catalog*, 14th Edition, Cover; *Sports Afield,* Aug. 1984, pg. 54; *Miniature Gazette,* Spring 1981, pg. 65

BIOGRAPHY:

Cliff is an Art graduate of Riverside City College. He owned and operated two separate graphic business. He has been selling his artwork, including watercolors and oils, since 1972. He started Small Accomplishments in 1978. Cliff is well versed on weapons and all technical aspects of them. He is currently compiling a portfolio of illustrations for freelance contracts.

ARTISAN: FERGUSON, ANNELLE

BUSINESS NAME: Mini Stitches

IDENTIFICATION MARKS:

Back of framed needlework

Back of chairseats

FERGUSON, ANNELLE continued

CATEGORY:
Kits: needlework; Needlework; Samplers

HONORS:
IGMA Fellow

RECOGNITION:
Miniature Collector, No. 69, Summer 1990, pg. 32; *Country Living*, Vol. 15, No. 3, Mar. 1992, pg. 102

AUTOBIOGRAPHY:
I am a self-taught needleworker, never having done needlework in full-size. I began doing needlepoint rugs for my daughter's dollhouse over 12 years ago. I credit Barbara Cosgrove for my interest in researching antique needlework and designing adaptations in miniature. I especially enjoy providing the collector with one-inch scale pieces adapted from 18th and 19th century originals. For the needleworker, I provide historical designs in kit form.

ARTISAN: **FINN, JOHN WILSON, F.C.A.**

BUSINESS NAME: John Finn

IDENTIFICATION MARKS:

With year

CATEGORY:
Furniture: period

AUTOBIOGRAPHY:
I started making miniature furniture after my retirement, and am self-taught in what I do.

ARTISAN: **FISHER, OBADIAH**

BUSINESS NAME: The Obadiah Collection

IDENTIFICATION MARKS:

Sterling [O][F]

925 [O][F]

CATEGORY:
Goldsmith; Reproductions; Silver: reproductions; Silversmith

HONORS:
IGMA Artisan 1983, Fellow 1989; Miniature Makers Society Award 1982; National Geographic Society Exhibition, 1987; Exhibit: Toy & Miniature Museum of Kansas City

RECOGNITION:
Nutshell News, Vol. 13, No. 7, Jul. 1983, pg. 64; Vol. 14, No. 4, Apr. 1984, pg. 64, Show Scene; Vol. 14, No. 11, Nov. 1984, pg. 81; *Miniature Collector*, No. 32, Aug. 1982, pg. 44-46; *Historic Preservation Magazine*, Aug. 1985, pg. 32-33; *Smithsonian Magazine*, Dec. 1988, pg. 122; *Television*, The Morning Exchange, Cleveland, Ohio, Aug. 18, 1989

FISHER, OBADIAH, continued

BIOGRAPHY:

Obadiah Fisher was born in Cleveland, Ohio. His original interest was in sculpture in which he excelled as a student and won several awards. It was in Cleveland that he first took up the designing and making of custom jewelry.

He came to New York in 1966 where he continued to work as a jewelry designer, working for several commercial companies. This work included the manufacturing and design of expensive commercial pieces such as wedding rings and necklaces, etc. During this first period in New York he pursued his interest in classical pieces of all cultures.

Obadiah subsequently left the commercial industry in order to freelance in custom jewelry and wax model making. In 1977, Obadiah was commissioned by the Metropolitan Museum of Art to produce wax models of Egyptian jewelry for the King Tut Show. He has done Egyptian models for the Brooklyn Museum and a Peruvian motif for the Philadelphia Museum of Art. Upon doing this work for the museums it also produced a number of artisans and craft people seeking to learn more about wax carving. Thus started his own private school of wax model making. Here he taught his own methods of carving wax for a few years.

In 1979, Mrs. E. Andrews of Alexandria, Virginia aroused his interest in miniatures and antiques and also in her own work of beautiful porcelain reproductions. With her assistance he chose several early American and English silver pieces to copy in miniature. This was the beginning of what has become a devotion to excelling in this field. Obadiah found the problems of hidden hinges, hollow vessels and engraving on such small scale, to be a very challenging business. He insists on as much accuracy as possible, and this requires a magnification of 7x in the original carving of the wax to make the tiny objects visible. He controls each step of the lengthy procedures; the carving, casting, making of the mold, and soldering of the casting pieces. The polishing is done by hand with the aid of a tumbling machine in order to reach areas that would be in other ways inaccessible. After the final hand polishing, some of the pieces such as tea and coffee pots are given a hand carved ebony handle. These special wooden handle pieces are added to the collection to upgrade the quality of the miniatures.

Obadiah Fisher's work has appeared in the August 1992 issue of the *Miniature Collector* magazine. He has also shown his work in several miniature shows. His miniature collection is sold by several dealers across the country; Washington Dollhouse & Toy Museum, Washington, DC, Maison des Maisons, of Colorado. Obadiah is also a member of the International Guild of Miniature Artisans in New York.

ARTISAN: **FISHER, PERRY**

BUSINESS NAME: Scale : of Twelve

IDENTIFICATION MARKS: (Submitted by William R. Robertson)

P. Fisher Hand written script in ink

Scale : of Twelve, Gold stick on label

CATEGORY:

Furniture; Tools: dovetail jig

HONORS:

Exhibit: Toy & Miniature Museum of Kansas City

RECOGNITION:

Nutshell News, Jul/Aug. 1979, pg. 36-39, 58; Jan. 1980, pg. 68; Mar. 1980, pg. 51, "Where the Stars Come Out," Sarah Salisbury; Jun. 1980, pg. 36; Nov. 1980, pg. 72-77, "The Workbench - Perfecting the Dovetailed Joint" Perry Fisher

ARTISAN: **FJARE, ORVIN**

BUSINESS NAME: Fjare Miniatures

IDENTIFICATION MARKS:

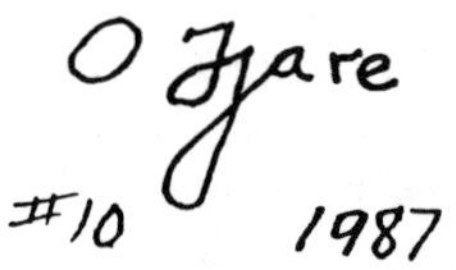

July 1985 to Sept. 1991

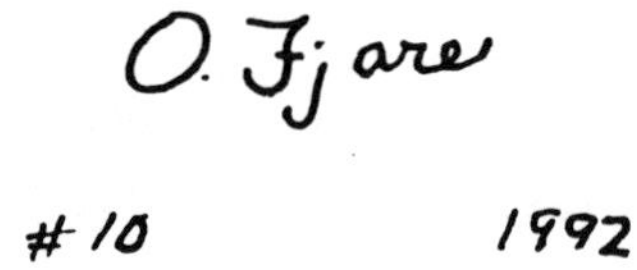

Sept. 1991 to present

CATEGORY:

Clocks: working; Furniture; Musical Instruments; Pianos

BIOGRAPHY:

Orvin Fjare was born in 1918 in Big Timber, Montana. He graduated from Sweet Grass County High School in 1937. In 1940, he enlisted in the Army and eventually served as a pilot of a B-24 in the Far East. After returning to Big Timber in 1945 he worked in a clothing store and started building furniture for his home. He became active in city government and several local organizations.

Orvin served on the Montana Welfare Board, as Representative to the Montana Legislature from Sweet Grass County, a Congressman from the Eastern district of Montana in Washington DC, and director of Advertising and Tourist Promotion for the State of Montana. He retired after eight years as Montana Director of Housing and Urban Development in Helena.

Upon returning to Big Timber, Orvin discovered the hobbies of gardening, orchard growing, and hand-crafting miniatures. His miniature dollhouses and furniture are distinctive in their use of beautiful hard woods, attention to detail and fine workmanship and are popular at miniature shows.

ARTISAN: **FLEMING, JOHN L.**

BUSINESS NAME: Seneca Baskets

IDENTIFICATION MARKS:

Mark used with Red, White and Blue dots

Currently using only Red, White and Blue dots

CATEGORY:

Baskets: wicker

RECOGNITION:

Nutshell News, Apr. 1974, pg. 48

ARTISAN: **FLOOR, JERRY**

BUSINESS NAME: Treasures in Porcelain Etc.

IDENTIFICATION MARKS:

1976 to present

FLOOR, JERRY, continued

CATEGORY:

China: handpainted; Houses: cigar box; Porcelain: handpainted

HONORS:

NAME AOH

RECOGNITION:

NAME National Souvenir Book, Cover, Jul. 1980; *Nutshell News*, Jun. 1980, pg. 69; Jun. 1981, pg. 32; Aug. 1981, pg. 8; Oct. 1982, pg. 92-93; Nov. 1983, pg. 36; Dec. 1983, pg. 62; Jun. 1989, pg. 42; *Miniature Gazette*, Winter 1987, pg. 54; Spring 1988, pg. 35; Summer 1988, pg. 17; *Miniatures Showcase*, Fall 1987, pg. 12, 14, 18, 19, 34, 42, 44, 46; *This Side of Yesterday in Miniatures*, Catherine B. MacLaren, 1975, pg. 37; *Our Miniature World*, Marie Dettling 1984, pg. 77

AUTOBIOGRAPHY:

I have collected and made miniatures for over 30 years. I specialize in handpainted china and making Cigar Box Houses. I have taught classes in the construction of these houses to many students, also taught miniatures at the College of Miniature Knowledge in Sacramento, California. I have chaired Theme Luncheons at NAME Houseparties, and had workshops numerous times. I was formerly a buyer of fine china and gifts for a chain of 15 stores. I have a certificate in retailing from the University of Indiana, which I completed in 1958. My interest in the making of china came from my job as buyer of fine china, and I had a television show in the fifties about entertaining. As I became interested in miniatures I decided to make china in miniature. I went to school to learn china painting, and I make all my molds.

Besides my husband, two children, two grandchildren, two great-grandchildren, miniatures are the love of my life!

ARTISAN: **FORCE, KATHY**

BUSINESS NAME: Kathy's Kuties

IDENTIFICATION MARKS:

CATEGORY:

Dolls: babies

AUTOBIOGRAPHY:

I have been interested in miniatures as far back as I can remember. Many years ago I wanted a realistic baby for my dollhouse. I joined a miniature club and one of the members showed me a fimo baby she bought at a show. I was quite interested in it but wanted to make some changes. I started experimenting with different materials and came up with my own mixture of super Sculpy, Fimo and Cernet. I made several and my friend asked me if I wanted to sell them at her table. They all sold and I had orders for more and have been selling them ever since. I sell my babies through many dealers in the United States and sell to collectors in Australia, Japan and Europe. I have taught school for 20 years and shared my miniatures with my students.

ARTISAN: **FORSLUND, CARL**

BUSINESS NAME: Hillery House

IDENTIFICATION MARKS:
Some unmarked

Carl Forslund
Stamped in ink

CATEGORY:
Furniture

ARTISAN: **FOTHERGILL, ELIZABETH**

BUSINESS NAME: Elizabeth Fothergill

IDENTIFICATION MARKS:

1985 to present

CATEGORY:
China: Dresden-style; Porcelain

BIOGRAPHY:
Elizabeth Fothergill was born in 1950. She studied at the Ruskin School of Drawing at Oxford University from 1967 to 1970. She attained the University of Oxford Certificate of Fine Arts, and spent the next 20 years in the Antiques trade. In 1985, Elizabeth continued using her Fine Arts background making miniatures professionally, having been a collector for many years.

ARTISAN: **FRAHNER, CHARLES A.**

BUSINESS NAME: Small Wonder

IDENTIFICATION MARKS:

or signature, 1986 to present

CATEGORY:
Accessories; Furniture; Houses; Roomboxes

RECOGNITION:
Miniature Collector, No. 68, Spring 1990, pg. 22; *Garden Railways*, Vol. 8, No. 1, Jan/Feb. 1991, pg. 58

ARTISAN: **FRANCO, DE LA PARRA VICTOR**

BUSINESS NAME: Miniatures Victor Franco

IDENTIFICATION MARKS:

CATEGORY:
Accessories

HONORS:
IGMA Artisan 1993

RECOGNITION:
Nutshell News, Jan. 1992, pg. 21; *Miniatures Showcase*, Winter 1990, pg. 14, 33; Spring 1990, pg. 31; Summer 1990, pg. 10, 18, 26, 32-34, 37-38; Fall 1990, pg. 20, 25-26, 39, 46; Spring 1991, pg. 22-23, 26-27; Summer 1991, pg. 20, 22-23, 28-29; Fall 1991, pg. 23, 25, 35, 38, 41, 43, 45, 47; Winter 1992, pg. 34, 39, 40-41; *Miniature Catalog*, 13th Edition, Cover; 14th Edition, Cover

AUTOBIOGRAPHY:
I was born in Mexico City in 1944 and since I was 4 years old, I have been making miniatures. I still have my first piece which is a carpenter's tool box made out of balsa wood and cardboard. So most of my life I have been working on miniatures, as a hobby, making many things including carvings on Ivory, wood, bone, and amber. I am a Mechanical Engineer graduated in Mexico City in 1968, working since that time in the air conditioning field.

Five years ago, I displayed some of my pieces at a miniature show in Mexico City, and since that time have been making miniatures to sell. My line has increased up to more than 150 different pieces. I have sent samples to *Miniatures Showcase* magazine starting in 1990, and since then they have pictured some of my pieces in many issues, they have also been in the *Miniature Catalog* and *Nutshell News*. In January 1992, I attended the CIMTA Show in Anaheim, California, and started selling wholesale in the US market. All my production now goes to CIMTA customers in the US and Europe. All of my pieces are 99% handmade by me and therefore my production is limited, but on the other hand the quality is very controlled.

ARTISAN: **FRICK, LESLIE**

BUSINESS NAME: Custom Creations by Rika

IDENTIFICATION MARKS:

Rika

1987 to 1991 hand sculpted

1992 to present, molded

CATEGORY:
Animals: original, wildlife, woodland

HONORS:
IGMA Artisan

RECOGNITION:
Nutshell News, May 1989, pg. 48-51; *The Miniature Catalog* 12th Edition, Cover, Pg. 9; *Miniatures Showcase*, Vol. 4, No. 3, Summer 1989, pg. 27, 40; *Dolls in Miniature*, Vol. 1, Issue 1, Cover

ARTISAN: **FRIEDMAN, MARIE** (Deceased)

BUSINESS NAME: Marie Friedman, Miniaturist

IDENTIFICATION MARKS:

MF Marie Friedman

CATEGORY:

Ceramics; Dinnerware; Dishes: ceramics, porcelain; Lighting; Porcelain; Pots: flower

HONORS:

NAME AOH

RECOGNITION:

Nutshell News, Fall 1978, pg. 42; Sept. 1981, pg. 8; *Miniature Collector; Creative Crafts; The Scale Cabinetmaker; Inside The World of Miniatures and Dollhouses*, Rosner & Beckerman, Mc Kay Press, 1976

AUTOBIOGRAPHY:

When my children grew up and left home, I decided it was time to build the dollhouse I had always wanted as a child, one in which everything "worked." At the time, very little was available in miniature. I needed door hinges, so I learned to form metal. I needed lumber, so I learned to operate a small table saw. I needed furniture legs, so I learned to use a Unimat lathe, which also came in handy for turning parts for chandeliers. Of course the lighting fixtures were all electric, for everything had to "work!" I wanted flowerpots and tiles and dishes that were truly fine authentic miniatures, so I learned to make molds, work with ceramic and porcelain clays, make ceramic decals, etc. In the course of all this, I met others interested in miniatures, and they learned that I could "do things." Within a very short time, my hobby had turned into a business as I began doing these things for others. The demand, especially for dinnerware, was so great that I worked 12 and 14 hours a day, seven days a week, for about 12 years. I also wrote articles and feature columns about other miniaturists in *Nutshell News* and *The Miniature Magazine*. For six years, I did a series of limited edition plates (250 in each edition) for Mother's Day and Christmas, in addition to the dinnerware sets, individual pieces, and flower pots. My most difficult project was ½-inch scale dinnerware, footed and handled just like their larger counterparts. I had to devise holding devices to be able to put on handles, apply glaze, decorate, etc. Only two dinnerware sets and a few individual pieces were made in this scale, everything else was in one-inch scale.

It was great fun, but I got tired. I have now returned to my earlier occupation, computer programming, which I can usually keep down to 40 or 50 hours a week. I still make flower pots, as some of my wholesale customers rely on them for their flower creations, but have discontinued everything else.

ARTISAN: **FRITZ, DIANE E.**

BUSINESS NAME: Fantasy Fabrications

IDENTIFICATION MARKS:

FF
Diane Fritz

Logo on all stationary, brochures and signs

CATEGORY:

Furniture; Lamps; Lighting; Roomboxes

RECOGNITION:

Artsnews, Mid-Valley Arts Council, Salem Oregon, Oct. 1992

FRITZ, DIANE E., continued

AUTOBIOGRAPHY:

The dollhouse I received for Christmas in the late 1940's was my favorite toy for many years. As an adult, I re-entered the miniature world in 1980, by attending a miniature show in Portland, Oregon. I began as a collector progressing into creative work in 1989, and established Fantasy Fabrications.

My philosophy is to interpret the style of a particular period, capture the essence of the era, and the situation in the scene I'm designing. Any furnishings developed as the result of creating a roombox are then added to the line that is marketed. Although my miniature skills are totally self-taught, I have a past that includes as many art classes that could be worked into my schedule in school. In the 1960's, I attended a few drawing classes at the Toledo Museum of Art educational facility. I've done commercial illustrations, primarily in pencil and pastel, with an emphasis on realism and detail. However, I fully intend to work entirely on miniature designs after I retire as a CPA.

ARTISAN: FROSETH, NANCY

BUSINESS NAME: Tierneys Tiny Tiles

IDENTIFICATION MARKS:

Some unmarked

CATEGORY:

Ceramics; Tiles

HONORS:

IGMA Fellow

RECOGNITION:

Miniature Collector, Fall 1988, pg. 24-25; *Nutshell News*, Apr. 1988, Cover; *Miniatures Showcase*, Winter 1992, pg. 47

AUTOBIOGRAPHY:

I received a BA degree from Concordia College, Moorhead, Minnesota having majored in Music and Art. I did graduate work in Art at the University of Minnesota, and independent research was accomplished in England and other countries.

ARTISAN: FULLWOOD, VIC

BUSINESS NAME: Thomas V. Fullwood

IDENTIFICATION MARKS:

CATEGORY:

Metalwork; Resin Work

RECOGNITION:

The Home Miniaturist, Issue No. 62, Aug. 1992, pg. 16; Issue No. 63, Oct. 1992, pg. 49

FULLWOOD, VIC continued

AUTOBIOGRAPHY:

I have had 46 years in engineering which consisted of eight years full-scale experimental model-making with Hotpoint, Ltd. United Kingdom; I worked with scale wind tunnel models at Hawker Siddeley Aviation (The Red Arrows HSA Hawk.) In my childhood, during the war years I built model airplanes and ships. I entered and won many competitions and looking back, they were very small-scale, miniatures in fact, which must have fascinated the adjudicators.

ARTISAN: FUNNELL, ANNE

BUSINESS NAME: Lenham Pottery

IDENTIFICATION MARKS:

Some unmarked

LENHAM POTTERY
NORWICH

On bellies of horses

1970 only

1971 1993

Lower letters change yearly to 1995

CATEGORY:

Bathroom; China; Harnesses; Horses: harnessed; Kitchen

RECOGNITION:

Miniatures Catalog

AUTOBIOGRAPHY:

I make my own originals in many materials. I have been making scale models for 25 years, beginning in 1968, with dogs, progressing through horses for model horse drawn vehicle makers, and the harness to go with them, coming to one-inch scale domestic china in the mid 1980's.

ARTISAN: FUTVOYE, JERI

BUSINESS NAME: JAF Miniatures

IDENTIFICATION MARKS:

JAF
MINIATURES
JEWELRY FINDINGS SELECTED ESPECIALLY FOR THE MINIATURIST

Kadeli Kits

Kadeli Kits
Professionally Designed with Pride in Mind

CATEGORY:

Accessories; Chandeliers; Designer; Kits: chandelier, lighting; Lamps; Lighting; Publications: How-to

G

ARTISAN: **GAFFNEY, JOYCE**

BUSINESS NAME: Gaffney Crafts

IDENTIFICATION MARKS:
Most unmarked

JL

CATEGORY:
Animals: bunnies in hutch, pets; Aquarium; Flowers and Plants

RECOGNITION:
Nutshell News; Miniatures Showcase

AUTOBIOGRAPHY:
My miniature mania started as a hobby and grew into a business. I am a charter member of CIMTA and have participated in all CIMTA Shows, kind of growing along with the organization. I am self-taught having no special education or background in miniatures.

ARTISAN: **GAINES, LILLIAN** (Deceased)

BUSINESS NAME: Lillian Gaines

IDENTIFICATION MARKS:
Woven label – used from 1972 to 1984

Handwoven by
Lillian Gaines

CATEGORY:
Needlework; Weaving: coverlets

RECOGNITION:
Nutshell News; Independence, Kansas Reporter

BIOGRAPHY:
Ellen Krucker Blauer, my daughter, had been a hand weaver for several years before I made miniatures. I started hand weaving because of Ellen's encouragement. Since she had become so busy working with chandeliers and other items in brass, she suggested I make miniature coverlets which were sold through the Miniature Mart as well as to individuals.

Editor's note: Lillian Dakan Gaines passed away December 14, 1993.

ARTISAN: **GALLERANI, BEVERLY**

BUSINESS NAME: Puffer Lane Petites

IDENTIFICATION MARKS:
1991 to present
Unmarked (beverages, most glass containers)

Bev 3/91 BG 8/91 Bev '92

GALLERANI, BEVERLY, continued

CATEGORY:

Beverages; Flowers and Plants; Food

HONORS:

IGMA Artisan 1994

RECOGNITION:

Miniatures Showcase, Fall 1991, pg. 13; Spring 1992, pg. 30; Winter 1992, pg. 31; Nov. 1992, pg. 36

ARTISAN: GANZER, CHARLES "CHARLIE" (Deceased)

(Submitted by Jan Johnston and Barb Stetz)

IDENTIFICATION MARKS:

CG '89' CG '89 CG '89' 1/12 CG '89 1/12

Limited edition

CATEGORY:

Furniture: Shaker

HONORS:

Exhibit: Toy & Miniature Museum of Kansas City

RECOGNITION:

Nutshell News, Vol. 14, No. 6, Jun. 1984, pg. 65, Show Scene; *Miniature Collector*, No. 38, Aug. 1983, pg. 38, Show Stoppers

BIOGRAPHY:

Charles Ganzer had a Master's Degree of Fine Arts from one of the Ivy League universities. His career was primarily in television, basically as set production and cameraman. He worked several years at WGN in Chicago. His last 10 years were out of corporate America, and creating and teaching miniatures was his sole income. Jan Johnson worked very closely with him on the MMTA Board and committees, as well as represented his work as a dealer. He enjoyed teaching and creating, but did not wish to handle the business end, so never sold at miniature shows. He chose to wholesale to a select few dealers that he knew personally.

He could almost always be found at the Chicago area shows, offering to help any dealer who needed it carrying boxes in and out for set up and break down. Charlie may never have attended a NAME function, but was generous in donating furniture pieces for NAME fund-raisers, as a silent member.

Charlie was first introduced to miniatures in 1982 when he happened into a shop in Sandwich, Illinois, owned by Barb Stetz and discovered our "small world." Barb was very instrumental in encouraging him to try his hand at making furniture and, in turn, selling pieces for him. Charlie often said that "he owed a lot to Barb for helping him find a direction for his life." For the first couple of years he used only an X-Acto knife, emery boards and sand paper, specializing in Shaker reproductions. From approximately 1981 to 1987, he worked in one-inch scale and later added ½-inch scale, using mostly basswood. His staining process made the pieces look like Colonial Pine, cherry or whatever wood or stain color he chose. They were of a quality that dealers could always be proud to present. In March of 1990, Charlie passed away. Charlie's passing was very sad for those of us who had known him and worked with him those last several years, not just for losing a very fine miniature artist, but also a compassionate and helpful friend.

ARTISAN: **GARDNER, MARCIA**

BUSINESS NAME: Yesterday's Charm

IDENTIFICATION MARKS:

CATEGORY:
Furniture

HONORS:
IGMA Artisan

RECOGNITION:
Nutshell News, Sept. 1988, pg. 68-69; Aug. 1989, pg. 67; Dec. 1993, pg. 61; *Miniatures Showcase*, Winter 1990, pg. 20, 35

AUTOBIOGRAPHY:
My fascination with miniatures began in 1976 when I saw a completed dollhouse at a toy store, but I didn't really become hooked by the "mini-bug" until I joined the Stark Mad Miniaturists in Canton, Ohio, in 1982. One of the members showed us how to use basic power tools and construct a piece of furniture from plans. From then on my basement workshop became my hideaway, giving me a chance to create from wood (I'd tried to take shop in high school, but girls weren't allowed!)

By 1987, I'd decided not to return to teaching junior high when my children were all in school, but instead to devote my time to making furniture to sell at miniature shows. Researching furniture pieces, creating them in miniature, and then selling them to someone who also enjoys my hobby has brought me much satisfaction. My goal is to create a quality piece of furniture at a price affordable to the average buyer. I enjoy being a dealer and do several shows a year.

ARTISAN: **GARFEN, CAREN LYNN**

BUSINESS NAME: Caren Garfen – Samplers

IDENTIFICATION MARKS:

CATEGORY:
Needlework; Samplers

HONORS:
Exhibit: "The World of Miniature" Museum at Oban in Scotland

RECOGNITION:
International Dolls' House News, Vol. 21, No. 1, Spring 1992, pg. 20

AUTOBIOGRAPHY:
I had the idea to produce miniature samplers around July 1991, and produced designs and made up samplers and took them directly to Caroline Hamilton of the London Dolls' House Festival at Kensington Town Hall, in November 1991. She accepted me for the May 1992 show. I then contacted Bob and Muriel Hopwood for Miniatura Birmingham at a later date, and was accepted for their September 1992 Show. I am working hard to become well known as the foremost British artisan in fine miniature samplers, using my own designs based on traditional full-sized samplers. My primary objective is to produce an authentically styled product with top quality as my main priority.

ARTISAN: **GARMIZE, SHARON**

BUSINESS NAME: Needlepoint Designs by Sharon Garmize
Sharon Garmize Needlepoint Designs
Designs by Sharon Garmize

IDENTIFICATION MARKS:
All faces have green eyes

Framed pieces, reverse side of rugs

Embroidered backs of pillows

CATEGORY:
Needlepoint; Needlework

HONORS:
IGMA Artisan, Fellow; NAME AOH 1988; Best of Show, Monaco & London Chapters, group show, American Needlepoint Guild, 1982; Exhibit: Toy & Miniature Museum of Kansas City

RECOGNITION:
Nutshell News, Aug. 1982, pg. 9, "In a Nutshell;" Sept. 1982, pg. 64, Shows Galore!; Mar. 1983, pg. 81, Show Scene; Jun. 1983, pg. 53, Show Scene; Feb. 1984, pg. 26, "Needlepoint Bellpull;" Apr. 1984, pg. 64, Show Scene; Aug. 1984, pg. 65, Show Scene; *Miniature Collector*, No. 29, Feb. 1982, pg. 28, Show Stoppers; No. 44, Jul/Aug. 1984, pg. 24-27, "Master Miniaturist: Sharon Garmize," Lillian Wachtel, pg. 51, Show Stoppers; *Miniature Gazette; Star Magazine*, Aug. 9, 1988, pg. 23; *American Period Interiors in Miniature*, Kate Doordan Klavan, 1984; *The Andrews Collection*, Personal Treasures, Anne Day Smith, 1988; *Masters in Miniature, 12 Artisans At Work, Volume 1*, Anne Day Smith, Kalmbach Publishing, 1987; *Who's Who of American Women*, 16th, 17th, 18th, 19th editions

ARTISAN: **GARNETT, LARRY**

BUSINESS NAME: Larry Garnett Miniatures

IDENTIFICATION MARKS:

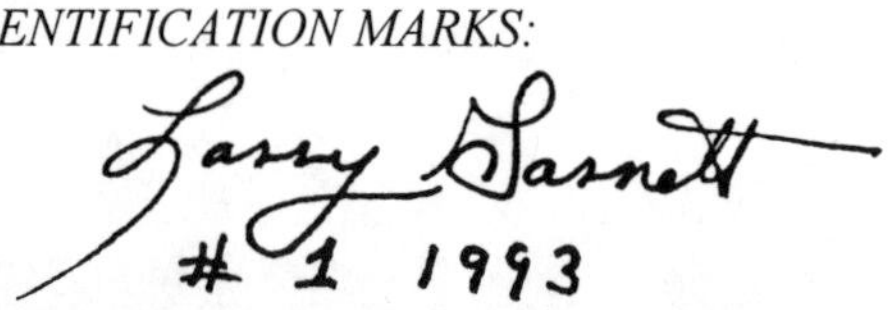

No. limited to 5 pieces a year

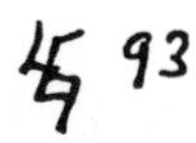

On smaller pieces

CATEGORY:
Furniture: antique, period, Shaker

HONORS:
IGMA Artisan

RECOGNITION:
The Richmond Times-Dispatch, Sept. 1991, "This is the house that Larry built;" Aug. 1993; *Blades; Fighting Knives; Knives* (magazines)

AUTOBIOGRAPHY:
My interest in woodworking spans many years and in different fields. As a child I made a lot of my toys from wood, my Dad as my teacher. I had three years of woodworking shop in high school, nine years of

woodworking and craft instruction in the Boy Scouts, and nine years as a master carpenter and prop manager for the Concert Ballet of Virginia. I still receive credit for sets and props used in "The Nutcracker" today.

I started making miniatures in 1968. My first exhibit was a copy of my dining room which was entered in the 1971 Virginia State Fair, winning a first place. From this exposure I met a number of people interested in miniatures. In 1972, ten of us formed the Virginia Miniature Enthusiasts, chartered under NAME in September of that year. I have been treasurer and registration chairman for the club ever since.

I work in one-inch and ½-inch scale furniture. One of my specialties is duplicating a home from a picture in ¼-inch scale or less, it can be lighted or can be a music box. All the furniture I make is hardwood and limited to five pieces of any one item each year, signed, numbered, and dated. My September 1991 exhibit was a copy of the famous Beacon Hill House, in ¼-inch scale, and was shown that year at the Virginia State Fair. The Richmond Times-Dispatch had a color picture of the Beacon Hill House, with a write up about me and my background in miniatures. This was an anniversary for me, 20 years ago I first exhibited at the Virginia State Fair.

In March 1988, I met a man who makes miniature knives, Dale Ballew. Dales' knives are three inches or smaller. We teamed our talents, making one of a kind sets. My specialty in this endeavor was to make boxes of wood lining them with felt and custom fitting his knives into them. Our displays have won two 1st place awards for Best of Show, one of which was presented at "The Worlds Largest Knife Show." Both Knives Magazine and Blade Magazine had pictures and write ups of our displays. I have also done miniature work for Terry Ward, who is known as "The Amazing Terry" a magician for Disney.

In December 1989, I took an early retirement from the telephone company. Since then I have acquired various tools and materials providing me with a state-of-the-art workshop. Now I spend four to six hours a day working on furniture or houses. Of all the things I have done for pleasure, miniatures have far outweighed them all.

ARTISAN: **GEORGE, MEGANNE E.**

BUSINESS NAME: Designs By George
Capital Ideas – A Creative Co-Op, prior to 1987

IDENTIFICATION MARKS:
Limited editions numbered above year

CATEGORY:
Accessories; Clowns; Dolls

BIOGRAPHY:

Meganne discovered miniatures filling a printer's tray and started doing roomboxes as set designs for a drama program in high school. She then joined her mother, Sharon S. George, in making miniatures for sale, and teaching classes at shows, in 1983. Meganne graduated from Baylor University with a BA in Theatre with emphasis in directing/technician, set designs, in 1989. She attended Ohio University Theatre Graduate School from 1990 to 1993 with dual emphasis in costume and set design.

ARTISAN: **GEORGE, SHARON S.**

BUSINESS NAME: Designs By George
Capital Ideas – A Creative Co-Op, Prior to 1987

IDENTIFICATION MARKS:
Limited editions numbered above year

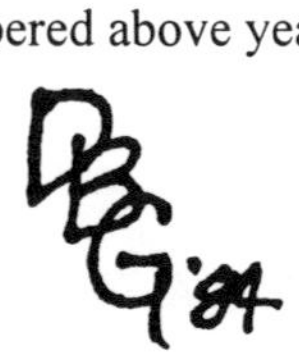

GEORGE, SHARON S., continued

CATEGORY:

Accessories; Clowns; Dolls

BIOGRAPHY:

Sharon graduated from the University of Oklahoma with a BS in education and minors in English Literature & Art in 1963. She entered the interior design business in 1970. She attended Scottsdale Community College and was a teaching assistant in interior design. Sharon discovered dollhouses because of her daughter's activities, after moving to Texas in 1978. She made miniatures for sale from 1980 to 1988, teaching classes locally and at shows. Sharon formed Capital Ideas, a creative co-op, with Dianne Jones and Su Andrews.

ARTISAN: GERARDI, FRANCES M.

BUSINESS NAME: La Petite Potpourri

IDENTIFICATION MARKS:

 Initials used from 1993

CATEGORY:

Accessories; Containers: scenes; Furniture; Room Settings

AUTOBIOGRAPHY:

I have been collecting miniatures since 1974, and making them since 1979, first for myself and then family and friends. In March of 1992, I decided to go into business. I haven't been in business long, and only sell at shows in my general area. I hope, in the near future, to travel to shows all over the country.

I make furniture and accessories but mostly furniture in all three scales, but my passion is in ¼-inch scale. My goal is to have every miniaturist in the United States own at least one piece of furniture made with loving care by "me."

ARTISAN: GERLINGS, CHARLOTTE

BUSINESS NAME: Pocket People

IDENTIFICATION MARKS:

G

Incised into back of neck © **G 1990;** Approximately 3mm high; Date refers to year model & mold was created originally; Earliest 1988

CATEGORY:

Dolls: character, original, porcelain; Kits: doll

RECOGNITION:

BBC TV Series *Handmade*, 1988, 1989

ARTISAN: **GIESLER, ALICE M.**

IDENTIFICATION MARKS:

 1989 to present

CATEGORY:

Landscaping

AUTOBIOGRAPHY:

My interest in dollhouses and miniatures began in the early 1970's. In 1973, I purchased a Walmer dollhouse which was the beginning of my devotion to miniatures. In 1978, I joined NAME and discovered shows and workshops. I began taking workshops at the Handcrafters of Miniature Shows in Andover, Massachusetts. Presently, I make plants, flowers and landscaped ponds for local shops. I enjoy making special occasion vignettes for family or donations to different organizations. For my granddaughter's birthday I built a Girl Scout craft house using the Houseworks Porch.

ARTISAN: **GILBERT, MARLENE**

BUSINESS NAME: Marlene Gilbert

IDENTIFICATION MARKS:

Plants unmarked

 Paintings initialed on front

CATEGORY:

Flowers and Plants; Paintings: watercolor

RECOGNITION:

Los Angeles Times Magazine, August 28, 1988, Vol. IV, No. 34, pg. 24-25; *Irvine World News*, July 11, 1991, pg. A8-A9

AUTOBIOGRAPHY:

My college education was a BA Degree from the University of Maryland in 1965, majoring in Government and Politics. I have been in the miniature business since 1983, and am a member of the Costa Mesa Art League.

ARTISAN: **GILL, APRIL D. & RON**

BUSINESS NAME: Wildwood Dollhouse & Miniature Shoppe

IDENTIFICATION MARKS:

CATEGORY:

Buildings; Dollhouse; Houses: custom; Roomboxes; Structures

GILL, APRIL D. & RON, continued

HONORS:

IGMA Artisan 1983, Fellow 1991

RECOGNITION:

Nutshell News, Oct. 1985, pg. 84-87; *The Andrews Collection*, Personal Treasures, Anne Day Smith, 1988, pg. 60, 68, 77, 88; *Treasures In Miniatures*, Jeanne Delgado, Mary Durland Fields, and Anne Day Smith

AUTOBIOGRAPHY:

In a time long ago, and far away, Ron and I would visit my parents and always have to see what Mom, Ruth Cavanaugh, was doing to her dollhouse or what she had just made for it. We would always tell her how "cute" it was, all the while wondering to ourselves if she was losing it! At that time we lived in the real world, owning a pet store and a wedding flower business. Ruth came to us one day and asked us if we would please carry miniatures in just one little corner of the shop. So much for the real world! Little by little the miniatures took over more of our lives.

Our world now is miniature homes, shops and roomboxes in all scales. Two of our daughters also live in this world. Laura builds country painted furniture in one-inch scale, and Beth builds country painted furniture in ½-inch scale.

Ron and I became Artisans of IGMA in late 1983 and when we felt our work was good enough in 1991 we applied for IGMA Fellow and were honored with the cubes that same year. We also are members of NAME and have attended many nationals and regionals.

We are very happy to be part of two books, *The Andrews Collection* by Anne Day Smith, and *Treasures In Miniatures* by Jeanne Delgado, Mary Durland Fields, and Anne Day Smith, edited by Sybil Harp.

We are very proud that Jackie Andrews, Eileen Godfrey, Sarah Salisbury, and June Neher each have more than one "Wildwood" piece in their collections. Living in this world has helped us to look at the real world with all its detail a little differently. We have met and been befriended by some of the most wonderful people.

ARTISAN: **GILL, BETH**

BUSINESS NAME: Wildwood Dollhouse & Miniature Shoppe

IDENTIFICATION MARKS:

CATEGORY:

Furniture: country, handpainted

ARTISAN: **GILL, LAURA**

BUSINESS NAME: Wildwood Dollhouse & Miniature Shoppe

IDENTIFICATION MARKS:

CATEGORY:

Furniture: country, handpainted

RECOGNITION:

The Andrews Collection, Personal Treasures, 1988, Anne Day Smith, pg. 61, 69

ARTISAN: **GOANS, ANN**

IDENTIFICATION MARKS: (Submitted by William R. Robertson)

AG with year

CATEGORY:

Furniture

HONORS:

Exhibit: Toy & Miniature Museum of Kansas City

RECOGNITION:

Nutshell News, Vol. 14, No. 8, Aug. 1984, pg. 82-84, "Annie's Happy Niche"

ARTISAN: **GOLDSBERRY, BILL**

BUSINESS NAME: B. & L. Miniatures

IDENTIFICATION MARKS:

Bill & Leona   Bill & Leona

CATEGORY:

Buggies; Furniture: lawn; Hospital Items; Toys; Wagons

ARTISAN: **GOOD, EMILY**

BUSINESS NAME: E. Good Heirloom Replicas

IDENTIFICATION MARKS:

Eg 248	Furniture	Eg	Accessories
#2 of 3	File No. Edition		
1992	Date		

CATEGORY:

Accessories: brass, bronze, silver; Furniture: reproduction

HONORS:

Exhibit: Toy & Miniature Museum of Kansas City

RECOGNITION:

Nutshell News, Jan. 1981, pg. 69-72; Nov. 1981, pg. 44-47; Feb. 1982, pg. 66-67; Dec. 1985, pg. 84-85; Jun. 1989, pg. 48-51; May 1990, pg. 68-71; Aug. 1992, pg. 84-87; *American Period Interiors in Miniature*, Kate Doordan Klavan, Scribners, 1984, pg. 10, 190; *Reproducing Period Furniture and Accessories in Miniature*, Merrill & Richardson, Crown Publishers, 1981, pg. 54E; *A Baker's Dozen in Wood*, Emily Good, Nutshell News Plans Service, Boynton III

AUTOBIOGRAPHY:

I have a BS in Physics from the University of Alabama; an MS in Physics from the University of North Carolina and did additional graduate work at the University of North Carolina. My professional experience consists of a Physicist at Thiokol Corporation, Huntsville, Alabama, from 1950 to 1952; Instructor of Physics,

University of Alabama, Huntsville from 1953 to 1954 and from 1955 to 1956 I was an instructor in Mathematics, at the University of Alabama, Tuscaloosa. From 1957 to 1985, I was a Physicist and Applied Mathematician, Physical Science Laboratory, New Mexico State University, and a Mathematician at White Sands Missile Range, New Mexico, from 1986 to 1989.

I have made miniatures since 1972, in limited editions for collectors since 1976. I started making only furniture, all accurately scaled and finely detailed replicas of actual antiques, primarily on a custom basis. Prompted by a need for metal accessories, I took a course in jewelry making. In addition to furniture, I began making lost wax castings. I make a wide variety of andirons, cloisonné, bronze with faux finishes, and silver hollowware, but, as with furniture, only in limited editions.

ARTISAN: **GOODRICK, JANET**

BUSINESS NAME: Janet Goodrick Miniatures

IDENTIFICATION MARKS:

Most unmarked

1981 to present

CATEGORY:

Accessories: personal; Christmas; Holiday Items; Toys

RECOGNITION:

Home Miniaturist, May 1991; *Dolls House & Miniature Scene*, Nov. 1993

AUTOBIOGRAPHY:

I was born in Pudsey, West Yorkshire, England in the 1950's. I left school at 15 but have since qualified from "the university of life!"

I came to live in the beautiful historic city of York, upon my marriage to Roger, and we now have two grown sons. The introduction to miniature making was in 1980 through my hobby of embroidery. I was asked to make a miniature sampler for a dollhouse, the results were pretty primitive but after trial and error a pretty sampler evolved. I am self-taught and work with many mediums but mostly I use fabrics, papers, card and Fimo, out of which I like to make some unusual items.

The majority of my work is distributed through miniature shops in Europe, but I love attending fairs, which I look upon as "sanity preservers," and receive great pleasure from selling "hands on" and meeting friends old and new.

ARTISAN: **GRABER, JANE**

BUSINESS NAME: Country Miniature Stoneware

IDENTIFICATION MARKS:

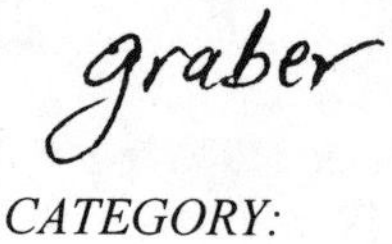

CATEGORY:

Pottery: Early American

HONORS:

IGMA Artisan, 1st Place, Crafts, Chatauqua of the Arts, Sept. 1992

RECOGNITION:

Nutshell News, Jul. 1993, pg. 44; *Ceramics Monthly*, Nov. 1984; *Miniature Collector*, 1981; *Studio Potter*, Summer 1992

GRABER, JANE, continued

AUTOBIOGRAPHY:

In 1973, I received an AA in Art at Hesston College, Hesston, Kansas, and in 1976 I achieved a BA in Art at Goshen College, Goshen, Indiana. From 1976 to 1980, I was a full-time potter at Sauder Museum in Archbold, Ohio. I have been a full-time miniaturist from 1981 specializing in Early American designs in stoneware and redware in one-inch scale and ½-inch scale.

ARTISAN: GRAHAM, NATALIE

IDENTIFICATION MARKS:

CATEGORY:

Furniture: period

HONORS:

IGMA Artisan

ARTISAN: GRAVELLE, SANDI A.

BUSINESS NAME: SG Enterprises

IDENTIFICATION MARKS:

SG

CATEGORY:

Flowers and Plants: cactus

AUTOBIOGRAPHY:

I have been interested in miniatures all my life, but never made any until about 1978. While living in the Boston area, I went to a show where I bought Ruth Hanke's book on making miniature house plants from florist tape. I was very impressed with how realistic mine turned out as were my family and friends. I gave some as gifts and kept others for show. I did not have a dollhouse. I moved to El Paso in 1982. I was encouraged to enter my plants in a local flower show, that had a miniature category for artificial plants and flowers. I won some ribbons, but more importantly, was introduced to the local miniature club. I became a member, and my life has been "ruled" by miniatures ever since! I like to make everything, foods, kits, furniture, etc., but my passion is plants and flowers. I make very realistic ones mostly from paper that I paint and cut or punch shapes from. I teach classes, sell to fellow club members, and through dealers who travel to shows.

I am single, living on a half acre in El Paso, Texas, with my cats, dogs and horse, loving every minute of my country life. I work full-time as a bookkeeper near home, and can even ride my horse to work! My goal is to work less hours at bookkeeping and more at miniatures, to make it a full-time business. I served two terms as president of our El Paso Mini-Makers Club.

ARTISAN: **GRAY, CAROLYN**

BUSINESS NAME: Carolyn Gray

IDENTIFICATION MARKS:
1984 to present

CATEGORY:
Accessories; Boxes: jeweled; Christmas; Eggs: jeweled; Holiday Items; Jewelry

HONORS:
Honorary Chairman 1994, "10th Anniversary Reunion Celebration," Gulf South Miniature & Dollhouse Event, New Orleans, Louisiana

RECOGNITION:
Nutshell News, 1987, 1989, 1990; *Miniature Collector*, Fall 1988; *Bright Star Publications*, Summer 1993; *Miniature Gazette*, Vol. 22, No. 4, Summer 1994, "Roses;" *The Andrews Collection*, Personal Treasures, Anne Day Smith, 1988

AUTOBIOGRAPHY:
I was born November 23, 1927. I attended Harcum Jr. College, Bryn Mawr, Pennsylvania. In 1947, I married Richard and we have three sons, Richard, Don, and James. I am a member of NAME, IGMA, SAM, and Dollhouse Museum of the Southwest. I served on the board of SAM for three years. Among some of the materials that I use are Austrian crystals, sterling silver, gold, precious and semi-precious gems, and silk ribbon. Working with miniatures is enjoyable, but most of all I cherish the friendships I have made throughout the United States.

ARTISAN: **GRAY, NANCY L.**

IDENTIFICATION MARKS: (Submitted by William R. Robertson)

Incised into wood with date

CATEGORY:
Accessories; Art: tramp; Furniture

HONORS:
Exhibit: Toy & Miniature Museum of Kansas City

ARTISAN: **GRAY, PHYLLIS "JOY"**

BUSINESS NAME: "J" Designs

IDENTIFICATION MARKS:

GRAY, PHYLLIS "JOY", continued

CATEGORY:

Accessories; Animals: dogs; Art: fine; Birdhouses; Cottages: English; Furniture; Landscaping; Mailboxes; Paintings; Trunks

RECOGNITION:

Nutshell News, Dec. 1988, pg. 80; *Miniatures Showcase*, Spring 1990, pg. 23, 31, 37, 42, 64; Spring 1989, pg. 30, 33, 42; Winter 1989, pg. 33, 37, 44; *Daily News*, L.A. Life Section, Sun. Feb. 23, 1992, pg. 14-15; *Miniature Gazette*, Vol. 18, No. 3, Spring 1990, pg. 45; Vol. 21, No. 1, Fall 1992, pg. 59; *Simple Pleasures Magazine*, Vol. 1, No. 2, Oct. 1990, pg. 2

AUTOBIOGRAPHY:

I lived most of my life in Oxford, Ohio and graduated there from Miami University with a BFA in 1957. I became interested in miniatures in 1976 when I joined the newly formed Oxford Society of Miniature Enthusiasts. In 1977, I joined NAME and later IGMA. A friend and I formed a partnership of "J & K Designs" to make and sell miniatures. We sold paintings and furniture at many shows in the Ohio area. When the partnership dissolved I continued as "J" Designs. In 1984, I sold at the NAME National Mini Mart, in Cincinnati, Ohio. In 1986, I moved to Los Angles, and joined Miniature West Club in Culver City in September 1986, The Mid-Valley Mini Maniacs in 1988 and Min-U-etts in 1991. I sell at many shows in the California and Nevada area. My paintings, trunks and dogs have appeared in many publications. I also make landscaped ponds, mail boxes, bird houses, & English Cottages three-inchs by one-inch. My latest items are English Silent Butlers in one-inch and ½-inch scale.

ARTISAN: **GREENBERG, SHIRLEE**

BUSINESS NAME: Shirlee Greenberg

IDENTIFICATION MARKS:

CATEGORY:

Carpets; Needlework; Roomboxes; Rugs

HONORS:

IGMA Fellow

RECOGNITION:

Nutshell News, Jan. 1994, pg. 54; *Miniatures Showcase*, Fall 1988, Cover, pg. 9, 46

AUTOBIOGRAPHY:

I am a graduate of Pratt Institute, Brooklyn, New York and also studied at Rhode Island School of Design, Providence, Rhode Island, and Art Students League in New York. I then designed greeting cards, textiles and wallpaper. I am a fine arts painter and have exhibited my work nationally including on Madison Avenue in New York. I have been involved in miniatures since about 1981 and in addition to making rugs, I also create roomboxes from scratch.

ARTISAN: **GREENWOOD, MARLEEN DODGE**

IDENTIFICATION MARKS:

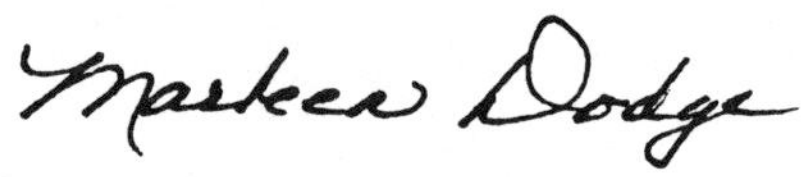

1970 to 1981 needlework, some furniture

1981 to present, samplers, French knot rugs
signature worked into petit point rugs

CATEGORY:

Needlework; Rugs: French knot; Samplers

HONORS:

IGMA Artisan 1993

ARTISAN: **GREGORY, ANDREW M. S.**

BUSINESS NAME: Andrews Miniature World

IDENTIFICATION MARKS:

Unmarked prior to 1993

AG Stamped into piece

CATEGORY:

Accessories: personal; Furniture: garden; Kitchen: appliances; Military Items; Nursery Items; Scientific Instruments; Sports Equipment; Tools: garden; Toys; Weapons

RECOGNITION:

Dolls House and Miniature Scene, Vol. 1, No. 1, 1992, pg. 7; *Dolls House World*, No. 26, 1993, pg. 12-13, 15

AUTOBIOGRAPHY:

Making miniature objects has been part of my life since the age of about eight or nine. In fact I started in the stone age. The roof of my school was slate and the winter frosts would crack off small slivers which fell to the ground. These pieces were simple to chip into ax heads which when bound with cotton into cleft twigs produced quite effective Paleolithic weapons. At the same time I was painting tiny figurines made from sun dried clay from a nearby riverbank. It was, however the weapon theme that was to dominate what I was to make in miniature until I became aware of the dollhouse scene as a potential outlet for my work.

A typical schoolboy's fascination with the implements of mayhem taught me the basics of miniature making. Lacking the equipment to manufacture the full-size articles it seemed natural to construct them in a size manageable with basic tools. Through the years I progressed from primitive swords and polearms until in my late teens I was making working miniature guns.

At college I studied architecture which, although it was not to become my career, did help me with skills including technical drawing and photography which have proven invaluable in later life. I was also taught the art of architectural model making, the application of which is of self evident utility in the world of miniatures.

Despite an almost exclusively arts background, my working life until spring 1990 was spent as a scientist in a government food research establishment. This was not as haphazard a change of direction as at first it must seem since, to me at least, both Art and Science are equally concerned with problem solving. Miniature making is of course a mixture of artistic skill and technological competence and in my case the objects are made in my head before even approaching the workbench.

In 1980, an article in a local newspaper featured the opening of dollshouse shop in my nearest city, Bristol, England. I contacted the owner and showed her some of the weapons I had made in the past and some tentative experiments in one-inch scale of household objects. She was very encouraging and for the next 10 years I supplied this shop exclusively while remaining anonymous to the purchasers. My full-time employment meant that I had financial freedom to make whatever seemed interesting without the pressures of time or repeat orders. I was thus able to develop an ever, and still, expanding range of different items.

Unfortunately my employment came to an end due to cutbacks in government research funding which left me with no job but a considerable sum in severance pay. I chose to spend it on travel. Since it was 1990, the obvious place to start was a marathon tour of Eastern Europe. I used a camper van to explore the whole area when the momentous events of the time were still inspiring an atmosphere of relief and optimism. Returning in the autumn I flew to Bombay and commenced a fairly routine round the world trip as a backpacker. Unhampered by the financial constrictions of the youngsters half my age on similar odysseys it was not a grueling adventure. The option to pop into the nearest Hilton was always there when things became a little too grubby. Throughout my travels I sought out the local craft skills with an eye for their future application in miniature.

On my return the world was in deep recession and there was little prospect of employment in my former field of research into computerized data capture systems. My hobby therefore had to become my business and I now enjoy the freedom of traveling in another sense; exploring the possibilities of what can be made in the world of miniatures.

ARTISAN: **GRIFFITHS, KAREN**

BUSINESS NAME: Stokesay Ware

IDENTIFICATION MARKS:

SW   SW.

CATEGORY:

Ceramics; China; Dinnerware; Kitchenware; Stoneware; Terra Cotta

HONORS:

IGMA Artisan 1992

RECOGNITION:

Miniature Collector, Fall 1990

AUTOBIOGRAPHY:

I attended the Harrow School of Art between the years of 1968 to 1972 where I received diplomas in Foundation Studies and Graphic Design. In 1974, I entered Hornsey School of Art and graduated in 1978 with a Bachelor of Arts Degree with first class honors having specialized in ceramics with three-dimensional design. Continuing in 1978, I attended the Royal College of Art and received a Degree of Master of Design in ceramics, having completed my study in 1981. In 1982, I established my own business under the name of "Stokesay Ware." In 1983 to 1985, I was a visiting lecturer at Eastbourne College of Art, teaching drawing and from 1984 until 1987, I was also a visiting lecturer at the Farnham School of Art where I taught BA Degree students ceramics. In 1988, I entered into a partnership with Peter Armstrong who carries a BA (Hons), and it has proved to be a most successful venture.

ARTISAN: **GUÉNO, JEFFREY G.**

BUSINESS NAME: Le Chateau Interiors

IDENTIFICATION MARKS:

Printed

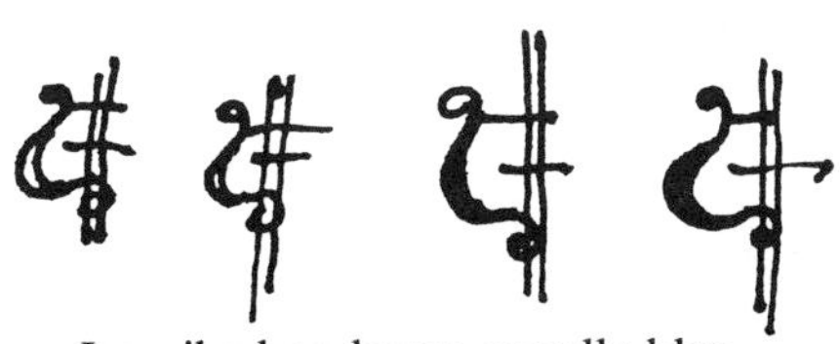

Inscribed or drawn, usually blue

GUÉNO, JEFFREY G., continued

CATEGORY:

Art, fine; Furniture: handpainted, period; Paintings: oil, watercolor; Period Settings; Porcelain; Pottery; Roomboxes; Room Settings

HONORS:

IGMA Fellow; Exhibits: Toy & Miniature Museum of Kansas City; Angels Attic, Santa Monica, California; The Carole & Barry Kaye Museum of Miniatures, Los Angeles, California; Miniature Museum of the Southwest, Dallas, Texas; Denver Museum of Miniatures; El Mondo de Max, Alicanté, Spain; 1976, Lafayette Natural History Museum, Lafayette, Louisiana; 1981, Mansur Museum of Art, Monroe, Louisiana; 1982, Museum of Art, Huntsville, Alabama; 1983, University Southern Louisiana Foundation; 1985, 1986, 1987, The Lafayette Museum, Lafayette, Louisiana; 1987, 1988, Pink Palace Museum of Art, Memphis, Tennessee; 1989, International Festival de Miniatures - Montelimar, France; 1989, Natchez Historical Society, Stanton Hall, Natchez, Mississippi; 1991, UFDC National Convention, New Orleans, Louisiana; 1992, IGMA Annual Meeting, New York City (This is a traveling exhibit to Pennsylvania, California, Colorado, Texas, Wisconsin, and Paris, France)

RECOGNITION:

Articles written about Jeffrey Guéno and Frank Hanley

Clarion Herald, Vol. 14, No. 44, Dec. 23, 1976, New Orleans, Louisiana, "Creche Art Sings Lovely Carol," photos, Frank Methe; *Town & Country*, May 1988, pg. 218, Nan Tillson Birmington, photos, John Lewis Stage; *Gazette*, Vol. 4, No 8, Jun. 1988, "18th Century Neapolitan Creche - Magnificent," Jackie McDaniel Alford; *Louisiana Life*, Mar. 1989, Cover, pg. 44-48, "Cypress and Collectibles in a Post-Bellum Palace," Bonnie Warren, photos, Charles Nes; *Nutshell News*, Apr. 1989, Cover, pg. 54-59, "The Renaissance Men of Lafayette," Phyllis Tucker; *Miniature Collector*, Summer 1989, "Past Perfect," Ann Bahar; *Le Magazine de la Maison de Poupée*, Paris, Autumn 1989, Cover, pg. 4-5, "Past Perfect," reprint from Miniature Collector in French; *The Best of Lafayette*, 1987, pg. 18-51, "Le Trio de Louisiane," Anne Simpson; *Smithsonian Magazine*, Dec. 1991, Cover, pg. 100-105, "Art Imitates Life in the Small World of Baroque Crèches," Diane Bolz, photos, Philip Gould; *Times of Acadiana*, Vol. 12, No. 12, Dec. 11, 1991, Cover, pg. 25-26, "Small is Beautiful - Museum in Miniature," Richard Baudouin

Articles written by Jeffrey Guéno and Frank Hanley

Nutshell News, Dec. 1981, Cover, pg. 28-31, "Antique Art in Miniature;" *Miniature Collector*, Winter 1993, Cover, pg. 30-35, Part 1, "Elements of Style;" Spring 1994, pg. 20-25, Part 11, "Elements of Style;" *Hobbies - The Magazine for Collectors*, Dec. 1976, Cover, pg. 115-117, "The Historical Creche;" *Doll News*, Vol. XXV11, No. 1, Winter 1977, Cover, pg. 14-21, "Creche Legacy For the Ages;" UFDC *30th Annual Convention Journal*, New York City, Aug. 1979, pg. 38-41, "A Closer Look;" UFDC *Regional Journal*, New Orleans, LA, 1984, pg. 41-50, "A Heritage in Wax," and "Creche in Louisiana - A Thoughtful Collection;" *Doll Collectors Manual*, Hobby House, 1983, pg. 22-28, "Presepio Figure and Environment," and pg. 40-43, "Inclination of the Age"

Featured Presentations

Aug. 1979, "The Art of the Nativity," UFDC National Convention, New York City; Aug. 1980, "Les Images de Noel," UFDC National Convention, Washington, DC; Nov. 1984, "Silk Purses and Sows Ears," DCA Annual Meeting, Rockport, Massachusetts; Nov. 1984, "Silk Purses and Sows Ears," UFDC Regional Meeting, New Orleans, Louisiana; Aug. 1985, "Small Things in Life," UFDC National Convention, Atlanta, Georgia; Apr. 1987, "Sow's Ears and Silk Purses," IGMA Annual Meeting, New York City; Apr. 1988, "The Small Things in Life, and Sows Ears and Silk Purses," Handorf, South Australia; Nov. 17, 1988, "Art of the Nativity," Natchez Historical Society, Natchez, Mississippi

BIOGRAPHY:

Jeffrey G. Guéno is a native of the Acadian Region of Louisiana. He received his Fine Arts degree from the University of Southwestern Louisiana. He is an accredited interior designer, artist, author, lecturer, art connoisseur, collector and museum consultant. Examples of his work can be found in private collections throughout the United States, Canada, England, Germany, France, Spain, and Mexico.

see "Frank Hanley"

ARTISAN: **GUKICH, MARY DALLAS**

BUSINESS NAME: Mary Dolls

IDENTIFICATION MARKS:

Mary
dolls

CATEGORY:

Dolls: molds, originals

HONORS:

Rocky Mountain Doll Fantasy, three Best of Show (Miniature Category) one in 1990, two in 1992

RECOGNITION:

Nutshell News, Mar 1991, pg. 78; Jun. 1991, pg. 63; Aug. 1992, pg. 21; *Dolls in Miniature*, Vol. 1, No. 4, pg. 72-76; *Doll Crafter*, Oct. 1992, pg. 84-103; *Contemporary Doll*, Nov. 1992, pg. 48-49

AUTOBIOGRAPHY:

I do not have a formal education in art but I have always enjoyed doing crafts. In 1980, I took a class in porcelain dollmaking and began making and selling dolls for profit. Around 1987, I began making reproduction miniature dolls and then handcrafted my own original dolls in 1991. Besides selling my original finished dolls I also started selling the molds of my originals.

ARTISAN: **GUTHEIL, ROGER L.**

BUSINESS NAME: Roger L. Gutheil, Inc.

IDENTIFICATION MARKS:

1962 to 1977 Chestnut Hill Studio Unmarked

1977 to present Stamped **R.L.Gutheil** -'92

Smaller pieces hand signed RG -'92

CATEGORY:

Accessories; Furniture: period, reproduction; Roomboxes; Shadow Boxes

HONORS:

IGMA Fellow; Exhibits: Toy & Miniature Museum of Kansas City; Gibbes Museum of Art, Charleston, South Carolina

RECOGNITION:

Nutshell News, Dec. 1981, pg. 63; Oct. 1982, pg. 65; Nov. 1982, pg. 26-27; Apr. 1983, pg. 41; Jul. 1983, pg. 64; Jul. 1984, pg. 35, 37; Aug. 1984, pg. 50, 71; Jan. 1995, pg. 82; *Miniature Collector*, No. 39, Oct. 1983, pg. 37, Show Stoppers; No. 44, Jul/Aug. 1984, pg. 51, Show Stoppers; No. 46, Nov/Dec. 1984, pg. 52, Show Stoppers; *Miniature Gazette*, Vol. 6, No. 3, Spring 1978, pg. 10; Vol. 7, No. 3, Spring 1979, pg. 9, 75; Vol. 9, No. 2, Winter 1980, pg. 89; *House & Garden*; *Masters in Miniature, 12 Artisans At Work, Volume 1*, Anne Day Smith, Kalmbach Publishing, 1987

GUTHEIL, ROGER L., continued

BIOGRAPHY:

Roger L. Gutheil started making miniatures in 1962, for Chestnut Hill Studio. His knowledge of woods and woodworking helped him, and his wife Nancy, solve the technical problems and master the art of miniature making. With the retirement of Chestnut Hill in 1977, the Gutheils decided to form their own business and offer a new line of miniature furniture and rooms to collectors. Their research and travels has enabled them to design and produce fine miniature reproductions.

ARTISAN: **HAAS, CLIFF**

BUSINESS NAME: Heirloom Toys

IDENTIFICATION MARKS:

CAH

118706015 [1]

Serial number is a code stating that this particular piece was made in November 1987, a Duncan Phyfe style piece, and was the 15th Duncan Phyfe piece made. The boxed number states that this is the number of the piece in a series of up to 25 pieces.

CATEGORY:

Accessories: kitchen; Furniture; Weapons

HONORS:

IGMA Artisan

RECOGNITION:

Nutshell News, May 1987; *Rocky Hill News,* Connecticut, Jun. 21, 1985; *Hartford Courant,* newspaper, Connecticut

ARTISAN: **HAGEY, ADRIENNE F. & DONALD W.**

BUSINESS NAME: Mt. Fanny Cottage Crafts
Hagey Dollhouse –Toybox

IDENTIFICATION MARKS:

A
Hagey
Original

CATEGORY:

Furniture

RECOGNITION:

Miniature Gazette, Vol. 1, No. 2, Dec. 1972, pg. 17, "Miniature Making in a Deep Freeze?"

ARTISAN: **HAGUE, BETTY**

BUSINESS NAME: Betty Hague

IDENTIFICATION MARKS:

B. HAGUE

CATEGORY:

Dolls

RECOGNITION:

Nutshell News, Nov. 1985, pg. 84; Dec. 1985, pg. 65; Jun. 1986, pg. 85

ARTISAN: **HAIGH, JOAN C.**

BUSINESS NAME: Joan Haigh

IDENTIFICATION MARKS:

Initially with DOT over J of JH combination
RED heart replaces dot

CATEGORY:

Bears: teddy; Dolls

HONORS:

Golden Teddy Award, 1988

RECOGNITION:

Nutshell News, Mar. 1983, pg. 84; Nov. 1983, pg. 58; *Teddy Bear Review*, Fall 1988, pg. 22

AUTOBIOGRAPHY:

I began making miniatures in 1978, and enjoy working in many mediums, especially fabrics, Fimo, and paint. I took classes whenever possible and taught myself a lot of things, but feel that I learned the most from generous fellow artisans. I try to follow in their footsteps and share the techniques that I have learned. I love what I do and enjoy sharing something that gives me such pleasure.

Although I would like to create more miniature people, the tiny teddies seem to take up most of my creative time. I prefer creating one-of-a-kind bears or very limited editions. My teddies are entirely hand sewn turned and jointed. They average 1-inch to 3-inches tall. I am very interested in period costume and my bears often reflect that.

ARTISAN: **HAIRRELL, HELEN JOAN**

BUSINESS NAME: Helen Joans' Art

IDENTIFICATION MARKS:

CATEGORY:

Paintings: oil, watercolor

ARTISAN: **HALL, EVELYN M.**

BUSINESS NAME: Evelyn's Little Things

IDENTIFICATION MARKS:

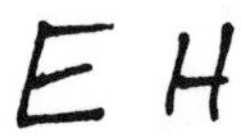

1979 to 1985

1985 to 1989

1989 to present

CATEGORY:

Flowers and Plants; Food; Wicker

HALL, EVELYN, M, continued

RECOGNITION:

Nutshell News, Apr. 1982, pg. 10-11, 58-59; Oct. 1984, pg. 76; Feb. 1986, pg. 65; Oct. 1986, Cover; Jan. 1987, pg. 75; Jul. 1989, pg. 64; Nov. 1989, pg. 94; Oct. 1990, pg. 66; Jul. 1991, pg. 63-64; Nov. 1991, pg. 76; May 1992, pg. 66; *Miniatures Showcase*, Fall 1986, pg. 11, 30, 36; Spring 1987, pg. 11, 13, 18-19, 42-45, 49; Winter 1992, pg. 30, 41; *Miniature Gazette*, Roses Section

AUTOBIOGRAPHY:

My miniature life began in 1978 with a visit to a bookstore and the purchase of a book on making dollhouse furniture. I helped to form and served as the first president of a local miniature club. I attended my first miniature show in Atlanta, in 1979, and have been totally committed since then.

ARTISAN: HALL, LORI L.

BUSINESS NAME: Lori L. Hall

IDENTIFICATION MARKS:

Back of head

Logo, stationery, mailing labels

CATEGORY:

Animal: dolls; Bears; Toys

RECOGNITION:

Nutshell News, Vol. 19, No. 4, Apr. 1989, pg. 71, Show Scene; Vol. 19, No. 9, Sept. 1989, pg. 69; *Miniatures Showcase*, Fall 1989, pg. 5; *Miniature Gazette*, Vol. 19, No. 2, Winter 1990, pg. 28; Vol. 19, No. 4, Summer 1991, pg. 53; *Miniature Collector*, No. 74, Winter 1991, pg. 22-23

AUTOBIOGRAPHY:

The critters simply presented themselves and demanded to be made. I have received no training, no instruction, except what the critters have given me through trial and error. It is fortunate, indeed, that they are patient little masters. Both the critters and I are very grateful to our kind customers for showing us such wonderful support. We couldn't have done it without them.

ARTISAN: HALLEY, CHARLOTTE

BUSINESS NAME: Cats by Charlotte

IDENTIFICATION MARKS:

All information located on bottom of cat, each pose has specific name written in **BLOCK LETTERS**, each cat numbered, all have painted foot pads, exception is "Skitter" pose whose largest pad is size of "**o**"

CATEGORY:

Animals: cats, pets

RECOGNITION:

Miniature Gazette, Spring 1990; *Nutshell News*, Jun. 1991, Show Scene

HALLEY, CHARLOTTE, continued

AUTOBIOGRAPHY:

I was born and raised in Southern California. In my early childhood I enjoyed doing arts and crafts. My major was fine and graphic arts in college. I lived with and always loved cats. Using my cats as live models whenever possible, and having an extensive library of reference materials made sculpting a natural for me. I used to do my own mold making and casting, but now have a specialist who does a much better job, so I just do the sculpture and send it to him. I get back beautiful cats ready to paint fur on. I keep a record of the purchasers and the numbers.

ARTISAN: HALLSTED, KENT

IDENTIFICATION MARKS: (Submitted by Toy & Miniature Museum of Kansas City)

Hand signed in black ink with number of piece, edition number and year

CATEGORY:

Accessories; Clocks

RECOGNITION:

Nutshell News, Vol. 12, No. 8, Aug. 1982, pg. 25

ARTISAN: HAMILTON, R. E. JR.

IDENTIFICATION MARKS:

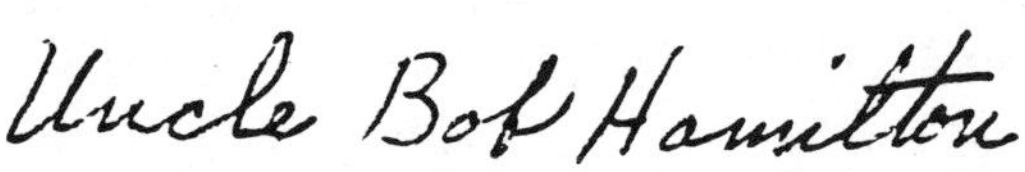

Larger pieces with number and date

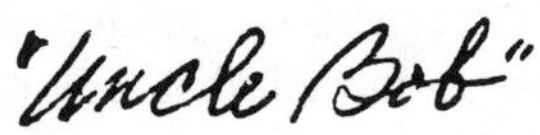

Smaller pieces with number and date

Given away, not sold

CATEGORY:

Furniture: cabinet

AUTOBIOGRAPHY:

I graduated from Huntington High School, West Virginia, Huntington Trade School and attended Greenbrier Military School, and the University of Arizona. My grandfather required all the boys in the family to have a trade plus a formal education.

While growing up I made model airplanes and race cars. After World War II while a patient in the VA Hospital, I made models including HO Trains. I operated a family owned mobile home business for 45 years. In addition to sales, we repaired mobile homes plus rebuilding some units.

I started making miniature furniture in 1987. If the letter "G" is on the item it means I gave it away rather than selling it. Numbers one and two are usually given away as they are mock-ups. I find you have to give the family at least one piece before you can sell any!

ARTISAN: **HANLEY, FRANK L.**

BUSINESS NAME: Le Chateau Interiors

IDENTIFICATION MARKS:

Printed

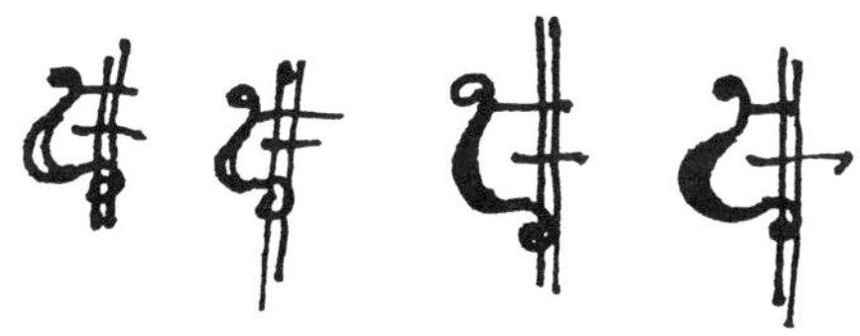

Inscribed or drawn, usually blue

CATEGORY:

Art: fine; Furniture: handpainted, period; Paintings: oil, watercolor; Period Settings; Porcelain; Pottery; Roomboxes; Room Settings

HONORS:

IGMA Fellow; Exhibits: Toy & Miniature Museum of Kansas City; Angels Attic, Santa Monica, California; The Carole & Barry Kaye Museum of Miniatures, Los Angeles, California; Miniature Museum of the Southwest, Dallas, Texas; Denver Museum of Miniatures; El Mondo de Max, Alicanté, Spain; 1976, Lafayette Natural History Museum, Lafayette, Louisiana; 1981, Mansur Museum of Art, Monroe, Louisiana; 1982, Museum of Art, Huntsville, Alabama; 1983, University Southern Louisiana Foundation; 1985, 1986, 1987, The Lafayette Museum, Lafayette, Louisiana; 1987, 1988, Pink Palace Museum of Art, Memphis, Tennessee; 1989, International Festival de Miniatures - Montelimar, France; 1989, Natchez Historical Society, Stanton Hall, Natchez, Mississippi; 1991, UFDC National Convention, New Orleans, Louisiana; 1992, IGMA Annual Meeting, New York City (This is a traveling exhibit to Pennsylvania, California, Colorado, Texas, Wisconsin, and Paris, France)

RECOGNITION:

Articles written about Frank Hanley and Jeffrey Guéno

Clarion Herald, Vol. 14, No. 44, Dec. 23, 1976, New Orleans, Louisiana, "Creche Art Sings Lovely Carol," photos, Frank Methe; *Town & Country*, May 1988, pg. 218, Nan Tillson Birmington, photos, John Lewis Stage; *Gazette*, Vol. 4, No 8, Jun. 1988, "18th Century Neapolitan Creche - Magnificent," Jackie McDaniel Alford; *Louisiana Life*, Mar. 1989, Cover, pg. 44-48, "Cypress and Collectibles in a Post-Bellum Palace," Bonnie Warren, photos, Charles Nes; *Nutshell News*, Apr. 1989, Cover, pg. 54-59, "The Renaissance Men of Lafayette," Phyllis Tucker; *Miniature Collector*, Summer 1989, "Past Perfect," Ann Bahar; *Le Magazine de la Maison de Poupée*, Paris, Autumn 1989, Cover, pg. 4-5, "Past Perfect," reprint from Miniature Collector in French; *The Best of Lafayette*, 1987, pg. 18-51, "Le Trio de Louisiane," Anne Simpson; *Smithsonian Magazine*, Dec. 1991, Cover, pg. 100-105, "Art Imitates Life in the Small World of Baroque Creches," Diane Bolz, photos, Philip Gould; *Times of Acadiana*, Vol. 12, No. 12, Dec. 11, 1991, Cover, pg. 25-26, "Small is Beautiful - Museum in Miniature," Richard Baudouin

Articles written by Frank Hanley and Jeffrey Guéno

Nutshell News, Dec. 1981, Cover, pg. 28-31, "Antique Art in Miniature;" *Miniature Collector*, Winter 1993, Cover, pg. 30-35, Part 1, "Elements of Style;" Spring 1994, pg. 20-25, Part 11, "Elements of Style;" *Hobbies - The Magazine for Collectors*, Dec. 1976, Cover, pg. 115-117, "The Historical Creche;" *Doll News*, Vol. XXV11, No. 1, Winter 1977, Cover, pg. 14-21, "Creche Legacy For the Ages;" UFDC *30th Annual Convention Journal*, New York City, Aug. 1979, pg. 38-41, "A Closer Look;" UFDC *Regional Journal*, New Orleans, LA, 1984, pg. 41-50, "A Heritage in Wax," and "Creche in Louisiana - A Thoughtful Collection;" *Doll Collectors Manual*, Hobby House, 1983, pg. 22-28, "Presepio Figure and Environment," and pg. 40-43, "Inclination of the Age"

Featured Presentations

Aug. 1979, "The Art of the Nativity," UFDC National Convention, New York City; Aug. 1980, "Les Images de Noel," UFDC National Convention, Washington, DC; Nov. 1984, "Silk Purses and Sows Ears," DCA Annual Meeting, Rockport, Massachusetts; Nov. 1984, "Silk Purses and Sows Ears," UFDC Regional Meeting, New Orleans, Louisiana; Aug. 1985, "Small Things in Life," UFDC National Convention, Atlanta, Georgia; Apr. 1987, "Sow's Ears and Silk Purses," IGMA Annual Meeting, New York City; Apr. 1988, "The Small Things in Life, and Sows Ears and Silk Purses," Handorf, South Australia; Nov. 17, 1988, "Art of the Nativity," Natchez Historical Society, Natchez, Mississippi

HANLEY, FRANK L., continued

BIOGRAPHY:

Frank L. Hanley is a native of Acadian Region of Louisiana and has now retired as Chairman of Keyboard Studies and Professor of Piano at The University of Southwestern Louisiana in Lafayette. He is an artist, author, lecturer, art connoisseur and collector. Examples of his work can be found in private collections throughout the United States, Canada, England, Germany, France, Spain, and Mexico.

see "Jeffrey Guéno"

ARTISAN: HANSEN, CATHY

BUSINESS NAME: Cathy Hansen

IDENTIFICATION MARKS:

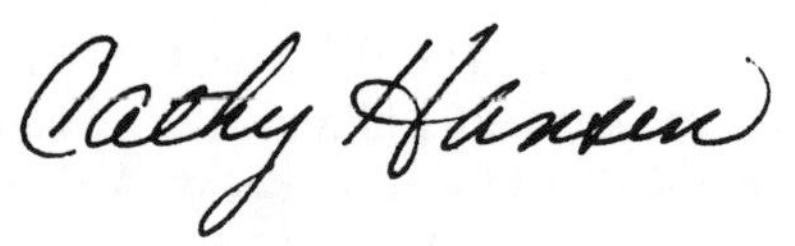

with year

CATEGORY:

Dolls: original

RECOGNITION:

Nutshell News, Vol. 13, No. 1, Jan. 1983, pg. 52; Vol. 14, No. 12, Dec. 1984, pg. 71, Show Scene; *Contemporary Dolls*, 1993

AUTOBIOGRAPHY:

My husband and I opened a miniature store in 1976. Since I had been interested and loved old dolls for some time, I decided to start making dollhouse size dolls. I took several lessons in painting dolls and purchased what molds were available at the time. I then expanded my stock of molds by taking my antique dolls and making my own molds from them, reducing them to dollhouse size. Since that time, I have sculpted my own original dolls. Many of my original dolls have been featured in *Nutshell News*.

ARTISAN: HANSEN, ROSEMARY & JIM

BUSINESS NAME: Mini-Fab

IDENTIFICATION MARKS:

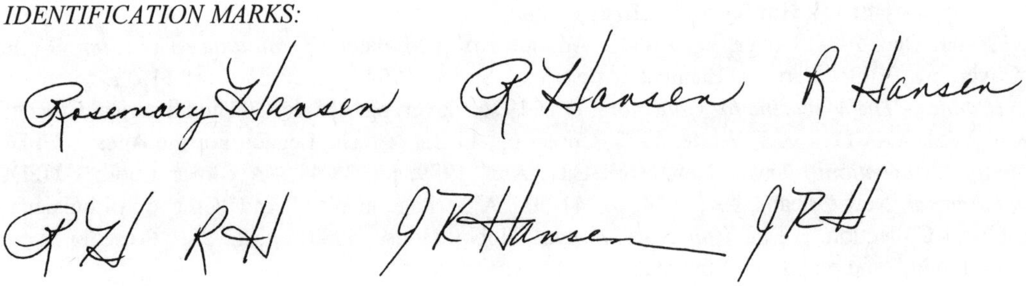

Initials and date hidden in needlepoint

CATEGORY:

Accessories; Dollhouse; Furniture: upholstered; Needlework; Roomboxes

HONORS:

IGMA Artisan (Rosemary)

HANSEN, ROSEMARY & JIM, continued

RECOGNITION:

Miniature Collector, No. 48, pg. 12-15; *Hobbies*, Jun. 1983, pg. 53-56; *Nutshell News; Miniature Collector*; *American Period Interiors in Miniature*, Kate Doordan Klavan, Scribners 1984

BIOGRAPHY:

Rosemary Hansen studied at the University of Washington and the University of Geneva, Switzerland, as a French major. She has lived in Europe and extensively traveled and studied in Europe and Russia, and has contacts with European artists. Rosemary is a needlework artist in both full-size and miniature, she designs many of the patterns and also has taught needlework since the 1970's. She started working seriously in miniatures in 1975.

Jim Hansen a mechanical and electrical engineer, has traveled extensively in Europe since the 1970's. Through his travels he has close contacts with many European artisans. During the late 1970's and 80's he built in excess of 400 Victorian dollhouse shells. He also builds miniature furniture, some of which have petit point upholstery made by Rosemary. Jim has also built roomboxes which have been featured in museums in Northwestern United States and his completed rooms have won many show awards.

ARTISAN: HANSON, ALICE

IDENTIFICATION MARKS:

CATEGORY:

Needlework; Quilts

RECOGNITION:

Miniatures Showcase, Winter 1992, pg. 30; Jan. 1993, pg. 39, 63

ARTISAN: HARDIN, LOUIS T.

BUSINESS NAME: The Wee House Enterprise

IDENTIFICATION MARKS:

Wee House Enterprise

Specializing in Doll House Dreams

SN: 00000

Logo on all stationary

CATEGORY:

Dollhouse: original

RECOGNITION:

Television interview WBSG-21, Brunswick, Georgia

AUTOBIOGRAPHY:

Since 1972, I have built dollhouses as a hobby. At the time I retired from my job I thought I would start building houses as a business. All of my houses are original designs, not kits. I treat the houses as real property. To accomplish this, I have three divisions of the company: Wee House Construction, for house construction; Wee House Realty, my sales division; and Wee House and Associates, for closings and issuing my warranty deeds which are legal and binding. Each transaction is treated as if you were purchasing a real house.

ARTISAN: **HARDY, CAROL**

BUSINESS NAME: Antiques in Miniature

IDENTIFICATION MARKS:
1976 to present, all signed on bottom in ink

Carol Hardy '94

C. Hardy '94
#1
Number of edition

C.S.H. '94
Smaller pieces

CATEGORY:
Accessories: sewing; Furniture: period; Roomboxes; Sleighs

HONORS:
IGMA Fellow

RECOGNITION:
Nutshell News, Aug. 1982, pg. 68-70; Jul. 1985, pg. 34; Feb. 1995, pg. 54-57, "Smaller Than A Breadboard," Anne Day Smith; *Miniature Collector*, Jul/Aug. 1984, pg. 44, 52; Fall 1989, pg. 24; Winter 1990, pg. 19-21; *Miniatures Showcase*, Winter 1987, pg. 36, 52; Spring 1987, pg. 50; *The Scale Cabinetmaker*, Vol. 4, No. 4, Aug. 1980, pg. 29-34; *Hobbies Magazine*, Dec. 1984, pg. 50-53; *Little Things*, Vol. 2, No. 1, Jan. 1983, pg. 20-21; *Country Living Magazine*, Mar. 1992, pg. 102-105; *Puppen Magazine*, Germany, Jan. 1991, pg. 67; *Chevron USA Odyssey Magazine*, Winter 1986, pg. 23

BIOGRAPHY:
Carol Hardy was born in Chicago and moved to California at the age of eight. While on a summer vacation in Los Angeles, Carol was fascinated by the Mott Miniature Collection. With a love of books, a rich imagination and an eye for detail, Carol began a lifelong involvement in miniatures. In the mid 1970's, she began making one-inch scale miniatures for her own enjoyment, and as therapy for being a mother of three little children. Soon people in the miniature world wanted to buy her little treasures, and with her husband's encouragement Carol found herself in business. She enjoys researching for authenticity, scouring libraries, museums, and historical buildings for inspiration. Frequently she is able to measure the actual pieces she wants to produce. She specializes in 18th century furniture, sleighs, sewing accessories and historical reproduction roomboxes. She also loves teaching miniature woodworking and has taught at the IGMA Guild school in Castine, Maine since 1985.

ARTISAN: **HARLEY, BILL & JULIE**

BUSINESS NAME: Anglesey Dolls Houses

IDENTIFICATION MARKS:

Bill & Julie Harley

Anglesey
Dolls Houses

(DATE)

CATEGORY:
Dollhouse: period; Roomboxes; Shops; Structures

RECOGNITION:
The Chronicle, Sept. 7, 1989, pg. 5; *Holyhead & Anglesley Mail*, Aug. 28, 1989 pg. 15; Sept. 20, 1989, pg. 30; Oct. 2, 1991, pg. 14; *International Dolls House News*, Vol. 19, No. 2, Summer 1990, pg. 37; *Dolls House World*, Issue No. 10, 1990, pg. 60; Issue No. 18, 1992, pg. 16; Issue No. 21, 1992, pg. 19; *The Home Miniaturist*, Nov. 1990, pg. 17; *The Times* Business Section, Jun. 28, 1991, pg. 34; *Wales in Action*, Oct. 1992, pg. 18; BBC Radio Wales, Feb. 25, 1992, Mar. 1, 1992; "Change of Direction;" H.T.V. News Jul. 15, 1992

ARTISAN: **HARRISON, JESSIE A.**

BUSINESS NAME: Jessie's Mini Needleworks
JAH Enterprises

IDENTIFICATION MARKS:
Some unmarked

CATEGORY:
Knitting; Needlework; Quilts

HONORS:
IGMA Artisan, Fellow 1994

AUTOBIOGRAPHY:
I started working in miniatures about 1988, thinking it would be a challenge to do miniature knitting. I have since branched into other areas of needlework. My mother taught me to knit when I was a little girl. In all other areas of needlework and miniatures I am self-taught.

Professionally, I am a Mathematician and Computer Scientist. I graduated from the University of California, San Diego in 1975 and worked as a computer specialist for 12 years. I quit working full-time to join my husband who is retired. I now do a little computer consulting under the name JAH Enterprises.

ARTISAN: **HART, WES**

BUSINESS NAME: Wes Hart Miniatures

IDENTIFICATION MARKS:
Very small pieces unmarked

CATEGORY:
Chandeliers; Clocks: working; Fabergé; Goldsmith; Instruments: scientific; Silversmith; Weapons

HONORS:
IGMA Artisan 1986; Exhibits: Toy & Miniature Museum of Kansas City; Carnegie Museum, Pittsburgh, Pennsylvania; The Favell Museum, Klamath Falls, Oregon

RECOGNITION:
The Robb Report, Christmas Catalog, Dec. 1986; *Nutshell News*, Jan. 1983, pg. 55; Jan. 1986, pg. 25

BIOGRAPHY:
Wes Hart was born in Spokane, Washington in 1954. His interest in miniatures began with sailing ship models in elementary and high school. That led to an interest in miniature cannons, and later to working miniature firearms. On completion of high school Wes began a career in the jewelry manufacturing and repair trade. He apprenticed in a large wholesale trade shop where he gained his journeyman status. Wes is now a master of his craft. He owned and operated a jewelry store for seven years where he created costume jewelry and fine miniatures. His work can be seen in the Carnegie Museum, Pittsburgh, Pennsylvania, The Favell Museum, Klamath Falls, Oregon, and the Toy and Miniature Museum, Kansas City, Missouri. Wes and his family currently reside in the Phoenix, Arizona area. He is a member of the Miniature Arms Society.

ARTISAN: **HASTINGS, MARTHA**

BUSINESS NAME: Miss Elaineous, Inc.

IDENTIFICATION MARKS:

Miss Elaineous, Inc.
M. HASTINGS

CATEGORY:
Dollhouse: custom, replicated; Furniture: upholstered

AUTOBIOGRAPHY:
Since the early 1980's, I have worked with the Southern Christmas Show, a two-week show, developing the "Enchanted Village," an exhibit of dollhouses, roomboxes and scenes. The "Village" has become a focal point of the show, which draws approximately 150,000 people each year. I have also worked with the Charlotte Miniature & Dollhouse Show & Sale since about 1980, and more recently as the show promoter.

Eight years ago, about 1985, I opened a miniature shop, Miss Elaineous, Inc., offering a complete line of dollhouses & miniatures, workshops and demonstrations. I welcome custom work on furniture and dollhouses. I have used the "Miss Elaineous" logo since 1961, when I was involved in arts & crafts.

ARTISAN: **HASTRICH, JAMES**

BUSINESS NAME: James Hastrich Fine Miniatures

IDENTIFICATION MARKS:

James Hastrich
James Hastrich — 1985 to present

Uncle Jim Hastrich — 1980 to 1985

CATEGORY:
Furniture: handpainted, period

HONORS:
IGMA Artisan

RECOGNITION:
Early American Life, Oct. 1991, pg. 28-33; *Colonial Homes*, Oct. 1991, pg. 63-64, 68-71

AUTOBIOGRAPHY:
I started out making full-size furniture; after eight years, I was introduced to miniatures and quickly became totally engrossed. I terminated my full-scale furniture business in 1977 and have devoted my time to Early American painted furniture in both one-inch and two-inch scale since that time. I have taken numerous decorative painting workshops and have fine tuned my eye for good design and color by studying New England antique furniture and accessories.

ARTISAN: **HASWELL, APRIL**

BUSINESS NAME: Angel's Accessories

IDENTIFICATION MARKS:
Unmarked

HASWELL, APRIL, continued

CATEGORY:

Crocheting; Needlework

HONORS:

IGMA Artisan

AUTOBIOGRAPHY:

I began my hobby in miniatures in December 1977 when my husband gave me a seven room dollhouse kit for Christmas. Over the next few years as I put the kit together and started decorating it, I began looking for accessories. With my talent in crocheting, I began to make doilies and table cloths. I looked at life-size pieces, pictured them reduced to scale and began making my own. I use a size 15 hook, which I filed with a jewelers file, and thread.

The items I made were admired by friends and fellow club members, and I sold a few pieces to them. I bought a few doll kits to put in my house. Since I really do not like sewing, I decided to crochet their costumes. Again, everyone admired them. I have done work for doll and teddy bear artists, and also made items for private collectors. After receiving Artisan Status in IGMA, I thought I might try starting a business selling my miniatures. My work is unsigned and is well received.

ARTISAN: HAW, DOROTHY

BUSINESS NAME: Abigail's Fantasy

IDENTIFICATION MARKS:

HAW 1983 to 1991 Haw 1991 to present

CATEGORY:

Costuming; Dolls: babies, character, children, original, porcelain

HONORS:

IGMA Fellow 1989; Exhibit: Toy & Miniature Museum of Kansas City

RECOGNITION:

Nutshell News, Vol. 18, No. 1, Jan. 1988, pg. 67; Vol. 18, No. 2, Feb. 1988, pg. 48-51; Vol. 18, No. 4, Apr. 1988, pg. 70; Vol. 18, No. 6, Jun. 1988, pg. 62; Vol. 19, No. 11, Nov. 1989, pg. 91, 95; Vol. 20, No. 6, Jun. 1990, pg. 64; Vol. 20, No. 12, Dec. 1990, pg. 67; Vol. 21, No. 4, Apr. 1991, pg. 56; Vol. 22, No. 3, Mar. 1992, pg. 70-71; Vol. 22, No. 5, May 1992, pg. 63; Vol. 22, No. 6, Jun. 1992, pg. 66; *Miniatures Showcase*, Vol. 2, No. 2, Spring 1987, pg. 20; Vol. 3, No. 2, Spring 1988, pg. 33-35; Vol. 4, No. 4, Fall 1989, pg. 35; Vol. 6, No. 4, Fall 1991, pg. 38; Vol. 7, No. 4, Nov. 1992, pg. 32; *Dolls In Miniature*, Vol. 2, No. 3, Fall 1992, pg. 21-25

AUTOBIOGRAPHY:

I studied Fashion design at Fashion Institute of Technology and designed upscale children's clothing. My interest in miniatures started with my daughter's dollhouse. I received my IGMA Fellow cube in 1989.

ARTISAN: HAY, G. EARL

IDENTIFICATION MARKS:

G E Hay GEH

HAY, G. EARL, continued

CATEGORY:

Furniture: period, rustic twig, Shaker

HONORS:

IGMA Artisan

RECOGNITION:

Miniature Collector; No. 65, Summer 1989, pg. 24-25, "The Will Of the Withe," Stephen L. Cronk

AUTOBIOGRAPHY:

My current miniature interest started when my wife, Margaret, needed a scale bed for a miniature needlework coverlet she had stitched. I copied our four-poster bed, and went on to do other period pieces. I had known about Adirondack rustic from my youth, and started making twig pieces following styles developed by the caretaker/guides in Adirondack Great Camps. Green woods are used. Shaker and period pieces follow measurements taken from existing pieces or measured drawings using woods which I cut in scale with the original pieces.

ARTISAN: **HEDRICK, LOUISE**

BUSINESS NAME: L H Studio

IDENTIFICATION MARKS:

All marks 1980 to present

Embroidered on female's underwear
Signed on bottom of wicker & male's shoes

Label sewn in female's clothes for limited edition dolls

Label placed on bottom of wicker, wood plaques, and doll stands; for limited edition figures

CATEGORY:

Costuming; Dolls; Wicker

HONORS:

IGMA Artisan 1994

RECOGNITION:

Nutshell News, Sept. 1985; Nov. 1985, Apr. 1986, pg. 76-79, "Louise Hedrick – Fairy Godmother," Jeanne Delgado; Jun. 1988; Mar. 1991; Nov. 1991; Sept. 1992; Dec. 1992; Mar. 1993; Jun. 1993; Sept. 1993; Dec. 1993; Mar. 1994; Jun. 1994; Dec. 1994

AUTOBIOGRAPHY:

My interest in miniatures began one day in 1978 when my aunt and I happened into a local miniature shop. As with many people, it took over my life. I really did not plan the business part of it. It evolved! The owner of this shop asked me to make a few things, then teach a few classes, and this was the beginning of L H Studio.

My background in fabrics and design was not a formal education, but an outgrowth of many classes and seminars at the Embroiderer's Guild of America and The Smocking Arts Guild of America. Countless trips to museums and devouring the contents of fashion publications from the 19th century led me to creating these small historical replicas. My interest in heirloom sewing has led me to first construct these garments in accurate sewing techniques, and then to teach others to do it. This includes not only miniature dolls, but the larger antique and reproduction dolls, and children's clothing.

ARTISAN: **HELTON, JOAN**

IDENTIFICATION MARKS: (Submitted by William R. Robertson)

Helton

with date

CATEGORY:
Boxes: decorative, jewelry

HONORS:
Exhibit: Toy & Miniature Museum of Kansas City

ARTISAN: **HEMMINGS, LINDA**

BUSINESS NAME: Linda Hemmings Miniatures

IDENTIFICATION MARKS:

LH   LH   On back

LINDA HEMMINGS MINIATURES   Swing tag logo

CATEGORY:
Dolls: character, porcelain

RECOGNITION:
Dolls & Dollhouses, Issue No. 1, Nov. 1988, pg. 24-26; *Dolls House World*, Issue No. 6, 1990, pg. 47, 49; *The Home Miniaturist*, Sept. 1988, pg. 29-31

AUTOBIOGRAPHY:
I studied Fine Art and Design for five years at Oxford, England. I have been making dolls since approximately 1979, initially being larger dolls, and latterly since 1985 dollshouse dolls, originally from bought molds, but more recently from molds that I developed myself. My dolls have been exhibited in Japan as well as in exhibitions in Great Britain, and have been bought for sale through Major British Fairs, in Munich, Germany; Sydney, Australia; Paris, France; and America to name a few. All my dolls are marked with my initials on the back, and have a swing ticket carrying my logo attached to their left arm.

ARTISAN: **HENDERSON, SYLVIA V.**

BUSINESS NAME: Wee-R-Crafts

IDENTIFICATION MARKS:

Sylvia V. Henderson   SVH   WEE-R-CRAFTS

CATEGORY:
Dollhouse; Roomboxes; Vignettes

RECOGNITION:
Miniature Gazette, Vol. 12, No. 1, Fall 1983; Vol. 16, No. 4, Summer 1988; Vol. 20, No. 2, Winter 1991; *Prince Georges County Independent,* Maryland, Dec. 26, 1984; *Prince Georges County Sentinel,* Maryland, Vol. 59, No. 31, Sept. 12, 1991; *Miniature Collector*, No. 38, Aug. 1983

ARTISAN: **HENDRICKS, ANN R.**

BUSINESS NAME: La Casa Photos

IDENTIFICATION MARKS:
Unmarked

Business logo

CATEGORY:
Books; Cameras; Frames; Memorabilia: movie; Photographs; Photography; Stationery: postcard; Stereoscope

AUTOBIOGRAPHY:
My interest in photography goes back to my childhood and teen years. After my girls left home I studied photography by taking workshops through the Extension division of the University of California, Santa Cruz as well as numerous seminars and classes through other institutions like Friends of Photography, etc. I started a small one-man photo lab operation specializing in Cibachrome printing and copy work and did commercial work for a number of clients.

I have also always had a love of miniatures so I decided to start offering miniature vintage photographs to the general public through various stores. This small business has expanded to the point where I now have buyers all over the country and some in Europe and as a consequence have given up printing for other people. Books, cameras, stereoscopes, frames, movie memorabilia, and a large line of one-inch scale postcards now make up the bulk of my business. I am at present a member of IGMA, NAME, CIMTA and MIAA.

ARTISAN: **HENRY, AUDREY**

BUSINESS NAME: A & H Porcelain Petites

IDENTIFICATION MARKS:

AH '92

Dolls 1981 to present, marked or inscribed in greenware on back of neck or shoulder plate
Pins signed on back with name and year, cats signed underside with above mark and year

CATEGORY:
Animals: cats; Dolls: porcelain; Pins

RECOGNITION:
Nutshell News

ARTISAN: **HEPLER, RALPH**

BUSINESS NAME: The Village Blacksmith

IDENTIFICATION MARKS:

Ralph Hepler
Village Blacksmith

HEPLER, RALPH, continued

CATEGORY:

Barns: woodshed; Buildings; Metalwork; Structures: weathered

AUTOBIOGRAPHY:

My hobby as a Blacksmith Miniaturist, derives from a lifetime of experience as a machinist, tool maker, and woodworker. I started the hobby miniature business in August 1989.

ARTISAN: HERBILLON, PATRICIA

BUSINESS NAME: Herbillon
Meubles Miniatures

IDENTIFICATION MARKS:

CATEGORY:

Furniture: inlaid, period

HONORS:

IGMA Artisan

RECOGNITION:

La Vie, Nov. 1984, pg. 76; *de Collectionneur Français*, Mar. 1987, pg. 22; *Femmes d'aujourd'hui*, No. 9, Mar. 1987, pg. 6; *France Soir*, Mar. 17, 1987, pg. 11; *Courrier de l'Ouest*, May 26, 1988; Jul. 25, 1988; Sept. 1992; *Le Nouvelle Republique*, Jun. 25, 1988; *Miniature Collector*, Winter 1989; *Magazine de la Maison de Poupees*, No. 6, pg. 19-20

AUTOBIOGRAPHY:

Nothing predisposed us to make miniatures in as much as one of us was an architectural assistant and the other stayed home as mother and housewife. In 1983, we were simply having a look at a dollhouse in a shop and were so stricken by its neatness we wanted to make one. We started making miniatures, drawing at first on our inspiration from our own "real" pieces of furniture. Later, this leisure activity turned into a real job, thanks to much work and encouragement from Mrs. Riesser, French Miniatures Club's chairman.

ARTISAN: HERGET, SUZANE

BUSINESS NAME: Petite Petits and Tiny Tattings

IDENTIFICATION MARKS:

Unmarked – tatted pieces

Petit point

CATEGORY:

Accessories; Needlework

HONORS:

IGMA Artisan

ARTISAN: **HERMES, JOSEPH**

BUSINESS NAME: J. Hermes

IDENTIFICATION MARKS:

J. HERMES

J. Hermes

CATEGORY:

Gift Wraps; Wall: coverings, murals; Wallpaper

HONORS:

NAME AOH; Exhibit: Los Angeles County Museum of Art

RECOGNITION:

Miniatures Showcase, Nov. 1992, Cover; *Dollhouse Miniatures Calendar*, Cover; *Nutshell News*, Dec. 1992, pg. 37

AUTOBIOGRAPHY:

While in high school, Elder, Cincinnati, Ohio and college, University of Washington, Seattle, Washington, I contributed as an artist to high school publications and yearbooks. At the University of Washington, I majored in Business Administration, and also took courses in art and design. I did post-graduate work at the University of Cincinnati, and at the Jepson Art Institute and Cal State, in Los Angeles, California. I worked as an artist for the American Laundry Machinery Mfg. Co., in Cincinnati, and for *Motor Trends* magazine in Los Angeles. Later, I designed fabrics and fashion yardage for men and women's clothing in my studio on Wilshire Blvd., also in Los Angeles. Some of my work is in the Los Angeles County Museum of Art.

In addition to being a commercial artist, I was also a fine artist, working in serigraph, better known as silk screen printing. I have exhibited my work nationally. With my knowledge of art and design, and the ability to put a design in repeat, it was an easy transfer from fabric to miniature wallpapers. I have done a great deal of research in authentic wallpapers of the past, so most are actually miniaturized copies of wallpapers from various periods such as Colonial, Federal, Victorian, and Craftsman. I actually started in miniatures before NAME was organized, creating furniture for my daughter, Heidi, who had a collection of Troll Dolls. Some of the first miniatures I made were pieces of furniture. Jackie Andrews, Bob VonFliss and Judy Berman are some of the people who have them, these pieces are unsigned.

My wife, Janet, and I were original members of the Mott's Miniature Club, which later became NAME. I was one of the organizers of IMA which later became AOH, and a founding member of MIAA. After my term as president of NAME, I served as editor of the Gazette for a number of years. I did the art work and calligraphy for our NAME membership charter.

ARTISAN: **HICKLING, JAMES E.**

BUSINESS NAME: Masterpiece Miniatures

IDENTIFICATION MARKS:

J E H included within Hallmark on gold and silver pieces

CATEGORY:

Brasswork; Goldsmith; Kitchenware; Silversmith

AUTOBIOGRAPHY:

I am a retired goldsmith. I took up miniature making in 1990 as a hobby and have turned it into a very small business.

ARTISAN: **HILL, EDWARD**

BUSINESS NAME: Glassblowing of Greenwich

IDENTIFICATION MARKS:
Unmarked

CATEGORY:
Glass: handblown

HONORS:
IGMA Artisan; Fellow 1994; Winner, all categories, Save The Children Competition 1987

RECOGNITION:
Miniature Collector, Spring 1991, pg. 30-32; *International Dolls House News*, Vol. 20, No. 4, Winter 1991, pg. 30-31

AUTOBIOGRAPHY:
From 1973 to 1974, I worked in glass factories in Venice, Italy, learning full-scale glass techniques. In 1975, I took a three month course in Scientific Glassblowing to learn techniques for working over a small gas flame. In 1976, I established my own workshop with a furnace for full-scale work and a burner for lampworking. I produced my first miniatures in response to a customer's request. From 1976 to 1992, there was a gradual development of the lampworking side of the workshop so that the furnace is now used quite rarely, and then mostly for special tubing etc. which I use on my miniatures.

ARTISAN: **HILLHOUSE, JIM & SHIRLEY**

BUSINESS NAME: Hillhouse

IDENTIFICATION MARKS: (Submitted by Esther R. Robertson)

HS

CATEGORY:
Folk Art; Furniture: handpainted, stenciled

RECOGNITION:
Nutshell News, Vol. 12, No. 12, Dec. 1982, pg. 32; Vol. 13, No. 6, Jun. 1983, pg. 36; Vol. 14, No. 4, Apr. 1984, pg. 68, Show Scene; Vol. 14, No. 8, Aug. 1984, pg. 54; *Miniature Collector*, No. 2, Jun. 1977, pg. 26, Show Stoppers; No. 11, Feb. 1979, pg. 39, Show Stoppers; *Miniature Gazette*, Vol. 5, No. 4, Jun. 1977, pg. 73; Vol. 6, No. 1, Sept. 1977, pg. 47; Vol. 7, No. 3, Spring 1979, pg. 9

ARTISAN: **HILLMAN, DENIS E. W.**

IDENTIFICATION MARKS:
DEW
H
HANDMADE — 1971 to present, number of piece
1972
12

CATEGORY:
Furniture: period

HILLMAN, DENIS E. W., continued

HONORS:

IGMA Fellow; Maître Ebonist A Miniature Meubles (Française)

RECOGNITION:

Nutshell News, Vol. 13, No. 8, Aug. 1983, pg. 47, Show Scene; *Miniature Collector*, No. 37, Jun. 1983, pg. 39; *Miniature Gazette*, Vol. 7, No. 3, Spring 1979, pg. 86; *Art & Antiques*, Vol. 33, No. 12, Oct. 7, 1978; Vol. 41, No. 8, 1980; *Antiques & Collecting* (Hobbies), Oct. 1986, pg. 44-47; Nov. 1986, pg. 44-46, 50; *Le Magazine de la Maison de Poupee*, 9, 1989, pg. 4-6, 8-9; GB-ITV, 1975; GB-BBC2 Small World series, 1980; ZDF (Germany) 1985

AUTOBIOGRAPHY:

I completed my apprenticeship for cabinet making in 1940. I was trained in precision model making by the British Admiralty and Air Ministry in 1941. I subsequently joined a group of professional model makers engaged in highly technical models for the Ministries in conjunction with the war effort. I joined the Royal Air Force early in 1944, until 1947. I was a member of a small group of specialists designing and manufacturing toys from 1951 to 1955. Then I commenced the making of miniature furniture in 1971 as a full-time profession, and have covered all periods of English furniture since 1979. I have specialized in the French periods of Louis XV and XVI.

I have pioneered miniature furniture and introduced miniature inlay, and was the first miniaturist to show in London and later in America. I've also held seminars in Britain, France and America, and taught at the IGMA school, Castine, Maine where I held the first master class. I have exhibited my miniatures many times in London, Paris, Monte Carlo (their first show), Frankfort, New York, Chicago and Anaheim, California.

Since approximately 1985, I have withdrawn from the commercial world in order to concentrate on the building of a collection of Louis pieces for a very special purpose and exhibitions, researching this project in the Louvre (Paris) Versailles and in London museums. I am a member of Le Club de la Miniature Française. All my miniatures are entirely handmade by myself. I do not use other peoples pieces or fitments. Every piece I make is constructed out of the correct woods, fully jointed and accurate down to the finest detail. The locks are made by myself as are all the brass and mechanical parts, including the minute screws which hold the ormolu in place.

ARTISAN: HIMES, RANDY

BUSINESS NAME: Miniatures By Randy Himes
Dogwood Miniatures

IDENTIFICATION MARKS:

CATEGORY:

Furniture: period

HONORS:

NAME AOH 1989

RECOGNITION:

Nutshell News, Aug. 1981, pg. 40; *Miniature Collector*, No. 46, Nov/Dec. 1984, pg. 52-53, Show Stoppers; *The Andrews Collection,* Personal Treasures, Anne Day Smith, 1988, pg. 14; *Miniature Gazette,* Vol. 8, No. 2, Winter 1979, pg. 86-87, "A Cincinnati Sampler – Jeffersonian Dining Room;" Vol. 20, No. 3, Spring 1992, pg. 28

AUTOBIOGRAPHY:

I began building miniatures with my wife, Barbara, in 1972. The first that I built was a rather crude music stand of my own design. Barbara made a flute case of balsa wood and velvet and purchased a silver charm flute. This was the beginning of our hobby and was for our daughter, who plays the flute.

I became more seriously involved in building furniture for Barbara and for our three children, and occasionally built pieces to give to friends. Next, I began giving workshops at Jean Ellsworth's miniature shop, and later was asked to give a workshop at the 1981 NAME National in St. Louis. Since then I've given many workshops at both National and Regional Houseparties, State Days, Shows, and for clubs.

In 1981, we started Dogwood Miniatures. Its name was changed to Miniatures By Randy Himes in 1992. In other joint efforts Barbara and I built souvenirs for two NAME Region A-3 Houseparties.

I found out from the music stand that I am not a designer and from then on I started building reproductions of antiques. Most every piece is a copy of a museum piece, from published plans or from Antiques magazine. I favor the Federal Period.

Barbara and I are founding members of the Miniature Society of Cincinnati and active members of NAME. We have served on both National and Regional Houseparty steering committees and chaired the 1990 National in Cincinnati. Also, we have been active on various MSC show and sale committees, chairing the event for two years.

We have a lot of fun building roomboxes. Barbara designs, plans and executes the boxes and I build the furniture.

ARTISAN: HINKEL, GLORIA R.

BUSINESS NAME: Gloria R. Hinkel
Proprietor: Delaware Toy & Miniature Museum, Wilmington, Delaware

CATEGORY:
Antique Miniatures; Antiques

BIOGRAPHY:

Gloria R. Hinkel, collector and dealer in antique miniatures, started collecting in 1967, and started producing shows in 1974 in the Philadelphia area. Gloria acquires her antiques through purchases from other dealers, but primarily through buying collections of many notable persons. One of her collection purchases was from Mrs. Jean Austin duPont, Newtown Square, Pennsylvania, who was also a member of the Philadelphia Miniature Enthusiasts, a NAME club. Gloria's collections include also miniature dolls, children's furniture, doll size furniture and accessories, trains, toys and sample size furniture.

Gloria is CEO of Hinkel Equipment Rental Associates, Inc., a plant maintenance contractor, and secretary-treasurer of Hinkel Engineering Products Corporation, a business involved with engineering and patents. Her interior design business is in conjunction with new construction by the two parent companies.

The Delaware Toy & Miniature Museum, which opened in September 1994, was founded by Gloria R. Hinkel and Beverly J. Thomes. It features private collections from Europe and the United States, such as Miriam Wentworth, Helena Rubenstein, the (Singer Sewing Machine) Strassburger family, and Mrs. Jean Austin duPont.

ARTISAN: HINKLE, JULIE

BUSINESS NAME: Poco Pots

IDENTIFICATION MARKS:

CATEGORY:
Ceramics

RECOGNITION:
Nutshell News, Jun. 1991, pg. 65; *Miniatures Showcase*, Winter 1988, Cover, pg. 3, 9, 40, 42, 44-45, 48; Spring 1991, pg. 21; Summer 1991, pg. 28; *Miniature Collector*, Nov/Dec. 1986, pg. 22

HINKLE, JULIE, continued

AUTOBIOGRAPHY:

I became interested in miniatures in 1977 when I went to St. Louis to help my mother sell our house. My dollhouse furniture had been stored there since 1953. I decided to build a house for my furniture and also wanted to do all the accessories, myself. Well, I got stuck on ceramics. I did a few pots for myself and friends until 1985, then I decided to do it as a business. I take classes offered at our museum each year and also workshops that are offered by visiting artists. I also took a 12 day Anasazi workshop in the summer of 1992. I have a degree in Secondary Education from the University of Missouri. I never took any formal art classes beyond seventh grade. The classes at the museum are casual and very informing. I feel lucky to do something I enjoy so much, traveling and meeting so many nice people.

ARTISAN: HIPWELL, BARRY

IDENTIFICATION MARKS:

Hallmark registered at Goldsmith's Hall, London, England
Stamped into small brass plate

CATEGORY:

Furniture: carved, English, European, inlaid, Japanese, period

HONORS:

IGMA Artisan; Exhibit: The Carole & Barry Kaye Museum of Miniatures, Los Angeles, California

RECOGNITION:

Nutshell News, Sept. 1991, pg. 29; Nov. 1991, pg. 39; Jan 1992, pg. 30; Jul. 1992, pg. 74; Apr. 1993, pg. 65, 67; Nov. 1993, pg. 46-49, 63; Jan. 1994, pg. 8, 50-51, 78; *Miniature Collector,* Winter 1990, pg. 44; Spring 1992, pg. 21, 24; *Doll's House World*, Issue No. 9, 1990, pg. 48-53; Issue No. 16, 1991, pg. 14-17; Issue No. 18, 1992, pg. 7, 25; Issue No. 22, 1992, pg. 11; Issue No. 24, pg. 57; Issue No. 30, pg. 48; Issue No. 32, pg. 40; *Home Miniaturist*, Jan. 1990, pg. 10; May 1990, pg. 5; Jul. 1991, pg. 19, 36-37; Sept. 1991, pg. 19; *Le Magazine de la Maison du Poupée*, No. 16, Spring 1991, pg. 14-15; No. 18, Autumn 1991, pg. 10; No. 19, Winter 1991, pg. 16, 20; No. 22, Autumn 1992, pg. 11-12; No. 23, Winter 1992, pg. 29; No. 24, Spring 1993, pg. 16; No. 25, Summer 1993, pg. 11-13; No. 27, Winter 1993, pg. 3-4, 6, 20; No. 29, Spring 1994, pg. 11, 24; *Country Life*, Jun. 25, 1992, "Not to be Toyed With," Caroline Clifton-Mogg; Le Dauphiné, Aug. 15, 1991 (Daily newspaper SE France) pg. 5; *Waukesha Journal,* Wisconsin, Sept. 7, 1994, pg. 1, 5; *The Secrets of the Dolls' House Makers*, Jean Nisbett, 1994

BIOGRAPHY:

Early practical education was in the family's tinsmithing business, making special and short-run items. Barry then moved to bigger things, making stage sets and props at London's Mermaid Theatre. A brief period as a silversmith and jeweler and a spell with the UK's top architectural model-making firm ended when Barry joined percussionist Stomu Yamash'ta's *Red Buddha Theatre*, in Paris, as an actor. He returned from this to make props and scenery for a touring theatre company in central England and then went into dealing in books and antiques. Eventually he decided to combine the two things he enjoyed most, model-making and fine furniture. Barry has pieces in various museums and has on loan pieces in exhibitions in Scandinavia, France, Belgium, Switzerland, and Japan.

ARTISAN: **HOCKEY, ISOBEL**

BUSINESS NAME: Isobel Hockey

IDENTIFICATION MARKS:

Unmarked, knitting

IH On packaging

DESIGNED AND HAND MADE BY ISOBEL HOCKEY

Sticker on back of packaging

CATEGORY:

Knitting; Needlework

RECOGNITION:

Workbox, Autumn/Winter 1987/88, pg. 35; *Dolls' House World*, Sept/Oct. 1991, pg. 37-38; *International Doll's House World*, Summer 1988, Cover; Autumn 1991, pg. 18; Spring 1992, pg. 23; Autumn 1992, pg. 2; *Doll Reader*, Apr. 1990, pg. 270-273; *Antiques & Collecting*, Dec. 1987, pg. 45; *Miniatures Showcase*, Fall 1991, pg. 82; Winter, 1991, Cover, pg. 40, 58, 82; Nov. 1992, pg. 41-42; *Dolls in Miniature*, Winter 1992, pg. 12; Spring 1992, pg. 62-65; *Decorative Dolls' Houses*, Caroline Hamilton, Ebury Press, London 1990, pg. 36, 77-78, 81; *Making Miniatures in 1/12 Scale,* Venus & Martin Dodge, pg. 67, 72-73, 122

AUTOBIOGRAPHY:

I have always loved creating things using the needle arts, knitting, sewing, embroidery or petit point. I have always loved doll's houses and small dolls. This love of doll's houses and miniatures took a back seat during my teens, early twenties, marriage and first son. In 1972, at the age of 27, I started collecting in earnest and used my skills to make miniature furnishings, clothes and carpets for my houses. In 1981, I was inspired by a picture to design and knit a traditional Shetland lace baby shawl with a crochet picot edging in one-ply Shetland wool. This was rapidly followed by complete layettes in either one ply wool or fine 80 lace cotton thread for babies aged new-born and six months, using one-mm and ½-mm needles.

This led to a commission from David Kilpatrick for a complete Shetland lace baby layette for his museum in Oban, Scotland, and also to an invitation to exhibit at the 1st London Dollshouse Festival in 1985. By this time my range had developed to include garments to fit all sizes up to senior citizens and now also includes accessories, knitted bedspreads and crochet Granny Square Afghans.

I design my own patterns, and I use natural yarns, wool, silk and cotton. My garments can be worn, buttons fastened, pockets can be used, bedspreads and afghans will drape, stockings and socks can be worn as they are knitted on four needles with correctly turned heels.

ARTISAN: **HODGSON, JOHN J.** (Submitted by William R. Robertson and Beth Stark)

BUSINESS NAME: E L F Miniatures
John J. Hodgson

IDENTIFICATION MARKS:

19 JJH 93 Some undated, incised into metal legs or bottom of tables

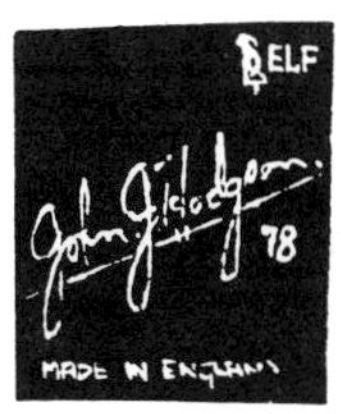

Handwritten signature in white or black ink on paper label glued on bottom of metal pieces
Signature in gold or black ink on wooden furniture

CATEGORY:

Furniture: English

HODGSON, JOHN J., continued

HONORS:

Exhibit: Toy & Miniature Museum of Kansas City

RECOGNITION:

Nutshell News, Vol. 12, No. 11, Nov. 1982, pg. 62, "Show and Tell," Judy Davis; Vol. 14, No. 8, Aug. 1984, pg. 64, Show Scene; *The Ultimate Doll's House Book*, pg. 48-51; *Dollhouse Furniture*, pg. 72; *Les Maison de Poupeés*, pg. 20-27, 84

BIOGRAPHY:

John J. Hodgson has been building miniature furniture since the 1970's. Most of his pieces are from the Queen Anne or Georgian periods. Chippendale ribbon back chairs are among his best work with their carved backs and legs. Dealers including Paige Thornton and Flora Gill Jacobs sold his work through shows and shops. Lately John has been working almost exclusively for the Guthrie Collection at Hever Castle in Edenbridge, Kent, England. He has been building and furnishing houses for a permanent exhibit. They include medieval, Stuart and Georgian houses. The Georgian house furnishings are patterned after those at Sledmere House in Yorkshire. John has also produced a group of cast metal gilded furniture for sale to collectors.

(Submitted by William R. Robertson)

ARTISAN: HOELTGE, SUSAN

BUSINESS NAME: Susan Hoeltge, Inc.

IDENTIFICATION MARKS:

S. Hoeltge 1992

CATEGORY:

Furniture: period; Kits: dollhouse

RECOGNITION:

Nutshell News, Mar. 1981 pg. 54-56; *Chagrin Herald Sun*, Ohio, Aug. 27, 1992, Community Life Section

AUTOBIOGRAPHY:

I have been involved in miniatures as a collector and as a craft person from about 1976. I design and make all that I sell. I currently, since about 1982, work exclusively in ½-inch and ¼-inch scale. I offer approximately 150 different items of furniture and upholstery. In addition, I offer dollhouse kits in ¼-inch scale and a line of toys in sub-scale. I work in different periods but prefer Queen Anne style.

My educational background as a Registered Nurse, now retired, did not prepare me for miniatures, other than to give me discipline and organizational skills. I have always done craft work, sewing, painting, needlework or woodworking. My collecting nature spurs me on to learn about all sorts of hobbies.

ARTISAN: HOERLE, SANDRA FRANCES

IDENTIFICATION MARKS:

S, F, H, prior to 1993 S. f. H. 1993 to present

CATEGORY:

Ceramics

RECOGNITION:

Miniatures Showcase, Spring 1991, pg. 21, 23, 27, 29, 31, 34; Winter 1991, pg. 33; Nov. 1992, pg. 32, 34; Winter 1992, pg. 33, 41, 58

AUTOBIOGRAPHY:

Since my childhood, I have drawn, painted and made things with clay. I've done full-size portraits, still life, and landscapes for years, in oils, watercolors and pastels. I left school in the tenth grade to marry at 15 and received no additional education. Over the years, my art knowledge has been self-taught. I became interested in ceramics, through a friend, and soon found out by experimentation I could make my own pieces out of wet clay. I purchased a kiln, did my own firing, and painted them by hand. I am starting to experiment with glazes and hope to learn how to make my own molds.

I've built an 18 room dollhouse and wanted some pieces to put in it. I sent some pieces to Miniatures Showcase which they featured in some of their magazines. I've received letters and some orders from people all over the world, which I find exciting.

I love doing miniatures as I always liked sculpting, even more than painting. This way I get to do both. I work full-time at a factory, so can only do miniatures in my spare time. With three sons and grandchildren, I don't have as much time as I'd like. I have signed smaller items with SH or SFH, before now. On larger pieces like my grandfather clocks I sign my full name and year. I am now signing everything with S.F.H.

ARTISAN: **HOFFMAN, GEORGE V., JR.**

BUSINESS NAME: The Hoffman Collection

IDENTIFICATION MARKS:

CATEGORY:

Furniture: period; Roomboxes

HONORS:

IGMA Fellow; Exhibit: Toy & Miniature Museum of Kansas City

RECOGNITION:

Nutshell News, Vol. 13, No. 1, Jan. 1983, pg. 28-30, "The Class of '82," Jane Mitchell; *Miniature Collector*, No. 2, Jun. 1977, pg. 27, Show Stoppers; No. 29, Feb. 1982, pg. 16-17; *Miniature Gazette*, Vol. 6, No. 1, Sept. 1977, pg. 47; Vol. 6, No. 3, Spring 1978, pg. 35; Vol. 7, No. 1, Fall 1978, pg. 81; Vol. 9, No. 2, Winter 1980, pg. 89; *Inside the World of Miniatures & Dollhouses*, Rosner & Beckerman, Mc Kay Press, 1976; American Period Interiors In Miniature, Kate Doordan Klavan, 1984

ARTISAN: **HOFFMAN, MARK S.**

BUSINESS NAME: The Hoffman Collection

IDENTIFICATION MARKS:

CATEGORY:

Furniture: period; Roomboxes

RECOGNITION:

Miniature Collector, No. 2, Jun. 1977, pg. 27, Show Stoppers

ARTISAN: **HOFFMAN, SARA J.**

BUSINESS NAME: The Hoffman Collection

IDENTIFICATION MARKS:

CATEGORY:

Furniture: period; Roomboxes

HONORS:

IGMA Fellow; Exhibit: Toy & Miniature Museum of Kansas City

RECOGNITION:

Nutshell News, Vol. 13, No. 1, Jan. 1983, pg. 28-30, "The Class of '82," Jane Mitchell; *Miniature Collector*, No. 2, Jun. 1977, pg. 27, Show Stoppers; No. 11, Feb. 1979, pg. 38; No. 29, Feb. 1982, pg. 16-17, Show Stoppers; *Miniature Gazette*, Vol. 6, No. 1, Sept. 1977, pg. 47; Vol. 6, No. 3, Spring 1978, pg. 35; Vol. 7, No. 1, Fall 1978, pg. 81; Vol. 9, No. 2, Winter 1980, pg. 89; *Inside the World of Miniatures & Dollhouses*, Rosner & Beckerman, Mc Kay Press, 1976; American Period Interiors In Miniature, Kate Doordan Klavan, 1984

ARTISAN: **HOFMAN, STACY ANN**

BUSINESS NAME: Hofman Doll Works

IDENTIFICATION MARKS:

1990 to present

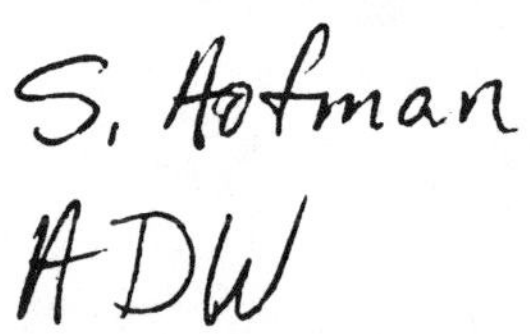

CATEGORY:

Dolls: children, costuming, figures, original, period, porcelain, reproductions

HONORS:

IGMA Artisan; Exhibits: The Carole & Barry Kaye Museum of Miniatures, Los Angeles, California; Rosalie Whyel Museum of Doll Art, Bellevue, Washington

RECOGNITION:

Nutshell News, Vol. 21, No. 3, Mar. 1991, pg. 66-69, "Fairy Tale Talent," Kathleen Zimmer

AUTOBIOGRAPHY:

My mother is the large doll artist, Jan Doehring, of New Orleans, Louisiana. She taught me how to make dolls when I was 13. Under her tutelage, I continued making porcelain dolls from about 1976. I have also experimented with wax dolls, costumed antique dolls, and designed costumes for other doll makers. In 1990, I bought my first miniature doll molds, and have devoted myself to small dolls since then. I am a featured artist in the Rosalie Whyel Museum of Doll Art, and the The Carole & Barry Kaye Museum of Miniatures.

ARTISAN: **HOOKER, GLENDA Y.**

BUSINESS NAME: Little Things Mean A Lot

IDENTIFICATION MARKS:

G.Y.H. with year

CATEGORY:

Dolls: costuming, hand sculpted, original

HONORS:

Letter from Colin Powell, Chairman of the Joint Chief of Staff, USA; Original Doll Artist Council of America; 3rd Place, Los Angeles County Fair, Miniature Competition

RECOGNITION:

Nutshell News, Sept. 1981, pg. 46; Vol. 12, No. 8, Aug. 1982, pg. 25; Vol. 14, No. 8, Aug. 1984, pg. 39, 54; *Miniature Collector,* No. 32, Aug. 1982, pg. 25; No. 37, Jun. 1983, pg. 42; No. 41, Jan/Feb. 1984, pg. 28; No. 43, pg. 38, May/Jun. 1984; *Miniature Gazette*, Fall 1979, pg. 23; *Dolls,* Summer 1984, pg. 90; *Collection*, Jul/Sept. 1991, pg. 10; *Sage Artist & Artisans*, Vol. IV, pg. 10; *Contempory Doll*, Summer 1991, pg. 86; *Doll House World*, Issue No. 22, 1992, pg. 35; *Small Talk*, Christmas 1981, pg. 6

BIOGRAPHY:

Glenda Hooker is the second child of five, raised in the Bronx, NY, where she attended elementary and high school. Marrying and starting a family, shortly after graduating high school, she focused most of her time into raising her four children, Sharon, Tanya, Martin, and Aaron. She actually discovered her talent quite by accident.

In 1978, Glenda ventured into the world of miniatures. Her interest in miniatures was ignited when she assisted a family member with furnishing a dollhouse. Having no knowledge of furniture making, she began with miniature furniture kits, but quickly shifted to her own designs, because of the limited selection of furniture available in kit form. After completing that project, she went on to design and build a dollhouse, entered it into the Los Angeles County Fair, Miniature Competition, and won third prize. This naturally led her to try her hand at making miniature dolls. Glenda Hooker Dolls have now become a unique and respected art form in the ever growing world of miniature collectibles.

Glenda, who has had no formal art training, sculptures each of her dolls from a low firing clay. The dolls, which are one-inch scale, are one-of-a-kind lifelike mirror images of people we all seem to know. The bodies, which are built on wire armature, are flexible and poseable, adding to the realistic scenarios she is able to create. She specializes in sculpting miniature people of African decent but does not limit herself to that genre alone. Her exhibits are always multi-racial and multi-cultural. Because of her passion for realism, an eye for detail, each piece seems to take on a life and personality of its own. Her work has been on display at shows across the United States and in Europe. She has been featured in all of the national miniature publications, doll magazines in the United States, Doll Collector Magazine in the United Kingdom, and countless local newspapers across the country. A large collection of her work was purchased by The Carole & Barry Kaye Museum of Miniatures, California. She has done likenesses of many famous people, including, Sammy Davis, Jr., Dionne Warwick and General Colin Powell, who sent her a letter praising her work.

In 1975, Glenda relocated to Southern California where she is currently living with her youngest son. She now has grandchildren, Wade, Deva, and Falon, whose frequent visits keep her busy. In spite of the demands of being a single parent, an active grandparent, and producing each doll one at a time, she still manages to do several shows a year. Her work can be seen at miniature shows throughout the United States and the United Kingdom. Glenda is a member of NAME, IGMA, and ODACA.

ARTISAN: **HOOKER, JUNE**

BUSINESS NAME: June's Things

IDENTIFICATION MARKS:

Some unmarked, 1980 to 1991

1980 to 1991

1981 to present

CATEGORY:

Dolls

HONORS:

Certificate of Merit from Doll Castle News, May 19, 1989

RECOGNITION:

Doll Castle News, May/Jun. 1989; Sept/Oct. 1993; *Dolls In Miniature*, Winter 1992

ARTISAN: **HOOT, MARY**

BUSINESS NAME: Mary Hoot Miniatures

IDENTIFICATION MARKS:

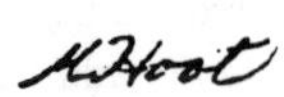

CATEGORY:

Animals: cats, dogs, domestic, original, painted, wildlife

RECOGNITION:

Nutshell News, Vol. 11, No. 10, Oct. 1981, pg. 58; Vol. 13, No. 9. Sept. 1983, pg. 64-66, "Mary Hoot's Really Loveable Babies," Jane Mitchell; *Toledo Blade,* "Something About A Siamese," Dec. 22, 1974; *Perrysburg Messinger*, Nov. 1975, "Nostalgia That's In;" *Petite Portraits,* Carol-Lynn Waugh; *Santa Dolls Historical to Contemporary,* Ann Baher, Hobby House, 1992, pg. 143, 146

AUTOBIOGRAPHY:

I received my art training at Bowling Green State University, Ohio, Toledo State University, and the Toledo Museum of Art. I have taken refresher courses through the years, most recently Arrowmont School, Gatlinburg, Tennessee.

I have had many years working with paint and fabric and finally arrived at the correct medium for the miniature soft sculpture animals which I have done from about 1978. I started with six different cats and dogs and now can do most in the animal kingdom. My listing includes over 70 domestic and wild animals, and I keep adding to the list upon request. The animals are original in design and skillfully painted in such a way that they are little fine works of art! I give the animals as much life as I can, working with this medium by turning heads and bodies, where possible. There was a big need for animals of any kind when I started doing miniatures. I first made large seven-inch to 12-inch animals, and upon request from a miniaturist friend, I transferred large to mini designs successfully.

In the beginning, my miniatures included dolls made of polymer resin. They included tiny bears, toddlers, and Santas, in a range of skin and hair colors. They were one-of-a-kind, and hand sculpted. It was difficult to do both animals and dolls with an overpowering demand for the dolls, so in 1984 they were temporarily put on hold while I concentrated on the animals. I have had such fun with the animals and strive to make them collectibles and real.

ARTISAN: **HOPWOOD, MURIEL**

BUSINESS NAME: Muriel Hopwood

IDENTIFICATION MARKS:

H.

CATEGORY:

Porcelain

ARTISAN: **HOSKINS, DOROTHY ALLISON**

BUSINESS NAME: We Two

IDENTIFICATION MARKS:

DAH with date Dorothy Allison Hoskins larger dolls

CATEGORY:

Dolls: original, porcelain

HONORS:

IGMA Fellow 1990; ODACA 1987; NIADA 1990; Exhibit: Rosalie Whyel Museum of Doll Art, Bellevue, Washington

RECOGNITION:

Nutshell News, Vol. 16, No. 7, Jul. 1986, pg. 68-72, "Portraiture in Miniature," Anne Day Smith; *Doll Reader*, Apr. 1990; *Contemporary Doll Magazine*, Mar/Apr. 1992; *Dolls – Collectors Magazine*, Aug. 1993; "Most Beautiful Dolls in the World"

AUTOBIOGRAPHY:

I came to Alaska in 1981. I was on my way to Texas, a slight detour to visit a friend in Fairbanks, Alaska took me seven days and 4,500 miles from Ohio. I drove the entire way by myself. This was the first time driving outside of my small hometown in Ohio. Snow was falling so I decided to stay in Alaska for the winter, and have been here ever since. My friend Pauline Chamness and I are still friends as well as business partners in We Two.

I got my first doll house as a kit in 1983. By 1984, we were in business and I had begun to sculpt my own dolls for the dollhouse we built. We also made roomboxes and I made one-of-a-kind dolls out of Super Sculpy. Recently I made my first porcelain miniature doll. I had been making larger, 19-inch to 21-inch, porcelain dolls for about three years. This was my first attempt at one-inch scale dolls, using the same method. "The Little Princess & the Pea" is on exhibit at the Springfield Museum in Oregon, "Dolls of the 21st Century."

I have been so fortunate to discover this talent for dolls late in my life. I can't imagine life better than this!

ARTISAN: **HOWARD, PHYLLIS**

BUSINESS NAME: Butt Hinge Pottery

IDENTIFICATION MARKS:

 Most pieces

 Larger pieces

CATEGORY:

Accessories: country, period; Pottery: thrown; Stoneware

HONORS:

Exhibit: Tiffany's, Atlanta, Georgia, 1986 Holiday Season

RECOGNITION:

Nutshell News, Jun. 1983, Cover, pg. 32, 37; Apr. 1984, pg. 56; Jun. 1984, pg. 41; Jul. 1984, Cover; Nov. 1985, pg. 73; Aug. 1986, pg. 70; Oct. 1986, Cover; *Miniatures Showcase*, Vol. 1, Fall 1986, pg. 31; Vol. 2, Spring 1987, pg. 49; Winter 1990, pg. 18, 57, 64, 72; *Miniature Gazette*, Vol. 15, No. 3, Spring 1987, pg. 27-30, "Miniatures at Tiffany's," Carol Friedrichsen; *The Miniature Magazine*, 1978, "Collector's Corner," Kathey Sevebeck; Winter 1979, "Feat of Clay," Marie Friedman; Summer 1980; "Small Talk," Faith Rogers; *American Period Interiors in Miniature*, Kate Doordan Klavan, Charles Scribner's Sons, New York, 1984, pg. 200, 213

BIOGRAPHY:

Phyllis Howard graduated from Goucher College with a degree in philosophy. She developed an interest in pottery and began producing hand thrown stoneware for gift shops and greenhouses as well as teaching. One of her students sparked her interest in the miniature world and she began to make miniature reproductions of traditional New England stoneware. After a few years of selling locally and at miniature shows, she confined her work to wholesale production for miniature shops. With the help of several sales representatives over the years, her work has been sold throughout most of the United States and in several foreign countries.

Phyllis Howard's specialized miniature throwing technique allows for fine detail and aesthetically well balanced pieces. Well fitted lids, finely turned spouts and unusual handles enhance many of the pieces. Because of the difficulty of reproducing certain techniques in miniature, a great number of the items are unique to Butt Hinge Pottery.

ARTISAN: **HOYT, HAZEL**

BUSINESS NAME: Hody's Individuals

IDENTIFICATION MARKS:

1957 to present

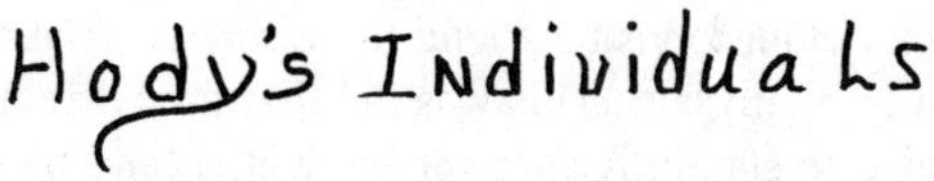

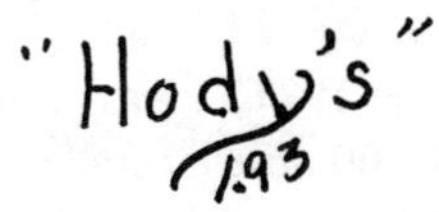

CATEGORY:

Accessories; Carriages; Dolls

HONORS:

15 Rosettes and four Best of Show at Doll Shows

RECOGNITION:

Nutshell News, Sept. 1985, pg. 82; *Needlework Times*, 1980

HOYT, HAZEL, continued

AUTOBIOGRAPHY:

From 1957, I worked as a psychiatric nurse, in rehabilitation, at Milwaukee Psychiatric Hospital. I became a Wisconsin Registry Art Therapist, W.A.T.R., in 1971, working with the mentally disturbed in hospitals using art as therapy for hospitalized patients. I am a member of the Milwaukee Miniature Club, Wee World Miniature Club, Hobby Club, Sunbonnet Bebes Guild of United Federation Doll Clubs, Inc., The China Doll Artisan Society of Wisconsin, and Micromaniacs Miniature Club.

ARTISAN: **HUBBLE, RON**

BUSINESS NAME: Hubble Miniatures

IDENTIFICATION MARKS:

CATEGORY:

Accessories; Sculptures; Structures

HONORS:

Exhibit: The Carole & Barry Kaye Museum of Miniatures, Los Angeles, California

RECOGNITION:

Nutshell News; Miniature Dealer

ARTISAN: **HUDSON, BILL**

BUSINESS NAME: Bill Hudson Miniatures
The Wm Hudson Carriage Co.

IDENTIFICATION MARKS:

Smaller items

The Hudson Carriage Co.

On packaging for kits

Items partially manufactured

CATEGORY:

Buildings; Tinware; Toys; Vehicles

HONORS:

IGMA Fellow; Exhibits: Toy & Miniature Museum of Kansas City; Georgia Pacific Logging Museum, Portland, Oregon; Oregon Historical Museum, Portland

RECOGNITION:

Nutshell News, Jan. 1985, pg. 60; *Eugene Register Guard,* (newspaper) Dec. 10, 1972; *Georgia Pacific Timber Line*, Portland, Oregon, Issue No. 24, Dec. 1925

HUDSON, BILL, continued

AUTOBIOGRAPHY:

I have been building miniatures most of my life, at least as long as I have been able to pick up a hammer and mash my thumb! Any old board and bent nail was a new toy for me. They may not have looked like much to anyone else, but I knew what they were. I learned to use a hammer and coping saw in the first grade when I built my first sailboat. My mother helped me build my first stick and paper model airplane, when I was about six or seven.

We moved to the California Desert during World War II. During that time I made dollhouses for my sisters from old boxes and all kinds of toys for myself from recycled apple and orange crates. We moved to Oregon a week after V. J. Day living about 10 miles from town and over a two mile walk to school and friends. It was there I started carving airplane models from pine wood using a WW II airplane identification book for pictures. I also built a scale logging truck using broom handle sections for wheels.

After serving four years in the Navy, during the Korean War, I took up model building again. I was fascinated by the variety of plastic models on the market. I feel fairly safe in saying I had built every plastic model on the market up until 1958. I had an agreement with a hobby shop to trade them a built model for a new kit. Pat and I were married in 1958 and model making took a back seat for a while. Our apartment was just a few blocks from the University of Oregon where Ivan Collins, a world renowned miniature carriage maker, had his shop and museum. I spent a lot of time hanging around looking in disbelief that anyone could work at such fine detail, and tried to emulate him but my scale was very loose and mostly eyeball work. After several years at the museum, Ivan finally showed me his secret measurements and methods of getting them. I learned how to take correct measurements and photographs. More importantly I learned to build each part as a separate miniature then assemble them as a whole working unit. In 1965, I built my first fine miniature and have been striving to keep up excellence ever since.

I started in one-inch scale about 1978, attending my first miniature show in Anaheim, California, in 1983. I sold everything I had and was taking orders by the middle of the first day. I am a Fellow in the Guild and have been teaching at the Guild School for several years, which is something I enjoy tremendously. I actually work in several scales and have done some large commercial models of whole saw mill complexes for both Georgia Pacific and Weyerhaeuser Timber Co.

Several of my ½-inch scale miniatures were included in a showing at the National Geographic Society Museum, in Washington, DC. I owe my thanks for this show to Bill Robertson, whom I have never met, for recommending me. My large scale models have been shown throughout Oregon. They were housed at the Georgia Pacific Logging Museum in Portland, Oregon until the museum was closed and moved to Atlanta. They were later shown at the Oregon Historical Museum in Portland, Oregon, with the late Ivan Collins collection for the opening of the Ivan Collins gallery. I have been trusted to repair two of Ivan's carriages that had become damaged over the years. I restored his covered wagon to get it ready for a world tour. I am presently working in one-inch scale miniatures and producing ¼-inch scale kits for model railroaders.

ARTISAN: **HUET, ROGER**

BUSINESS NAME: Roger Huet

IDENTIFICATION MARKS:

All book limited editions

Copy number 5/150 Total issue number

CATEGORY:

Books: miniature; Publications; Publisher; Writer

HONORS:

Distinguished Book Award 1990; Grande Medaille of the City of Paris 1981

RECOGNITION:

Book of Records of Quebec, Canada - *Who is Who in Miniature Books*

HUET, ROGER, continued

AUTOBIOGRAPHY:

I have been a publisher and bookbinder since 1978. I have done studies of Graphic Arts in Spain in 1958, and in France in 1980, and in Canada from 1983 to 1986.

ARTISAN: HUGHES, SCOTT

BUSINESS NAME: Scotts Lighting

IDENTIFICATION MARKS:

Some pieces unmarked

SCOTT'S LIGHTING

Logo on kettles

CATEGORY:

Chandeliers; Lighting; Lighting Devices

HONORS:

IGMA Artisan

RECOGNITION:

Nutshell News, Jul. 1988, pg. 38; Dec. 1988, pg. 82; Apr. 1989, pg. 69; Oct. 1990, pg. 66, 68, 70; Apr. 1991, pg. 54; Nov. 1991, pg. 73; *Miniatures Showcase*, Winter 1992, pg. 32, 40, 58; Jan. 1993, pg. 22, 31-33; *Los Angeles Times Magazine*, Nov. 15, 1992, pg. 41

AUTOBIOGRAPHY:

Before miniatures I was in the aircraft business. I designed planes and started my own aircraft company. Suddenly the aviation industry for ultra-light aircraft's went for a nose dive! One of my friends, an aviation engineer, showed me some miniature items his mother collected. I was so impressed with the quality of those miniatures, from that time on, it became my hobby and eventually my full-time occupation.

ARTISAN: HULSBUS, RUTH POLLOCK

BUSINESS NAME: Ruth Pollock Miniatures

IDENTIFICATION MARKS:

Burnt into wood at base

Burnt onto paint at base

CATEGORY:

Furniture: decorated, period

RECOGNITION:

Nutshell News; *Miniature Collector*, Spring 1992, pg. 22-23; *Costa Brava News*, Jan/Feb. 1990, pg. 30; *Dolls House World*, Issue No. 16, Nov/Dec. 1991, pg. 27, "Ruth Pollock's Painted Furniture;" Issue No. 21, Sept/Oct. 1992, pg. 34

HULSBUS, RUTH POLLOCK, continued

AUTOBIOGRAPHY:

I started making my miniatures in 1988, finding that I could put into full use the eight years of studies at the Art High School in Argentina, Escuela Nacional de Bellas Artes, that included drawing, painting & sculpture. I also did three years of ceramics, and I learned woodworking from my husband who made model ships as a hobby.

ARTISAN: HUNT, CHARLOTTE

BUSINESS NAME: Charlotte Hunt Miniatures

IDENTIFICATION MARKS:

1988 to present

Marks on painted furniture in gold or black ink

CATEGORY:

Chandeliers; Furniture: handpainted; Hardware

RECOGNITION:

Dove, Italy, Issue 1 1992; *The Complete Dolls' House Book*, Joan Nisbett, 1993; *The Dolls' House Source Book*, 1993

AUTOBIOGRAPHY:

I have always been fascinated by miniatures whether they are snuff boxes, painting or ornaments of silver and glass. When I discovered the world of dolls' houses and their contents I became totally hooked on this hobby. It all started one cold winter's day in my home town of Stockholm, Sweden. I was returning home to London, that afternoon and feeling rather melancholy at the thought of leaving my family. This was in the early years of the 1980's and I had no idea, at the time, that this fast growing hobby existed. I approached a shop window and there was a stove, a writing desk and arm chair, all in the now familiar Swedish Gustavian style. I stood there just dreaming! There was a card, near by, with a name and phone number. This was the start of a long and successful liaison with the famed Swedish miniaturist, Carin Backlund.

I became Carin's United Kingdom distributor. At that time there were very few painted pieces of furniture in the French Louis XV and XVI style. Most collectors were quite interested in the Victorian and Georgian periods. We were, after all in England. I was very gratified to receive my first orders. I became more interested in the period and the market that I had tentatively identified, and started to research more deeply into its history. I was helped by the glossy magazines of the time, which were responding to the increasing interest of the real world in Swedish Castles and Manor Houses, and whose articles featured their romantic neo-classical interiors. I was determined to create my own furniture.

By this time, I had become increasingly sure of the discerning collector's taste. I started to bring together an immensely talented team who could interpret what I wanted and who helped me in the many aspects of furniture making, which I could not manage myself. Now, having learned many more skills, through previous training in painting real world furniture with different finishes and learning miniature upholstery, we have become known as much for these attributes as any other.

I say, we, because without my talented team, my dreams standing outside in the cold in Stockholm, would never have materialized into this absorbing work.

ARTISAN: **HURST, NORMAN F. C.**

BUSINESS NAME: Castle Miniatures

IDENTIFICATION MARKS:

Month & Year printed under signature

CATEGORY:
Furniture; Tunbridgeware

RECOGNITION:
Dolls House and Miniature Scene, Issue No. 1, 1992, pg. 67

AUTOBIOGRAPHY:
My interest in modeling started many years ago at school when I used to make models of aircraft using Sky Bird kits which were solid wood you have to carve. I learned draftsmanship at school and often designed and made my own models. During my service in the army, both in bomb disposal and the Royal Marine Commandos, I was an NCO instructor and often used models and figures, which I made, to help in my training methods. After many years of exhibiting model vehicles, etc. I was informed that I was now considered an Artisan model-maker and no longer eligible to enter open competitions but could still exhibit. When, through ill health and other problems, probably related to my army service, I could no longer do a full-time job. I decided to take my love of modeling and toy making and turn it into a business which I have been doing since 1989, with gradual success.

ARTISAN: **HYDE, JOSEPHINE A.**

BUSINESS NAME: Min-i-kin

IDENTIFICATION MARKS:

J.A.H. '93

CATEGORY:
Animals

I

ARTISAN: **IACONO, ANTHONY W.**

BUSINESS NAME: Sir Thomas Thumb

IDENTIFICATION MARKS:

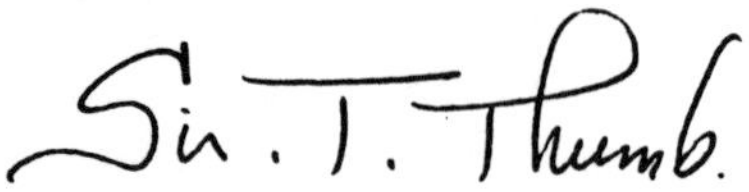

CATEGORY:

Accessories: kitchen; Furniture: country, kitchen; Garden: supplies; Sports Equipment; Tools: garden, woodworker

RECOGNITION:

Nutshell News, Vol. 17, No. 1, Jan. 1987, pg. 54, "A Slice of History;" *Miniatures Showcase*, Vol. 2, No. 2, Spring 1987, pg. 14, 19, 40, 43; Vol. 3, No. 1, Winter 1988, Pg. 40-41, 46; Vol. 4, No. 4, Fall 1989, pg. 28-29, 40, 45; Vol. 4, No. 2, Summer 1989, pg. 27, 30; Vol. 5, No. 2, Spring 1990, pg. 10, 42, 47, 49, 56, 62, 64, 66-67; Vol. 5, No. 3, Summer 1990, pg. 36; Vol. 5, No. 4, Fall 1990, pg. 20, 43; Vol. 5, No. 1, Winter 1990, pg. 51, 57; Vol. 6, No. 3, Summer 1991, pg. 23, 29, 47, 62; Vol. 6, No. 4, Fall 1991, pg. 22-23, 29; Vol. 6, No. 1, Winter 1991, pg. 32-33, 59; *Country Living*, Mar. 1992, pg. 102-105; *Miniature Gazette*, Vol. 6, No. 2, Winter 1977, pg. 54-56, "Sir Thomas Thumb"

BIOGRAPHY:

Anthony W. Iacono graduated from the City University of New York, majoring in Studio Fine Arts. In 1976, he joined his brother, Thomas, to start Sir Thomas Thumb, a wholesale business, and relocated to Lancaster County, Pennsylvania. Presently they are still partners in their business.

A number of custom pieces were created for the following customers:

Enchanted Dollhouse of Manchester, CT — Garden hoe for a farm girl doll, 1991
Sauder Farm & Craft Village of Archbold, OH — Crosscut saw for a carpenter doll, 1991
Smith & Hawkins of Mill Valley, CA — Jewelry pin, garden shovel, 1992

ARTISAN: **IACONO, THOMAS J.**

BUSINESS NAME: Sir Thomas Thumb

IDENTIFICATION MARKS:

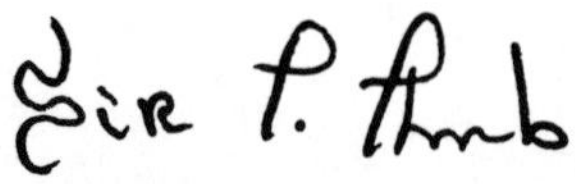

CATEGORY:

Accessories: kitchen; Furniture: country, kitchen; Garden: supplies; Sports Equipment; Tools: garden, woodworker

RECOGNITION:

Nutshell News, Vol. 17, No. 1, Jan. 1987, pg. 54, "A Slice of History;" *Miniatures Showcase*, Vol. 2, No. 2, Spring 1987, pg. 14, 19, 40, 43; Vol. 3, No. 1, Winter 1988, Pg. 40-41, 46; Vol. 4, No. 4, Fall 1989, pg. 28-29, 40, 45; Vol. 4, No. 2, Summer 1989, pg. 27, 30; Vol. 5, No. 2, Spring 1990, pg. 10, 42, 47, 49, 56, 62, 64, 66-67; Vol. 5, No. 3, Summer 1990, pg. 36; Vol. 5, No. 4, Fall 1990, pg. 20, 43; Vol. 5, No. 1, Winter 1990, pg. 51, 57; Vol. 6, No. 3, Summer 1991, pg. 23, 29, 47, 62; Vol. 6, No. 4, Fall 1991, pg. 22-23, 29; Vol. 6, No. 1, Winter 1991, pg. 32-33, 59; *Country Living*, Mar. 1992, pg. 102-105; *Miniature Gazette*, Vol. 6, No. 2, Winter 1977, pg. 54-56, "Sir Thomas Thumb"

IACONO, THOMAS J., continued

BIOGRAPHY:

Thomas J. Iacono graduated from Millersville State College, Millersville, Pennsylvania with a teaching degree in Industrial Arts in 1974. He built custom dollhouses from 1974 to 1976, both to order and on speculation. In 1976, he started a wholesale business with a line of miniature stone and brick fireplaces, and operated a full-time miniature shop in Lancaster, PA until 1981. During this period he built many custom and standard dollhouses as well as roomboxes and store front displays. In 1978, a line of rifles and fishing rods were created to accompany the wholesale fireplaces. The retail shop was closed in 1981 so Mr. Iacono could concentrate on the wholesale business, which was expanded creating more wholesale items, between 1981 to present.

A number of custom pieces were created for the following customers:

Enchanted Dollhouse of Manchester, CT — Garden hoe for a farm girl doll, 1991
Sauder Farm & Craft Village of Archbold, OH — Crosscut saw for a carpenter doll, 1991
Smith & Hawkins of Mill Valley, CA — Jewelry pin, garden shovel, 1992

ARTISAN: IDUCOVICH, LUCY

BUSINESS NAME: Lucy Iducovich
Rugs, Etc.

IDENTIFICATION MARKS:

1992 to present

CATEGORY:

Accessories: needlework; Kits: needlework; Needlepoint; Needlework; Rugs

HONORS:

IGMA Artisan

RECOGNITION:

Nutshell News, Dec. 1990, Cover; Jun. 1992, pg. 63; *Miniatures Showcase*, Fall 1988, pg. 28; Summer 1989, pg. 34, 40, 42; Summer 1990, Cover; Spring 1991, pg. 26; Fall 1991, pg. 39; Winter 1992, Cover, pg. 19, 25, 36, 39, 40; Nov. 1992, pg. 36; Jan. 1993, pg. 19, 38-39

BIOGRAPHY:

The main focus for Lucy Iducovich from about 1981 in the field of miniatures has been the development of petitpoint rugs, pillows, chair seats and accessories. These are offered in both kit and finished form, along with other finished needlework items.

ARTISAN: INGALL, CAROLA

BUSINESS NAME: Carola Ingall

IDENTIFICATION MARKS:

Some pieces unmarked

CATEGORY:

Accessories; Ornaments: mantle

INGALL, CAROLA, continued

BIOGRAPHY:

Carola, living in Hampshire, England, has been working with miniatures since 1972. She specializes in mantle ornaments. Originally, these were all cottages, castles and other miniature buildings, but recently she has expanded her range to include animals such as pigs, sheep, cats and dogs. Other figures will be brought in as time goes on. Most items made so far are of Victorian inspiration, including Staffordshire figures, but Carola will shortly be producing miniatures which portray ornaments from Georgian times. Most are miniatures of genuine antiques, whose original size of course varies greatly, but some are to her own design.

Each piece is modeled uniquely, exact copies are then made, and hand-painted individually. Most often, the original modeling material used is Fimo, as Carola is very experienced in its use, having held workshops, demonstrations and tutorials working with Fimo. She has also written a book on the subject. Carola's father is a US citizen living in California, she visits him whenever she can.

ARTISAN: **IRVIN, AUDREY**

BUSINESS NAME: Edwards House

IDENTIFICATION MARKS:

Edwards House

Rubber stamp impression

CATEGORY:

Rugs: braided

AUTOBIOGRAPHY:

A lifetime love of miniatures and longtime hobby, braided rug making converged in 1987 with miniature braided rugs. A few shows, a few orders and I was hooked. It didn't occur to me to sign them until 1990. Improvising with bondex and a rubber stamp, I made tiny iron-on labels. The name Edwards House was inspired by a Victorian dollhouse my husband gave me for a birthday. I must confess the dollhouse is still under construction! It seems there's always a flock of little rugs demanding completion.

ARTISAN: **ISABELLE, RENEE**

BUSINESS NAME: Renee Isabelle

IDENTIFICATION MARKS:

RENEE ISABELLE

CATEGORY:

Furniture: handpainted

ARTISAN: **ISON, JIM**

BUSINESS NAME: Jim Ison Miniatures

IDENTIFICATION MARKS:

J.I. - '92 1976 to present

#7/25 Limited Edition, piece number and edition number

ISON, JIM, continued

CATEGORY:

Accessories; Furniture; Roomboxes

HONORS:

IGMA Fellow; Exhibit: Toy & Miniature Museum of Kansas City

RECOGNITION:

Nutshell News, Vol. 12, No. 9, Sept. 1982, pg. 63; Vol. 12, No. 10, Oct. 1982, pg. 65; Vol. 13, No. 1, Jan. 1983, pg. 28; Vol. 13, No. 6, Jun. 1983, pg. 35; Vol. 14, No. 9, Sept. 1984, pg. 73, Show Scene; Vol. 21, No. 11, Nov. 1991, pg. 54-57; *Nutshell News Miniatures Calendar*, 1992; *Miniature Collector*, No. 6, Mar. 1978, pg. 8; No. 10, Dec. 1978, pg. 38, Show Stoppers; No. 28, Dec. 1981, pg. 14-16; No. 44, Jul/Aug. 1984, pg. 53, Show Stoppers; *Miniature Gazette*, Vol. 7, No. 3, Spring 1979, pg. 9

BIOGRAPHY:

Jim Ison's college major was in architecture. He worked in residential design, trade show exhibits and store planning. He has constructed models of automobiles, ships, railroads and airplanes for over 50 years. Jim has been a full-time miniature artisan since 1982 and has taught classes for the Guild School, Castine, Maine, NAME and also for area clubs.

J

ARTISAN: **JACKMAN, CAROL & JEFF**
JAGO, PAUL

BUSINESS NAME: Recollect Studios

IDENTIFICATION MARKS:
Glass & Metal unmarked   Painters mark in Red; Makers marks Inscribed

CATEGORY:
Animals; Bears: jointed, soft; Dolls: babies, original, porcelain; Glassware; Kitchenware; Knitting: patterns; Kits: doll; Molds; Ornaments: mantel; Porcelain

RECOGNITION:
Nutshell News; Making Miniatures, Venus Dodge, David & Charles Press, England, 1989; *Making & Dressing Doll's House Dolls in 1/12 Scale,* Sue Atkinson, David & Charles Press, England, 1992

AUTOBIOGRAPHY:
I have always loved miniatures. I can remember at the age of four looking at a friend's very old dollhouse and longing to take out all the furniture, but all she would let me do was watch her as she briefly switched on the lights! In 1963, when my daughter was born, I was determined to get her a really interesting old dollhouse. I put a wanted advertisement in the local paper and kept on getting replies. In the end I had bought six houses, as each time I went to see one it was better than the previous one. Fortunately, I had a shop selling antique and collector's items and sold off the other five which started my business of selling miniatures, made at the time by other crafts people. Jeff, my husband, and I traded under the name of Minutiques and after a mention in *Nutshell News*, in 1970, we were inundated with orders and inquiries. Over the next few years I became more interested in making miniatures, particularly in porcelain and recently in wax. Porcelain wares and dollhouse dolls in porcelain and wax are now my main areas, together with creating miniature soft teddy bears.

Paul Jago is Carol's son-in-law, in 1983 he came to work in the family business and has been trained by Carol in all aspects so that he can carry on the family business. Paul is a talented sculptor and mold maker and has sculpted a series of three bears in sizes ranging from one-inch to 2½-inch as well as a golliwogg, dog and rabbit for the nursery. His next projects are a range of dollhouse dolls. Recollect Studios sell finished miniatures as well as their own miniature molds. They also hold teaching courses in miniature making each year which are taught by Carol and Paul.

ARTISAN: **JACKSON, JEAN**

BUSINESS NAME: Dolly Daydreams

IDENTIFICATION MARKS:

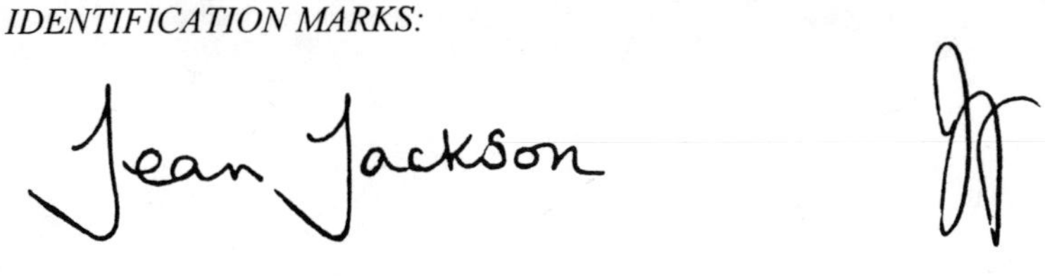

CATEGORY:
Dolls

ARTISAN: **JARBOE, PATSY JO HOCKADAY**

BUSINESS NAME: Memories in Miniature

IDENTIFICATION MARKS:

1986 to present

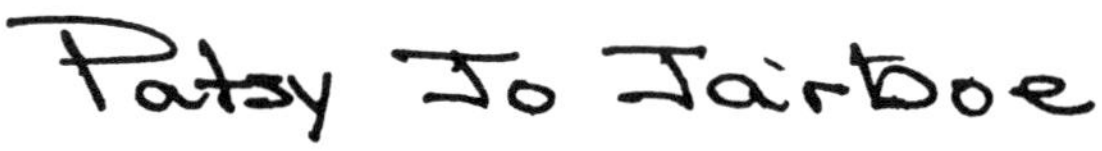

Smaller pieces

CATEGORY:

Accessories

HONORS:

Bernice Stevens Miniaturist of the Year

RECOGNITION:

Nutshell News, Vol. 17, No. 1, Jan. 1987, pg. 75; Vol. 17, No. 6, Jun. 1987, pg. 63; Vol. 17, No. 10, Oct. 1987, pg. 77; Vol. 18, No. 7, Jul. 1988, pg. 39; *Miniature Gazette*, Vol. 16, No. 2, Winter 1987, pg. 54; Vol. 18, No 3, Spring 1990, pg. 49

AUTOBIOGRAPHY:

My interest in miniatures stems from an early age, as I had my first dollhouse at age four. I became involved again in 1978 after a hiatus of many years. I am both a collector and craftsman. I have no formal education or training in anything pertaining to art, architecture, etc. I have an MS degree in Geology and have taught at both the secondary and college levels and attended Law school. I did attend the IGMA school in Castine, Maine, one summer. Perhaps my technical training did give me an appreciation of scale.

ARTISAN: **JENKINS, BARBARA**

BUSINESS NAME: Barbara Jenkins

IDENTIFICATION MARKS:

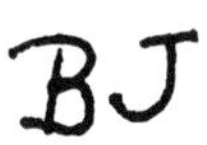

with year

Back of breast plate

CATEGORY:

Dolls: original, porcelain

HONORS:

Original Doll Artist Council of America

RECOGNITION:

Nutshell News, Nov. 1982, pg. 59-60; *National Doll World,* Sept/Oct. 1984, pg. 56-59

AUTOBIOGRAPHY:

I have been making original miniature porcelain dolls since about 1977. My background includes a BA in English Literature and History and a Masters Degree in Early Childhood Education and Teaching Credential. I have always been involved in needlework and crafts and when I discovered the world of Miniatures, I found a niche that encompassed all my interests. I am a member of ODACA and participate in miniature shows throughout the country.

ARTISAN: **JENSEN, BETSY & CLARK**

BUSINESS NAME: Bcj Miniatures

IDENTIFICATION MARKS:

Bcj Betsy's mark BCJ Clark's mark

CATEGORY:

Accessories; Furniture; Kits; Tools

RECOGNITION:

Nutshell News, Oct. 1986, pg. 77; Apr. 1987, pg. 32; Aug. 1987, pg. 69; Aug. 1991, pg. 21; Jan. 1992, pg. 67; *Miniature Gazette,* Summer 1990, pg. 53-54; *Miniatures Showcase,* Summer 1987, pg. 17, 22, 32; *The Scale Cabinetmaker,* Winter 1989, pg. 46; Fall 1990, pg. 23

AUTOBIOGRAPHY:

We were always "Artsy-Craftsy" people. Clark made reproductions of full-size antique tavern signs and Betsy did various other crafts. In 1975, we started making miniatures for printer's drawers which, very unintentionally, were one-inch scale, such as canister sets, spoon racks and coffee grinders, etc. From this evolved other accessories and then furniture pieces which we continue to make today.

ARTISAN: **JENSON, DEAN**

BUSINESS NAME: Rainbow Design by Dean Jenson

IDENTIFICATION MARKS:

Dean Jenson DJ

CATEGORY:

Accessories: kitchen, sewing; Display Cases; Fixtures: store; Shelves; Toys

ARTISAN: **JENVEY, DENNIS**

IDENTIFICATION MARKS:

Dennis Jenvey signature in script, gold pen, with year DJ etched

CATEGORY:

Furniture

RECOGNITION:

Nutshell News, Vol. 13, No. 7, Jul. 1983, pg. 48, Show Scene; *Miniature Collector*, No. 40, Dec. 1983, pg. 36-39, "Jenvey of Nottingham," Ann Bahar

ARTISAN: **JOHNSON, BOBBIE**

BUSINESS NAME: Dollhouse Interiors by B.J.

IDENTIFICATION MARKS:

Some unmarked

B. Johnson B.J.

Some pieces dated and signed

CATEGORY:

Accessories; Animals; Clothing; Costuming; Dolls: porcelain; Furniture; Indian

HONORS:

IGMA Artisan 1994; Twelve 1st. Place Ribbons, costuming mini-dolls; Miniaturist of the Year Award, Bernice Stevens 1993

RECOGNITION:

Nutshell News, Jun. 1991, pg. 65

AUTOBIOGRAPHY:

After my second child was born, it was necessary for me to stay home with him due to an illness. I was always trying to think of ways to generate an income from our home.

My sister-in-law got her first dollhouse as a Christmas present in 1988. Always wanting one myself, I decided to make things for hers. I made a toy doll for her bed and some little pillows and a basket of sticks to sit by her fireplace. After which a few friends and family said I should make more miniatures. That was when I went to my first dollhouse store. Wow, what a shock! The interest was there, but not my craftsmanship. Ideas came easy but it took several years before my work became saleable. With much patience and encouragement from family and friends, and a strong desire to create little things, I continued to improve. I had small showings of my work in my home.

I took my creations to Norm's Dollhouse, in Denver, and he bought many of them, which inspired me to push even harder for perfection. In this short time I have done local shows and sell to many dealers nationally. It is wonderful to do what I love from home and still be with my children. My passion for miniatures grows daily.

ARTISAN: **JOHNSON, DONNA & JIM**

BUSINESS NAME: Donna & Jim Johnson

IDENTIFICATION MARKS:

D-JJ

CATEGORY:

Beds; Dolls; Furniture; Game Table: poker, pool; Pianos

RECOGNITION:

Nutshell News, May 1983, pg. 55; Oct. 1985, pg. 76; Sept. 1986, pg. 77, 79-80; Dec. 1986, pg. 64; Jun. 1987, pg. 59; Jul. 1987, pg. 62; Aug. 1987, pg. 70; Jun. 1988, pg. 59; Jul. 1988, pg. 60; Sept. 1990, pg. 65; Apr. 1991, pg. 56; Jul. 1991, pg. 61; Feb. 1993, pg. 71

AUTOBIOGRAPHY:

Our introduction to miniatures came about in a fairly common way. We bought a dollhouse for our daughter and proceeded to completely take it over! She moved on to boys, swimming, college and a career but we are still working on "her" dollhouse! It is an 18 room Colonial that fills a 4 foot by 8 foot sheet of plywood and will probably never be finished. We started making our own furniture after taking her to our first miniature show where she wanted to buy a chess table. The table was $75.00 and she only had $35.00, so her father said he would make her one. He proceeded to spend $500.00 on tools and we've been using them ever since! We have taken classes with some outstanding teachers and love to share what we've learned both from them and on our own, by giving workshops ourselves.

ARTISAN: JOHNSON, JENIFER K.

BUSINESS NAME: The Tree Trunk Studio

IDENTIFICATION MARKS:

1984 to present

JKJ Name initials
TTS Business initials
1992 Year

JKJ\TTS '92 On small items

Business logo
On printed matter

CATEGORY:

Furniture: Colonial, custom, period, reproductions, Shaker

RECOGNITION:

Nutshell News, Jun. 1987, pg. 60; Dec. 1987, pg. 69; *Miniatures Showcase,* Summer 1990, pg. 24, 33-34; Winter 1990, pg. 49, 60; *The Shaker Messenger,* Vol. 9 No. 2, pg. 13

AUTOBIOGRAPHY:

I have been working as a professional miniaturist since 1984. I began with Shaker reproductions because I have always admired the dignified simplicity of their designs. Although I have branched out into other furniture periods, notably American Colonial, Shaker continues to be my area of specialty. In all my work, I strive to achieve precise scale and historical authenticity.

I have exhibited at many shows which feature the work of handcraft artisans, but now concentrate on museum shops and private collectors and enjoy researching special orders for hard-to-find items.

I have a degree in management, which is useful in the administrative aspect of The Tree Trunk Studio; my woodworking and research skills are a result of extensive self-study and interaction with museums and fellow artisans in miniatures and full-scale woodworking. I am an active member of the Western Shaker Study Group and have conducted workshops for miniatures and woodworking groups. In addition to crafting miniature reproductions, I also provide editorial services to publishers of books on miniatures and other crafts.

My work continues to increase in challenge and diversity and I look forward to many years of miniatures to come.

ARTISAN: JONAS, PENNI JO ELOUISE

BUSINESS NAME: Penni Jo's Originals
United Design Corporation (staff sculptor/designer)

IDENTIFICATION MARKS:

1982 to present

Jo

Handwritten on bottom in black ink or sculpted into piece

Not sculpted into piece

Penni jo Jonas Penni jo Penni jo

JONAS, PENNI JO ELOUISE, continued

CATEGORY:

Accessories; Bears: teddy; Christmas; Designer; Dolls; Figurines; Holiday Items; Sculptor

HONORS:

Bell Designs nominated by Collector Editions for Award of Excellence; PenniBears™ nominated for Miniature of the Year, NALED

RECOGNITION:

Nutshell News; Miniature Collector; Miniature Gazette; Collector Editions, Dec. 1990, pg. 12, 37, 57; *Collectors Mart,* Sept/Oct. 1990, pg. 10; Oct. 1992, pg. 12-13, "Fun and Names;" Feb. 1993, pg. 25; *Giftware News,* Mar. 1992, pg. 83-84; *Doll Reader,* Dec. 1991; Jan. 1992, pg. 232; *Collectors Mart Magazine*, Apr. 1992, pg. 34, Previews & Reviews, Marjorie M. Rosenberg; *Plate World*, Jan/Feb. 1992, pg. 53-56, "A Matter of Inches," Tina Panoplos; *Gifts International*, Oct. 1990, pg. 14; *Gifts & Decorative Accessories,* Nov. 1990, pg. 140; *International Collectible Showcase,* Vol. 91; *Daily Oklahoman*, Oct. 4, 1983, pg. 2S, "Her Tiny Art Work Booms," Katie Fellows; *Norman Transcript,* Norman, Oklahoma, newspaper Feb. 4, 1990; *Collectibles Market Guide & Price Index*, Vol. 7, pg. 263; Vol. 8, pg. 263; Vol. 9

BIOGRAPHY:

"I have to pinch myself every once in a while to make sure I am not just dreaming!" says Penni Jo Jonas.

Finding herself surrounded by enthusiastic, admiring fans may seem like a dream to Penni Jo, a talented miniature artist. Just a few short years ago, Penni Jo was a homemaker with no idea she would have such a successful artistic career. But the phenomenon of PenniBears™, a limited edition series of tiny teddies created by Penni Jo in 1983, has propelled her into the national spotlight among collectible figurine artists.

Penni Jo's first creations were made in her kitchen, using colored clays she mixed in her food processor and baked in her toaster oven. A miniature teddy bear she made for her daughter's dollhouse became the inspiration for a series of similar bears. The little bears were soon sculpted with clothes and accessories and eventually became known as PenniBears. Her local following of collectors blossomed into a national following and in 1989 Penni Jo joined the staff of United Design, where all the intricate detail of PenniBears are now reproduced by talented production artists and craftsmen.

In addition to PenniBears, Penni Jo designs and sculpts several other collectible miniature figurine editions, including miniature angels, figurines, ornaments bells and Itty Bitty Critters™.

Delightfully open and candid about her transition from homemaker to nationally renowned artist, Penni Jo loves to meet collectors and fans as much as they love her and the exquisitely detailed miniatures she sculpts.

ARTISAN: JONES, ALIOUISE H.

IDENTIFICATION MARKS:

1975 to present

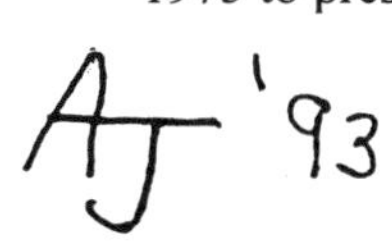

CATEGORY:

Needlework

AUTOBIOGRAPHY:

My miniature and needlework career started as a very little girl, when I had to stand to use the sewing machine because I couldn't reach the pedal. I had a dollhouse, which I decorated and redecorated, but in all the family moves it just disappeared.

In 1967, about the time of the last of our five children started to school, I began thinking about a hobby. After trying several things; collecting thimbles, spoons, etc. I saw an advertisement somewhere for *Nutshell News*, Vol. 4, No. 1 and I was hooked. If these people could make and do such lovely miniatures, so could I!

JONES, ALIOUISE H., continued

After reading, for about three years, about miniaturist Back to College Weekend at Randolph Macon College in Ashland, Virginia, about 50 miles from here, I finally got up my nerve and sent in my reservations. The very first person I met and who turned out to be my suite mate, was Carol Schobert from Des Plains, Illinois, who has become my very best friend.

My husband started a dollhouse for me soon after. Now I have seven one-inch scale dollhouses, roomboxes, and breakaway boxes, including ½-inch scale, ¼-inch scale and 1/144-inch scale houses and boxes.

Because I love needlework, I thought I would try something in miniature. My first project was a needlework rug and I haven't stopped since then. I have designed six cross stitch bedspreads that look very much like the Bates "George Washington" spreads in full-size. My friend Carol, who is a dealer at several shows in the Midwest, sold my kits and patterns for several years. Now I sell only by word of mouth.

My first design was "Carter's Grove" designed especially for the miniature Carter's Grove then owned by Jackie Andrews in Ashland, Virginia, now exhibited at The Carole & Barry Kaye Museum of Miniatures, Los Angeles, California. Jackie had more than six of my spreads in her houses.

Because of progressively worsening arthritis and other ailments, I only do work for friends. My friends say, "How do you do such miniature needlework or build all those Mini-things with arthritis?" I say "Thank God for tweezers and the will to keep my fingers moving."

Thank God for miniatures, my therapy, and for Virginia Miniaturist Back to College Weekends, which have given me confidence, many good friends and so much joy.

ARTISAN: JONES, HORACE B.

BUSINESS NAME: Horace B. Jones

IDENTIFICATION MARKS:

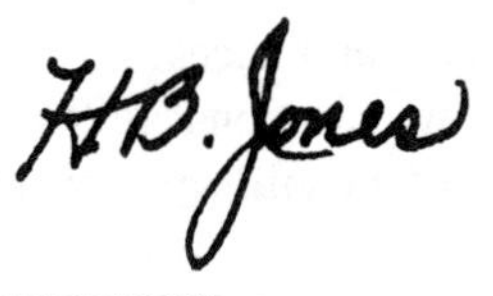

Date and Year

CATEGORY:

Bathrooms: components, fixtures; Kitchen: appliances, cabinets, components

HONORS:

IGMA Artisan

RECOGNITION:

Miniatures Showcase, Winter 1989, pg. 31

AUTOBIOGRAPHY:

I have a background in the construction trades as a carpenter-cabinet maker, draftsman and director for 40 plus years prior to my retirement I have been in miniatures since approximately 1982 making my standard design contemporary kitchens and bath fixtures in both one-inch and ½-inch scales, including custom work.

ARTISAN: JOUVENEL, MONIQUE

BUSINESS NAME: Monique Jouvenel

IDENTIFICATION MARKS:

JOUVENEL, MONIQUE, continued

CATEGORY:

Etching: acid; Glass: handpainted; Glassware; Porcelain: handpainted

HONORS:

IGMA Artisan 1989, Fellow 1992; Certified IPAT Artist 1992

RECOGNITION:

Nutshell News, Dec. 1990, pg. 33, 67, Show Scene; Feb. 1992, pg. 64, Show Scene; Mar. 1992, pg. 27, 71, Show Scene; Jun. 1992, pg. 65, Show Scene; *Dolls House World,* Issue No. 14, 1991, pg. 58-59; *Le Magazine de la Maison de Poupee,* No. 15, Winter 1990/91, pg. 14; No. 17, Summer 1991, pg. 6-7; No. 22, Autumn 1992, pg. 27; *Miniature Gazette,* Vol. 17, No. 4, Summer 1989, pg. 28-29

AUTOBIOGRAPHY:

I am largely self-taught since 1987. I learned the basics from Halfmoon Ceramics, Halfmoon Bay, British Columbia and therefore embarked on miniature work as a specialty. In 1988, in competition with full-size entries, I won 19 first prizes out of a possible 21 in Vancouver Island (West Coast) major show and repeated the performance in 1989. After joining IGMA in 1989, I became an Artisan in the same year and showed in the IGMA Show and in Paris in 1990. I contributed to the IGMA Showstopper display in both 1990 and 1992. I was elected to IGMA Fellowship status in 1992 and certified as IPAT Artist in the same year. Now I am specializing in European 18th and 19th Century porcelain museum pieces reproduced in one-inch scale from original drawings and production specifications. I also am a member of NAME, Club Miniature de France (CMF) and Porcelain Artists Society, Victoria, British Columbia, Canada.

ARTISAN: **JUNKE, SHEILA**

BUSINESS NAME: Memphis Miniatures

IDENTIFICATION MARKS:

CATEGORY:

Accessories; Bears; Linens

K

ARTISAN: **KAIGLER, CATHY**

BUSINESS NAME: Miniature Dreams

IDENTIFICATION MARKS:

CATEGORY:

Flowers and Plants; Landscaping

RECOGNITION:

Nutshell News; *Miniature Showcase*

ARTISAN: **KANZE, JOEN ELLEN & ROBERT**

BUSINESS NAME: Joen Ellen Kanze

IDENTIFICATION MARKS:

CATEGORY:

Flowers and Plants; Furniture; Leather Work; Luggage; Patios

RECOGNITION:

Nutshell News, Vol. 23, No. 1, Jan. 1993, pg. 44-48, "Divining Woman," Anne Day Smith; *Good Housekeeping* 1971; *New York Times; Miniature Gazette*

AUTOBIOGRAPHY:

I have been involved in miniatures since 1965 when my husband built my first dollhouse. In 1969, I started a mail order business which went on to 1978 when I dropped commercial advertising and decided to do shows only.

I put on the first all miniature show in 1971 with Caye Mac Laren, and later Caye started *Nutshell News* using the mailing list from my mail order business. After 23 in the business I've had so much fun and satisfaction, and met so many marvelous people.

ARTISAN: **KARNEY, VIRGINIA M.**

BUSINESS NAME: Miniature Gallery of Art

IDENTIFICATION MARKS:

V.M.Karney '86 — 1986 to 1990 Lower left front corner , scratched in paint over red acrylic.

V.M.Karney '90 — 1990 to 1992 Signed, dated, name of picture, on back

VK — 1992 Marked with logo and dated when space allows.

VKarney '92 — 1992 May also be used with any other work of art, signed on front with date, logo/signature

Paintings numbered

CATEGORY:

Art: fine; Painting

HONORS:

1st Place Blue Ribbon, Miniature Oil & Collectors Choice Ribbon, 17th National Art Show, La Luz, New Mexico "Bright Roses," Mini Spatula Painting, 1991; 1st Place and Honorable Mention, Blue Ribbon and Cash Award, Maddington Square Art Show, Riverside, California

AUTOBIOGRAPHY:

My educational background took place in Philadelphia, Pennsylvania at Catherine St. Free Art School, and Moore Institute of Design, and in Riverside, California at Riverside City College, and Arlington Art Guild. From 1944 until 1987, I worked in standard size scale oil, pen and ink, and watercolor. My works were commissioned as well as sold in shows in Riverside, California, as well as Eau Claire, Wisconsin. At the Maddington Square Art Show, I won 1st Place and Honorable Mention and have illustrated two books for Hazelden, Minnesota, and American Guidance Services, and "Conversations," a game which is a tool for psychologists to use in working with children and families designed by Rich Boardman of Eau Claire, Wisconsin.

Due to an injury to my right arm, I switched from standard size to miniature painting which was much easier to handle. From 1988 through 1992, I have worked in one-inch scale exclusively. I have shown and sold my work many times throughout the Upper Mid West, and at the Gallery La Luz in New Mexico. I did not work or sell miniatures during 1993. I needed a breather, for a year, and in 1994 continued my miniature work.

ARTISAN: **KAROBLIS, EVE**

BUSINESS NAME: Spotlight Miniatures

IDENTIFICATION MARKS:

Eve year — EVE date — Eve Spotlight Miniatures date

CATEGORY:

Furniture: aged, garden; Landscaping

HONORS:

IGMA Artisan, Exhibit: City of Long Beach, City Hall, Mayor's Office

KAROBLIS, EVE, continued

RECOGNITION:

Nutshell News, Vol. 20, No. 12, Dec. 1990; Vol. 21, No. 6, Jun. 1991; Vol. 21, No. 7, Jul. 1991; Vol. 21, No. 8, Aug. 1991; Vol. 21, No. 12, Dec. 1991; *Home Miniaturist*; *Miniatures Showcase*, Winter 1991, pg. 20-23, "A Bit Unusual You Bet!", Geraldine Willems; Spring 1992, pg. 46-47; Vol. 8, No. 4, Jul. 1993; *Miniature Gazette*, Dec. 1981; *Gardens By Eve*, Guide to Landscaping in Miniature

BIOGRAPHY:

Eve began life as a miniaturist in the second grade in a California school. Each year the class made a 2-inch miniature adobe of a California Mission. Eve was assigned mud and straw brick making. In her late 20's, a Sunset Magazine design and plan was built by Eve for her children. Holding a BA in Early American Folk Art from Portland State, 1970, helped with color, scale, and interiors. By the late 1970's, after marriage to Ed Mabe, Eve and Ed began in earnest to develop settings and roomboxes geared to NAME Houseparty themes.

Their work as full-sized Hollywood set painters precludes a full sales tables as dealers at miniature shows, but private commission work has been completed for collectors, museums, and movies. In 1984, Eve continued her teaching career as well, adjusting to miniatures classes only. How-to articles are written for *Nutshell News*, only after extensive development through classes. Eve and Ed take advantage of their free lance schedule in Hollywood to plan classes and research trips throughout the US and Canada. Their IGMA Artisan status has helped them to teach from Castine, Maine to New Orleans, Western Canada, and across the United States Eve is a certified fund raiser for non-profit organizations, and a certified meeting planner, CSULB. This advanced education is put to use for miniatures only!

ARTISAN: KASZA, LORETTA

BUSINESS NAME: Loretta Kasza
Fond Memories

IDENTIFICATION MARKS:

Some pieces unmarked

CATEGORY:

Costuming; Dolls

HONORS:

IGMA Artisan

RECOGNITION:

Doll Crafter, May 1991, pg. 82-84; *Miniatures Catalog*, 15th Edition, Cover; *Miniatures Showcase*, Nov. 1992, Cover, pg. 15, 30, 38-39; *Dolls in Miniature*, Cover, Fall 1992

ARTISAN: KAY, PATRICIA JOYCE

BUSINESS NAME: Brentwood Decor Miniatures

IDENTIFICATION MARKS:

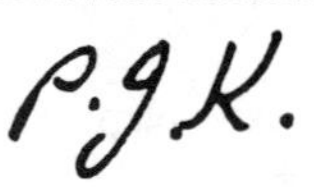

CATEGORY:

Furniture: handpainted, period; Toys

RECOGNITION:

Doll's House World; Poppenhuis Magazine; International Dolls House News

ARTISAN: **KEETON, BEVERLY**

IDENTIFICATION MARKS:

B. Keeton – date   Inside back seam of slips

CATEGORY:

Costuming; Dolls: period, porcelain

AUTOBIOGRAPHY:

My miniature background began in the spring of 1976, at which time Jack (Jackie) Andrews asked me to help her a few days a week in their miniature business. I had met Jack just a short time prior to this. Not only did a very special friendship develop, she also introduced me to the world of miniatures, and a whole new wonderful way of thinking. During the five years I worked for them, I learned many things about miniatures and the one-inch scale hobby.

Jack taught me how to make a lot of different things, one of which was how to take a porcelain doll kit and develop it into a dressed dollhouse doll. I expanded on this and made dolls to sell. All of these were one-inch scale, 18th century and Victorian era. They were sold at Little World in Williamsburg, Virginia, and Joe Andrews purchased and sold my dolls at his shows. I also had special orders I did for customers. I assembled the parts, dressed and styled the wigs from the kits that I bought wholesale, during the years from approximately 1981 to 1986.

ARTISAN: **KELLEY, KATHLEEN C.**

BUSINESS NAME: Kay's Bears

IDENTIFICATION MARKS:

KAY'S BEARS   Cloth label sewn on

CATEGORY:

Bears: teddy

HONORS:

IGMA Artisan

RECOGNITION:

Teddy Bear and Friends, Apr. 1992, pg. 93

AUTOBIOGRAPHY:

I began making and selling miniature fabric bears seven years ago, in 1986. I am originally from Massachusetts and have traveled extensively with my military husband before retiring to Florida. I have always been interested in miniatures and joined NAME in 1977.

ARTISAN: **KELLY, JEAN A.**

BUSINESS NAME: The House That JAK Built

IDENTIFICATION MARKS:

NUMBER jaKelly DATE

KELLY, JEAN A., continued

CATEGORY:

Decorating: exterior, interior; Roomboxes

HONORS:

IGMA Artisan, Fellow 1993

RECOGNITION:

Nutshell News, Dec. 1980; Feb. 1981; Jul. 1983; Aug. 1990; *Doll Castle News,* Mar. 1977; *McCall's Needlework,* Fall 1975; Fall 1977; Winter 1979; *McCall's Big Book of Dollhouse & Miniatures*, 1983; *Luck of the Irish*, Nutshell News Plan Service, Jean A. Kelly, Boynton, 1984; *Through the Looking Glass*, Boynton and Associates, Inc., Ann Ruble, 1984

ARTISAN: KELLY, KEVIN & THERESA

BUSINESS NAME: Kelly Studios

IDENTIFICATION MARKS:

1978 to 1980 + OKELLY

1980 to 1982 T. KELLY K. KELLY

1982 to 1991 © KELLY ©KEVIN + TERRY KELLY •|•<

1991 to present © KELLY STUDIOS •|•<

This mark not on every handcrafted piece

CATEGORY:

Animals; Dolls; Figurines; Resin Work; Vignettes: bell jar

BIOGRAPHY:

Kevin and Theresa Kelly began sculpting together shortly after their wedding in 1976. After discovering both Super Sculpy and miniatures in 1979 they began supplying the miniature market with one-of-a-kind wizards, unicorns and dragons.

By 1991, they could no longer keep up with demand for their one-of-a-kind pieces which had grown to include not only fantasy people and animals, but also period and contemporary pieces as well as portrait sculptures. In 1992, Kelly Studios began to cast their art work in a resin and glass formula of their own making. This medium allows limited reproductions of the finely detailed ½-inch scale and one-inch scale art pieces. All work is still hand done at the studio.

There art is sold worldwide. The Kelly Bears™, a line of about 50 miniature bears portraying all types of situations and professions was produced by several English manufactures between 1989 and 1992. These little bears have now come home to the studio and will be produced in the USA with some new pieces added.

The Kelly's live in a small mountain community in Northern California with their three children, Brieston, Ashley, and Taylor.

ARTISAN: KENDALL, DALE R.

BUSINESS NAME: Jeannetta Kendall Miniatures

IDENTIFICATION MARKS:

Unmarked, laser cut signature on sheet connected to piece

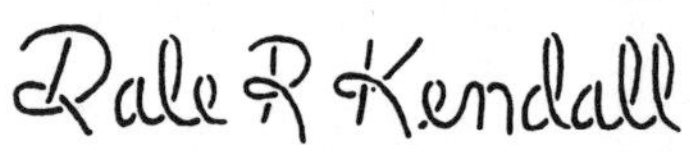

KENDALL, DALE R., continued

CATEGORY:

Accessories; Linens: laser cut, paper

AUTOBIOGRAPHY:

I was born and raised in Los Angeles, California. I was first exposed to miniatures in high school while working part-time in a miniature shop. After graduating high school, I decided I would like to open my own business. In 1983 in Torrance, California, my mother, Jeannetta Kendall, and I opened Petite Designs, a retail shop specializing in hand crafted miniatures. As our business grew, we became associated with some of the finest artisans in the industry and were fortunate enough to have Cece McGough, one of the most creative people I have had the privilege of knowing, working with us. In conjunction with the shop, we also did miniature shows. The success of Petite Designs was due to a strong partnership between myself and my mother and our relationship with many artisans.

In 1989, we sold Petite Designs to Susan Garfield, who moved the shop to West Los Angeles, and we continued to do miniature shows under a new name, Jeannetta Kendall Miniatures, based in Los Angeles.

Around 1990, after years of collecting and handcrafting miniatures, I decided to try my hand at designing miniatures. In 1991, I came out with my first sheet of doilies. Since then, I have designed place mats, napkins, runners, shelf edging and more doilies. All of my designs are laser cut from acid-free archival paper and available in one-inch scale; some of my designs are available in ½-inch scale. I am delighted whenever I learn that other artisans have incorporated my doilies in their work. I look forward to many years of designing, creating and collecting miniatures. I feel we are fortunate to have a common scale, which gives people around the world the opportunity to work together.

ARTISAN: **KENNARD, ANTHONY**

BUSINESS NAME: Anthony Kennard

IDENTIFICATION MARKS:

AK
1992

CATEGORY:

Furniture: period

AUTOBIOGRAPHY:

I started making miniature period furniture in 1983, the reason being a granddaughter who was given a dollhouse. Having finished my granddaughter's dollhouse I was completely hooked on the miniature hobby and have continued ever since. I am now 78, and wondering how much longer I will be able to continue. I show my work at a major fair in the West of England and also at the London Dollhouse Festival.

ARTISAN: **KENNEDY, BART**

BUSINESS NAME: E & BK Originals
The Kennedys Ellen & Bart

IDENTIFICATION MARKS:

BK Burned into wood

HANDMADE BY
BART KENNEDY No._______

© 1989 O. B. K.

KENNEDY, BART, continued

CATEGORY:

Musical Instruments; Phonographs; Pianos; Radios

HONORS:

Bernice Stevens Texas Miniaturist of the Year 1990

RECOGNITION:

Nutshell News, Jul. 1991, pg. 65; *Miniature Gazette,* Vol. 21, No. 2, Winter 1992, pg. 54; *El Paso Times,* Jan. 3, 1991; *Amarillo Daily News,* Jan. 11, 1991; *Dallas Times Herald,* Jan. 13, 1991; *Houston Chronicle,* Jan. 13, 1991; *Baldwin Piano and Organ,* company newsletter, Dec. 1990

AUTOBIOGRAPHY:

I graduated from the University of Texas, El Paso, with a BM in music education, with piano as my principle instrument. I taught choir, guitar, and general music until my school district de-emphasized the music, art, foreign language, and PE programs. The teachers in these classes were told if we were not re-certified by May of 1986, we would lose our jobs. My school district was very nice, they paid us for going back to college, and now I can also teach elementary school, reading, and computer literacy. I am currently teaching computer literacy at Indian Ridge Middle School

My avocation for building miniature pianos came about from visiting many miniature shops, with my wife Ellen, and being very impressed with the miniature musical instruments, except the pianos. I have been playing the piano since I was six years of age. I grew up playing on a Wurlitzer Spinet piano and was very excited every time I could play on a grand piano. When I graduated from the University of Texas in El Paso one of my first goals was to buy a grand piano. At the university every studio had Steinway Grands and compared to my piano at home, they were very hard to play. When I was in college we would present piano festivals. This would require going to different music stores where there were enough pianos on the floor so 20 or more people could play at one time. When we went to the store where they had Baldwin pianos, these brand new pianos had keys that were as easy to push down as mine at home. At the university, in my senior year, we received a new Steinway Concert Grand. The keys were so hard to push down, that your arms would burn. They sent a factory technician, but the piano was still a bear to play. My former professor is now a Baldwin Artist and his reasoning for using a Baldwin Grand is, they are more consistent from piano to piano. Naturally, when I purchased a new piano it was a Baldwin Grand. I have a 6 foot 3 inch model L with a dark mahogany finish.

My first miniature piano is a copy of my piano at home. I measured every part of the piano, drew plans, and started construction. My miniature pianos are *true to scale* miniature copies of real Baldwin Grands. For the 5 foot 2 inch, 6 foot 3 inch, and 7 foot pianos I used Baldwin literature, with those specifications for the measurements of these three pianos. For the concert grand I went to the local Baldwin dealer. It took me three days going after school everyday to complete the measurements. The local dealer, Mr. Schorder, thought my miniature was good enough that the Baldwin Piano and Organ Company in Ohio, might allow me to use their logo. I have been working with Mr. John Simpkinson, advertising manager of that company, who really likes the miniatures, and granted me permission to use their logo. I was asked by the company to make one for them to display at the 1990 piano and organ convention in Anaheim, California. It was shipped on a big semi along with the real pianos. I was told by the local district sales manager that Mr. Simpkinson carried the miniature in his hand for three days showing it to everyone. It is now on display at the main Baldwin offices. Mr. Simpkinson said Baldwin would like to present their *longtime* artists with a miniature piano for supporting the company, and allowing Baldwin to use their name. The names mentioned were Leonard Bernstein and Liberace. Unfortunately both of these artists are now gone, we waited too long!

I use bass wood for the white and black lacquer finish pianos. I use real miniature mahogany or walnut for the wood finishes, they are finished with a high gloss clear lacquer. As mentioned above, the measurements are taken from the real pianos. The rim for the case of the miniature piano is made just like the real one. The wood is bent around a form, clamped and baked so it will remain in the proper shape when it is released from the form. The plate, the metal part that holds the tuning pins and strings, is made from my own original molds. Since July 1992 I have been casting the plate in white metal using the lost wax method which is the same way jewelry is made. The keys are also made from my molds and are cast using polyester resin. The pedals are also from my original molds and cast in brass using the lost wax method. The longest process is sanding the wood and then sanding the lacquer when the pianos are nearly completed. The hinges and casters are the only parts I do not make.

In December of 1990, Baldwin Piano and Organ Company sent out a two page newsletter to all of their US and International dealers which showed photos of my pianos. In addition to the miniature Baldwin Grand

Pianos, I make miniature console and table model phonographs from 1905 and also console radios from the 1930's and 40's. I have also made the console, the keyboard part, of a 1930 Wurlitzer theatre pipe organ. I have started plans and drawings on a 1946 model 1015 Wurlitzer juke box.

The most asked question about the pianos is, and I take it as the highest compliment, “Do they really play?”

ARTISAN: **KENNEDY, ELLEN J.**

BUSINESS NAME: E & B.K. Originals
The Kennedys Ellen & Bart

IDENTIFICATION MARKS:

CATEGORY:
Accessories

RECOGNITION:
Nutshell News, Jul. 1990, pg. 60; Jan. 1991, pg. 75

AUTOBIOGRAPHY:
I have always loved miniatures and have dabbled in crafts since childhood. I have a BA in Art Education and Elementary certification and am teaching first grade.

I made my first miniatures for sale in local gift shops in the early 1970's. Later on I discovered Fimo and became fascinated with the caning process, used to make miniature candy. From this I started collecting samples of miniature gingerbread houses and tried to develop my own style. I took private lessons in the canning process, from Tess Goodier, who lives in Virginia. I sell to three miniature shops in Colorado, Dallas and Virginia. I try to attend at least two miniature shows a year.

ARTISAN: **KETCHUM, SUE ANN**

BUSINESS NAME: Sue Ann Ketchum

IDENTIFICATION MARKS:

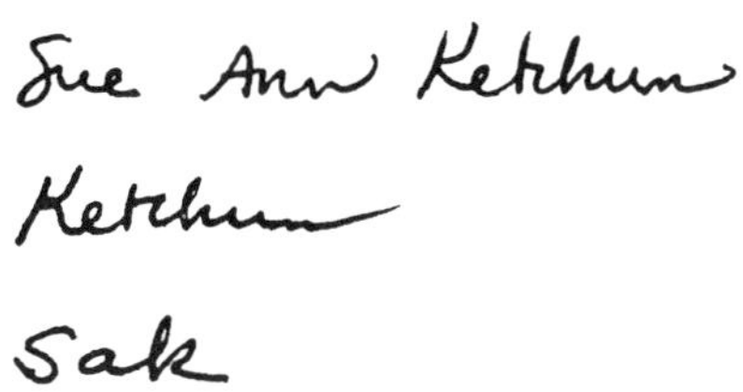

CATEGORY:
Accessories: household; Animals: pets; Flowers and Plants; Furniture; Gazebo; Holiday Items; Roomboxes; Toys

RECOGNITION:
Miniatures Showcase, Fall 1991, pg. 82; Nov. 1992, pg. 30, 72

AUTOBIOGRAPHY:
I received my first dollhouse at age 3, the 1960's metal and cardboard type with plastic furniture that did not open. I played with that for years, adding homemade household accessories. As a young child, I replaced the

furniture with cardboard furniture of my own design which opened and as a teenager with my own handcrafted balsa wood furniture. At age 16, I scratch-built a one-inch scale dollhouse from my own plans, which has since been remodeled and several additions have been added.

After college, marriage, two children, a major addition to my home and my dollhouse, I joined a miniatures club. Several members of the club are dealers and pushed me into making and selling my miniatures. I have been doing so since approximately 1989. I have attended one Regional NAME Houseparty and one National NAME Houseparty and have taken several workshops and taught roundtables and one registered workshop. I am also a member of IGMA.

ARTISAN: **KEUKER-HARDENBERG, ELSE**

BUSINESS NAME: Else Keuker Miniatures

IDENTIFICATION MARKS:

EH — Silver

E.K. — Bottom of stone bowls

CATEGORY:

Bowls: semiprecious stone; Silversmith

HONORS:

IGMA Artisan

RECOGNITION:

Nutshell News, Apr. 1988, pg. 30; *Miniature Gazette*, Fall 1992, pg. 34

BIOGRAPHY:

Else Keuker has been a lapidary and silversmith since 1970. She took five years of private silversmithing lessons. In 1983, her daughter started building a dollhouse and asked her to make some silver miniatures. That brought her into miniatures and into the business. Else makes many kinds of silver items, stone bowls, sometimes on a silver stand, and plants, which are sold only in Holland. Some of her silver items are shown in the Denver Museum of Miniatures.

ARTISAN: **KIDDER, BEVERLY**

BUSINESS NAME: Bev Kidder's Doll Works

IDENTIFICATION MARKS:

Some unmarked

B. Kidder
Date

BJK
Date

CATEGORY:

Dolls

RECOGNITION:

Nutshell News, Oct. 1991

ARTISAN: **KI-KYDD, PAUL M.**

BUSINESS NAME: Escutcheon

IDENTIFICATION MARKS:

 Burned into wood

 Printed and signature

CATEGORY:
Furniture

ARTISAN: **KILKENNY, JANE WINSTON**

BUSINESS NAME: Kilkenny Miniatures

IDENTIFICATION MARKS:

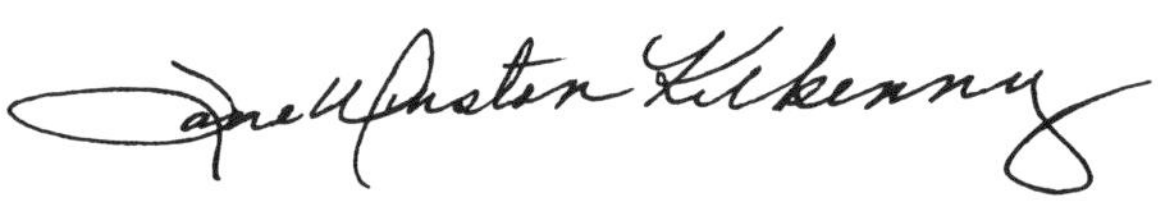 Nov. 1978 to present

Original Floral Design by
 1979 to present
Jane Winston Kilkenny

CATEGORY:
Floral Arrangements; Flowers and Plants; Kits: floral

RECOGNITION:
Miniature Gazette; Nutshell News

ARTISAN: **KIMBLE, GERALDINE**

BUSINESS NAME: Jeri's Junk

IDENTIFICATION MARKS:

CATEGORY:
Crocheting; Cross Stitch; Embroidery; Needlework; Roomboxes

AUTOBIOGRAPHY:

My father was a career military man which meant we moved often while I was growing up. I have always had a love of miniatures and was fortunate enough to have a talented mother who built my first dollhouse and furnished it with furniture made by her out of cheese boxes. The dollhouse was lost but she saved the furniture and returned it to me after my children were older. She kept it safe all those years!

KIMBLE, GERALDINE, continued

I do cross stitch, crocheting, embroidery work and knitting in real life and have found it easily adapted to miniatures. I enjoy the needlework but am also interested in building roomboxes. I sell those as well as needlework and other items. I try different areas and enjoy them, but keep coming back to my first love, cross stitch and crocheting.

I went back to school after my children were grown and became a registered nurse, attending college in San Jose, California. I have been employed, since then, as a full-time rehabilitation nurse with the VA Medical Center, Palo Alto, California. Working on miniatures is a relaxing way to unwind after a rough day. I have interested many people in miniatures as I bring them to the ward for display purposes. The patients, visitors and staff all love them.

I began my business in 1979 and have continued to sell at shows only due to my inability to build a large inventory of items ahead of time. Just recently I began making roomboxes for people. This gives me a chance to design and make a scene that is personal to the one receiving it.

ARTISAN: **KING, BOBBI**

BUSINESS NAME: Handmades

IDENTIFICATION MARKS:

 month/year (era)

B KING month/year (era)
Etched on windows

Code of era's

V - Victorian	C - Contemporary (Current)
E - Edwardian	A - Art Deco
2 - Twenties	N - Art Noveau
3 - Thirties	O - Original
4 - Forties	

CATEGORY:

Building Components: doors; Furniture; Glass: stained; Windows

HONORS:

IGMA Artisan 1994

RECOGNITION:

Miniatures Showcase, Winter 1992, pg. 28, 30, 58; Spring 1992, pg. 31, 38; Jan. 1993, Cover; *Milwaukee Journal*, Feb. 27, 1992, Sec. B, pg. B1

AUTOBIOGRAPHY:

After a lifetime of handcrafting I became involved in miniatures, through my sister, after a visit to a local miniature museum in 1989. I purchased several magazines, tracked down our local shops, and started purchasing kits and taking classes. Once I realized there isn't enough time in the world to do it all myself I settled on my favorite, stained glass.

I usually make my mark on the wood frame of the component, although many customers give me their insert to complete. I will then etch a mark on the window itself if there is an inconspicuous corner.

ARTISAN: **KING JANE**

BUSINESS NAME: Jane King Miniatures

IDENTIFICATION MARKS:

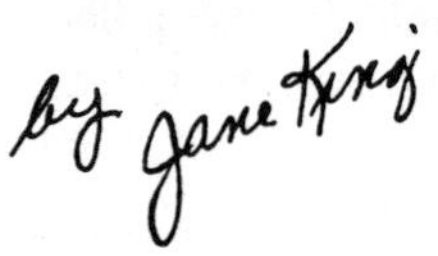

KING, JANE, continued

CATEGORY:

Confectionery; Food

AUTOBIOGRAPHY:

I have had no formal training in the art field. I have come from a very creative family and found in miniatures all the interests I had over the years compiled in one form. I have been making miniatures since 1978 and started marketing them shortly thereafter. A local shop, Granns, was very supportive of my work and started buying things for resale. I have been doing shows since 1981 and have sold nationally and to Japan. I also supply other artisans with items they use with their work. The miniatures I make are everyday food items that would be used in any setting.

ARTISAN: KINGHORN–DICKINSON, BARBARA

BUSINESS NAME: B. K–D Miniatures

IDENTIFICATION MARKS:

B. K-D 98'92 Last number is year

CATEGORY:

Dolls: original

RECOGNITION:

International Dolls House News, Vol. 20, No. 4, Winter 1991, pg. 28

AUTOBIOGRAPHY:

Denied the opportunity to study full-time at art college upon leaving school, I have attended evening classes for about 25 years to study pottery, portrait painting, sculpture and silversmithing. I have also made my own clothes since I was a teenager. When I discovered miniatures in 1980, all my skills came into focus. I have made furniture, rugs and silver etc. for my dollhouse, but came almost by accident to doll making in 1990. I had bought a porcelain lady at about the same time that I copied an antique bisque doll in miniature in my possession. I realized that my doll's face looked more like a child than a doll and had far more life and character than the porcelain lady with her expressionless face and silly little hands and feet. Since then I have been sculpting individual people with character and realistic limbs, using a mix of Fimo and Super Sculpey. I have a few faithful fans and sell only at two local fairs being determined to keep output low and to remain fresh and original in my efforts.

ARTISAN: KLEIN, JANICE S.

BUSINESS NAME: Janice Klein Porcelain Dolls

IDENTIFICATION MARKS:

1986 to present

jsk 1993 jsk '93

On shoe soles or back of heels

CATEGORY:

Dolls: original, porcelain

RECOGNITION:

Nutshell News, Jun. 1986, pg. 88; Jun. 1990, pg. 65; *Miniatures Showcase*, Spring 1987, pg. 42, 44-46; Fall 1987, pg. 44; Summer 1987, pg. 44-45, 64-65; Summer 1989, pg. 44; Fall 1989, pg. 12; Winter 1990, pg. 48; Spring 1990, pg. 63; Summer 1991, pg. 20; *Miniature Dealer*, Sept. 1990, pg. 23

KLEIN, JANICE S., continued

AUTOBIOGRAPHY:

My profession is teaching which has always included arts and crafts activities. Although I no longer teach school full-time, I've taught craft classes especially doll making for more than 20 years. I've worked with people ages four to 80 and love to make it possible for each to feel successful.

I have also worked part-time in a large department store in both the display and gift wrap areas. From this I've acquired many additional skills.

ARTISAN: **KNIGHT, SONDRA**

BUSINESS NAME: Some Like It Small

IDENTIFICATION MARKS:

CATEGORY:

Furniture: upholstered, wicker; Wicker: reproductions

AUTOBIOGRAPHY:

I have been involved with miniatures since 1981 and started making reproductions of original antique wicker pieces in 1988. The overstuffed upholstered furniture became a part of my line in 1992. I was inspired towards excellence after a personal tour from Eugene Kupjack while 81 of his roomboxes were on tour in Norfolk, Virginia. My extensive knowledge of period wicker is self-taught after acquiring every book on it I could find. I am an IGMA and NAME member.

ARTISAN: **KNOER, SUSI**

BUSINESS NAME: Gryphon's Den

IDENTIFICATION MARKS:

CATEGORY:

Needlework

HONORS:

IGMA Artisan

RECOGNITION:

Nutshell News, Dec. 1986, pg. 68; Oct. 1990, pg. 70; *Miniatures Showcase,* Fall 1986, pg. 11, 20; Fall 1988, pg. 8, 24, 40; Winter 1991, pg. 27, 29; Winter 1992, pg. 28, 30, 33

AUTOBIOGRAPHY:

I have been doing needlework since age six. I graduated college with a BA in Education. My professional career included theatrical costume designer, researcher and miniaturist.

ARTISAN: **KNOWLES, WINK**

BUSINESS NAME: The Squirrel's Nest

IDENTIFICATION MARKS:

CATEGORY:

Brasswork; Furniture; Structures

HONORS:

IGMA Artisan 1991

AUTOBIOGRAPHY:

My educational background is a BS Degree from Trinity University in 1970, and an MBA from Southern Methodist University in 1971. I worked in the graphic arts industry all through my professional career. In 1987, my wife purchased our daughter a very expensive cardboard and plastic dollhouse for Christmas. This led to the all too much heard phrase, "I can do better than that!" Within one year of uttering these fateful words, my wife and I had opened up our own retail miniature store in Pittsburgh, Pennsylvania, The Squirrel's Nest. The rigors of retail did not allow me adequate time to pursue miniatures as an art, as I desired, so the retail store front part of the operation was closed in 1991. The Squirrel's Nest began operating then, as it does today, as a retail source of museum quality hand crafted one-inch scale miniatures, dealing only through miniature shows and our catalog.

In October of 1991, I was awarded artisan designation by the International Guild of Miniature Artisans, Ltd., in the category of furniture. This award means more to me, and is much more rewarding and fulfilling than any other award or degree that has been bestowed on me.

ARTISAN: **KOCEVAR, GLENDA**

BUSINESS NAME: Designs by Glenda

IDENTIFICATION MARKS:

CATEGORY:

Confectionery; Holiday Items

ARTISAN: **KOCH, F. WHITNEY**

BUSINESS NAME: What's Next

IDENTIFICATION MARKS:

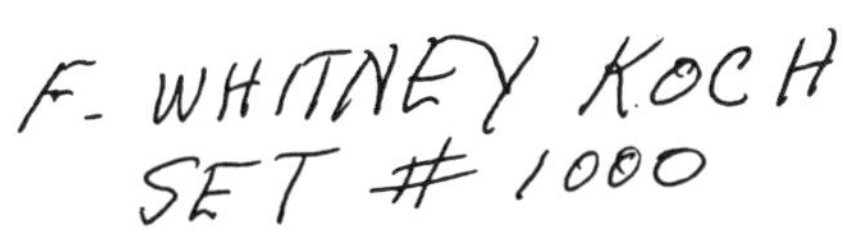

CATEGORY:

Bathroom: fixtures

KOCH, F. WHITNEY, continued

AUTOBIOGRAPHY:

I am an inventor and hold patents on 24 fluidics, electronic, mechanical and chemical inventions. I invented asphalt shingles on a belt for roofing dollhouses. I expanded into bath sets making them of porcelain and 24K gold and black walnut. Because they are expensive I have only made 1,236 sets since 1982.

ARTISAN: KOTHE, ELAINE

BUSINESS NAME: Elaine's Petite People Plus
Petite People Plus

IDENTIFICATION MARKS:

Some unmarked, marks 1992 to present

E.K. Landscaping

PPP Dolls

CATEGORY:

Dolls: porcelain; Landscaping

RECOGNITION:

Nutshell News, Oct. 1990; Nov. 1993, pg. 62; *Miniatures Showcase,* Spring 1990, pg. 28; Fall 1991, pg. 27; Jul. 1993, pg. 31; *Miniature Collector*, Spring 1989; Spring 1994, pg. 40; *Dolls in Miniature,* Fall 1993, Cover

AUTOBIOGRAPHY:

My interest in miniatures evolved when I received a dollhouse at age five and proceeded to design clothespin dolls and furniture for my favorite toy.

I graduated college with a degree in art and married my college sweetheart, Dan. When my two children were toddlers, I taught classes in miniatures at a local dollhouse shop and taught ceramics, painting crafts and miniatures for the Huntington Town program and after school activities.

At a NAME club meeting I met Joan Cremins, a talented lady who dressed dolls and the idea formed that we would establish the business "Petite People Plus" and specialize in reasonably priced porcelain dolls. Joan costumes and I pour and paint the dolls. Recently I branched out into landscaping "unique animal houses," for relief from the tediousness of painting doll faces.

We try to use humor in the making of the dolls and hope that people will smile when they see our works.

see "Joan Cremins"

ARTISAN: KOTT, DOLORES

BUSINESS NAME: Kott Kreations

IDENTIFICATION MARKS:

KOTT

Sewn on clay flower
back of bears

Color denotes year.

White	1991
Red	1992
Blue	1993
Green	1994

CATEGORY:

Accessories; Bears: teddy; Needlework; Rugs: French Knot

KOTT, DOLORES, continued

RECOGNITION:

Nutshell News, Apr. 1987, pg. 44

AUTOBIOGRAPHY:

I have been making miniatures since the late 1970's working in a variety of media. I work with cernit making items from fruit and veggies to teddy bears, simulated wood, driftwood, old logs and stumps; with fiber in creating French knot hooked rugs, copies of antique rugs or my own designs, wooden folk art pieces and Santa's. I use organic naturals, growing my own herbs to create mini wreaths and floral arrangements. I'm also known for my small teddy bears, all hand sewn from vintage plush ranging in size from 3½ inches to ¾ inch.

Most items are marked Kott or D. Kott on the bottom. I like combining media such as landscaped vignettes, featuring landscaping material, dried flowers, clay for logs or driftwood, resin ponds and sewn bears completing the setting.

ARTISAN: KOWALKE, NORMA & FRED

BUSINESS NAME: Miniatures From The Aviary

IDENTIFICATION MARKS:

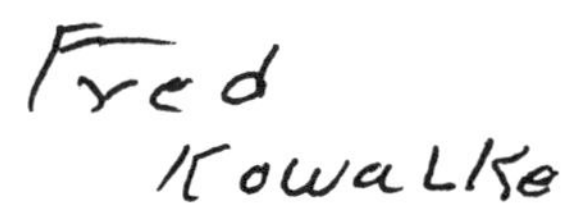

CATEGORY:

Bears: teddy; Dolls: porcelain; Furniture: period; Jewelry: box; Kits: bear; Perfume Sets

HONORS:

1st Place, Canada, Upholstered Furniture; 1st Place, Columbus, Ohio, Row House

RECOGNITION:

Nutshell News

AUTOBIOGRAPHY:

I was an antique doll collector and dressed dolls for antique dealers in the Saginaw, Michigan area. I started collecting after two eye operations made it impossible for me to continue my old life style of antiquing. When Judeé Williamson came to the doll club as a guest speaker I changed to miniatures. Judeé has always been such an inspiration to all of us!

I went into business when Fred had to quit work at age 47 and we had to move to Florida. I have been in business since 1976 and have been all over this country on selling and buying trips.

ARTISAN: KRAEGER, VERL

IDENTIFICATION MARKS: (Submitted by Dorothy Midgett, "Midge")

verl kraeger usa Blue stick on label, white lettering

CATEGORY:

Furniture: period, plant stands

RECOGNITION:

Nutshell News, Vol. 13, No. 12, Dec. 1983, pg. 80; Vol. 14, No. 4, Apr. 1984, pg. 41

ARTISAN: **KRAFT, BETTY JEAN**

BUSINESS NAME: "Kraft's" by Betty Jean

IDENTIFICATION MARKS:

CATEGORY:

Accessories; Ceramics; Rubber Stamps

RECOGNITION:

Miniatures Showcase

AUTOBIOGRAPHY:

I am a high school graduate, but more or less self-taught in miniatures. My interest in crafts began when I first worked with Brownie Scouts and later with Cub Scouts, when my sons were old enough. I have done some craft shows and learned ceramics. My first miniature show was in Wichita, Kansas, and I was hooked! I have done shows in Wichita, Kansas City, Dallas, Little Rock, Oklahoma City and the NAME National in Denver.

I started out with different ceramic accessories and have recently added rubber stamps to use for printing borders on towels, curtains, place mats, etc. I also have greetings for Christmas cards and welcome signs.

I taught a class at Playfest in Salado, Arkansas in 1992 and have also taught crafts for our local summer youth program for many years. I enjoy crafts, but the little person in my head is always trying to figure out how to make it dollhouse scale. I am a member of NAME and SAM.

ARTISAN: **KRAUSS, CHRISTINE**

BUSINESS NAME: Krauss House Miniatures

IDENTIFICATION MARKS:

CATEGORY:

Dolls: porcelain

RECOGNITION:

Nutshell News, Apr. 1992, pg. 38-41, "Chateau La Chaille," Jeanne Delgado; *Dolls in Miniature*, Vol. 1, Issue No. 4, Winter 1991/92, Cover, pg. 18-22; Vol. 2, Issue No. 2, Summer 1992, pg. 10; *Miniatures Showcase*, Winter 1992, pg. 61

AUTOBIOGRAPHY:

I became a doll maker of miniature dolls because my mom and dad were building a 22 room French Chateau and my mom needed elegant dolls in modern evening attire and could not find any easily. She purchased a doll undressed and I dressed it for her, thus beginning a new love and hobby. I purchased books on the subject and spoke with people in the trade learning all I could in a short period of time. I am still learning and have been making miniature dolls since about 1990. I have always had a love for art although I never pursued it educationally. All art endeavors have been self-taught. I strive to make each doll creation the finest I can achieve. I work out of my home most often at night because I have two small children.

ARTISAN: **KRAUSS, KENTON**

BUSINESS NAME: Krauss House Miniatures

IDENTIFICATION MARKS:

CATEGORY:

Furniture

RECOGNITION:

Nutshell News, Apr. 1992, pg. 38-41, "Chateau La Chaille," Jeanne Delgado; *Miniatures Showcase*, Winter 1992, pg. 60

AUTOBIOGRAPHY:

I have always had a special fascination with building unusual articles from wood. As with many others, my introduction to wood working came during high school. This interest took a turn towards the smaller when I became interested in building radio controlled model airplanes.

A number of years after marrying my wife, Christine, her parents, James and Audrey Goodwin, were finishing up a dollhouse project of immense proportion. She felt that she could fulfill the project's needs for fine porcelain miniature dolls. Likewise, I realized that the creation of miniature furniture pieces, was yet another extension of a hobby I already enjoyed and I felt compelled to become involved as well.

To this day, I like to create articles of furniture that are out of the ordinary. Most notable is my fantasy swan bed, as featured in *Miniatures Showcase*. Hand carved from a single block of poplar, the bed is finished with gold leaf and adorned with real silk and ermine.

I like to draw my own plans, primarily from reference photographs or from my imagination. All of my articles are built entirely from scratch, including milling of raw lumber into thicknesses suitable for miniatures. My wife's natural talent for painting allows me to offer extraordinarily detailed handpainted furniture pieces, as well as articles which highlight the natural finishes of many exotic woods.

I have a Bachelor's degree in Management Science, have completed post-graduate work towards an MBA in Information Systems Management, and currently work as a Systems Analyst for a Southern California computer engineering firm.

ARTISAN: **KRONBERG, DANIEL PHILLIP**

BUSINESS NAME: Daniel Phillip Kronberg Miniature Statuary
D.P.K. Miniature Statuary

IDENTIFICATION MARKS:

1989 to 1991

1991 to present

CATEGORY:

Accessories; Bronzes; Goldsmith; Silversmith; Statuary

HONORS:

IGMA Artisan, Fellow 1993

KRONBERG, DANIEL PHILLIP, continued

RECOGNITION:

Miniatures Showcase, Jul. 1993, pg. 38-41

AUTOBIOGRAPHY:

Most artists can't remember the first piece of art that would eventually lead them into this very special career of carving in miniature. In 1960, when I was about seven years old, I picked up a piece of boxwood, part of a fruit crate from the fruit store next to my grandfather's grocery store in Essex Street Market on the lower East Side of New York City and with a safety edge razor I began carving my first of many totem poles. The design was simple and not very deep, but I do remember how much I enjoyed cutting the wood and how proud I was with the results.

As the years passed, I carved many totem poles, horses and other designs. As a child, I never thought this love that I had for carving wood could be anything more than a hobby.

My enthusiasm for working with wood, metals, tools and machinery continued in high school. I received a scholarship to New York University's Industrial Arts Program, hoping to become a teacher. One afternoon in the industrial design class, I saw some miniature pewter statues, (charms) the professor had brought in. I was captivated by their small size and detail.

That summer I needed to make a very important decision: stay in school and pursue a career that I was sure was not for me or give up a full scholarship to study a craft I knew very little about.

In September 1964, I began a four year apprenticeship program with the Danish Silversmith, Inc. in Providence, Rhode Island. It wasn't long before I was certain I had made the right decision. As an apprentice, I needed to learn all related aspects of manufacturing so I worked as a waxer, moldmaker, caster, production model cleaner and primarily as a modelmaker. Perhaps most important of all, I made lifelong friends, honest, hardworking and generous people, all master craftsmen.

I also enrolled at The Rhode Island School of Design at night to study jewelry design. In the evening and weekends I would do wood carvings, and sculpt in clay, making latex rubber molds and castings in plaster. I learned a great deal during those years, but it was only the beginning.

Many times, as a child, my father told me that whatever I chose as a profession to be sure it was something that I enjoyed, because I would be spending a great deal of my time and energy at it. It has been 15 years since I began my own business, in 1977, and 28 years since I began my apprenticeship. Looking back, I can honestly say, I made the right choice.

I believe that every artist and craftsman has a philosophy that guides their every move and thought while creating works of art and perhaps even in their everyday decision making. Every decision, no matter how large or small, has results which can be judged to be in some degree, good or bad, constructive or destructive. I made a conscious choice and chose to be constructive: to be a builder, to work in some small way to be a positive, creative force.

ARTISAN: KRUCKER, DANIEL GAINES

IDENTIFICATION MARKS:

Brass birdcages 1978 to 1982

Furniture 1978 to 1982

CATEGORY:

Birdcages; Furniture

HONORS: Exhibit: Toy & Miniature Museum of Kansas City

RECOGNITION:

Nutshell News; Miniature Collector

AUTOBIOGRAPHY:

I had been traveling with a disco band in the 1970's. This was a dead-end profession. I left the band and moved to San Francisco for a respite with my parents.

They needed help with their businesses, The Miniature Mart, and The Peddler's Shop. Since I was out of work, had no money and needing a job I was willing to work for reasonable rates.

My mother, Ellen Krucker Blauer, asked me to make some bird cages. She also encouraged me to try new things, in wood and brass. I liked the wood. She and John also wanted other new products and gave me pictures with license to try what seemed right. I worked for five years before starting my own company.

At first, all of my work was for The Peddler's Shop, but more and more the projects became life-size. Now I employ five people in the burgeoning custom casework industry. No miniatures at all!

My mother has said that people are still writing and calling to ask if I could make more birdcages.

ARTISAN: KRUEGER, TODD

BUSINESS NAME: T. K. Designs

IDENTIFICATION MARKS:

1984 to 1986

small pieces, current

current

CATEGORY:

Animals: primates; Bears: teddy

RECOGNITION:

Nutshell News, Jan. 1989, pg. 60-61

ARTISAN: KRUG, CHARLES

BUSINESS NAME: C. Krug Miniatures

IDENTIFICATION MARKS:

CATEGORY:

Furniture: carved, period

HONORS:

IGMA Fellow 1989; Red Ribbon, Philadelphia Flower Show, 1983; Exhibit: Toy & Miniature Museum of Kansas City

RECOGNITION:

Nutshell News, Jan. 1984, Cover; Mar. 1992, pg. 29, 71; Oct. 1992, pg. 63; Feb. 1993, pg. 72

AUTOBIOGRAPHY:

In 1980, I started to make miniatures as a hobby. In a joint venture with another miniaturist, my wife Jane and I entered a roombox in the Philadelphia Flower Show in 1983, winning a red ribbon. The box was on display later at the IGMA Show in New York City and was shown on the cover of *Nutshell News*, January 1984 issue. I joined IGMA in 1986 and started working in miniatures full-time. I received the honor of becoming Fellow in 1989.

ARTISAN: **KRUPICK, BARBARA**

BUSINESS NAME: Krupick Miniatures

IDENTIFICATION MARKS:

BK Bottom of flower containers

CATEGORY:

Floral Arrangements: bouquets; Flowers and Plants: seashells

RECOGNITION:

Nutshell News

ARTISAN: **KRUPICK, DAVID**

BUSINESS NAME: Krupick Miniatures

IDENTIFICATION MARKS:

Some unmarked

DK

small pieces

David Krupick

CATEGORY:

Birdcages; Furniture; Kitchenware; Toys

HONORS:

Exhibit: Toy & Miniature Museum of Kansas City

RECOGNITION:

Nutshell News

BIOGRAPHY:

David Krupick was born into a family of furniture makers and custom home builders. In 1976, after visiting a miniatures show he turned a hobby of ship model building into a career of making a great variety of fine quality miniatures. After these many years, his work is located in museums and collections around the world.

ARTISAN: **KUBESH, CAROL**

BUSINESS NAME: Carol's Creations In Miniature

IDENTIFICATION MARKS:

Carol
Nov. 1987 to Jun. 1992

Kubesh
1988 to present
Rocking horses

CMK
Jul. 1992 to present

CATEGORY:

Dolls: original; Rocking Horses; Toys

KUBESH, CAROL, continued

HONORS:

IGMA Artisan 1991

RECOGNITION:

Nutshell News, Aug. 1988, pg. 54; *Dolls In Miniature*, Vol. 1, Issue No. 2, pg. 88-93

AUTOBIOGRAPHY:

My interest in miniatures began in 1980 when I acquired a dollhouse kit. I learned to make many of the accessories that furnished the house. I fell in love with miniature dolls when I started putting people in them, progressing from dressing doll kits to sculpting my own dolls from Fimo and Sculpy. In November 1987, I sold my first doll, a Father Christmas doll, and have been making and selling ever since. I was awarded IGMA artisan status in figures and costuming in March 1991.

ARTISAN: **KUHNS, JOHN**

BUSINESS NAME: Handcrafted Dollhouses by John Kuhns

IDENTIFICATION MARKS:

John C Kuhns
BUFFALO NY
(DATE)

CATEGORY:

Dollhouse: reproductions

AUTOBIOGRAPHY:

My introduction to miniatures began as a Christmas suggestion from a daughter in law for a dollhouse. In 1982, I checked out one of the local miniature shops and found a country farmhouse that I thought would be a perfect gift. After seeing the quality of the kits I felt I could build a better house. The easiest thing was the one-inch scale. I built a farmhouse and through friends seeing it, I sold it before actually finishing it. I discovered a market, and being retired from the US Army, I made what originally was a pastime into a business. I have made more than 239 dollhouses including 19 reproductions and uncounted roomboxes, breakaway boxes, etc. I have been doing approximately ten miniature show annually, from Boston to Florida and including Chicago. I have been a member of NAME during this time and have made the dollhouse door prize for eight of the 12 shows the Western New York Miniature Enthusiasts Club has sponsored.

ARTISAN: **KUMMEROW, BARBARA**

BUSINESS NAME: Kummerows
Kummerow's Studio of Miniature Design

IDENTIFICATION MARKS:

BK

KUMMEROW, BARBARA, continued

CATEGORY:

Lamps: Tiffany; Screens

HONORS:

IGMA Artisan

RECOGNITION:

Nutshell News; Miniature Collector; Maison de Poupee

AUTOBIOGRAPHY:

I graduated from the University of California, Santa Barbara with a BA in Art. I have been working with miniatures for 20 years, 1972, and as a full-time occupation for the last 16 years.

ARTISAN: KUMMEROW, LEW

BUSINESS NAME: Kummerows
Kummerow's Studio of Miniature Design

IDENTIFICATION MARKS:

CATEGORY:

Accessories: household; Appliances: household; Birdcages; Furniture; Houses; Reproductions; Toys; Trains

RECOGNITION:

Nutshell News; Miniature Collector; Hobbies; Maison de Poupee; Santa Dolls, Historical to Contemporary, Ann Bahar, Hobby House, 1992

AUTOBIOGRAPHY:

I graduated from the University of California, Santa Barbara with a BA in Industrial Arts. I have been teaching high school drafting and architecture for 15 years, and have been working with miniatures for 20 years, 1972, of which the last 16 were full-time.

ARTISAN: KUNZ, LYNDA

BUSINESS NAME: Lynda's Teddies

IDENTIFICATION MARKS:

Paper tag sewn to back of bear

Other side of tag has bear's name, if limited edition, bear's number

KUNZ, LYNDA, continued

CATEGORY:
Bears: teddy; Toys: stuffed

HONORS:
IGMA Artisan; 2nd Place, Original Small Bear Design, 1992

RECOGNITION:
Teddy Bear Review, Vol. 7, No. 4, Jul/Aug. 1992, pg. 41; *Dolls In Miniature*, Vol. II, No. 3, Fall 1992, pg. 69-72; *Teddy Tribune*, Apr. 1993

AUTOBIOGRAPHY:
My interest in miniatures came from my love of teddy bears, especially miniature ones. I've been making bears since 1980 and collecting bears since 1977.

My bears range from 1½ inches to 2¾ inches tall. They are sewn, turned and stuffed. All the bears are five way jointed, arms, legs and head.

Dolls in Miniature referred to them as museum quality.

ARTISAN: **KUPJACK, EUGENE J.** (Deceased)
(Submitted by Henry Kupjack)

BUSINESS NAME: Kupjack Studio
E. J. Kupjack Associates Inc.

IDENTIFICATION MARKS:

Mass produced pieces

Antique Silver Miniature Reproductions

Commenced production 1967
Ended production 1985

Total line of 87 pieces

Sterling Silver with Rhodium plate
Some pieces Sterling Silver with 22 carat Gold plate
Line included 3 pieces of furniture — Safety Pewter, wood with various paints

French Gilt Miniature Reproductions

Commenced production 1976
Ended production 1985

Total line of 51 pieces

Bronze with 22 carat Gold plate
Bronze with Rhodium plate
Sterling Silver with Rhodium plate

Fabergé Miniatures

Commenced production 1976
Ended production 1985

KUPJACK, EUGENE J., continued

Silver with 22 carat Gold plate, various enamels, some containing Diamonds or Sapphires

Victorian Plate Miniatures

Commenced production 1977
Ended production 1985

Total line of 20 pieces

Bronze with Rhodium plate
Sterling Silver with Rhodium plate (marked Sterling)
Bronze with 22 carat Gold Plate

Miniature Tole, Flowers and Figurines

Commenced production 1979
Ended production 1983

Total line of 56 pieces

Safety Pewter with various paints, some Bronze as base metal,
very limited number silver with various paints

IDENTIFICATION MARKS:

United Federation of Doll Clubs, Inc.

Produced 1985

Commemorative Comb, Brush and Mirror set in plush red box

1610 sets produced, dies destroyed

IDENTIFICATION MARKS:

Winterthur Museum Collection
produced for Winterthur Museum exclusively

Commenced production 1982
Ended production 1985

Total line of 22 pieces

Sterling Silver with Rhodium plate
Brass
Safety Pewter
Safety Pewter with Gold leaf
Safety Pewter with various paints

KUPJACK, EUGENE J., continued

IDENTIFICATION MARKS:

Collection Cabinets:

18th Century Silver Curio Shop
French 18th Century Shop

Commenced production 1968
Ended production 1981

Early cabinets unsigned
Middle years some signed: **E. Kupjack**
Late signed: Logo card with **E. J. Kupjack**

Georgian Shop Fronts

Commenced production 1986
Still in production

Logo card on back
Limited production

Miniature Rooms and Furniture

Miniature Rooms

1936 – 1940

All rooms done in conjunction with Mrs. James Ward Thorne and signed by her.

1948 – 1964

Rooms and other work done in conjunction with Mrs. James Ward Thorne, signed by her.
Rooms made solely by Eugene J. Kupjack, signed (printed) **E. J. Kupjack**

1964 – 1968

All rooms done solely by Eugene J. Kupjack, signed (printed) **E. J. Kupjack**

1968 – 1991

Rooms signed: **E. J. Kupjack**
H. C. & E. J. Kupjack
Kupjack Studio
Kupjack
Henry Kupjack

1991 – Present

Rooms signed: **Kupjack Studio**
Henry Kupjack

KUPJACK, EUGENE J., continued

Furniture

Individual pieces made separate from rooms, signed: **E. J. Kupjack**
some logo mark
some not signed

CATEGORY:

Accessories: personal; Bronzes; Collection Cabinets; Fabergé; Furniture: period, reproductions; Pewter; Roomboxes: furnished; Room Settings; Silversmith; Silver: reproductions

HONORS:

Exhibits: Thorne Miniature Rooms, The Art Institute of Chicago, Illinois, The Phoenix Museum of Art, Phoenix, Arizona, and the Dulin Gallery of Art, Knoxville, Tennessee; The Carson Pirie Scott Miniature Rooms, Illinois State Museum, Springfield, Illinois; Kupjack Miniature Rooms, Winterthur Museum, Winterthur, Delaware, Children's Museum, Indianapolis, Indiana, The Forbes Magazine Gallery, New York City, Gibbs Museum of Art, Charleston, South Carolina, The Carole & Barry Kaye Museum of Miniatures, Los Angeles, California; The Cheney Collection of Kupjack Miniature Rooms, The Baltimore Museum of Art, Baltimore, Maryland; The Leo S. Singer Collection of Kupjack Miniature Rooms, The Palm Springs Desert Museum, Palm Springs, California; The Serta Imperial Bedrooms Collection of Kupjack Miniature Rooms, The Furniture Discovery Center, High Point, North Carolina

RECOGNITION:

Nutshell News, Vol. 11, No. 1, Jan. 1981, pg. 42-43; Vol. 12, No. 11, Nov. 1982, pg. 57; Vol. 13, No. 1, Jan. 1983, pg. 53; Vol. 13, No. 2, Feb. 1983, pg. 34; Vol. 13, No. 5, May 1983, pg. 47; *Miniature Collector*, No. 10, Dec. 1978, pg. 34, Show Stoppers; No. 29, Feb. 1982, pg. 12, "Winterthur Collection Pieces being Reproduced in Miniature," No. 41, Jan/Feb. 1984, pg. 32-34, "Miniature Masterpieces, The Kupjack Rooms;" *Miniature Gazette*, Vol. 3, No. 1, Sept. 1974, pg. 11, "Elegance on a Small Scale;" Vol. 6, No. 3, Spring 1978, pg. 34; Vol. 9, No. 4, Summer 1981, pg. 64; Vol. 10, No. 2, Winter 1981, pg. 28; Vol. 11, No. 1, Fall 1982, pg. 26; Vol. 12, No. 4, Summer 1984, pg. 14-16, "Eugene Kupjack: A Public Appearance with 30 of His Rooms," Father Arthur Edward Norton

BIOGRAPHY:

Eugene J. Kupjack was born in Chicago in 1912. He attended Crane College, The Art Institute of Chicago and the American Academy of Art. He passed away on November 8, 1991.

While working as a designer of convention and window displays in 1936, Mr. Kupjack became interested in Mrs. James Ward Thorne's first collection of miniature rooms. He worked with Mrs. Thorne for three and a half years to produce her collection of 37 American period rooms. The Thorne Miniature Rooms now are on permanent display at The Art Institute of Chicago.

During World War II Mr. Kupjack served for six years in the United States Navy. As a Commander in the Office of Naval Research in Washington, DC, he created orthopedic instruments, 13 of which were patented. Following the war he entered the surgical instruments business, while still continuing to create miniatures for Mrs. Thorne. In 1959, he built 17 miniature rooms depicting the work of contemporary designers for the annual convention of American Institute of Decorators. A number of commissions followed, and his full-time career in the field was launched.

The work of Eugene J. Kupjack is saturated with enthusiasm for excellence. His diminutive re-creations are dominated by a sense of convincing realism, heightened by a theatrical use of light and design, and brought to life by precise details. Using a scale of one inch to a foot, he constructs rooms either line to line (exact copies) or as eclectic assemblages of his own creation. Objects are constructed through the imaginative use of a variety of materials, ranging from patterned fabrics reproduced in miniature through photographic etching, to lathe turned wood, metal castings and carved Lucite.

By re-creating rooms from various periods, each hand-crafted miniature offers a nostalgic glimpse into the past, and as a group they provide a survey of stylistic differences on interior and architectural design.

ARTISAN: **KUPJACK, HENRY**

BUSINESS NAME: Kupjack Studio
E. J. Kupjack Associates Inc.

IDENTIFICATION MARKS:

EK

HENRY KUPJACK with date

On rooms

1968 – 1991

Rooms signed: **E. J. Kupjack**
H. C. & E. J. Kupjack
Kupjack Studio
Kupjack
Henry Kupjack

1991 – Present

Rooms signed: **Kupjack Studio**
Henry Kupjack

CATEGORY:
Furniture: period, reproductions; Roomboxes: furnished; Room Settings

HONORS:
Exhibits: Kupjack Miniature Rooms, Winterthur Museum, Winterthur, Delaware; Children's Museum, Indianapolis, Indiana; The Forbes Magazine Gallery, New York City; Gibbs Museum of Art, Charleston, South Carolina; The Carole & Barry Kaye Museum of Miniatures, Los Angeles, California; The Cheney Collection of Kupjack Miniature Rooms, The Baltimore Museum of Art, Baltimore, Maryland

RECOGNITION:
Miniature Collector, No. 41, Jan/Feb. 1984, pg. 32-34, "Miniature Masterpieces, The Kupjack Rooms;" *Goldbook*, 1993 Annual Edition, Beverly Hills, California, pg. 162-167; *Chicago Tribune Sunday Magazine*, Aug. 24, 1986; *The New York Times*, Jan. 15, 1984

BIOGRAPHY:
Henry Kupjack graduated high school in 1969. He attended The University of Illinois, majoring in architecture. He has been immersed in the world of miniatures from childhood, first accompanying his father, Eugene Kupjack, to Mrs. Thorne's studio as a child, then becoming increasingly involved in the work throughout his youth. Having received something of a unique, lifelong master's class, it was fitting that he would ultimately join his father full-time, which he did, in 1974. In the 20 years since the partnership was formed, Kupjack Studios has solidified and expanded its reputation for unparalleled mastery of the art of miniaturization. After Henry's father passed away the Kupjack Studios continued on with Henry taking on his father's work and Jay, Henry's brother, still producing photography for the studio. Many hours and possibly days of research is collected for the historical and architectural accuracy of the pieces he makes.

(Goldbook, 1993 Annual Edition, Beverly Hills, California)

ARTISAN: **KURESMAN, A. JACK**

IDENTIFICATION MARKS:

CATEGORY:

Furniture: period; Roomboxes; Vignettes

HONORS:

NAME AOH; Taft Museum, Cincinnati, Ohio, 1984/85; 1989/90

RECOGNITION:

Nutshell News, Vol. 13, No. 9, Sept. 1983, pg. 50-52; Vol. 18, No. 11, Nov. 1988, pg. 94; Vol. 19, No. 11, Nov. 1989, pg. 92; *Miniature Collector*, No. 46, Nov/Dec. 1984, pg. 32; *Cincinnati Post,* Nov. 15, 1984; Apr. 5, 1986; *Nutshell News Calendar,* 1985

AUTOBIOGRAPHY:

My childhood interest in miniatures was rekindled in 1976 with membership in the Miniature Society of Cincinnati. Since then, in addition to creating miniature rooms, shops, and furniture, I have served MSC as Treasurer, Board Member, and as Treasurer and as Co-Chairman of the annual show. In addition I have served as Treasurer of two NAME National Houseparty Steering Committees.

In 1986, I elected early retirement as an operating Vice President of Federated Department Stores, responsible for investor relations.

After election to two terms as Treasurer of the National Association of Miniature Enthusiasts, I served as an appointed board member of that organization.

L

ARTISAN: **LACY, ALICE, PH.D.**

BUSINESS NAME: Alice Lacy, Ltd.

IDENTIFICATION MARKS:

Logo

Alice Lacy, Ltd.

Iron Wire Wicker & Software

Alice Lacy, Ltd.
Iron Wire Wicker & Software

CATEGORY:
Designer; Furniture: wicker; Wicker: iron wire

RECOGNITION:
Miniatures Dealer, Apr. 1987

AUTOBIOGRAPHY:

As a child, I went after school and Saturdays to the Maryland Institute of Art. Indeed, in the summer when I was only 12, I was allowed to take an adult course in portrait painting in oils. Relating to that experience, I was awarded a four year scholarship at the art institute. My father was dogmatic in his insistence that I return to more prosaic studies in the seventh grade.

My classical art career was revived briefly after high school when I studied medical art and, followed the tradition of Michelangelo, dissected a human cadaver in the medical school in order to learn muscle attachments. After this, my studio art was always there but only as an adjunct to academic work.

I graduated from University of California, Berkeley where I was accepted into Phi Beta Kappa and began graduate studies. In addition to seminars in social psychology and cross cultural work leading to a Ph.D. in sociology, I continued to study painting and to paint. During this time and later when I taught at American University, I exhibited my art. I won various prizes and had a one man show at a gallery in Georgetown.

It was just eight years ago, approximately 1984, that I discovered miniatures, by accident. Traveling in mainland China, I came across an artisan winding wire over wire threads to make little temples and other small pieces. He called them curios. I thought they would make nice toys for children.

On my return I learned that they, if properly scaled, were miniatures. It was after this that I began to work with the artists and craftsman there to produce the little pieces which are now known as "Iron Wire Wicker." Probably of equal importance to my art in the design of the furniture is my basic appreciation of cross cultural similarities and differences in improving the quality of the work.

Our miniature wicker is made from iron wire. A thread of wire is wound around the core wire to make a strong structural frame. Other wires are braided, flattened with a mallet, looped, or woven, before they are soldered together.

In 1989, we began copyrighting our distinctive designs. In creating new pieces I strive for beauty as well as strength, always asking myself the question, "Would I like this in the large size in my home?" On reviewing my designs, from early to recent, the higher numbers are the later designs, I observe a trend towards simplicity, a little more woven and a few less curves.

As an American artist, developing miniature wicker, I feel myself identified with the past of wicker. Just as it was by chance that we found the small curios while traveling in China, so it was by accident that the wicker industry developed in America. And both are linked to the Clipper trade. The small coastal village of Bath, Maine, where we live, was known for its ship building industry. Our house was the office of the Sewall ship yard. On the living room wall are mahogany boxes with gilded names of the raked masted sailing ships built here for the China trade. On their return voyage, the Clipper ships discarded the bamboo poles used as dunnage to steady the cargo. A Boston grocery clerk, Cyrus Wakefield, began weaving the jettisoned reeds. His story as the founder of one of the largest industries in Victorian America parallels that of Horatio Alger. Later there were inexpensive Chinese copies of American wicker.

Wicker is the generic name for woven furniture. It can be made of any material capable of being bent. In its endless variety, used inside or on a patio, in a large house or dollhouse, wicker adds a warm nostalgic aura.

Here in Maine, some of my iron wire wicker was exhibited in the gallery at the Center of the Arts, where my painting had hung. I understand that my creative art continues, only the medium has changed.

I feel that all my past, which is long and varied, culminates in my present work with miniatures.

ARTISAN: **LAKES, ARTHUR & LYNN**

BUSINESS NAME: A. L. L. Small

IDENTIFICATION MARKS:

Jan. 1990 to present

CATEGORY:

Beds: dressed; Drapes; Furniture: upholstered

HONORS:

IGMA Artisan 1994 (Lynn)

RECOGNITION:

Nutshell News, Oct. 1991, pg. 79; *Miniatures Showcase*, Winter 1992, pg. 24, 33; Jan. 1993, pg. 39; *Dolls In Miniature*, Summer 1991, pg. 26-30

AUTOBIOGRAPHY:

We began our miniature business in 1990 after collecting for several years. Arthur does all the woodwork, as he has had a lifelong interest in drafting and woodworking. He uses computer-aided design programs in his work. Lynn has worked with textiles for many years and does all the miniature fabric work.

ARTISAN: **LAMB, ELENA**

IDENTIFICATION MARKS:

Elena signed in script **Elena** or printed

CATEGORY:

Furniture

RECOGNITION:

Nutshell News, Vol. 12, No. 10, Oct. 1982, pg. 64; Vol. 13, No. 5, May 1983, pg. 49; Vol. 13, No. 8, Aug. 1983, pg. 46, 48, Show Scene; *Miniature Gazette*, Vol. 10, No. 2, Winter 1981, pg. 29

ARTISAN: **LANCASTER, JUDY**

BUSINESS NAME: Judy Lancaster

IDENTIFICATION MARKS:

Some unmarked, all 1979 to present

Larger pieces, may also have date

Needlework: initials worked into design
Small items: initials embroidered in a patch or printed on bottom

CATEGORY:

Beds: dressed; Dolls; Furniture; Glass: stained; Lamps: stained glass; Lighting; Quilts: Victorian; Roomboxes; Rugs

RECOGNITION:

Dolls In Miniature, Summer 1993, pg. 63-68

AUTOBIOGRAPHY:

I am a native of Southern California and I met John, my husband of 29 years, at the University of California, Santa Barbara where I earned my degree in English. While our two sons were little, I was very involved in community affairs and scouting, but I always found time for various forms of needlework and sewing as well as occasional other arts and crafts. Soon after moving to Washington State in 1977, I rediscovered the world of miniatures, thinking back to my metal 1940's dollhouse filled with plastic furniture, my favorite toy! While in Washington, I formed a club which met twice a month, and later began teaching classes to new miniaturists and selling lamps and accessories through a local shop.

When we returned to California in 1987, I immediately joined two clubs and have been very active in both ever since. I have also established a small business finishing dollhouses for people and teaching classes at various shops and NAME Houseparties. In addition, I have sold stained glass lamps, tiny dolls, Victorian crazy quilts and other accessories on a limited basis to stores, dealers, individuals and at a few shows.

ARTISAN: **LANG, JAMES E.**

BUSINESS NAME: Langlass

IDENTIFICATION MARKS:

Unmarked

CATEGORY:

Glassware

AUTOBIOGRAPHY:

After a varied scientific/decorative glassblowing career, I started working for myself in 1987. Almost immediately I started making designs of miniature glassware, but only in the last year have I taken it more seriously. I am making many new contacts and friends and am always pleased to help with any information to further the ends of the miniaturists cause.

ARTISAN: **LANKFORD, BILL**

BUSINESS NAME: Creative Accents

IDENTIFICATION MARKS:

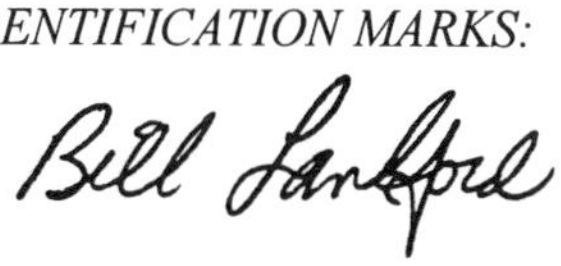

LANKFORD, BILL, continued

CATEGORY:

Buildings; Landscaping

HONORS:

Exhibits: Toy & Miniature Museum of Kansas City; The Carole & Barry Kaye Museum of Miniatures, Los Angeles, California; Miniature Museum of the Southwest, Dallas, Texas; Denver Museum of Miniatures

RECOGNITION:

Nutshell News, Vol. 20, No. 4, Apr. 1990, pg. 62; Vol. 21, No. 5. May 1991, pg. 44-46, "Faded Glory," Sybil Harp; Vol. 22, No. 10, Oct. 1992, Cover, pg. 40; Vol. 23, No. 2, Feb. 1993, pg. 44-45, 49; *Miniature Collector*, Vol. 17, No. 1, Cover, pg. 50; *Le Magazine de la Maison de Poupée*, Paris, Vol. 17, 1991, pg. 22

ARTISAN: LA ROCHE, LINDA

BUSINESS NAME: Linda La Roche
Linda La Roche Museum Reproductions

IDENTIFICATION MARKS:

All marks 1979 to present

CATEGORY:

Furniture

HONORS:

IGMA Fellow; 2nd prize Handcrafted Furniture, Tiny Treasures Society, Boston, 1979, 1980; 2nd, 3rd, 4th Honorable Mention Prizes, GNOME, 1st Annual Juried Show, 1986; Exhibit: Toy & Miniature Museum of Kansas City

RECOGNITION:

Nutshell News, Vol. 11, No. 6, Jun. 1981, Pg. 28-31; *Arlington Advocate* Massachusetts, Mar. 20, 1980; *Art Week Boston*, Massachusetts, 1980, Exhibit Government Center

AUTOBIOGRAPHY:

I began making miniature furniture in 1978 at the Old Schwamb Mill in Arlington, Massachusetts, in a class offered by Bill Bromell, noted ship builder, whose work is represented in nautical museums both in this country and abroad. I had never worked with wood before although I had worked with my hands since childhood. Originally, I became interested in dollhouses and miniature furniture when I was given a dollhouse shell and began to read about the brilliant and sophisticated collections around the world, including Queen Mary's Dollhouse and the Thorne Rooms.

I have taught miniature furniture building for over 12 years, beginning in 1980, at the Schwamb Mill, the Little Red Schoolhouse in Concord, Massachusetts, Yankee Artisans in Needham, Massachusetts, and the Guild School in Castine, Maine. I have also spoken to many groups about my work at various places in Massachusetts, including the Cooper Hewitt Museum of Design, a division of the Smithsonian, in New York.

I work exclusively in one-inch scale, specializing in carved furniture of the 18th and 19th centuries. Pieces are usually exact scale models of full-sized furniture found in books, museums, or private collections. I exhibit at shows around the country and accept commissions for special orders. I have achieved the rank of Fellow of The International Guild of Miniature Artisans and am a member of the National Association of Miniature Enthusiasts.

I graduated from Grinnell College with a BA in English and have done graduate work in reading rehabilitation. I have two sons, Joe and Chris.

ARTISAN: **LARSEN, GARY**

BUSINESS NAME: Gary Larsen

IDENTIFICATION MARKS:

GL

CATEGORY:

Furniture

AUTOBIOGRAPHY:

I learned the art of making miniature furniture from Warren Dick. I started making miniatures as a full-time occupation in July 1987, at the age of 55.

ARTISAN: **LASCH, WAYNE & SALLY**

BUSINESS NAME: Shaker Miniatures

IDENTIFICATION MARKS:

WL
W. Lasch

SL
S.LASCH

W+S LASCH

CATEGORY:

Furniture: Shaker

HONORS:

NAME AOH (both)

RECOGNITION:

Articles written by Wayne and Sally Lasch

Nutshell News, May 1980; Jul. 1980; Nov. 1980; Mar. 1981; Aug. 1981; Nov. 1988; *Miniatures Showcase*, Sept. 1993; *Miniature Gazette*, Winter 1982; Spring 1983; *Miniatures Magazine*, May 1976; *Hobbies Magazine*, Apr. 1973; Mar. 1974; *Creative Crafts*, Jun. 1973; *The Scale Cabinetmaker*, Vol. 14, No. 1; Vol. 14, No. 3; Vol. 15, No. 1; Vol. 16, No 1; Vol. 16, No. 3; Vol. 17, No. 1; *Dollhouse Miniatures*, Carstens, 1975

Articles written about Wayne and Sally Lasch

General Electric News, Sept. 12, 1975; *General Electric Monogram*, Nov/Dec. 1976; *Miniature Entrepreneur's Newsletter*, Jul/Aug. 1977; Sept. 1977; *Miniatures Dealer*, Mar. 1986; *Shaker – The Community Newsmagazine*, Mar. 1987; *The Cleveland Plain Dealer*, Jul. 1972; *Linn's Stamp News,* Post Office Picture, Apr. 29, 1974; *Miniature Room Settings*, Helen Ruthberg, 1978; *This Side of Yesterday in Miniatures*, Catherine B. MacLaren, 1975; *The Book of Miniatures*, Helen Ruthberg

AUTOBIOGRAPHY:

Wayne and I graduated from Case Western Reserve University, in Cleveland. Wayne has a Masters degree in Science and Sally has a BS degree in Nursing. Wayne has just retired from General Electric where he worked as a chemist. Sally works part-time as a RN at University Hospitals, Cleveland.

We have been collecting and making miniatures since the late 60's. Our business, Shaker Miniatures, started in 1971, when we began making grocery store counters and display cases and then branched into Shaker items. Our most notable customer was Disney World in Florida who ordered items for their gift shop soon after they opened. We have been involved with NAME and with our local club since 1974 and 1971 respectively. We have sold at many miniature shows around the country and have taught workshops at many of them. Wayne teaches on the proper use of hand tools.

ARTISAN: **LAST, CATHERINE**

BUSINESS NAME: Fantasy Finishes by Catherine Last

IDENTIFICATION MARKS:

CATEGORY:

Finishes: faux, painted

HONORS:

IGMA Artisan; Journeyman & Masters Awards, Isabel O'Neil Studio Workshop, New York City

RECOGNITION:

Nutshell News, Dec. 1981, pg. 66-68; Feb. 1983, pg. 33-34; *Miniature Collector*; *House Beautiful*, 1988; CNN Cable News, Elsa Klensch, 1994

AUTOBIOGRAPHY:

I've studied painted and faux finishes, in full-scale, at the renowned Isabel O'Neil Studio Workshop in Manhattan from 1971 to 1994. As a teacher there since 1983, I've received both the Journeyman and Masters awards from the Studio, which is based on the Renaissance guild system. My full-scale faux finishes have been exhibited in Tiffany's spring bridal vignettes and in a window of Gucci's Fifth Avenue Shop, as well as in our yearly Sotheby's auction and as part of an annual May fund raising event for the Studio Workshop.

Some time in 1978 I entered a small shop to purchase a gift for a friend's daughter, and left entranced by the world of miniatures and intrigued by the possibility of using my training, to reduce marble, malachite, lapis, tortoise, chinoiserie, glazing, antiquing and gold leaf techniques to miniature scale. Unacquainted at the time with The Thorne Rooms or any of the famous miniature artisans, I started experimenting with commercial furniture, some of which I revised by reshaping and refining legs, tops or cabinet doors. Later I had a limited supply of furniture, mostly French 18th century, made for me by Robert A. Chucka of Milwaukee, who was all of 18 at the time. This furniture, when the painted finish was completed, was signed by me "R.A. Chucka" and the date Bob made it, and "Catherine Last" and the date I finally completed the piece.

My first show in Mt. Kisko, possibly in 1979, resulted in no sales, but I met the Dearing Tracys, who urged me to enter the IGMA show the following spring. That started my brief career in miniatures, which ended with my husband's death in 1983. Although I have felt stirrings of late to complete some of Bob's beautiful pieces, I have not yet committed myself to any future shows. But possibly the Guild show in the future, who knows!

ARTISAN: **LATANÉ, THOMAS & CATHERINE**

BUSINESS NAME: T & C Latané

IDENTIFICATION MARKS:

Small pieces unmarked

TL	TL TL TL	TLC LATANÉ
Burned into wood	Stamped or chiseled into metal	Joint projects: initials or name

On houses and some furniture name was written out

CATEGORY:

Accessories; Dollhouse; Furniture; Metalwork; Roomboxes

LATANÉ, THOMAS & CATHERINE, continued

HONORS:

IGMA Fellow (Thomas); IGMA Artisan (Catherine)

RECOGNITION:

Nutshell News, Apr. 1981, pg. 84; Oct. 1981, pg. 22-27; Nov. 1981, pg. 92-96; Dec. 1982, pg. 101; *Miniature Collector*, No. 30, pg. 20-22; No. 32, pg. 51-55; No. 33, pg. 57-60; No. 37, pg. 8; No. 75, Spring 1992, pg. 28-32

AUTOBIOGRAPHY:

Thomas M. Latané, born Baltimore, Maryland October 16, 1955

I built my first model house in a high school architecture class. The sale of this model in a Baltimore consignment shop, "The Calico Cat" got me started. I worked for eight years in my parents' basement and in a backyard smithy I erected, producing full-size and miniature items which I sold at local craft shows and to local miniature collectors and dealers.

The only higher education I received were three metal smithing and jewelry classes at Towson State University, from goldsmith John Fix. This developed my sense of detail in both miniature and full-size metal work.

Catherine Hillman Latané, born Minneapolis, Minnesota February 27, 1954

I married into the business in 1981. After two years in Minnesota we settled into our shop in Pepin, Wisconsin. My interest in fiber arts which involved me in dressing beds and similar activities gave way to tin work as we both focused more on metals, cutting out the furniture construction.

We team taught at the Guild school in Castine, Maine five sessions teaching 48 hours of class some years. We have taken a break from the trip to Maine to raise our daughter Frances, but hope to go back when she is older.

Our miniatures business has taken a back seat the past few years to our full-size work, a change dictated by the custom orders received. In either size the work is the same, except for houses, Medieval to Early American rustic furnishings and hardware made with traditional techniques.

ARTISAN: LAUER, MARY J.

BUSINESS NAME: J. J. 's Miniatures

IDENTIFICATION MARKS:

On bottom of paw

CATEGORY:

Animals; Bears: jointed, stuffed, teddy

RECOGNITION:

Nutshell News, Jun. 1991, pg. 65

AUTOBIOGRAPHY:

My mother was a seamstress and taught me to sew when I was about nine. I always loved stuffed animals, mainly teddy bears. My occupation is secretarial.

ARTISAN: **LAUGHON, FRED T.**

BUSINESS NAME: Fred T. Laughon

IDENTIFICATION MARKS:

Some pieces have initials and date

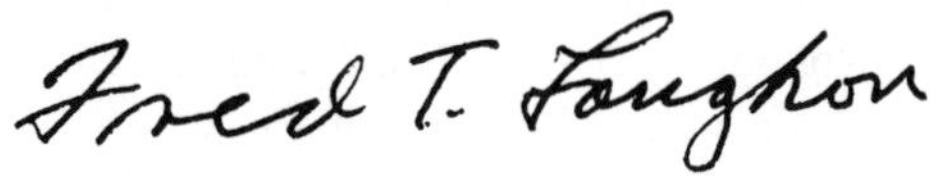

Signature burned into wood with date printed

CATEGORY:

Dolls: wooden; Furniture: salesmen samples

HONORS:

IGMA Fellow

RECOGNITION:

Traditional Home, Fall/Winter 1986, pg. 34, 46; *Doll Reader*, Sept. 1992, pg. 50; *Doll News; Richmond Times Dispatch*

ARTISAN: **LEE, JANICE**

BUSINESS NAME: Creative Hearts

IDENTIFICATION MARKS:

CATEGORY:

Accessories: nursery; Furniture: nursery

RECOGNITION:

Nutshell News, Apr. 1991, pg. 55; May 1992, pg. 64

ARTISAN: **LE GUERRIER, LÉON**

BUSINESS NAME: Miniatures L. Le Guerrier

IDENTIFICATION MARKS:

CATEGORY:

Furniture: unpainted

RECOGNITION:

Miniature Gazette, Spring 1989, pg. 60-61

ARTISAN: **LEISOREK, FAY**

BUSINESS NAME: Fay–vourite Crafts Co.
My Fay–vorite Dollhouse

IDENTIFICATION MARKS:
Small pieces unmarked

Fayvourite Crafts | My Fay-vorite Dollhouse | Fay

1979 to present | 1991 to present

CATEGORY:
Floral Arrangements; Food; Judaica

HONORS:
IGMA Artisan; Greater Niagara Original Miniatures Enthusiasts juried show

RECOGNITION:
Nutshell News, Mar. 1989, Cover; *The Canadian Jewish News,* Oct. 17, 1985, pg. 35, Art Section, "Miniature Creations Have Artist Thinking Big;" Oct. 5, 1989, pg. 32, Organizations & People, "Chabad Lubavitch Centre Receives Miniature Mikvah;" *Hands Magazine,* Canadian Crafts, Nov/Dec. 1985, pg. 52-53, "Judaic Miniatures;" *Miniature Gazette*, Vol. 17, No. 3, Spring 1989, pg. 57-58, see Fay Mernick; *Miniature Collector*, No. 72, Spring 1991, pg. 7-9; No. 75, Spring 1992, pg. 5, see Fay Mernick; *LittleThings*, Canadian magazine, Vol. 1, Issue 4, Jul. 1992, Cover

BIOGRAPHY:
Fay Leisorek was born in Mexico City in 1957. She graduated from the New School of Science & Humanities. Fay's love for miniatures developed when she was four, with her first visits to the local markets with her mother. There she came in contact with artisans displaying their hand made miniatures that were exact replicas of the utensils her mother used in the kitchen. Years later, she realized that these miniatures were one-inch scale.

She still has her first dollhouse, which she received when she was five years old, that included the original furniture and dolls, and all those market miniatures.

During her father's business trips to the provinces, she learned first hand how to make different kinds of miniatures from the local crafts people.

As the years past, she developed diverse interests, but her love for miniatures was always there. Even while she attended dental school she would make miniature figurines in wax and cast them in silver.

Since she was unable to continue her dental studies when she came to Canada in 1977, she devoted her time to crafts. It was then she got involved with the miniaturist community in Toronto, Ontario, Canada, joining the Toronto East Area Miniaturists Club, serving as program chairman for three years and president for two years.

In 1979, after attending a number of shows, she realized there were no miniatures for Jewish dollhouses, so she started her own line of Judaica.

Fay is recognized in Canada and the United States with her line of Judaic miniatures, holiday roomboxes and prize winning flower and food arrangements. She gives workshops at schools and is a promoter of miniatures as an art form. Fay is a member of NAME and an IGMA Artisan.

Her work has been exhibited in different synagogues in Toronto, libraries, art galleries, schools, miniature shows and Judaic miniature shows. Fay has also taken part in special exhibits at the Royal Ontario Museum, the Museum of Civilizations in Hull, Quebec, and the Jewish Museum in New York City.

Fay is in partnership with two architect model makers, runs a miniature store and studio and does commission work. Her work is sold in Canada and the United States. She is a single parent of two.

ARTISAN: **LEONARD, ANNE LUREE**

BUSINESS NAME: Anne Luree Originals
Anne Luree Dolls

IDENTIFICATION MARKS:

On original dolls

On reproductions of Commercial molds

On tags

CATEGORY:

Dolls: original, reproductions

HONORS:

Original Doll Artists Council of America

RECOGNITION:

Contemporary Doll, Jan. 1993, pg. 38, 40; Dec. 1993, pg. 64; *California Collector; Petite Portraits*, Carol-Lynn Waugh, Hobby House Press 1980, pg. 47-49; *Dolls In Miniature*, Viola Williams & Alice Smith, Vol. 2, Issue 4, Winter 1992/93, pg. 10; *The Doll Catalog,* Hobby House Press, 1980, 1981, 1982

BIOGRAPHY:

Anne Luree is a charter member of ODACA, belongs to the Pioneer Doll Club, UFDC, Doll Artisan Guild, NAME and Small but Mighty, a miniature club in Sacramento, California. She currently holds office in two clubs and is Secretary of ODACA. She has been collecting most of her life and has the first doll ever given to her. She developed one of the early slide programs on sculpting basic dolls and has taught many workshops. She professionally restored bisque, porcelain and composition for many years before retiring to concentrate on making and dressing dolls. She likes to prepare and present workshops, where the students make or finish a project.

She is mostly self-taught, though she majored in art in school, and has a "DDT," Doctor of Doll Technology, from Lifetime Career Schools, and has taken several seminars with noted teachers.

She has been married to a super guy for 28 years, they have two sons. She was born in Los Angeles, moved to Reno when she was 10, lived in Phoenix, Arizona for four years after marriage and has lived in Sacramento since approximately 1973.

She likes to travel and is permitted to do so at least once a year for the national doll conventions, and sometimes other meetings. She has hopes of visiting Prague, the home of her ancestors, in the next few years.

ARTISAN: **LEONARD, KATHY**

BUSINESS NAME: K L Miniatures

IDENTIFICATION MARKS:

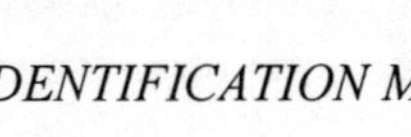

CATEGORY:

Furniture: wicker; Needlepoint; Needlework

HONORS:

IGMA Artisan, 1989

LEONARD, KATHY, continued

RECOGNITION:

Nutshell News; Miniatures Showcase

AUTOBIOGRAPHY:

My introduction to the world of miniatures was in 1981 when I started building a doll's house, and furniture from kits. I learned how to do the basics of weaving wickerwork from Millie August How-to Book, but aside from the stock pattern, I've made my own designs and patterns.

I applied to IGMA for artisanship and received it in two categories, needlepoint and wicker furniture, in October 1989.

I've taught classes at several shows, and at the Guild School, Castine, Maine. In 1989 and 1992, I was a dealer at the London Doll's House Festival, and have enjoyed making friends internationally.

ARTISAN: LE ROUX, MARIUS

BUSINESS NAME: Marius Miniatures

IDENTIFICATION MARKS:

CATEGORY:

Furniture; Roomboxes; Shadow Boxes

HONORS:

IGMA Artisan; Honorary Award March 8, 1983, Cape Tercentenary Foundation

RECOGNITION:

Die Kaapse Kopersmid, Stellenbosch, 1981; *The Cape Copper-smith,* Stellenbosch, 1981

AUTOBIOGRAPHY:

I was born January 11, 1938 in Witbank, South Africa, attending junior and high school in Cape Town, earning a Cape Senior Certificate, First Class in 1955. My higher education was obtained at the University of Stellenbosch where I received a BA in 1965, a BA with honors in 1975 and an MA in 1980. At the present time my occupation is Director of the Stellanbosch Museum. I worked for four years in sales promotion at the head office of the Old Mutual Life Assurance Society, and spent a one year residence in London, England. For five years I was in the service of the Rembrandt Group of Companies as Head of the Rembrandt Van Rhyn Art Foundation, Peter Stuyvesant Foundation & Public Relations Officer.

I have lectured at the Department of Afrikaans Cultural History and was a part-time lecturer for a post-graduate course in Museum Science since 1977. I've held the positions of Vice-President, 1981-1983 of the Council of the Southern African Museum's Association of which I was a member from 1977 to 1984; Chairman of the Cultural History section of SAMA, 1974-1975; and Chairman Heads of Cape Provincial Museums' Meetings, 1975-1979. The Cape Tercentenary Foundation bestowed upon me an Honorary Award on March 8, 1983.

I became involved in the making of miniature furniture in 1989.

ARTISAN: LEVI, OTILIA

BUSINESS NAME: Otilia Originals

IDENTIFICATION MARKS:

LEVI, OTILIA, continued

CATEGORY:

Accessories: bridal, personal; Clothing; Floral Arrangements; Millinery; Pictures; Trunks; Vignettes; Wreaths

RECOGNITION:

Nutshell News, Aug. 1982, pg. 40-42 "Symphonies In Bloom;" *Miniature Gazette*, Winter 1980; Summer 1988, pg. 29; *Miniatures Showcase,* Spring 1988, pg. 11, 18, 28, 31

AUTOBIOGRAPHY:

I was born in Romania but the family moved to France in 1937. Since early age I loved to work on designing crafty items. While in France World War II broke out and times were bad for everybody. Yet I found myself helping in refugee causes. At night I would sit at the kitchen table and paint with watercolors which I sent with letters to my friends left in my native land. Living in Lyon I wanted to study textiles and fashion designing, since Lyon was the place for textiles. But we had to fight for our survival, so my dreams and my youth have been buried in a troubled world.

In 1956, I emigrated to America with my husband and little boy, after many years of pains, deprivation mentally and physically hurt. After arriving in the States, I felt in my heart a new wave of hope and happiness.

I made up my mind to do something with my buried talents. We lived in Maryland from 1958 to 1983 when we moved to Florida. In Maryland I had an antique shop, specializing in growing little flowers and preserving them, using them in decorating wedding invitations, in full-size.

Soon a customer of mine introduced me to the world of miniatures. I registered for the NAME Houseparty in Washington, DC in the summer of 1980, and entered an exhibit made of little flower arrangements. I enjoy doing a large variety of pieces that I decorate with antique items I find, fabrics and my home grown miniature roses.

ARTISAN: **LEVINGER, STEVE**

BUSINESS NAME: Scale Builders

IDENTIFICATION MARKS:

CATEGORY:

Structures

HONORS:

IGMA Artisan

AUTOBIOGRAPHY:

My education is a Bachelor Degree in Construction Management from Colorado State University, where I graduated in 1985.

I've been involved in model making most of my life. Professionally I started building architectural models in 1985. Through this I received commissions to build miniature buildings. When things slow down, I build miniatures to sell. I have built mostly log cabins and rustic barns. I enjoy custom work.

I currently work mostly for a pewter casting studio. I make mold patterns for a variety of miniature items including cars and buildings.

Most of my model building experience has been learned on the job as I work.

ARTISAN: **LEVY ERNIE**

BUSINESS NAME: Ernie Levy Museum Quality Furniture and Clocks

IDENTIFICATION MARKS:

With month and year, or month, day, and year.

CATEGORY:

Clocks: working; Furniture: period

HONORS:

IGMA Fellow; Exhibit: Toy & Miniature Museum of Kansas City

RECOGNITION:

Nutshell News, Vol. 8, No. 2, Summer 1978, Pg. 15; *Architectural Digest; New York Times*, Sunday, Oct. 12, 1977, The Living Section

AUTOBIOGRAPHY:

My miniature background started when I built model aircraft, boats, ships, trains and cars from 1935 to 1974. In 1958, I graduated from the Chicago School of Watchmaking using my legal name of Isaac Levy. From 1975 to the present, I have been a builder of miniature furniture and clocks.

ARTISAN: **LEWANDOWSKI, SHERI**

BUSINESS NAME: Sheri Lew
Environmental Design

IDENTIFICATION MARKS:

CATEGORY:

Carvings: wood; Sculptures

AUTOBIOGRAPHY:

Since high school, I have taken art classes including fine art oil and acrylics, tole painting, and rosemaling. I have taken bird carving classes between 1986 and 1992 with Jack Bayman at the National Carvers Museum, Monument, Colorado. I entered my work in two competitions, winning two blue ribbons for bird and duck carving, in the decorative category.

I began experimenting with one-inch scale carvings in 1987. In April of 1991, I started selling at shows, a certificate of authenticity accompanies most of my pieces. In 1992, I graduated from the Guild School in silversmithing. My educational background is in registered nursing.

ARTISAN: **LEWIS, STAN**

BUSINESS NAME: Stan Lewis – Artist in Fine Miniatures

IDENTIFICATION MARKS:

With number and date.

LEWIS, STAN, continued

CATEGORY:
Furniture: J.H.Belter, period

HONORS:
IGMA Fellow

RECOGNITION:
Nutshell News, Sept. 1981, pg. 66; Oct. 1982, pg. 50; Sept. 1984, Show Scene; Nov. 1985, pg. 70; Aug. 1986, pg. 25; Nov. 1986, Show Scene; Oct. 1987, Show Scene; Jul. 1988, pg. 61; Oct. 1988, pg. 73; Nov. 1988, Show Scene; *Miniature Collector*, No. 33, Show Stoppers; No. 44, Show Stoppers

ARTISAN: LEWIS DeMET, THELMA

BUSINESS NAME: Thelma Lewis DeMet

IDENTIFICATION MARKS:

Hang Tag

CATEGORY:
Clothing; Millinery

HONORS:
IGMA Artisan

RECOGNITION:
Nutshell News, Jul. 1990, pg. 59; *Miniatures Showcase*, Fall 1990, pg. 19; Spring 1991, pg. 35, 60; Summer 1991, pg. 33; Winter 1992, pg. 29, 39, 40

AUTOBIOGRAPHY:
I basically "fell" into miniatures in 1990 as a schoolhouse volunteer trying to make changes in a bureaucratic system that affects children. My first miniature house was completed inside and out within eight months, but I found that working with wood was not as exciting for me as working with fabrics. I have a dressmaker background and decided that I would try to create some contemporary clothing and accessories from fine upscale fabrics, as I shopped at miniature stores and shows there wasn't anything contemporary. I then decided to preserve today's fashions and create history for tomorrow.

ARTISAN: LICHTENHAN, GARNET

IDENTIFICATION MARKS:

CATEGORY:
Furniture: period, tufted

RECOGNITION:
Nutshell News, Jan. 1983, pg. 53, 55; 1989; *Miniature Gazette*, 1983; *Miniature Collector*, Spring, 1983, pg. 38-39; *American Architecture,* 1983; *Small Talk,* Dec. 1978, pg. 4-9

LICHTENHAN, GARNET, continued

AUTOBIOGRAPHY:

I started producing Victorian tufted sofas and chairs in 1978. They are all handcrafted on walnut bases. The tufting is accomplished exactly like its full-sized counterpart, charted by a retired upholsterer and made from all pure silk. All of the upholstery work is completely hand sewn with the only glue being used on the frame itself, although the cushions are glued in.

ARTISAN: LITTLEJOHN, MARION

BUSINESS NAME: Littlejohn's Wee Magic

IDENTIFICATION MARKS:

Some unmarked

ML

CATEGORY:

Animals: cats; Flowers & Plants; Linens; Needlework

AUTOBIOGRAPHY:

I got a late start in the miniature field. I worked with computers for 30 years, and in my middle 50's I discovered that there was a miniature world! I had done a lot of crafts, and handwork, teaching youngsters in small groups and for my own children.

In 1976, I saw my first miniature show in a mall, and the following month joined the Mile High Miniature Club. I also belong to two more clubs, and am a volunteer at the Denver Museum of Miniatures, Dolls and Toys. I do sell at local shows and miniature sales.

I make a lot of items, but I mainly make and sell paper flowers, which I have no way of marking. I do use paper labels, but of course they don't stay with the flowers. Bill Lankford has used them in several of his displays, and they are in some museums.

I tat doilies, big and tiny, originally using larger cotton thread, but have graduated to using smaller cotton thread for some of the tablecloths. Now I am working with the tiny silk threads. These cannot be marked but do start out with my name on a label. The flowers and tatting are sold at shows by dealers, throughout the country.

I have made and painted cats with Sculpy, which I have signed with the ML and date, and Cernit swan centerpieces, also with the ML, but most of my things have been unmarked.

My dollhouse, which I inherited, has been featured and shown along with several of my roomboxes, in magazines, which of course are not all my work, but have been put together by me.

I was born in 1921 and am now enjoying a second childhood, that has lasted for 18 years! My first was during the depression, so you can see that I am having a lot of fun now.

ARTISAN: LITTWIN, HARRY G. (Deceased)

(Submitted by Helen Littwin)

BUSINESS NAME: Copper Corner

IDENTIFICATION MARKS:

H L

CATEGORY:

Accessories; Coppersmith; Dioramas; Metalwork

HONORS:

IGMA Fellow

LITTWIN, HARRY G., continued

RECOGNITION:

Nutshell News, Vol. 12, No. 11, Nov. 1982, pg. 57; Vol. 14, No. 10, Oct. 1984, pg. 57; *Miniature Collector,* No. 2, Jun. 1977, pg. 30; No. 14, Aug. 1979, pg. 20; *Miniature Gazette*, Vol. 6, No. 3, Spring 1978, pg. 9, 52-53, "The Master of Copper Miniatures;" Vol. 7, No. 1, Fall 1978, pg. 81; Vol. 10, No. 3, Spring 1982, pg. 54, "Copper Master Celebrates 13 Years"

BIOGRAPHY:

Harry was a retired businessman when he discovered the world of miniatures. Years ago he went into The Elder Craftsman in New York City to browse around. He was interested in making full-size Colonial furnishings. When he overheard the store manager tell a customer that she was looking for someone who could make copper kitchen miniatures, Harry stepped in and volunteered.

Within a week, he had made 31 different pieces - trays, mugs, cups, and suffered many burnt thumbs in the learning process! When he took the items back to the store, the owner loved them. She asked him to make miniatures for her the year round and Copper Corner was born. A stickler for detail, Harry researched various periods in history for authenticity in his designs.

The curator of the Museum of the City of New York liked Harry's work well enough to display it. Many items are still popular sellers in the museum gift shop. His work has been exhibited in shows throughout Florida, Atlanta, Boston, Pennsylvania, New York, Connecticut, Ohio and California. He worked in both one-inch and ½-inch scale. Harry was known as the Master of Copper Miniatures.

ARTISAN: **LLOYD PATTI ANN**

BUSINESS NAME: Patti's Little Women Boutique
Patti's Classes Unlimited

IDENTIFICATION MARKS:

AN ORIGINAL BY PATTI LLOYD

1/8 inch wide silk ribbon glued or sewed inside costume

CATEGORY:

Costuming; Figures

HONORS:

IGMA Artisan

RECOGNITION:

Nutshell News, Apr. 1989, pg. 71; Jul. 1989, pg. 64; Jun. 1990, pg. 60-62; Jul. 1990, pg. 60; *Miniature Collector*, Fall 1992

AUTOBIOGRAPHY:

My field was Audio Disorders and sign language. I worked with non-verbal and hearing impaired children. Believe it or not, my miniature world began with a foot operation. At the time, it really didn't matter if I had only 20% hearing, now I'm considered profoundly deaf, as needless to say, I didn't need to hear my miniature dolls. My eyes and those of others told me the story. I left a 10 year teaching job and ended up designing costumes and making dolls full-time. I am self-taught in this area with much I still want to learn. Later I took an extensive course in doll repair and restoring.

I made a few large dolls before deciding to "think small," one-inch scale was just right. I didn't need a big work table and they were suitable for a lovely dollhouse, roombox, or simply to collect.

In teaching and sharing my skills with others, I've traveled as far as Australia. You might say I never left my teaching job. Might I add that in the miniature world I found much warmth, love and many friends for a lifetime.

ARTISAN: **LODDER, CAROL**

BUSINESS NAME: Carol Lodder

IDENTIFICATION MARKS:

CATEGORY:
Pottery; Porcelain

HONORS:
IGMA Artisan

RECOGNITION:
Nutshell News, Vol. 18, No. 9, Sept. 1988, pg. 46-48, "Posset Pots & Posy Plates," Lauran Stevens; *Dolls House World*, Issue No. 10, 1990

AUTOBIOGRAPHY:
I studied at Bournemouth and Poole College of Art and gained my diploma in Art and Design, and Licentiateship of the Society of Designer-Craftsmen, both in ceramics.

I have workshop experience with Michael Cardew and Marianne de Trey. In 1980, I set up my own workshop after working for other potters and teaching pottery summer school for six years. I now specialize in high quality hand-thrown and hand painted miniature ceramics. I am an IGMA Artisan. My mark is also on the country furniture I make with my father, Nigel Lodder.

ARTISAN: **LOGAN, BARBARA**

BUSINESS NAME: Barbara Logan

IDENTIFICATION MARKS:

CATEGORY:
Toys: antique reproductions

HONORS:
IGMA Fellow

RECOGNITION:
Nutshell News, Vol. 15, No. 5, May 1985, pg. 58-60; *Dolls: The Collectors Magazine*, Vol. 7, No. 6, Nov. 1988, pg. 98-99

ARTISAN: **LONG, PEGGY**

BUSINESS NAME: Mini Millinery

IDENTIFICATION MARKS:
Unmarked

CATEGORY:
Accessories: ladies

RECOGNITION:
Nutshell News; Miniatures Showcase

ARTISAN: **LOPÉZ, LAURA E.**

IDENTIFICATION MARKS:

CATEGORY:
Dolls: character, fantasy, portrait

ARTISAN: **LOSCAR, ERNIE**

BUSINESS NAME: Saloon Originals

IDENTIFICATION MARKS:
1990 to present

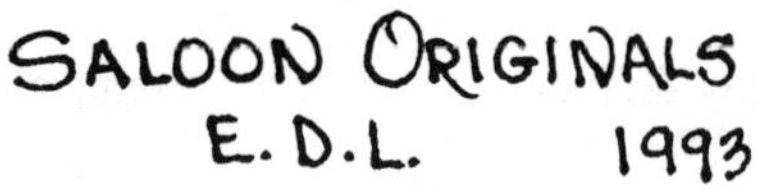

CATEGORY:
Bars; Saloons

RECOGNITION:
Nutshell News, Jun. 1992, pg. 21; *Miniature Collector*, Mar. 1993, pg. 56

ARTISAN: **LOSCAR, NANCIE**

BUSINESS NAME: Nancie's Millinery Plus

IDENTIFICATION MARKS:
1988 to present

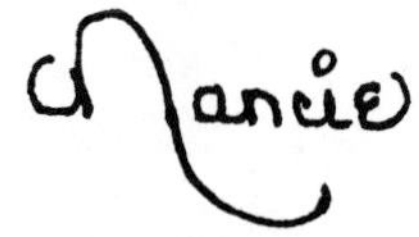

CATEGORY:
Millinery; Shoes

RECOGNITION:
Dolls In Miniature, Winter 1992/93, pg. 77-81

ARTISAN: **LOWE, KAREN**

BUSINESS NAME: The Mini Maniac

IDENTIFICATION MARKS:

CATEGORY:
Accessories: country

LOWE, KAREN, continued

RECOGNITION:

Nutshell News, Oct. 1984, pg. 73; Feb. 1986, pg. 65; Dec. 1986, Cover; Jan. 1987, pg. 58; Jul. 1987, pg. 58; Nov. 1989, pg. 93-94; *Miniature Collector*, Winter 1991, pg. 31; *Miniatures Showcase*, Fall 1986, pg. 34-40; Spring 1987, pg. 18, 21, 49; Summer 1987, pg. 43; *Miniature Gazette*, Spring 1987, pg. 27

AUTOBIOGRAPHY:

About 1979, one of my craft magazines featured a dollhouse and plans, and I decided to make one. While visiting our local shop for supplies, I learned they would be offering a furniture making class, and eagerly signed up. I thought it would be fun to make all the furnishings for my house when it was finished.

At the class, I met some dealers who attended miniature shows, and invited me along. I never knew there were miniature shows, but I was hooked with the first one. I was encouraged to make a few things to take, which I did, and eventually became a dealer. That furniture class gave me the basics, and the rest is self-taught, trial and error education.

Although it took years, my house finally did get finished, but it is still completely devoid of furniture.

ARTISAN: **LUCAS, ANN & ROBIN**

BUSINESS NAME: World Of My Own

IDENTIFICATION MARKS:

"Ann Lucas"

Sewn inside clothing

CATEGORY:

Accessories: garden; Dollhouse; Dolls; Furniture; Houses; Kits: doll

RECOGNITION:

Nutshell News, Vol. 23, No. 4, Apr. 1993, pg. 64-65; *Dolls House World*, Issue No. 6, 1990, pg. 53; Issue No. 9, 1990, pg. 52-53; Issue No. 10, 1990, pg. 9; Issue No. 15, 1991, pg. 18; Issue No. 22, 1992, pg. 62; *Dollhouse & Miniature Scene*, Issue No. 1, 1993, pg. 20; *International Dolls House News*, Vol. 17, No. 3, 1988, pg. 37; Vol. 19, No. 2, 1990, pg. 26

BIOGRAPHY:

In 1985, Ann set up business making and dressing dolls full-time, trading under the name World Of My Own. Ann dresses dolls in costumes ranging from Tudor to modern day and specializes in commissions working from photographs and reference books. Her dolls can be seen at many British dolls house fairs.

Robin started making dolls houses full-time in 1990 and informal training in building, landscape gardening and architecture helped him to develop his own style. Designs are based on real buildings, usually timber framed houses found in Sussex and Kent, England, and great attention is paid to detail. Robin also makes simple old English furniture. He exhibits at many fairs in England.

ARTISAN: **LUTJENS, BETH LANE**

BUSINESS NAME: Beth Lane Creations

IDENTIFICATION MARKS:

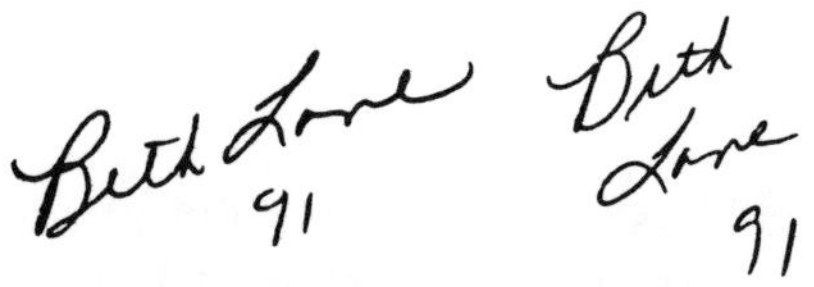

Back of head with year
1981 to present

Carved behind Right ear
1993 to present

CATEGORY:
Dolls

HONORS:
Dolls Exhibited with Binder Collection, Palace of the Governors Museum, Santa Fe, New Mexico, Jun/Aug. 1992

RECOGNITION:
Nutshell News, Sept/Oct. 1984

AUTOBIOGRAPHY:
I started miniatures in 1979 by building a dollhouse. I could not find any dolls I liked, so I started making them myself. I made mostly Old West Characters but will make all types. I love teaching dollmaking and teach classes across the United States.

ARTISAN: **LYONS, SYLVIA**

BUSINESS NAME: Sylvia Lyons
Porcelain People

IDENTIFICATION MARKS:

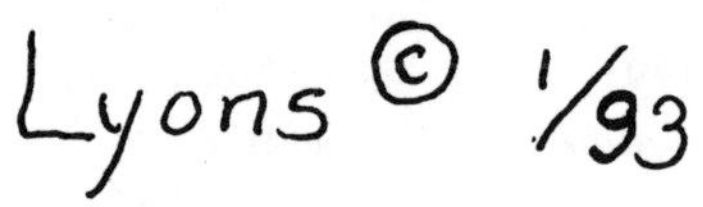

Number of piece in edition
Year of edition

CATEGORY:
Animals; Dolls; Figures: historical

HONORS:
IGMA Fellow; NAME AOH; Original Doll Artist Council of America; Exhibit: Toy & Miniature Museum of Kansas City

RECOGNITION:
Nutshell News, 1991; *Contemporary Doll*, Fall 1991, pg. 86; *Dolls*, Feb. 1994

ARTISAN: **LYTLE, BILL**

BUSINESS NAME: The Workshop

IDENTIFICATION MARKS:

1985 to present

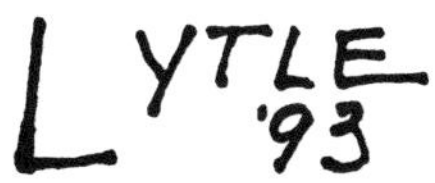

CATEGORY:

Costuming; Dolls: costuming

HONORS:

IGMA Artisan, Fellow

M

ARTISAN: **MABE, ED**

BUSINESS NAME: Spotlight Miniatures

IDENTIFICATION MARKS:

CATEGORY:

Furniture: art deco, art nouveau riche, faux; Roomboxes; Structures

HONORS:

IGMA Artisan

RECOGNITION:

Nutshell News, Vol. 24, No. 4, Apr. 1994, pg. 84; *Miniatures Showcase*, Vol. 5, No. 2, Spring 1990, pg. 52; *Miniature Gazette*

BIOGRAPHY:

Ed Mabe was born and raised a beach kid and surfer in Long Beach, California. He has an Engineering Degree in Mechanical Engineering from Long Beach State University. Ed engineered and raced off road cars, after growing up on a family owned car lot, he specialized in custom cars of the 1950's and 60's era.

His miniature career began in self defense, after marrying Eve Karoblis and three children. He has been a Hollywood set painter since 1976 working on feature films, television shows, and commercials.

Over the years Ed has used his experience and product knowledge of paint and design, and applied them to miniatures. He specializes in Faux Marble and aging techniques.

Ed enjoys the challenge of developing and teaching these techniques to miniaturists across the country.

ARTISAN: **MALON, CINDY**

BUSINESS NAME: Cindy's Workshop

IDENTIFICATION MARKS:

CATEGORY:

Furniture

HONORS:

IGMA Artisan

RECOGNITION:

Nutshell News; Miniatures Showcase; Country Living, Vol. 15, No. 3, Mar. 1992, pg. 102-103

AUTOBIOGRAPHY:

I have been producing and selling my work at national shows since approximately 1985. I began by making furniture for my own enjoyment and due to local requests for my work, began to sell at shows. I was entirely self-taught until 1989 when I began to attend the Guild school in Castine, Maine. This experience greatly expanded my awareness of what fine miniatures should be, helped me to expand my skills and the quality of my work. I have been fortunate to study there for three years and will continue to return in the future.

My work has appeared from time to time in *Nutshell News* Show Scene, and in issues of *Miniatures Showcase. Country Living* magazine has also featured my work along with those of several other artists in the March 1992 issue.

ARTISAN: **MANDERS, NANCY**

BUSINESS NAME: Nancy Manders Originals

IDENTIFICATION MARKS:

○

Nancy
Manders
ORIGINALS

CATEGORY:
Accessories: doll

HONORS:
IGMA Artisan 1989

AUTOBIOGRAPHY:

My interest in miniatures increased dramatically after my children were grown, and I decided to resume work on a long neglected dollhouse. This project eventually led to a toy shop and, of course, toys and dolls to fill it. My first attempt was a nondescript character doll and it was awful. But I kept going. My Scottish American husband suggested a Highland dancer which turned out much better. I was so proud of her that I took her to a club meeting and to my absolute surprise people wanted to buy her. That's when my business started, in 1983. Before long, in 1985, I was making hats and accessories, which I dearly love. I have been a CIMTA member since 1984 and was awarded IGMA Artisan in 1989. Miniatures have been a pure joy for me, not only as a creative outlet but also in the wonderful people I have met.

ARTISAN: **MANISCALCO, SYLVIA**

BUSINESS NAME: Maison Mini

IDENTIFICATION MARKS:
Unmarked

CATEGORY:
Accessories

AUTOBIOGRAPHY:

I was a home economics teacher in the New York City School system, complete with training in architecture, decorating houses, costuming, etc. On a vacation to Europe I discovered the wonderful dollhouses in the Dutch museums. It was a natural to combine the two interests. Returning home I started researching castles and built a thirteenth century castle dollhouse. I was immediately hooked on miniatures.

Before I knew it I was in business building dollhouses and dollhouse accessories. Now, after having been in business since 1974, and with the help of my daughter, Robin, we manufacture over 700 accessories in one-inch, ½-inch and doll's dollhouse scales. Most of our accessories are in the toy/classroom line; general store merchandise, Judaica and hobby items for the dollhouse.

When I lived in Holland, I published *Maison Mini Miniature Magazine*, about dollhouses and miniature events in Great Britain and Europe. It was wonderful traveling around and sharing with my readers all the unusual and wonderful miniatures I was privileged to see.

ARTISAN: **MANN, CAROL**

BUSINESS NAME: Carol Mann

IDENTIFICATION MARKS:

CATEGORY:

Earthenware; Porcelain; Pottery: wheel thrown; Stoneware

RECOGNITION:

Dolls' House World, No. 20, 1992, Cover, pg. 34-35; *International Dolls House News,* Vol. 20, No. 4, 1991, pg. 19

AUTOBIOGRAPHY:

I graduated from Manchester Polytechnic in July 1970, after studying 3D design in wood, metal and ceramics. I specialized in ceramics and after a post graduate course went on to teach full-time for the next 20 years.

I have always loved throwing small pots, but was not aware of one-inch scale and dolls' house "mania" until 1990 when I set up my workshop and made my first few pieces. I began potting full-time in January 1991. Encouraged by Caroline Hamilton, I worked for my first "big" show in May 1992 at the London Dolls' House Festival. Here I met buyers nationally and internationally, and have been kept very busy. I still make normal sized pots and have just exhibited in a gallery in Northamptonshire.

My pots are individually thrown on the potters wheel, and using a wide variety of techniques and materials I hand decorate with slips, glazes, oxides and lusters, pieces are fired up to several times in an electric kiln. My range of traditional and contemporary pieces is constantly expanding, including commissioned work.

ARTISAN: **MANN, RICHARD L.** (Deceased)

IDENTIFICATION MARKS:

CATEGORY:

Furniture: period; Musical Instruments; Pianos: Harpsichord, Spinet; Roomboxes

HONORS:

NAME IMA and AOH

RECOGNITION:

Nutshell News, Vol. 12, No. 11, Nov. 1982, pg. 67; *Miniature Gazette*, Vol. 5, No. 1, Sept. 1976, pg. 23-24; Vol. 9, No. 1, Fall 1980, pg. 91-92, "I.M.A. Report," Thomas Devereux

BIOGRAPHY:

Richard L. Mann was born in Buffalo, New York on August 13, 1888. After attending Nichols School he entered Yale, Sheffield Scientific School, and after graduating from Yale he studied Mechanical Engineering at Cornell for two years. Upon leaving Cornell, Richard pursued a career in Engineering and during World War I he was engaged in war work, making Industrial Furnaces, and spent some time in the Field Artillery Corps Officers Training School during the war.

He married Margaret Green in 1934 and later became involved with miniatures when he created a dollhouse for his granddaughter. During WW II, he worked for the Barden Company making precision Ball Bearings for the Norden Bomb Sight. About that time he began making miniature furniture for Beth Martin, who then had an antique and miniature shop on New York's Madison Avenue. Richard continued with miniatures well into his 90's when he passed away at his retirement home in Hawaii.

(IMA report, by Thomas Devereux; AOH profile, by Ferbie Claudon, authorized reprint by NAME)

ARTISAN: **MANNING, K. R.**

BUSINESS NAME: The Ken Manning Collection

IDENTIFICATION MARKS:

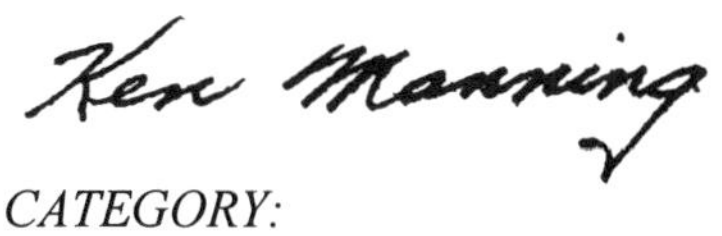

CATEGORY:

Musical Instruments

HONORS:

IGMA Artisan, Fellow 1987

RECOGNITION:

Nutshell News, Dec. 1983, pg. 71; Oct. 1989, pg. 76-77; Feb. 1990, pg. 46; Feb. 1992, pg. 64; Apr. 1992, pg. 40; *Hobbies Magazine*, Aug. 1983, pg. 64-65; *Western Living*, Vancouver, British Columbia, Feb. 1984, pg. 38; *Doll Reader*, May 1985, pg. 209; *Miniature Collector*, Fall 1989, pg. 23; *Miniatures Showcase*, Spring 1991, pg. 35

AUTOBIOGRAPHY:

I was born February 2, 1921. During World War II from 1942 to 1945 I served in the Royal Canadian Air Force.

I worked at various jobs including house building and cabinet making, and built several miniature one-inch scale model houses for building contractors in the 1940's.

As a hobby, I started making miniature musical instruments about 1980. Subsequently, I joined IGMA and eventually received my Fellowship in the Guild in 1987. I am self-taught in all fields.

ARTISAN: **MANNING, M. E..**

BUSINESS NAME: The Small Touch

IDENTIFICATION MARKS:

1977 to present

CATEGORY:

Accessories; Furniture: Country

HONORS:

State Fair Awards

RECOGNITION:

Nutshell News; 5th Edition Miniature Catalog; Miniature Collector

MANNING, M. E., continued

AUTOBIOGRAPHY:

For Christmas 1976, my one and only response to my husband's inquires, regarding my desires for a Christmas present was a dollhouse. Although thoroughly convinced that I had flipped my wig, he hid his embarrassment at buying one for an adult, and my first dollhouse, a nine room Williamsburg, made its appearance. Trying to furnish my new toy proved to be a challenge, and after one or two kits I knew designing my own furniture was the only way. Struggling to furnish my house led to many trips to the local dollhouse shop and on one such trip I met a shop owner from New Jersey, now one of my best friends. I was showing off my new creations and she followed me out of the shop and offered to buy some on the spot. My very first customer and a new career.

Miniature enthusiasts in Montgomery, Alabama in 1978 were as scarce as hens' teeth and anyone with teaching ability was non-existent. In an effort to meet others interested in miniatures and to further interest in my new hobby, I consented to teach a class in furniture construction at the local shop. Little did I realize how many classes would follow, or how many interested people would surface. Soon a local mini club was formed and continues today. The South Alabama Fair, held each October, due to our mini club efforts, now has an annual exhibit devoted to miniatures. What a joy to see the finished product, the imagination, ideas, and totally different exhibits produced from a single theme is fantastic!

Creating original miniatures gives one a feeling of ecstasy, which is reward enough, but the real joy and love comes from the fellow miniaturists. No group of people ever existed that are more congenial, caring and lovable.

Working with wood, which I dearly love, has led to a newly acquired hobby. Wood carving is really a carryover from the miniatures as many items in my collection are hand carved. While working on wood carvings I still do my miniatures as time permits.

My husband has now retired and we are traveling, cruising, doing as we please. Five children and seven grandchildren make for a busy day. Miniatures will always have a very special place in my life, thank goodness Santa gave me the dollhouse, back in 1976.

ARTISAN: MANWELL, SALLY

BUSINESS NAME: Sally Manwell Miniatures
The Three of Us

IDENTIFICATION MARKS:
Most unmarked

SALLY MANWELL	1992 to present Name tag back of right leg

CATEGORY:
Dolls: costuming, figures: Toys

HONORS:
IGMA Artisan

RECOGNITION:
Nutshell News, May 1992, pg. 64; *Miniatures Showcase*, Spring 1992, pg. 28, 58

AUTOBIOGRAPHY:

I joined a newly organized miniature club in our area in 1974 and began to make dolls for the little girl in the dollhouse so I could feed my miniature habit. From this it grew into a small business. Story-book type dolls were developed and then character and period-dressed dolls added. As ¼-inch scale became popular, several of the dolls fit into this scale as people.

Researching costume and period clothes is what I've always enjoyed most. I am always searching for fine fabrics, small trims, costume books, and ways to refine the dolls.

Of course one of the main elements of the hobby is the association with so many other miniaturists, many of whom have become very good friends.

ARTISAN: **MARBLE, NICOLE WALTON**

BUSINESS NAME: Williamson Walton Marble

IDENTIFICATION MARKS:

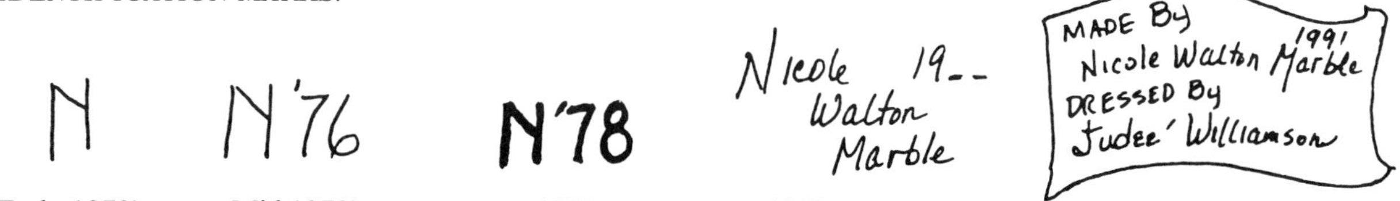

Early 1970's	Mid 1970's	1978 Branded into wood	1979 to present	1986 to present

CATEGORY:

Carvings: carousel, ivory, wood; Designer: exterior, interior; Furniture: period; Roomboxes; Rooms

HONORS:

IGMA Artisan

RECOGNITION:

Nutshell News, May/Jun. 1979, pg. 48; Mar. 1980, pg. 33, 53; Jan. 1982, Show Scene; Jul. 1982, pg. 98, "Who's Who in Small Scale Miniatures;" Jan. 1983, Show Scene; Jun. 1983, pg. 36; Jul. 1984, pg. 35-36; Sept. 1986, pg. 72; Nov. 1986, pg. 54-55, "To Windsor and Beyond;" Apr. 1987, Show Scene; Oct. 1987, pg. 78; Sept. 1988, pg. 36-37; *Miniatures and Doll Dealer Magazine*, May 1983, pg. 57; Nov. 1983, pg. 43; Jun. 1985; *Miniature Gazette*, Fall 1981, Cover; Summer 1983, pg. 29-30; *Honolulu Star-Bulletin*, Newspaper, Aug. 9, 1982, Front Page

Williamson Walton Marble "Nicole Walton Marble and Judeé Williamson"

Nutshell News, Oct. 1987; Jan. 1988, pg. 67, 70; Jul. 1988, pg. 32-33; Nov. 1988, pg. 90; Apr. 1989, Cover, pg. 73; Jun. 1989, pg. 68; Jul. 1990; May 1991, pg. 65; Sept. 1991, Cover, pg. 69-70; Nov. 1991, pg. 72; Jun. 1992, Show Scene; Jan. 1993, Product Review; Jul. 1993, Show Scene, pg. 66; Nov. 1993, Product Review, pg. 26-27; Jan. 1994, Show Scene; Mar. 1994, pg. 77-78, Build Your Dollhouse, Part 6, Sydnie Wagner; Jun. 1994, pg. 22, 33, 35; Oct. 1994, pg. 63; *Miniatures Showcase*, Spring 1988, pg. 16-17; Winter 1989, pg. 13; Summer 1990, pg. 26-27, 29, 46; Spring 1992, pg. 31; Mar. 1993, More Minis, pg. 52; Sept. 1993, pg. 20, Exciting Decorating Styles; *Contemporary Doll Magazine*, Summer 1991, pg. 62-63; Feb. 1994, pg. 100; *Miniature Collector*, Winter 1993, pg. 33; Spring 1994, pg. 24; Nov/Dec. 1994, pg. 28; *Dallas Life Magazine*, Sept. 5, 1993, pg. 23

BIOGRAPHY:

Nicole Walton Marble, now an Arizona resident, has spent most of her life in California. Nicole has had a varied career having been a housewife, worked as a library assistant, as a zoo keeper in Ft. Worth, Texas and Los Angeles, California, a manager of several pet stores, and then as a designer and craftsman in stained glass. Drawn to miniatures in the early 1970's, Nicole specialized in Windsor chairs and related English and American period furniture, and normally works in one-inch and ½-inch scales, but has also made French and Windsor pieces in ¾-inch, 1 ½-inch and two-inch scales.

After forming Williamson Walton Marble with Judeé Williamson in 1985, Nicole has been able to explore many furniture styles, working both in hardwoods and gilt. The styles include Chinese Ming styles, French Louis XV furniture, French Provincial, high Victorian, fantasy furniture, Stickley, and any other styles that look interesting. She also enjoys wood and ivory carving, and has made carousel carvings in both mediums and in various scales. Nicole has been a full-time professional miniature maker since 1987.

Nicole has taught furniture classes for many years. Now that Judeé and Nicole are partners in their work and in classes, they travel and teach classes all over the United States, and on the Mini Cruise. Nicole and Judeé have also been developing various new kits and tools.

Nicole is an Artisan in the International Guild of Miniature Artisans, and has been a member of the National Association of Miniature Enthusiasts, for many years.

See "Judeé Williamson"

ARTISAN: **MARCH, WILLIAM C.**

BUSINESS NAME: Cape May Miniatures

IDENTIFICATION MARKS:

CATEGORY:

Structures

HONORS:

IGMA Artisan

AUTOBIOGRAPHY:

I have been a historic restoration contractor for 29 years and started plying my trade in miniatures since 1990. I have concentrated exclusively on miniatures since the spring of 1993, when I opened a full-service miniature shop in Cape May, New Jersey. Up until that time my business was solely by mail.

I have been interviewed and my work photographed by *Victorian Homes* magazine.

My experience and expertise in the restoration field serves me well in creating scale miniatures.

ARTISAN: **MARCUS, ARTHUR & PAUL**

BUSINESS NAME: Miniatures Unlimited

IDENTIFICATION MARKS:

Unmarked

MINIATURES UNLIMITED

Logo

CATEGORY:

Accessories; Furniture

RECOGNITION:

Miniatures Showcase; Miniature Needlepoint and Sewing, "Projects for Doll Houses," Kathryn Falk, Hawthorn Press 1977, pg. 128

BIOGRAPHY:

Arthur Marcus first became interested in miniatures in 1976. He saw a dollhouse and noticed that there weren't many items to put it together; no staircases leading up to the second or third level nor too many items for the windows. He created his first staircase, which was the typical straight stairs that most buildings have. At that time there was a miniature store located on the Upper East Side of New York City. It was the only miniature store known on the East Coast and most items were handcrafted and limited. The store, Mini Mundus, was the start. They loved the staircase and placed an order. He spoke with the owner and she was interested in other items; i.e. a non-working window shade. His son Paul studied for two years as a fashion major was able to sit at a factory sewing machine and experiment. In very little time a non-working window shade in ecru was created. That led to more orders and designs for staircases. Arthur was creating and building dollhouses.

Arthur has been a talented craftsman for a long time, doing all the detailed construction work on his own home, so it wasn't too difficult for him to scale any item down to dollhouse scale. As a youngster, Paul Marcus, attended the Saturday Art School at Pratt Institute in Brooklyn. After high school he attended the Traphagen School of Fashion majoring in Fashion Design. Designing and creating clothes enabled him to use his many talents to learn different aspects of assorted fabrics. He was doing visual merchandising for many years while always creating miniatures. He plays a major role in the many aspects of Miniatures Unlimited.

ARTISAN: **MARKS, KATE** (Deceased)

IDENTIFICATION MARKS:
Unknown

CATEGORY:
Needlepoint; Needlework

HONORS:
NAME AOH

RECOGNITION:
Nutshell News, Nov. 1980, pg. 32; Jul. 1982, pg. 41

BIOGRAPHY:

After retiring as a medical secretary, Kate did extensive research into needlework and textile design. She made her first dollhouse rug about 1942. It was a gift to a friend who was furnishing a dollhouse for her grandchild. She made several after that, each one becoming more polished. In the early 1970's she met Betty Valentine who asked her to do some petit point rugs for her miniature rooms. This time they were pictured in *Nutshell News*, and Kate was behind in orders from then on. She passed away in 1979.

(AOH profile, by Ferbie Claudon, authorized reprint by NAME)

ARTISAN: **MARSHALL, ANDEE**

BUSINESS NAME: Andee M Miniature Originals

IDENTIFICATION MARKS:

CATEGORY:
Accessories; Animals: cats; Dolls; Food

RECOGNITION:
Nutshell News, Vol. 19, No. 3, Mar. 1989, pg. 66; *Miniatures Showcase*, Vol. 5, No. 3, Summer 1990, pg. 82; Vol. 7, No. 2, Spring 1992, pg. 30

AUTOBIOGRAPHY:

I had a brief stint at the Art Center, Los Angeles, California. I always have been interested in miniatures but marriage and nine children caused a delay in being serious. In 1985, the children bought me a dollhouse and since I love cats and didn't want dolls for my house, I made a few for myself. They were shown to the owner of the local miniature shop, and a business was born!

ARTISAN: **MARSTON-ROBINSON, MARY LEE**

BUSINESS NAME: Marston Miniatures

IDENTIFICATION MARKS:

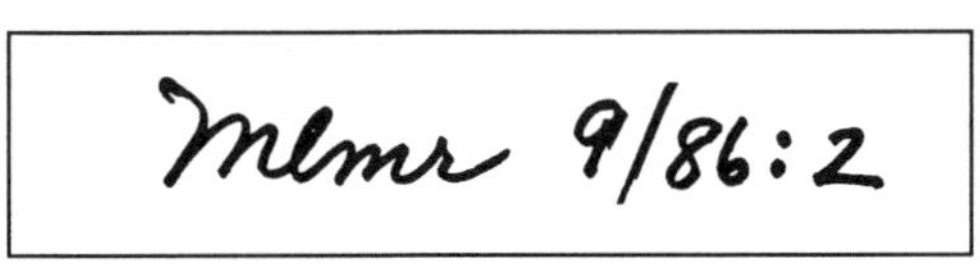

Month & Year first piece started
Number of edition

Brass plaque engraved in old English Script

MARSTON-ROBINSON, MARY LEE, continued

CATEGORY:

Furniture: wicker; Reproductions; Wicker: Antique, Victorian

HONORS:

Exhibit: Toy & Miniature Museum of Kansas City

RECOGNITION:

Nutshell News, Vol. 21, No. 6, Jun. 1991, pg. 38-41, "The Golden Age of Wicker," Anne Day Smith; *Miniature Collector,* Spring 1989, pg. 25-27, "Working With Wicker," Ann Bahar

AUTOBIOGRAPHY:

I am self-taught in making Victorian wicker replications. I've always been interested in tiny things and as a child I experimented with trying to make things out of left-over bits and pieces around the house. I crafted a dollhouse at the age of seven using toothpicks and scraps of corrugated cardboard. At the age of nine, I made a one-inch scale guitar out of balsa wood, but complete with strings, pegs and even a delicate inlay around the sound hole. All of this was left behind, however, through the remaining school years and college.

Upon graduation from college, I entered into a career in banking but before long, the world of fine and applied arts beckoned again and I spent my evenings after work in the financial world as an artist in Greenwich Village, New York. It was an eerie double life style and about 1990, I finally decided to become wife, mother and artist.

At the time I made this decision, there was no one making line-for-line replicas of Victorian wicker furnishings and since I loved the nostalgia, history, fussy detail, and intricate design involved in reproducing such wicker projects, I decided there was definitely a place for me in the miniature world.

All of my pieces are carefully researched and when I'm really stumped, I call a friend who is an expert in the field of period wicker. Wicker is normally the use of any one of a number of fibers from rattan to willow twigs, but since all of these fibers are out-of-scale for my work, I substitute a "look alike" fiber which is available in bundles which have to be separated into thin strips similar to cane but comparable to the thickness of a heavy duty sewing thread. I also make my own fabric coverings from scratch by weaving threads of the untwisted fiber or sewing thread on a homemade loom.

My line now covers nearly 40 different Victorian wicker designs to include tables, settees, beds, picture frames, and bird cages complete with working doors, birds, cuttlebones, perches and swings. I thoroughly enjoy testing my abilities by doing one-of-a-kind designs also. I feel I am finally accomplishing a life long dream by being a part of the miniature art community.

ARTISAN: **MARTIN, ALLEN** (Submitted by William R. Robertson)

BUSINESS NAME: Martin's Miniatures

IDENTIFICATION MARKS:

Signed **Martin's Miniatures**, with year, piece number, and ©

CATEGORY:

Furniture

RECOGNITION:

Nutshell News, Vol. 13, No. 8, Aug. 1983, pg. 46-47, Show Scene; Vol. 14, No. 6, Jun. 1984, pg. 49

ARTISAN: **MASCALL, NICOLA**

BUSINESS NAME: Nicola Mascall Miniatures

IDENTIFICATION MARKS:

N.M.

CATEGORY:

Needlepoint; Needlework; Samplers

RECOGNITION:

Dolls House World, Issue 18, 1992, pg. 19; *International Dolls House News,* Vol. 21, No. 1, Spring 1992, pg. 20

AUTOBIOGRAPHY:

I received a diploma in Art and Design, and worked in design for several years, then as a freelance illustrator. Having enjoyed embroidery as a hobby I combined this with the illustration, and produced several illustrative embroideries which were bought by Gordon-Frazer for greeting cards.

I enjoy the challenge in working on very fine fabric and it was by accident that I became familiarized with dolls house miniatures.

ARTISAN: **MASCH, ALFRED T.**

BUSINESS NAME: Masch Miniatures

IDENTIFICATION MARKS:

Unmarked

CATEGORY:

Accessories: outdoor; Furniture: patio; Wrought Iron

HONORS:

IGMA Artisan, Fellow 1987

RECOGNITION:

Nutshell News, Feb. 1982, pg. 25-26, "On the Practical Side," Harry D. Larson; Jul. 1991, Cover; *Miniature Collector*, Fall 1987, pg. 31, Show Stoppers

AUTOBIOGRAPHY:

Shortly after a *Nutshell News* article appeared in the February 1982 issue under the title, "On The Practical Side," and with encouragement from Sybil Harp, I thought I would try my hand in the art of miniatures. I had been an enthusiastic model airplane maker in my younger years and it seemed a natural thing for me to do.

As a graphic artist for Price Waterhouse and having taken specialized courses at Cooper Union, Phoenix Art Institute, and Indiana University, it provided me with a good background to design and handcraft my own creations.

I joined IGMA and was soon ranked as an Artisan and in 1987 given Fellow status.

I was not too encouraged at first and thought that I had made a mistake in choosing patio furniture as my specialty. Although comments were very complimentary at my first shows sales were less than spectacular. In surveying the situation I began to see that many miniature buffs seemed only to be interested in the Victorian era and my work was strictly contemporary. However, I think that most collectors have now thought to add patios to their projects so I can only hope that I have been the catalyst in spurring the addition of patios to their handiwork.

ARTISAN: **MASTERMAN, JOHN** (Submitted by Pat Arnell)

IDENTIFICATION MARKS:

Marks in black ink

MASTERMAN with month and year
Smaller pieces

JOHN MASTERMAN with month and year
Larger pieces

CATEGORY:

Furniture: dolls' dollhouse, period; Houses; Musical Instruments; Pianos; Structures

RECOGNITION:

Nutshell News, Vol. 12, No. 11, Nov. 1982, pg. 31-32; Vol. 13, No. 5, May 1983, pg. 37, 39; Vol. 13, No. 10, Oct. 1983, pg. 62-65; *Miniature Collector,* No. 42, Mar/Apr. 1984, Cover, pg. 25-31, "A True Master (man)," Mary Durland Fields; *Miniature Gazette*, Vol. 11, No. 4, Summer 1983, pg. 29-30

ARTISAN: **MATHIAS, LEONA**

BUSINESS NAME: B. & L. Miniatures

IDENTIFICATION MARKS:

CATEGORY:

Buggies; Furniture: lawn; Hospital Items; Toys; Wagons

ARTISAN: **MATTER, FRANK** (Deceased)
(Submitted by John & Ellen Blauer)

IDENTIFICATION MARKS:

Stamped on pieces

**Miniatures
by
MATTER**

CATEGORY:

Accessories: household; Architect: drafting tools; Art: objects: supplies; Cameras; China; Clocks; Firearms; Furniture: office; Games; Pipe: smoking; Shoes; Tools; Toys

RECOGNITION:

Nutshell News, Vol. 5, No. 4, Winter 1975, pg. 50; Vol. 12, No. 9, Sept. 1982, pg. 43; Vol. 12, No. 11, Nov. 1982, pg. 67; *Miniature Collector*, No. 4, Dec. 1977, pg. 25; No. 6, Mar. 1978, pg. 22-23; *Miniature Gazette*, Vol. 5, No. 4, Jun. 1977, pg. 11-15, "The King is NOT DEAD – Long Live the King," John M. Blauer

BIOGRAPHY:

Joseph H. Gray, the late collector and dealer in miniatures, once stated: "There is no miniature artist alive or dead that could ever equal Frank Matter." This statement, I know, is quite challenging; but as a lifelong collector myself, I most certainly agree with Mr. Gray. Mr. Matter was a commercial artist for 25 years. He began his long career as a miniature artist when he read an ad in a hobby magazine which he had borrowed from the Public Library. Until then he had made miniatures for fun. Following the lead of a fellow craftsman, he published an announcement:

"MINIATURE COLLECTORS: I make miniature portfolios and books of water colors, miniature mechanisms and objects of many kinds. Tell me what you want and I will quote a price."

His first order came from Jack Norworth, famous vaudeville and stage star and composer of "Shine on Harvest Moon" and "Take Me Out to the Ball Game." For Norworth he created a book of 24 water colors. The leather-bound, hand-stitched book was one-inch by 1¼-inch in size. The pictures themselves (done with unbelievable detail) measured ½-inch by 5/8-inch. Norworth was delighted, and thus started a long and successful career as the world's top miniature craftsman.

Frank Matter had retired when I first started to deal with Mr. Gray. However, a few of his treasures were available, among them a working eggbeater, a meat grinder that would grind hamburger into a paste, a coffee grinder that would grind celery seeds to a fine powder, and a tiny barber clippers that would clip the fuzz from a peach. He made furniture, china, stemware, musical instruments, toys, boots, shoes, guns, smoking pipes, games, and clocks. You name it – he could produce it. He worked in one-inch scale and ¼-inch scale.

His greatest challenge was a Boston Beacon Hill Mansion built for Mrs. Frederick Hammons of Seattle. This was done in ¼-inch scale. He created every item down to the silverware, with the exception of the micro stitch petit point rugs, which were done by the famous Mrs. Ethel Forbes Harding. The ¼-inch scale masterpiece was valued at $10,000.00 in 1959, and took Mr. Matter four years of painstaking labor. One of the tiny drawing rooms contains a mantel copied from the Pierce Nichols house in Salem Massachusetts. In the dining room there is a fireplace mantel in delicate green Wedgwood, a sideboard – the original of which was owned by Paul Revere, and a sterling tea set. A grandfather clock 1 ½" high stands in the banqueting hall keeping perfect time. This Mr. Matter reproduced from one designed by Eli Terry, who worked between 1795 and 1812.

Winding continuously from the first to the third floor is a staircase copied from one in the John Pierce House, Portsmouth, New Hampshire. It connects the lower and upper halls. The house is approximately 13" high, 12" across, and 9" deep.

A few months ago (quite by accident) I learned that Mr. Matter was still alive and well. I contacted him by phone and explained that I had been a long-time fan of his. After 11 years of retirement he had somewhat lost contact with the world of miniatures, and was surprised to learn of the current Renaissance. I asked him if he would consent to an interview and he agreed. Before saying good-by, I asked if he had by chance any of his creations available. "No" he replied, "only my personal collection." "Would you consider selling it," I asked. "Yes" he replied. So Ellen and I took the tape recorder, the camera, and the checkbook and set off to meet the "King of Miniatures" in person.

As a life-time collector and a nut on microscopic perfection, to meet Frank Matter was to me what would be to most people like meeting the President, a King, or a movie star.

A widower, Mr. Matter lived alone in a nice cottage style home surrounded by his and his wife's paintings. At 85 he kept in shape riding a bicycle and playing the organ. One of the most remarkable things to me – principally because I work with three pairs of glasses – was the fact that he did not need them. However, when working on micro miniatures, he used a magnifying glass. An enlisted cavalry soldier in World War I, he had had a varied career and many achievements to his credit, among them naming the famous soup company's "Campbell Kids." No challenge seemed too great for his genius. If a tool was not available, he made it – jigs, templets, dies, punches, stamps, lathes, drill presses, and even a pantograph.

Before Joseph Gray was the leading dealer in fine miniatures, R.V. Fisher had had an excellent reputation as the source of fine tiny works of art. Frank Matter had made many items for Mr. Fisher's collection and for Mr. Fisher's customers. One of Mr. Fisher's weaknesses was miniature pipes. He had dozens of them – meerschaums, calabashes, corncobs, and briars – all under one inch in length and made with open bowls and pierced stems, exact reproductions of larger pipes. Mr. Matter made a new pipe perfect in every detail – 1/8-inch long – the smallest one in Fisher's collection.

At once Mr. Fisher ordered five more. "I have five collector friends" he wrote, "who will never let me rest until they, too, have one of the smallest pipes in existence." Mr. Matter filled the order but wrote back: "I am going to have the smallest pipe in the world. I am working on it now." And as is true of all things he pursued, it was accomplished. The completed pipe is 3/32 of an inch long, and the hole that pierces the stem and bowl measures .003 of an inch in diameter. The pipe – the thinnest in the world – can only be viewed through a ten-power glass and is something to behold.

Our day with Frank Matter concluded with the packing of his personal collection, which is now on display at our studio. A day never passes that Ellen and I, along with our collector friends, do not stop and marvel at the skill and creative genius of this remarkable artist. A 1/8-inch padlock and key that actually works, a retractable tape line, chess sets, a checker set with tiny checkers (each checker embossed with a crown), toothpaste tube with toothpaste and tiny screw cap, safety razor with removable blade, and so much more. Yes, this was a King of making miniatures.

(Written by John M. Blauer for *Miniature Gazette,* June 1977, authorized reprint)

ARTISAN: **MATUSCHAK, GEORGIA**

BUSINESS NAME: Georgia's Studio
It's A G.A.S.

IDENTIFICATION MARKS:

Smaller pieces **G** or **M**

CATEGORY:
Accessories; Dolls; Pocketwatch Scenes

HONORS:
IGMA Artisan; NAME AOH

RECOGNITION:
Nutshell News, Vol. 24, No. 5, May 1994, pg. 36-39, "A Peach In A Pair," Anne Day Smith; *Contemporary Doll Magazine*, Jul/Aug. 1992

AUTOBIOGRAPHY:

I became interested in miniatures many years ago after seeing the Colleen Moore Fairy Castle. It's been a love since that first day.

I collect as well as craft, of course, to support my habit. Sculpting was an instant love and my dolls have been my expression of the art in me. I work in extremely small scale, especially in the pocketwatch scenes; structures and accessories are my newest challenges. Quite early on, it became apparent that trial and error would be my teacher in obtaining the results I was seeking.

ARTISAN: **MAYES, SALLY M.**

BUSINESS NAME: Auntie Em's Victorian Treasures

IDENTIFICATION MARKS:
Smaller pieces unmarked

On puppet theaters

CATEGORY:
Accessories; Clothing; Marionettes; Puppets: theaters; Quilts; Toys

RECOGNITION:
Nutshell News

AUTOBIOGRAPHY:

I started as an antique doll collector. Two members of our Denver Dollers started a miniature club of which I was an early member. After buying a large dollhouse I soon learned filling it was very expensive, so I started, with the aid of the few books available, to make things myself. Few materials were available, as they are now. My interest and talent have now centered on the more whimsical and accessories such as toys, puppet theaters, marionettes, crazy quilts, chatelaines, sewing baskets, purses, capes with hats, and whatever else strikes my fancy. I am a retired registered nurse.

ARTISAN: **MAZUR, RUTH L.**

BUSINESS NAME: Masterpieces in Miniature

IDENTIFICATION MARKS:

All 1981 to present

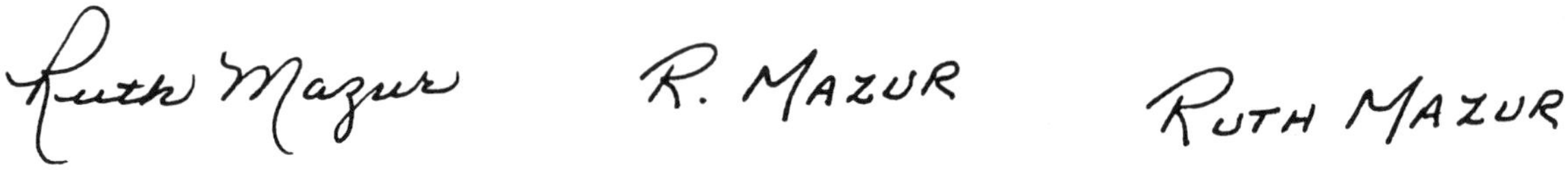

CATEGORY:

Art: fine; Paintings: oil

RECOGNITION:

Nutshell News, Oct. 1984, pg. 66; Jan. 1985, pg. 78; Sept. 1986, pg. 73, 101; Sept. 1991, pg. 76; Nov. 1991, pg. 72

BIOGRAPHY:

Ruth's interest in painting began at age seven when her great grandmother, an artist, handed her a brush and canvas. Her paintings were full-size until 1981 when she pursued the challenge of miniatures. Each frame is hand made and finished to complement the painting.

As you review her work, you will see spring meadows, streams flowing through stands of trees, quaint old barns, floral and misty forests.

Many of her inspirations came from nature itself, representing a serene place where you can walk with her and share the tranquillity.

ARTISAN: **McCABE, STUART**

BUSINESS NAME: Stuart McCabe

IDENTIFICATION MARKS:

On all pieces

Other marks are
English Hallmark
925 (sterling silver) and date

CATEGORY:

Silversmith

HONORS:

IGMA Artisan; Exhibit: Toy & Miniature Museum of Kansas City

ARTISAN: **McCORMICK, JAYNE**

IDENTIFICATION MARKS:

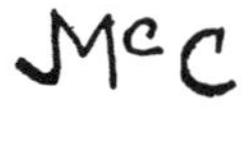

CATEGORY:

Accessories; Furniture: handpainted

McCORMICK, JAYNE, continued

RECOGNITION:

Nutshell News; Miniatures Showcase

AUTOBIOGRAPHY:

I was born in West Chester, Pennsylvania and grew up there. All of my married life has been spent in Delaware. I've been involved in miniatures since 1983 when I quit smoking and needed something constructive to do with my hands. My husband, Ben, and I began participating in the Miniature Settings exhibits at the Philadelphia Flower Show in 1989, winning three seconds, two thirds and one honorable mention.

I've been painting furniture and accessories, for sale, since 1988. I was the NAME Delaware State Representative for five years, the Region M-1 Newsletter Editor and the Centerpiece Chairperson for both the M-1 Atlantic City Regional and the 1992 Philadelphia National Houseparty.

ARTISAN: **McGRATH, MARY**

BUSINESS NAME: Mary McGrath, Ltd.

IDENTIFICATION MARKS:

CATEGORY:

Birds: wildlife; Sculptures

HONORS:

IGMA Fellow; NAME AOH

RECOGNITION:

Nutshell News, Oct. 1986; Apr. 1989; *Miniature Collector*, No. 20, Aug. 1980, pg. 27-29; *Creative Crafts & Miniatures*, Jun. 1985

AUTOBIOGRAPHY:

My interest in art probably started in high school when I entered some soap carving contests. My father was a very talented artist and although I hadn't had any formal training I think I inherited and absorbed some talent from him.

I married young and had four children so I didn't have much time for art when they were growing up. I was able to do three or four paintings a year to enter into a local art show and sale. Sometime in the 1970's, I happened to go to an eggery show and decided that this might be an outlet for me to venture into. I started by painting birds and flowers on egg shells. My painting skills increased with trying to keep enough stock for these egg shows. I had the good fortune that they were well accepted. I am thankful to God for his beautiful creations, especially the birds and flowers which I love. I began venturing into sculpting some of these and incorporated them into and around the eggs.

It was a matter of being in the right place at the right time that I found out about miniature shows, and friends encouraged me to try them. I think I knew then I had found my niche and gradually I decided to do the sculptured pieces by themselves. I feel very blessed that I have found an outlet for work that I enjoy doing and for the success I have in selling it. It very quickly became a full-time job. I have a wonderful husband who has encouraged me all along the way, and without him this very shy person would not have gotten into this fulfilling venture.

ARTISAN: **McINNIS, ELIZABETH**

BUSINESS NAME: Mere Trifles

IDENTIFICATION MARKS:

Most pieces unmarked

Gold mark top of jewelry boxes

Oil paintings signed on back
All Bronzes one-of-kind, signed on bases

CATEGORY:

Animals; Bronzes; Furniture: contemporary; Jewelry: boxed; Masks; Metalwork; Paintings: oil

HONORS:

Exhibit: Toy & Miniature Museum of Kansas City

RECOGNITION:

Nutshell News; Miniature Collector

AUTOBIOGRAPHY:

I have been interested in drawing and sculpture all of my life, but used them for entertainment purposes only, never intending to make art a career. I was primarily interested in the sciences, although I eventually changed my focus to writing and was graduated from college with a degree in Communications. For a number of years I worked as a journalist for a medium size midwestern newspaper, covering everything from murder to political corruption. Eventually, however, my interest palled and I began to look for something else to do. At about the same time, I moved to Raleigh, North Carolina and made friends with several people who collected dolls and miniatures. I had no idea such things really existed! I quickly began to put my art background to work making miniatures, starting with contemporary furnishings and jewelry, and eventually moving on to oil paintings, carnival masks and bronzes. My biggest success, though, and the things for which I am most known are my carved furred animals.

ARTISAN: **McKIRDY, ALAN**

BUSINESS NAME: Alan McKirdy

IDENTIFICATION MARKS:

Small pieces unmarked (accompanied with description card signed in same manner)

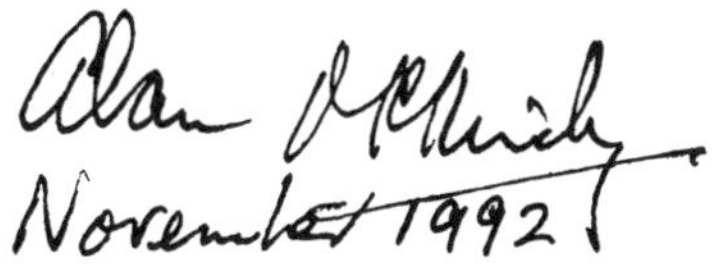

Instruments signed in black ink

CATEGORY:

Furniture; Musical Instruments

AUTOBIOGRAPHY:

I make a number of pieces of furniture for a very close friend as Christmas presents; she then showed these to Bob Hopwood, the organizer of Miniatura in Birmingham, England, who immediately suggested I should take a stand at one of their fairs. Having visited quite a number of dolls house and miniatures shows, it was obvious that there were quite a few makers of fine quality furniture, but no one producing quality keyboard instruments, and as I had the requisite knowledge at my finger tips, being in the business of making and restoring keyboard instruments, it seemed the natural way forward.

McKIRDY, ALAN, continued

Where ever possible, I use correct materials subject only to the grain texture looking right and having sufficient strength. Keyboards are covered in real ivory reclaimed from old piano keys. All casters and hinges work correctly. All instruments are supplied with full details of the original on which it's based. I exhibit at the larger, more important Fairs, but due to the amount of time each instrument requires to complete, I am unable to make enough to supply the retail trade.

I find making miniatures very satisfying, and although extremely exacting a great deal less hard work than heaving about full-size instruments, as strictly speaking, I am well past retiring age.

ARTISAN: McKNIGHT, DEBORAH H.

BUSINESS NAME: Deborah McKnight

IDENTIFICATION MARKS:

CATEGORY:

Ceramics; China; Pottery

HONORS:

IGMA Fellow; NAME AOH; Exhibit: Toy & Miniature Museum of Kansas City

RECOGNITION:

Nutshell News, Vol. 14, No. 6, Jun. 1984, pg. 44, 46, 49; Vol. 14, No. 11, Nov. 1984, pg. 80; *Miniature Collector*, No. 1, Apr. 1977, pg. 46; No. 10, Dec. 1978, Cover, pg. 9, 36, Show Stoppers; *The Doll House & Miniature News*, Vol. X11, Nov. 1979, pg. 12

BIOGRAPHY:

Deborah McKnight has been producing miniature pottery and china since 1974. She has made a wide variety of things ranging from foods to Canton and Chinese Export china.

She is a charter member of the International Guild of Miniature Artisans, and taught at the Guild school, in Castine, Maine, for five years. She is a NAME AOH member. Deborah's work has been exhibited in a number of museums.

Two artists do underdecoration on some of her pieces, they are – Priscilla Lance, who is a talented craftsperson and designer and also does eggs, decoupage and other crafts. Priscilla is an IGMA Fellow and signs her work P. LANCE. Nancy H. Warner is a lithographer and painter and signs her pieces NHW. Their marks are on pieces they have decorated.

ARTISAN: McLEAN, JOAN

BUSINESS NAME: Joan McLean

IDENTIFICATION MARKS:

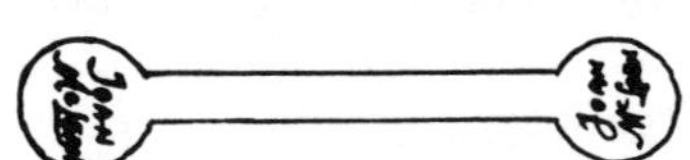

Gold wrist tag

McLEAN, JOAN, continued

CATEGORY:

Dolls: porcelain

HONORS:

IGMA Artisan

RECOGNITION:

Nutshell News, Mar. 1991, pg. 64-65, 74; *Miniatures Showcase*, Spring 1992, Cover; Nov. 1992, pg. 50-51, "Collections –Create Miniature Illusions," Anne Day Smith; *Dolls in Miniature*, Spring 1992, pg. 23-26

AUTOBIOGRAPHY:

I have taken oil painting classes in San Francisco and Southern California. This was before I became interested in miniatures. I have taken classes from Georgia Matuschak, Madelyn Cook, Brooke Tucker, Judeé Williamson, D. Anne Ruff and Charles Claudon.

I have taught classes and round tables at several NAME National Houseparties. I also teach at miniature shows and on crusises.

ARTISAN: **McNARY, ANITA**

BUSINESS NAME: Anita McNary Originals
Minute Miracles

IDENTIFICATION MARKS:

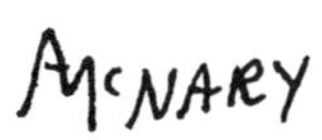

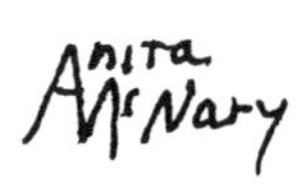

CATEGORY:

Accessories; Dolls: original, porcelain; Furniture; Porcelain

HONORS:

IGMA Artisan

RECOGNITION:

Nutshell News; Dolls in Miniature; Miniatures Showcase

AUTOBIOGRAPHY:

I received my first dollhouse at age two and still have all my Tootsie Toy furniture. I was an insurance agent for 15 years retiring in 1988. At this point I finally had time to start doing the things I've always wanted to do in miniature.

Dolls have always been a love of mine. I've wanted to do my own that looked like real people and not just another pretty face, but one with character and heart. In 1988, I began sculpting with Sculpy, trying to find a way to make molds for doing the piece in porcelain. With the information from club member, Hermania Anslinger, I was able to construct a simple mold.

I took a short class at a NAME National Houseparty, Fiesta De Los Amigos, in California, and shortly after that from Dawn Adams, a very talented artist. Most of my art training has been trial and error, but I've had a force greater than I guiding me in this and I feel quite happy with the people I've created.

One thing leads to another and in order to have proper accessories, I've learned many skills from creating tiny squash blossom necklaces from sterling silver and real turquoise to constructing musical instruments.

The love of tiny things got me into ¼-inch scale items including furniture and tiny dolls.

ARTISAN: **McNEELY, PAUL**

BUSINESS NAME: China Bull

IDENTIFICATION MARKS:

1944 to present

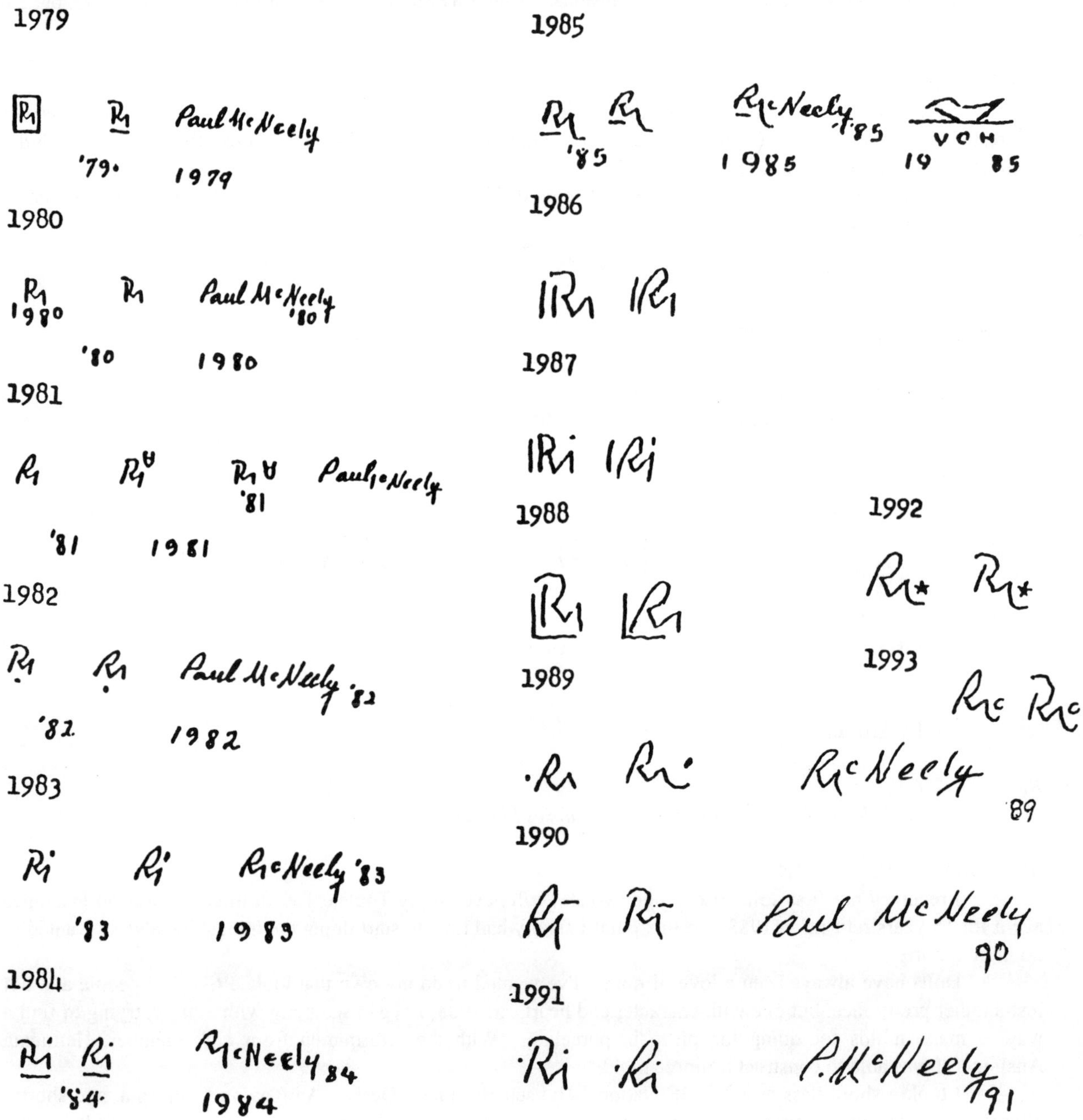

CATEGORY:

Accessories; Ceramics

HONORS:

Exhibits: National Geographic Society, Oct. 1988; Explorers Hall, Smithsonian Institution, Washington DC; Toy & Miniature Museum of Kansas City; The Dollhouse Museum of the Southwest; Liberty Historical Society Museum, Liberty, Missouri

McNEELY, PAUL, continued

RECOGNITION:

Nutshell News, Fall 1973, pg. 33-34; Fall 1976, pg. 13; Dec. 1982, pg. 15; Jan. 1983, pg. 53; Aug. 1984, pg. 70, 83, 96; Mar. 1984, pg. 56; Sept. 1985, pg. 58-62; Oct. 1986, pg. 78; Jan. 1988, pg. 48; Oct. 1991, pg. 4, 92; *Miniatures Showcase*, Winter 1991, pg. 18-19; Spring 1991, pg. 68; Summer 1992, pg. 33; *Miniature Collector*, No. 1, Apr. 1977, Cover; *Passport - Society Magazine*, Jun. 1982; Aug. 1982; Apr. 1983; May 1983; Dec. 1983; Apr. 1984; Jun. 1984; Dec. 1984; Apr. 1985; Aug. 1985; Oct. 1985; Dec. 1985; Feb. 1986; Jun. 1986; *The Illuminator*, Castellano and Seneschals of Turreted Little Edifices, Denver, Colorado, Vol. 2, No. 1; Vol. 2, No. 4; Vol. 4, No. 3; Vol. 4, No. 4; *Kansas City News Press*, Dec. 5, 1949, Isis Theater Features Attractive Christmas Displays in Miniature; *Newsstar*, Shawnee, Oklahoma, Dec. 27, 1945, Whole Native Village, Roy McNeely; Jan. 12, 1947, Starology; Nov. 8, 1948, Artist; *The Complete Book of Making Miniatures*, Thelma Newman & Virginia Merrill, 1975, pg. 289; *American Period Interiors in Miniature*, Kate Doordan Klavin, 1984, pg. 181; *The Andrews Collection, Personal Treasures*, Anne Day Smith, 1988, pg. 66; *Lehner's Encyclopedia of U.S. Marks on Pottery, Porcelain and Clay*, Lois Lehner, 1988, pg. 91; *The Kansas City Star*, Art and Artists, Jan. 18, 1970; Dec. 6, 1979, "He's a Giant in the World of Miniatures;" Feb. 21, 1982; *Who's Who in the Midwest*, 1970-1971; 1972-1973; *Tulsa Daily World*, Oct. 18, 1976, "Creator of Miniatures Looks at World Through Tiny Keyhole," Yvonne Litchfield; *Doll Reader,* Aug. 1977, "Miniature from Findings," "Camelot;" Joan Meshirer *Chicago Tribune*, Feb. 15, 1984, "Antiques," Turning Over an Old Leaf May Pay Off, Anita Gold; Jul. 10, 1988, "Collectibles," Getting a Reading on Tea Leaf Decorated China in all its Various Forms, Anita Gold

AUTOBIOGRAPHY:

I was born in Hammond, Oklahoma and graduated from high school in Bowlegs, Oklahoma. At the age of four I started collecting and making miniatures. In the years between 1944 and 1951, I started a Christmas Village in one-inch scale. In 1948, I made farm buildings for sale, in one-inch scale and in 1949 I made them in ½-inch scale. In 1955, I graduated from the Kansas City Art Institute and School of Design. Between 1970 and 1971 , at Miniature World, Rolla, Missouri, I made displays, a Back Yard, Western Museum, Blacksmith Shop, General Store, Artist Studio, Fortune Telling Shop, Attic, Stained Glass Workshop, and Toy Shop, of which several have movement. Between 1971 and 1976, I started a mail order business called Bespoke Miniatures. Between 1976 and 1979, I published the Miniature Forum and in 1977, I wrote Miniatures From Findings published under Leotaur Publications, and in 1979 I started China Bull. Between 1982 and 1984, I was on the Board of Directors and Education Director for Society of American Miniatures. I have shown in various miniature shows throughout the United States.

ARTISAN: **McNEIL, DANIEL L.**

BUSINESS NAME: The Lawbre Company

IDENTIFICATION MARKS:

CATEGORY:

Furniture; Roomboxes

RECOGNITION:

Miniatures Showcase; Nutshell News

BIOGRAPHY:

Daniel McNeil is co-founder and creative director of The Lawbre Company, founded in 1974. His fine arts background includes sculpture, painting, and printmaking with an ongoing pursuit of Art History and

Architectural Design. His historical and contemporary reproduction rooms and furniture have found their way to museums and private collections in this country and abroad. Through the years he has been challenged by virtually every architectural style with a strong emphasis in English and American 18th Century. The range has been wide from Frank Lloyd Wright to Chinese to Art Deco. Each project is carefully researched and rendered as closely as possible to the original room or in the spirit of the period.

ARTISAN: **McNULTY-BOWERS, EILEEN**

BUSINESS NAME: Dovetail Miniatures

IDENTIFICATION MARKS:

Limited Edition pieces numbered 2 / 250 (2nd piece of 250)

CATEGORY:
Accessories; Furniture: antique, reproductions

RECOGNITION:
Miniatures Showcase

ARTISAN: **McPEAK, KATE**

BUSINESS NAME: Fox Hollow Miniatures

IDENTIFICATION MARKS:

CATEGORY:
Holiday Items

ARTISAN: **McVAY, LYNNE**

BUSINESS NAME: Lynne McVay, Porcelain Art Studio

IDENTIFICATION MARKS:

Smaller pieces

CATEGORY:
Porcelain

McVAY, LYNNE, continued

RECOGNITION:

Nutshell News, Sept. 1992, pg. 75; *Miniature Collector*, Summer 1992, pg. 24

AUTOBIOGRAPHY:

Since 1986, I have traveled taking classes to continue my education in the area of porcelain art, and have been painting miniature porcelain since 1990. I teach classes in my home on painting porcelain in full-size scale.

ARTISAN: MEEHAN, FRAN & DON

BUSINESS NAME: Fran & Don Meehan Lighting
Fran's Miniatures

IDENTIFICATION MARKS:

Fran & Don Meehan 8/24/94   F&D.m 8/94   or certificate with name, date and engraved seal

CATEGORY:

Carpets; Fixtures; Lighting; Rugs

HONORS:

IGMA Artisan (both)

RECOGNITION:

New York Times, Jan. 16, 1983; *Asbury Park Press*, New Jersey, Feb. 17, 1984; *Windsor Heights Herald*, New Jersey, Mar. 3, 1983; Apr. 22, 1987; May 1994; *Philadelphia Enquirer*, Aug. 1983; *National Enquirer*, Feb. 1984

BIOGRAPHY:

Fran and Don Meehan came into miniatures in 1976 after receiving the first patent granted in needlework by the US Patent Office in over 40 years. Utilizing a tiny (miniature) latch hook, they devised a way to do miniature latch-hooking and made the first miniature latch hooked rugs. Next, they combined latch hooking with needlepoint and created "Hook-Point" and received a registered trade mark from the Patent Office.

Not satisfied with the scale of these rugs, they ultimately experimented with combining hooking with punch embroidery and called it "Punch-N-Hook." Using the "Punch-N-Hook" technique, they introduced very intricate rug kits to the miniature world with a simplification of complicated Persian rug designs and clipped the stitches with hair clippers. The result was the most realistic, and in scale carpets on the market at the time.

In 1982, Fran and Dan went "from the floor to the ceiling" when they discovered that their miniature talents were more suited to researching, designing and making miniature lights and chandeliers. The punched Persian type carpets and several very intricate limited edition sconces and chandeliers, including one with over 2,500 Austrian crystals, won them Artisan status in the International Guild of Miniature Artisans.

Fran and Don met on the ocean liner "France" in 1971, and married in 1972. After having raised four of Don's children, by another marriage, Crystina was born to them. They left miniatures for a short while, devoting most of their time to her, their most precious little "miniature!" In 1992, they came back to miniatures with a full line miniature shop in Hightstown, New Jersey (Fran's Miniatures), fulfilling a long time dream of Fran's.

Having the shop has, again, rekindled their interest in miniature lighting. They have succeeded in redesigning and fine tuning some of their earlier lighting fixtures, and have also introduced more than a few new designs to the world of miniatures, which certainly gives all the others a fair amount of competition.

Fran and Don spend a considerable amount of time researching period designs. They owe their great success with miniature lighting to teamwork and utilizing each other's artistic talents. Thus the unique nature of their fixtures. There are no marks on the works of Fran and Don Meehan, however, their lights are usually recognizable by their look of authenticity in relation to certain periods, including Colonial, Federal, Victorian and Contemporary, as well as their great attention to scale and quality.

Don also specializes in photographing miniatures with heavy concentration on realism and perspective, which he feels is ignored or overlooked by the majority of photographers. In 1982, he visited the Art Institute of Chicago study the famous Thorne Rooms in relation to the published black and white photos of those rooms. At the time, he believed that these were probably the best and most realistic photographs of miniature rooms ever to be taken.

Don studied the camera angles, lenses, distance and lighting used in these photos. Holding them next to the actual rooms enabled him to solve the unique close-up and wide angle problems involved. He was able to determine the exact placement of the camera on the original photos. Don returned to New Jersey and continued to perfect his miniature photo skills from these studies.

At one point, Don photographed an intricately carved Belter chair by a well known miniaturist, and Fran enlarged the final print to near full life size. Everyone who saw the photo thought it was a photograph of a full-size chair – not a one-inch scale.

Combining these skills with their miniature lighting, Fran and Dad Meehan now photograph their tiny creations and display the almost life size prints in the same manner. Of course, this procedure magnifies any flaws or unbalance, but according to Don, "keeps us attentive to detail and excellence."

The couple is presently writing a book on the technique and art of miniature photography.

ARTISAN: **MELTON, VERNA J.**

BUSINESS NAME: Verna J. Melton

IDENTIFICATION MARKS:

Unmarked

CATEGORY:

Dolls: costuming

ARTISAN: **MEMMER, TILLIE**

BUSINESS NAME: Tillie ®

IDENTIFICATION MARKS:

CATEGORY:

Dolls; Wicker

HONORS:

IGMA Fellow

RECOGNITION:

Nutshell News, Vol. 15, No. 8, Aug. 1985, pg. 70-72, "Tillie's Loveable Bratz" Anne Day Smith; *Miniatures Showcase*, Summer 1987, Cover; Nov. 1992, pg. 34; *Through The Looking Glass,* Boynton and Associates, Inc., Ann Ruble, 1984

AUTOBIOGRAPHY:

I have a BA in Interior Design.

ARTISAN: **MENA, GILBERT**

BUSINESS NAME: Gilbert Mena

IDENTIFICATION MARKS:

CATEGORY:
Furniture

RECOGNITION:
Nutshell News, Vol. 18, No. 10, Oct. 1988, pg. 44-46; *Miniature Collector*, Spring 1992, pg. 37-41

ARTISAN: **MERCY, ROSALIND**

BUSINESS NAME: Rosalind Mercy and Isabel

IDENTIFICATION MARKS:

Silver hallmark, Rosalind Mercy, 1959

Isabel Fisher marks, tree dwellings

CATEGORY:
Dwellings: root tree; Porcelain

AUTOBIOGRAPHY:
Rosalind Mercy

In 1953, I took a basic pottery course at Lime Grove, London this was followed by a three year working silversmith apprenticeship in the city of London. In 1959, I was granted the use of my own silver hallmark. My growing interest in small things lead me to start making miniature porcelain items in 1972. Drawing on my own skills and those of my husband, a dentist, I developed and perfected my techniques. My work is now recognized and appreciated worldwide.

Isabel Fisher

I am the daughter of Rosalind Mercy. Between the years 1980 to 1983, I attended a modeling course at Midway College of Design and attained a college diploma with credit. From the years 1984 to 1989, I ran my own model making company employing five people, working in film, television and architectural model making. By 1989, I joined my mother making miniature porcelain. I use my mother's mark for the porcelain. I also make street trees.

ARTISAN: **MERRILL, VIRGINIA**

BUSINESS NAME: The Blue Swan Studio

IDENTIFICATION MARKS:

MERRILL, VIRGINIA, continued

CATEGORY:

Furniture; Roomboxes; Rooms: period; Room Settings; Vignettes

HONORS:

IGMA Fellow; IGMA Charter Member; Exhibit: Gibbes Museum of Art, Charleston, South Carolina

RECOGNITION:

Miniature Collector, No. 1, Apr. 1977, pg. 18, 22, 24; No. 4, Dec. 1977, pg. 28; *Miniatures Showcase*, Summer 1992, pg. 50; *The Complete Book of Making Miniatures*, Thelma Newman and Virginia Merrill, 1975; *Reproducing Period Furniture and Accessories in Miniature*, Virginia Merrill, Susan Merrill Richardson, Crown, 1981; *CBS Television*, Mar. 5, 1978, Charles Osgood

AUTOBIOGRAPHY:

After visiting the Art Institute in Chicago, (Mrs. Thornes' Miniature Room Collection) 25 years ago, and being so inspired I took up the challenge of becoming a miniature maker; with no supply sources available at that time. I set out in a search for woodworkers who would be willing to pare down the proper wood, thin enough for my needs, and with the proper grains. Lucky was I, to find a friend in Paul Runyon who not only prepared the wood, but as a full-size cabinet maker also helped me understand the procedures for making furniture, paring it down to my size of one-inch scale. I proceeded slowly and precisely to accomplish my goal, miniature rooms.

I wrote three books on the subject, *The Complete Book of Making Miniatures, Needlework in Miniature,* and my favorite, *Reproducing Period Furniture and Accessories in Miniature* with my daughter Susan Richardson. This led to teaching classes in miniature making for eight years, 15 students all year, one day a week, and no one willing to give up his or her space to accommodate a new student. With the great interest and enthusiasm for miniatures, television network CBS and Charles Osgood made an appointment for March 5, 1978 to come to my home to televise my class in action. Six attractive young men including cameraman, news persons etc. descended on my home in the countryside of New Jersey to view the 15 lady carpenters who were building such enchanting miniatures. And so, the miniature craze took a step forward with this program being viewed on national TV.

I was accepted in the prestigious Appraisers Association of America, and included in the publication *Who's Who in the Southwest.* Being a charter member of IGMA with the Tracys, Buttfields, and Bloomfields my interest grew in creating a place for outstanding miniatures and their makers in the category of collectible art of museum quality. I taught a class at the Guild School in Castine, Maine on reproducing a miniature bird cage. I am proud to say one of my Louis XV1 style drawing rooms is on permanent exhibit in the Gibbes Museum of Art, Charleston, South Carolina.

ARTISAN: **MESSER, SONIA**

BUSINESS NAME: Sonia Messer Imports, Inc.

IDENTIFICATION MARKS:

Made in Colombia
Exclusively for
Sonia Messer Imports
Los Angeles, California

Label on bottom of each piece

CATEGORY:

Accessories; Furniture; Lighting; Roomboxes; Rugs; Shadow Boxes

MESSER, SONIA, continued

RECOGNITION:

Wilshire Independent Sun Living, Vol. 6, No 49, Nov. 6, 1985, "Eleven-Twelfths Shrunk," photo, Delmar Watson; *Wilshire Press,* Vol. 62, No. 47, Nov. 6, 1985, "Miniatures Popularity is Her Dream Come True," K.T. VanDeGraaff; *Glendale News-Press*, Aug. 17, 1984, People section, pg. A-7, "Safe" and "Friendly" get gussied up, Wanda Owen; *Glendale Federal Intercom*, California, Nov/Dec. 1984, pg. 7; *Pasadena Today*, Vol. 7, No. 4, Nov. 1984, pg. 16, "Big Business on a Miniature Scale," Barbara Backley

BIOGRAPHY:

Born in Los Angeles, California, Sonia had a reputation with her family and friends of having very refined taste. This love of beautiful things took her to South America in 1965 to start a business, Sonia Messer Imports. The idea was to develop Folk Art skills into saleable merchandise for the United States market. On one of her trips to South America, she discovered a factory that had made some pieces of dollhouse furniture for a New York toy company as an experiment. Things had not gone well for the Colombian firm and the toy company, so all plans were discontinued. However, Sonia simply could not let an opportunity like this pass her by. She began to work with the Colombian firm designing a line that would be later known as the Sonia Messer Imports, The Queen Anne Colonial Line. This would be the first of approximately 450 pieces that were designed and manufactured by the Sonia Messer Company. The line was sold through all major stores who specialized in dollhouse miniatures, including Marshall Fields, in Chicago. In 1980, Sonia Messer also created a line of porcelain dolls for the wholesale market. Two of these dolls were sold through the Bullocks, Wilshire catalog. Three of the dolls were featured and sold through the Smithsonian catalog. Currently, Sonia Messer has a display of all her prototype pieces in room-setting display shadow-box vignettes in her home in Los Angeles. She shows the collection for charity frequently.

ARTISAN: METCALF, JOYCE B.

BUSINESS NAME: Joyous Originals

IDENTIFICATION MARKS:

1989 to present

JO-92

CATEGORY:

Dolls: originals

HONORS:

IGMA Artisan

RECOGNITION:

Miniatures Showcase, Spring 1992, pg. 30-31

AUTOBIOGRAPHY:

My miniature background didn't start until I was over 55 years old and then it just sort of happened. It all started when I had a group of church women meet to make clothespin dolls for the bazaar. I made some and went from bazaars to craft shows, to doll & toy shows. It was at the doll & toy show that I met my first miniature dealers.

Since clothespin dolls weren't to scale I decided to dress other artists' dolls, but I couldn't put my business tag on them since my business name is Joyous Originals - and the work wasn't all mine. After considerable encouragement I took a sculpting doll class, then an adult education class in sculpting. From here on it's learn as you go with help from another doll maker. Now I sculpt, make molds, fire, paint etc. etc. It is truly a Joyous Original!

ARTISAN: **MEYER, BARBARA**

IDENTIFICATION MARKS:
Unmarked

CATEGORY:
Flowers and Plants; Food

RECOGNITION:
Nutshell News; Small Talk

AUTOBIOGRAPHY:
I started crafts when my daughters were in school and scouts. We made earrings, necklaces, mushroom plaques, etc. and sold them at street fairs. One customer suggested going into miniatures and that was our start. The four girls had a "sandwich bar" at a Wee C show and wanted to earn new bicycles. After several years they had a four-page menu. Five books are published on bread dough flowers, fruits and vegetables, bakery and homemade meals. Barbara Ann has her own book on toy figures and animals.

About 24 years ago John Zweifel contacted us to do the White House floral arrangements and I've been doing them ever since. I've had no special training, just the mother of five children and currently five grandchildren. I garden, cook and bake and love duplicating what I see in miniature.

ARTISAN: **MEYER, JOYCE M. & CURTIS**

BUSINESS NAME: Miniatures By Joyce

IDENTIFICATION MARKS:
1980 to present

J.M. Meyer 1992

CLM 92 Curtis Meyer

J.M.M. '92 Smaller pieces

J.&C. Meyer '92 Made by both

CATEGORY:
Aquariums; Flowers & Plants; Landscaping

RECOGNITION:
Nutshell News, Oct. 1986, pg. 77; Jan. 1992, pg. 66; *Miniatures Showcase*, Spring 1989, pg. 32-35, 40; Summer 1989, pg. 28, 30, 41-42; Winter 1989, pg. 24, 34-38, 40, 44; Spring 1990, pg. 42, 63-64; Summer 1990, pg. 27, 30, 34, 36; Spring 1991, pg. 34-35; Summer 1991, pg. 22, 30-31, 37-38

AUTOBIOGRAPHY:
I have been making and showing my plants since 1980. This is my job. I have not had training for this , but am self-taught through my love of miniatures.

My husband, Curtis, also has the miniature bug. He makes aquariums and sells them under Miniatures By Joyce.

ARTISAN: **MEYER, MARJORIE**

BUSINESS NAME: Marjorie Meyer

IDENTIFICATION MARKS:

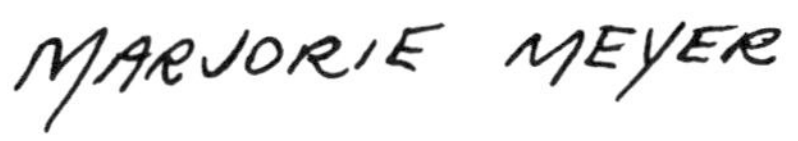

Smaller pieces

CATEGORY:
Flowers & Plants; Wicker

HONORS:
IGMA Artisan; NAME AOH

RECOGNITION:
Nutshell News, Apr. 1986, pg. 60-62; *Miniature Collector,* 1988, pg. 20-22; *Masters in Miniature, 12 Artisans At Work, Volume 1*, Anne Day Smith, Kalmbach Publishing, 1987, pg. 78

ARTISAN: **MIDDLEBROOK, JANET**

BUSINESS NAME: The Miniature Mademoiselle

IDENTIFICATION MARKS:
1987 to present

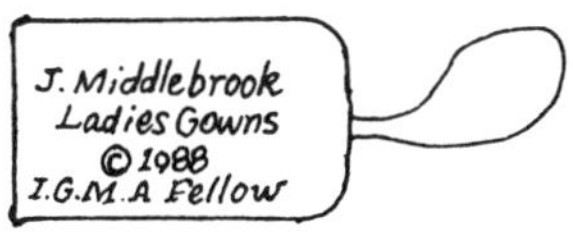

Black printing on Gold tag; same on both sides
Attached to costume

CATEGORY:
Clothing: period; Costuming

HONORS:
IGMA Fellow; Exhibits: Toy & Miniature Museum of Kansas City; The Carole & Barry Kaye Museum of Miniatures, Los Angeles, California; Denver Toy & Miniature Museum

RECOGNITION:
Nutshell News, Jul. 1988, pg. 60; Apr. 1989, pg. 29; Jun. 1989, pg. 64; Aug. 1989, pg. 66; Oct. 1990, pg. 66, 68; Sept. 1991, pg. 79; Mar. 1992, pg. 71; May 1992, pg. 62; *Miniatures Showcase*, Fall 1988, pg. 40, 42; Summer 1990; Spring 1991; Fall 1992; Winter 1992, pg. 42, 44; *Miniature Collector*, Fall 1988; *Miss Marples Cottage*, video tape, Jason Getson

AUTOBIOGRAPHY:

I've always loved dolls and doll clothes. Even as a small child, I remember making dresses for my dolls, and my nieces' dolls. In fact much of this came from my mother, who sewed for me all those years before leaving home. I still remember one Christmas, about 1956, receiving a Betsy Wetsy doll, and a box of home made baby doll clothing. In my mind's eye, I can still see the sweet pink coat, a bonnet, draw string night gown, dress, bunting and sunsuit. If only I had them now!

Having to work my adult life, the florist trade became my creative outlet. I was a designer for 16 years, and also free lanced for awhile.

My first encounter with miniatures came when I was about eight. A family member gave me a set of Tootsie Toy cast iron doll house furniture, circa 1920, and my sisters played with the same set. It was well loved! Years later I took it out of the box and displayed it in a "memory box," the hobby "rage" of the 1970's. What a hard time I had trying to find and make finishing touches for my box. At that time nothing could be bought, everything had to be improvised, using all kinds of odds and ends.

Several years went by, and I attended my first miniature show. I've never been the same, and I wondered how I could ever afford my new hobby!

One day it came to me; I collect real antique dinnerware, could it be made in miniature? And the "ball" started rolling. For six years I made handpainted porcelain dinnerware in one-inch scale. I was delighted at how well they were received at miniature shows. By the end of the six years, I found, I could no longer work with porcelain. Still wanting to stay in the miniature field I remembered seeing miniature children's clothing but no adult clothes. I started with a tea gown on a hanger, then all types of ladies clothing, dresses, gloves etc. Next I made men's clothing, as no one else was, I soon found out tailoring is not easy. Baby clothes followed, and so it goes.

At this time my show tables include many styles, and types of costumes. I have a time frame from 1400-1960, and also include custom work. Period costumes, movie stars, famous people and fairy tales are a real challenge, and I always welcome new ideas. So here I am back to where I started, making little clothes. What fun, I love it!

ARTISAN: MIDGETT, DOROTHY W.

IDENTIFICATION MARKS:

D.W. MIDGETT

D.W.M. Smaller pieces

MIDGE On pieces given as gifts

CATEGORY:

Furniture: handpainted

HONORS:

NAME AOH

RECOGNITION:

Nutshell News, Vol. 9, No. 2, Mar/Apr. 1979, pg. 76-78; Vol. 2, No. 10, Oct. 1981, pg. 62; Vol. 13, No. 10, Oct. 1983, pg. 71; Vol. 14, No. 6, Jun. 1984, pg. 45; *Miniature Magazine*, No. 1, May 1976, pg. 30; *Creative Crafts & Miniatures*, Vol. 9, No. 10, Oct. 1985, pg. 17; *Miniature Catalog*, 2nd Edition, 1980, pg. 16; *Miniature Gazette*, Vol. 19, No. 3, Spring 1991, pg. 38; *The Andrews Collection, Personal Treasures*, Anne Day Smith, 1988, pg. 18, 19, 40, 82; *Wish Booklet*, Vol. XXIII, pg. 17

BIOGRAPHY:

Dorothy, or as her friends refer to her, Midge, is a highly talented lady who is also a very avid collector. Midge's miniature collections are extensive and she crafts a number of items, most notably her painted furniture.

Midge has always been a collector. Her earliest collections began in the 1950's and were children's toys and books. Her interest in miniatures began in the 1970's when she agreed to help her friends, Joe and Jackie Andrews, arrange a display for their new line of Williamsburg Style wooded pocketbooks. Later Midge helped refurbish an antique French dollhouse belonging to the Andrews. Midge drew on her talent and skills learned during her studies to earn her BFA, Bachelor of Fine Arts Degree, in art education. A number of pieces of painted furniture followed, from Shackman pieces, then from more challenging kits.

Midge's work has been featured in the *Andrews Collection, Personal Treasures*, Anne Day Smith, 1989; Susan Sirkis' *Wish Booklets; Nutshell News*, Mar/Apr. 1979.

In 1974, Midge became a member of the Virginia Miniature Enthusiasts. In 1980, she joined the club and served on the Steering Committee for the 1980 National Houseparty for NAME. She was a member of the Steering Committee for the NAME Regional Houseparty in Williamsburg, Virginia in 1985.

Midge has taught art in public school, been a resident stage designer and business manager for Barksdale Dinner Theatre, designed an exhibit of puppets and marionettes for the University of Richmond's permanent collection, done volunteer work for Richmond's Valentine Museum, and worked in an antique shop. She has worked for 28 years as state employee and determiner for social security. Her college education was from Richmond Professional Institute, now Virginia Commonwealth University.

(AOH profile by Ferbie Claudon, authorized reprint by NAME)

ARTISAN: **MIERZEJEWSKI, ELIZABETH (LIZ)**

BUSINESS NAME: Kingdom Critters

IDENTIFICATION MARKS:

Liz Mierzejewski
Kingdom Critters
1994

LM KC 94

CATEGORY:

Animals

HONORS:

IGMA Artisan

AUTOBIOGRAPHY:

I have always been artistic, since I was small. I was a natural at most any art form I tried, except sculpture. All through school and college, I mastered the techniques of drawing and painting. I never really explored sculpture.

I got married in 1983 and started my career as a paste-up artist for a newspaper and went on to become a sign designer and manufacturer. In 1987, expecting my first child, I knew I would have to come up with a new career that I could do in my home. My sister-in-law, Betty Martin (King's Harvest), was at the time experiencing great success as a miniature artist of fruits and vegetables. I spent some time with her, and out of boredom and desperation, made a small sampling of cats and dogs, which she kindly took with her to Tiny Treasures in Boston. Much to my surprise, my work was a rousing success, selling all that I had given her. The customers seemed to appreciate the individually hand-sculpted design of my animals. Over the next few years, I did several shows with her in Massachusetts, in New York, and Connecticut. My work was getting better and better and I was starting to build up clientele and fans. Betty quit to move onto other things. Scared and unsure, I stepped out on my own. I have since started making many kinds of North American wildlife, along with the myriad of cats and dogs.

Seven years and three children later I am pleased to say that Kingdom Critters is thriving. Here I am succeeding in a form of art I thought would never be mine. It is my hope that my work will continue to improve, as it has so drastically over the years.

ARTISAN: **MILLER, ANN W.**

BUSINESS NAME: Ann W. Miller

IDENTIFICATION MARKS:

Ann W. Miller

AWM

Ann Miller Handcrafted Miniatures

CATEGORY:

Accessories; Floor Coverings: painted floor cloths; Rugs: braided

HONORS:

IGMA Artisan

MILLER, ANN W., continued

AUTOBIOGRAPHY:

Always having an interest in interior design and architecture, doing the same in miniature seemed logical. After receiving a dollhouse for a Christmas gift from my husband, I was hooked. After designing the house then looking for furniture and accessories, I began to make things myself. But after seeing artisan's work I became more of a collector which has evolved back into making things for myself and others that I could not find at shows.

ARTISAN: MILLER, JOHN ANTHONY

BUSINESS NAME: John Anthony Miller Etchings & Engravings

IDENTIFICATION MARKS:

CATEGORY:

Engravings; Etchings

HONORS:

Creative Excellence Award , 1981; Carnegie Art Museum, Oxnard, California, Dec. 19, 1992 to Mar. 28, 1993; Clark Humanities Museum, Scripps College, Claremont, California, Nov. 12, to Dec. 15, 1993, Picturing Wonderland, illustrations for Carroll's Alice

RECOGNITION:

Miniature Collector, No. 29, Feb. 1982, pg. 52-53, "The Etchings of John Anthony Miller," Dana Gearhart

AUTOBIOGRAPHY:

I was born in Tacoma, Washington and attended Fresno State University, graduating with a BA, Magna Cum Laude, having done my post-graduate work in physics working with electron microscopes.

I am self-taught in the field of art, having done wall murals in oil, and a limited number of bronze figures in one-inch scale using the lost wax casting method. I have concentrated my efforts primarily, however, in the art of etching and engraving, producing numerous numbered, framed, limited editions in miniature which are in many well-known collections throughout the miniature collecting field. In the late 1980's, I produced Tiffany-like stained glass windows for the dollhouse utilizing special designs of my own creations, having developed a method of applying a silver leading compound directly onto micro-thin glass in fine line and using thinned-down glazed enamels to produce jewel-like color detail. It was a unique style and yielded a stunning effect.

I maintained my gallery and studio in Ventura, California in combination with an antiquarian bookshop in an adjacent suite. I've done special commissions for Renaissance Antiques in Solvang, California and Books of Wonder in Beverly Hills, California as well as replication work for exhibit sale at the Art Institute of Chicago and the Museum of Science & Industry, Chicago in conjunction with the Thorne Rooms and Colleen Moore's Fairy Castle respectively.

ARTISAN: MINNICK, NICOLE

BUSINESS NAME: Ni-Glo ® Lamps

IDENTIFICATION MARKS:

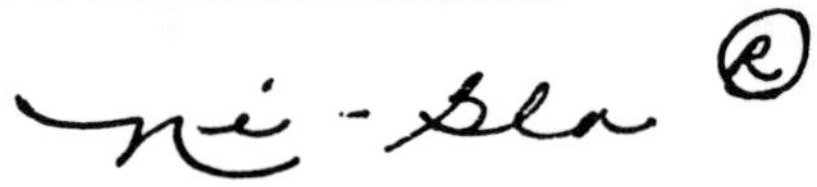

MINNICK, NICOLE, continued

CATEGORY:
China: handpainted; Dinnerware; Lamps; Lighting; Vases

RECOGNITION:
Nutshell News, Calendar, 1993, 1994; *Miniatures Showcase*, Spring 1988, Cover, pg. 18, 28-29, 33-35, 42; Winter 1989, pg. 40; Fall 1990, pg. 34-35, 40; Summer 1990, pg. 10-11, 19-21, 70

BIOGRAPHY:
Producing and painting fine porcelain pieces is nothing for Nicole. Being part of a family that has been associated with the ceramic arts, for nearly three generations, she has traveled throughout Europe and Great Britain studying the fine art of china painting. Her porcelain pieces are in collections throughout the world. The Ni-Glo ® Collection of lamps, vases, dinnersets are individually hand designed and hand china painted. Each piece is signed and represents a truly fine example of porcelain art.

ARTISAN: MITCHELL, CHARLES & DOROTHY

BUSINESS NAME: The Tinker's Box

IDENTIFICATION MARKS:
Most unmarked

CJM with year

CATEGORY:
Accessories; Brasswork; Coppersmith; Metalwork

HONORS:
IGMA Fellow (Charles)

ARTISAN: MITCHELL, SHANNON

BUSINESS NAME: Shannon's Miniature Manuscripts

IDENTIFICATION MARKS:

~Scriba~
Shannon Mitchell
© MCMXCIII

~Scribe~
Shannon Mitchell
© 1993

שֶׁנָן מִיטְשֶׁעל
תשנ״א

CATEGORY:
Art: fine; Books: binder, hand-scribed, miniature; Calligraphy; Designer; Illustrator

RECOGNITION:
Nutshell News, Apr. 1983, pg. 91; *Doll Reader*; Feb/Mar. 1987, pg. 202; Television Station KXLY, Spokane, Washington, Feb. 24, 1987, News Interview; *Miniature Collector*, Winter 1987, pg. 39; Fall 1989, pg. 39-40; *Antiques & Collecting,* Dec. 1989, pg. 60-63; *Portland Society for Calligraphy Newsletter*, Winter 1990-1991, pg. 2-3; *Miniature Book Society Newsletter*, Jan. 1991, pg. 5-6

AUTOBIOGRAPHY:
While living in Spain back in the 1960's, I accumulated two or three large parchment sheets of music which had been cut from an ancient church missal. These proved to be portions of Gregorian chants from one of the Masses of the Catholic Church. Years later, 1981, I received a set of calligraphy pens for Christmas, and while

experimenting with them, reproduced the sheets of music in miniature. They turned out rather nicely, and I became curious about Gregorian chants in general and did some research about them. One thing led to another, and pretty soon I was hand-scribing miniature books containing individual Latin Masses in their entirety. These I illuminated and bound in leather, using the same techniques that the monks did in the Middle Ages. My husband hand-crafted and attached brass or silver hasps.

As time went by, I replicated 15 or so different ancient books. Examples of these are: a *Book of Hours* in Latin; the *Passover Haggadah* in Hebrew; an *Erstes Lesebuch fur Kinder* (First Reader for Children) in old German script; and the *Biblia Pauperum* (poorman's Bible) on olde English. I incorporated illuminations and/or illustrations appropriate to the text into each of the miniature volumes.

Most of my books are in languages other than English. I am able to do this, since foreign languages have been a hobby of mine for more years than I care to remember. I began with French and other Romance languages and later delved into Russian, Chinese, Greek, Japanese, German, Latin, Hebrew and ancient Egyptian hieroglyphics. I don't pretend to speak all of those languages, but I am familiar enough with their script, grammar and vocabulary to know precisely what I'm putting into my books.

I have had no formal training or instruction in calligraphy or other art forms. Over the years, however, I have produced some regular-sized works in pen-and-ink and pastels. The same is true of my study of foreign languages; all of my knowledge of them has been gained from books, exposure and usage. Incidentally, my interest in languages was stimulated by practical considerations as well as intellectual curiosity, as we spent almost half of my husband's 30-year career with the U S Government on resident assignments in other countries. These included Mexico, Spain, Greece and Germany.

ARTISAN: **MOBLEY, SYLVIA P.**

BUSINESS NAME: Pine Rose Studio 1994 to present
Miniatures in Porcelain 1977 to 1993

IDENTIFICATION MARKS:

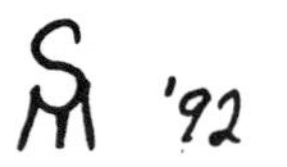

1985 to present; animals, figurines, smaller pieces
Limited editions additionally marked with piece number & edition quantity

Dolls; letter **S** carved on back of shoulder plate
and overwritten with name and year

CATEGORY:

Animals: carousel, cats, dogs, pets; Christmas; Dolls; Figurines: Christmas; Holiday Items; Kits: dolls; Mermaids; Porcelain: houses

HONORS:

IGMA Fellow, 1984

RECOGNITION:

Nutshell News, Vol. 2, No. 7, 1981, pg. 84-87; Jun. 1986, Cover

AUTOBIOGRAPHY:

I've always collected tiny things. In 1973, I received a BFA in ceramics from the Rhode Island School of Design. Three years later I studied china painting and miniature doll making in Connecticut with several local artisans. When we moved to Virginia, that same year, I met Bob and Jean Porter of the Mountain Valley Miniature Shop. With their guidance I was able to turn an interest into a business. Within the first couple of years I expanded from dolls to animals and figurines, and a little later carousel horses and mermaids.

ARTISAN: **MONSON, CRYSTAL D.**

BUSINESS NAME: Just A Little Something
Apple Valley Baskets

IDENTIFICATION MARKS:
Unmarked

CATEGORY:
Baskets; Food

HONORS:
IGMA Artisan

RECOGNITION:
Miniatures Showcase, Summer 1990, pg. 21, 34, 36, 38; Summer 1991, pg. 22

AUTOBIOGRAPHY:
My miniature background includes one year of art in college although my food making skills are completely self-taught. I have been making food since about 1984. I use real food for my models although I cannot cook, bake or can fruits and vegetables in real life. I borrow some models from my mother who is a very good cook. In May 1991, I purchased Apple Valley Baskets from Elsie's Exquisiques. I am also a self-taught basket maker.

ARTISAN: **MOORE, ETHEL L.**

BUSINESS NAME: Harvest Miniatures

IDENTIFICATION MARKS:

With date

CATEGORY:
Accessories; Furniture; Needlepoint; Needlework

HONORS:
Charter/Founding Member CIMTA

RECOGNITION:
Nutshell News, Sept. 1990, pg. 65, Show Scene; *Sewickley Herald*, Sewickley, Pennsylvania, Aug. 1985

AUTOBIOGRAPHY:
My interest in miniatures started when I worked for the Girl Scouts as Public Relations Director. I had graduated from Penn State with a BA in recreation, and had taken PR courses at a local college. As a PR Director, I was responsible for scale displays for special events, such as models of campsites, etc. A Girl Scout volunteer friend introduced me to the world of miniatures, and we decided to try several local shows.

I attended the first trade show of CIMTA and became a Charter Member, serving on the Board of Directors as Supporting Membership Chairman. Since then I have attended shows in many different parts of the country.

My main line is furniture decorated with Friesland Carving, an incised form of woodcarving. Since all the work is handcrafted, I concentrate more on quality than quantity, and each carved design is unique. I have also done a number of custom made orders from photographs of full-sized furniture.

ARTISAN: **MOORE, PAUL D.**

BUSINESS NAME: Paul D. Moore, Miniature Artisan

IDENTIFICATION MARKS:
All 1979 to present

PAUL D. MOORE   PAUL MOORE   P. D. MOORE

Printed on bottom or back in gold, black or white

CATEGORY:
Buildings; Furniture; House Boxes; Roomboxes

HONORS:
IGMA Artisan, 1984; Fellow, 1987

RECOGNITION:
Nutshell News, Jun. 1985, pg. 64; Feb. 1986, pg. 62; Nov. 1989, pg. 62; Sept. 1991, pg. 68; *Miniatures Showcase*, Vol. 2, Winter 1987, pg. 36; *The Miniature Magazine*, Spring 1981, pg. 44

AUTOBIOGRAPHY:

As a child, Paul Moore built miniature houses and furniture as an expression of his architectural tastes. Later, he worked as an architectural model maker and a designer of commercial interiors, work experiences which helped him in 1979 when he became a miniature artisan. At first, Paul built only houses and roomboxes, but soon started building furniture; primarily 18th Century mahogany and walnut case pieces.

In 1984, Paul was awarded artisan status with the International Guild of Miniature Artisans, and in 1987 he became a Guild Fellow. Paul served on the IGMA Board of Trustees from 1987 to 1993, was on the Membership, Nominating, and Publication Committees and was third Vice-President his last year on the board.

Currently, Paul builds Georgian style houses of his own design and custom houses as well as roomboxes and furniture.

ARTISAN: **MOORE, SHANNON**

BUSINESS NAME: Shannon Moore

IDENTIFICATION MARKS:

S Moore   SM

CATEGORY:
Furniture; Roomboxes; Structures

HONORS:
IGMA Artisan

RECOGNITION:
Nutshell News, Sept. 1992

AUTOBIOGRAPHY:

I graduated from Iowa State University with a BS in mathematics. I taught high school mathematics for one year and worked as a road designer for two years, then retiring to be a mother and housewife. I was a docent at the Toy and Miniature Museum of Kansas City before we moved to Florida.

ARTISAN: **MOREY, GAIL**

BUSINESS NAME: Morey's Miniatures
Gail Morey's "Mutts"

IDENTIFICATION MARKS:

With year

21 - 105
Series Number in series

Certificate accompanies most animals

CATEGORY:
Animals: cats, dogs

HONORS:
IGMA Fellow, 1987; NAME AOH, 1988; Miniaturist of the Month, *Nutshell News*, Nov. 1986; Honorary Chairman 1992, "It's Carnival Time," Gulf South Miniature & Dollhouse Event, New Orleans, Louisiana; Exhibits: Toy & Miniature Museum of Kansas City; The Carole & Barry Kaye Museum of Miniatures, Los Angeles, California

RECOGNITION:
Nutshell News, Oct. 1985, Cover; Vol. 16, No. 11, Nov. 1986, pg. 44-45, "Gail Morey's Canine Crowd," Bonnie Schroeder; *Nutshell News Calendar,* Nov. 1986; *Miniatures Showcase*; *Unadilla, NY,* newspaper, Nov. 28, 1984; *The Andrews Collection, Personal Treasures*, Anne Day Smith, 1988

AUTOBIOGRAPHY:
I am a self-taught miniaturist with a natural talent for drawing, painting, and sculpting. In 1974, I made accessories, furniture and figures for my first dollhouse, out of scraps of materials, boxes, etc. This sparked my interest in miniatures.

I owned and operated a craft store, 1975 to 1980, carrying craft supplies and a line of commercial miniatures. To my amazement I discovered I could actually make these tiny little pieces and was having fun doing it. The experience working with the clay improved my ability to sculpt my very first dog. The interest and enthusiasm of the collector for my canine crowd was quite gratifying. It was 1980 when I decided to branch out and sculpt pedigree dogs as a full-time pursuit.

My work has been nationally and internationally accepted, with special features in *Nutshell News, Miniatures Showcase*, other various miniature magazines and local newspapers. I am a Fellow of the International Guild of Miniature Artisans and a member of the National Association of Miniature Enthusiasts. I am also a member of the NAME Academy of Honor.

My goal is to be able to supply the collector with a choice of their favorite pedigree dogs. I have 70 one-inch scale breeds in stock along with several ½-inch and ¼-inch scale at this time, and want to continue creating a larger selection.

ARTISAN: **MORGAN, JOHN**

BUSINESS NAME: Simply Shaker

IDENTIFICATION MARKS:
1991 to present

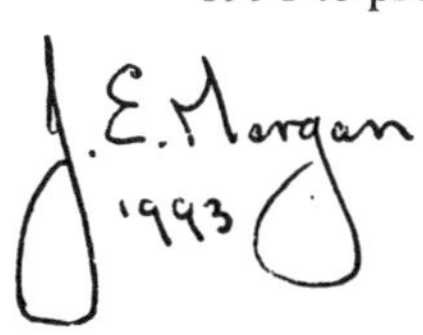

Smaller pieces

CATEGORY:
Furniture: period, Shaker

MORGAN, JOHN, continued

HONORS:

Brittish Toy Makers Guild, Sept. 1991

RECOGNITION:

Woodworking Today, Oct. 1991, pg. 34-35; *Miniatures Showcase*, Sept. 1993, pg. 19, 26-28, 32, 34, 39, 66; *Dolls House World*, No. 20, pg. 4; *The Complete Dolls House Book*, Jean Nisbett, 1993, pg. 4

AUTOBIOGRAPHY:

My career prior to making miniatures full-time, was in the plastics and paint industries working in research and development laboratories and latter in marketing and management positions. I started making miniatures in various styles as a hobby in 1989. I began making Shaker style furniture full-time, in mid 1990. My exhibiting and selling, at the major British shows, started at the end of 1990. I was accepted as a full member of the British Toy Makers Guild, September 1991. In October 1993, I attended my first international show in Holland. I have received no formal training in woodwork. The chair seating, rugs and textiles are produced by my wife Jean.

ARTISAN: **MORLEY, FRANKLYN J.**

BUSINESS NAME: Morley Miniatures

IDENTIFICATION MARKS: (Submitted by William R. Robertson)

CATEGORY:

Furniture

RECOGNITION:

Miniature Collector, No. 1, Apr. 1977, pg. 22; No. 3, Aug. 1977, pg. 28-30, "Franklyn Morley's Collectible Victorian Miniatures," Bernard Rosner; No. 4, Dec. 1977, pg. 25; *Miniature Gazette*, Vol. 9, No. 4, Summer 1981, pg. 72

ARTISAN: **MORMAN, JIM**

BUSINESS NAME: J.D. Morman Miniatures

IDENTIFICATION MARKS:

Rugs unmarked

J • D • MORMAN

Incised into wood with knife on inside or underside of furniture parts

J • D • M •

Some frames initialed

CATEGORY:

Frames; Furniture: period; Rugs: French Knot

HONORS:

Exhibit: Toy & Miniature Museum of Kansas City

MORMAN, JIM, continued

BIOGRAPHY:

Jim Morman has a Fine Arts education from the Kansas City Art Institute. He majored in graphic design, and has a minor in painting. Jim worked for nine years as a lettering artist at Hallmark Cards. He has done extensive research in the art history of seventeenth and eighteenth century France.

ARTISAN: MOROZ, FRANK
BAUDER, PAT

BUSINESS NAME: Bauder-Pine, Ltd.

IDENTIFICATION MARKS:

Most unmarked

Frank Moroz:

FJM
Earlier pieces

Cassidy Creations
½-inch furniture kits

Pat Bauder:

Bauder-Pine, Ltd.
Limited Edition houses
signed & numbered

Cassidy Creations
½-inch furniture kits

CATEGORY:

Dollhouse; Kits: furniture

HONORS:

NAME AOH (both)

RECOGNITION:

Nutshell News, Vol. 12, No. 9, Sept. 1982, pg. 55; Vol. 14, No. 2, Feb. 1984, pg. 79, "Kit-Crafting Tip A Cassidy Creations Nursery in Two Scales", Bob Porter, (Pat Bauder); Vol. 14, No. 9, Sept. 1984, pg. 71, Show Scene; *Miniature Collector; The Miniature Magazine; Miniature Gazette*

AUTOBIOGRAPHY:

Pat Bauder

I started with a dollhouse for my daughter Kim, and as she broke pieces I started repairing them. Repairing led to making and making to selling. I worked in one-inch scale for several years and got tired of toting around big houses, so tried ½-inch scale as a sample of one-inch scale. The houses couldn't remain empty so making furniture was the next logical step. Miniatures have always been fun to me. Many of the houses Frank Moroz and I have designed over the years are copies of historical homes. I feel that miniatures are an enjoyable way to preserve and study architecture, since historic preservation is important to me. I have served as president of our local historic association. I have chaired the Borough Planning Commission, and served on the Boards of both IGMA and NAME. I've been nominated for Volunteer of the Year, in Bucks County, Pennsylvania, and have served on the Langhorne Borough Council.

When I retired from Bell of Pennsylvania I turned to miniatures, and a miniature business full-time. I am also a collector; collecting sample sized furniture, toys and ½-inch scale pieces.

My husband, Joseph, and I have two children and grandchildren.

ARTISAN: **MOSER, SUZANNE A.**

BUSINESS NAME: This Olde House

IDENTIFICATION MARKS:

SM SM

Sometimes with date

CATEGORY:

Accessories: country, handpainted; Baskets; Bears: quilted; Birdhouses; Fimo; Fireplaces: accessories; Furniture; Rugs

RECOGNITION:

Nutshell News; Miniatures Showcase

AUTOBIOGRAPHY:

I first became involved with miniatures in 1984, when I opened a country gift shop. We began to carry miniatures and in a relatively short period the shop converted to a miniature shop, featuring some gifts. I became possessed by the hobby and that mixed with my artistic nature is how I began creating little things.

One day while paging through *Country Living* magazine, I saw a willow chair and attempted to make it in one-inch scale for myself. It turned out rather well and friends asked me to make one for them, and then their friends, and so on. I began designing more and soon put together a list with photos which I advertised in *Nutshell News*. The response was overwhelming.

I use willow and wire to create my designs. All my learning was by trial and error, but now that I've formulated my designs I'm proud to say that each piece is one hundred percent my creation. I now make furniture in one-inch, ½-inch and ¼-inch scales. I also work with Sculpey to make my quilted bears. Each bear takes one full day to paint as my detail is very small. I also use my painting talents to produce my fire screens and handpainted birdhouses.

I've seen many changes with my business since 1989. I gave up my shop to stay home and raise my three boys. Having developed my mail order business made the transition easier, as I was able to take my miniature hobby home with me. It has proven to be a good move, as business has grown while at the same time I've been able to be with my children.

For the future, I hope to continue to develop my line, I have many new ideas. As my children enter school, I would like to join CIMTA and attend more shows.

ARTISAN: **MOSQUEDA, ROBERT E.**

BUSINESS NAME: Fantasy Fabrications

IDENTIFICATION MARKS:

FF

Robert Mosqueda

CATEGORY:

Furniture; Lamps; Roomboxes

RECOGNITION:

Artsnews, Mid-Valley Arts Council, Salem Oregon, Oct. 1992

MOSQUEDA, ROBERT E., continued

AUTOBIOGRAPHY:

As a child, I assembled and painted plastic airplane kits. After several years I tried balsa wood kits with tissue paper coverings. At the age of 12, I switched to plastic boat kits, at 15 or 16, I went to a wooden model of the "Cutty Sark," three feet long and three feet high with cloth sails. In my 20's I started and continue to do leather tooling.

For the past 30 years I have experimented with close up lenses and macro lenses, etc. Now I photograph miniatures in addition to creating miniature furniture. I was enticed into miniatures when a friend was making a Halloween roombox and asked me to make a trick or treat bag for her. All the skills I have as a miniaturist were developed long ago assembling plastic model kits.

Miniatures will become a full-time occupation after retirement from being a computer consultant and an accountant.

ARTISAN: MOTT, ALLEGRA & DeWITT (Deceased)

BUSINESS NAME: Mott's Miniatures

IDENTIFICATION MARKS: (Submitted by Elizabeth Mott)

Allegra

Dewitt

CATEGORY:

Accessories; Furniture; Houses; Roomboxes; Structures

HONORS:

IGMA Crystal Award, 1992 (Allegra)

RECOGNITION:

Nutshell News, Vol. 13, No. 2, Feb. 1983, pg. 26; *Miniature Collector*, No. 2, Jun. 1977, pg. 32-37, "The Marvelous Legacy of Allegra Mott," Virginia DeMoss; No. 39, Oct. 1983, pg. 53, "Projects & Plans;" *Miniature Gazette*, Vol. 1, No. 1, Sept. 1972, pg. 3, "Allegra's Dream," A. Mott; Vol. 1, No. 2, Dec. 1972, pg. 18-19, "Mrs. Mott is just Wild about Dolls, Dolls, Dolls," Ray Rhoads; *Daily News Tribune*, News of North Orange County, Monday Jul. 4, 1977, pg. A-3, "For the Motts, at Knotts, It's a Small Small Small World," Tony Long

BIOGRAPHY:

This miniature collection began when Allegra was just eight years old and started collecting Cracker Jack prizes. She met Dewitt when they were both just teenagers and six years later, in the early 1920's, they were married. Soon after they married, Dewitt, who shared his wife's enthusiasm for miniatures, started to build exact replicas of their antique furniture. Perfectly detailed and in miniature, his pieces were used to display Allegra's Cracker Jack prizes and tiny party favors. Today, the collection includes the original prizes, miniature party favors, antique furniture, and books among others. The collection was housed at Knott's Berry Farm in Buena Park, California for some time and numbers more than 300,000 pieces.

The Mott's collection traces the history of America from the 1760's to the present with scenes that are historically correct down to the finest detail. Dewitt created the realistic settings modeled after toy stores, Oriental and Scandinavian shops, a pharmacy, and an early American home at Thanksgiving to show off their best pieces, including a 1750's Eastern cabin that is a replication of the one Dewitt Mott's father owned, and a 1900's Des Moines home of Allegra Mott's family and in which their three children were raised, and many more. The Motts paid particular attention to the exactness of their displays. In fact more than 5,000 school children every year have seen the collection used as an aid in learning their history lessons.

MOTT, ALLEGRA & DeWITT, continued

The Motts had three children of their own, Barbara, Elizabeth, and Bill, who did not have the same passion for miniatures as the rest of the family. The girls have continued to grow the collection along with Elizabeth's two children. Today the collection, starting with Allegra's Cracker Jack prizes, has been active for more than 60 years.

Today the collection includes pieces such as an entire tea set made from dimes which won first prize at the Silversmith's Convention at the 1893 World's Fair, a perfect set of porcelain false teeth that rest in a glass, and the smallest printed miniature book ever type set, at that time, made for a printer's convention in the 1920's.

The Motts also played a significant role in the creation and development of the National Association of Miniature Enthusiasts. In 1972, Allegra expressed a dream that she had to several other collectors. That same year the organization was chartered. The first club meetings were held at the Mott's home. Today, NAME has grown to include more than 10,000 members worldwide and sponsors at least six yearly major miniature collector's conventions around the United States.

(Kenneth L. Frank, Reference to *Miniature Collector*, Jun. 1977, *Miniature Gazette*, Sept. 1972)

ARTISAN: **MOTT, BARBARA** (Deceased)

BUSINESS NAME: Mott's Miniatures

IDENTIFICATION MARKS: (Submitted by Elizabeth Mott)

CATEGORY:

Accessories

RECOGNITION:

Nutshell News, Vol. 13, No. 2, Feb. 1983, pg. 26; *Miniature Collector*, No. 39, Oct. 1983, pg. 53, "Projects & Plans;" *Daily News Tribune*, News of North Orange County, Monday Jul. 4, 1977, pg. A-3, "For the Motts, at Knotts, It's a Small Small Small World," Tony Long

BIOGRAPHY:

One of the founders of the Mott Miniatures Museum in 1949, Barbara Mott played an active role in collecting, displaying, and teaching other artisans in the world of miniatures.

Barbara helped to build the museum to 75 different exhibits most of which were created by her family; her parents Allegra and Dewitt Mott, her sister Elizabeth and Elizabeth's two children.

In 1972, Barbara helped to co-found the National Association of Miniature Enthusiasts. Additionally, Barbara served as the first president of NAME.

In 1976, Barbara and Elizabeth co-wrote the *Mott Miniature Workshop Manual*, one of the first books dedicated to the miniature hobbyist.

(Kenneth L. Frank, Reference to *Miniature Collector*, Jun. 1977, *Miniature Gazette*, Sept. 1972)

ARTISAN: **MOYNIHAN, LINDA**

BUSINESS NAME: Rastus

IDENTIFICATION MARKS:

Most work unmarked

1982 to present

RASTUS

MOYNIHAN, LINDA, continued

CATEGORY:

Accessories: country, Victorian

RECOGNITION:

Nutshell News, Jan. 1986, pg. 70, Show Scene; *Miniatures Showcase*, Fall 1988, pg. 36, 42, 47; *Miniature Gazette*, Summer 1992

ARTISAN: **MUCK, KATIE**

BUSINESS NAME: Mother Muck's Minis

IDENTIFICATION MARKS:

Prior to 1990

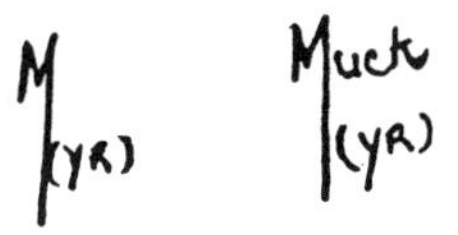

1990 to present

CATEGORY:

Accessories

AUTOBIOGRAPHY:

As long as I can remember, I have worked with my hands in every craft known to man. In 1983, Chevron closed their refinery in our native New Jersey, and transferred us to Utah. Suddenly I found myself 2,000 miles from home, no friends or family, one car and two little boys ages three and four. I was losing my mind fast until my husband came to the rescue and made a lifelong dream come true. A dollhouse under the Christmas tree! I had finally found my niche and a way to do all my crafts in one compact unit. Who knew that the entire house would eventually be overrun with compact units! Within six months I was teaching workshops and selling my accessories at a local shop.

In 1987, I began my own mail order business, became a member of CIMTA in 1988 and a member of NAME in 1989. About the same time, I discovered that one-inch scale wasn't challenging enough and I much preferred ½-inch and ¼-inch scales. During the past five years, I have been expanding my smaller scale line of accessories and foods while phasing out one-inch scale. As of June 1993, I work in the smaller scales exclusively.

ARTISAN: **MURPHY, MARK**

BUSINESS NAME: Mark Murphy

IDENTIFICATION MARKS:

CATEGORY:

Furniture: American, English, Japanese

HONORS:

IGMA Artisan

MURPHY, MARK, continued

RECOGNITION:

Nutshell News; Miniature Collector

AUTOBIOGRAPHY:

I have a BFA in woodworking and furniture design from the Philadelphia College of Art, now the University of Arts. I started doing miniatures about 1982.

ARTISAN: MURPHY, MARY AGNES

BUSINESS NAME: Mary Agnes Murphy Handcrafted Miniatures

IDENTIFICATION MARKS:

CATEGORY:

Accessories; Clothing; Furniture; Knitting; Paintings; Toys

RECOGNITION:

Miniatures Showcase, Nov. 1992, pg. 72; *Miniature Catalog*, 13th Edition, Cover; *Miniature Dealer*, 1989, 1991

AUTOBIOGRAPHY:

I received a BA from the University of Massachusetts, Amherst in 1964 with art as my major, and an MFA in Graphic Design from the University of Massachusetts, Dartmouth in 1969.

From 1964 to 1981, I taught art in grades K through 12. During this time I developed an interest in miniatures and started making furniture and accessories. I also taught miniature craft classes in my home.

From 1982 to the present, I have been actively involved in the miniature market, and have been a member of CIMTA since 1987.

ARTISAN: MURPHY, STEVE

BUSINESS NAME: Glass Blowers Workshop

IDENTIFICATION MARKS:

1968 to present

Logo

CATEGORY:

Accessories: crystal

RECOGNITION:

Nutshell News, Vol. 14, No. 8, Aug. 1984, pg. 86; *Miniature Gazette; Miniatures Showcase*

AUTOBIOGRAPHY:

I began my career in 1963. A glass blower by the name of Nick Leopardi, (shop located inside of the Pottery Shack, in Laguna Beach, California) moved in next door to me. As we became friends he began showing me the tricks of the trade. I would spend countless hours watching him at his shop, then I would spend more countless hours trying the same things at home. As time passed, and after I had accomplished a few designs Nick introduced me to Harold Hacker, the original glass blower at Knotts Berry Farm in Southern California. Harold taught me how to create even more items using different techniques. During this training period I joined the National Guard and was attending school to become an architectural engineer. Needless to say I never finished my schooling in that field. In 1968, I married Kandy and at the same time we bought the business (Glass Blowers Workshop) from Nick Leopardi and operated it from 1968 to the present time. We left the Pottery Shack and moved to Arkansas. I work at home, travel to miniature shows and do mail order. I have been a member of NAME since 1973, and a member of CIMTA since 1989. We also run a trophy and engraving business. Between the two, glass and trophies, we stay very busy.

ARTISAN: **MURTER, JOE**

IDENTIFICATION MARKS: (Submitted by Esther Robertson, Vivian Stoddard)

All marks with year. Piece number in edition/edition quantity

CATEGORY:

Furniture: period

RECOGNITION:

Nutshell News, Vol. 14, No. 3, Mar. 1984, pg. 37, 56; Vol. 14, No. 4, Apr. 1984, pg. 42, 69

BIOGRAPHY:

Joseph A. Murter was born in Delaware County, Pennsylvania in 1946 At an early age he showed a bent toward nature and art, along with a very good way with animals both domestic and wild.

Around the age of 15 he obtained a paper route, with the money he made he took a course in Taxidermy from the Northwest School of Taxidermy. He then apprenticed with J. Mackrel in Pennsylvania. After getting his license in Delaware he practiced that art until he moved to Pennsylvania.

Joe's interest in creating miniature furniture was influenced, though not taught by, his uncle E.L. Murter (Lou). By 1976 a friendly rivalry had developed between them. For about ten years Joe produced limited editions of many fine pieces, mostly Chippendale style.

He anticipates he may again get back into producing in the future. In the meantime, he remains in his job with the railroad and will soon have put in 30 years. During this time he raised four girls, and a lot of handyman work for himself, his parents, and his friends. He also obtained his pilot license in small aircraft.

(Submitted by Ruth Murter)

ARTISAN: **MURTER, LOU** (Deceased)

IDENTIFICATION MARKS: (Submitted by Vivian Stoddard)

All marks with year. Piece number in edition/edition quantity

CATEGORY:

Furniture: period

MURTER, LOU, continued

RECOGNITION:

Nutshell News, Vol. 13, No. 7, Jul. 1983, pg. 48, Show Scene; *Miniature Gazette*, Vol. 7, No. 3, Spring 1979, pg. 9

BIOGRAPHY:

Eugene Louis Murter, Jr. was born on Sept. 15, 1924 in Wallingford, Connecticut, the third child in a four child family. His father was an electrician on the Pennsylvania Railroad. When he was a young lad he received a pair of boots with a penknife in a little side pocket as a gift. He started whittling animals, etc. in soap, then on to wood. He had a God given talent and never hesitated to give God the glory for it. He whittled for years before starting miniature furniture. One of his loves was whittling large eagles for gifts and to give as prizes for charity. He would whittle copies of old guns for display and for our children to play with later. He would make HO railroad cars from scratch. He never sold any of his work, but gave it to those who admired it. Lou became very involved with Cub Scouts and Boy Scouts and made many many neckerchief slides as awards as well as plaques, scenes, etc.

I can't begin to describe his giving nature and pure pleasure he derived from knowing that people liked and had his work in their homes. Lou started making miniatures by copying a rocker that we had in our home. It wasn't scale but it was so much fun that he made several more non-scale before finding out that there was such a thing as scale. Everybody like them and told him that he should go into business. Charging for them was still very much against his grain, but kids getting ready to go to college helped change his mind about that, although he would have always rather given them away. He took them to a couple of outlets and was very pleased that the public seemed to like them also. He held free classes in his home to try to pass the art on to others. About this time he met Vivian Stoddard, she was a dealer and had seen his work and this started a great friendship as well as a business relationship. His great joy in the business was going to the shows (which he didn't have to do) and talking to the people about his craft. Lou loved meeting the people who cared enough about his furniture to want it in their homes. I still run into people everyday, both young and old, that remember him for his genuine interest in his art and in them as human beings. Till the day he died, Oct. 17, 1985, his greatest joy in his craft was not the money, but the people he met and the craft living on. He left us with great memories.

(Submitted by Dorothy Murter)

N

ARTISAN: **NAKOA, CHARLOTTE**

BUSINESS NAME: Charlie's Chimney Corner

IDENTIFICATION MARKS:

Ch   char   Char Nakoa   Nakoa

CATEGORY:

Accessories: handpainted; Christmas: Cards; Holiday Items; Paintings: watercolor

RECOGNITION:

Nutshell News, Jul. 1990, pg. 58, Show Scene

AUTOBIOGRAPHY:

I was born in Valparaiso, Indiana, which is still my hometown. As a child I fashioned little fabric and wire stick people to dwell in a secret village inside a lilac bush. I would peek in upon them from time to time, and prop them back up after a storm.

I received a B Ed as an Art Major from the University of Hawaii in 1972. I developed a hand for fine detail through employment with a jewelry firm where I painted miniatures on gold-framed mother-of-pearl pendants.

In 1986, I took my first one-inch scale watercolor originals to shows in the Chicago area. I also paint full-size, and have prints with Arts Uniq' of Tennessee.

ARTISAN: **NALVEN, RUTH E.**

BUSINESS NAME: R. E. Nalven

IDENTIFICATION MARKS:

R.E.N. With date
1990 to present

1993 to present
limited edition pieces numbered & dated

CATEGORY:

Carpets; Needlepoint; Needlework; Rugs

HONORS:

IGMA Artisan

AUTOBIOGRAPHY:

I have a BFA majoring in textile design at the College of Fine Arts, Syracuse University, New York. I have taken workshops and seminars at the following institutions; Museum of Natural History, New York; New England Wildflower Society and the Connecticut Botanical Society in the fields of Herbariums, Lepidopterology and Botany. In various topics pertaining to work as either a curator or museum trustee I was also schooled at New England Museum Association, Museum of Fine Arts Boston, Massachusetts, and Clark Institute, Williamstown, Mass.

I have been employed as a crafts instructor, YMCA, Harrisburg, Pennsylvania, Junior Designer for Lily Dache, New York, Advertising Manager, Window Display for Mary Sachs Stores, also in Harrisburg, Textile Designer for Robert Gentile, Inc., Salinger Textiles both in New York and including self-employment. I have been Curator for Gunn Historical Museum in Washington, Connecticut, and crafts designer and producer, also self-employed, making needlework design in miniature as well as using pressed flowers, seaweed and feathers to make cards and bookmarks.

I have enjoyed many community service programs in the capacities of Board member, The League of Women Voters; Trustee, The Gunnery School; Trustee and Co-Founder, The American Indian Archeological Institute all in Washington, Connecticut, to include Chairperson on a committee for Handicapped Accessibility; Fundraising and Collections Committees, and have researched, developed, collected and catalogued for the Ethno-Botanical Herbarium.

ARTISAN: **NASH, JACK & JINNY**

BUSINESS NAME: The House That Jack Nash Built

IDENTIFICATION MARKS:

CATEGORY:

Dollhouse; Structures

ARTISAN: **NEAVES, MARY K.**

BUSINESS NAME: Mama Bear Creations

IDENTIFICATION MARKS:

CATEGORY:

Bears; Toys

HONORS:

IGMA Artisan

RECOGNITION:

Nutshell News, Nov. 1988, pg. 96-97; Mar. 1989, pg. 71; Apr. 1989, pg. 69, Private Eye; Dec. 1990, pg. 25; Mar. 1991, pg. 25, 82; Apr. 1991, pg. 56; Jul. 1991, pg. 60, 65; Dec. 1991, pg. 27; Jan. 1992, pg. 67; May 1992, pg. 63; Jun. 1992, Cover, pg. 41-42; *Miniature Gazette*, Fall 1987, pg. 20; Spring 1987, pg. 58; Fall 1988, pg. 46; Fall 1989, pg. 24, 56; Spring 1990, pg. 44; Winter 1990, pg. 32; Fall 1991, pg. 19; Spring 1992, pg. 36; *Miniatures Showcase*, Fall 1987, Cover; Summer 1987, Cover; Winter 1990, pg. 44; Winter 1991, pg. 24, 68; Summer 1991, pg. 25; Fall 1991, pg. 12, 17, 35; Nov. 1992, Cover, pg. 32, 38; *Teddy Bear Artist's Annual*, Issue No. 1, pg. 89

AUTOBIOGRAPHY:

My degree is in Cosmetology, but I prefer miniatures. I started making miniature flowers in 1981, but always loved sculpting and child's toys, so changed to sculptured bears and tiny figures. I started selling at shows in 1986 and now do eight to 10 shows nationally each year.

I feel the "Talent to Create" is a gift, I only supply the patience.

ARTISAN: **NEILL, GINNIE**

BUSINESS NAME: Noah's Country Ark

IDENTIFICATION MARKS:

CATEGORY:

Fimo; Sculptures

HONORS:

Seven Ribbons in show competition

RECOGNITION:

Nutshell News, Vol. 20, No. 6, Jun. 1990, pg. 56-58, "A Gift of Hope," Sybil Harp; *Miniatures Showcase*, Summer 1992, pg. 54

ARTISAN: **NEI – NEI**

BUSINESS NAME: The Desert Indian

IDENTIFICATION MARKS:

1986 to present

CATEGORY:

Pottery: American Indian

HONORS:

Honorable Mention, Best of Category, Best of Division Trophy, National Date Festival, Indio, CA 1974-1978; Best of Show, Palm Springs Convention, CA

RECOGNITION:

Desert Sun Newspaper, Palm Springs, CA Feb. 26, 1988, Sec. D, Part V; Oct. 28, 1988, Sec. B, Part V; Jul. 4, 1989, Sec. D, Part V

AUTOBIOGRAPHY:

After a good, hard rain my Indian grandmother would take a pinch of earth and molded small people and horses. These were very private little toys with which I played within her barricaded lot. No one would see and no one would laugh or ridicule. The toys were never baked and always destroyed. The images stayed ingrained in my mind and my heart.

Decades later and after becoming a professional clay artist, I realized that an interest was growing in Native American Art. Size and price were sometimes a problem for collectors so miniatures from my distant past came back to mind.

At first a token price was tagged to miniatures, but demand became too great to continue my "give-away hobby". Casting was out of the question for me, for the pottery would then not be genuine. In 1987, I began to become more intricate with the design and appearance of each vessel. To my amazement collectors continued to pay the price. The smaller the item, the more interest there was. I found great satisfaction and pleasure in the challenge to produce micro-miniatures. I could see my grandmother's face smiling at me as I produced each little pot.

I make miniatures for my gratification, not for serious production. As pieces are accumulated, they are displayed for the public to view.

ARTISAN: **NEISWENDER, BETTY**

BUSINESS NAME: Keramos Ceramics

IDENTIFICATION MARKS:

Smaller Dolls unmarked; Larger Dolls marked on back of head

K year   BN year   Both marks incised & painted

ST   Sandy Turner

LL   Linda Locke

SM   **SMS**   Susan Moriera Sheridan

MK   Mott-Keramos, in 1977 - 1984

CATEGORY:

Dolls; Figurines; Porcelain; Toys: dolls

HONORS:

IGMA Artisan

RECOGNITION:

Contemporary Doll Magazine, Issue No. 1; *The Nevadan*, Newspaper, Las Vegas, Nevada, Sunday supplement Review Journal, 1976, 1988

AUTOBIOGRAPHY:

I have always loved miniatures and all kinds of arts and crafts. When I was 12, my parents bought me a plaster casting set with rubber molds of Indian figurines. I was so intrigued, I learned how to make rubber molds, and soon I was making molds of anything that would hold still long enough! Plaster craft enjoyed great "fad" status in the late 1940's and early 1950's. I made figurines, plaques, etc. and sold some to friends during my high school years. After graduation, I married and had four children. When they were still quite small, I took classes in painting, sculpting and ceramics at a local high school, and taught classes to senior citizens. I studied interior decorating through a correspondence school while working part time in a furniture store. In 1973, I bought my first kiln, and began doing ceramic miniatures for local gift shops. In 1977, I met Sandy Turner, who became my partner and encouraged me to attempt porcelain. We helped to found the Las Vegas Miniature Enthusiasts and put on a NAME Regional here in 1981. Sandy left the business in late 1981 and I have continued on my own since then, selling mold designs to a number of mold companies and doing some mold manufacturing myself between 1982 and 1987.

I collect antique dolls, and have made some very accurate reproductions of them as one-inch scale toys. I have sculpted originals of a number of characters from literature and television shows, notably five characters from TV's "Beauty and the Beast" "Phantom of the Opera" and "The Wizard of Oz." I have won ribbons and trophies in our local ceramic show, including the highest award in the professional category, and a Judges Choice Trophy. My work has been pictured at various times in *Nutshell News* and *Miniatures Showcase*, and an article on my "Beauty and the Beast" dolls appeared in *Contemporary Doll* magazine; premier issue.

My children are grown and I am a widow. What began as a hobby is now my living! I still love miniatures, and always will.

ARTISAN: **NICHOLS, KAREN MARKLAND**

BUSINESS NAME: Karen Markland Studio

IDENTIFICATION MARKS:

Karen L Markland KLM

CATEGORY:

Accessories; Folk Art; Furniture: handpainted

HONORS:

IGMA Fellow

RECOGNITION:

Nutshell News Calendar, 1986; *Nutshell News,* Jul. 1986; *Miniatures Showcase*, Summer 1987, Cover; *Miniature Gazette*

AUTOBIOGRAPHY:

Miniatures has been my most fervent and enduring passion that began when I was four when I pleaded with Mother to buy me the tiniest and most perfect miniature coffee grinder at Colonial Williamsburg, Virginia. I avidly collected and cared for the antique dollhouse furnishings that had belonged to her and to my grandmother. I continuously guarded and repaired them after the onslaught of my little sister who lost ice tea glasses, bent and twisted all the pewter castings and cut & bobbed all the dolls' wigs to various stages of baldness.

All through teenage years, college, marriage and early motherhood, I packed away my precious miniatures. Finally, at thirty something, when I grew restless and knew I needed to satisfy this creative and unfulfilled yearning, I was able to unpack the boxes. From them I received the inspiration and direction for the small business I wanted to start. My Fine Arts degree from the University of Colorado, and my interest in all forms of large scale crafts and sculpture was my background. I had taught art for years at all levels, primary grades through adult education and knew teaching was not a career option for me. For many years my hobby has been my business; how lucky I am to still love my hobby!

ARTISAN: **NICHOLS, NIC & LINDA**

BUSINESS NAME: Nic's Creative Workshop

IDENTIFICATION MARKS:

Most pieces numbered with date

Nic Nichols On furniture and roomboxes

NIC Floss or ink on right heel

NCW N.C.W.

On accessories

CATEGORY:

Accessories; Bears: teddy; Furniture: period; Roomboxes

HONORS:

IGMA Fellow 1979 (Nic); Exhibit: Toy & Miniature Museum of Kansas City

NICHOLS, NIC & LINDA, continued

RECOGNITION:

Nutshell News, Vol. 16, No. 8, Aug. 1986, Cover, pg. 56-57, "Victorians at Heart," Bonnie Schroeder; Vol. 20, No. 2, Feb. 1990, pg. 40-41, "St. Nic's Workshop," Jeanne Delgado; *Reproducing Period Furniture and Accessories in Miniature*, Virginia Merrill, Susan Merrill Richardson, Crown 1981, pg. 103; *Through the Looking Glass*, Boynton and Associates, Inc., Ann Ruble, 1984, back cover, pg. 77; *American Period Interiors in Miniature*, A Style and Source Book, Kate Doordan Klavan, Scribner's, 1984, pg. 153, 155, 161, 163, 166, 182

BIOGRAPHY:

Nic Nichols is an internationally recognized artisan in the "world of miniatures". For over 10 years he has specialized in the miniaturization of the Victorian era. His miniature Victorian pieces in one-inch scale as well as his complete room environments have delighted collectors around the country.

Nic's work is part of the permanent collection of the Toy & Miniature Museum of Kansas City and other museums and established collections throughout the country and Europe. He is a graduate of the duCrete School of the Arts in Plainfield, New Jersey.

A Fellow of the International Guild of Miniature Artisans, Board member and 1st Vice President, he was Founding Director as well as a full professor at the Guild's school in Castine, Maine. One of Nic's most popular miniatures has always been his interpretation of the classic jointed American Teddy Bear, which he is now featuring in many of his new room settings.

He is currently creating full-sized and miniature bears and teaching the art of "bear making" to hundreds of students in his workshop in New Jersey and at various schools. He is chief designer for Bear Beginnings™, a mail order company for Teddy Bear kits and supplies. Nic was responsible for forming a "Bear Giving Guild" within his local Teddy Bear Club, which supplies teddy bears to the local charities in their work with children, i.e., Ronald McDonald House. In his local area he is fondly referred to as "Doctor Nic" for his care and restoration of ailing bears of all ages.

In 1990, Nic went to South Africa to give a week long series of lectures and slide programs on the 20th Century art form of Miniaturia.

Nic enjoys teaching more than anything; he feels by teaching people to make quality room environments that his students will then collect quality miniatures to furnish them with. He also hopes that someday miniatures will be accepted by the art world as a viable art form!

ARTISAN: NICKEL, TINA SELDEN

BUSINESS NAME: Tina Selden Nickel Originals

IDENTIFICATION MARKS:

With year

CATEGORY:

Animals: figures

HONORS:

IGMA Artisan; Exhibit: Toy & Miniature Museum of Kansas City

RECOGNITION:

Dolls in Miniature, Vol. 1, No. 4, Winter 1991/1992, pg. 63-66

AUTOBIOGRAPHY:

I was born and raised in Raytown, Missouri a suburb of Kansas City. My senior year in high school I was the year book editor. I graduated from the University of Missouri, majoring in Interior Design. I became interested in miniatures teaching my two sons about the Old West, first making a stage coach, then a general store. Initially I started making "look-alike" dolls and stationary figures. Now I am concentrating on "look-alikes" of pets and wildlife animals. All my work has been signed Tina.

ARTISAN: **NIELSEN, ROGER G.**

BUSINESS NAME: Custom Miniature Homes

IDENTIFICATION MARKS:

CATEGORY:

Buildings; Structures

HONORS:

IGMA Artisan

AUTOBIOGRAPHY:

I studied commercial and fine art at California College of Arts & Crafts, Oakland, California for two years before entering the Army Air Corps in 1943. After spending three years in the Air Corps as a pilot, I returned to my art studies for another year after which I free-lanced in commercial art for a short time.

I had also had a great interest in building design and construction and I became involved more deeply in this field to a point where it became my vocation and for over 31 years I worked for two different large corporations in building design and construction management. During all of this time I continued in my hobby of miniatures, especially buildings, and upon retirement in 1987, my background and interests created a natural evolution into full-time construction of miniature buildings of all descriptions and at present my work is limited to primarily commission work only.

ARTISAN: **NINE, MARGARET**

BUSINESS NAME: Miniatures By Margaret

IDENTIFICATION MARKS:

CATEGORY:

Paintings: oil, originals, reproductions

HONORS:

IGMA Fellow

RECOGNITION:

Nutshell News, Dec. 1984, pg. 70; Oct. 1988, pg. 67; *Knoxville Lifestyle*, Dec. 1982, pg. 16; *Miniature Collector*, No. 48, Mar/Apr. 1985, pg. 30-31; *Miniature Gazette*, Winter 1985, pg. 19; Winter 1989, pg. 44; *Miniatures Showcase*, Spring 1990, pg. 40; *Action 10 News*, Television, Knoxville, Tennessee, 1984

AUTOBIOGRAPHY:

I worked in an art gallery for 14 years and began doing small paintings in 1969. I became interested in miniatures in 1978 and from that time, I painted in miniature and am participating in shows each year from 1981 until the present.

ARTISAN: **NISSEN, PHYLLIS**

BUSINESS NAME: Phyllis N. Miniatures

IDENTIFICATION MARKS:

All marks 1984 to present

CATEGORY:

Chandeliers; Curtains; Dolls; Drapes; Furniture; Kits; Lighting; Quilts

AUTOBIOGRAPHY:

I have worked with dolls and miniatures since I was six years old but didn't have time to become totally involved until 1984 when I joined NAME and the San Diego Miniature Crafters Club. I taught myself from books with the exception of attending a few classes. I especially enjoy miniature shows and teaching classes. I make and have taught the following classes: crystal chandeliers, electrical table lamps, leather chairs and silk Victorian chairs, quilts, both in kit form and quilting techniques, gold leafing, etched glass, doll costuming for both men and women, ½-inch scale upholstered furniture, and curtains.

I am a member of NAME and IGMA, San Diego Miniature Crafters Club, Mission Minis Club, Society of American Miniaturists and Friends of Miniatures. I especially enjoy the Gulf South Miniature & Dollhouse Event, which is held in New Orleans, Louisiana the week prior to Memorial Day.

ARTISAN: **NOBIS, RUDI & BARBARA**

BUSINESS NAME: B B Fine Miniatures

IDENTIFICATION MARKS:

 Prior to 1988  1988 to present

CATEGORY:

Christmas; Dioramas; Eggs: scenes; Holiday Items

RECOGNITION:

Nutshell News; The Miniatures Catalog, 6th Edition, pg. 11, "Farrow Industries Four Story Department Store," pg. 413, "Bookcase by Farrow Industries;" *Miniatures Showcase*, Vol. 1, Fall 1986, pg. 52, "Country Doctor's Office"

AUTOBIOGRAPHY:

I founded Farrow Industries which was incorporated in August 1980, and after my husband, Gene Farrow died in March of 1986, I sold the wholesale end of the business, as it was more than I wanted to handle at the time. I kept the retail division, "BB Fine," my maiden name being Barbara Bradway. I was the first to gain written permission and licensing agreements from many major companies in the United States to authentically re-produce their boxes, labels, cans, bottles and jars in miniature. A box, label or picture was photographed, reduced to one-inch scale and then went through a 4-color processing the same as its larger counterpart, and scored when necessary for easy folding. Among our accomplishments we created a 5 foot long supermarket complete with carts and check out counters, a two story toy store and a four story department store, each of these winning 1st place and best of show in competition.

I have since remarried and am presently decorating and doing miniature vignettes and dioramas in real eggs from finch to ostrich size. My husband, Rudi and I are presently doing shows in the Eastern part of the US.

ARTISAN: **NORMAN, HELEN** (Deceased)

BUSINESS NAME: Hudson River Doll Houses

IDENTIFICATION MARKS:

Accessories unmarked

Built by Andy + Helen Norman
Palisades N.Y. With date

Dollhouses built between 1966 – 1979

CATEGORY:

Accessories; Dollhouse; Structures

HONORS:

Exhibits: Blauvelt Historical Society, New York, 1974; Bear Mountain Museum, New York, 1984

RECOGNITION:

Nutshell News, Vol. 13, No. 12, pg. 80; *Miniature Collector*, No. 41, Jan/Feb. 1984, pg. 42-44, "Shedding the Bag Lady Label", James van Maanen; *Miniature Gazette,* Vol. 6, No. 1, Sept. 1977, pg. 47; *New York Times*, Saturday, Jan. 18, 1975, "Doll Houses: From Memory," Lisa Hammel

ARTISAN: **NORTON, EDWARD G.**

BUSINESS NAME: Edward G. Norton

IDENTIFICATION MARKS:

CATEGORY:

Furniture: period

HONORS:

Founding member IMA now NAME AOH; Mell Prescott Memorial Award 1987

RECOGNITION:

Nutshell News, Jul. 1982, pg. 47; Jan. 1989, pg. 80-81; *New York Times*, Sunday, Oct. 30, 1977; *Connecticut Public TV, CPTV,* May 28, 1978; *Hobbies Magazine*, Sept. 1973, pg. 138-139; *American Period Interiors in Miniature*, Kate Doordan Klavan, Scribner's, 1984, pg. 48, 60, 80, 105, plate #30

AUTOBIOGRAPHY:

After working as a plumber for 15 years , I was forced to leave that work because of a back ailment in 1972. I started making miniatures as a part-time hobby in 1970 and went into it full-time in 1972. In the beginning, I received much aid and encouragement from Mrs. Mel Prescott and also Mr. Carl Anderson. My interest is mainly in American Queen Anne and Chippendale furniture as well as Windsor chairs. I have made a few dollhouses which are from Colonial background.

ARTISAN: **NUSSBAUM, PAM**

BUSINESS NAME: Pam Nussbaum's Minis
Country Workery

IDENTIFICATION MARKS:

CATEGORY:
Dolls: costuming; Needlepoint; Needlework

HONORS:
IGMA Artisan

BIOGRAPHY:
Pam Nussbaum has been involved in miniatures since 1982. Having done needlepoint her whole life as well as embroidery, cross stitch, quilting, hook rugs, appliqué and other forms of fabric arts it was a natural ease into miniature dress making and miniature needlework. Pam likes small pieces of work best, working on 84 screen as well as 72 and 60. She hasn't been working for many years but has recently returned to what she does best. Miniatures have always been a large part of her life, and will continue to be in the future.

ARTISAN: **NUTTER, TERRIE LYN**

BUSINESS NAME: Tiny Needlework Treasures in Miniature

IDENTIFICATION MARKS:
Most unmarked

Some have initials worked into piece; may include a detailed signed certificate with photograph.

CATEGORY:
Needlepoint; Needlework

HONORS:
IGMA Artisan

AUTOBIOGRAPHY:
I have been doing needlework since 1978, and miniature needlework in counted cross stitch and micro petit point since 1983. I have lectured at my local EGA chapter on micro petit point and have taught classes on the subject. My micro petit point miniature pieces have won many first place and best of show ribbons at local and state fair needlework shows. I am currently working on my master craftsman status with the Embroidery Guild of America in counted thread. I have also written a small book entitled "First Steps in Micro Petit Point on Silk Gauze."

O

ARTISAN: **OADES, JACK & JOY**

BUSINESS NAME: JoJay Crafts

IDENTIFICATION MARKS:

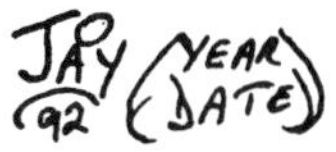

CATEGORY:

Furniture; Knitting; Linens

ARTISAN: **OAKES, MARILYN**

BUSINESS NAME: Little House on the Table

IDENTIFICATION MARKS:

Knit pieces unmarked

CATEGORY:

Accessories; Fimo; Food; Knitting; Needlework

RECOGNITION:

Miniatures Showcase

AUTOBIOGRAPHY:

My love of miniatures began very, very early. I have a sister who is four years older than I. She had a dollhouse that I was not allowed to play with or even touch. When I was grown and had children of my own I discovered the Colleen Moore Fairy Castle at the Museum of Science and Industry in Chicago. I took my children to see it and found it hard to drag myself away!

Later, my husband was trying very hard to think of a gift for our 25th wedding anniversary. We had observed some retired men working on dollhouses at a senior citizens clubhouse several years earlier. Without my knowing anything about it, he contacted them and asked them to build a custom Victorian house. On the day of our anniversary he took me to see the unfinished shell. I couldn't believe it! For three days and nights I cried every time I thought about "my" house.

I began immediately making cross-stitched rugs and Fimo foods. I made almost everything that went into that first house. By then my granddaughter was about two years old. Whenever she spent the night at Grandma's house, the dollhouse was her night light. Later, when Amy was four and a half, I made a dollhouse for Christmas, for her very own.

I loved making foods and other things for my house and always seemed to make several of each thing that I made. This led to selling miniatures at shows. I have continued to learn new ways of working with Fimo and sell many Fimo foods. I also make some accessory items in both one-inch and ½-inch scale. I started crocheting and knitting items for that first house and now make knitted items to sell and give to friends.

I organized our local miniature club and have been president for about eight years. I also formed a Ship and Share Miniature Club that exchanges projects by mail. I am currently the NAME State Rep for South Carolina. I enjoy getting together and sharing with my "miniature" friends at home, shows, or houseparties. I like to design and teach workshop projects. I work full-time as an occupational health nurse but spend most of my spare time working with miniatures.

ARTISAN: **O'BRIEN, MARY GRADY**

BUSINESS NAME: Mary Grady O'Brien
Yankee Notions

IDENTIFICATION MARKS:
All pieces dated

1st mark

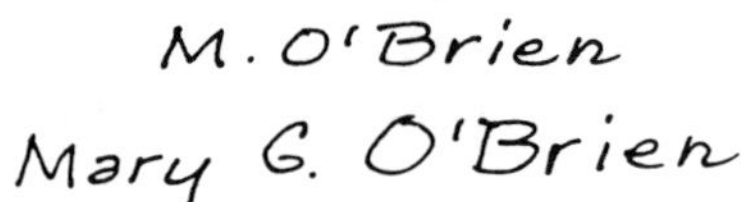

2nd mark

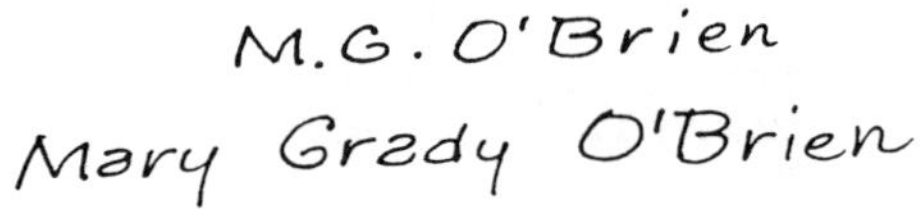

Present mark

CATEGORY:
Dolls: figures, porcelain; Folk Art; Furniture: handpainted

HONORS:
IGMA Fellow; NAME AOH

RECOGNITION:
Nutshell News, Mar. 1986; Apr. 1986; Sept. 1987; Oct. 1989; Dec. 1990; Mar. 1992; Mar. 1994; *Logos, Ursuline Academy Magazine*, Dallas, 1988; Video tour of *Shanunga*, a tiny Nantucket Whalers Cottage, Pam Throop; *A Mansion in Miniature*, Bets O'Meara, O'Meara Publications, 1979; *American Period Interiors in Miniature*, Kate Doordan Klavan, Scribner's, 1984, color plate 3, 25, pg. 126, 188

AUTOBIOGRAPHY:
I am a Home Ec major who became a self-taught miniature artist. Perhaps after raising six children, I was ready for a less domestic turn in my life. It has been a very satisfying path and I continue to grow and learn, and have also enjoyed seven years of teaching at the Guild School in Castine, Maine. I try to do two shows a year. I feel very fortunate to be able to work in a field that gives me so much pleasure – and make such wonderful friendships.

ARTISAN: **O'CONNOR, SUSAN W.**

IDENTIFICATION MARKS:

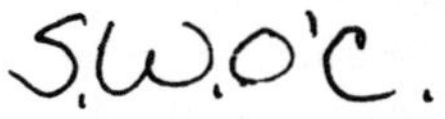

CATEGORY:
Landscaping; Wicker

AUTOBIOGRAPHY:
My passion for miniatures started in 1987 while I was discovering my childhood dollhouse. It started with kits, then bashings, any and all workshops offered by the local shops. I do what I like to call "reading and deeding," how-to and do-it-yourself books. Since then I've taken many workshops given by the Hoffmans; Pat & Frank (Bauder-Pine), Bob Bernhard; Nic Nichols; Bill Langford and George Passwater and have plans for many more.

Now I'm giving workshops and exhibiting. I belong to NAME, and am a charter member of the Philly Miniatics. I enjoy using a variety of unusual containers, but my favorite is my Landscaped Birdcages.

ARTISAN: **OHANIAN, JUDITH G.**

BUSINESS NAME: Judith G. Ohanian

IDENTIFICATION MARKS:

JGO

Stitched into needlework, signed on the reverse side in same style lettering
Printed on back of picture or bottom of chair seat

CATEGORY:
Kits: needlework; Needlepoint; Needlework

HONORS:
Exhibit: Toy & Miniature Museum of Kansas City

RECOGNITION:
Nutshell News; Miniatures Showcase, Vol. II, Winter 1987; *Miniature Gazette; The Scale Cabinetmaker*

AUTOBIOGRAPHY:
I started working in miniature in February, 1975. Out of necessity, I am mostly self-taught. I work in almost all phases of miniatures, building furniture and roomboxes, making most of what I need. I am a dedicated devotee of the many wonderful books and plans and magazines, telling me how-to "do it myself." My needlework was a natural to try in miniature since I have done sewing of all kinds, most of my life. I so enjoyed my needlework that I manufactured a small line of needlepoint carpets. Then over the years I added more than 25 kits for smaller pieces, pictures, pillows etc. In 1985, Boynton Publishing published a "Plans Service" book of needlepoint designs, which is still in print. I am married and have a daughter, neither my husband or daughter are involved in miniatures.

ARTISAN: **OLDHAM, BERT & NORMA**

BUSINESS NAME: Oldham Studio

IDENTIFICATION MARKS:

OLDHAM STUDIO
CALIFORNIA

Numbered and dated

CATEGORY:
Accessories; Furniture: period

HONORS:
IGMA Artisan, 1989 (both); IGMA Fellow, 1992 (both); Miniature Maker's Society, Excellence in Miniature Artistry, 1986; Boston Tiny Treasures, 3rd Prize Furniture, 1987; 1st Prize Furniture, 1988; 3rd Prize Furniture, 1989

RECOGNITION:
Nutshell News, Dec. 1980, pg. 58-60; Jul. 1982, pg. 51; Sept. 1984, pg. 62-63; Apr. 1985, pg. 22-24, Private Eye; Mar. 1986, pg. 61, Private Eye; Apr. 1986, pg. 55; Jun. 1986, pg. 22, Private Eye; Sept. 1986, pg. 81; Apr. 1987, pg. 31, Private Eye; Jun. 1987, pg. 60, Show Scene; Jul. 1987, pg. 61, Show

Scene; Aug. 1987, pg. 31, Private Eye; Apr. 1988, pg. 71, Show Scene; Jul. 1988, pg. 59, Show Scene; Oct. 1989, pg. 79, Show Scene; Jun. 1990, pg. 31, Private Eye; Oct. 1990, pg. 66, Morningside Cottage; May 1991, pg. 31, Private Eye, pg. 63, Show Scene; Nov. 1991, pg. 72, Show Scene; May 1992, pg. 30, Private Eye; Jun. 1992, pg. 65, Show Scene; Sept. 1992, pg. 40-43, Warp & Weft; Oct. 1992, pg. 64-65; *Nutshell News Calendar*, Feb. 1986; *Miniature Gazette*, Winter 1980, pg. 19-21; Summer 1988, pg. 16; Fall 1988, Cover; Spring 1992, pg. 36, Roses; *Miniature Collector*, No. 23, Feb. 1981, pg. 43, Show Stopper; No. 50, Fall 1985, pg. 35-36, Show Stopper; *Creative Crafts & Miniatures*, Dec. 1985, pg. 9, 12; *Miniatures Showcase*, Sept. 1986, pg. 11; Spring 1988, pg. 18, 31, 42; Winter 1988, pg. 14, 28, 30, 44; Fall 1989, Celebrating the U.S.A.; Fall 1990, pg. 71; Spring 1991, pg. 11, 12, 22, 23, 26; Winter 1991, pg. 31; *Miniatures Catalog*, 1988, Cover; *Threads Magazine*, Feb/Mar. 1992, Back Cover; *Working in Miniature*, Becky Schaefer, pg. 2

BIOGRAPHY:

Bert and Norma Oldham are retired teachers and artists who have had several joint shows of their paintings prior to devoting all their time to miniatures in 1986. Both are graduates of the University of California, Berkeley, with Art majors. Bert has a Master's Degree in Art and has had 22 one-man shows of watercolors and prints in Northern California, including a 20 year retrospective at Shasta College, Redding, California, prior to his retirement as Art Department Chairman.

Oldham Studio specializes in Early American furniture of the Colonial period in both one-inch and ½-inch scale. The wood is primarily pine with hardwood dowels. Featured pieces include cider, cheese & butter presses, cranberry picker & harvester, kitchen bowl & work table from Monticello, fire screen from Mt. Vernon, baby walker, Stockbridge, Mass., a wash stand, Johnson City, Texas, cricket leg candle stand & several decorated chests. Many are based on pieces from the Shelburne Museum, Vermont, Winterthur Museum, Delaware and the Philadelphia Museum and Lancaster Heritage Museum, Pennsylvania. They also have a line of contemporary watercolor paintings and Indian style decorated pottery in one-inch scale, and braided rugs in both scales.

The Oldhams received Artisan Status in the International Guild of Miniature Artisans in 1989 and were named Guild Fellows in 1992. Bert and Norma share a love of history and travel and are continually seeking new and unusual historical items to duplicate in miniature on their visits to museums and historical points of interest around the United States.

ARTISAN: **OLIVER, ANITA**

BUSINESS NAME: Anita Oliver

IDENTIFICATION MARKS:

Unmarked

CATEGORY:

Bears: teddy

RECOGNITION:

Nutshell News, Dec. 1989, pg. 60; *Antique & Collectors*, Fayre, Feb. 1989, pg. 43; *Dolls and Dolls Houses*, May 1989, pg. 8-9; *Teddy Bear Times*, Winter 1990/1991, Issue 3, pg. 25; *Daily Express*, Sept. 21, 1990, pg. 21

AUTOBIOGRAPHY:

I trained at Canterbury College of Art as a Graphic Designer, then worked in magazine and book publishing, making soft toys and dolls in my spare time. In 1976, my book *Making Dolls For Pleasure And Profit* was published. The book was successful and I decided there was a market for making dolls and other toys so I went into it full-time.

In 1980, I made my first tiny teddy bear and have continued ever since, selling nationally and internationally.

ARTISAN: **OLIVER, CURTIS & HARRIET**

BUSINESS NAME: The Clever Hand

IDENTIFICATION MARKS:

CATEGORY:

Dollhouse; Dolls: porcelain, soft body; Furniture

AUTOBIOGRAPHY:

We were stationed in Europe when we both became interested in porcelain dollmaking. We came back to the States and did it as a hobby, as we were involved in another business. Curtis was in the Army ready to retire in 1973, we bought a home and place for our business in 1977, and have been making dolls both in miniature and all sizes since. This is our sole occupation and we both love it, making dolls everyday.

ARTISAN: **OLSON, NORAL D.**

BUSINESS NAME: Noral D. Olson

IDENTIFICATION MARKS:

1970 to present

CATEGORY:

Furniture: reproductions

HONORS:

IGMA Artisan, Fellow 1994; Exhibit: Toy & Miniature Museum of Kansas City

RECOGNITION:

Nutshell News, Jun. 1984, pg. 52-54; Apr. 1994, pg. 42-45; *Better Homes & Gardens*, Wood, Dec. 1987. pg. 40-43

AUTOBIOGRAPHY:

My career as a furniture designer for manufacturers was an excellent background for making miniature furniture. I especially enjoy doing complicated pieces with lots of drawers and doors. Since 1970, I have produced over 700 pieces. In 1989, I did a French building complete with furnishings, for Barbara Marshall's Museum in Kansas City. I then completed 16 pieces of Biedermeier for Ingeborg Riesser in Paris, France.

I have taught at the College of Miniature Knowledge in Ashland, Oregon and at the Guild school in Castine, Maine.

ARTISAN: **OLSZEWSKI, ROBERT**

BUSINESS NAME: Olszewski Studios

IDENTIFICATION MARKS:

Printed material and hand signed miniature figurines

OLSZEWSKI, ROBERT, continued

CATEGORY:

Art: figurative; Bronzes: handpainted; Designer; Figurines: bronze; Sculptor

HONORS:

White House, Washington, DC 1982, Miniature Art Display; Grolier Enterprises, 1985, 25th anniversary of Snow White, 7 Dwarfs; First National Olszewski Convention Toledo, Ohio 1991; Gift and Collectible Industry 1985, 1992, Miniature of the Year; Carnegie Art Museum, Oxnard, California 1993, 30 year museum retrospective, 15 years of painting, 15 years of miniature art; The Carole & Barry Kaye Museum of Miniatures, Los Angeles, California; Dollhouse Museum of the Southwest, Dallas, Texas; Gift and Collectible Industry, 1993, International Collectible Artist of the Year; From 1980 to 1994 worked interpreting in miniature under license the works of *M. I. Hummel, Walt Disney, Bialosky, Norman Rockwell, Ted DeGrazia,* and executed commission work for *Grolier Enterprises, Danbury Mint, Franklin Mint;* Carnegie Art Museum, Oxnard, California, Dec. 19, 1992 to Mar. 28, 1993

RECOGNITION:

Nutshell News, 1978; *Collector's Editions*, Fall 1987; *Collector's Mart,* Aug. 1991; *Antique Trader*, Jul. 1992; *Gift Reporter*, Feb. 1989; *Miniature Collector*, 1982; Nov/Dec. 1994; *Toy and Hobby*, Fall 1993; *Toy Box,* Winter 1993; *Figurine Collector*, Summer 1984; *Masters in Miniature, 12 Artisans At Work, Volume 1*, Anne Day Smith, Kalmbach Publishing, 1987; *The Goebel Miniatures of Robert Olszewski,* An Authoritative Reference And Price Guide, Dick Hunt; *The Wizard of Oz Collectors Treasury*, Jay Scarfone & William Stillman; *Limited Edition Collectibles*, Paul Stark; *M. I. Hummel*, Price Guide, Carl Lucky; *Today Show*, 1982, Jane Pauley; *People Are Talking*, 1985, Philadelphia, Penna. Interview; *P.M. Magazine*, 1986, Western US from Salt Lake City

BIOGRAPHY:

Robert Olszewski was born in 1945 in a small town north of Pittsburgh, Pennsylvania. His natural interest in art developed early and was first demonstrated in painting and drawing. At age 16, he began winning awards for his work at local art shows, and was encouraged to pursue a career in art. Robert graduated in 1968 with a BS in Art Education, married, and moved to Southern California in the same year to live near a major US art center and teach. While teaching he painted in the summers and at night. The security of teaching plus the free time, allowed him to experiment freely and develop his skills. He had his first one-man show at the Ryder Gallery on La Cienega Boulevard in Los Angeles at the age of 27. At the same time he enjoyed his young family and made toys for his children to play with. Along with toys, he built a dollhouse for his daughter and this was his introduction to the world of miniatures. His interest in miniatures turned from playful to a serious exploration of miniature figurative works as a new medium of expression.

After 11 years, Robert left teaching in 1978 and pursued miniature figurative work full-time. Within a year his work was receiving national attention. In 1979, at age 34, Robert was brought under exclusive contract with the major European porcelain company, Goebel, maker of the world famous M.I.Hummel figurines, and was co-founder of the Goebel Miniatures Studios. As master artist from 1970 to 1994, Robert oversaw the development of the modeling and painting studios, and watched the company grow from a staff of four painters in 1979 to 65 painters in a studio numbering 95 personnel.

In 1993, a 30-year museum retrospective of his work was mounted at the Carnegie Art Museum in Oxnard, California, and in the same year Robert was named "International Collectible Artist of the Year."

In 1994, Robert re-established privately owned Olszewski Studios and began exploring his art in a smaller studio to enable him to devote more time to his personal artistic growth. This new direction will follow his personal artistic interests and will reflect his love of working in the small scale, his interest in European figurative porcelain, and his love of exploring and combining new materials. At 49, his move to an independent status will leave more time to pursue in depth his art and address those areas he has been waiting to explore.

He is a member of the National Association of Miniature Enthusiasts, a continuous member since 1977; International Guild of Miniature Artisans; American Decorative Arts Council; Miniature Industry Association of America, National Association of Limited Edition Dealers, artist member, and Manufacturing Jewelers and Silversmiths of America.

ARTISAN: **O'MEARA, BETS**

BUSINESS NAME: Maison des Maisons

IDENTIFICATION MARKS:

Bets O'Meara

CATEGORY:

Books; Christmas; Holiday Items; Roomboxes; Rugs; Writer

HONORS:

3rd Place, Trees, Art Reach Festival, 1992; Exhibits: Denver Museum of National History, 1988, 1989; Western Museum of Wickenburg, Arizona, 1990, 1991

RECOGNITION:

Nutshell News; 1978; *Miniature Collector*, 1978; *Durango Herald*, Durango, Colorado, 1986, 1991; Alamosa Valley Courier, Colorado, 1979; Denver Post, 1978, 1979, 1980; Rocky Mountain News, Denver, Colorado, 1980; ABC & NBC TV, Denver, Colorado, Show coverage, 1978, 1979, 1980, 1986, 1987; *A Mansion in Miniature*, Bets O'Meara, O'Meara Publications, 1979

ARTISAN: **O'NEILL, ELEANOR**

BUSINESS NAME: O'Neill's Mini Knittery

IDENTIFICATION MARKS:

Certificate of Authenticity
O'Neill's Mini Knittery
Certificate Number ______ for
______
issued to
______
Date: ______ ______
Bill & Eleanor O'Neill

CATEGORY:

Crocheting; Knitting

HONORS:

IGMA Artisan, Fellow

RECOGNITION:

National Doll World, Mar/Apr. 1987, pg. 12-13; Kathleen Taylor, Doll Pattern Review; *Washington Post*, 1988, Marriage of Miniatures; *Collectible Doll Calendar*, Apr. 1988

ARTISAN: **ORR, JUDITH A.**

BUSINESS NAME: Judy Orr Miniatures

IDENTIFICATION MARKS:

JAO JO Judith A. Orr JOrr

CATEGORY:

Dolls: original, porcelain; Fimo

HONORS:

IGMA Artisan; Best in Class Fantasy Division, West Coast Doll Competition, Seeley Company 1992

ORR, JUDITH, continued

RECOGNITION:

Nutshell News, Mar. 1991, pg. 72

AUTOBIOGRAPHY:

My career in miniatures began in the fall of 1981. I began by making a miniature cake for a neighbor's child to have in her new dollhouse. Through lots of encouragement, I made more and began selling them to local shops. I met a knowledgeable miniaturist through a close friend. She taught me about Fimo, lycopodium, and how to make things tiny by using everyday objects.

I went on to develop 16 Christmas ornaments. Through my sales I paid for lessons in porcelain work. I apprenticed under the following teachers: Marigold Hogan, (The China Doll); Ricky Macias, lace draping and carving; Shirley Harless, Antique Reproduction China Painting; and Dawn Adams, sculpturing and anatomy.

Through the last 12 years, I have designed 52 Christmas ornaments, Renaissance Jesters and accessories, porcelain doll originals as well as tiny antique reproduction dolls. I also have a line of kits for Christmas decorating. porcelain originals include Christmas elves, woodland elves and fairies and characterizations.

I have always been interested in art, interior design, fantasy, children's books and the Victorian Era, as well as the Renaissance period. I have two years of college in design.

ARTISAN: **ORTHAUS, DORIS J.**

BUSINESS NAME: D J O's Porcelain Dolls

IDENTIFICATION MARKS:

Behind left ear, bottom right foot, left hip

CATEGORY:

Dolls: original, porcelain; Indian: American

HONORS:

IGMA Artisan 1992

RECOGNITION:

Nutshell News, Mar. 1991, pg. 84; Nov. 1992, Cover; *Miniatures Showcase*, Summer 1988, pg. 26; Winter 1988, pg. 28; Spring 1991, pg. 60; *Doll Castle News*, Jul/Aug. 1988, pg. 23; Sept/Oct. 1989, pg. 16

AUTOBIOGRAPHY:

I have always had a love for small things. As a Girl Scout leader our troop exhibited small scenes of woodland trails, camp scenes and made "peep boxes" with miniature scenes inside that were given to children in the hospital.

In the early 1940's, I became involved in ceramics which gave me the basics for making the porcelain figures. The miniature dolls became my greatest interest and the American Indian fascinated me. I have exhibited the dollhouse that I made from a kit, and at different times roomboxes with Indian scenes.

ARTISAN: **O'SHAUGHNESSY, LYNN**

BUSINESS NAME: The Hurricane Room

IDENTIFICATION MARKS:

1990, 1991

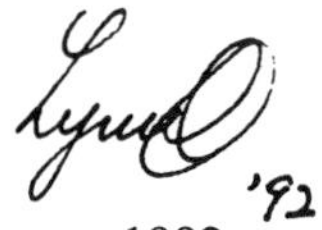

1992

Sailor's Valentines, with initials and date in pen

CATEGORY:

Baskets; Bears; Photography; Valentines: Sailor's

RECOGNITION:

Nutshell News, Nov. 1992, pg. 73; *Princeton Packet,* Princeton, New Jersey, Mar. 21, 1990, pg. 27, "Time Off"

ARTISAN: **OSTENDORF, JOHN H., SR.**

BUSINESS NAME: J & J Woodesign

IDENTIFICATION MARKS:

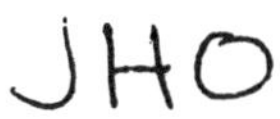

CATEGORY:

Dollhouse; Roomboxes; Structures

AUTOBIOGRAPHY:

I have been a carpenter, cabinetmaker and have made custom furniture, working for display and architectural woodworking firms. I started doing miniature structures in 1983. I am working on a series of Historical US Miniature Structures.

ARTISAN: **OTTEWILL, JOHN G.**

BUSINESS NAME: John G. Ottewill

IDENTIFICATION MARKS:

Signed, dated, numbered in limited editions

CATEGORY:

Furniture

RECOGNITION:

Nutshell News, May 1985, pg. 50; *Miniature Gazette*, Winter 1981, pg. 87; Vol. 17, No. 3, 1989, pg. 59; *Miniature Collector*, No. 44, Jul. 1984, pg. 34; No. 74, Winter 1991, pg. 28-31, "John Ottewill, Master Carver," Pat Ostovar; *Hobbies Magazine*, Aug. 1983, pg. 63

OTTEWILL, JOHN G., continued

AUTOBIOGRAPHY:

I trained and was employed in England as a professional model maker and wood carver, producing prototype models of various Industrial Design products. I emigrated to Canada in 1957 and until 1979, in addition to full daytime employment with an architectural firm, was self-employed as an architectural model maker receiving commissions from various architects for models. Since 1979, I have been self-employed making miniature furniture.

P

ARTISAN: **PAGEL, JAMES B.**

BUSINESS NAME: Wooden Rainbows

IDENTIFICATION MARKS:

1989 to present

CATEGORY:

Furniture

RECOGNITION:

Miniatures Showcase, Fall 1991, pg. 13, 22, 26, 38; Mar. 1993, pg. 33, 38-39; Sept. 1993, pg. 18-19, 33-34, 39, 66

AUTOBIOGRAPHY:

I began my interest in full-size furniture, collecting, refinishing and reproducing antique furniture for our home. But our small house began to fill quickly, and as a way to maintain my fascination with furniture I turned to creating scaled miniature reproductions.

ARTISAN: **PALMER, JOHN**

IDENTIFICATION MARKS:

J P Initials printed in white with year

CATEGORY:

Accessories

ARTISAN: **PALMER, KEN**

BUSINESS NAME: Ken Palmer

IDENTIFICATION MARKS:

Hallmark punch on precious metals

Metallic pieces

CATEGORY:

Automata; Clocks; Porcelain; Silversmith

RECOGNITION:

Dolls House World

PALMER, KEN, continued

AUTOBIOGRAPHY:

I was trained as a teacher at Birmingham College of Arts and Crafts as a qualified silversmith and cabinet maker. I taught arts and crafts until taking an early retirement. I was introduced to miniature making by Muriel Hopwood, the miniature ceramist, and began to make miniature silver pieces. I now have a range of over 60 sterling silver artifacts and use the Birmingham Assay Office for the hallmarking.

Recently I have branched out into making clocks; one with a working pendulum, and am also into automata. I wrote articles for *Dolls House World* magazine covering the less usual miniature items.

ARTISAN: **PAPKE, BUNNY**

BUSINESS NAME: Distinctive Needlework "Heirlooms in Miniature"

IDENTIFICATION MARKS:

Some unmarked

CATEGORY:

Kits: needlework, rugs; Needlework

HONORS:

IGMA Artisan

RECOGNITION:

Nutshell News, Feb. 1989, pg. 27, 31; *Miniatures Showcase,* Summer 1990, Cover, pg. 10-11, 26-27; Winter 1990, pg. 33, 36-37, 82

ARTISAN: **PARDINA, JEAN**

BUSINESS NAME: Jean Pardina Dolls and Molds

IDENTIFICATION MARKS:

CATEGORY:

Dolls: molds

RECOGNITION:

Nutshell News, Sept. 1984; Jan. 1985; Dec. 1988; Aug. 1989; Nov. 1991; *Miniature Gazette*, Spring 1981; Winter 1983; Summer 1985; Fall 1986

ARTISAN: **PARKER, JOHN WATSON**

BUSINESS NAME: Swallowhill – J. Parker

IDENTIFICATION MARKS:

1993 to present

PARKER, JOHN WATSON, continued

CATEGORY:

Figures; Sculptures

RECOGNITION:

Making & Dressing Doll's House Dolls in 1/12 Scale, Sue Atkinson, David & Charles Press, England, 1992

AUTOBIOGRAPHY:

Throughout most of my life I have been involved in miniatures through my parents' business. This meant that when it came to summer jobs, I was gainfully employed in the miniatures field, manufacturing and producing porcelain dolls.

I attended Art College with a view to becoming an active partner in Swallowhill. After graduation I entered the art field through drafting, sign painting and free lance art work. I now work full-time running the manufacturing end of Swallowhill. I am sculpting a new series of dolls for our business.

ARTISAN: **PARKER, JOY ANN**

BUSINESS NAME: Swallowhill – J. Parker

IDENTIFICATION MARKS:

1993 to present

CATEGORY:

Costuming; Dolls: porcelain

RECOGNITION:

Nutshell News, 1982; *Miniature Collector*, 1985; *Miniature Gazette; 1987; Making & Dressing Doll's House Dolls in 1/12 Scale*, Sue Atkinson, David & Charles Press, England, 1992

AUTOBIOGRAPHY:

My mother, and her family for three generations back, have been Art Teachers. I have always painted in oils and acrylics. I started making cloth dolls when I was about 10 years old and continued making them for many years. In 1975, I attended the International Doll Makers Association convention in Atlantic City, and discovered porcelain dolls. I bought a mold and brought it home in my suitcase. Then I had to buy a kiln and accessories so I could use the mold!

At that time porcelain slip was not commercially available here in Canada, and I learned, with the help of a potter friend, how to make my own porcelain slip from materials available at a pottery supply shop. I was actually quite successful, but am glad I can now buy the slip already made up and don't have to spend the time mixing it myself.

I started by making larger reproduction porcelain dolls, being entirely self-taught as there was no one in Canada to teach me. In 1978, I made my first miniature doll using "large doll" techniques, which I soon found did not work with miniatures. I developed special painting techniques which I still use today.

I began a mail order business selling porcelain doll kits, and very soon my husband, Wayne, joined me in the business. For some years we were the largest supplier of miniature porcelain doll kits in the world, selling sometimes more than 1,000 kits per month. Sue Atkinson, of London, England, became our European distributor, and she still sells Swallowhill dolls.

With the help of my husband we started adding original dolls to our line. Although Wayne can no longer work because of rheumatoid arthritis, our son John is now working with me. John is interested in sculpting originals and I expect great things of him!

ARTISAN: **PARKER, LAURIN**

BUSINESS NAME: Parker Carriage Works

IDENTIFICATION MARKS:

CATEGORY:

Buggies; Carriages; Carts; Harnesses; Horses: harnessed; Vehicles: horse drawn

HONORS:

IGMA Artisan

RECOGNITION:

Nutshell News, May 1992; *Dolls in Miniature*, 1992

AUTOBIOGRAPHY:

Parker Carriage is proud of its myriad of horse drawn vehicles: carriages, buggies, carts and sleighs. All are fashioned after actual antique vehicles or reduced from existent working carriage plans and photos. All are accurate one-inch scale with working springs and fifth wheels where applicable. Upholstery is carefully attended to, and hand tufted. The painted finish on the vehicles is created in exactly the same manner as that found on actual horse drawn vehicles in full-scale, this is to say a multi-step process of priming, filling, sanding, sealing and painting. This creates a high gloss finish with no visible wood grain.

All vehicles are created from various woods and brass, wood for the body and wheel construction and brass for the springs and hardware.

The original Parker Carriage Works, owned and operated by my husband, Michael, is involved in building and restoration of full-sized horse drawn vehicles both for show and family heirloom. I personally drive and show miniature horses, having developed a number of national champions (some of whom are seen annually driven in the Pasadena Tournament of Roses Parade on New Year's morning).

When I decided that a one-inch scale vehicle would enhance the house and barn I built for my niece, I found a lack of available vehicles which were accurate, with proper turning radius, running gear and springs. In the interest of creating a vehicle which was similar to the full-sized vehicles, I took carriage plans from my husband's shop and with calculator in hand, designed my first miniature gig.

Since that time, I have imported carriage plans from England, measured and photographed vehicles in working carriage shops and private collections, and acquired as many historical reference books as possible. With the able advice of my husband to verify the mechanical correctness of running gear and construction, I have set a goal to create miniature vehicles capable of actually being driven, if you could find something small enough to pull them!

ARTISAN: **PARKS, IRMA**

IDENTIFICATION MARKS:

Signed paper label — **NIADA Irma Parks ®**

Printed — **Hand made by Irma Parks** with year

CATEGORY:

Dolls

ARTISAN: **PARRAIN, GENEVIEVE**

BUSINESS NAME: Genevieve Parrain

IDENTIFICATION MARKS:

Carpets unmarked, 1993 to present, label sewn on back, Creations Genevieve Parrain

Linen Samplers and year

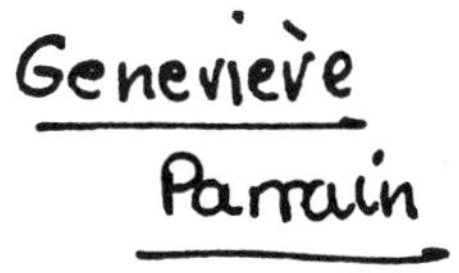

Silk Gauze and year

CATEGORY:

Carpets; Kits; Samplers

RECOGNITION:

The Catalogue of the Festival International de la Miniature Monte'limae, 1991, pg. 11; 1992, pg. 12; *The Catalogue of the Miniatures Exhibition at Domaine De Beloeil, Belgium*, 1991; *La Nouvelle République*, Newspaper, Tuesday, Aug. 11, 1992; FR3 Centre TV, Mar. 21, 1992

AUTOBIOGRAPHY:

I have been a collector of miniatures and dollhouses for many years. My activity, making and creating carpets really started in 1988. I have not studied in this field but I had always seen my grandmother do needlework. I first started making carpets for myself to put in my dollhouses. It was showing them to the owner of a miniature shop that started my selling and I added samplers, bundles of towels etc. I also sell them in kit form.

ARTISAN: **PARTELOW, RALPH E., JR.**

BUSINESS NAME: Miniature Grand Pianos

IDENTIFICATION MARKS:

Prior to 1981

1981 to present

CATEGORY:

Furniture; Musical Instruments; Pianos

RECOGNITION:

Nutshell News, Feb. 1996, pg. 38-39, "Partelow = Piano," Anne Day Smith; *Miniature Collector; Creative Crafts; Dollhouse and Miniature News; The New York Times*, 1978; *The Rocky Mountain Miniatures Magazine; Pierce Piano Atlas*, Edition 7; *Masters in Miniature, 12 Artisans At Work, Volume 1*, Anne Day Smith, Kalmbach Publishing, 1987

AUTOBIOGRAPHY:

Interest in miniature piano making began when I was a child, about 11 years old. It was sometime during that year that I began taking piano lessons and we got our first upright piano. Lessons accelerated under the tutelage of Earyle Browne, a retired concert pianist near Fishkill, New York for 3 years (between my 14th and 17th years.) Mr. Browne introduced me to the Steinway family in New York where I met the late John Steinway, who later was a tremendous inspiration and help in providing Steinway specifications for my miniatures. Mr. Steinway was an ardent supporter and friend until his death in 1990. We exchanged miniature pianos and I currently own a one-inch scale concert grand that he hand made (one of very few) inscribed with a message of friendship from him.

PARTELOW, RALPH E., JR., continued

Mr. Browne, my very strict, but capable, piano teacher further ignited my interest in pianos, music, and art by his counsel and fabulous antique collection at home. His two large Steinways were always a joy to play. Mr. Browne's teacher was a student of the great Franz Liszt who could trace his student-teacher relationship back to Mozart through Beethoven. I am proud of this heritage.

My interest in pianos and keyboard instruments of almost any description has remained strong through the years since my childhood. When visiting England, France, Germany and Italy, I have taken the opportunities to visit instruments museums, to gather photos and books, specifications and details for the purpose of replicating beautiful 18th century harpsichords and clavichords for my collector-customers.

For many years, since 1978, we were in and out of the US doing missionary work in Kenya, E. Africa as teachers at the Scott Theological College, training African seminary students. The interim years were spent doing further studies in theology and making miniature pianos. In 1992, we returned to the US more or less permanently due to my wife's failing health with multiple sclerosis. Earlier in our career, she was of inestimable help in doing the finishing on all the instruments. Our 19 year old son now does all of the art work on our instruments with painted lids.

Since February 1993, I have pastored the Zion Lutheran Church in Worland, Wyoming, a congregation of about 500, which enjoys good music! And, I still build miniature pianos in limited number. To date, I have made 2010 pianos and have sold them internationally as well as within the US. We have been making miniature pianos for sale since 1976.

ARTISAN: **PASIC, PAULA**

IDENTIFICATION MARKS:

CATEGORY:

Costuming; Dolls; Landscaping

RECOGNITION:

Nutshell News, Vol. 23, No. 2, Feb. 1993, pg. 44-50, "Going Places, Petite Elite," Jeanne Delgado

BIOGRAPHY:

Raised in the rolling hills of Northern California, Paula Pasic's varied works in miniature, scenic paintings and set design all reflect the natural hues and picturesque atmosphere of her childhood. It was in the rustic community of Lincoln, California, that Paula established herself as a professional artist, selling her first work at 16, and working on commission only two years later. After high school Paula began studying art at the local community college. During this time she chose to devote much of her time and creativity to promoting the college with animated shorts, light shows and other applications of graphic designs. In addition, Paula was instrumental in a program that provided environmental education to the local community, helping others to discover and appreciate the natural beauty which she so enjoyed.

Paula became seriously involved with the world of miniatures when she began studying with the noted miniaturist, Martha Farnsworth. Under Mrs. Farnsworth's guidance, Paula learned the intricacies of pouring, painting and ornamenting dolls. This experience opened a whole new facet of art to her and she has ever since been fascinated with the Lilliputian world.

While continuing her formal education at the Art Center in Pasadena, Paula was able to employ her artistic talents in Hollywood's motion picture industry. Her work in this field included background scenes, set design in both miniature vehicles and landscape. Working behind the scenes, Paula could make her wondrous world of make believe come to life, not only for her, but for moviegoers across the country.

In early 1992, Paula became art director of The Carole & Barry Kaye Museum of Miniatures, Los Angeles, California. The position has been both challenging and fulfilling, requiring her to draw upon both her talents and experience. In addition to creating new pieces for display at the museum, Paula has provided both interior and exterior settings for period pieces, developed arrangements of multiple works, and inspired a new standard of artistic realism in miniature displays.

ARTISAN: **PASSWATERS, GEORGE R.**

BUSINESS NAME: George R. Passwaters

IDENTIFICATION MARKS:

G.R.P. JR.   G.R.P

CATEGORY:

Furniture: period, reproductions

HONORS:

IGMA Fellow

RECOGNITION:

Nutshell News; Miniature Collector; Philadelphia Inquirer, This Week magazine; *Camden Courier Post; American Period Interiors in Miniature*, Kate Doordan Klavan, Scribner's, 1984

BIOGRAPHY:

George Passwaters is a modelmaker developing industrial prototypes for electronic, space, and motion picture industries. Many of his creations are exhibited in museums around the country. He teaches individuals and workshops at many miniature shows. He is a member of NAME and IGMA and has served on both the Artisan and Fellow Selection Committees of IGMA.

ARTISAN: **PATERSON, MELINDA SMALL**

BUSINESS NAME: Smallworks

IDENTIFICATION MARKS:

MSP '93   Melinda Small Paterson '93

CATEGORY:

Accessories; Dolls: character, doll's dolls, fantasy, porcelain; Furniture: wicker; Toys: clowns, dolls

HONORS:

IGMA Artisan; 1st Place, Wicker Vignette, Oct. 1984, Portland, Oregon; Mar. 1985, Seattle, Washington; 1st Place, Sept. 1986, King Arthur Doll, Best of Division, Modern Doll Convention; 1st Prize, Oct. 1987, Doll Store Exhibit, Portland, Oregon; Best of Show, Mar. 1988, Doll Store, Seattle, Washington

RECOGNITION:

Nutshell News, Jul. 1984, Aug. 1987, Private Eye; May 1985; Sept. 1988, pg. 62-65, "Melinda's Magic," Catherine McGuire; Feb/Mar. 1988, pg. 80; Aug. 1992, pg. 24; Jan. 1993, pg. 26; Feb. 1993, pg. 71, 75; *Miniatures Showcase*, Apr. 1987, pg. 12-13, 14, 18-19; Apr. 1988, pg. 47; Summer 1988; Jan. 1993, pg. 48-49, "Artisan Creates A Touch of Fantasy," Melinda Wolf; *Atlanta Journal,* newspaper, Jun. 26, 1986; *Oregonian,* newspaper, Jan. 21, 1987; *Doll Reader* magazine, Feb/Mar. 1988, pg. 199-204, "Doll Making in Fimo, Arthurian dolls," Susanna Oroyan; KATU Channel 2, Portland, Oregon, Jul. 1990, Evening News, Pat Wilkins; KOIN Channel 6, Portland, Oregon, Jan. 5, 1989, Evening News, Ray Summers; *Miniature Collector*, Summer 1992, pg. 23, Showstoppers; Northwest Women's Art Show, Oct. 1990, Forestry Center, Portland, OR; Beaudet Gallery, Nov/Dec. 1988, Eugene, Oregon

PATERSON, MELINDA SMALL, continued

AUTOBIOGRAPHY:

I grew up with creative parents and siblings. My father was a scale model builder and graphics artist when I was a child he is now a sculptor. I never finished my Art degree but my summer, college days, job was working for a character doll company in Colorado Springs, Colorado.

I've done dolls, doll furniture and dollhouses all my life and began doing it for a living, in 1982. I also do 18 inch fairy dolls and sell at doll shows as well as miniature shows. I thank my mother for teaching me to sew, in 6th grade, and for showing me how to be creative with materials at hand. Recycling second hand items into new usefulness has been a way of life for my whole family.

ARTISAN: **PAUL, PATRICIA**

IDENTIFICATION MARKS:

CATEGORY:

Folk Art; Paintings; Toys

HONORS:

IGMA Fellow

RECOGNITION:

Nutshell News, Nov. 1992, Show Scene; Jun. 1993, pg. 38-41, "Carving Her Niche," Mary Kaliski; *Miniatures Showcase*, Winter 1990

AUTOBIOGRAPHY:

I've been making miniatures since about 1982, having started as a collector. My education is in art which is definitely a way to express myself, creatively. Currently I have a young son and work around his schedule. I prefer working in wood and enjoy carving and painting. My work generally has an animal theme. I have done several Noah's Arks and keep finding new and different ones to do.

ARTISAN: **PAYNE, BRAXTON**

BUSINESS NAME: Braxton Payne Miniatures

IDENTIFICATION MARKS:

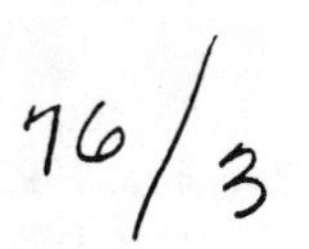

©
BRAXTON
PAYNE

© 1992
BRAXTON PAYNE

Year, and month

Copywrite varies

CATEGORY:

Architectural Reproductions: facades; Fireplaces; Greenhouses; Mantels; Pottery; Roomboxes

HONORS:

IGMA Artisan; NAME AOH; Honorary Chairman 1996, "The Magnificent Mini-A-Tour," Gulf South Miniature & Dollhouse Event, New Orleans, Louisiana; Exhibit: Atlanta Dollhouse and Toy Museum, 1986

RECOGNITION:

Nutshell News, May, 1981, Cover; *Miniature Gazette*, Spring 1990, pg. 34-35; Winter 1993, pg. 42; *Miniatures Showcase*, Winter 1992, Cover; *Our Miniature World*, Marie Dettling, 1984, pg. 91; *Inside The World of Miniatures and Dollhouses*, Rosner & Beckerman, Mc Kay Press, 1976, pg. 59

BIOGRAPHY:

Braxton was born in Birmingham, Alabama, on September 20th, 1943, and has always lived in the South. In 1973, he received his Bachelor of Architecture Degree from The Georgia Institute of Technology, and became interested in miniaturing the following year when his mother, who had begun making miniature flowers and plants for some of her friends, asked him to make clay pottery for her. He formed his business in 1974, and soon began marketing his first miniatures: greenhouses and roomboxes. Over the years he has concentrated on two general areas for his handmade miniatures: fireplaces and architectural details, and greenhouse and garden accessories, including kiln fired clay pottery, in all scales. Since 1979, he has taught many workshops and seminars at miniature shows, at National and Regional NAME Houseparties, at the Guild school in Castine, Maine, and at the College of Miniature Knowledge at Ashland, Oregon.

He created souvenir fireplaces for the 1981 St. Louis NAME National Houseparty, and the 1992 Atlanta Regional, and the 1993 San Jose Regional Houseparties. He also created souvenirs for the 1994 Virginia Miniature Enthusiasts "Miniaturists Back To College," in Ashland, Virginia, and the Gulf South Miniature & Dollhouse Event in New Orleans, beginning in 1991.

Braxton joined NAME in 1978 and served on the Board of Directors from 1980 to 1990 including one term as President from 1986 to 1988. In 1989 he was elected to the NAME Academy of Honor.

ARTISAN: **PAYNE, MARY**

BUSINESS NAME: Posy Patch Originals

IDENTIFICATION MARKS:

CATEGORY:

Flowers and Plants; Kits: flowers and plants

HONORS:

NAME AOH 1986; Exhibit: Atlanta Dollhouse and Toy Museum, 1986; National Geographic Society, "Small Wonders," Washington, DC, Oct. 1987 - Jan. 1988

RECOGNITION:

Miniatures Magazine, May 1976, pg. 38-39; *Creating in Miniature*, Mar/Apr. 1976, pg. 4-5, "V.I.P.;" *Newsweek*, Dec. 9, 1974, pg. 87; *Our Miniature World*, Marie Dettling 1984, pg. 95; *Inside The World Of Miniatures & Dollhouses*, Rosner & Beckerman, McKay Press, 1976, pg. 58

BIOGRAPHY:

Mary was born and grew up in a small North Georgia town where her love of flowers was nurtured by her mother's lovely gardens; her mother had a "green thumb," and even today continues to be Mary's constant inspiration. Her earliest miniature memories are of a dollhouse made from an apple crate, with cutouts from a Sears, Roebuck catalogue for decoration.

Mary married and attended Auburn University to study Art and Interior Design, but left after two years when WWII erupted, to have the first of her four sons (see Braxton Payne). Most of her business career was spent drafting roads and interstate highways, and she retired in 1981.

Her miniatures career began in 1973 with the forming of her business, Posy Patch Originals. She began by creating her flowers and plants from bread dough, eventually switching to a variety of art papers which allowed a much greater variety of shapes and textures. In the late 1980's she developed and began marketing her line of hand made flower and plant kits under the same business name.

From 1979 through 1984, working under the direction of curator Alice Pirie Hargrave, Mary assisted in the restoring of the flowers and plants in the Thorne Rooms Miniature Collection in the Art Institute of Chicago. Her work has been featured locally and internationally on television, in magazines and in a variety of miniatures exhibits.

Mary is a Charter Member of NAME, and was elected to the NAME Academy of Honor.

ARTISAN: **PEARSON, ERIC** (Deceased)

IDENTIFICATION MARKS: (Submitted by William R. Robertson)
Most pieces unmarked

MADE BY ERIC H. PEARSON

CATEGORY:
Furniture; Needlepoint; Needlework

HONORS:
Exhibit: Toy & Miniature Museum of Kansas City

RECOGNITION:
Nutshell News, Vol. 1, No. 3, Fall 1971, pg. 15; Vol. 4, No. 3, Summer 1975, pg. 33, "Eric Pearson," Gretchen Deans; Aug. 1980, pg. 37; Nov. 1980, pg. 29, 32; Mar. 1981, pg. 29; May 1981, pg. 40, 43; Vol. 13, No 3, Mar. 1983, pg. 42; Vol. 13, No. 10, Oct. 1983, pg. 54; *Miniature Collector*, No. 1, Apr. 1977, pg. 19; No. 6, Mar. 1978, pg. 22; *Miniature Gazette*, Vol. 4, No. 2, Dec. 1975, pg. 51; Vol. 7, No. 1, Fall 1978, pg. 14

BIOGRAPHY:
Eric H. Pearson was born in Gothenberg, Sweden, where he subsequently studied art and learned his trade at a craft school. He originally made fine antique reproductions in full-scale. When Eric came to America, he went to Montana wanting to be a cowboy, but finding the broncs not wooden enough, he returned to New York City.

Eric was commissioned by Mrs. James Ward Thorne in the 1930's to make much of the furniture in her European and American room collections. In the mid 1950's, he had a small basement shop in New York City that featured his furniture and also offered select pieces of fine silver and porcelain accessories. Mrs. Pearson served the customers until about 1960 when the shop was robbed and the Pearsons then moved upstate where one could phone for an appointment or order by mail.

Mr. Pearson took special delight in making to-scale pieces from actual photographs of furniture and the results precluded any hesitation in buying sight unseen. His workshop in a small outbuilding was almost totally destroyed by fire in the late 1960's and shortly thereafter he chose to retire.

Eric Pearson had always been a perfectionist as to details such as wood grain even when these became difficult to obtain. He made all his own hardware with jeweler's tools, all closures, hooks and bolts function. Many of his drawers were dovetailed and his hand-rubbed finish had the same patina as a full-sized 18th century piece. He would work with any wood, scale or style that a customer specified.

(*Nutshell News*, Summer 1975, "Eric Pearson," Gretchen Deans, authorized reprint)

ARTISAN: **PENFOLD, FAY DOREEN**

BUSINESS NAME: Mainly Men Minis

IDENTIFICATION MARKS:

FAY.

PENFOLD, FAY DOREEN, continued

CATEGORY:

Dolls: character, original; Fimo

RECOGNITION:

Nutshell News, Jun. 1990; *Miniature Gazette*, Vol. 17, Spring 1989; *Dolls' House World*, Issue 11, 1991; *Dolls in Miniature*, Vol. 1, Issue 1, 1991; *International Dolls' House News*, Vol. 23, 1992; CHCH TV, Ontario, Canada, Spring 1991, "The Best is Yet to Come"

ARTISAN: PERCEVAL, DAVID

BUSINESS NAME: Maquette

IDENTIFICATION MARKS:

M A Q U E T T E

CATEGORY:

Castles; Fortifications; Structures

AUTOBIOGRAPHY:

David Perceval was born at Poole, Dorset, England. His family heritage is Scottish and Black Irish, with a strong genealogical line of industrialists and innovators in the field of leather goods, steam engines and metallic high pressure packings. He continues a family tradition of enjoying the athletic pursuits and having an interest in art, architecture, history, anthropology and archaeology.

He began his career in the architectural field, spending five years as a surveyor-draftsman before entering civil engineering where for seven years, he specialized in public health and road engineering. David studied construction technology and management at the Bournemouth and Poole Technical College. In 1973, he became a member of the Chartered Institute of Building, and in 1976 joined the Faculty of Building.

In 1977, he began professionally making miniatures trading as "Maquette," and has incorporated, with their kind permission, the front elevation design of the English National Trust Dorset Folly, Bond's Folly, otherwise known as Creech Grange Arch, into his trademark. In 1990, he joined the newly formed English Society, The Folly Fellowship, which studies these unusual and mysterious structures.

David enjoys traveling, and before he came to the United States he spent some time in the United Arab Emirates as a pipe location surveyor at the Bu-Hasa Oil Field.

David is a "Castellolohist" and a member of the International Castle Institute, The Fortress Study Group, and the Coastal Defense Study Group. His surname, although spelled with an 'E', is well known for its association with "Sir Percival and the King Arthur Legend." Ironically, "Percy-Val" a medieval French warrior, was an expert at besieging castles, while his 20th century counterpart is devoted to building them in miniature.

ARTISAN: PERKINS, DON E.

BUSINESS NAME: Don Perkins Miniatures

IDENTIFICATION MARKS:

PERKINS, DON E., continued

CATEGORY:

Furniture: period; Needlepoint

BIOGRAPHY:

Like many miniaturists, Don Perkins first became interested in miniatures when his daughters were youngsters playing with dollhouses. He built several pieces of furniture for them and found it was thoroughly enjoyable. His interest continued and at the urging of friends, offered his work for sale through Iowa's Living History Farms craft shop in 1971. Since then his work has been sold by selected miniature shops and dealers, through mail order, and at miniatures shows.

In 1983, he left his work as rehabilitation counselor/supervisor with Iowa's Vocational Rehabilitation Agency to devote full-time to miniatures. His wife Gladys Courtney Perkins shares his interest in miniatures and replicates early period American needlepoint work, designs new pieces representative of the period as well as Southwestern Indian motifs. She offers many of her designs in kits. Together they have given workshops around the country in weaving rush chair seats.

Don did his undergraduate work at St. Ambrose University, Davenport, Iowa, and at Drake University, Des Moines, Iowa. His masters degree in counseling is from the University of Iowa, 1965. Don and Gladys have two daughters, one son, two sons-in-law, and grandchildren.

ARTISAN: **PETERSEN, NANCY**

BUSINESS NAME: Katy Nan's Minis

IDENTIFICATION MARKS:

KTY NAN'S — Engraved on dolls

M.L. Petersen — Book roomboxes

Nancy Petersen Kty Nan's — Inside petticoat starting 1993

Logo

CATEGORY:

Dolls: porcelain; Roomboxes: book

RECOGNITION:

Nutshell News; Miniatures Showcase; Doll Crafter Magazine, Sept/Oct. 1987, pg. 70-71, "Basics of Dollmaking", Nancy Edwards; Mar. 1991, pg. 36-37, 47, "Dressing Mini People", Nancy Edwards

ARTISAN: **PFEIFFER, URSULA G.**

BUSINESS NAME: Pied Piper Petites

IDENTIFICATION MARKS:

1980 to present

Ursula

PFEIFFER, URSULA G., continued

CATEGORY:

Accessories; Dolls

HONORS:

The Museums at Hartwick College, Oneonta, New York, Exhibition, "A-Fair of the Heart," Dec. 1992-Jan. 1993

RECOGNITION:

The Buffalo News, New York, Nov. 22, 1992, Social Events, "Little things capture fancy of collector," Erna P. Eaton

ARTISAN: **PFLUEGER, LU**

BUSINESS NAME: It's A Lulu

IDENTIFICATION MARKS:

Both marks 1981 to present

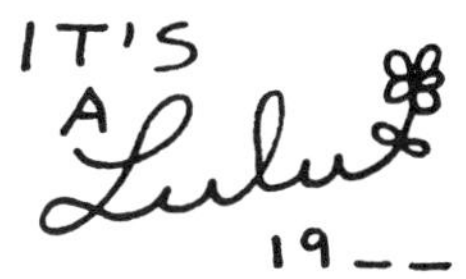

On Dolls

CATEGORY:

Dolls; Roomboxes; Vignettes

HONORS:

Exhibit: 3 Vignettes, New Orleans Museum of Art, Christmas 1990

RECOGNITION:

Nutshell News, Vol. 19, No. 3, Mar. 1989, pg. 74; Vol. 22, No. 10, Oct. 1992, pg. 75; *Miniature Gazette*, Vol. 16, No. 1, Fall 1987, pg. 41; Vol. 18, No. 4, Summer 1990, Back Cover; *Miniatures Showcase*, Summer 1988, pg. 26, 30; *Dolls in Miniature Magazine*, Vol. 1, No. 3, Fall 1991, pg. 88-93; WWL TV Ch. 4, New Orleans, 1990, Frank Davis' Naturally N'awlins; WDSU TV Ch. 6, New Orleans, Dec. 1990, Alec Gifford, The Morning Show

AUTOBIOGRAPHY:

I have always done arts and crafts. I did many class room bulletin board displays in grade school, and took art classes in high school. I graduated from Texas Woman's University, Denton, Texas, in 1960, with a BS Degree in Fine Arts.

I entered the miniature world in 1979, taking classes and making things at home, my first sale was in 1981. I have been teaching classes since 1988. Most of what we make are finished roomboxes and occasionally dolls.

The first contest I entered I won a Blue Ribbon for my "Camp Naturally N'awlins" vignette, and second place for "Cille's Sno-Balls" vignette. I volunteer as exhibit chairman for the Gulf South Miniature & Dollhouse Event, miniature show held by the National Kidney Foundation of Louisiana in May. I am a member of NAME and belong to the Elegant Elves club, and am also a member of a casual group called "Monday Bring & Brag."

ARTISAN: **PHILLIPS, BRUCE H.**

BUSINESS NAME: Bruce H. Phillips

IDENTIFICATION MARKS:

PHILLIPS, BRUCE H., continued

CATEGORY:

Furniture

HONORS:

IGMA Fellow

RECOGNITION:

Nutshell News, Sept. 1988, pg. 58-61, "Tools are his Toys," Anne Day Smith

ARTISAN: PHILLIPS, LORETTA

IDENTIFICATION MARKS:

Some pieces unmarked

Some hand signed in script in ink with year and piece number

CATEGORY:

Furniture

HONORS:

Exhibit: Toy & Miniature Museum of Kansas City

ARTISAN: PICKETT, ROBIN ALBERT

BUSINESS NAME: Robin A. Pickett, Miniaturist

IDENTIFICATION MARKS:

 Year made

Logo stamped or burned into back of pieces, with signature 1993 to present

CATEGORY:

Furniture: period

AUTOBIOGRAPHY:

I was born January 29, 1944. As a schoolboy, I was always top in my class of woodwork and art. When I left school, I went into the building trade as a painter and decorator, furthering my skills to carpentry and plastering.

I then served 12 years with the British Army. Some of this time was with the "Territorial Army Volunteer Reserves," which are units similar to the National Guard in the United States. While in the army and for some time after, I had a very great interest in model soldiers and dioramas which are miniature sceneries. This led me for some reason into making dolls houses. After I found out that a lot of people were making dolls houses, but not many people were making the furniture. This gave me the idea, being that I had the basic knowledge of carpentry, I started to do furniture research, learning about the cabinet side of carpentry. Although there were a lot of kits available to make miniature furniture, I found that they were not true one-inch scale. So I set about the task of producing my own.

I carried on this as a hobby for a period of 10 years or more. After finding that the more I made, the more I could sell. I decided when in 1989 the building trade in England went into deep decline I started making the miniature furniture as a full-time profession.. I now sell at miniature fairs as well as mail order and have some six to eight shops which buy from me.

ARTISAN: **PIERCE, DAVID G.**

BUSINESS NAME: Ain't No Big Thing
Pierce Graphics

IDENTIFICATION MARKS:

Smaller pieces

CATEGORY:

Animals; Art: objects; Figures; Masks

HONORS:

IGMA Artisan; Award Winning Woodcarver, Onandoga Woodcarvers Association; John F. Kennedy Award for Excellence in Art

BIOGRAPHY:

Dave Pierce owes his materials expertise and eye for detail to his career in advertising graphics, illustration, and jewelry making. After high school where Dave won several awards in art, including the John F. Kennedy Award for Excellence, Dave became an artist for the Air Force, and after discharge moved to his adopted home in Anchorage, Alaska. While there, Dave was Alaska's youngest Art Director, working at a local advertising agency. Many years and campaigns later, he moved to upstate New York and is exploring broader artistic horizons, noting that it was time to quit the commercial "rat race" and create art for his own pleasure.

Dave was bitten by the miniature bug after discovering the rich range of mediums and crafts that were involved in miniature collecting. Working in everything from airbrush, to wood, to antique ivory, plus many materials not normally seen in an artist's studio. Dave loves challenges! While his expertise is in figures, animals and "objets d'art," Dave will take on almost any challenge to create new and unusual miniatures. Among his creations are a dog in full gallop with only one foot touching the ground, and a perfectly scaled smoking pipe, made in two pieces exactly like the real thing, including ashes in the bowl. Most recently, Dave has begun a series of authentically scaled and fully researched African masks and artifacts. He has served as President of Syracuse Area Miniature Enthusiasts and is experienced in miniature photography.

ARTISAN: **PIERRE, GINA**

BUSINESS NAME: Lovely Little Things from Oregon

IDENTIFICATION MARKS:

CATEGORY:

Accessories; Beds: dressed; Costuming; Dolls: dolls' dolls; Roomboxes; Toys

AUTOBIOGRAPHY:

I've been involved in miniatures seriously since about 1978. My primary thrust is the design and execution of theme rooms and designing of room and houses to display special collections of customers. Prior to miniatures I made exquisite egg art for Designs Unlimited of Wisconsin. Some items were used on the White House Tree for two years and regularly supplied to the National Cathedral Gift Shop in Washington DC.

I am a professional couturier, shop owner, specializing in "party" clothes for women and girls and costumes in general.

ARTISAN: **PIPPIN, SUSAN J.**

BUSINESS NAME: Small Things Bright & Beautiful

IDENTIFICATION MARKS:

SP With year

CATEGORY:
Ceramics; Porcelain; Stoneware

AUTOBIOGRAPHY:
I started painting designs on miniature ceramic pieces in 1990. I currently work with stoneware and porcelain, in addition to ceramic. I also make miscellaneous miniatures in other mediums or combined with ceramics, such as bonsai trees, plants, and food, but usually don't sign those. I have mainly done shows in the South Eastern US and sometimes am in the Mini Mart at the NAME National Houseparty. I love doing miniature shows but am somewhat limited in the distance I can travel being a single parent of two children. I also love to give workshops.

ARTISAN: **PIRO, ROYCE**

BUSINESS NAME: Royce Piro Miniatures

IDENTIFICATION MARKS:

RP

CATEGORY:
Costuming; Dolls: original, porcelain; Kits: doll; Sculptures

HONORS:
NAME AOH 1995

RECOGNITION:
Nutshell News, Dec. 1985, pg. 40; *Miniatures Showcase*, Spring 1987, pg. 34, 36, 44-45; Summer 1987, pg. 37-39, 50; Spring 1988, Cover, pg. 8, 22-23, 34-35, 36-37; *Miniature Catalog*, 1987, Cover; 1991, Cover

AUTOBIOGRAPHY:
My interest in miniatures started as a hobby in 1979. Dolls and period costumes have always fascinated me and, gradually, I became interested in trying my hand in these two areas.

In 1983, I was brave enough to try selling my creations at miniature shows, and I've been doing so ever since. I am primarily self-taught. None of my formal education prepared me for this profession. In 1990, I did master sculpting and now all my dressed dolls, men and women, are my own sculptures.

ARTISAN: **PLATT, TREVOR "TIM"**

BUSINESS NAME: Tim Platt, Miniaturist

IDENTIFICATION MARKS:
1987 to present

Inlaid in veneer underside of piece, black serial number right of monogram

PLATT, TREVOR "TIM" continued

CATEGORY:

Accessories: parquetry; Boxes: decorative; Furniture: veneered

AUTOBIOGRAPHY:

I retired as a mechanical engineer in 1988, having been an amateur woodworker several years. I sold a few items to Miniature World and took the owner's valuable advice to concentrate on decorative veneer work. I've attended two shows a year since 1989 and made 419 items in limited editions of 100. I have sold 375, mostly Georgian caddies, needlework boxes, writing slopes, decanter boxes, etc., as well as some specific commissions. I am now researching new items to replace completed limited editions.

ARTISAN: **PLUNKETT, SALLY**

BUSINESS NAME: The Knitting Lady

IDENTIFICATION MARKS:

1985 to present

Printed on silk ribbon, sewn inside garment

CATEGORY:

Clothing; Knitting; Needlework

HONORS:

IGMA Fellow

RECOGNITION:

Nutshell News, Mar. 1986, pg. 78; *Knitters*, No. 25, Winter 1991, pg. 24

ARTISAN: **POITRAS, TOM**

BUSINESS NAME: Thomas Creations in Wood
Tom Poitras

IDENTIFICATION MARKS:

CATEGORY:

Art: prints; Engravings; Furniture: period

HONORS:

IGMA Artisan; 1st Place, Graphics and Printmaking, Georgia Miniature Art Society, 1991; 3rd Place, Graphic Arts, "The Miniature Painters," Sculptors and Gravers Society of Washington DC, 1991 and 1992; 3rd Place, Birds and Animals, Miniature Art Society of New Jersey, 1992; 3rd Place, Prints and Drawings, Edmonds 35th Annual Arts Festival, Edmonds, Washington, 1992; 1st Place Graphics, 18th Annual National Miniature Art Show, Gallery La Luz, La Luz, New Mexico, 1992; Exhibit: Toy & Miniature Museum of Kansas City

RECOGNITION:

Nutshell News, Feb. 1985; *Miniature Collector*, Spring 1986; *Seattle Post-Intelligencer*, Sept. 1, 1984; *American Period Interiors in Miniature*, Kate Doordan Klavan, Scribner's, 1984

POITRAS, TOM, continued

BIOGRAPHY:

Tom Poitras began working in miniature in the early 1980's after having worked as a mathematician and computer programmer. He has built miniature furniture of many periods, including Early American, Queen Anne, Chippendale, Hepplewhite, and Louis XV. Due to an interest in wood carving, many of his pieces have carved surfaces. The use of gravers to carve brass and gold ormolu for French furniture lead him to try making prints using the engraving method. Several of his engravings have received awards at national and international art shows. Some of his miniature furniture is included in the permanent collections of several museums in the United States. His miniature furniture has also been included in museum and gallery shows featuring miniatures.

ARTISAN: POTTER III, M.D., WILLIAM W. "BILL"

BUSINESS NAME: Miniatures By Potter

IDENTIFICATION MARKS:

With date

CATEGORY:

Furniture

RECOGNITION:

Nutshell News, Mar. 1994, pg. 46, Show Scene; May 1994, pg. 42-45, "Rx: Miniatures," Jeanne Delgado; *Fine Woodworking*, Vol. 100, May 1993, pg. 100; *Citizen Tribune*, Morristown, Tennessee, Sunday, Jan. 7, 1990, Section C-1

AUTOBIOGRAPHY:

I have been a model builder forever; airplanes, ships, railroads etc. After the US Navy, on submarines, college, medical school, internship and residency, I began building full-size furniture for relaxation and pleasure. In the fall of 1987, my wife requested a dollhouse for our daughter's 11th birthday. I constructed this from a kit. Furniture was purchased for two rooms and I built several pieces from kits. I was displeased with both the purchased and kit built pieces. With my model and furniture building background, the logical next step was to scale down furniture plans to "model" size; thus miniature furniture. I am still "practicing" medicine and miniatures.

ARTISAN: POTTS, LORI ANN

BUSINESS NAME: Mustard Seed Miniatures

IDENTIFICATION MARKS:

Some unmarked

CATEGORY:

Crocheting; Fimo: character; Toys

HONORS:

IGMA Fellow, 1992

POTTS, LORI ANN, continued

RECOGNITION:

Nutshell News; *Miniatures Showcase*

AUTOBIOGRAPHY:

I have been involved with crafting miniatures since about 1978 and have no special training in the arts.

ARTISAN: **POWEL, JOHN S.**

BUSINESS NAME: Miniatures of Merritt

IDENTIFICATION MARKS:

Unmarked

CATEGORY:

Furniture: spinning wheel; Household Accessories; Indian: implements; Machines: farm; Weapons: medieval; Tools: blacksmith, Early American, hand, occupational

HONORS:

NAME AOH, 1979; International Miniature Artists Achievement Award

RECOGNITION:

Crafts & Decorating Ideas, Vol. 10, No. 5, Jun. 1979, pg. 44

AUTOBIOGRAPHY:

I was born January 25, 1921 in Buffalo, New York, and lived there for most of my life (with the exception of five years in Crystal Beach, Ontario, Canada) in the early 1930's. It was here in Canada that I started carving miniatures around the age of 10 or 11. There wasn't much else to do in a summer resort in the winter. We moved back to Buffalo in 1935.

I finished high school and went to work as a riveter in an aircraft factory, and worked my way up to a branch of Engineering (with some night school) called the mold loft. There we made precision full-scale layouts of almost every single part of the aircraft except the mechanical parts to a ±.500 tolerance. I took some more night classes at the University of Buffalo.

Then the Navy got me for a few years during World War II!. When I came home after being discharged at the end of the war, the aircraft plant was making telephones. So I went back to college and got a teaching degree in Industrial Arts. I taught boys and girls in grades one through six how to make things in wood, metal, ceramics, textiles, and showed them varieties of techniques. The program I taught, however, was not a skills program as such, but an enrichment program designed to make their classroom studies more meaningful.

Since their coordination and dexterity was still not too well developed, I devised ways and tools so they could be successful (i.e. I made them a potter's wheel from a discarded 45 rpm phonograph.) Throwing a piece on a regular wheel was very hard for them and the mini wheel was even worse, so I made it a jiggering wheel. With this process all who did it succeeded. We also made tools and equipment for a variety of trades, home and farm in miniature.

I showed a small collection of these that I had made to our local library on Merritt Island, Florida, and have been making miniatures ever since. My teaching took place on Long Island, New York, for 26 years. During this time and while working for my Masters degree and Ph.D. credits I took courses in jewelry work. During one of these classes I met a young woman who worked for the Metropolitan Museum of Art in New York City. She had me reproduce some 1700's dollhouse miniatures for sale in the museum gift shop. I also made some for the Museum in Wilmington, Delaware.

ARTISAN: **POWELL, MIKE**

BUSINESS NAME: LM Period Miniatures

IDENTIFICATION MARKS:

LM

CATEGORY:

Clocks: working; Room Settings

HONORS:

IGMA Artisan; Exhibit: A World In Miniature, David Kilpatrick, Oban, Scotland, 6 Grandfather Clocks

RECOGNITION:

Nutshell News, Feb. 1984, pg. 48; Jul. 1990, pg. 36; *Through The Looking Glass*, Boynton and Associates, Inc., Ann Ruble, 1984, pg. 44

BIOGRAPHY:

After running a restaurant first in Portugal and then in Spain, Mike Powell moved to Vancouver, Canada, in 1978, and made room settings. In 1986 he moved to England for four years, where he started making working clocks and in 1990 he moved back to Vancouver, where he presently lives.

ARTISAN: **PRESCOTT, MELL** (Deceased)
(Submitted by Blake D. Prescott, M.D.)

BUSINESS NAME: Mell Prescott
Mell Prescott Miniatures

IDENTIFICATION MARKS:

Mell Prescott 1983
written by her in ink—
accompanied by the date

CUSTOM MADE BY
Mell Prescott
Blue on white

Mell 1983
On very small pieces

Custom Made by
Mell Prescott
Black on gold

Important additional
comments were written
directly on the piece by
her, eg, Old Williamsburg
cotton on a sofa bottom.

Original by
Mell Prescott
Elaine Prescott Wonsavage

Mell Prescott, IMA
Red lettering

CATEGORY:

Beds; Candlestands; Chairs; Furniture: antique, period, upholstered; Mirrors; Musical Instruments; Paintings: transfer: Pianos; Roomboxes; Rooms; Room Settings; Tables: end

PRESCOTT, MELL, continued

HONORS:

NAME IMA; AOH

Progenitor of the Academy of Honor Mell Prescott Award given by NAME Academy of Honor annually to that individual artisan miniaturist who has shown excellence in miniatures and who has exemplified the highest standards of the AOH as well as having contributed significantly to the growth and enjoyment of miniatures. A medallion is presented with this award. Each large medallion has Mell's silouette on it.

RECOGNITION:

Nutshell News, Vol. 1, No. 1, Mar. 1971, pg. 5; Vol. 12, No. 11, Nov. 1982, pg. 52; Vol. 13, No. 3, Mar. 1983, pg. 82, Show Scene; Vol. 13, No. 7, Jul. 1983, pg. 48, Show Scene; Vol. 13, No. 10, Oct. 1983, pg. 70, Show Scene; Vol. 14, No. 6, Jun. 1984, pg. 46-47; Vol. 14, No. 8, Aug. 1984, pg. 71; *Miniature Gazette*, Vol. 8, No. 2, Winter 1979, pg. 26; Vol. 9, No. 3, Spring 1981, pg. 32; Vol. 11, No. 1, Fall 1982, pg. 26; *Miniature Collector*, No. 29, Feb. 1982, pg. 15

BIOGRAPHY:

Born and raised in the west, Mell Prescott found this to be no deterrent to her love affair with New England. She adapted quickly and combined her artistic ability, intelligence, and determination with an initial focus on collecting antiques. Working with a limited budget in the depression years, she understandably focused on those pieces needing repair or refinishing. She and her husband, Blake D. Prescott, Sr., M.D., spent much of their "leisure" time restoring these fine pieces of furniture.

This served her very well in future years when she made her own miniature reproductions of antiques.

Mell was able to select those pieces which were exceptional. She was intuitively able to distinguish good and faulty design. Moreover, she was able to envision how pieces would complement one another. She combined this with her knowledge of craftsmanship, beautiful woods, and college education in art. Thus, she was able to combine pieces and accessories into rooms which were never frozen in time or confined by artificial barriers, but were representative of an art form. Even then, doing the unexpected became an extension of her personality, resulting in a unique and natural looking product – something envied by others.

At a time when few women attended college, Mell entered college before completing high school, and she naturally selected Utah State where her father, a geologist, was president for a number of years. It was there that she studied art, and it was there that she met a young man working his way through college by selling books. When he asked her where the office of the president was, she told him that she didn't think that the president would see him. This was illustrative of her wonderful sense of humor. The president was her father, and the young man was Blake Prescott who subsequently married Mell and went on to get a Master's degree at Columbia prior to completing his education in medicine and then in psychiatry.

Mell continued her education throughout her life. She was an avid reader and much of that which she acquired was self-taught. In her early years in Connecticut, the early 1940's, she took courses under Esther S. Brazier in antique decorating. Mell became a consummate artist: eventually not only producing her own beautiful works but also sharing her talent with others through teaching and lecturing throughout many states, with emphasis on illustrating the creative interfaces between such art forms as antiques, flower arrangements, antique reproductions and the fine arts. Here it was that her diverse abilities were reflected in a variety of methods such as reverse painting on glass, painting on velvet, tole painting, stenciling, and, of course, painting with brush. She had hundreds of students. and even with her teaching over many years and receiving a variety of awards, little did she realize how this would facilitate her later work with miniatures. One of her dicta to students was, "Don't copy anyone else's mistakes." This illustrated her dedication to the art and to excellence rather than to a frozen reproduction – no matter how accurate.

Mell had a great interest in flowers and was able to use this to enhance her decorating. Indeed, she did this so well that she soon found herself in great demand to lecture throughout New England (and later, to many states beyond) on decorating with flowers and antiques, showing the native New Englanders how to enjoy their heritage to a greater degree.

With an ever broadening interest, she started collecting dolls, and, soon thereafter, miniatures. She never stalled, and was rarely slowed by adversity, even in her advanced years. She noted a cradle that she wished to purchase; but the owner refused to sell that particular piece. Undaunted, this led to Mell's returning home, and fulfilling her determination by making just such a piece herself. In turn, this burgeoned into Mell's making many different pieces, combining them into rooms, and complementing them with carefully selected pieces of others. The oriental rugs and samplers furnishing these rooms were generally made by her daughter, Elaine Nondia Prescott Wonsavage. She acquired a table saw, jig saw, jeweler's lathe, dental drills, and whatever else was necessary in order to make her beautiful pieces. She would buy old combs to make piano keys. old cloth for her upholstered pieces, and even cut up old jewelry to complete her unique furniture. Just as her products resulted in the amazement of others, so she would quickly recognize talent in those about her. She encouraged others to pursue their interests and excellence, and she promoted this through using their pieces in her rooms. Starting with miniature reproductions of antiques in the one-inch scale, she was in her seventies when she went further with ½-inch scale. Such was the quality of her work that her pieces now are housed in a variety of museums.

Sundays were generally reserved not to fulfill orders but to create. It was then that she would try something new, making a few different examples of that which she chose to make, but discarding all but one at the end of the day. That one would go on to be perfected and to join her other creations.

She had been an officer of a number of different organizations affiliated with the arts. She was recognized as uniquely adept in decorating with such a mix of art forms just as she was recognized as not only being gifted in her own creations by in her ability to teach others to make the most of their abilities. Mell Prescott died in her early eighties. She was indomitable up to the end, looking for new avenues. and creating new masterpieces. She set an example for us all; and just as we thoroughly enjoyed Mell as a unique individual, so we shall treasure and enjoy those creations that she left behind.

Editor's note: Mell lives on today through her unique miniature creations, some of which her children are so generously donating for charitable fund raisers, and always through the Mell Prescott Award.

ARTISAN: PRITCHETT, DENISE S.

BUSINESS NAME: D–leprechaun

IDENTIFICATION MARKS:

D

Green paint on bottom of horse hoof
bottom of rocking horse rocker
bottom of dish or basket

CATEGORY:

Animals: horses; Food

HONORS:

IGMA Artisan

RECOGNITION:

Nutshell News, Vol. 19, No. 3, Mar. 1989, Cover, Centerfold, pg. 87; Vol. 19, No. 5, May 1989, pg. 44-47, "Horses, Hats & Hors d'oeuvres," Kim Remesch; *Miniatures Showcase*, Vol. 3, No. 3, Summer 1988, Cover, pg. 6, 46; Vol. 4, No. 1, Winter 1989, Cover, Centerfold

AUTOBIOGRAPHY:

I was interested in arts & crafts at an early age and always tried many mediums. Then I found miniatures, the perfect way to play with a lot of different crafts and decorate even more rooms than 20 years of military moves had given me.

In 1984, I started selling mini foods and hats since I enjoyed making them the most. But I had always had a passion for horses, and when I found others liked them too, I knew I'd found my special place in miniatures. I'm always trying new techniques to see how realistic a horse I can create.

It's fascinating to back up the craft techniques with research. My library background taught me useful reference skills, and I enjoy researching the miniatures I make to improve them.

ARTISAN: **PURDY, HARRIET**

BUSINESS NAME: Harriet's House

IDENTIFICATION MARKS:

1980 to present

HP

CATEGORY:

Furniture: upholstered, wicker; Needlepoint; Needlework; Roomboxes; Rugs

AUTOBIOGRAPHY:

My miniatures education owes so much to so many talented people, beginning with my father, who taught me that I could do anything I really put my mind to. He built a large dollhouse and helped me build furniture for it when I was very young. He also turned a portion of our basement into a theatre, whose projection screen raised to reveal a marionette stage. I dressed marionettes and built crude stage sets and furniture. Later, an HO train layout replaced the theatre and there were buildings and scenery to do. He discovered a school of costume design in Detroit, which I attended for 1½ years, learning pattern making, draping and fashion illustration, as well as clothing construction and French hand sewing techniques. My college major in textiles, clothing and related arts continued these interests.

In 1976, my interest in miniatures resurfaced when my husband gave me a Dremel saw so I could make a dollhouse for our granddaughter. I met Barbara Nancarrow, who had a miniature shop in a downtown mall and was teaching a class in Exquisite Dollhouse for the adult education department. We discovered we had grown up within five miles of each other with many similar interests and became best friends, an association which has endured. We organized a miniature club and obtained our NAME charter. Barb's classes taught me all manner of wondrous things she was learning from Judeé Williamson at Miniature Maker's Workshop in Birmingham, Michigan. Trips down there introduced me to more wonders, especially petit point rugs, which I embraced with a passion, with thanks to Barbara Cosgrove, Harry Whalon, and Sharon Garmize. "Miniatures Back to College," sessions at Randolph Macon College in Ashland, Virginia, introduced me to more talented people; Mell Prescott, Faith Wick, Wayne Lasch and Joe & Jackie Andrews, who shared their expertise in their chosen fields. John Murphy, a friend from my father's model railroad days, taught me lost wax casting and lathe work and built a lathe for me. I also owe a large debt of gratitude to Helen and Jim Dorsett whose *Scale Cabinetmaker* magazine and plan books have been a constant inspiration and source of helpful techniques.

During those high energy years, before my husband retired, I helped plan and execute miniatures exhibits at Jacobson's store, area libraries, historical museums, and art galleries. We moved Barb's shop inventory to my house when she moved to Florida and I was suddenly in business. I have taught classes at club meetings, and in my shop.

A long and pleasant relationship with Sister Pauline Boyd resulted in some of my best efforts. She did exquisite petit point on silk gauze and I made the furniture and mounted her work on chairs, tables, and pictures. She convinced me to apply for a scholarship at the Guild school in Castine, Maine, where George Passwater's class was a great learning experience in using jigs and dial calipers to ensure exacting perfection. I returned to Castine the following year when Linda Wexler and Don Dube added vast amounts of new knowledge and techniques in French furniture construction, faux marble and gold leaf. Classes at Miniature Makers' Workshop gave me the privilege of learning from other gifted miniaturists; Judeé Williamson, Nicole Walton Marble, Barbara Blaumann, Chris Goad, and Sandra Henry Wall. Exhibitions at shows and museums and books have also added greatly to my appreciation of this fascinating art form.

Currently my work is confined to retail sales and custom work. I build and decorate dollhouses and roomboxes and do individual furniture pieces. My favorite projects are glove leather, wing chairs, and upholstered furniture.

ARTISAN: **PUTNAM, JANE**

IDENTIFICATION MARKS:

Tag accompanying piece, 1978 – 1984

Some cactus unmarked
Initials on bottom of pots
1987 to present

On bottom of Cactus Garden pots
1987 to present
2 digit year or 4 digit year

CATEGORY:

Accessories; Flowers & Plants: cactus, garden

HONORS:

Prize Ribbons, Tucson Miniature Society Shows, 1978-1988; Exhibits: Denver Museum of Miniatures, Dolls and Toys, 1989-1993; Tucson Children's Museum, 1989-1992

RECOGNITION:

Nutshell News, Vol. 21, No. 12, Dec. 1991, pg. 48-51, "New England Barns," Jane Putnam; Vol. 22, No. 11, Nov. 1992, pg. 40-43; Vol. 23, No. 7, Jul. 1993, pg. 64, Show Scene

AUTOBIOGRAPHY:

My mother gave me my first dollhouse miniature at Christmas 1929, when I was just five months old. Obviously she had plans! More came at birthdays and any-excuse times, and eventually when I was about four my dad built a dollhouse. I learned a lot of new words as he cut the glass for the windows! It was not perfect scale, of a sort of egg box construction, but I loved it. My friends and cousins and later my son played with it too.

He and I had both outgrown it when, in 1961, we moved from Connecticut to Tucson, Arizona, and my dollhouse was sold to a distant cousin. It broke my heart, but the responsibilities of single-parenting prevailed.

With son in college and a new marriage in hand, in 1975 I re-discovered dollhouses as an adult pursuit! I managed to get my dollhouse back, much vandalized but with "possibilities." Some of the old furnishings my parents had made were even in scale enough to be usable. So I set out to achieve a restored Pre-Revolutionary Connecticut home. The key word here is "restored," for it contains many periods of furniture and a modern kitchen, just as a real house of its kind would today.

All my endeavors during those intervening years seemed aimed at preparing me for this project. A burgeoning teenage interest in art had taken me to a Westchester County, New York, junior college major in interior decoration; then to the Ringling School of Art in Sarasota, Florida, for advertising art, fashion illustration and fine arts; and later to one handcraft after another, some of which I taught in Adult Education and YWCA programs. My watercolor paintings and several crafts were being shown in galleries in five Eastern states by 1961.

It soon became evident that I could not buy everything I wanted for my "little house;" some things were simply not available, others too expensive, and some did not fit my scheme to have everything in the house relate to my parents and to my own early life. So my dollhouse and the nearly 60 buildings and vignettes I've designed and built in the past 15 years are liberally salted with my own creations. Everything from books and kites to kitchen sponges and credit cards, from dried arrangements and Oriental scrolls to framed paper samplers and all sorts of wall plaques; inkwells, yardsticks, toy sailboats; shell framed mirrors, cone wreaths and centerpieces, Christmas ornaments, bird houses, shopping bags, greeting cards; Sculpey gourds, chili peppers, cattails and pumpkins; orange crates, footstools, tables and benches–whatever kind of wooden furniture I wanted and couldn't find anywhere.

As I made for myself I also made to sell, so many of these items have found their ways into other collections as well. But it is my lifelong love of gardening and all the many facets of nature, along with a need for miniature Southwest landscaping, which eventually evolved into simple cactus plants and then the Cactus Gardens, all made from natural dried materials, for which I'm best known at present.

I've traveled much of the world; North & Central America, the Caribbean Islands, 10 European countries, the Orient, Hawaii and many islands of the South Pacific, Malaysia and Indonesia. I've been on two miniatures tours to England/Scotland, 1980 and 1992, have attended shows in five US states, and have visited hundreds of shops, bazaars, native markets, and other places where "little things" can be found.

I have twice installed exhibits of my toys, dolls, and miniatures in the Tucson Children's Museum from 1989 to 1992, and am a member of the Denver Museum of Miniatures, Dolls & Toys, from 1989 to 1993. A true packrat, my home is filled with nearly two hundred collections, of which miniatures are an ever growing part!

ARTISAN: **QUINBY, A. J. & NANCY**

BUSINESS NAME: Nantasy Fantasy Creations

IDENTIFICATION MARKS:

CATEGORY:
Antiques: Victorian; Cameras; Luggage; Optical

HONORS:
IGMA Artisan (A.J.)

RECOGNITION:
Nutshell News; Miniatures Showcase; Miniature Gazette

BIOGRAPHY:

For more than 12 years, A.J. and Nancy Quinby have been creating reproductions of the Victorian era, specializing in carefully researched replicas of authentic Americana in the 1800's and early 1900's.

In 1979, principal artist, A.J. Quinby, began his career in miniatures when he constructed 40 pieces of dollhouse furniture as a Christmas gift for his daughters. His enormous talent is enhanced by an eye for fine detail and patient pursuit of quality. He has been recognized by the International Guild of Miniature Artisans in the category of Victorian Antiques.

Years of art education leading to a degree in Fine Arts are the foundation for Nancy Quinby's contribution to the artwork presented by Nantasy Fantasy. A graduate of the Cooper School of Art, she constantly employs her unique gifts of color sense and design.

These one-inch scale miniatures are historically accurate representations of life in America at the turn of the century. The one-inch scale is practical yet aesthetic. It is large enough to capture fine detail but small enough to be magical.

The Quinby's works are exquisite museum quality artistry. Each piece is carefully executed using steel, brass, aged leathers and hardwoods, simple materials treated with Nantasy Fantasy magic.

ARTISAN: **QUINTANAR, ENRIQUE**

BUSINESS NAME: Enrique Quintanar

IDENTIFICATION MARKS:

CATEGORY:
Silversmith

HONORS:
IGMA Artisan

QUINTANAR, ENRIQUE, continued

RECOGNITION:

Nutshell News, Nov. 1986, pg. 77; Jun. 1987, pg. 61; Sept. 1991, pg. 75; Nov. 1991, pg. 73-74; Dec. 1992, pg. 72; Oct. 1995, pg. 32; *Miniatures Showcase*, Summer 1990, pg. 27, 46, 70; Spring 1992, pg. 61; Nov. 1992, pg. 18; Jan. 1993, pg. 33-34, 53; Sept. 1993, pg. 55; Nov. 1993, pg. 61; *San Francisco Examiner*, newspaper, Sept. 8, 1993, pg. 1, Habitat section

AUTOBIOGRAPHY:

Born and raised in Mexico City, I started my journey towards becoming a metalsmith after graduating from the Universidad Autónoma de México in Mexico City in 1983. From childhood on I have always enjoyed working on projects involving scale models and prototypes.

In 1984, I started crafting miniatures on a part-time basis to see how well this work would be received in my country. Due to the fact that the hobby of collecting miniatures made to scale was not understood in Mexico, the market for my work was limited there.

Soon I moved to the US and began going to miniature shows to discover the extent and understanding and appreciation of this kind of work. I started my business on a part-time basis soon after. In 1989, I opened a full-time studio where I work on miniatures as well as creating custom jewelry.

My miniatures are modern looking, with an antique flavor. Due to the fact the pieces are individually fabricated yet often of the same design, they are never quite the same. This makes each coffee set, Menorah and picture frame “one-of-a-kind.”

R

ARTISAN: **RAHEB, BARBARA J.**

BUSINESS NAME: Barbara J. Raheb

IDENTIFICATION MARKS:

Mudlark Miniatures, TM., 1975-1976
The Littlest Library, 1976-1977
Collector Editions in Miniature, 1977-1980
The Pennyweight Press, 1980 to present
Barbara J. Raheb, 1980 to present

All of the above are printed on the information page, title page and/or the Limited Edition/Colophon page, within time frame indicated.

Handwritten signature is printed on the Limited Edition or Colophon page.

CATEGORY:

Accessories; Artist; Author; Books: binder, designer, instructional, miniature, reference; Calligraphy; Illustrator; Publications: how-to; Publisher; Writer

HONORS:

IGMA Fellow; Exhibit: International Miniature Book Exhibit, 1984-1985, Ljubljana, Yugoslavia, Dr. Martin Znidersic

RECOGNITION:

Nutshell News, Winter 1976; Vol. 8, No. 3, Fall 1978, pg. 26-27, "A Few of My Favorite Things – A Rainbow of Books," Ginny Schoonover; Jul/Aug. 1979, Cover, pg. 51-52, "Creative Displays," Dee Snyder; Nov/Dec. 1979, pg. 76-79, "A dividend In Your Dollhouse,"; Vol. 21, No. 9, Sept. 1991, pg. 38-41, "Barbara Raheb's Volumes of Talent," Jeanne Delgado; *Miniature Collector*, Feb. 1980, pg. 14; No. 36, pg. 41-44, "Great Books in Miniature," Ann Bahar; Vol. 17, No. 6, Jan/Feb. 1995, Cover, pg. 30-37; *Miniature Gazette*, Winter 1978, pg. 40-42; *Wilson Library Magazine*, 1978; Feb. 1981; *Doll Reader*, Feb/Mar. 1986; Feb/Mar. 1987; *American Libraries Magazine*, Mar. 1980; *American Times*, Summer 1995, "Itty Bitty Lit," Grote Publishing; *Jente Magazine*, Apr. 1993, Chesare Bonatza, European distribution, Milano, Italy; *Sorrisi e Canzoni TV*, Oct. 1993, pg. 11; *Focus Magazine*, May 1993, Tokyo, Japan; *People Magazine*, May 10, 1993; *Globe Magazine*, Vol. 40, No. 18, May 4, 1993; *Storyworks*, Vol. 1, No. 2, Oct. 1993, Scholastic, Inc., Publishers; *Boy's Life*, Boy Scouts of America publication, Oct. 1994, pg. 14; *Hobbies Magazine*, Mar. 1983; *Two on the Town,* CBS-TV, Apr. 10, 1981; KABC-TV, Jul. 18, 1993, national news; Jul. 18, 1993, World News Now, picked up by International TV Syndication Service and shown world-wide on CNN-TV, Jul. 20, 1993; *Bayerischer Rundfunk*, Bavarian Broadcasting, Munich, Germany (interview by Thomas Woldhaf for radio with German over-dubbing); *Los Angeles Times*, Oct. 16, 1986, Metro Section; Feb. 18, 1993, two page color article released over syndicated news wire to 600 newspapers throughout the US; *Scandanavian News Service*, Apr. 1993, Neal Bjorns, Oslo, Norway; *News of the World*, May 1993, Sunday Magazine, E. Sanderson, London, England; *Daily News*, May 10, 1993, Valley Section, Los Angeles, California; *Smat Er Smukt*, May 1994, Copenhagen, Denmark; *National Enquirer*, Jun. 22, 1993; *Daily Camera*, Nov. 25, 1993, Boulder, Colorado; *Miniature Book Society Newsletter*, Fall 1993; *Moscow Miniature News Letter*, 1992, Moscow, Russia, Dr. Pavel Pochtovik; *Mikrobibliofilok*, Apr. 1986; Vol. 21, 1991, Budapest, Hungary, Dr. Lajos Bajos; *Microbibliophile*, Jan. 1978; Mar. 1979; Nov. 1993; *Miniature Book News*, Jun. 1993; Jun. 1994, Julian Edison, Quarterly; *Select Guide to Sources for Miniature Books, 1879-1992*, Msgr. Francis F. Weber, Lorson's Books, 1992; *Little Books By Big People*, Msgr. Francis J. Weber, Opuscula Press, 1991, pg. 36-38; *Miniature Books*, Louis Bondy, Sheppard Press, London, England, 1981, English Edition, pg. 172, German Edition, pg. 169; *Discovering Miniature*

Sherlockian Books, Robert F. Hanson, Opuscula Press, 1982; *The Contemporary Miniature Book Scene in the U.S.A.*, Kal Levitan, Kaycee Press, 1984

AUTOBIOGRAPHY:

Born in lowa in 1933, we moved to California in 1941. I joined the Women's Army Corps in 1951 where I was schooled as a Still Photographer and Photo Lab Technician. Upon discharge, I worked for Drewry Photocolor Corp. as an Executive Secretary, pitch-hitting in the lab and doing freelance artwork for point-of-sale material while attending college at night. In 1965, I began work with Raheb Color Corp. in the same capacity. When my husband sold the business in 1972, he added a studio to the house so I could concentrate on my art. I returned to school, this time attending the West Valley College of Art.

I was introduced to miniatures in 1974 and was completely enchanted. I subsequently built my own dollhouse from scratch. It had a decided English orientation and was named "Poppins Cottage" after the Mary Poppins books. I wrote and illustrated its history in book form, from concept through construction, interweaving at the same time a fantasy around its inhabitants. The house was sold eventually, together with its little history.

In 1975, I developed a line of miniature accessories under the registered trademark Mudlark Miniatures. It was quite innovative for those early years with four-color printed-litho boxed game boards and cast metal pieces, a complete artist's line, working handpainted silk fans, etc. In a very short time, I was so inundated with orders, I realized I would have to find a solution for keeping up or drown in the process. The business was ultimately sold to another miniaturist within 6 to 8 months of its inception.

I decided to specialize. We had seen Queen Mary's Dollhouse on a 1972 trip to England and I was fascinated by its library. Being a bibliophile at heart with a large library of standard-sized books, including an extensive collection of both antiquarian and contemporary First Edition children's books, I decided to produce a library concept of "real" books in miniature of the world's great classic literature; audacious concept, but in my ignorance and zeal, I proceeded. (I have since been recognized as the world's most prolific publisher of miniature books in history!) I am, however, self-taught in this area and have destroyed my line twice in an effort to achieve the best possible. (Those books from the earlier attempts now sell for more than ten times their original published price). It was a period filled with trial, error, and expense, but I gained knowledge and experience through perseverance. I had by now also discovered that miniature book collecting was a separate collecting field with a history reaching back to the 13th century.

Today the little books are sold world-wide to both serious dollhouse collectors and miniature book collectors. They are represented in the Rare Book Section of such notable libraries as the Huntington Library, San Marino, California, State Library at Sacramento California, UCLA Library, Los Angeles, California, University Of Minnesota Library, Des Moines Library, Iowa, and Occidental College Library, Special Collections Dept., Los Angeles, California, as well as representation in prominent personal collections throughout the world. Two of the books were ordered by the Westpoint Military Academy, Literature Dept., and went up in the space shuttle Discovery in August, 1984 before returning to earth to repose in a glassed display case with other literary mementos in the department.

I have lectured to academic and bibliophile groups about miniature books and their history. In 1993, I introduced the first "popup" book in miniature when Haunted House was released. It was out-of-print within five weeks of release and has since doubled in price on the secondary market. I'm constantly striving in my work and always look forward to the next challenge.

I am a Miniature Book Society Charter Member and served on the Board of Governors of the Society from 1993 to 1995. In 1986, I wrote and illustrated a how-to book entitled Jewelry Making In Miniature, a standard-sized instruction book. establishing at the same time, a business for my sister, Claudette Priddy, for supplying the tiny Victorian beads and various component parts required to produce miniature jewelry.

ARTISAN: **RAINBOW HAND**

BUSINESS NAME: Mini Moons Ago

IDENTIFICATION MARKS:

Also seen on pottery

RAINBOW HAND, continued

CATEGORY:

Artifacts: American Indian

HONORS:

Exhibits: Toy & Miniature Museum of Kansas City; Gene Autry Western Heritage Museum, Los Angeles, California, Oct. 1993

RECOGNITION:

Nutshell News; Miniatures Showcase, Vol. 8, No. 3, May 1993, pg. 40-43, "Rainbow Hand - Dedicated to Authenticity," Melinda Wolf; *Miniature Arts of the Southwest*, Schiffer Publishing 1991

ARTISAN: RANKIN, BOB & NAN

BUSINESS NAME: Rankin's Tiny Treasures

IDENTIFICATION MARKS:

1989 to present

CATEGORY:

Accessories; Furniture: wicker; Wicker

ARTISAN: RASMUSSEN, ANKER & CAROLE

BUSINESS NAME: Anker Manufacturing

IDENTIFICATION MARKS:

CATEGORY:

Furniture; Tools: miniature making

RECOGNITION:

Nutshell News; The Scale Cabinetmaker

AUTOBIOGRAPHY:

Carole started in miniatures in 1976. Anker became interested in miniatures in 1978. Not finding any small precision power tools, he soon developed a small line of miniature power tools. We found that other miniaturists wanted them, so started manufacturing and selling these tools under the name of Anker Manufacturing. In 1992, Anker retired and the tools are now being manufactured and sold through Klein Design of Renton, Washington.

We made the Saturday Banquet gifts for the NAME National Houseparties in Seattle, Washington in 1985 and Orlando, Florida in 1993. Other pieces of furniture we have made, have been given as gifts.

RASMUSSEN, ANKER & CAROLE, continued

We have given numerous demonstrations on the use of power tools. We have taught hands-on classes in building furniture and finishing roomboxes and miniature houses using small power tools. We taught several years at the College of Miniature Knowledge.

ARTISAN: **RATAJESAK, KIRK G.**

BUSINESS NAME: The Fretworker – Kirk Ratajesak

IDENTIFICATION MARKS:

Some unmarked, 1973 to present

CATEGORY:

Accessories: wall; Building Components: scroll trim; Furniture: scroll trim

HONORS:

IGMA Artisan; Exhibit: Toy & Miniature Museum of Kansas City

RECOGNITION:

Nutshell News; *Miniature Collector*, Jun. 1983; *Creative Crafts*, Aug. 1981, pg. 8; *The Scale Cabinetmaker*, Vol. 6, No. 2, 1982; *Scrollsaw Fretwork Patterns*, Patrick Spielman, Sterling Publishing, pg. 224-226, 1989; *Scrollsaw Fretwork Techniques & Projects*, Patrick Spielman, Sterling Publishing, pg. 200-206, 1990

AUTOBIOGRAPHY:

All my life I have enjoyed miniatures, small things, scroll work and working by myself. I started scroll sawing as a hobby/business in 1973. My products have found homes in all 50 states and at least a dozen countries. They are also exhibited in a number of museums.

My miniature scroll trim business started in 1978 and furniture in miniature in 1980. I have sold at NAME National and Regional Houseparties as well as at CIMTA and other shows across the country.

Now I'm also getting into carving on my fretwork furniture, as well as larger projects.

ARTISAN: **RAWDING, DOLORES V.**

BUSINESS NAME: D V R

IDENTIFICATION MARKS:

Early pieces marked in gold; most black; Large pieces dated

CATEGORY:

Furniture: period

RECOGNITION:

Nutshell News; The Scale Cabinetmaker, Vol. 8, No. 2

RAWDING, DOLORES V., continued

AUTOBIOGRAPHY:

I have been creating miniatures in one-inch scale since 1976. I have taught at two museum schools and an Arts & Crafts Society in Massachusetts. I have done shows mostly along the Northeast Seaboard. I have also conducted workshops on tool handling and woodworking at NAME Shows and Tiny Treasures in Boston, Miniature Makers Shows and others, as well as for private clubs. I have had hundreds of students, some of whom have gone on to establish businesses of their own.

ARTISAN: **REED, ROSLYN J.**

BUSINESS NAME: Roslyn Reed Miniatures

IDENTIFICATION MARKS:

All marks 1976 to present

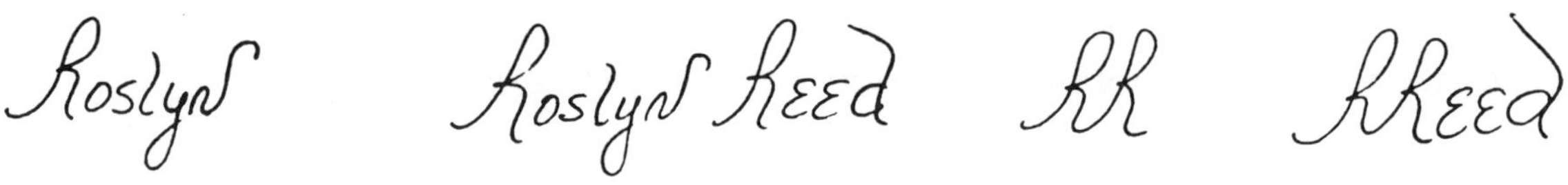

CATEGORY:

Accessories: personal, Victorian; Furniture: handpainted; Roomboxes; Shops

ARTISAN: **REEVE, SHARON LeDOUX**

BUSINESS NAME: Sharon Reeve Interiors
European Environs

IDENTIFICATION MARKS:

Very small pieces unmarked, 1978 to present

Mark usually includes year, '92

CATEGORY:

Accessories: floral; Beds; Drapes; Fabrications: custom; Furniture: handpainted; Roomboxes; Upholstery

AUTOBIOGRAPHY:

Born and raised in the San Francisco Bay Area, I attended public schools there, including the University of California at Berkeley. I graduated in 1958 with a major in Decorative Arts. I have been a professional interior designer, with my own business since 1978. About the same time, I became interested in miniatures as an enjoyable shared hobby with my 10-year old daughter. The evolving sophistication of products and materials made possible a cross-over into business, creating model rooms as visual aids for design clients. Searching my wholesale resources at the design center for even more sophisticated wallpapers and fabrics to use in the models, and selling the remnants and accessories to other miniaturists eventually led to a miniatures business.

I am an active member of NAME, belonging to three clubs and having chaired several houseparty committees, both regional and national. In 1991, Bluette Meloney and I decided to pool our talents to expand the business. We sell our products and teach classes locally and at regional and national houseparties. Together, we strive to achieve quality miniature interiors and furnishings with a realistic, "Old World" look.

ARTISAN: **RENNINGER, DOLORES & JOHN**

BUSINESS NAME: d. j. miniatures

IDENTIFICATION MARKS:

1986 to present
½-inch pieces

1987 to present
one-inch pieces made by W. Spencer Clinger and finished by d.j.miniatures

CATEGORY:
Furniture

ARTISAN: **REYNOLDS, DELIA**

BUSINESS NAME: Miniatures Limited

IDENTIFICATION MARKS:
Chandeliers unmarked

CATEGORY:
Chandeliers; Lamps; Lighting; Sconces

RECOGNITION:
Nutshell News, May 1982, pg. 64-67; Nov. 1988, pg. 86-87, "Delia Reynolds' Tribute To Our Lady"; Dec. 1988, pg. 71, 73; Sept. 1991, pg. 67, 69; *Miniatures Showcase*, Fall 1988, Cover; *The Atlanta Journal-Constitution*, Sat., Oct. 10, 1981, pg. 3; Wed., Apr. 13, 1983, Sec B, pg. 1, 3; Sat., Oct. 19, 1985, pg. 52; *Our Miniature World*, Marie Dettling, 1984, pg. 94; *Through The Looking Glass*, Boynton and Associates, Inc., Ann Ruble, 1984, pg. 136; WXIA TV, NBC Ch. 11, Atlanta, Apr. 15, 1983, Noon News; Oct. 17, 1985, Noon News; Jul. 8, 1987, 6 pm News; WAGA TV, CBS Ch. 5, Atlanta, Oct. 17, 1985, AMS and greenhouse contest; Cable News Network, CNN, Atlanta, July 28, 1987, Evening News, Looking Up; North Dekalb Cable TV, Atlanta, August 17, 1987, Just Hobbies; *NAME Limited Edition Victorian Christmas Note Cards*, Houseworks, 1992; Victorian Christmas, Santa's Christmas House

AUTOBIOGRAPHY:

I have always had an interest in art work and crafts, however, the spark which ignited my miniature career was a dollhouse which one of my sons built for me in the fall of 1976. I've always loved working with my hands, and tools intrigue me. Studying an object to ascertain how it is put together and, in the case of an electric light fixture, how to make it work fascinates me.

I attended Wesleyan College in Macon, Georgia for two years as a music major and then completed my work on my BA degree in English at Emory University, 1958, after which I became a grammar school teacher. Except for a knack for teaching, I have no formal education in arts and crafts, or design, just teaching experience and on the job training as the mother of three sons; two avid railroad modelers and one a miniature enthusiast. A healthy curiosity and a desire to create have been the motivating factors in my miniature vocation.

I began selling my work in 1979. Chandeliers and lamps are my first love, however, I build houses, roomboxes, and vignettes, teach workshops, design and make quilts, and work one on one with clients to decorate and finish their dollhouses. I prefer working in one-inch scale, but will work in both ½-inch and ¼-inch scales.

ARTISAN: **RICHARDS, NÄDA**

IDENTIFICATION MARKS:

Näda

year

CATEGORY:

Buildings: period; Decorating: exterior, interior; Structures

HONORS:

IGMA Artisan

RECOGNITION:

Nutshell News, Oct. 1982; Aug. 1982

AUTOBIOGRAPHY:

I started miniatures in 1976 and became addicted immediately. I have finished 34 buildings for my town, and 10 houses for others who liked my work. I have two ½-inch houses in Europe, one in England and one in Denmark. I have copied seven buildings from the "Painted Ladies" book for my collection. The boxes are built for me, then I customize them by doing all of the decor on the exterior and interior including the flooring and electrical wiring and room planning. I've filled three bedrooms and have finished the "Carson Mansion," the last of my collection. I make miniatures for others, and love every minute of it.

ARTISAN: **RICHARDSON, J. NEILL**

BUSINESS NAME: Samuel Halfpenny

IDENTIFICATION MARKS:

1980 to 1985 unmarked

Samuel Halfpenny 1986 to present, also stamped

CATEGORY:

Dollhouse; Structures

RECOGNITION:

Miniature Collector, Fall 1987, Cover, pg. 14-17; *International Doll's House News*, Vol. 12, No. 4, Winter 1983/84, pg. 14; Vol. 13, No. 1, Spring 1984, pg. 6-7; Vol. 14, No. 1, Spring 1985, pg. 10; Vol. 18, No. 2, Summer, 1989, pg. 11; *Woodmaker*, Mar. 1989, pg. 226; *House and Garden*, Jan. 1986, pg. 94; *Traditional Homes*, Aug. 1989, pg. 61; *Decorative Dolls House*, Caroline Hamilton, Ebury Press, London, 1990, pg. 8-9; Cable TV, S4C, Wales, 1988, "Neill Richardson, Dolls House Maker"

AUTOBIOGRAPHY:

I was born in 1938 in Nottingham, England. I received a degree in Theology and was trained as a teacher. In 1961, I married and moved to Unst, the most northerly island of the Shetland Isles where I taught in an island school. I learned the skills of furniture maker from an old crafter, Magnus Clarke. My wife died in 1961 and I returned to England with a 1 year old son.

RICHARDSON, J. NEILL, continued

For 15 years I worked exclusively in Education and subsequently qualified as a Child Psychologist. I published several books and papers in the field of mental handicap.

My interest in fine woodwork was rekindled in 1978 when I built a dollshouse for my own daughter. I have since specialized in building high quality dollshouses in solid hardwoods, polished in beeswax. I currently build exclusively to commission only. One of the most ambitious projects was a 36 room Palladian mansion built in solid mahogany. One of the most interesting houses I've done was for Vivien Greene based on a house in Totnes, which she and Graham visited in 1952.

ARTISAN: **RICHARDSON, SUSAN MERRILL**

IDENTIFICATION MARKS:

CATEGORY:

Needlework

HONORS:

IGMA Fellow

RECOGNITION:

Nutshell News, Vol. 12, No. 11, Nov. 1982, pg. 42; *Miniature Collector*, No. 4, Dec. 1977, pg. 28; *Reproducing Period Furniture & Accessories in Miniature*, Co Author; *Cooper Hewitt Museum of Design*, New York City, Slide lecturer

AUTOBIOGRAPHY:

As my mother, Virginia Merrill, began creating miniatures in the 1970's, I became intrigued with the challenge of miniaturization. In her rooms, twigs became logs in the fireplace, art stamps coated with small strokes of varnish became oil paintings, buttons with hands and numerals seen on the faces of clocks became the face of miniature clocks. Why couldn't I reduce the needlework I enjoyed to one-inch scale?

Needlepoint designs were worked at first on 28–count canvas. The bulkiness was eliminated by changing to silk gauze. This new material also allowed for a finer count, 28–count became 38–count. Thirty-eight count became designs worked 48 stitches to the inch.

Mother and daughter worked as a team. I created rugs, pillows, slippers, upholstery and accessories for mother's rooms. As we worked on period pieces, we realized that a great deal of research was required to marry period needlework to period furniture and room settings. Thus, we wrote a book for Crown Publishers in 1980, sharing our research and designs in the context of historic authenticity.

At the Guild School in Castine, Maine, I taught students to reproduce designs by reducing the original work to its basic format and adding details as the scale permitted. Bargello was replicated by using a tent stitch. Students were taught to paint with thread.

Early in the life of the organization, in the 1980's, I served for two years as president of the International Guild of Miniature Artisans. We worked to make the organization professional and to bring fine miniatures into the arena of art.

Today I am only a collector, as other professional demands leave little time to design and stitch miniature needlework. I am very proud of the work that my mother and I produced during our creative years. We were strong advocates of quality, authenticity and understanding the artistic value of fine miniatures.

ARTISAN: **RICHMOND, GERI**

BUSINESS NAME: Tom Thumb's Treasures

IDENTIFICATION MARKS:

GR

CATEGORY:

Accessories: knickknack's; Boxes: jewelry; Dolls: porcelain

AUTOBIOGRAPHY:

I've been doing miniatures off and on for about twenty years. I got into miniatures heavily about 1989. I make porcelain dolls, jewelry boxes, perfume bottles and porcelain knickknack's such as houses, boxes, makeup kits etc. for sale at shows. I've had no special education in art. Enjoyment is the name of the game and I think that miniatures has really broadened my horizons.

ARTISAN: **RIMER, BETTY**

BUSINESS NAME: Pussy Cat Company

IDENTIFICATION MARKS:

Gold Rimer '92' Betty Rimer '92'

Gold + Betty Rimer "92"

1986 to present

Gold Rimer / Robert Bugue '91'

1989 to present

Logo used on first pieces in place of signature, also used on packaging and letterhead

CATEGORY:

Flowers and Plants; Food; Furniture; Landscaping

RECOGNITION:

Miniatures Showcase, Fall 1988, pg. 26, 36, 38; Winter 1989, pg. 29; Winter 1990, pg. 32-33

AUTOBIOGRAPHY:

In 1977, my husband and I closed an Interior Decorating business due to health problems. As I missed the decorating, I turned to the miniature field to begin a collection hobby of dollhouses and accessories. This was great and led to a large collection of houses and related items.

Our talents became known through our local club and we were soon being asked to make many different items for our friends. Hence the beginning of the Pussy Cat Company. We began doing shows, just a few during nice weather. In 1986, we opened the shop and added models, trains, and planes to the miniatures. We did more shows and traveled even further. Then we joined CIMTA, and began wholesaling our items throughout the US. In 1990, we shipped the first order out of the country. Thus our international trade began. We are members of NAME and Mini Magic.

ARTISAN: **RINARD, VIRGINIA**

BUSINESS NAME: Omniarts of Colorado

IDENTIFICATION MARKS:

VR

CATEGORY:

Accessories; Jewelry; Kits: furniture, wicker

RECOGNITION:

Nutshell News; Miniatures Showcase, Summer 1987, pg. 16, 20, 36; Fall 1990, pg. 23

AUTOBIOGRAPHY:

I graduated from the University of Missouri, Columbia, with a degree in Home Economics, in 1961. The next 15 years were spent as a homemaker, wife and mother with various handicrafts as diversions.

In 1976, I discovered miniatures and embraced them with great enthusiasm. I could do all my crafts in miniature! Initially I created little accessories from beads and findings and soon expanded to selling manufactured as well as other handcrafters' items. My husband suggested I should make more things to sell. One item I was selling was the "Millie August Wicker Book." I decided I would make kits for the furniture in the book. When the kits seemed to be popular, I decided to add tables which I had to design and write instructions for. One thing led to another, and I now have over 50 different wicker furniture kits in one-inch and ½-inch scales, using either cotton cord or waxed linen. One feature of all these kits is clear, easy to follow instructions which I learned how to write while in college. I also make a limited number of finished pieces of wicker furniture. In addition to the wicker, I make tiny jewelry that can be placed on a doll or displayed on a table, and other tiny accessories.

ARTISAN: **RINEHART, DEE JAY**

BUSINESS NAME: Creative Enterprizes

IDENTIFICATION MARKS:

©DJR

CATEGORY:

Animals; Dolls

RECOGNITION:

Nutshell News, Vol. 17, No. 12, Dec. 1987, pg. 86-87

AUTOBIOGRAPHY:

I began my miniature career making little candy dishes, perfume bottles, lamps and such in 1979. I soon switched to sculpting miniature dogs, cats, toys and babies. I enjoyed seeing how much detail I could put into my little critters such as pads on their toes, whiskers, tufts of hair in cats' ears, and eyes that glowed in the dark. All pieces were individually hand sculpted, I used Sculpey at first then Super Sculpey. After they were baked they were hand painted with acrylics. Then, depending on the order, flocking or fur could be added for a fuzzy or furry finish. The flocking or fur could be blended to achieve a wide range of colors and subtle shading effects.

I had customers from all over the United States, Canada, and Japan. I did mostly mail order but several shops carried my animals and Judeé Williamson took them to many shows and used them in a number of her projects.

ARTISAN: **RIPLEY, DON W.**

BUSINESS NAME: Virdon Company

IDENTIFICATION MARKS:

CATEGORY:

Accessories; Furniture; Kits: furniture

HONORS:

IGMA Artisan

RECOGNITION:

Tucson Citizen, Arizona, Newspaper, Oct. 25, 1989; *Rocky Mountain Miniature Journal*, Nov/Dec. 1984; *Kimberly Corner*, Issue No. 8, Dec. 1990

AUTOBIOGRAPHY:

I have done miniature work all my life.

ARTISAN: **RIPLEY, VIRGINIA A.**

BUSINESS NAME: Virdon Company

IDENTIFICATION MARKS:

CATEGORY:

Accessories; Kits

RECOGNITION:

Kimberly Corner, Issue No. 8, Dec. 1990

ARTISAN: **RITTER-PEACOCK, NANCY E.**

BUSINESS NAME: Peacock's "Tinker-Belles"

IDENTIFICATION MARKS:

Month - Year   Signature may be hidden by clothing

Peacock tails in multi-color

Peacock's
Tinker-Belles

Original Hand-Crafted Collectors Miniatures by Nancy Ritter Peacock

Folded tag on Dolls

RITTER-PEACOCK, NANCY E., continued

CATEGORY:

Beds; Clothing; Dolls: original; Millinery

AUTOBIOGRAPHY:

All of my little people, clothing, bonnets, and beds are one-of-a-kind. The little people are sculpted, painted, dressed and wigged by me. Most are made of Sculpey over a wire armature to make them poseable. A small number were made of Super Sculpey. Hair is made of hand dyed silk. Each is signed and dated, usually under their garments and has a gold embossed tag. All garments are historically accurate for periods ranging from 1800 to 1905 and are hand made by me. Many of the costumes are silk and antique lace.

I began making the miniatures because I couldn't afford any real looking people for the dollhouse I was making about six years ago, 1987. After doing a few of them I understood why they were so expensive. I loved making them; each takes on its own personality as I work. People started asking for consignments, so I began making them to order. Then I did a few doll and miniature shows locally and sold some through local retail miniature shops. I have kept a catalog of all the little people I have made and sold. Recently, I have made some 10 inch to 30 inch one-of-a-kind people in period costume. I've been sewing for 35 years and have had some art training but the sculpting is self-taught. Currently some of my work is on display at The Rikki Schaefer Gallery, in West Bloomfield, Michigan.

ARTISAN: **ROBBINS, ALICE**

BUSINESS NAME: Alice's Wonderland

IDENTIFICATION MARKS:

CATEGORY:

Accessories; Dolls: original, porcelain

RECOGNITION:

Miniatures Showcase

AUTOBIOGRAPHY:

My husband was the first in the family to be fascinated with miniatures. A friend of his owned a toy store and carried some miniatures. He gave me pieces on every occasion for a number of years. It wasn't until I'd accumulated enough that I decided to try to build a house for all the furniture. That was it! I could find very little in the way of accessories, so began to make my own. By 1973, I began selling to shops and doing shows. My four children were all involved in helping me at shows and today I have my eldest granddaughter as my assistant. Wow, that even amazes me. For over twenty years I have been making miniatures and each new project excites me still. Hope to say that in another 20 years!

ARTISAN: **ROBERSON, COLIN & YVONNE**

BUSINESS NAME: Colin and Yvonne Roberson Miniatures

IDENTIFICATION MARKS:

ROBERSON, COLIN & YVONNE, continued

CATEGORY:

Beds; Bicycles; Buggies: baby; Carriages: baby; Furniture: bamboo; Metal; Stoves

RECOGNITION:

Dolls House World, Issue No. 8, 1990, pg. 51-53, "Shades of Brighton Pavilion;" *Decorative Dolls House's*, Caroline Hamilton, Ebury Press, London, 1990

AUTOBIOGRAPHY:

Colin attended art school in London but apart from painting pictures, mostly for his own pleasure, it wasn't until he began making miniatures that he used his artistic skills full-time.

Yvonne has no artistic background but quickly learned the art of patiently painting and finishing off the miniatures; as well as dealing with the administrative and dispatch side of the business.

Our two man operation has been in existence since about 1979. It began in a very modest way, selling to one private local customer and an established shop in London. After taking part in our first London Show the business grew and grew and we now sell to many European countries as well as America, Canada, Australia and South Africa.

ARTISAN: **ROBERTS, JO ANNE**

BUSINESS NAME: JoAnne Roberts

IDENTIFICATION MARKS:

Most unmarked

JBR
Dedicated to Nick

1985 to 1986

JR

1986 to present may be marked

CATEGORY:

Dolls: costumed, porcelain

RECOGNITION:

Nutshell News, Jan. 1986, pg. 70, Show Scene; Sept. 1986, pg. 77; Apr. 1988, pg. 70, Show Scene; Jul. 1991. pg. 60, Show Scene; Oct. 1993, pg. 71, Show Scene; Jun. 1994, pg. 58, Show Scene; *Morning Call Newspaper*, Neighbor's Section, Mar. 8, 1990

BIOGRAPHY:

JoAnne Roberts is a native of Northeastern Pennsylvania. As a child, she attended The Baum Art School in Allentown. After graduating from high school, she received her beauty operator's license in cosmetology. She was married in 1972 to Clark Roberts. They have two children, Shane and Quinn. It was her daughter's dollhouse that started JoAnne on her very busy career in doll dressing.

While working on the dollhouse, JoAnne quickly found out that this undertaking was quite expensive. An alternative to this was to start making her own things. One thing led to another and she began selling her handicrafts to shops. One day one of the shop owners asked if she would put together and dress a miniature porcelain doll kit. This was the start of a new love affair and career that allowed her to design and create. The rest, as they say, is history.

JoAnne works only in the finest materials - silk taffetas, silk satins, fine batiste, etc., - and combs through antique shops and fairs for old laces. It is because of her constant search that many of her dolls are one-of-a-kind. She has an eye for design as well as an uncanny ability to determine which fabrics and laces will drape just the way she requires. Victorian era dolls are among her favorites.

JoAnne is doing more and more shows now that the children are older, as well as workshops both in her home and on the road. You will find her husband, Clark, at her side, being her best helper as well as her biggest fan. JoAnne has taught classes in both the Regional and National levels in miniatures. She belongs to UFDC, Twin County Doll Collectors of Pennsylvania, NAME and Small on Scale.

ARTISAN: **ROBERTS, GUY T.** (Deceased)

(Submitted by Tom Roberts)

IDENTIFICATION MARKS:

CATEGORY:

Buildings; Dollhouse; Furniture; Houses; Roomboxes; Rooms; Room Settings

HONORS:

Exhibits: The Carole & Barry Kaye Museum of Miniatures, Los Angeles, California; "Miniature Perspectives," Fullerton Museum Center, Fullerton, California, 1988; "Small Wonders," National Geographic Society, Washington, DC, 1987

RECOGNITION:

Nutshell News, Jan. 1988, pg. 46; May 1988, Cover, pg. 56-60; Jun. 1988, pg. 30-34; *Nutshell News Calendar*, 1989, Jan., May, Sept., Nov.; *The Miniatures Catalog*, 12th Edition; *Miniatures Showcase*, Jan. 1993, pg. 30-35; *Hobbies*, Jul. 1983, pg. 61-62; Aug. 1985, pg. 55-59; Sept. 1985, pg. 46-50; *This Side of Yesterday in Miniatures*, Catherine B. MacLaren, 1975, pg. 38, 44, 136, 137; *American Period Interiors in Miniature*, Kate Doordan Klavan, Scribner's, 1984, pg. 136, 189, 211, 222, plates, 27, 28, 29, 31

BIOGRAPHY:

Early in 1966, the year my dad retired from an active business career, my mother, Ruth, said to me in mock, I think, despair. "What am I going to do? Your father's going to be home all day!" I suggested we get out the miniature furniture Guy had made for me years before and see if we could renew his interest in making miniatures. To sweeten the inducement I designed a 1/12 scale kitchen that was my childhood remembrance of his mother's kitchen on their farm in Iowa. My memory wasn't very accurate, but the project intrigued him and from then on the making and collecting of miniatures became a joy. a challenge and a full-time commitment. Only the lure of lunch and dinner could get him away from his workbench.

He and I very shortly settled into a nice working relationship: I'd design something and he would make it. Whether it was a three story house, a roombox or a piece of furniture. he took all my suggestions and plans with good grace and enthusiasm. He loved woodworking but occasionally felt his pieces were not as good as he would have liked, but everyone, especially the ladies. thought he and his work were wonderful and how he loved the attention. I believe my parents truly enjoyed all aspects of the field of miniatures. The social as well as the artistic. Guy would be embarrassed to have me write that he "contributed" to the art and the craft, but I know he did as do all the miniaturists who knew and admired him through the years.

Guy T. Roberts 1900–1993

ARTISAN: **ROBERTS, TOM (GUY T. ROBERTS, JR.)**

BUSINESS NAME: Winfield Design Associates, Inc.
Winfield International

IDENTIFICATION MARKS:

Unmarked

CATEGORY:

Buildings; Dollhouse; Furniture; Houses; Roomboxes; Rooms; Room Settings

ROBERTS, TOM (GUY T. ROBERTS, JR.), continued

HONORS:

Macy's 39th Annual Easter Flower Show, 1985; Exhibits: Toy & Miniature Museum of Kansas City; The Carole & Barry Kaye Museum of Miniatures, Los Angeles, California; "Miniature Perspectives," Fullerton Museum Center, Fullerton, California, 1988; "Small Wonders," National Geographic Society, Washington, DC, 1987

RECOGNITION:

Nutshell News, Jan. 1988, pg. 46; May 1988, Cover, pg. 56-60; Jun. 1988, pg. 30-34; Jan. 1995, pg. 55-58, "Le Plaiser De Venise," Tom Roberts; *Nutshell News Calendar*, 1989, Jan., May, Sept., Nov.; *The Miniatures Catalog*, 12th Edition; *Miniatures Showcase*, Summer 1989, pg. 12; *Hobbies*, Jul. 1983, pg. 61-62; Aug. 1985, pg. 55-59; Sept. 1985, pg. 46-50; *Miniature Collector*, Summer 1986, Cover, pg. 22-25; May/Jun. 1994, pg. 32-37; *The Franklin Mint Almanac*, Oct/Nov. 1992, pg. 16-21; *Le Magazine De La Maison De Poupée*, No. 17, Summer 1991, pg. 4-5; *San Francisco Chronicle*, Dec. 1978; *This Side of Yesterday in Miniatures*, Catherine B. MacLaren, 1975, pg. 38, 44, 136, 137; *American Period Interiors in Miniature*, Kate Doordan Klavan, Scribner's, 1984, pg. 136, 189, 211, 222, plates, 27, 28, 29, 31

AUTOBIOGRAPHY:

When I was nine or 10, I discovered some Life Magazine pictures of eight of Mrs. Thorne's miniature rooms in Chicago. That article, which I still have over a half-century later, ignited a love of – almost a physical craving for – miniatures and for which I am at a total loss to explain. But anyone who has been bitten by the miniature bug knows what I mean. I think miniatures, I dream miniatures. Mrs. Thorne got me going.

After that illuminating discovery I guess I must have begged, coaxed, and whined until my dad, Guy Roberts, made me some simple pieces of early American Colonial furniture and a roombox to put them in...which I also still have. He thought the whole experience would be a good way for me to learn about woodworking tools. His plan was doomed. I was far more interested in the results than in the process...an attitude I regret today.

Anyway, time passed, miniatures were put away, four years of college at the University of California, Berkeley, a year of graduate work and a Masters in painting, two years in the Army stationed in the pentagon and then the beginnings of a graphic design career in San Francisco. More years passed and while the attraction of miniatures dimmed, it never died. Then, when my dad retired we began a wonderful father/son relationship involving miniatures: I designed things and he made them; simple as that. And for at least 15 years we enjoyed a close and respectful partnership which, at the time, I didn't think of as anything special but now realize it was.

By the time this Guide is published I will have retired from a 38-year career as a graphic and wallpaper designer. I plan now to devote a minimum of 24 hours a day to miniatures. I don't "make" miniatures as much as I "assemble" them; that is, I gather together the best work I can find and afford and combine it in what I hope is a pleasant setting. I'll probably concentrate on roomboxes because they take up less space than houses and are far easier to move about. My only worry is that there won't be enough time to accomplish all that I'd like.

ARTISAN: ROBERTSON, ESTHER

IDENTIFICATION MARKS:

CATEGORY:

Needlepoint; Needlework

HONORS:

Exhibit: Toy & Miniature Museum of Kansas City

RECOGNITION:

Nutshell News, May 1988, pg. 38; *Miniature Collector*, Winter 1987, pg. 33; *Threads*, Oct/Nov. 1987, Back Cover; *Traditional Homes*, Dec. 1991

ROBERTSON, ESTHER, continued

AUTOBIOGRAPHY:

My work in miniatures has been primarily needlepoint and most of that in connection with my son, Bill Robertson, for "Twin Manors." All needlework and upholstering in Twin Manors is my work. My part of Twin Manors also included the painting, not the wallpaper or drawing room scene, and repetitive work such as flooring, siding, shingles etc. Almost all the needlework pieces that I have sold also carry Bill's name as he has done the wood work.

ARTISAN: **ROBERTSON, FERNE A.**

BUSINESS NAME: Ferne's Miniature Treasures

IDENTIFICATION MARKS:

FERNE

CATEGORY:

Flowers and Plants; Food; Paintings: oil; Rugs; Wicker

HONORS:

1st Place, General Federation of Womans Clubs, Columbia, South Carolina 1989, rug; Foothills Festival, Easley, South Carolina 1991, rug; Best of Show, General Federation of Womans Clubs, Columbia, South Carolina 1990, rug; Spring Water Festival, Williamston, South Carolina 1991, wicker furniture; Foothills Festival, Easley Art Gallery, Easley, South Carolina, 1991; Festival of Flowers, Greenwood, South Carolina 1992, wicker & rug; Division winner, Spring Water Festival, Williamston, South Carolina 1990, rug; Spring Water Festival, Williamston, South Carolina 1992, flowers

RECOGNITION:

Anderson Independent, Newspaper, Oct. 16, 1988; Nov. 10, 1989; *The Easley Progress*, Newspaper, Nov. 8, 1989; Apr. 4, 1990; *The Greenville News*, South Carolina, Jul. 24, 1991; *The Monitor*, Jun. 17, 1992

AUTOBIOGRAPHY:

I attended the Van Emberg School of Art in Plainfield, New Jersey and studied oil and watercolor painting privately for most of 20 years. I began miniature furniture construction in 1972. I built my first dollhouse in 1985, it is 5½ feet wide by 6 feet tall containing 20 rooms. I now have a small museum of houses, vignettes, and curiosities, with a small sales area. My museum is on the tour for Foxwood Hills, a resort area, and Clemson University Seniors. I also have Church, School, Garden, Scout & Womens Club Tours averaging one a week. My miniatures have been on display in stores, museums and libraries and country clubs. I've won several awards.

I am a member of IGMA, NAME, Foothills Area Miniature Enthusiasts, and Mini Tonga Society.

ARTISAN: **ROBERTSON, WILLIAM R.**

IDENTIFICATION MARKS:

WM. R. ROBERTSON

W.R.R.

Brass plate on larger pieces; engraved on bottom of smaller pieces; 1992 to present stamped in .012" high letters on brass plate; usually followed by year

Some pieces signed in same manner as original full-size counterpart

ROBERTSON, WILLIAM R., continued

CATEGORY:

Accessories; Furniture: American, English, period

HONORS:

IGMA Artisan; Exhibit: Toy & Miniature Museum of Kansas City; Academy Hall, Philadelphia, 1981, 1982; National Geographic Society, Explorers Hall, "The Enchanting World of Dollhouses" 1984, "Small Wonders, The Delightful World of Miniatures" 1987

RECOGNITION:

Nutshell News, Mar. 1980, pg. 33, 38-43; May 1989, Cover, pg. 38-41, "A Is For Accuracy," Kim Remesch; Feb. 1996, pg. 28-31, "Architect's Classroom," Jeanne Delgado; *Nutshell News Calendar*, 1989, Cover; *Miniature Showcase*, Winter 1987, pg. 54-55; *Miniature Collector*, Winter 1987, pg. 31-33; *Miniature Gazette*, Fall 1985, pg. 32-33; *Threads*, Oct/Nov. 1987, Back Cover; *Carpenter*, May 1985, Back Cover, pg. 16-17; *Le Magazine De La Maison De Poupée*, No. 26, Cover, pg. 21-23; No. 27, pg. 23-25; *Workbench Magazine*, Apr. 1990; *The Washington Post*, Nov. 8, 1981; Sept. 9, 1985; *Washington Times*, Jan. 17, 1985, Home section, Cover; *Historic Preservation*, Aug. 1985; *Amtrac Express*, Oct/Nov. 1986; *Fine Woodworking*, Nov/Dec. 1994, Back Cover; *National Geographic,* 1981, pg. 75-77, "How Things are Made;" *Traditional Homes*, Dec. 1991; CBS Evening News, Mar. 2, 1991; *Allentown Art Museum*, brochure, 1981, Cover; *Portsmouth Museum*, poster, 1986

AUTOBIOGRAPHY:

I've always had a high aptitude for mechanics. In the early 1970's I worked in a hardware store, was foreman of a production shop and built everything from sophisticated electronic equipment to race cars. I always enjoyed building things, especially the unusual. When I was self-employed in 1977, I discovered and began making miniatures. I like to make things that work and since 1980, I've rarely made more than 10 of any one piece. On larger items I usually do only two or three. Most of the projects I do are by commission.

Having seen many dollhouses I wanted to build one my way, after spending over 10,000 hours during nine years I completed a pair of houses named "Twin Manors." Each contain about 75,000 pieces with details like working locks with oval knobs and handmade moldings.

Research is very important to making fine miniatures so I spend considerable time going to museums and libraries. I collect original books on design and techniques from the 18th and 19th centuries as well as the tools to copy the work as accurately as possible.

I've been Guest Curator for the National Geographic Society's Explorers Hall Museum for two miniature exhibits with attendance over 100,000 people. Other major museums I have worked with and exhibited at include the National Trust, Smithsonian Institution and the Toy and Miniature Museum in Kansas City, Missouri. Teaching at the Guild School in Castine is one way I share my knowledge of miniatures, and by slide shows given across the US and abroad. I write articles on old tools and miniatures for a number of magazines.

I have most records of where all my pieces were sold, and I also handle the resale of earlier pieces.

ARTISAN: **ROBINSON, AMY W.**

BUSINESS NAME: All Through The House

IDENTIFICATION MARKS:

Some pieces unmarked
All marks 1982 to present

ROBINSON, AMY W., continued

CATEGORY:

Accessories: outdoor; Christmas; Holiday Items

RECOGNITION:

Nutshell News, Oct. 1987, pg. 5; Feb. 1990, pg. 57; Apr. 1992, pg. 70; *Miniatures Showcase*, Spring 1987, pg. 48; Fall 1987, pg. 42-43; Summer 1989, pg. 39; Winter 1992, pg. 19

AUTOBIOGRAPHY:

I've had a life long interest in miniatures beginning with admiring my grandmother's exquisite ¾-inch scale collection and spending countless hours playing in my mother's childhood dollhouse. In a high school drafting class, I drew up plans for an English Tudor Dollhouse as a class project. More than 10 years later, I took out those plans and built that dollhouse, without help, from scratch. That was in 1982, and that house launched me into the miniature business I conduct today under the name of "All Through the House." I make every item myself and I sign or initial most of them. I was souvenir gift artist for the NAME M-2 Houseparty in 1991.

ARTISAN: **ROCHE, CARIDAD M.**

BUSINESS NAME: Miniatures By Caridad M. Roche

IDENTIFICATION MARKS:

1986 to present

CATEGORY:

Accessories; Dioramas; Paintings; Roomboxes

HONORS:

Exhibits: Toy & Miniature Museum of Kansas City; The Carole & Barry Kaye Museum of Miniatures, Los Angeles, California

RECOGNITION:

Nutshell News

AUTOBIOGRAPHY:

I have always admired miniature items whatever they may be of. I did not realize until 1977 that there was actually a specific scale for these wonderfully small pieces which was used and accepted world wide. This awakening was due to a publication named *The Miniature Magazine* which is not in existence any longer.

Since then I started to create one-inch scale furniture and accessories. I still have my original scratch built pieces. One is a Colonial hutch made of balsa wood and the other is a fireplace made out of a dismantled cigar box.

Thanks to my persistent and persuasive husband Gary and son Gary, Jr., I started to do shows while I resided in New York. I have become known for my room cases, dioramas, paintings, 1/87th scale Victorian homes and other accessories in many scales.

ARTISAN: **ROGAL, TERRY**

BUSINESS NAME: Roof Top Studios

IDENTIFICATION MARKS:

T. Rogal with year in black or gold ink;
Brass plate engraved **Terry Rogal** with year
White and Black stick-on label with printed name, year, number of piece, with roof tops

ROGAL, TERRY, continued

CATEGORY:
Furniture

HONORS:
IGMA Fellow; Exhibit: Toy & Miniature Museum of Kansas City

ARTISAN: **ROGERS, FAITH & TOM**

BUSINESS NAME: "Precious Little Things"(TM) by The Fieldwood Co., Inc.

IDENTIFICATION MARKS:
Some unmarked

Faith B. Rogers

Thomas E. Rogers.

FBR

PLT

Fieldwood Co., Inc.

"Precious Little things" (TM)

Precious Little Things®

Trademark registered 1975

CATEGORY:
Accessories: seasonal; Dollhouse; Food; Furniture; Medical; Roadside Stands; Roomboxes

RECOGNITION:
Nutshell News; Country Living, Mar. 1992; *Creative Crafts; Miniature Gazette; Miniatures Dealer; Home Miniaturist; House Beautiful; Miniature Collector; Dollhouse News*

ARTISAN: **ROGERS, MAY**

BUSINESS NAME: May Rogers Miniature Needlework

IDENTIFICATION MARKS:

MR

CATEGORY:
Needlework

HONORS:
IGMA Artisan 1989, Fellow 1994

ROGERS, MAY, continued

RECOGNITION:

Nutshell News, Vol. 17, No. 2, Feb. 1987, pg. 84-85; Vol. 17, No. 8, Aug. 1987, pg. 68; Vol. 22, No. 4, Apr. 1992, pg. 70-71; *Miniature Collector*, No. 73, Summer 1991, pg. 23; *Miniatures Showcase*, Vol. 8, No. 1, Jan. 1993, pg. 38-39

AUTOBIOGRAPHY:

I learned to do needlework as a child growing up in rural Massachusetts, in an old-fashioned family that regarded sewing as a basic life-skill for all girls. I began sewing in miniature around 1975 for a friend's dollhouse, and from that friend and those early attempts I "caught the fever" and began to pursue miniature needlework seriously. It became a business in 1981.

In the real world I am a professional librarian. I am married and have two children.

ARTISAN: ROSE, IPHIGENIA

IDENTIFICATION MARKS: (Submitted by Toy & Miniature Museum of Kansas City)

IPHIGENIA

Capital printed letters in pen on bottom of piece

CATEGORY:

Furniture: wicker; Wicker

HONORS:

Exhibit: Toy & Miniature Museum of Kansas City

RECOGNITION:

Nutshell News, Vol. 12, No. 9, Sept. 1982, pg. 60

ARTISAN: ROSENTHAL, HANK & JOHN

BUSINESS NAME: Mini Graphics, Inc.

IDENTIFICATION MARKS:

Unmarked

CATEGORY:

Drapes; Furniture: upholstered

ARTISAN: ROULEAU, PAUL E.

BUSINESS NAME: Rouleau Reproductions

IDENTIFICATION MARKS:

P.E.R.

ROULEAU, PAUL E., continued

CATEGORY:

Accessories: general store, kitchen; Furniture: country, Shaker; General Store; Kitchen

HONORS:

NAME AOH; Mell Prescott Award 1995

RECOGNITION:

Nutshell News, Jun. 1983; *Country Living*, Mar. 1992

ARTISAN: ROUNTREE, SYLVIA

BUSINESS NAME: The Dolls' Cobbler

IDENTIFICATION MARKS:

Some unmarked

The Dolls' Cobbler

CATEGORY:

Accessories: leather; Leather Work

HONORS:

IGMA Fellow; NAME AOH; Exhibit: Toy & Miniature Museum of Kansas City

RECOGNITION:

Nutshell News, 1978; *Miniature Collector*, 1979; 1983; *Miniature Gazette*, Spring 1981

AUTOBIOGRAPHY:

My mother was a lifelong miniaturist, so I grew up thinking it was perfectly normal to have two dollhouses in the family, one for my mother and one for the kids. And in keeping with family tradition, when I had a daughter and three sons we had a dollhouse too. That was about 1967. Soon we had a barn, country store, log cabin, etc. Once you start fooling around with miniatures, it becomes an addiction. Then I became interested in antique dolls, too, and I was really in trouble! A school librarian from Cuyahoga Falls, Ohio, who is raising four children by herself has to find ways of supporting her hobby. In my case, it turned out to be costuming antique dolls for the Bradley Doll Hospital in Stow, Ohio. I learned to make leather shoes to go with the outfits. Soon I was busy just making doll shoes and began to sell them mail-order. Hence, the name "The Doll's Cobbler." In 1973, I attempted to make some miniature shoes. The Bradleys took them to the Cleveland Miniature Show and that one day changed my life.

Since that day in August, 1973, I have made so many thousand little shoes that I've lost count, plus lots of other leather miniatures such as saddles and suitcases and I'm still creating new items.

My children are grown up now and I have left the school library and Ohio. I now live near Ocean City, Maryland, in a place called Ocean Pines. I have a studio in my home and I work many hours each day as a full-time miniature craftsman. When I want to relax and stretch a bit, I work outside in my cottage garden, or feed the goldfish in my lily pool or tend the orchids in my greenhouse.

ARTISAN: **ROWBOTTOM, DEREK RICHARD & SHEILA ANN**

BUSINESS NAME: Torbay Model Workshop

IDENTIFICATION MARKS:

CATEGORY:

Author; Dollhouse: plans; Roomboxes; Rooms: corner; Writer

RECOGNITION:

Miniature Collector, Winter 1989, pg. 14; *Dolls & Dolls' Houses*, Nov. 1988, pg. 10-13; May 1989, pg. 30-35, 56-60; *Model & Miniature Crafts*, Issue No. 7, pg. 70-74; *Dolls House World*, Issue No. 2, 1989, pg. 32-34, 36; Issue No. 3, 1989, pg. 38-41; Issue No. 7, 1990, pg. 12; Issue No. 12, 1991, pg. 55; Issue No. 14, pg. 33

BIOGRAPHY:

Derek has been a modeler of many subjects for the past 50 years and his daughter Sheila has also modeled for most of her life, approximately, thirty years.

A serious illness at the age of 11 cut short Derek's formal education until the age of 16 when some improvement in his health allowed him to continue his education at the Bolton College of Art. His illness gave him the time to read anything and everything and he also discovered that he had a talent for drawing and art in general. When confined to bed he would carve small figures from pieces of wood and a safety razor blade, his only tool!

As the illness began in war time his interest soon turned to airplanes and he would draw these and later turned to carving scale models, dozens were made during this period. Later he turned to model galleons and from this became interested in the 15th and 16th century which brought about his interest in architecture of the period, Tudor and Elizabethan buildings. These he drew and also modeled from cardboard.

Any hopes of becoming a professional painter or sculptor had to, however, be set aside for the more serious consideration, that of making a living! He became a tailor which in a small way was artistic, creating a garment from scratch.

Marriage and two children meant art had to be put on one side although he did continue learning about the subject at Salford University in the evenings and models were still made in his spare time.

It was almost by chance he became a professional modeler. Sheila was instrumental in this change. She had always loved to paint, draw and model and some 12 or 13 years ago began construction on one-inch scale model period furniture. Sheila always loved antiques and this was one way to afford them! The furniture collection grew and grew and because of the detail these were greatly admired by all who saw them.

Derek then recalled the model houses he made during his illness and decided to build a Tudor Manor House so that the furniture could be viewed in a proper setting. Building the house took almost two years but when finished, complete with rich wood paneling, beamed and plastered ceilings and period lights Derek was pleased with the results. Sheila provided the paintings, flowers, and food to complete the model.

The president of the Devon Guild of Craftsmen inspected the model and informed Derek and Sheila that this was worth a considerable amount of money. This came as a great surprise as the model was not built for sale. Derek was advised to show the house at the London Doll's House Festival and so more models were required. Derek and Sheila decided to construct a model each, both the same period, based on actual houses, but both completely different designs.

A small show was tried first, Exeter, and they both had a feeling of trepidation in case the models were not favorable to the visitors. This feeling disappeared after a couple of hours as it became obvious that the models were being well received and both houses were sold at the end of the show for over £1,000 each and two commissions had been received. The year was 1985 and such was the demand for the houses and furniture that Derek turned professional modeler at the age of 56.

In 1988, he was invited to write an article for *Model & Miniature Crafts,* a magazine published by the Guild of Master Craftsman Publications, further articles followed and he was then commissioned to write a book on *Making Tudor Dolls' Houses* which he did, with great excitement. This was published by the Guild in 1990 and proved a best seller for the publishers, it was re-printed in 1992 and will shortly be re-printed again. In fact so successful was the book that two more were commissioned, *Making Georgian Dolls' House* and *Making Period*

Doll's House Furniture, the second was published in 1992 as was the third book. Both proved very successful and the latter has been re-printed again. Both Derek and Sheila are very busy with commissions, writing and the publication of full-scale plans for houses.

ARTISAN: **RUCKER, MARITTA**

BUSINESS NAME: Nimble Fingers

IDENTIFICATION MARKS:

CATEGORY:

Flowers and Plants; Landscaping; Outdoor Accessories

HONORS:

IGMA Artisan; Exhibit: Toy & Miniature Museum of Kansas City

RECOGNITION:

Nutshell News, Nov. 1987, Show Scene; April 1987, Show Scene; Sept. 1988, pg. 24; Oct. 1990, Show Scene; Dec. 1990, Show Scene; May 1991, pg. 31; Nov. 1991, Show Scene; May 1992, Show Scene; Aug. 1992, pg. 65; Oct. 1992, Show Scene; Nov. 1992, Show Scene; Feb. 1993, pg. 49; May 1993, Cover; Jun. 1993, Show Scene; Sept. 1993, pg. 13; Oct. 1993, pg. 25; Dec. 1993, Show Scene; Mar. 1994, pg. 46; Apr. 1994, pg. 61; *Miniature Gazette*, Fall 1985, Cover, pg. 27-28; Spring 1986, pg. 27-28; Spring 1987, pg. 36-37; Summer 1987, pg. 28-29; Winter 1987, pg. 21-25; Fall 1988, pg. 24-27; Winter 1988, pg. 24; Winter 1990, pg. 60-63; Winter 1986, pg. 31; *Miniature Collector*; Fall 1990, Show Report

AUTOBIOGRAPHY:

I was born in Koblenz, Germany and lived there until I was eight. We lived in the country, and between the heavenly countryside and forests, and a grandmother who had green fingers, I could not help but develop a passion for growing things. It was in Germany, also, that I played with my first miniatures.

When I came to America miniatures were forgotten as I tried to make a new life with my father, brother, new mother and brothers.

Making things was a driving force throughout my developing years and encouraged by art and shop teachers. My high school art teacher in particular helped to mold my creative skills by encouraging me in every medium.

During my 20's and early 30's, I had little time to persue my creativity. I was busy building a career, nourishing a home and husband, and raising two sons. My re-acquaintance with miniatures came when I was 29, when my mother-in-law bought me a dollhouse kit. I loved making it and the furniture and just had to have flowers in the yard. Everything was fun to make. And I was able to dabble in every medium.

I began to sell some of my work locally to defray the cost of my hobby. Local miniaturists were very supportive and I found the whole experience very gratifying. I began doing shows and workshops within driving distance and eventually began flying to shows. I now do about six shows per year across America and teach workshops whenever possible.

The most important thing I have gotten from miniatures, however, is friends. I have met many wonderful folks, many of whom I now cannot live without. What a hobby! I just hope I live long enough to do half the things I want to.

ARTISAN: **RUEMELI, BARBARA J.**

BUSINESS NAME: B.J.R. Miniatures

IDENTIFICATION MARKS:

Carriages numbered and recorded

BJR

CATEGORY:

Carriages: wicker; Furniture: wicker; Wicker

RECOGNITION:

Nutshell News, May 1984; *Enchanted Doll House*, Catalog, 1984; 1985; 1986; 1987; *Miniature Gazette*

AUTOBIOGRAPHY:

B.J.R. Miniatures has been established since 1982. I am one of the very few artisans in the country that handcrafts wicker miniatures totally from natural reeds. My pieces are one-inch scale. Most of the pieces are copied from antique pieces. I use a variety of finishes and fabrics or will custom cover the piece. My carriages are copyrighted and have been sold in several countries in Europe, including Canada, Australia and New Zealand. I am a member of MIAA and CIMTA and do these shows yearly.

ARTISAN: **RUFF, DUREEN ANNE**

BUSINESS NAME: d. Anne Ruff

IDENTIFICATION MARKS:

d. Anne Ruff   d. Anne Ruff

CATEGORY:

Curtains; Drapes; Furniture: upholstered; Kits; Pleaters; Windows: dressing

HONORS:

IGMA Artisan; NAME AOH; Who's Who In America; Honorary Chairman 1987, "A Cajun Culinary Festival," Gulf South Miniature & Dollhouse Event, New Orleans, Louisiana

RECOGNITION:

Nutshell News, Dec. 1982, pg. 31; Vol. 13, No. 1, Jan. 1983, pg. 20, "Product Review – Pretty Pleat;" Oct. 1983, pg. 48; Apr. 1985, pg. 20, 24; Vol. 18, No. 7, Jul. 1988, pg. 64-69, "The Well Dressed Window," d. Anne Ruff; Vol. 19, No. 4, Apr. 1989, pg. 88-92, "The Well Dressed Window," d. Anne Ruff; Jan. 1996, pg. 12-15, "The Magic Touch," Anne Day Smith

AUTOBIOGRAPHY:

I received a BS in Art Education with a minor in Home Economics. My occupation before my involvement in miniatures was an art teacher in elementary and junior high school.

In 1969, I began making and selling one-inch scale upholstered furniture which I sold to a local children's shop. During the next few years I also supplied miniatures to Dayton's a Minneapolis department store chain. At this time I was not interested in greatly expanding my growing business because we had four young children that kept me busy. However, as the children became more independent, I had more time to devote to miniatures and began to ship my furniture to other miniature shops in this area.

In 1976, I went to my first miniature show as a dealer. That experience opened up a whole new world for me. One of the things I realized was that people not only wanted to buy miniatures, they wanted to make things themselves. With this in mind, I began creating kits and products for the crafts person as well as finished items for collectors. In 1980, I created the Pretty Point rug kits and, in 1982 the Pretty Pleat fabric pleaters, both of which have become staple items in most miniature shops.

In 1985, we added the window collection, a line of window dressings, cornices, draperies and curtains that coordinate with our upholstered furniture.

My lifelong interest in art and specifically in interior design has found a wonderful outlet in creating miniatures.

ARTISAN: RUMBLE, BRIAN

BUSINESS NAME: Rudeigin Beag

IDENTIFICATION MARKS:

Logo burned into piece; signed and dated in ink

CATEGORY:

Dollhouse: custom; Furniture: period

RECOGNITION:

Evening Telegraph, Jul. 16, 1982, pg. 4, "Brian's Prize-winning Chair Was Made in a Month;" Nov. 30, 1989, pg. 8, "East Neuk Cottage;" *Modelling and Miniature Crafts*, Issue No. 4, Jan. 1988, pg. 6-9, "Unique Highland Collection;" Issue No. 6, Jan 1989, pg. 52-54, "A Jointed Table;" Issue No. 7, Jul. 1989, pg. 37-40, "The Cottar's Hame;" *Dolls and Dolls' Houses*, Issue No. 2, May 1989, pg. 45-48, "Orkney Chair;" Issue No. 3, Nov. 1989, pg. 4-8, "Sarah's House;" *Sunday Post Magazine*, Feb. 4, 1990, "Just Like the Real Thing;" Dec. 1, 1990, pg. 38, "Making it Big in a Small World;" *Dolls' House World*, Issue No. 11, Jan. 1991, pg. 30-31, "Opening of a Shop Called Weirside;" *The Home Miniaturist*, Issue No. 62, Aug. 1992, pg. 20-25, "A Cottage Industry"

AUTOBIOGRAPHY:

I received a B Ed in Craft and Design at Oxford University Institute of Education in 1958. From 1958 to 1967, I taught cabinet making at high school and vocational education schools in the United Kingdom. From 1967 to 1968, I taught cabinet making in high school, in the USA. Returning to the UK in 1968 I spent two years teaching craft and design in high school and for further education. I graduated in Advance Diploma in Craft, Design and Technology at London University Institute of Education in 1971 and in 1972 I graduated M Sc in Industrial Arts Education at New York State University. I was back to teaching again from 1972 to 1975, cabinet making at masters level and ceramics, graphic arts, leather working and silversmithing at undergraduate level at Ohio State University, Columbus, Ohio.

In 1975 I graduated Ph.D. in Industrial Technology Education at Ohio State University, and in 1986 I accepted early retirement from full-time employment and set up business as a designer and maker of miniatures in one-inch scale houses and furniture.

ARTISAN: RUNYON, PAUL A.

IDENTIFICATION MARKS: (Submitted by Toy & Miniature Museum of Kansas City)

Some unmarked
Some dated

MADE BY PAUL A. RUNYON Brass plate, block letters
Stamped in ink, block letters

PAUL A. RUNYON Incised into wood, block letters

R Incised into wood, block letter

RUNYON, PAUL A., continued

CATEGORY:
Furniture

HONORS:
Exhibit: Toy & Miniature Museum of Kansas City

RECOGNITION:
Nutshell News, Vol. 14, No. 11, Nov. 1984, pg. 62; *Miniature Collector*, No. 4, Dec. 1977, pg. 14-17, "Paul Runyon, Cabinetmaker Turned Miniaturist," Virginia Merrill; *The Complete Book of Making Miniatures*, Thelma Newman and Virginia Merrill, 1975, pg. 154

ARTISAN: RUSSELL, ART

BUSINESS NAME: Russell Enterprises Reg'd

IDENTIFICATION MARKS:

Brass plaque

CATEGORY:
Clocks; Furniture

HONORS:
IGMA Artisan

RECOGNITION:
Nutshell News, May 1986, pg. 54-57; *Montreal Gazette*, Canada; *Hudson Gazette*, Quebec, Canada; *Our Miniature World*, Marie Dettling, 1984, pg. 85-86

AUTOBIOGRAPHY:
My miniature hobby came about when my son and daughter-in-law presented me with a granddaughter. I spent many years in tool design and building a successful aircraft business. When I retired miniatures gave me a new world to conquer.

ARTISAN: RUSSELL, GEORGE & ANNETTE

BUSINESS NAME: Rosiewood Miniatures

IDENTIFICATION MARKS:

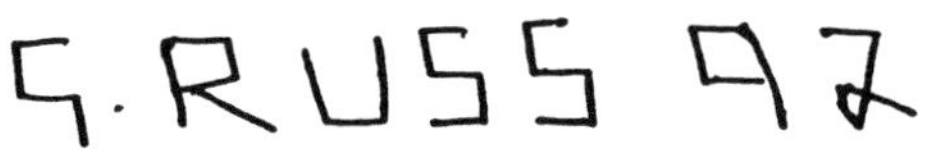

RUSSELL, GEORGE & ANNETTE, continued

CATEGORY:
Dolls; Furniture; Kits; Metalwork; Wrought Iron

RECOGNITION:
Dolls House World; *The Home Miniaturist*, 1992

ARTISAN: RUSSELL, JULIA ANN

BUSINESS NAME: Julia's Artwork

IDENTIFICATION MARKS:
1982 to present

Year when space available

CATEGORY:
Accessories: handpainted; Paintings: oil

RECOGNITION:
Nutshell News, Jul. 1986, pg. 22, Private Eye; *Miniatures Showcase*, Vol. 2, No. 4, 1987, pg. 36; *Memphis, Tennessee Commercial Appeal*, May 24, 1993, pg. A8

ARTISAN: RUSSELL, ROBERT

BUSINESS NAME: Nonesuch Miniatures

IDENTIFICATION MARKS:

CATEGORY:
Furniture: English, period

RECOGNITION:
International Dolls' House News, Vol. 21, No. 2, Summer 1992, pg. 51

BIOGRAPHY:
Robert Russell has been restoring antiques and making reproduction furniture since 1973, working to the very highest standard, having been trained in London. He has worked for stars of television and theatre, and Nobility. Now Robert has increased his repertoire to include miniatures, working to the same high standards using all original timbers and polishes, being authentic and correct in every detail.

ARTISAN: **RUSSO, SUSANNE** (Submitted by Pam Nussbaum)

BUSINESS NAME: Brasses by Susanne Russo

IDENTIFICATION MARKS:

S. Russo 1982

Sue Russo 1982 to 1983

Susanne Russo 1983 to Aug. 1984

CATEGORY:
Brasswork; Furniture; Kits

HONORS:
IGMA Fellow 1982

RECOGNITION:
Nutshell News, Aug. 1982; Vol. 13, No. 2 Feb. 1983, pg. 60, Show Scene; Vol. 14, No. 2, Feb. 1984, pg. 54, Show Scene; *The Scale Cabinetmaker; Through The Looking Glass*, Boynton and Associates, Inc., Ann Ruble, 1984; *American Period Interiors in Miniature*, Kate Doordan Klavan, Scribner's, 1984

BIOGRAPHY:

A Renaissance artisan, multi-talented in a wide variety of miniature mediums, Susanne is a designer of period furniture, authentic period brass hardware from furniture to exterior, including doll and clock accessories, and designer of period trunk kits.

She has shared her expertise throughout the nation giving classes and seminars for over a decade. Susanne is best noted for her Swan furniture, horn furniture, lawn furniture, brasses, trunk kits and various how-to articles.

S

ARTISAN: **SABELLA, LULIE NEWCOMB**

BUSINESS NAME: Lulie's Zoo

IDENTIFICATION MARKS:

Mark 1990 to present
Series number 1992 to present

Year, Number of piece

CATEGORY:

Animals; Dolls; Figures

HONORS:

IGMA Artisan

RECOGNITION:

Nutshell News, Vol. 20, No. 11, Nov. 1990, pg. 58-61; *Doll Artistry*, Nov. 1991, pg. 28-33; *Santa Dolls:* Historical to Contemporary, Ann Bahar, Hobby House, 1992, pg. 166-168, 171, 172

AUTOBIOGRAPHY:

I have been making portrait dolls since my teen years and larger size animal head dolls all through the 80's, finally scaling down to miniatures in 1990. I attended Cornish Institute of Allied Arts in Seattle, Washington, and helped run Earthworks and Artisans, a pottery shop in New York City before moving to Los Angeles. I am a member of NAME and CIMTA. I am also an actress who works on stage, TV and screen between doll shows.

ARTISAN: **SACK, RICHARD A.**

BUSINESS NAME: The Blacksmith Shop

IDENTIFICATION MARKS:

Some tools unmarked
1986 to present

Burned on wood
1/16 to 1/8 inch long

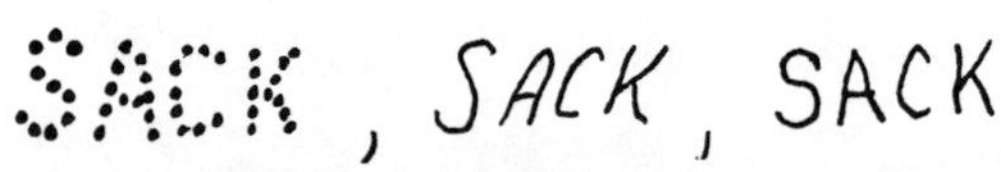

Guns, knives; some show year
3/16 inch long

CATEGORY:

Kitchenware; Tools; Weapons

HONORS:

Exhibit: Toy and Miniature Museum of Kansas City, Summer 1991

AUTOBIOGRAPHY:

I have been working with miniatures and toys since I was about five years old, when my grandfather gave me a knife and taught me how to use it. I have been working with "true" miniatures since 1985.

My profession is teaching. I have been an industrial arts teacher for over 27 years, and for most of those years I have used miniature building to teach construction methods. I also do construction work during the summer, and have often worked out problems by first building in miniature, but I was not aware of the "real" miniature world until 1985.

In 1985, I attended my first miniature show in Leavenworth, Kansas and found it very interesting. The houses, buildings and furnishings were wonderful, however the tools lacked a great deal. Because of my background, I started making tools and related items, and because most of the dollhouses at miniature shows were dated from the late 1800's to the early 1900's, my tools followed that era. Most of my trade came from people asking "If I made..." The most difficult "If I..." was guns. As with most miniature artisans, my goal is to make the most realistic pieces possible. I use steel, wood, brass, silver and even gold when ever possible.

The name "The Blacksmith Shop" came about because of making tools first. I had to have some method of showing the tools, and so I made a blacksmith shop to put them in. As I started selling items the name stuck, and for the most part, it still fits.

ARTISAN: **SALPEKAR, BETTY**

IDENTIFICATION MARKS:

1978 to present, some pieces unmarked between 1978 and 1983

BNS SALPEKAR BNS

CATEGORY:

Accessories; Furniture; Knitting

HONORS:

IGMA Artisan

RECOGNITION:

Nutshell News, Vol. 22, No. 9, Sept. 1992, pg. 79; Vol. 23, No. 5, May 1993, pg. 38-40; Vol. 24, No. 4, Apr. 1994, pg. 52-54

AUTOBIOGRAPHY:

I have been making miniatures since I was in my teens, though there were long intervals when other things such as family and career took precedence. I have no formal training in art or decorating and only a few classes in miniature making. Most of the miniatures I've made have been self-taught.

In the late 1970's and early 1980's I sold miniatures on consignment through a shop in St. Louis, Missouri. They were miscellaneous accessories such as sports equipment, skis and ski poles, crutches, ballet toe shoes and tutus, braided rugs, slippers, toy dolls, nesting blocks, wooden chess sets, and some modern style Queen Anne wing chairs. I accepted a few commissions locally and sold directly at a few local craft shows.

Since late 1991 I have made miniatures my full-time occupation, concentrating mainly on 1/144th-inch scale settings and one-inch scale knitting. I have sold these to a shop in Venarey, France. In the future I plan to produce mostly one-of-a-kind items or very limited editions, possibly selling them at one or two shows a year.

I attended the Guild School in Castine, Maine for the first time, in 1994, and plan to go back again. I enjoy broadening my miniature horizons.

ARTISAN: **SALTARELLI, DEBBIE**

BUSINESS NAME: Debbie's Designs

IDENTIFICATION MARKS:

Frames unmarked

DD

SALTARELLI, DEBBIE, continued

CATEGORY:

Boat; Frames; Nautical: ship models

AUTOBIOGRAPHY:

I worked with Paul, mostly office duty and with framing paintings, while our children were growing up. In 1993, I finally had the time to pursue an idea that was on my mind for months. I wanted to produce lightweight, durable, detailed picture frames. Once the frames were off to a good start I looked for other projects. The model ships started as a whim. First were one-inch scale, then I tried ½-inch scale. I really enjoyed the challenge of ¼-inch scale. My next planned project is to design ½-inch scale frames to add to my one-inch line.

ARTISAN: SALTARELLI, PAUL

BUSINESS NAME: Paul Saltarelli Paintings

IDENTIFICATION MARKS:

Paul Saltarelli	(SS) year
Paintings	1994 to present

CATEGORY:

Figurines; Furniture; Mirrors; Paintings; Shelves

HONORS:

IGMA Artisan, Permanent exhibit, Palm Springs Desert Museum

RECOGNITION:

Nutshell News, Vol. 18, No. 4, Apr. 1988, pg. 50-53, "Paul Saltarelli's Museum Masterworks In Miniature," Emile Zola; Vol. 21, No. 9, Sept. 1991, pg. 66-70

AUTOBIOGRAPHY:

I am self-taught and have no formal training in art. As a child I was exposed to art through my parents, often visiting museums. I also spent a lot of time drawing and painting.

After painting some miniatures for my daughter's dollhouse, Mary Pennoyer, a friend of my mother's, felt they were good enough to sell. This is when I dropped computer programming, the field I was trained in, and started a new business.

I learned as much as possible by visiting museums and reading as much as I could about art. I became familiar with the different artists, styles and techniques. I now paint in oil, acrylic and watercolor. I do full-size reproductions, portraits and miniatures for museums and collectors.

ARTISAN: SANDERS, JOHN & BELLA

BUSINESS NAME: Show & Tell

IDENTIFICATION MARKS:

JWS with label

CATEGORY:

Greenhouses; Houses; Kits: attic, fair stand, porch; Lamps; Lighting; Roomboxes; Store; Vignettes

SANDERS, JOHN & BELLA, continued

HONORS:

Best of Show Award, Maplewood, Minnesota, 1982, 1983, 1985

RECOGNITION:

Nutshell News, May 1990, Cover; Jun. 1990, pg. 66; Aug. 1990, pg. 40-43; *St. Paul Pioneer Press*, Minnesota, Mar. 1, 1985; *Twin Cities Magazine*, Jan. 1984, pg. 40-42

AUTOBIOGRAPHY:

John Sanders, a music teacher, and Bella Sanders, a school librarian, found the perfect retirement business that allowed them to travel and earn income. John's hobby of woodworking and Bella's ownership of an 1870 dollhouse (passed down through three generations of her family), initiated the thought of building scale-model dollhouses. In 1979, John took a five year leave of absence from teaching to develop and market his idea of modular dollhouses. The business was very successful and kept them busy.

In the early 1980's they added their unique "little house" table lamps, wood-crafted roomboxes, and leaded-glass greenhouses in anticipation of retirement travel with smaller items. Since retiring in 1984, John and Bella travel each year to selected miniature shows in the Midwest and on the east coast from Maine to Florida to show their unique items in one-inch and ½-inch scales. These items are sold through these few shows and a large mail-order business, while the dollhouses are now built by special-order only.

ARTISAN: SANFORD, BONNIE

BUSINESS NAME: Wee Whimsies by Bonnie Sanford

IDENTIFICATION MARKS:

Wee Whimsies by Bonnie Sanford	BJS	WW Bonnie Sanford
Dressed dolls inside clothing	Doll kits	Furniture

CATEGORY:

Dolls: costumed, porcelain; Kits

HONORS:

IGMA Artisan

RECOGNITION:

Nutshell News, Vol. 13, No. 4, Apr. 1983, pg. 54, Show Scene; Vol. 15, No. 4, Apr. 1985, pg. 62; Vol. 20, No. 12, Dec. 1990, pg. 66; Vol. 22, No. 3, Mar. 1992, pg. 71; *Miniature Collector*, No. 68, Spring 1990, pg. 23; *Dolls in Miniature*, Vol. 1, No. 1, Spring 1991, pg. 24

AUTOBIOGRAPHY:

I was raised by a very artistically talented mother, who both studied and taught several forms of art, including oil and watercolor painting and ceramics. Upon graduation from high school, I attended a fashion design school in San Francisco. Marriage, and two daughters sidelined my career ambitions for many years.

My interest in miniatures was sparked when my sister gave several pieces of fine old dollhouse furniture from her childhood, to my daughters. It seemed reasonable that a dollhouse should be built to hold these treasures. Of course, when the nine room house was completed, the half dozen pieces of furniture didn't go far towards filling it.

I started buying a few pieces of the Taiwan imports, but really wanted something nicer. The Realife kits for whole rooms of furniture fit my budget, and were fun to assemble. Out of the leftover scraps of wood, I started to whittle out a few pieces of my own furniture. My husband encouraged my endeavors by buying some small power tools.

It wasn't long before I was making furniture for a nearby miniature shop. Then, in 1978 I started doing a few miniature shows in Pennsylvania. It was at these early shows that I first noticed the one-inch scale dressed dolls that were available. I started doing a few of my own from purchased kits, but I wasn't thrilled with the way they were painted and wigged. My husband rescued me again by buying a kiln so I could pour, paint, fire and wig the dolls myself. The early instructions given by my mother in ceramics started me, and the rest I have learned through trial and error.

At last, all my interests and talents have come together, and a full career has developed.

ARTISAN: **SAUERS, ANDRÉE**

BUSINESS NAME: Pretty Penny

IDENTIFICATION MARKS:

Small pieces

CATEGORY:

Accessories: Southwest; Flowers and Plants; Food

RECOGNITION:

Nutshell News, Oct. 1987, pg. 76

AUTOBIOGRAPHY:

I've taken art lessons since age seven. I attended Rhode Island School of Design for two and a half years. Since the 1970's, I've been making miniatures for sale, first in Ohio, then in Rhode Island and now in New Mexico. I am a member of CIMTA and NAME.

ARTISAN: **SAUNDERS, WILLIAM FANT**

BUSINESS NAME: Fant's Miniatures

IDENTIFICATION MARKS:

CATEGORY:

Furniture

AUTOBIOGRAPHY:

I began making miniature furniture in 1982.

ARTISAN: **SAWHILL, JOAN M.**

BUSINESS NAME: Joan M. Sawhill

IDENTIFICATION MARKS:

Year

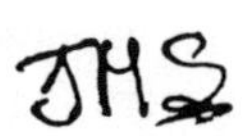

Year

CATEGORY:

Furniture: handpainted, upholstered; Paintings

SAWHILL, JOAN M., continued

HONORS:

IGMA Artisan

RECOGNITION:

Nutshell News

ARTISAN: **SCARBORO, JOANNA**

BUSINESS NAME: Joanna's Miniatures

IDENTIFICATION MARKS:

Joanna Scarboro

CATEGORY:

Furniture: country

HONORS:

IGMA Artisan; NAME AOH 1995

RECOGNITION:

Nutshell News, Jun. 1983, Cover; Dec. 1983, Cover; Oct. 1988, Cover; Jan. 1988, pg. 42-44, "Come to Scarboro Fair," Isabel Jerrold-Jones; *Miniature Catalog*, 7th Edition; 10th Edition; *Miniatures Showcase*, Vol. 1, Fall 1986

AUTOBIOGRAPHY:

I started making miniatures when I became involved in building a dollhouse for my granddaughter, after which, one thing led to another and before long, I was making furniture for friends which led eventually to selling my work at shows. I have always been interested in arts and crafts and decorating and refinishing furniture, so miniatures seemed something of a natural offshoot. I have taken many classes and have attended the Guild School at Castine, Maine. I served on the NAME Board from 1990 to 1994.

ARTISAN: **SCATES, KAREN**

BUSINESS NAME: Karen's Miniatures

IDENTIFICATION MARKS:

Made by
Karen Scates

Karen Scates

CATEGORY:

Birds: wildlife; Furniture; Musical Instruments

RECOGNITION:

Early American Life, magazine, Aug. 1990; *Guide to American Craftsmen*

AUTOBIOGRAPHY:

I have been making miniatures since 1968. I learned woodworking from my grandfather, but because of the tools required and the size of full-scale woodworking, I decided miniatures were for me. I have been an amateur guitar player for many years and have a passion for music as well as miniatures, so it was a natural evolution towards miniature musical instruments. I try to use full-scale techniques whenever possible and make my instruments as realistic as possible. I also have a great love for wildlife and all animals, and have been an avid bird and wildlife observer for many years, so I also do some wildlife and bird carvings. I make furniture, usually by special request, in several different styles including Shaker and Early American.

ARTISAN: **SCHAD, GENE** (Deceased)
(Submitted by Charles & Dorothy Mitchell)

IDENTIFICATION MARKS:

GENE SCHAD with year
In black print

GS

CATEGORY:
Furniture: Country

ARTISAN: **SCHAFER, MIKE**

BUSINESS NAME: Ki De Miniatures

IDENTIFICATION MARKS:
Unmarked

CATEGORY:
Baskets: Indian

RECOGNITION:
Miniatures Showcase

AUTOBIOGRAPHY:
I attended Ohio State University (1957). I have always loved crafts and once the family was raised I decided to become involved with dollhouses. I fell in love with miniatures and began trying to make my own. I tried selling them and quickly realized it was better to specialize. I sent for a kit on basket weaving and after experimenting, decided I liked it. I have been making baskets since about 1978, all coiled, raffia-type authentic adaptations of Indian designs.

ARTISAN: **SCHECK, JO ANN**

BUSINESS NAME: Willo Miniatures

IDENTIFICATION MARKS:

CATEGORY:
Accessories; Dioramas; Dolls: character; Furniture; Roomboxes

SCHECK, JO ANN, continued

RECOGNITION:

Nutshell News; Miniatures Showcase

ARTISAN: **SCHERER, BILL**

BUSINESS NAME: Shaker Carpenter Shop

IDENTIFICATION MARKS:

CATEGORY:

Furniture: Shaker

AUTOBIOGRAPHY:

My experience with one-inch scale miniatures has only been since October of 1992. I have been building Shaker furniture since 1980. For nine years of this time everything we did was full-size. Our reputation is very good. We then started adding four-inch scale; three-inch scale and finally two-inch scale. Now we are into the real one-inch scale miniatures!

We have been working with wood since 1958, so we know what we are doing. All of our pieces have always been signed and dated.

ARTISAN: **SCHIADA, LEONARD L. & KATHLEEN**

BUSINESS NAME: Schiada Miniatures

IDENTIFICATION MARKS:

Some unmarked

 Handpainted pieces, worked into foliage left side of design or on horizontal line Delft style at back

CATEGORY:

Chandeliers; Lighting

HONORS:

IGMA Fellow (Leonard)

RECOGNITION:

Nutshell News, Vol. 4, No. 2, 1974, pg. 25-26; Jul. 1986, pg. 74-75; *Miniature Gazette*, Vol. 4, No. 2, pg. 27; *Small Talk*, Feb. 1977, pg. 8-9, 16; *Miniature Collector*, No. 3, Aug. 1977, pg. 33; *Decorating & Crafts Ideas*, Oct. 1977, pg. 20-23; *Orange County*, newspaper, California, Sept. 1980, pg. 46-47; *Register Orange County,* newspaper, Mon. May 30, 1977, Sec. B-1, "Mrs. Parks House;" *This Side of Yesterday in Miniatures*, Catherine B. MacLaren, 1975, pg. 78

BIOGRAPHY:

Leonard's profession is in accounting, but he also enjoys many hobbies. It was in helping a daughter construct and furnish a miniature room that the first hanging oil lamps were made in 1970. Collecting antique lighting for our home has been another hobby and reducing the full-size examples to one-inch scale is a challenge he enjoys. Leonard has created over 50 different Victorian styles; hanging, table, wall and elegant chandeliers.

ARTISAN: **SCHLOSSER, GEORGE** (Deceased)

BUSINESS NAME: George Schlosser

IDENTIFICATION MARKS:

 1978 to 1994

CATEGORY:

Dummy Boards; Fireboards; Paintings: oil, watercolor; Signs: store front

HONORS:

IGMA Fellow 1985; NAME AOH 1979; Retailer of the Year Award, 1972; Who's Who in Advertising, 1968; Merit Award, Rotary Club of Meriden, Connecticut, 1991

RECOGNITION:

Nutshell News, Feb. 1982, pg. 24-25; Jun. 1983, pg. 37; Jan. 1984, pg. 42-45; Dec. 1989, pg. 80; Nov. 1990, pg. 78; Feb. 1993, pg. 68; Jun. 1993, pg. 66; *Miniatures Showcase*, Winter 1988, pg. 37, 41, 45; Fall 1991, pg. 16, 42, 82; *The Miniature Magazine*, Winter 1980, pg. 64, 68; *Miniature Gazette*, Winter 1990, AOH Profile; *The Star-Ledger*, Springfield, NJ, Jan. 15, 1981; *Record Journal*, Meriden, CT, Dec. 28, 1982; Feb. 15, 1983; Jun. 15, 1985; Jul. 30, 1988; *The Post*, Frederick, MD, Mar. 21, 1983; *Los Angeles Times Magazine*, Los Angeles, CA, Aug. 28, 1988

BIOGRAPHY:

George began specializing in miniature paintings in 1978, after 27 years as an executive in retailing. Since he had studied at the Paier (formerly Whitney) School of Art in New Haven, Connecticut, and spent much of his spare time researching, collecting and restoring antiques, most of his artwork had an historical ambiance. Earlier in his career he had become intrigued with one-inch scale when the sets and scenery he designed for the Connecticut Experimental Theater and New Haven's Television Channel 8 were initially produced as miniatures.

When asked by a small friend to do a painting for the dollhouse her grandfather had designed and built, he was captivated by the challenge of miniature scale and began a new career. George incorporated his love for antiques into his miniature paintings. He became especially interested in English and American folk art, particularly admired Edward Hicks, and reproduced a number of that Quaker minister's paintings.

Realizing that commercial materials were too coarse for miniatures, George developed his own methods for making stretched canvasses, canvas boards, wood panels and frames for his artwork. He frequently gives workshops teaching the techniques he has developed.

He also created a line of storefront signs, exhibiting his appreciation for the historical by reproducing signs that are authentic for a particular period. The pin for the September 1990 NAME M-1 Regional Houseparty in Atlantic City was designed by George. He also provided the boat backdrop for guests' souvenir photographs.

In 1992, he created the logo for the NAME National Houseparty in Philadelphia. He also reproduced one of Edward Hicks' Peaceable Kingdom paintings showing William Penn, the founder of Pennsylvania, signing a peace treaty with the Indians. Then he framed, numbered and signed prints of this miniature reproduction for one of the houseparty souvenirs.

George was elected an International Miniature Artist, (the forerunner of the NAME Academy of Honor) in 1979 and one of his paintings is on permanent loan to the AOH exhibit.

In 1985, he was recognized as Fellow by the International Guild of Miniature Artisans, Ltd. and served on the Board of Directors of the Guild. George felt very fortunate to have been able to make a second career as an artist specializing in miniatures.

ARTISAN: **SCHLUNZ, TERRY**

BUSINESS NAME: Terry Schlunz

IDENTIFICATION MARKS:

TS

CATEGORY:
Accessories: Victorian; Clocks: marbleized; Furniture: handpainted; Paintings; Paper Maché

RECOGNITION:
Miniature Showcase, Fall 1988, pg. 37, 46; *Daily Tribune*, Ames, Iowa

ARTISAN: **SCHMELTZLE, BARRY**

BUSINESS NAME: Schmeltzle Miniatures

IDENTIFICATION MARKS:

BLS B. Schmeltzle — Printed

B. Schmeltzle — Engraved on brass pieces

B.+S. Schmeltzle — Back/bottom jointly worked pieces including petit point

CATEGORY:
Cameras; Furniture; Kaleidoscope; Optical; Telescope

HONORS:
IGMA Artisan 1984, Fellow 1987; Exhibits: Toy & Miniature Museum of Kansas City; The Carole & Barry Kaye Museum of Miniatures, Los Angeles, California; The California Institute of Art Miniature Museum

RECOGNITION:
Nutshell News, Jan. 1985, pg. 79; Jan. 1987, pg. 94-95; Jul. 1994, pg. 43; *Miniature Gazette*, Fall 1983, pg. 56-57; *Focus Magazine*, San Luis Obispo Telegram-Tribune, Feb. 11, 1984, Cover, pg. 12-13

BIOGRAPHY:
Barry Schmeltzle attended Brooks Institute of Photography and has a BS in Graphic Arts from California Polytechnic State University. Barry has been making miniatures since 1981. Many pieces are joint efforts with his wife, Sharon, who does micro-petit point for furniture and room screens in one-inch and ½-inch scale.

ARTISAN: **SCHMELTZLE, SHARON**

BUSINESS NAME: Schmeltzle Miniatures

IDENTIFICATION MARKS:

SS — 1982-1984

SCS S — 1984 to present

B.+S. Schmeltzle — Back/bottom jointly worked pieces, including petit point

SCHMELTZLE, SHARON, continued

CATEGORY:

Needlepoint; Needlework

HONORS:

IGMA Artisan, 1984; Fellow, 1987; First place petit point, Golden Thimble Needlework Exhibition, Los Angeles, 1985; Exhibits: Toy & Miniature Museum of Kansas City; The Carole & Barry Kaye Museum of Miniatures, Los Angeles, California; The California Institute of Art Miniature Museum

RECOGNITION:

Nutshell News, Jan. 1985, pg. 79; Jan. 1987, pg. 94-95; Jul. 1994, pg. 43; *Miniature Gazette*, Fall 1983, pg. 56-57; *Focus Magazine*, San Luis Obispo Telegram-Tribune, Feb. 11, 1984, Cover, pg. 12-13

BIOGRAPHY:

Sharon Schmeltzle has been doing needlework since a 1973 visit to Greece and has been working on miniature needlework pieces since 1981. Much of her work is combined with husband Barry's woodworking on miniature furniture and screens.

Sharon has worked almost exclusively with silk thread on 60 mesh silk gauze since 1985. She has done a number of miniature double-sided screens similar to Chinese double-sided embroidery, as well as many other highly detailed delicate pieces.

ARTISAN: **SCHOENBERGER, YAHNA**

BUSINESS NAME: Imagineering by Yahna

IDENTIFICATION MARKS:

1979 to present

CATEGORY:

Art: folk; Folk Art; Holiday Items; Toys

HONORS:

IGMA Fellow

RECOGNITION:

Nutshell News, Nov. 1989, pg. 91, Show Scene; Jan. 1990, pg. 83, Show Scene; Jun. 1990, pg. 65, Show Scene; May 1992, pg. 63, 64, Show Scene; Jun. 1992, pg. 65, Show Scene; Oct. 1992, pg. 62, Show Scene; *Miniature Collector*, Vol. 16, No. 1, Spring 1993, pg. 12-15; *Miniatures Showcase*, Winter 1990, pg. 44, 46, 48-49, 71; Fall 1991, pg. 16, 35, 37; Spring 1992, pg. 21; Nov. 1992, Cover, pg. 38, 78

BIOGRAPHY:

Yahna Seip Schoenberger graduated from Drexel Institute of Technology with Bachelor of Science and Master of Science degrees. Her curriculum electives included courses in art education and interior design. It was while making interior design models that her interest in miniatures was originally kindled. For nine years she participated in the annual miniature room competition at the Philadelphia Flower Show. She has been both a collector and artisan of miniatures for more than 25 years.

Her affiliations include membership in the National Association of Miniature Enthusiasts since its founding year, and the International Guild of Miniature Artisans.

Her first endeavors concentrated upon wholesale production for some of the pioneer miniature specialty shops such as Beehive Studio and Miniature Makers Workshop. She has taught courses in miniature room construction and accessories, both as multi-evening classes and workshops/roundtables.

She started to wholesale her products in the early 1970's, and since 1980, she has limited her selling activity to retail shows and direct mail.

ARTISAN: **SCHOONMAKER, BOBBIE**

BUSINESS NAME: Small Ideas

IDENTIFICATION MARKS:

Some unmarked

Handprinted, black or gold ink

Metal stamp

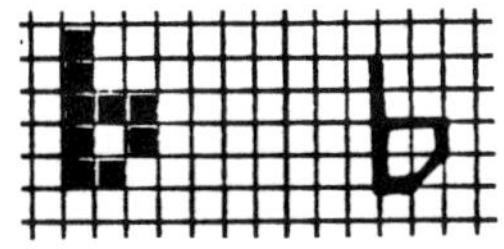

Stitched into design

CATEGORY:

Needlepoint; Needlework

HONORS:

IGMA Fellow 1987

RECOGNITION:

Nutshell News; Miniature Collector

AUTOBIOGRAPHY:

My early childhood was spent in a suburb of Chicago where I remember my parents taking me to the city to see Colleen Moore's Fairy Castle exhibited at the Museum of Science and Industry. I fell in love with the tiny things contained within it and that love has continued to this day. Collecting miniatures officially didn't begin for me until the late 70's, although diminutive objects were often safely tucked in my pockets as a child. I expect that if I had daughters instead of three sons I would have "been hooked" sooner. However, when choosing Matchbox cars for the boys, I always selected the ones with the finest detail!

In the late 70's, I attended my first miniature show and began collecting sterling silver pieces. I then decided to protect my investment and make a silver shop to house my pieces so they wouldn't get lost. Our dining room table was my workshop and I could tell by my husband's condescending tone each evening "That's very nice, dear," that he thought I was losing my mind!

In the meantime, my good friend, Maggie Urciuoli, and I started going to miniature shows together. It was at this point that I saw needlepoint worked in one-inch scale and really got excited. I had designed full-size needlepoint for years so this was something I could relate to much better than making furniture and roomboxes. Maggie, on the other hand, was making furniture for her daughter's dollhouse and loved it, so we teamed up and made a few pieces of furniture with petit point, supposedly for the dollhouse. In the spring we took these pieces to the IGMA Show in New York City to shop for wallpaper, fabric and accessories. Virginia Merrill, noted author and miniature craftsman, saw and admired our work and encouraged us to make pieces to sell. Thus, *Small Ideas* was born. In the coming months Gini was not only our first customer but our mentor. She inspired us and also helped us decide to which shows we should apply. The first show we ever did was the 1982 IGMA show. We were extremely nervous and simply couldn't believe that any one would want to buy what we made.

In 1983, I was awarded an Artisan certificate in the field of petit point and in 1987 honored with Fellow status. Our work has appeared in needlepoint magazines in the US and Europe, on postcards and in newspapers, miniature magazines and museums.

Answers to the most commonly asked questions: Constructing slippers not stitching them, is my most challenging task. The average amount of time to stitch a piece is about 10 hours, not counting finishing. I try to stitch an average of 5 hours a day. I work on silk gauze with mesh sizes from 40 to 72 stitches per inch (1,600 to 5,184 stitches per square inch) using silk or cotton thread and a quilting needle. Yes, I use a magnifying light and no, I'm not going blind!

See "Maggie Urciuoli"

ARTISAN: **SCHUCKMAN, BARBARA**

BUSINESS NAME: By Barb

IDENTIFICATION MARKS:

1978 to 1980–1980 to 1983
Stick on Dots

1st 3 1983 to 1992 — 1993 to 1994 — 1995
Header card attached to plastic bag with piece inside

CATEGORY:

Accessories; Ceramics; Dishes: ceramics; Food; Furniture: contemporary; Holiday Items; Judaica

RECOGNITION:

Nutshell News, Jul. 1983, Cover; Nov. 1988, pg. 48-51, "Judaic Miniatures 'By Barb'," Terry Yacona; Oct. 1994, pg. 54; *International Dolls House News*, Vol. 25, No. 1, Spring 1995, pg. 5, 25, "Passover - A Jewish Spring Festival," Barb Schuckman; *New York Times*, Jan. 1, 1989, pg. 5; *Washington Jewish Week*, Dec. 7, 1989, pg. 35; *The Jewish Week,* Feb. 3, 1995, pg. 19; *The Jewish Press*, Sept. 25, 1981, pg. 6; *Miniatures Showcase; The Miniature Magazine*, Winter 1991; *Gift Reporter*, Oct. 1989, pg. 46; *Creative Crafts & Miniatures*, Dec. 1982, pg. 63

AUTOBIOGRAPHY:

I majored in art in high school as well as Boston University, and received a BS degree in Education from Hofstra University in New York. I also attended Queens College where I started my Masters in art education. I received my first dollhouse in 1976 and started handcrafting miniatures and selling at shows in 1978. In 1979, I joined NAME and have since been a board member of the South Shore Miniature Enthusiasts Club, President of the North Shore Miniature Society, a founding board member of CIMTA, President of MIAA in 1991-1992, and founding member of the American Guild of Judaic Art.

ARTISAN: **SCOGIN, SUSAN**

BUSINESS NAME: Susan Scogin Miniature Figures, 1985 to present
Susan Scogin Editions, Ltd., 1992 to present

IDENTIFICATION MARKS:

1985 to present
Limited Edition pieces numbered (piece/edition)

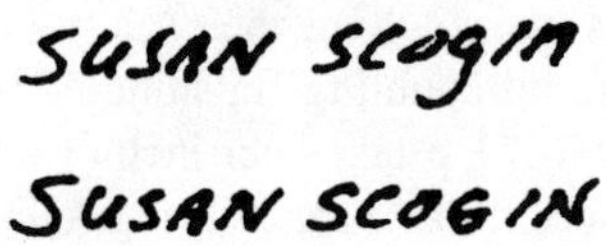

In black ink
Incised back diaper area, stomach area, or underside thigh area
Upper/Lower case letters may be mixed

In black ink
Incised bottom of foot

CATEGORY:

Dolls: babies, children, originals, porcelain; Figures

HONORS:

IGMA Artisan, 1988; Fellow, 1992; NIADA Artist; Bernice Stevens Award, 1987; Exhibits: Toy & Miniature Museum of Kansas City; The Carole & Barry Kaye Museum of Miniatures, Los Angeles, California; Society of American Miniaturists Collection, Dallas, Texas; Salon International Parisien de la Miniature

SCOGIN, SUSAN, continued

RECOGNITION:

Nutshell News, Vol. 18, No. 1, Jan. 1988, pg. 50-53; Dec. 1990; *Contemporary Doll*, Vol. 3, No. 2, Dec. 1992, pg. 78-80; *Miniatures Showcase,* Jun. 1987; Sept. 1989; *Miniature Collector*, Sept. 1989; *New Orleans Times Picayune*, Nov. 1991

AUTOBIOGRAPHY:

My educational background consisted of a BFA at Louisiana State University, Baton Rouge, LA, 1973 and Graduate study 1975; with additional education at U.N.O. New Orleans, LA, 1971-73; Atlanta School of Art, Atlanta, GA, 1968-69, and the University of Southwestern Louisiana, Lafayette, LA, 1967-68.

My work has appeared in the following shows which are juried or invitational, primarily sales events and I was either a regular or frequent exhibitor; IGMA, New York City, TAMS, Anaheim, CA and NIADA. I have attended miniature shows held in various parts of the country, including Gulf South Miniature & Dollhouse Event, New Orleans, LA, and Walt Disney World Doll and Teddy Bear Convention, Florida, and the National Institute of American Doll Artists annual exhibit.

ARTISAN: SCOTT, DEA

IDENTIFICATION MARKS:

Dea Tag sewn on back, Certificate of Authenticity included

CATEGORY:

Needlepoint; Needlework

HONORS:

IGMA Artisan 1992

AUTOBIOGRAPHY:

I have been sewing full-scale needlepoint and collecting museum quality miniatures since 1982. It was only natural for me to combine my two loves and to start sewing miniature museum quality needlepoint in 1989. My most famous pieces are "The Hunt," "Father Christmas," and "English Country Cottage," all 54 count needlepoint pillows 1 1/8 inch square. I received my artisan status with IGMA in March of 1992. My pieces can been seen at Auntie Bea's Miniatures in Calgary, Canada, and at shows.

ARTISAN: SCOTT, PAMELA R.

BUSINESS NAME: Pamela Scott Miniatures

IDENTIFICATION MARKS:

PAM SCOTT
1990-'92

CATEGORY:

Accessories; Art: folk; Folk Art; Furniture: handpainted; Holiday Items; Porcelain; Toys

SCOTT, PAMELA R., continued

RECOGNITION:

Miniatures Showcase, Vol. 6, No. 4, Fall 1991, pg. 82; Vol. 7, No. 1, Winter 1992, pg. 27; Vol. 7, No. 4, Nov. 1992, pg. 35, 41, 72

AUTOBIOGRAPHY:

Following a tradition of artists in my family, I became deeply involved with art and with crafts at a very young age, enthusiastically drawing everything I saw or imagined, creating puppets, painted glass, doll clothes, holiday decorations, whatever struck my fancy. After my husband and I purchased our first house in 1972 I began to indulge in my love of interior design, happily painting the walls, lampshades, curtains, and kitchen cabinets of our homes with a variety of florals, leaves and sea shells. I enrolled in a wide range of art courses, but soon discovered that my true love was decorative painting and folk art. The encouragement of others, however, had me designing and creating a line of painted and embellished clothing which I sold wholesale to a number of retail shops. I taught classes in this as well as other crafts for several years.

In 1988, I stepped into my local miniatures shop for the first time, picked up a copy of *Interior Design in Miniature*, and knew that I'd come home! After a period of absorbing everything I could and attempting to do it all, I settled comfortably once again into decorative painting and folk art, but this time in miniature. I began to sell my work in 1989, to miniatures giants, Ann Masselli and Judeé Williamson, as well as to several collectors, who encouraged me to offer my pieces at a wholesale trade show in early 1992. Today, my work is sold by dealers in the US, Canada, England, and New Zealand, and I am pleased to be one of the artisans featured in the miniatures catalog published by My Sister's Shoppe. I continue to teach miniature classes and to develop new techniques and new designs.

ARTISAN: **SCOTT-LANGLEY, DAVID**

BUSINESS NAME: Michael Martin Ltd. (1981-1986)

IDENTIFICATION MARKS:

Saddles & Harnesses unmarked

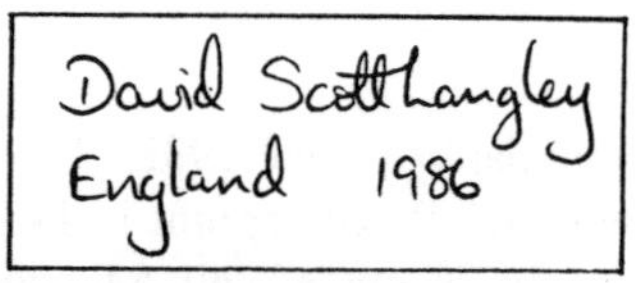

Furniture

CATEGORY:

Furniture; Luggage; Saddles

HONORS:

Highly Commended, Save The Children Fund Miniaturist Competition, 1987; Exhibit: A World in Miniature Museum, Oban, Scotland

RECOGNITION:

Nutshell News, Jul. 1985, pg. 68-70

AUTOBIOGRAPHY:

In 1981, the Saddlery Company for which I was bridle shop manager, Michael Martin Ltd. was hit by a recession. In our efforts to find other work for our craftsmen, we were introduced to the miniatures world and very quickly discovered that the one product missing was leather. We quickly developed a range of furniture incorporating leather; in particular our buttoned, leather upholstered sofas and chairs. We trained our craftsmen to be able to produce each other's ranges so that when there was a rush order, it could be produced with the minimum of delay. Our furniture went to the USA, Japan, and Europe as well as the UK and Australia.

Sadly, due to the illness of the proprietor, the company ceased trading in 1986 although I continued to make miniatures for sale until 1987. Since then I have made occasional pieces, mainly as gifts or for my own collection.

SCOTT-LANGLEY, DAVID, continued

In 1987, I was given a Highly Commended in the Furniture Section of the Save The Children Fund Miniaturist Competition. Several of my pieces were selected for the Wedding Day Dollhouse and for the AMREF Dollhouse. I also have some furniture and luggage on permanent display at A World in Miniature Museum, Oban, Scotland.

ARTISAN: **SCOTT-LANGLEY, HELEN**

BUSINESS NAME: Minikin Masters

IDENTIFICATION MARKS:

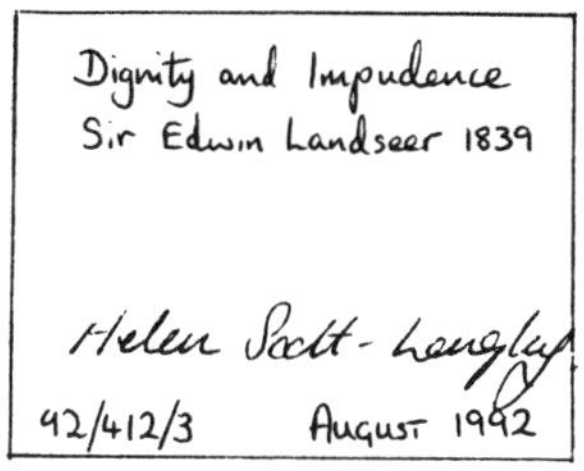

CATEGORY:

Paintings

HONORS:

2nd Prize, Save The Children Fund Miniaturist Competition, 1987; Exhibit: A World in Miniature Museum, Oban, Scotland

AUTOBIOGRAPHY:

I studied art up to the age of 16 at school. Apart from an occasional drawing, it was not until my husband suggested that I try some miniature paintings for his miniatures business in 1986 that I became hooked and have been painting ever since. My niche in the market was the reproduction in miniature of pictures by masters such as Landseer, Constable, Turner, Renoir, Monet, etc., studying and learning their techniques as I went along. Now, my pictures are sold in the UK, Europe and the USA. In 1987, I was awarded 2nd prize in the Paintings section of the Save the Children Fund Miniaturist Competition. Some of my paintings are also on permanent display at A World in Miniature Museum, Oban, Scotland.

ARTISAN: **SCRIBNER, JEAN**

BUSINESS NAME: Jean's Wee Things

IDENTIFICATION MARKS:

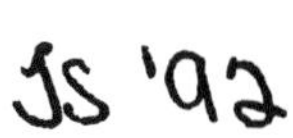

CATEGORY:

Accessories; Flowers and Plants; Kits; Leatherwork; Luggage; Photography; Toys

RECOGNITION:

Nutshell News, Feb. 1992, pg. 67

ARTISAN: **SCRIMGEOUR, MURRAY**

IDENTIFICATION MARKS:

 1985 to present   MS 1992 to present

CATEGORY:

Decoys; Furniture

HONORS:

IGMA Artisan

AUTOBIOGRAPHY:

I have been involved in miniatures since 1985 strictly as a hobby, however local people are now interested in buying my work. Carving is what I enjoy doing so most of my furniture is period furniture with carving. Carving and painting miniature decoys also is very enjoyable for me.

I have attended the Guild School, Castine, Maine, for several years and plan to continue.

ARTISAN: **SCULPHER, DAVID**

BUSINESS NAME: Objects and Things

IDENTIFICATION MARKS:

CATEGORY:

Art: objects

HONORS:

Institute of Theatre Designers, London

AUTOBIOGRAPHY:

I take the inspiration for my work from the many years designing decor and lighting for the Theatre, mostly in England. Venues include the Royal Opera House, the Royal Shakespeare Company and many Musicals and Plays. But possibly the most important lesson taken from all those years of experience was the art of creating atmosphere, which can now be applied to my models. All the work is placed heavily in Victorian and Dickensian London, my favorite period.

Since leaving the theatre and England in 1975, I find the charm of Amsterdam is the perfect environment in which to continue my work.

ARTISAN: **SEEBER, CARRIE**

BUSINESS NAME: Olde Mountain Miniatures

IDENTIFICATION MARKS:

Windows unmarked

OLDE MOUNTAIN MINIATURES

Printed ribbon label on backside

SEEBER, CARRIE, continued

CATEGORY:

Needlepoint; Needlework; Windows: leaded stained

HONORS:

IGMA Artisan 1991

RECOGNITION:

Miniatures Catalog, 13th Edition, Cover; *Miniatures Showcase*, Fall 1988, Cover; Winter 1988, pg. 36

AUTOBIOGRAPHY:

I have been making leaded stained windows since about 1984, and things have evolved to the point where I'm doing my own interpretations of some of the Tiffany style windows. I have been specializing in Navajo style needlepoint since 1988, and all the patterns are adapted from authentic rugs, some very old style and some more recent. I became an IGMA Artisan in 1991.

ARTISAN: SEEBER, KEITH DONALD

BUSINESS NAME: Olde Mountain Miniatures

IDENTIFICATION MARKS:

Furniture and Structures

Incised on reverse side
Hardware and Accessories

CATEGORY:

Accessories; Fireplaces; Furniture; Hardware; Kitchen; Lighting; Metal; Pewter; Structures

RECOGNITION:

Miniatures Showcase, Spring 1991, Cover

AUTOBIOGRAPHY:

As I have related to students, "It doesn't take any special aptitudes to produce the pieces to which I affix my signature." Basically a keen eye and steady hands, a lot of horse-sense, and a certain amount of re-creative imagination. The only plus I may have going for me is a lifelong desire to study and portray history on a small scale. My first love is model railroading. All my furniture pieces and structures are either actual piece replication or ideas for structures as they would have appeared at the time in history. Simplicity and authenticity will be found in my pieces. However, I am either going to have to work a lot faster in the miniature business or return in an after life to fulfill all of my mini dreams.

ARTISAN: SEGAN, RISA

BUSINESS NAME: Kew Gardens Miniatures

IDENTIFICATION MARKS:

Some unmarked

Smaller pieces

CATEGORY:

Accessories: floral; Floral Arrangements; Food

SEGAN, RISA, continued

RECOGNITION:

Nutshell News, Vol. 17, No. 7, Jul. 1987, Cover; Vol. 18, No. 10, Oct. 1988, Show Scene; Mar. 1989; Feb. 1992, Show Scene; Vol. 22, No. 2, Oct. 1992, Show Scene; *Miniature Collector*, No. 76, Summer 1992, Show Stoppers

AUTOBIOGRAPHY:

I was born in Brooklyn, NY in 1951. At age 10 my family moved to Glens Falls, NY. Artwork in all forms was encouraged as my mother was a painter and illustrator. However, I preferred modeling clay as a medium. By adolescence, my work in plasticine become smaller and smaller, as my budget and lack of work space, and unfortunately, I wanted to make everything! By high school age, I was creating whole villages in approximate HO scale in plasticine. The temporary nature of the medium eventually forced me to abandon it. I attended Syracuse University and Skidmore College where I acquired a BS degree in Art Education. It was during graduate school, in New York, when I found both my current occupation and miniatures. I received my MPS degree in Art Therapy and Creativity Development from Pratt Institute in 1978. However, it wasn't until 1986 that I began to show and sell my miniatures to any great extent. I have been Director of Activities at Greenpark Care Center in Brooklyn since 1975. It's not just a job, it's an "obsession!" Greenpark is a 400 bed nursing home. Over the years, I've made numerous miniature displays and have given slide shows for the residents. Eventually I hope to be able to travel more distance for shows. I love to travel, but for now, I only have done shows in the Northeast.

ARTISAN: **SELLERS, LUELLA M.**

BUSINESS NAME: Special Sellers

IDENTIFICATION MARKS:

1984 to present

CATEGORY:

Accessories; Candy and/or Sweets; Confectionery; Food

HONORS:

IGMA Artisan

RECOGNITION:

Miniature Gazette, Vol. 15, No. 3, Spring 1987, pg. 62; Vol. 21, No. 2, Winter 1992, pg. 26

AUTOBIOGRAPHY:

I have a BBA degree in accounting and a MBA degree in Business Administration from Memphis State University, Tennessee. Upon graduation, I was hired to work in a CPA office while at the same time, engaging myself in numerous craft projects as a hobby. In 1984, I became interested in miniatures and am now a full-time manufacturer, specializing in confectionery delights and foods in general.

ARTISAN: **SENFT, WILMER L.**

IDENTIFICATION MARKS:

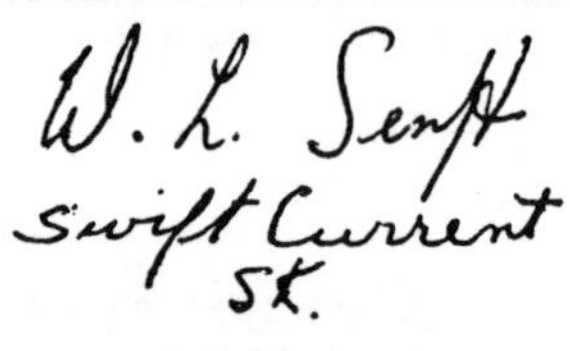

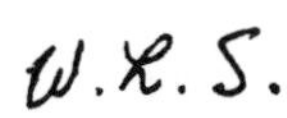

SENFT, WILMER L., continued

CATEGORY:

Lathe Work: hand turned

HONORS:

IGMA Artisan 1994

RECOGNITION:

American Turning Magazine, Sept. 1989

AUTOBIOGRAPHY:

I was born on a farm at Hodgeville, where I lived until I retired to Swift Current in 1993. I have always worked with iron and wood, often making some of the equipment needed on the farm. Making toys and furniture for my children, and now my grandchildren, has been a favorite hobby.

My turning career began in 1984. My work is all done on a general 160 lathe. I use chisels of my own making. Local woods such as caragana, elm, ash, chokecherry, saskatoon and alder are put to use, as well as fruitwoods. For variety, I use walnut, oak and imported hardwoods like African blackwood and Bloodwood. I use materials like bone, nut, some metals and alabaster. As well as doing regular sized pieces, I love to do miniature work. Some of my pieces are in the ¼-inch range.

I am a member of the Saskatchewan Crafts Council, The American Association of Wood Turners and the Swift Current Allied Arts Council. I have had work accepted for exhibition in "Dimensions" each year from 1986 to 1994. I received a Merit Award in 1993. This is the premier exhibition open to all crafts people in Saskatchewan.

In 1987 and 1988, I had three pieces accepted for exhibition for the "6x6x6 Metal and Wood Show" arranged by the Cartwright Gallery of Contemporary and Historical Crafts in Vancouver, BC., Canada. Also in 1988, I had three pieces accepted in the ITOS (International Turned Objects Show) held in the Port of History Museum in Philadelphia, Pennsylvania, and that same year I had two groups of work exhibited in the touring exhibition "Magic of Childhood" sponsored and arranged by the Saskatchewan Arts Council.

In 1989, I was privileged to be one of the few artists who worked on a commission for the Province of Saskatchewan – a gift for Princess Beatrice, daughter of Andrew and Sarah, Duke and Duchess of York. In 1989, I had three pieces in "Games People Play" arranged by the Saskatchewan Craft Council and Festival Saskatoon, which ran in conjunction with the Juex Canada Games in Saskatoon. In that year I contributed an article to the September issue of *American Woodturning Magazine.*

In 1991, The Saskatchewan Arts Board purchased five of my miniature pieces for their permanent collection. I had eight pieces in the 1991 "Thrown, Turned and Blown Goblets" show in the Northwest Gallery of Fine Woodworking in Seattle, Washington. In 1992, I had 16 pieces in the "Goblets" show in this gallery.

In 1993, one of my pieces owned by the Saskatchewan Arts Board was included in a show at the Dunlop Gallery in Regina entitled "Advancing the Media, Craft from the Collection of the Saskatchewan Arts Board."

In 1994, I received an Honorable Mention in "The Wood Show Competition" in Durham, Ontario for one of two pieces accepted to that juried show.

I have attended woodturning symposiums in Saskatoon, Saskatchewan, and Philadelphia, Pennsylvania. I have taken part in workshops conducted by Mike O'Donnel of Scotland and Vic Wood of Australia. In Philadelphia, I demonstrated miniature turning and have also conducted wood turning workshops.

The craft of wood turning has become a very satisfying part of my life.

ARTISAN: **SEQUEIRA, ROBERT G.**

BUSINESS NAME: Robert G. Sequeira – Custom Miniatures

IDENTIFICATION MARKS:

SEQUEIRA, ROBERT G., continued

CATEGORY:

Accessories: wooden; Brasswork; Cannon: Civil War; Kitchenware; Lighting; Metal: handpainted; Metalwork; Toys: wood

AUTOBIOGRAPHY:

I was a tool & die maker for 30 years in the electronics industry. I contracted for 10 years as tool designer in small electronic parts.

ARTISAN: SHAW, DONALD

BUSINESS NAME: Hand Carved By Don Shaw "The Bear"

IDENTIFICATION MARKS:

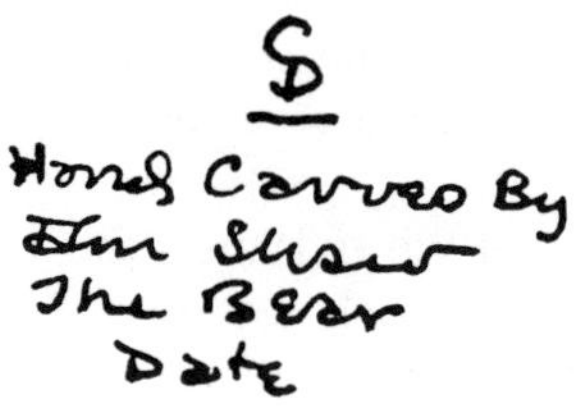

CATEGORY:

Accessories; Furniture

RECOGNITION:

Nutshell News, Sept. 1980, pg. 42; Oct. 1984, pg. 56; Aug. 1987, pg. 69; *Miniature Collector*, No. 20, Aug. 1980, pg. 25; *Miniatures Showcase,* Fall 1988, pg. 33-34, 38, 40, 42; Winter 1988, pg. 48-49; *Miniature Gazette*, Vol. 14, No. 3, Spring 1986, pg. 13

AUTOBIOGRAPHY:

When I was 6, I was sitting on the pump house platform trying to pry open a paint can with a wood carvers chisel I had inherited, when a neighbor, Oscar Peterson, a Swedish woodcarver, came by on his way to visit my folks. He looked at the tools I had and announced to my mother, "If that boy is going to have tools like that, he is going to learn to use them properly." For the next dozen years I learned to carve wood from Mr. Peterson and several of his friends who also taught me numerous and useful things.

For the next 30 years or so, I whacked away at any piece of wood that happened to come my way. So a hobby became a way of picking up a few odd dollars when I was in the service and school, but I never looked on it as much more than a diversion. In the late 1960's and 1970's, I was teaching at the University of Albuquerque when one of my students asked me if I had ever made any dollhouse furniture, as his wife, mother, and mother-in-law were miniature collectors and he would like to give them something special for Christmas. I made them each an 1880's drop front secretary. I didn't think too much about it again until suddenly people were asking if I would make something for them.

My wife and I decided to start a woodcarvers shop. For several years I made both full-size and miniature pieces until one day, when I was trying to load a full-size desk into my van by myself, it suddenly occurred to me that when you consider the cost of materials and the space required for standard size furniture, I could make a better profit on miniatures as well as have more fun producing them.

ARTISAN: SHEA, ROBERT E. & BEVERLY H.

BUSINESS NAME: Shea Miniatures

IDENTIFICATION MARKS:

SHEA, ROBERT E. & BEVERLY H., continued

CATEGORY:
Furniture: handpainted; Nautical: ship models

HONORS:
IGMA Artisan, Fellow (Robert)

RECOGNITION:
Nutshell News

ARTISAN: **SHEPHERD, ANTHONY**

BUSINESS NAME: Brentwood Decor Miniatures

IDENTIFICATION MARKS:

With number of piece

CATEGORY:
Furniture: period; Toys

RECOGNITION:
Doll's House World; International Dolls' House News; Poppenhuizen Magazine

ARTISAN: **SHERRILL, SUSAN I.**

BUSINESS NAME: Miniatures By Sue Sherrill

IDENTIFICATION MARKS:

With year

CATEGORY:
China

HONORS:
Exhibit: Toy & Miniature Museum of Kansas City

RECOGNITION:
Nutshell News; *Miniature Collector; Ann Arbor News*, Michigan; *Hobbies,* Jul. 1982

ARTISAN: **SHERWOOD, ROY**

BUSINESS NAME: Roy Sherwood

IDENTIFICATION MARKS:

With number of piece

SHERWOOD, ROY, continued

CATEGORY:

Furniture: period

RECOGNITION:

Dolls House World, Issue No. 22, pg. 12

JS

ARTISAN: **SHOWALTER, JIM**

BUSINESS NAME: Jim & Sharon Showalter

IDENTIFICATION MARKS:

CATEGORY:

Furniture

RECOGNITION:

Nutshell News, Sept. 1986, pg. 85; May 1991, pg. 26; *Miniatures Showcase*, Mar. 1993, pg. 16

AUTOBIOGRAPHY:

In 1979, while in St. Louis for a doctors appointment, my wife Sharon and I attended our first miniature show. As we walked around with our eyes wide and our mouths open I told her I could make that kind of furniture. Her response was to say that I must be crazy. After we returned home I started to buy some of the Dremel tools and some basswood. A local shop in our area began to buy a few of my pieces off and on.

In 1984, Sharon was chairperson for the PANS club show in Peoria, Illinois. At this show I met Jackie Deiber and showed her a few of my pieces. One was an 11 drawer one-inch scale spice box of cherry. She offered to buy the few pieces I had with me. In 1985, I decided to go into business for myself and started doing a few shows. I now do several shows a year, working mostly in ½-inch scale and beginning in ¼-inch scale. I still do a few pieces in one-inch scale.

My only training was four years of woodshop in high school and some drafting in college, where I learned about scale!

ARTISAN: **SILVER, ROBIN & PATRICIA**

BUSINESS NAME: Mini Marvels

IDENTIFICATION MARKS:

MINI MARVELS

CATEGORY:

Carpets; Rugs; Signs: enameled advertising

ARTISAN: **SIMMS, RICHARD**

BUSINESS NAME: Simms Miniatures

IDENTIFICATION MARKS:

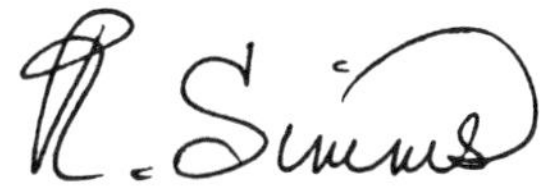

CATEGORY:

Furniture; Silversmith; Tools: hand, shop; Video Tape: how-to

HONORS:

IGMA Artisan

RECOGNITION:

Nutshell News; Miniature Collector, Fall 1986

AUTOBIOGRAPHY:

My father was apprenticed in England in 1922, to a cabinet maker, himself apprenticed in 1858. I came with the family to Williamsburg, Virginia in 1957 where my father did restoration work on the furniture for the Colonial Williamsburg Foundation. After leaving the College of William and Mary in 1970, having majored in Music, I apprenticed to my father, also doing restoration work for the foundation. My training included participating in the restoration of Guston Hall, the John Marshall House, Bacon's Castle and others. In 1975, my father and I started our own business doing both restoration work and miniature copies of furnishings we had either restored or worked on for the foundation.

I have been working on my own since 1984 when my father's health declined. Strangely, his signature and mine were virtually identical so that often I was unable to distinguish one from the other on the older work. I still have all of our acquired tools, including those of the men my father worked with, going all the way back to the 1850's. My work still requires the use of hand tools almost exclusively and most of my antique tools are in daily use. My miniature work is accomplished using the same antique woods as in the original pieces and this will continue as long as the supply we've acquired holds out. Some of these woods were acquired by my father in the 1920's in England while the rest are from a previously undiscovered amount that had been resting undisturbed in a warehouse in Richmond, VA since approximately 1900 or possibly earlier.

ARTISAN: **SIMONE, CONSTANCE**

BUSINESS NAME: Something Different Miniatures (1974 – 1977)

IDENTIFICATION MARKS:

Some unmarked

Brush stroke in color available when marked

CATEGORY:

Accessories: wooden; Books; Clocks; Fireplaces: accessories; Furniture; Mirrors; Tinsmith; Tinware; Toys: Victorian

HONORS:

1st Prize, 3rd Prize Ribbons, Hand Crafted Accessories, Doll House & Miniature Show, Sept. 11-12, 1976, Spring Lake, New Jersey; Exhibit: 27 tinware pieces, The Hitchcock Museum, Riverton, Connecticut, Sept/Oct. 1976

SIMONE, CONSTANCE, continued

RECOGNITION:

Miniature Collector, Jun. 1978, pg. 25; *The Miami Herald*, Feb. 20, 1977, pg. 17-BR; *Inside The World of Miniatures and Dollhouses*, Rosner & Beckerman, McKay Press, 1976, pg. 40-41; *American Period Interiors in Miniature*, Kate Doordan Klavan, Scribner's, 1984

AUTOBIOGRAPHY:

My childhood interest in dollhouses is pretty much covered in the poem "The Doll House" which I wrote in 1977 for the miniature book of my poetry which I put into my catalog that year. My adult interest began in 1971 when I elected to keep some of the more expensive items of dollhouse furniture I'd bought my daughter, then turned 17 and too old for such childish pursuits. I did this in case I should "ever feel the urge to do a dollhouse." It didn't take long to conclude that that dollhouse would be based on a Samuel McIntire house in Salem, Massachusetts but as it might appear in the early 1840's, and I decided that if I found anything was currently available for such a setting, I'd better go ahead and buy it.

I fell in love with life in the 1840's. And eight months into what started out in January 1974 as rather casual miniature making (perfume bottles), I found myself already turning out 20 of the 42 pieces of authentic miniature painted tinware that I eventually worked up just fine for "my period." Consciously or unconsciously, more often than not the miniatures I've made for sale, from the painted tinware and working jack-in-the-boxes I introduced in the 1970's to my more recent shelf clocks with their etched glass designs and empire bureaus added in the 1990's work out just fine for my dollhouse.

While my daughter claims she never did return to doll housing, when I stored my granddaughter's dollhouse things at my apartment because they were moving to Paris, I couldn't help but notice that her collection takes up at least as much space as my own!

ARTISAN: **SIMONS CAROL**

BUSINESS NAME: Medallion Miniatures

IDENTIFICATION MARKS:

Right shoulder plate or bottom of foot with year

Smaller pieces on right shoulder plate

CATEGORY:

Figures; Porcelain

RECOGNITION:

Dolls in Miniature, The Magazine, Vol. 11, No. 4, Winter 1992-1993, Cover, pg. 21-24

AUTOBIOGRAPHY:

My formal education includes a BS in Mathematics. I taught mathematics, mostly algebra, for eight years. I quit teaching to start an engineering firm in 1985, and ended this business in 1992 to work on miniatures full-time. My interest in doll making and miniatures began in 1982, after years of preoccupation in various art forms and mediums. I began teaching classes in making miniatures in 1985. A poetic profile appears with photos of my work on pages 21 through 24 of Volume 11, Issue 4 of *Dolls in Miniature, The Magazine.*

ARTISAN: **SIMPSON, JUNE**

IDENTIFICATION MARKS:

Marks may include date

June Simpson   J. Simpson

CATEGORY:

Furniture

HONORS:

IGMA Artisan, 1988; Fellow; Marjorie Naylor Award, Canada's Juried Show 1990, 1991; 5, 1st Place Ribbons, Canada's Juried Show 1990; 6, 1st Place Ribbons, Canada's Juried Show 1991; 2, 1st Place Ribbons, Markham Fair 1988, 1989, 1990

RECOGNITION:

Miniature Collector, Summer 1990, pg. 20-23; Winter 1990, pg. 26-29; Spring 1991, pg. 7-9; Spring 1992, pg. 4-5

AUTOBIOGRAPHY:

I am a teacher by profession and have nine years attendance at the Guild School, Castine, Maine behind me as well as attending workshops taught by John Ottwell, Jim Dorsett, Art Russell and Hal Watson. I've twice acted as a judge at Canada's Juried Show of Miniatures in 1989 and 1992. Throughout the years of 1987 to 1993 I've taught carpentry in miniature at the Haliburton School of Fine Arts, Haliburton, Ontario, Canada; Guild School, Castine, Maine; The Daisy House Dollhouse Shop, Toronto, Ontario; NAME Gathering, Region M, Ontario, Canada; M.E. London-B Spring Workshop; Miniature Makers Workshop, Royal Oak, Michigan; GNOME Club, and several Canadian Miniature Workshops as well as being represented in the following shows: Ridgehouse Museum, Wallaceburg Museum, Chatham Museum, MET Show Toronto, Canada's Juried Show, Markham Fair and the Guild School. I am a member of NAME, IGMA, and Miniature Enthusiasts of London, Ontario-B.

ARTISAN: **SIMPSON, POLLIE** (Submitted by Ellen Blauer, & Toy & Miniature Museum of Kansas City)

IDENTIFICATION MARKS:

Marks may include date

P. Simpson

Printed in gold

CATEGORY:

Clocks: handpainted; Dinnerware: handpainted; Furniture: handpainted, period; Screens, handpainted

RECOGNITION:

Nutshell News, Vol. 14, No 7, Jul. 1984, pg. 44-45, “Pollie Simpson's Golden Brush,” Kristin Helberg

ARTISAN: **SINNETT, DOREEN**

BUSINESS NAME: Doreen Sinnett
Doreen Sinnett Designs, Inc.

IDENTIFICATION MARKS:

© DS 1975 — Backward when hand screened

© DOREEN SINNETT DESIGNS 1975 — Both marks printed on fabric dolls

DS 1980 — Incised back of head below hair line with year

© SINNETT 1980 — Incised back of head under wig with year

© Doreen Sinnett 1986
© Doreen Sinnett Designs, Inc. 1978
Printed material

CATEGORY:

Books: clothes pin dolls, doll dress patterns; Dolls: clothespin, original, rag; Molds; Rugs: punch needle patterns; Supplies: doll making

RECOGNITION:

Nutshell News, Vol. 15, No. 10, 1985, pg. 88-90; *The Scale Cabinetmaker*, 1975; *Dolls In Miniature*, Vol. 1, No. 1, 1991, pg. 21-23; *Small Talk*, Vol. 5, No. 3, 1980, pg. 4-7, 12-13; *Doll Reader*, Feb/Mar. 1990; Musée de Poupées, *Poupées Créations d' heir et d'aujourd'hui*, Jun/Sept. 1988

AUTOBIOGRAPHY:

I majored in Art in Toronto, Canada in the 1940's. My husband, Jack, and I worked for large department stores in Los Angeles doing photo retouching, paste-up and production. When he passed away in 1973, I turned to creating miniature punch-needle rug patterns. I published a Dress Pattern Book in 1979, and then created original dollhouse dolls from Sculpy. Time did not allow me to learn from others, so all the mold making and porcelain techniques are completely self-taught. I have released some of my molds and patterns for others to use, but my finished porcelain dolls are sold only at shows.

ARTISAN: **SIRETT, PETER J.**

BUSINESS NAME: Quality Miniatures

IDENTIFICATION MARKS:

CATEGORY:

Furniture: veneered

ARTISAN: **SIRKIS, SUSAN B.**

BUSINESS NAME: The Wish Booklets

IDENTIFICATION MARKS:

SBS '93

CATEGORY:

Dolls: costuming, original, portrait; Publications: how-to; Researcher: material; Video Tapes: how-to; Writer

SIRKIS, SUSAN B., continued

HONORS:

NAME AOH; Honorary Chairman 1986, "Come to the Mini Mardi Gras," Gulf South Miniature & Dollhouse Event, New Orleans, Louisiana

BIOGRAPHY:

Susan has been a doll maker and collector since she grew too old to play with dolls. Her collection began when she refused to dispose of dolls she had played with. Susan makes miniature dolls of fabric and wire. As a fashion historian Susan has written more than 33 Wish Booklets of doll patterns and completed several videos. Susan is a consultant for several firms which manufacture collector and toy dolls. She was past President of UFDC.

ARTISAN: **SISSON, LAURIE H.**

BUSINESS NAME: L. Sisson – doll artist

IDENTIFICATION MARKS:

Incised back of head under wig, Letter of authenticity provided when requested

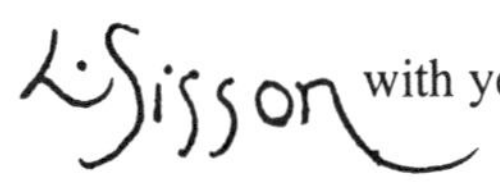
with year

CATEGORY:

Dolls: original

HONORS:

IGMA Artisan

RECOGNITION:

Nutshell News Jul. 1994, pg. 46-48, "Understanding Characters," Denise Pritchett; *Dollhouse Miniatures,* Calendar, Dec. 1993; *Dolls in Miniature*, Vol. 1, No. 4, Winter 1991/92, pg. 23-28; *Miniatures Showcase*, Fall 1989, pg. 12; Spring 1990, pg. 26; Fall 1990, pg. 82; Summer 1991, pg. 20-21

AUTOBIOGRAPHY:

The pieces I create are individually sculpted characters, one-of-a-kind. My goal was to produce a quality product. I wanted to improve the status of dolls to make it easier for miniaturists to place them in dollhouses since they would either fall over or look out of place as they stood on a doll stand.

I feel my invention, "The Foot" which allows dollhouse dolls to stand without a doll stand, wax or any attachment has been an advancement since it is part of the doll and has achieved the goal set. I produce The Foot in men's, women's and children's sizes, in three scales, and hands in two scales.

I graduated from the University of Alaska, but I remain a firm believer in our family motto, "Nothing you learn is ever wasted," as it was bits and pieces of knowledge which created The Foot.

ARTISAN: **SKINNER, AMANDA E.**

BUSINESS NAME: Amanda E. Skinner

IDENTIFICATION MARKS:

SKINNER, AMANDA E., continued

CATEGORY:

Animals: rocking; Dolls: porcelain

ARTISAN: **SLOMINSKI, NORMA**

BUSINESS NAME: Norma Slominski
Heirlooms in Miniature

IDENTIFICATION MARKS

CATEGORY:

Furniture

HONORS:

IGMA Fellow 1984

RECOGNITION:

Nutshell News, Mar. 1983, pg. 44; Jan. 1984, Cover, pg. 8; Sept. 1984, pg. 73, Show Scene; *Through The Looking Glass*, Ann Ruble, Boynton and Associates, Inc., 1984, pg. 67, 84

AUTOBIOGRAPHY:

In 1979, my husband and I decided to attend the IGMA show to see what miniatures were all about. It was love at first sight! It seemed impossible that people could make such wonderful things. I went home and decided to build a dollhouse, then it came time to furnish it. Knowing next to nothing about it, I spent many hours reading woodworking books and seeking advice from local miniature shops. After making a few pieces, I took them to the shop and they asked me if I'd be interested in selling them. The furniture sold well and thus began my career. I established my own business, "Heirlooms in Miniature," did a few shows a year and to my surprise was accepted as an artisan in the Guild. The following year, I was elected as a Fellow. I sold my work from 1979 to 1985, until I needed a steady income to put my son through college. My last son graduated in June 1992, and now I'm working to re-establish my career in furniture building, again.

ARTISAN: **SMITH, ALICE M.**

BUSINESS NAME: Alice in Miniature Land
ALi – J's Originals

IDENTIFICATION MARKS:

And dated where space available

CATEGORY:

Crocheting; Dolls; Furniture; Roomboxes

AUTOBIOGRAPHY:

I discovered miniatures late in life, through a friend. She was a neighbor when we lived in Virginia. She talked me into buying the dollhouse she had built from a kit, and like so many others, the rest is history.

I have always been creative. As a young girl I was already painting with oils and watercolors. My parents had paintings hanging on their walls, framed, that I had painted at age 5. From that, I quite naturally expanded my interests. Knitting, crocheting, sewing, needlepoint, cross stitch and almost any other craft you can think of, anything and everything that was artistic held my interest.

I guess I can blame Jackie Caron, of House of Caron, for my miniature doll mania. I bought my first kit from her, just to see if I could do it. I was hooked after that! Soon I had to have a kiln and molds so I could do them completely by myself. I also had to try my hand at sculpting original dolls, and I do have a few molds now, of my own sculpting, but I use commercial molds as well.

I thoroughly enjoy everything about miniatures and nothing is too challenging for me to try, but the dolls are my big love and I hope to get some molds or kits of my own sculptures on the market sometime in the near future.

Loving miniature dolls as I do, quite naturally led to my next adventure, and that is publishing a magazine about the miniature dolls, doll artists and collectors. I am the founder of *Dolls in Miniature the Magazine*, which keeps me so busy I have very little time left for making or sculpting my own dolls. I do only about three shows a year, now.

ARTISAN: **SMITH, ALTHEA J.**

BUSINESS NAME: A. J. S. Productions

IDENTIFICATION MARKS:

1990 to 1991

1992 to present

CATEGORY:

Christmas; Confectionery; Dolls: fairies; Holiday Items; Nativity Sets; Porcelain: Santas; Snow Babies

AUTOBIOGRAPHY:

The primary types of miniatures I make are dolls, creatures, and fairies. I also make porcelain Santas, Snow Babies, and Nativity sets. In my spare time, I help my daughter, Christy Davison with some of her projects. I make the roses for her wedding cakes, and help her with many of the other items that she makes.

I became interested in miniatures because of my daughter. Christy is an avid collector of miniatures and used to be a cake designer. When she became very ill and was confined to a wheelchair, she could no longer make full-size cakes and decided to make them in miniature. Because of her condition, she could not do shows by herself, so I accompanied her, and the miniature business started.

My dolls, creatures and fairies are made primarily from Jean Pardina and Parker Levi molds, but I am working on some original sculptures, and hope to be able to patent some of them soon. My name is Althea Joan Smith, and consequently the name of our company, A.J.S. Productions, however, my mark is AJV, Althea J. Valentine, my maiden name.

see "Christy L. Davison"

ARTISAN: **SMITH, GRACE S.**

BUSINESS NAME: Grace S. Smith, Botanicals

IDENTIFICATION MARKS:

All 1989 to present

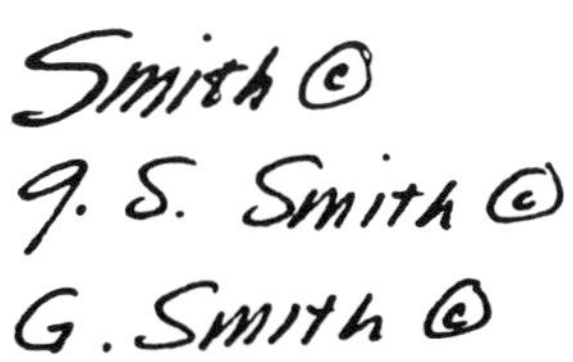

Front of piece, with year

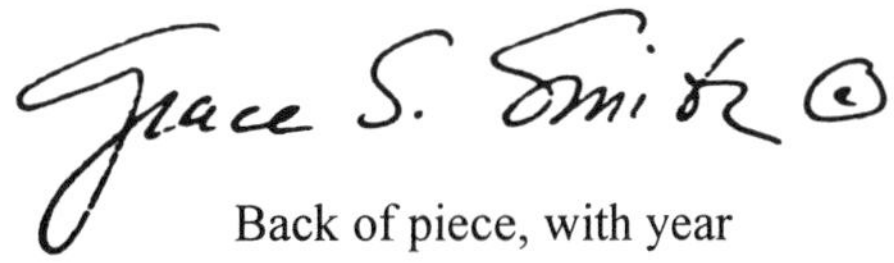

Back of piece, with year

SMITH, GRACE S., continued

CATEGORY:

Art: fine; Paintings

HONORS:

IGMA Artisan 1991

RECOGNITION:

Nutshell News, Nov. 1991

ARTISAN: SMITH, HARRY

BUSINESS NAME: Barnstable Originals

IDENTIFICATION MARKS:

On early painted pieces, clear decal showing business name and address of Perrysville, Indiana

Silver

Furniture

CATEGORY:

Author; Books; Furniture: period; Illustrator; Room Settings; Silversmith; Writer

HONORS:

NAME AOH; Who's Who in American Art; Contemporary Authors; Exhibits: Coe-Kerr Gallery, New York City; Farnsworth Museum of Art, Rockland, Maine; Toy and Miniature Museum of Kansas City, Kansas City, Missouri; Gibbes Art Gallery, Charleston, South Carolina; Mystic Seaport, Mystic, Connecticut; Essex Institute, Salem, Massachusetts; Evansville Museum of Art, Evansville, Indiana; Marshall Field Art Gallery, Chicago, Illinois; Colby College Museum of Art, Waterville, Maine; Indianapolis Museum of Art, Indianapolis, Indiana; Maine State Museum, Augusta, Maine; Public House, Sturbridge, Massachusetts; Kokusai Art Galleries, Tokyo, Japan; Ellis Memorial Show (Center for Arts), Boston, Massachusetts; Neiman Marcus Galleries, Dallas, New York, Chicago, and San Francisco

RECOGNITION:

Nutshell News, Jan. 1990, pg. 70-78; *Nutshell News Calendar*, 1992, Cover & Nov.; *Miniature Collector*, Spring 1990, pg. 29-31, Cover; *Architectural Digest; New York Magazine; McCall's; Better Homes and Gardens; Grit; Hobbies; Creative Crafts; Art in Auction; Washington University Magazine*; *The Art of Making Furniture in Miniature,* Harry Smith, Kalmbach; *Down East*, Dec. 1989, pg. 56-57; *Crafts of America*, Harper & Row; *Complete Book of Miniatures*, Crown; *Yankee Way With Wood*, Berkshire House; *Miniatures*, Houghton Mifflin; *Brown Co. Artists,* Northway & Reinwaldt; *American Period Interiors in Miniature*, Kate Doordan Klavan, Scribner's, 1984; *Traditional Crafts in America*, Random House; *The World of Miniatures*, McKay

BIOGRAPHY:

Harry Smith has studied art at St. John's Academy, architecture at Washington University, Goldsmithing at The Gemological Institute of America and fine art at The Chicago Academy of Fine Arts.

He began creating miniatures in 1959, selling to stores such as Marshall Field and F.A.O. Schwarz. In 1960 he and his wife, Marsha, published his first retail catalog and he has since created miniatures for many of the nation's major museums and numerous collectors world wide.

Mr. Smith has written and illustrated several books including *The Art of Making Furniture in Miniature.* This definitive work is known as the bible in the miniature world.

In 1989, Harry began making a line of miniatures cast in precious metals. These works are delicately carved sculptures in sterling silver, bronze and gold, several of which are encrusted with precious stones.

Since beginning his career in the 1950's, he has been a major force in bringing miniatures to an accepted art form. His works not only appear in museums but his one man shows at galleries such as the prestigious Coe Kerr Gallery in New York City have introduced miniatures to the fine art collector. Berry Tracy, curator of New York's Metropolitan Museum of Art, has described Harry's miniature creations as, "Unequaled in his generation of miniature furniture artists. His meticulous attention to detail has the gem like quality and mechanical intrigue of the precious works of Carl Fabergé." Most recently he was chosen by *Early American Life* as one of the nation's top 100 traditional craftsmen.

Through out his career Harry Smith has strived to make each of his creations better than the last. If you ask him what piece is his best, he replies, "The next one."

ARTISAN: **SMITH, JUDY**

BUSINESS NAME: Judy's Littles

IDENTIFICATION MARKS:

All 1984 to present

JUDY'S LITTLES YR J/S YR JAS YR

CATEGORY:

Figures: fantasy

HONORS:

IGMA Artisan

RECOGNITION:

Nutshell News, Feb. 1989, pg. 69; Dec. 1990, pg. 54-56; *Miniatures Showcase*, Winter 1989, pg. 24; Fall 1991, pg. 72; Spring 1992, pg. 42-43; *Miniature Gazette*, Fall 1991, pg. 20; Fall 1992, pg. 60

AUTOBIOGRAPHY:

I started working with Fimo and Sculpey about 1980, making bears as jewelry. From there I was asked to do a sleeping baby, followed by little girls for a year or so, finally settling into the fantasy world of Bunnies and Mice, about 1987.

I am self-taught for the most part, picking up hints from very generous people here and there. I have been getting my work finer and thinner as time passes and am continuing to learn new things each time I sit down to work out a problem with a new critter.

ARTISAN: **SMITH, KAYE**

BUSINESS NAME: Kaye Jones Originals, (Pre 1985)
Smith-Halverson Enterprises, (1987 to 1992)
Kaye Smith's Miniatures, (1992 to Present)

IDENTIFICATION MARKS:

KJ '81 Kaye 1992

SMITH, KAYE, continued

CATEGORY:

Flowers and Plants; Kits: plant; Plants: handpainted; Porcelain: wheel thrown

RECOGNITION:

Nutshell News, May 1990, Cover; Jun. 1991; Jul. 1992; Jan. 1993, pg. 77; *Miniatures Showcase*, Summer 1990, pg. 4, 18, 26, 30, 37, 68; Fall 1990, Cover; Spring 1991, pg. 62; Summer 1991, pg. 28, 63; Nov. 1992, pg. 30-31; Jan 1993, Cover, pg. 3, 16, 30-33, 38-39; *Miniature Dealer*, Apr. 1991, pg. 14; Jun. 1991, Cover

AUTOBIOGRAPHY:

I began my career as a miniaturist by making plants almost as soon as I discovered miniatures. I was dazzled by the skill of the artists who made them. I was not happy with the available plants, so I bought a lovely book on making floral tape plants and set to work. I soon learned there were serious limitations to using floral tape, and was feeling frustrated until I noticed a roll of masking tape and that lovely creative little angel voice said, "I wonder if that will work." Well, it did and many years thousands of leaves and hundreds of plants later, I'm still reaching for the perfection of the exquisite miniatures created by other outstanding artists. I have learned there are no limitations to the realism that can be achieved. My hope is that I can help people notice the incredible detail and beauty of the plant kingdom.

Miniatures, their creators and collectors have given me so much in so many ways. My life is far better for the love, nurturing and incredible creativity of the miniature world.

ARTISAN: SMITH, PATRICIA

BUSINESS NAME: Nip and Tuck

IDENTIFICATION MARKS:

1987 to present

PS
92

CATEGORY:

Animals; Figures

RECOGNITION:

Miniatures Showcase, Vol. 3, No. 3, 1988, pg. 36; Vol. 5, No. 1, 1990, pg. 52; Vol. 5, No. 2, 1990, pg. 63; Vol. 6, No. 3, 1991, pg. 62

BIOGRAPHY:

Patricia Smith treasured and collected tiny things since childhood but it wasn't until 1987 that she discovered the hobby of miniatures. After receiving her BA in Journalism from the University of South Carolina, she was an editor/proofreader for 15 years. She now spends her time as a homemaker and miniature artisan, creating finely detailed whimsical clay characters. She is a member of NAME and the National Polymer Clay Guild.

ARTISAN: SMITH, TONI

BUSINESS NAME: Mini – Magic

IDENTIFICATION MARKS:

Toni Smith

Toni
Small clay animals

Mini Magic logo

SMITH, TONI, continued

CATEGORY:

Bears: teddy; Dolls

RECOGNITION:

Nutshell News, Mar. 1989, pg. 61; May 1992, pg. 71; Jul. 1992, pg. 68, 70; *Miniatures Showcase*, Winter 1989, pg. 14

AUTOBIOGRAPHY:

I have always made sketches of dresses whenever I had a pen or pencil and a piece of paper at hand. I was even doing it in school as far back as I can remember. I always wanted to be a dress designer having majored in art at school. However, instead of going to school to further a career in this area, I married. With two girls, I made a lot of doll clothes, from Betsy Wetsy to Barbies! When I got into miniatures in 1980 my husband and I started a business. After approximately three years in miniatures I began dressing porcelain dolls. I wanted to pose them, so I started making them from Fimo. I simply don't have the time to do everything I want to do!

ARTISAN: **SNYDER, PATRICIA**

BUSINESS NAME: Patricia's Garden

IDENTIFICATION MARKS:

CATEGORY:

Flowers and Plants; Landscaping; Ponds; Shrubs and Trees

RECOGNITION:

Nutshell News, Feb. 1986

AUTOBIOGRAPHY:

My first contact with miniatures was in my early teen years. I had gone to a friend's house and she had this beautiful dollhouse, but when I said let's play in it, she went into shock! "We don't play with it! It's only to look at!" That put "me" into shock. What possible use was a dollhouse you couldn't play with?

About the same time my mother had been collecting Popsicle sticks and was trying to figure out what to do with them. They finally evolved into miniature ladder back chairs. She got that down to a science, scaled it into one-inch scale, and became McIntyre Miniatures, manufacturer of authentic Early American furniture. She also made the first ladder back chair kit. Tom, my husband, had a compulsion to be a salesman and when I was making ming trees and they had accumulated to more than we needed, the kids took them out and sold them door to door. This was more than he could take, Tom decided that if the kids could sell them he most certainly could also. The ming trees scaled down into miniature beaded flower arrangements when we found a box of miniature colored blown glass vases at my mother's. When we moved to Oregon the holes in the tiny beads became so small I couldn't find them half the time. One day I told God that I needed a better more realistic flower that every one couldn't make. It wasn't five minutes that the answer came to me. It took about a year to go from the effect of a flower to a real recognizable flower.

I took the first batch to the Portland Oregon Miniature Show where I met Betty Martin and was invited to show my flowers at her new Top Artisan Miniature Show in Anaheim, California. It was through Betty that I became well known in the miniature world. Hank and Eleanor Taylor, The Carpenters Chest, were the first to carry my line of flowers and then later Dale and Jeanetta Kendall formerly of Petite Designs, became my distributor. It's been approximately fifteen years (1978), I have never been able to make enough flowers for everyone who wanted them. I have constantly taken more orders than I could fill because I have had a hard time saying no! My flowers have been sold all across the USA although I am better known on the West Coast.

I am giving all the information and secrets I have discovered through the years away now, as my family is not interested in carrying on with them. I am in the process of putting all this information into a book. The planned publication date was January 1994, and covers "how-to make" flowers, vines, wisteria, shrubs and trees, as well as ponds and little rock gardens.

The butterfly was my signature for a short while but I couldn't keep enough of them on hand to use, so only my signature on rock gardens and ponds, with the date, of course, will identify my work.

ARTISAN: **SOBOL, FERD**

BUSINESS NAME: Ferd Sobol Editions

IDENTIFICATION MARKS:

Initials branded

CATEGORY:

Furniture: period

HONORS:

IGMA Fellow

RECOGNITION:

Nutshell News, Mar. 1981, pg. 38; Nov. 1985, pg. 71; Jun. 1988, pg. 61; Apr. 1989, pg. 62; *Miniature Collector*, Aug. 1982, pg. 42; Fall 1988, pg. 47; *Miniature Gazette*, Summer 1984, pg. 51; *Santa Barbara Magazine*, California, Nov. 1984, pg. 70; *American Woodworker*, Mar. 1985, pg. 19; *Washington Post; Carpinteria Herald; Santa Barbara New Press; Milwaukee Journal*

AUTOBIOGRAPHY:

I was born in Green Bay, Wisconsin in 1924. As a young boy, I loved spending much of the winter months carving and inventing gadgets and found Christmas giving a joy, especially when being able to present self-made gifts to loved ones. I found myself excelling primarily in art and craft work throughout school years. Eventually, I became a teacher in drafting and manual arts. Most of my occupational life was as an owner and operator of a construction business, building and renovating schools, churches, and dwellings. Exclusively, when away from my crew, much of my personal devotion was relegated to customized projects that required fine detail, which I expressly relished. After the age of retirement, I sought to continue this passion of wood crafting, in miniatures.

ARTISAN: **SOBRERO, ETTORE**

BUSINESS NAME: Miniature Libraries And So On

IDENTIFICATION MARKS:

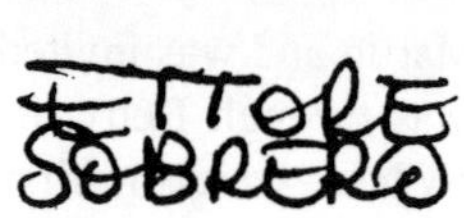

CATEGORY:

Shadow Boxes

HONORS:

Club Français de la Miniature, Paris; Libreria Messaggerie Modernissima, Rome 1993

SOBRERO, ETTORE, continued

RECOGNITION:

La Repubblica, Oct. 5, 1983, pg. 30; Dec. 28, 1983, Tuttoarte; *Casa Vogue*, Dec. 1983, Cover; *Panorama*, Dec. 24, 1984, pg. 166-167, Come e piccolo il mondo; Dec. 8, 1985, pg. 80; Jan. 11, 1987, Mi ha preso una libridine; Jun. 1987, pg. 131; *Gran Bazaar*, Jun/Jul. 1985, pg. 80, Accumulazioni; *Civiltà delle Macchine*, Jan/Apr. 1973, pg. 49-52; *Vitalità*, Jan/Feb. 1975, pg. 68-69; *Io, Gatto*, Pinuccia Ferrari, 1984, pg. 106; *Brava Casa*, Feb. 2, 1984, pg. 70; *L'Uomo Vogue*, Oct. 1984, pg. 266-273; *Corriere della Sera*, Oct. 9, 1984; *Bella*, Oct. 22, 1985; *Il Piacere*, Dec. 1986; *Tutto Gatto*, May 1987, pg. 34; *VerdEtä,* Jan. 1988, pg. 43-47; *Napoli Oggi*, Apr. 21, 1988, pg. 13; *ViviMilano*, Apr. 28, 1988; *Epoca*, May 22, 1988, pg. 183; *Ciga Hotels Magazine*, 1989, pg. 74-83; *Gioia*, Jun. 8, 1992; *Gap Italia*, Summer 1984, Title Page, Pg. 105-110; *La Peinture Italienne du Futurisme a nos Jours*, (Institute Europeen d' Histoire de l'Art) 1967, pg. 774, ; *Catalogo Generale Arte Italiana*, pg. 172; *Dictionnaire des Peintres, Sculpteurs, Dessinateurs et Graveurs*, (E. Benezit), Vol. 9, pg. 676; *Chicago Tribune*, May 29, 1994, Home Section 15, pg. 1, 4; *Minima Libraria ovvero*, Le biblioteche in miniatura di Ettore Sobrero

BIOGRAPHY:

Ettore Sobrero was born in Torino, Italy in 1924. Currently, he lives in the outskirts of Milano in a small villa chock-full of books, antiques, advertising ephemera, hats and miscellaneous, wonderful objects. He is quite proud of the grape vine that surrounds his house and produces a small strawberry grape from which he makes wine.

Although he studied the figure and drawing as a young man, he considers himself fundamentally self-taught. He has always been into "things of art." His first experiments in figurative painting go back to 1940. However, his first public exhibition was in 1955. His first one-man show was in 1960. Since then, he has had about 30 exhibitions, many introduced by Italo Calvino, in New York, Detroit, Paris and Italy. Towards the end of the 1970's he dedicated himself to printmaking, surrealist photography and bas-relief.

In the last several years, he has been making marvelous miniature objects that recreate reality on a reduced scale by the use of clever self-made devices and authentic things in very reduced proportions. Taking either small walnut furniture, 12" high, former typeset storage drawers or hollowed out period books, he packs the shelves, existing or added, full with familiar things made of wood, paper, glass and metal, tiny books, newspapers, etc. As well, minuscule period objects like bottles, photographs, labels, pieces of fabric and leather, dolls toys, and in some cases, made of valuable materials such as ivory, silver, rosewood and crystal, are placed in the remaining nooks and crannies on the shelves. Thus, "Miniature Libraries." However, sometimes he creates unusual "Maquettes" such as musicians' rooms, newspapermen's desks, mini-shoe racks, display cases for French perfume and Swiss Tobacco products.

Most of Sobrero's "miniature libraries" and "maquettes" are personalized and their themes are dedicated to the people in the worlds of culture, show business, finance, sports or politics. Their effect is intended to surprise the observer and recreate very often the atmosphere of a past era. Generally, never larger than a briefcase, a single work loaded with tiny books, vases and personal mementos can be easily lifted with one hand.

He is represented in Milano, Torino, Zurich, London and Buenos Aires. In America he is exclusively represented in Chicago by the Gallery Kate Khristianne.

ARTISAN: **SPACHER, CHESTER J.** (Deceased, 1987)
(Submitted by Alice Spacher Young)

BUSINESS NAME: Spacher's Studio

IDENTIFICATION MARKS:

CJS

SPACHER, CHESTER J., continued

CATEGORY:

Accessories: brass; Brasswork

HONORS:

IGMA Fellow 1984; Tiffany's, Christmas window display, 1978; Exhibit: Denver Museum of Miniatures; Toy and Miniature Museum, Kansas City

RECOGNITION:

Nutshell News, May/Jun. 1979, Cover; *The Andrews Collection*, Personal Treasures, Anne Day Smith, 1988

BIOGRAPHY:

Chester Spacher and his wife Alice graduated from Rochester Institute of Technology in 1933. He worked for Eastman Kodak Company for 12 years. After resigning he tried other professions including self-employment and being a sales representative. Eventually his inclinations towards the Arts won out and he became a sculptor for several years.

His clientele included Eastman Kodak, Bausch and Lomb, General Motors, and Xerox. In the year 1979 his youngest granddaughter Karen, received her first dollhouse for Christmas. Her Grandpa made 33 miniature pieces for her gift. That started the ball rolling! Chet and Alice visited the Washington Dolls' House and Toy Museum. After a gracious reception by Flora Gill Jacobs, who placed our first order, we were elated. We drove South towards Richmond, Virginia. Our idea was to stop at the Holiday Inn in Ashland, to see if we could find a miniature shop listed in the phone book. We explained our dilemma to the lady at the desk. She said "There are two miniaturists right here in Ashland. Wait a minute and I will call Mr. & Mrs. Andrews. You really should meet these two wonderful people". Thanks to that dear lady, we spent the next two hours sitting on Jackie and Joe's living room floor a whole new world unfolded to us from these wonderful loving and generous people. Needless to say we considered it a great honor to become their friends and we cherished a close relationship for many years.

Chet and Alice made a good team. Her responsibility was to keep tiny brass miniatures polished and packed ready to leave for a show in any of the states in the union. It was great fun as well as an education traveling and making so many wonderful friends. Many became collectors and loved to take home one or more of our little blue boxes with some precious goodie carefully packed inside.

Chet took great pride in his hand made brass miniatures, always made to one-inch or ½-inch scale. He often copied antiques, and because the design was not original he would not sign those pieces. His own designs were signed. He was honored by being elected a Fellow in the International Guild of Miniature Artisans, in 1984.

ARTISAN: **SPAIN, JANE**

BUSINESS NAME: Jane Spain

IDENTIFICATION MARKS:

Most unmarked

Brass tag; 1988 to present

CATEGORY:

Dolls: porcelain

HONORS:

IGMA Artisan

RECOGNITION:

Nutshell News, Sept. 1982, Cover; Jul. 1985, pg. 83; Jun. 1985, pg. 54-57; Jun. 1990; Nov. 1990; Jun. 1991, Cover; Jan. 1992, pg. 81; Oct. 1992, pg. 64; *Miniatures Showcase*, Fall 1986, pg. 11; Summer

SPAIN, JANE, continued

1989, Cover, pg. 44; Fall 1989, pg. 40; Winter 1989, pg. 29; Fall 1990, pg. 31; Spring 1991, pg. 26; Fall 1992, pg. 25; *Miniature Gazette*, Winter 1981, pg. 72-74; Spring 1989; Summer 1991, pg. 53; Summer 1992, pg. 51

ARTISAN: **SPANJAR, DEANNA**

BUSINESS NAME: Mini – tiques

IDENTIFICATION MARKS:

CATEGORY:
Accessories; Judaica; Needlepoint; Needlework

RECOGNITION:
Nutshell News, Nov. 1986

AUTOBIOGRAPHY:
As a child I remember having a tin dollhouse that always fell apart and an architectural model of a room that an aunt had given me. Both instilled a love of miniatures. However, neither were durable and I was left with a frustration that eventually got me into making and selling miniatures of quality.

I hold a BS degree from the School of Home Economics at the University of Wisconsin. I also have a master's equivalency and have obtained a certificate as a Learning Disabilities teacher. My current position is as a Kindergarten teacher in Milwaukee Public Schools.

For about fourteen years, since 1979, I have been making and selling my miniatures at regional shows and at the NAME Mini-Mart. In 1991, I opened a shop in Thiensville, Wisconsin. The shop is an extension of my show experience and my love of miniatures. I hope to retire to the shop in a few years.

My hand-made work features such items as needlepoint rugs, purses, pictures, slippers, book covers and Judaic items. I also crochet hats with silk roses added, afghans, and baby layettes. Other hand work includes placemats, ladies' hankies, bedspreads and tablecloths. In my earlier miniaturing I made wooden chests and sleigh beds.

At present I have been doing roomboxes for customers. Children's rooms and fairy tale themes interest me most.

ARTISAN: **SPARROW, MIKE**

IDENTIFICATION MARKS:
Registered, Sheffield Assay Office

CATEGORY:
Goldsmith; Silversmith; Silverware

HONORS:
IGMA Artisan

SPARROW, MIKE, continued

RECOGNITION:

Miniature Collector, Fall 1992, pg. 28

AUTOBIOGRAPHY:

Between the years of 1977 and 1980, I studied silver smithing at Medway College of Design in Chatham, England. Since that time, I have worked variously as a silversmith, goldsmith, and modelmaker. I've been increasingly specializing in miniature work over the last several years.

ARTISAN: **SPICE, BETTY**

BUSINESS NAME: Betty Spice

IDENTIFICATION MARKS:

THE MAN HATTER

Paper label pasted on brim of men's hats

CATEGORY:

Art: folk; Folk Art; Furniture: handpainted; Millinery; Paintings: oil; Screens; Toys: Bliss-like

RECOGNITION:

Nutshell News, Feb. 1990, pg. 59; *Miniatures Showcase*, Mar. 1993, pg. 36-37; *Make and Furnish Your Own Miniature Rooms*, Marian Maeve O'Brien, Hawthorne Books, Inc. NY 1978, pg. 81; *The Andrews Collection*, Personal Treasures, Anne Day Smith, 1988, pg. 51, 100

ARTISAN: **SPIREK, DENNIS & MARY**

BUSINESS NAME: Mary's Miniature Mansions

IDENTIFICATION MARKS:

CATEGORY:

Furniture

HONORS:

IGMA Artisan 1984 (Dennis)

BIOGRAPHY:

Dennis has been a member of the International Guild of Miniature Artisans, Board of Trustees, and served as second vice-president. He achieved Artisan status in 1984, and has served as *The Cube* editor since his election to the Board in 1990. He also has served on the Long Range Planning Committee. His specialty is carving one-inch and ½-inch scale Victorian furniture with his wife Mary, which is sold under the name "Mary's Miniature Mansions." Originally from Chicago, Dennis retired from the Army in 1988 and works full-time with the Department of Defense.

ARTISAN: **STAFFORD, PHYLLIS**

BUSINESS NAME: Phyllis Stafford
Sillyhp Creations

IDENTIFICATION MARKS:

CATEGORY:
Needlepoint; Needlework

HONORS:
IGMA Artisan, Fellow

RECOGNITION:
Nutshell News, Mar. 1987, pg. 40; Jun. 1987, pg. 40; *Nutshell News Calendar*, June 1989

ARTISAN: **STALBAUM, TERESA WELCH**

BUSINESS NAME: The China Closet

IDENTIFICATION MARKS:
All marks 1977 to present

CATEGORY:
Accessories; China: handpainted; Dinnerware; Porcelain

HONORS:
Exhibit: Toy & Miniature Museum of Kansas City

RECOGNITION:
Nutshell News, Jan. 1988, pg. 33; Jul. 1988, pg. 63; Mar. 1988, pg. 69; Sept. 1993, pg. 66; *Miniature Collector*, No. 36, pg. 39-40, "Like Mother, like Daughter: Passing on the Secrets of the Porcelain Trade," Louise A. Fecher; *American Period Interiors in Miniature*, Kate Doordan Klavan, Scribner's, 1984, pg. 61, 81, color plate 4

BIOGRAPHY:
In 1977, Jean Welch started The China Closet. She was joined by her daughter, Teresa. Teresa paints the intricate patterns, and Jean makes the raised floral pieces. Jean studied art at Nebraska University and Kansas City Institute. Teresa learned the trade working with Jean.

See "Jean Welch"

ARTISAN: **STALL, SPENCER**

BUSINESS NAME: Taos Sun Miniatures

IDENTIFICATION MARKS:

STALL, SPENCER, continued

CATEGORY:

Accessories: Southwest; Furniture: Southwest

HONORS:

IGMA Artisan

AUTOBIOGRAPHY:

I have been making Southwest miniatures since 1988. My background includes eight years as a carpenter and building model cars, planes, and ships since I was a young boy. I enjoy Southwest designs because of the clean and simple lines. My business evolved from making furniture for my daughter's dollhouse.

ARTISAN: STEBBINS, PATRICIA L. "PAT"

BUSINESS NAME: The Minikin Florist

IDENTIFICATION MARKS:

1990 to present

CATEGORY:

Baskets; Flowers and Plants; Floral Arrangements; Pots: handpainted, original

RECOGNITION:

Nutshell News, Vol. 21, No 12, Dec. 1991, pg. 67

AUTOBIOGRAPHY:

I have been doing Southern California miniature shows since January 1989, though I did not use a mark until 1990. I have no special training, only a love of gardening, and many years of drawing and painting. I have done crafts of all kinds, including needlework, jewelry, full-size floral arrangements, Christmas & other decorations and related items. Many of these I have sold at San Diego Craft fairs until I became possessed by miniatures. I am a member of NAME.

ARTISAN: STEELE, JEFFREY R.

BUSINESS NAME: Steele Miniatures

IDENTIFICATION MARKS:

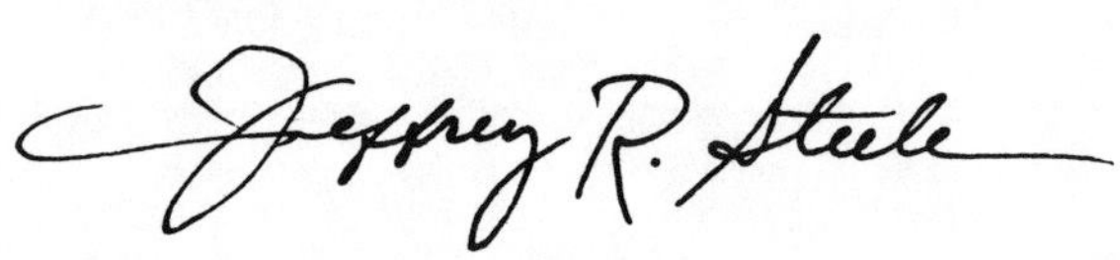

CATEGORY:

Furniture; Roomboxes; Room Settings; Video Tape: how-to

HONORS:

Exhibits: Holiday Window, Tiffany & Co., 1983, Chicago; The David Adler Cultural Center, 1987, Libertyville, Illinois, For the Love of Miniatures; Holiday Display, Saks Fifth Avenue, 1986, Chicago; The Chicago Botanical Gardens, 1988, A Holiday In Miniature; *Victorian Sampler Magazine*

STEELE, JEFFREY R., continued

RECOGNITION:

Nutshell News; Miniatures Showcase, Vol. 2, No. 4, Fall 1987; WBBM TV 2, Feb. 16 1986; *Pioneer Press Newspaper*, Oct. 27, 1983, "It's a Very Small World for Jeff Steele," Michael Bonesteel; *Chicago Tribune*, Sunday, Jan. 10, 1993, Sec 18, "Little Big Man," Dale Duda; Sunday, Mar. 1, 1992, Sec 15, "Scaling Down," Julie Morse; *Victorian*, Fall 1992, pg. 49, "A Perfect Little World," Debra Anton; WCIU TV 26, Chicago, Feb. 22, 1986, 10:30am; *Through The Looking Glass*, Boynton and Associates, Inc., Ann Ruble, 1984

AUTOBIOGRAPHY:

In 1979, I graduated from Northern Illinois University with a BFA degree in Fine Art Painting and a BSE degree in Art Education and Design. I've always had an innate interest in miniatures since high school although my college studies were directed towards painting in watercolor and art education. This led eventually to a position of decorator for the well known Marshall Field department store in Chicago, now owned by Dayton Hudson Corp. Minneapolis. I've been involved with the tiny world since 1972 through the inspiration given by the Beehive Studio in Deerfield, Illinois. That first step into their Victorian parlour room was the beginning.

I work on my designs in suites of four per item while smaller items are done in suites of 12. Custom work is actually the core of my production. I specialize in complete miniature "visions" or settings and the work is accomplished totally by hand and I always add an element of surprise as my ideas come from the heart and through the materials. I also have a line of video classes.

ARTISAN: **STEELE, PETE & JACKIE**

BUSINESS NAME: Coyote Minis

IDENTIFICATION MARKS:

CATEGORY:

Accessories: carvings, Southwest; Dolls; Fimo; Furniture: rustic twig; Kits; Paintings; Pottery

RECOGNITION:

Miniatures Showcase, Summer 1990, pg. 32-34, 38, 41-44

AUTOBIOGRAPHY:

We are members of NAME, IGMA, CIMTA.

ARTISAN: **STEELY, KAREN LYNN**

BUSINESS NAME: Karen Steely

IDENTIFICATION MARKS:

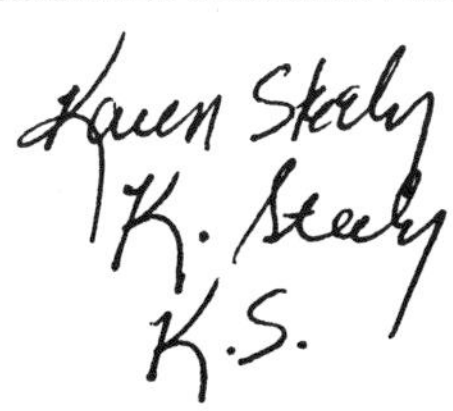

STEELY, KAREN LYNN, continued

CATEGORY:

Accessories: country, period; Furniture: country, period; Murals; Paintings: oil; Roomboxes; Signs

RECOGNITION:

Nutshell News, Mar. 1984

AUTOBIOGRAPHY:

I received my bachelors degree in art from Penn State University in 1971; my masters degree in Art Education, from Tyler School of Art in 1978; and have achieved 30 post graduate credits as of 1994, in art history, painting, and drawing from The University of Pennsylvania as well as Tyler School of Art.

I have taught art in public schools for 24 years, 23 of those years at Lower Moreland Sr. High School, in Huntingdon Valley, Pennsylvania. My home is shared with my husband, Jim Rosa, and our two sons Jeremy and Zachary.

Most of my time in miniatures, is spent traveling and selling my work as well as doing an occasional workshop, both at shows as well as clubs. I have been in business since 1983.

ARTISAN: **STEFFEY, GAIL**

BUSINESS NAME: Miniature Upholstery

IDENTIFICATION MARKS:

Certificate of authenticity with each piece

22554 Gail Steffey #B-15-6

22554	Gail Steffey	B	15	6
Zip code indicating place of origin		Color of piece (Burgundy)	Leather skin	Number of piece made from skin

CATEGORY:

Accessories: desk; Furniture: tufted, upholstered

HONORS:

IGMA Artisan

RECOGNITION:

Nutshell News, Apr. 1984, pg. 40, 42; Sept. 1990, pg. 67; *Miniatures Showcase*, Jan. 1993, pg. 36-37

AUTOBIOGRAPHY:

I became interested in miniatures in 1978 thru Bob and Jean Porter in Occoquan, Virginia Mountain Valley Miniature Shop. I did special order upholstery work for their customers. I started making, in about 1982 or 1983, upholstered pieces for their shop on consignment, but after the 1984 *Nutshell News* article, I started selling to others. I have done very few shows. I mostly sell wholesale and to shops. I know how to upholster in full-size, so therefore I think I excel in miniature upholstery. I think you have to be a woodworker as well as a fabric/seamstress worker. I wish I were a better woodworker and could make a Betty Valentine cabriole leg, but I feel I am truly an artisan in the field of upholstery.

ARTISAN: **STEIGER, THOMAS W.**

BUSINESS NAME: Concept Prime

IDENTIFICATION MARKS:

1987 to present

CATEGORY:

Furniture: period

HONORS:

IGMA Fellow; Best of Show, Canada Juried Show, 1991; Naylor Memorial Award, 1992

RECOGNITION:

Miniature Collector, Winter 1988, pg. 39-41; *Boca Raton Magazine*, Jun. 1990, pg. 80-84; *Antiques*, Aug. 1990, pg. 19-20, "The Shell Game;" *The Scale Cabinetmaker*, Summer 1989, Cover, pg. 5-9, "O Wondrous Wooton," serialized; Spring 1991, pg. 25; Summer 1991, pg. 25; Fall 1991, pg. 42

AUTOBIOGRAPHY:

I began designing and constructing miniature furniture in 1986, concentrating my work on a series of 25 secretaries in one-inch scale. Each secretary represents a major design period and all are museum quality pieces.

In 1970, I founded and became the President of an international marketing consulting firm which is headquartered in Ft. Lauderdale, Florida. I'm a graduate of Northwestern University.

ARTISAN: **STEORTS, LARRY** (Submitted by William R. Robertson)

IDENTIFICATION MARKS:

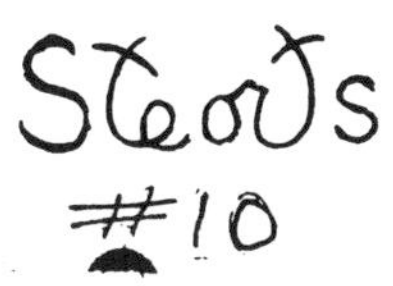

With number of piece

CATEGORY:

Dollhouse: doll's dollhouse; Houses: Victorian doll's dollhouse

HONORS:

Exhibit: Toy & Miniature Museum of Kansas City

RECOGNITION:

Nutshell News, Jan. 1981, pg. 32-34, "Cross Examining Larry Steorts;" Feb. 1983, pg. 27; *Miniature Collector*, No. 38, Aug. 1983, pg. 38

ARTISAN: **STEPHENSON, CAROLYN**

BUSINESS NAME: Miniature Lumber Shoppe

IDENTIFICATION MARKS:

CATEGORY:

Building Components: doors, moldings, windows; Furniture; Kits: house, store building

AUTOBIOGRAPHY:

I have been involved with miniatures since 1980. With my business partner, John Warner, I have designed and produced many miniature products, including several dollhouse kits in ¼-inch scale. I have degrees in education and business.

ARTISAN: **STEPHENSON, FRED**

BUSINESS NAME: Design Tecnics Miniatures

IDENTIFICATION MARKS:

Unmarked

CATEGORY:

Books: hand book; Dollhouse: blueprints, plans; Publications: how-to

RECOGNITION:

Nutshell News, "Architect's Angle," bi-monthly column, Fred Stephenson ; *The Scale Cabinetmaker*

AUTOBIOGRAPHY:

My interest in architectural miniatures for my model railroad in my youth led me to a career in architecture. I have a Bachelor degree in Architecture from the University of Michigan and a Masters in Architecture from the University of Kansas, where I also taught for eight years. I have been active in dollhouse miniatures since about 1979, working in all scales. My primary activity involves houses and buildings, but I also produce kits and finished furniture in ¼-inch scale. Much of my miniature work is done working with my wife, Carolyn, who is a partner in Miniature Lumber Shoppe.

ARTISAN: **STETKEWICZ, RON**

BUSINESS NAME: Ron Stetkewicz

IDENTIFICATION MARKS:

CATEGORY:

Accessories: brass; Boat; Brasswork; Hardware; Nautical: ship models

STETKEWICZ, RON, continued

HONORS:

IGMA Fellow

RECOGNITION:

Nutshell News; Miniature Collector; Miniature Gazette

BIOGRAPHY:

Ron Stetkewicz has been a miniaturist since about 1968. Originally a city boy, Ron along with his wife and children, moved to the mountains in New York State in 1971, looking for the peaceful life away from the hectic city. With an Associates in Landscape Architecture, and Photography, a craftsman at heart, Ron began making small pieces of furniture to decorate full-size desk sets. Jean Schramm of Enchanted Doll House in Manchester, Vermont, happened to see some of Ron's work on these desk sets, and contacted him. She advised Ron to go into the miniature business making his small pieces one-inch scale. From that day forward, Ron has made miniatures in every configuration and in every medium, from wood to porcelain to brass. He owns and works his own photo-etching business as well as doing his hand-carved and crafted miniatures which range from ship models to brass accessories to hand-carved and painted figures, not to mention his line of authentic brass hardware.

ARTISAN: STETZ, BARBARA J.

BUSINESS NAME: Barb Stetz – Miniatures

IDENTIFICATION MARKS:

1975-1985	**HANDMADE BY BARB**	ribbon glued to furniture or stamped on furniture
1982 to present	**BY BARB STETZ**	ribbon glued on dressed beds and mannequins
	B STETZ	hats and veils

CATEGORY:

Accessories; Beds; Furniture; Millinery

AUTOBIOGRAPHY:

I've collected miniatures since I was a child. While raising a family my hobby had taken a back seat. In 1975, miniatures re-entered my life and took over. Fabric seems to be my main medium. Curtains, bed spreads, beds, couch & chair sets, dressed manniquins, and many accessory pieces are among the many things that have materialized. All of these I sold to miniature stores throughout the Chicago area.

In 1977, I bought a miniatures store. I continued to wholesale my items. I did retail shows, taught at shows, houseparties, state days, and local stores. I've been written up in local papers. Since closing the store in 1987, I continue to teach and wholesale to stores throughout the United States while traveling with my husband. I'm a member of CIMTA, NAME, and SAM.

ARTISAN: STEWART, CAROL

BUSINESS NAME: Carol Stewart's Miniature Teddy Bears Inc.

IDENTIFICATION MARKS:

STEWART, CAROL, continued

CATEGORY:

Bears: teddy; Puppets; Toys

HONORS:

IGMA Fellow 1990; Golden Teddy Bear Award, 1988; Toby Nomination, 1990 & 1992

RECOGNITION:

Nutshell News, Oct. 1985; *Miniature Collector*, Fall 1989; *Teddy Tribune*, Aug. 1987; Feb. 1988; *Teddy Bear and Friends*, May/Jun. 1991; Dec. 1991; *Teddy Bear Times*, Summer 1991

BIOGRAPHY:

Carol was born in Indiana of German and English ancestry. She is married to an Irishman, has three grown daughters, and now lives in Stuart, Florida. Carol, always a multi-talented artist, built her first dollhouse in 1982 and began making miniature toys, specializing in wood carved puppets and stuffed teddy bears. She has become well known for her exquisitely designed Teddy Bears and her keen eye for exacting detail.

In 1990, Carol achieved the status of Fellow in the International Guild of Miniature Artisans. She is a member of the National Association of Miniature Enthusiasts and the Stuart Miniature Club both located in the USA. She has received the "Golden Teddy Award" and two of her Teddy Bears have been nominated for the "Toby Award". Also in 1990, she was licensed to make a miniature 3" Disney Classic Pooh bear and was a featured artist at the Walt Disney World Teddy Bear Convention. She was invited again in 1991 and was licensed to make a 6" Disney Classic Pooh bear.

ARTISAN: **STIEFEL, LYNDA**

BUSINESS NAME: Hearth and Home Miniatures

IDENTIFICATION MARKS:

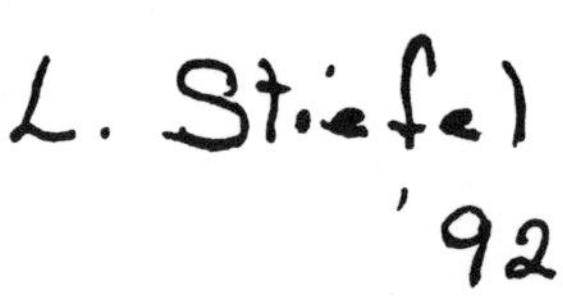

CATEGORY:

Lighting; Weaving: equipment, looms

HONORS:

IGMA Fellow

RECOGNITION:

Nutshell News; *Cleveland PM Magazine*, TV Show

ARTISAN: **STIMLER, RAE**

BUSINESS NAME: Rae Stimler
Big Time Minis

IDENTIFICATION MARKS:

Scribed into porcelain back of head or shoulderplate

STIMLER, RAE, continued

CATEGORY:
Dolls

RECOGNITION:
Nutshell News, Vol. 21, No. 3, Mar. 1991, pg. 72; Vol. 21, No. 10, Oct. 1991, pg. 85; Vol. 21, No. 11, Nov. 1991, pg. 77; *Miniatures Showcase*, Vol. 6, No. 3, Summer 1991, pg. 38, 40; Vol. 6, No. 1, Winter 1991, pg. 26-27; *Dolls in Miniature*, Vol. 1, No. 2, Summer 1991, pg. 75-77

BIOGRAPHY:
Although she has no formal art training, Rae Stimler apprenticed to Dawn Adams for six months of classes in miniature dollmaking. She took additional classes from Lorraine Garner, Master Bearmaker, who gave her guidance in dressing techniques.

ARTISAN: **ST LEGER, LAURENCE**

BUSINESS NAME: Angela – Laurence St Leger

IDENTIFICATION MARKS:
Most unmarked

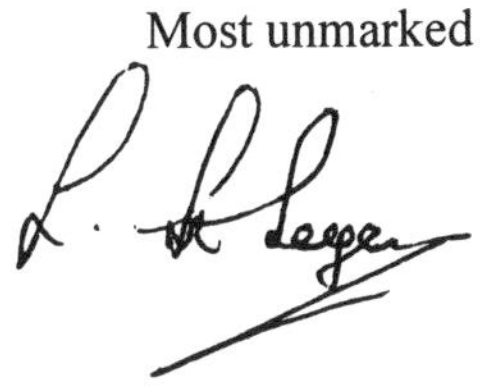 or name plate

CATEGORY:
Accessories; Metalwork; Toys

HONORS:
Exhibit: Toy & Miniature Museum of Kansas City

RECOGNITION:
Nutshell News

BIOGRAPHY:
Laurence has been a miniaturist for 19 years, since 1977. He was previously a watch maker who stumbled upon the world of miniatures by accident. It is now his full-time occupation, helped by his wife Angela. They work seriously both in wood and metal with mechanical toys being their fun element. They have also made a Miniature silver galleon for a BBC Screen 2 production called "Flea Bites."

ARTISAN: **STOCKTON, MARK & SHARON**

BUSINESS NAME: Mark and Sharon Stockton

IDENTIFICATION MARKS:

1982 to 1987 - Signed individually or jointly

1987 to present - Signed individually or jointly

STOCKTON, MARK & SHARON, continued

CATEGORY:

Accessories: church, school; Furniture

RECOGNITION:

Nutshell News, Apr. 1989, pg. 71; Aug. 1989, pg. 69; Sept. 1989, pg. 66; Sept. 1990, pg. 66; Mar. 1992, pg. 26, 69; Apr. 1992; May 1992, pg. 29, 65; Sept. 1992, pg. 75; May 1993, pg. 62-63; *Miniatures Showcase*, Spring 1990, pg. 5, 28, 30, 37, 42, 46; Winter 1992, Cover, pg. 5, 30, 32, 33, 41; *Miniature Gazette*, Summer 1991

AUTOBIOGRAPHY:

Our miniature career began in 1982 when Mark was asked by a local miniature shop in Sacramento, California if he could make some school desks. These first pieces were made with a hand saw and X-Acto knife. One thing led to another, and soon we were making other schoolhouse furniture; teachers desks, chalkboards, dunce stools, clocks, etc. That required the purchase of a Dremel table saw, scroll saw and router. We were now officially miniature artisans!

Since we both had full-time jobs, Mark was a small engine mechanic, and I was a bookkeeper, we only did an occasional show close to home. Our inventory was very limited, and we often had only eight or 10 different items on the table. We presently do 36 or more shows per year and have a catalog of over 300 items. Many pieces came about when a customer would ask, "Can you make such and such?" Our want list continues to grow.

Our pieces have always been a joint effort. Mark does all the saw work and I do all the finishing. We each have our own pieces that we assemble. We design our pieces by seeing an actual piece or a photograph and then scale it down.

From 1987 to March 1993, we were known as "the Gypsy Mini Makers" because we lived in our motor home and traveled the miniature show circuit throughout the United States. We also did mail order through a P.O. Box in Sacramento. Pieces had their origin in ghost towns, along rivers and the ocean, and many other interesting places around the country. In March 1993, we decided to buy a home in Waldron, Michigan, which is a central location for doing shows. Our business had grown so much that we had run out of space in the motor home. We are members of NAME and IGMA.

ARTISAN: STRANGE, RHEA

BUSINESS NAME: Rhea's Wicker in Miniature

IDENTIFICATION MARKS:

Rhea '92' — Year made
#1 — Number made
circa! 1880 — Circa (if known)

Logo – Wakefield 1870's overhang crib

CATEGORY:

Furniture: period; Wicker: Victorian

HONORS:

IGMA Artisan 1988; People's Choice Award, Santa Barbara Miniature Show, 1984

RECOGNITION:

Nutshell News, Oct. 1987, pg. 75; Apr. 1989, pg. 71; Feb. 1990, Cover; Jul. 1991, pg. 62; Jan. 1992, pg. 67; Nov. 1992, pg. 74, Show Scene; May 1994, pg. 58; *Nutshell News Calendar*, 1994, Jan., May; *Miniature Showcase*, Fall 1987, pg. 18-19, 30; Fall 1988, pg. 36; Winter 1990, Cover, pg. 26-28, 71; Winter 1992, pg. 32-33; Jan. 1993, pg. 51; Mar. 1993, pg. 52; Jul. 1993, pg. 26-27

STRANGE, RHEA, continued

AUTOBIOGRAPHY:

I guess I have to say that I have been an artist all of my life. I was always getting in trouble for drawing pictures in class. My parents evidently realized I needed direction and started me with a tutor in fine oil painting when I was 13 years old. It was then that I really learned to love painting. I continued as an oil painter until four children and a husband became too much work for the time needed to paint. Eventually I became involved in crafts of all kinds, some for extra money, but mainly as gifts for family and friends.

My family moved from Minnesota when I was a child, and I had to give away my dollhouse, and always promised myself that when my children were grown I'd have another. In 1979, my husband bought a kit which we worked on together for four years. I made 90% of its contents and was so proud that I showed it at a miniature show in Santa Barbara in 1984, and won their very first People's Choice Award, and also a 2nd Place Award from the judges.

When building my next dollhouse I started taking classes at Larrianne's Small Wonders, in Ventura, California, including Sylvia Rountree's leather, to clothes by Donna Johnson, ¼-inch scene from Jane Kilkenney, and a class in wicker from Leilani Warling and knew I had found my niche. I began researching antique wicker so I could make replicas of antiques. I now have 140 pieces of wicker.

I have come to love the challenge and intend to stay with it as long as possible. My next goal is to become an IGMA Fellow.

ARTISAN: **STRINGER, TERENCE**

BUSINESS NAME: Terence Stringer

IDENTIFICATION MARKS:

Registered London Assay Office

CATEGORY:

Accessories: bone, nursery, sewing, silver, wooden; Silver; Silversmith

HONORS:

IGMA Artisan

RECOGNITION:

Daily Telegraph Magazine, Jan. 25, 1992, pg. 37; *International Dolls House News*, Spring 1989, pg. 42-43; Winter 1990, pg. 44; Winter 1991, Cover, pg. 7

AUTOBIOGRAPHY:

We are a husband and wife team earning our living by making miniatures full-time. Our business was established in 1986. Terry is mainly self-taught, while Heather did a three year city-guild course in Fashion Design. Terry does the making and Heather does the painting of our decorated wooden miniatures.

ARTISAN: **STRUP, JEAN L.** (Submitted by Toy & Miniature Museum of Kansas City)

IDENTIFICATION MARKS:

J L STRUP

with year

CATEGORY:

Needlework

STRUP, JEAN L., continued

HONORS:

Exhibit: Toy & Miniature Museum of Kansas City

RECOGNITION:

Miniature Gazette, Vol. 9, No. 2, pg. 35-36, “Early American Crewel in Miniature”, Rita De Marco

ARTISAN: **SUDLER, CHUCK & MARGI**

BUSINESS NAME: C M S Creations
Margaret's Miniatures

IDENTIFICATION MARKS:

CMS

with date and numbered

CATEGORY:

Musical Instruments

HONORS:

Exhibit: Denver Museum of Miniatures

RECOGNITION:

Nutshell News; *Miniatures Showcase;* *Name Gazette;* *Denver Post*, 1982

AUTOBIOGRAPHY:

In 1973, I made a flea market purchase of a dilapidated dollhouse for my 11 year old daughter. We refurbished the house and made all the furnishings for it. When it was completed I found I couldn't stop the flow of ideas and making adorable one-inch scale dollhouse treasures.

In 1974, I joined NAME to expand my knowledge of the trade. My original business name was Margaret's Miniatures, and I flourished through the miniature trade shows, eventually making my first upright piano.

In 1979, Chuck joined me in the business. We married in 1980 and changed the business name to C M S Creations. We decided to specialize in keyboard and stringed instruments. Our success was phenomenal, and we loved every minute of our work. I had previously taught piano and organ from 1952 to 1972.

We researched all our instruments for authenticity. Measurements were taken from the actual full-size instruments found in museums, stores, libraries, and private homes. We made our own pattern in one-inch scale, and a few in ½-inch scale. All were popular.

In 1983, we made 410 upright pianos for the regional houseparty in Sacramento, California, in 1988, we made 1200 guitars for the national houseparty in Santa Clara, California, and we have been instructors at the College of Miniature Knowledge, in Ashland Oregon.

In 1994, our health failed and we had to give up our work. I have limited mobility due to arteriosclerosis. Chuck takes care of me, the house, and the yard. We work on scenes for music boxes as a hobby, and will always enjoy making little things.

ARTISAN: **SUTHERLAND, TAMMY C.**

BUSINESS NAME: Geppetto's
Tammy's Calico Crafts

IDENTIFICATION MARKS:
Many unmarked

Logo used as label

HANDCRAFTED BY
GEPPETTO'S

Burned into wood

CATEGORY:
Accessories: bath, bedroom, garden, kitchen, nursery, pet shop; Clothing; Dolls: character, children, doll's dolls, porcelain; Furniture: potting bench, workbench; Holiday Items; Millinery; Needlework; Sewing; Tools: garden

RECOGNITION:
Miniature Dealer, Mar. 1990, Cover; *Miniatures Showcase*, Spring 1990, Cover; *Jefferson City News Tribune*, 1981; TV, Cape Girardeau, Missouri, Mar. 1993, "Heartland Images"

AUTOBIOGRAPHY:

When I innocently walked into a small miniature shop in 1974, little did I know it would be a life-changing experience! At the time I was living in Branson, Missouri and making many full-sized "country" crafts using barn board, dough, calico, corn husks, etc. I immediately began incorporating miniature accessories into the full-sized items. Before long I realized I could convert all the skills used in full-sized crafts to miniature and switched to minis only, after all, there are only so many hours in a day.

My first business name was Tammy's Calico Crafts, selling to shops and at craft shows in the Branson area; then Tammy's "Small" Business in Jefferson City, a weekend only miniature and antiques shop and also some miniature shows. In 1984, I moved to Charleston, MO and became an isolated miniaturist. I continued doing a few shows and attending all I possibly could. In 1987, my husband and I purchased Geppetto's from its Florida owner and have been upgrading, changing, and adding ever since.

I have always been art and design oriented, majoring in Fashion Design in college, but never really liked the study of history until I discovered miniatures. Now I love researching for houses, scenes and dress, thanks, in part, to Dougless Bitler and her wonderfully interesting ways of presenting historical facts.

I am currently a member of IGMA, NAME, DAG (Doll Artisan Guild), the Mississippi County Historical Society and a "friend" to the Miniature Museum of St. Louis.

ARTISAN: **SYLSBERRY, MOLLY**

BUSINESS NAME: Treasures

IDENTIFICATION MARKS:

TREASURES

Rubber stamp, 1/16" high letters, upper case italics

CATEGORY:
Accessories: country; Furniture: country

RECOGNITION:
Miniatures Showcase, Fall 1991

SYLSBERRY, MOLLY, continued

AUTOBIOGRAPHY:

Hi! My name is Martha Sylsberry but everyone calls me Molly. I've been fascinated with miniatures as long as I can remember. I wish I still had some of the miniature furniture I played with, as a child. As I grew older, I put away the toys of a child and took up other hobbies. You might remember the "old Bottle" craze in the 60's and 70's! Well, that bug bit me too, and a girlfriend and I became avid bottle diggers. In amongst the bottles we were after, we found china miniatures of pitchers and bowls, plates, pots, etc. which I still have. Their discovery rekindled my fondness for miniatures, and I embarked on building myself a dollhouse. I went to toy stores and got what I could but I soon had pieces in mind that I couldn't find anywhere. Because I was fortunate to be born into a family who did things, I tried making my own. My dad built furniture from scratch and sold the pieces to antique dealers as reproductions. I have his copper-lined dry sink in my shop and I've copied it in miniature.

I enjoy working with wood, and try to do things that aren't currently on the market. However, to fill the empty spaces, I do a lot of accessories also. I'm real proud of my shrimp cocktail! I've been at this full-time since 1987 and feel I've not yet scratched the surface and what fun it is!

ARTISAN: SZUBA, DOLORES M.

BUSINESS NAME: Dolores Szuba Cromınds

IDENTIFICATION MARKS:

Crocheted pieces unmarked

CATEGORY:

Animals: crocheted; Clothing; Crocheting; Dolls: crocheted; Needlework; Publications: how-to

RECOGNITION:

Buffalo Evening News, Aug. 1, 1984

AUTOBIOGRAPHY:

After my marriage in 1954, I began crocheting as a hobby. Over the years there were many doilies and baby sweater sets which were given as presents. One day I wondered how a doily made from regular sewing thread would look, so I made one. It looked good, but small.

I'm sure you remember the old saying "Necessity is the mother of invention." Joe, my husband, was laid off from his job so I had to invent. My miniature business came about in a serendipitous way, late in 1979. My sister Gail brought a small crocheted Christmas tree to show me. She asked if I could make a miniature bell for her boss. I made one from regular sewing thread and that was the start of my crocheting business. I graduated from that little Christmas ornament and went on through miniature doilies to pot holders, formulating directions for each one and keeping a copy of each. I soon connected up with two dear friends in South Buffalo, Marge and Claire, who became interested in my miniatures. One day Claire asked if I could make a three dimensional doll, upon seeing one of my flat pot holders which had been made in the shape of a doll. After much trial and error, that stuffed doll came about. Each week I would come up with directions for something new, a doll, an animal, a cartoon character, a fairy tale character, and on and on until I now have probably 200 or more directions for my unique little stuffed creations which I call "Crominds."

Naturally when you have so many directions, you have to do something with them so I started going to local shows and fairs, selling my little dolls and creatures, then on to National ones like the MIAA and CIMTA Shows. I now have a backlog of orders.

T

ARTISAN: **TAG, ELMER A.**

BUSINESS NAME: Originals by Tag

IDENTIFICATION MARKS:

Stamped on some pieces 1976 to 1981

Hand signed 1980 to 1994

CATEGORY:

Houses; Memorabilia; Roomboxes; Shops

HONORS:

IGMA Fellow 1980; Exhibit: Toy & Miniature Museum of Kansas City

RECOGNITION:

Nutshell News, Jul/Aug. 1979; May 1980, Cover, pg. 26-29; May 1981; Sept. 1984; *Miniature Collector*, No. 22, Dec. 1980, pg. 13; Jun. 1981; Jun. 1988; *Miniature Gazette*, Vol. 21, No. 4, 1993; *The Craft Report*, Apr. 1989; *The New Jersey Herald*, Aug. 1982; Feb. 1987; *Daily Record of New Jersey*, Oct. 1982; *Sussex County Voice*, Jun. 1987; *Reproducing Period Furniture and Accessories in Miniature*, Virginia Merrill, Susan Merrill Richardson, Crown, 1981, pg. 264

BIOGRAPHY:

After graduating from Arts High School, Newark, New Jersey, a technical school for art majors, Elmer Tag served with the US First Cavalry in GHQ Special Services, traveling with USO Camp Shows throughout Japan. This experience with show production and design led to his entry into Yale University Department of Drama which prepared him for induction into the United Scenic Artist Union. Hired by NBC in 1950, he designed scenery for television shows from Howdy Doody in black and white, to Saturday Night Live, in "living color," in the 40 years that followed.

Much of the preliminary work of a set-designer is done "to scale" and in 3 dimensional models. So, when his wife, Jean, had need of a sales display for her miniature pottery and china, in 1976, it was with experience and skill that he designed and built miniature shops in which she could showcase her wares. Unexpectedly, the shops attracted so much interest that he found himself in the "miniature business" creating and customizing shops to meet the collector's needs. Roomboxes, and some houses followed – each with historical significance. In contrast to the demands of architectural detail, Elmer finds great satisfaction in depicting small items of nostalgic appeal to their finest detail – items such as a Flexible Flyer, a spinning piano stool, a rocking horse, a bird cage each in limited editions. Since his retirement from the television industry, Elmer continues to create in miniature, mostly for the Tag's own miniature collection. Occasionally, a new miniature reproduction of a sentimental item might show up in limited editions. He has many challenges still to be met!

ARTISAN: **TAG, JEAN C.**

BUSINESS NAME: Originals by Tag

IDENTIFICATION MARKS:

Stamp used on china & pottery
1976 to 1980

Stamp used on china & pottery
1980 to 1991

Hand signed
1991 to 1994

TAG, JEAN C., continued

CATEGORY:
China; Pottery

HONORS:
IGMA Fellow 1980; Exhibit: Toy & Miniature Museum of Kansas City

RECOGNITION:
Nutshell News, May 1980, Cover, pg. 26-29; Jun. 1981; Mar. 1984; Sept. 1984; Aug. 1986; Mar. 1987; Apr. 1988; Oct. 1988; *Miniature Collector*, Jun. 1988; *Decorating Craft Ideas*, Apr. 1981; *Ceramic Scope*, Dec. 1987, pg. 16-18; *New Jersey Herald*, Aug. 1982; Feb. 1987; *Daily Record of New Jersey*, Oct. 1982; *American Period Interiors in Miniature*, Kate Doordan Klavan, Scribner's, 1984, pg. 200-217

BIOGRAPHY:
As an art major graduate of Arts High School in Newark, New Jersey, Jean Tag turned her interest in art toward education and acquired the necessary degree and certifications to teach Art. After two years of teaching, Jean resigned, stayed at home to raise a family with her husband Elmer. During the 15 years spent at home she directed her talents to oil painting, completing many commissions of historical landmarks in northwest New Jersey.

When returning to teaching full-time, in 1966, she had to refresh her skills in many of the crafts once learned. It was the reunion with the potters wheel that captured her special interest. During the national bi-centennial preparations in, 1975, she participated in many community events demonstrating the early American craft of wheel-thrown pottery. Space and time were limited so by necessity pieces had to be small, so small, in fact, that some observers wondered if they were for dollhouses. They also revealed the need for one-inch scale china for miniature collectors. This became Jean's new pursuit. The journey to perfect this craft and produce what collectors wanted has seen no end. After being indoctrinated into the "world of one-inch scale" possibilities were countless.

Researching periods and styles of china became intriguing, but research and experimenting with clays, glazes, colors and paint became critical, and is on-going. Jean's blue and white pieces of Chinese export design as well as Delft and Meissen became her trademark. She also produces complete dinner sets as well as unique pieces with a history. Her more recent renditions of the turn-of-the-century majolica ware with textures and raised designs applied to the greenware are reminiscent of that period.

All of Jeans's wheel-turned pieces are of a white talc clay which has been kiln fired, decorated with underglaze, refired, glazed and fired again. The addition of gold trim or china paint requires a 4th firing.

Although Jean has retired from 25 years of teaching she continues to produce china to the collector's satisfaction and need.

ARTISAN: **TATE, MARVIN & BARBARA**

BUSINESS NAME: Tate's Collectables

IDENTIFICATION MARKS:

B.T.
M.T.

Fish may face right or left

BARBARA A. TATE
+
MARVIN L. TATE

M.L.TATE
B.A.TATE

BARBARA TATE
+
MARVIN TATE

Marvin Tate
Barbara Tate

TATE, MARVIN & BARBARA, continued

CATEGORY:
Accessories: country; Dolls: original, porcelain; Flowers & Plants; Food; Furniture: country, period, wicker; Trunks

RECOGNITION:
Miniatures Showcase, 1989

BIOGRAPHY:
Barbara Tate became interested in miniatures when her husband was on a tour of duty in Hawaii and they moved there. She was so turned on to them that she started making her own, and was told by a fellow club member that she should start selling them. Both Barbara and Marvin became more involved with miniatures as their travels progressed to California and ever since. They are both a great help to each other and find miniatures a fantastic hobby and business.

ARTISAN: **TAYLOR, PEGGY C.**

BUSINESS NAME: Peggy's Miniature Wicker

IDENTIFICATION MARKS:

CATEGORY:
Wicker

AUTOBIOGRAPHY:
I started in miniatures like so many people did because my 14 year old daughter wanted a dollhouse in 1978. We built a Victorian house together. Since our tastes were very different, we divided the rooms and did our own thing. It turned out to be a very interesting dollhouse. We bought most of the furnishings at a local shop and also attended a few shows, and I realized I could make miniatures. I decided to specialize in wicker and my first show was Ann Weiners Mini Mania Show in New Jersey. After that I did about five or six shows a year. That is about all I can handle, because I do everything myself. Now most of my business is wholesale to shops and show dealers, however I do like to do a few shows so I can talk to people and get their reaction. This has become my living, since I was divorced a number of years ago, and I consider it a blessing to be able to work in my home which I love so much.

ARTISAN: **TAYLOR, RANDI**

BUSINESS NAME: Randi Taylor Collectables
Randi Taylor & Company
Randi Taylor's Little Legacys

IDENTIFICATION MARKS:

CATEGORY:
Animals: mice; Bears: teddy; Dolls: character, fantasy

TAYLOR, RANDI, continued

HONORS:

1st Place, Family Circle & Smithsonian Contest, Elf; Exhibit: Trees of Christmas Display, Elf, 1992-1994, Smithsonian Museum of American Art History, Washington, DC

RECOGNITION:

ABC TV, 1976; *Orange County Register*, Apr. 1976; *Family Circle*, Dec. 22, 1992, pg. 92

AUTOBIOGRAPHY:

I have loved miniatures since I was a child, some 40 years plus. I was always fascinated by tiny things especially elves and fairies. I was determined someday I would make little people and critters. In 1976, I began experimenting in sculpting with Fimo. Being self-taught I had to learn everything the hard way, and I really enjoy passing on all the information and short cuts that might help someone else.

Over the years many miniaturists have collected my little people, and when I look at some of my earlier creations they really seem primitive compared to my work today. I am a member of NAME, IGMA and CIMTA.

ARTISAN: TAYLOR - GORE, VICTORIA

IDENTIFICATION MARKS:

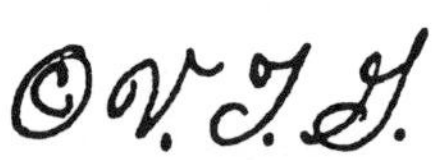

CATEGORY:

Christmas; Holiday Items; Paintings: pastels

RECOGNITION:

Nutshell News, Nov. 1992, pg. 70, "Designs on the Desert," Betty V. O'Meara

BIOGRAPHY:

Victoria Taylor-Gore earned an MFA in Painting & Drawing from the University of California, Santa Barbara in 1985, and a BFA in Painting & Drawing from the West Texas State University, Canyon, Texas in 1983. Her teaching experience was as a part time instructor of Drawing and Art Appreciation, West Texas State University, 1987-1991; Instructor of Pastel and Art Appreciation, Continuing Education Program, Amarillo College, Texas in 1988. She also instructed Adult Painting and Children's Painting at the Amarillo Art Center in Amarillo, Texas from 1980 to 1983, 1985 to 1986 and in 1988, and from 1983 to 1985 she was Teaching Assistant for Painting, Drawing, Intaglio and Color Theory at the University of California, Santa Barbara.

ARTISAN: TEBELMAN, CHARLES E.

BUSINESS NAME: Charles E. Tebelman

IDENTIFICATION MARKS:

CATEGORY:

Furniture; Lanterns: train scene; Roomboxes

HONORS:

NAME AOH; Exhibit, Taft Museum, Cincinnati, Ohio, 1984, 1989-1990

TEBELMAN, CHARLES E., continued

RECOGNITION:

Nutshell News, Vol. 13, No. 9, Sept. 1983, pg. 50-52; Vol. 16, No. 6, Jun. 1986, pg. 76-78; Vol. 17, No. 7, 1987, pg. 69; *Miniatures Showcase*, Vol. 4, No. 1, 1989, pg. 46; Vol. 4, No. 2, 1989, pg. 20; Vol. 6, No. 1, 1991, pg. 21

AUTOBIOGRAPHY:

I am a Certified Gemologist, and was introduced to miniatures in 1976, by a friend and have been working on them ever since. I have enjoyed learning various miniature crafting skills rather than specializing in one form, and consequently my work has ranged widely. Some favorites were a series of one-inch scale Grand Pianos made as gifts for friends, Miniature Trains in Lanterns, and ½-inch scale dollhouses and furniture.

I have also served on the Board of Directors of the Miniature Society of Cincinnati, as Co-Chairman of MSC's annual show, and on two NAME National Houseparty Steering Committees.

ARTISAN: THEDE, ALLAN

IDENTIFICATION MARKS:

A. THEDE with year

Block letters incised into wood

CATEGORY:

Furniture

HONORS:

Exhibit: Toy & Miniature Museum of Kansas City

RECOGNITION:

Nutshell News, Aug. 1982, pg. 48-50, "From Satellites to Spinning Wheels," Anne Day Smith; Oct. 1984, pg. 71, Show Scene

ARTISAN: THIBAULT, LEONA "LEE ANN"

BUSINESS NAME: Little Bow Teenies

IDENTIFICATION MARKS:

Business mark

CATEGORY:

Accessories; Christmas; Holiday Items; Needlepoint; Needlework; Toys

HONORS:

Founding member CIMTA

RECOGNITION:

Nutshell News, 1985; 1986; WTTW TV 11, Chicago, 1981 (Video tape donated to NAME); *Moreno Valley News*, California, 1986; *Miniatures Showcase*, Winter 1988; Fall 1990, pg. 67, "Turn of the Century;" *Chicago Tribune*, Du Page County Tempo Section, Jan. 26, 1992

THIBAULT, LEONA "LEE ANN", continued

AUTOBIOGRAPHY:

I started collecting miniatures in 1972 and started making miniatures for sale in 1974, because I couldn't find what I wanted and needed at stores.

I've had a year of college majoring in Home Economics, which has helped me in my specialty of needlepoint. I am self-taught and do mostly contemporary needlepoint. I will do rugs, fire screens, and chair seats on commission only, as I feel there are enough good needleworkers already on the market doing these items.

The company, Little Bow Teenies, has been in existence since around 1975, and was one of the original founding companies of the Cottage Industry Miniatures Trade Association. I have been a continuing and supporting member of the National Association of Miniature Enthusiasts since 1976, and have donated numerous needlepoint Houseparty Helpers to both National and Regional Houseparties.

I was a member of the Illinois Air National Guard as a full-time Medical Technician for 12 years, which allowed me to travel and meet fellow needlework artisans who inspired me to work harder and try new and unusual patterns.

ARTISAN: THIBAULT, ROBERT "BOB"

BUSINESS NAME: Little Bow Teenies

IDENTIFICATION MARKS:

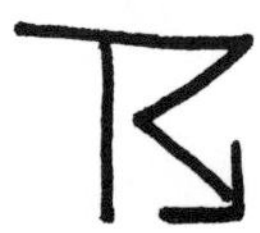

Business mark

CATEGORY:

Accessories: wooden; Christmas; Furniture; Holiday Items; Nutcrackers

HONORS:

Founding member CIMTA

RECOGNITION:

Miniatures Showcase, Fall 1990, pg. 67, "Turn of the Century"

AUTOBIOGRAPHY:

I started in miniatures by making special pieces my wife needed or wanted but could not find in any shop. She took these pieces to miniature shows, to show the dealers. The dealers liked what they saw and placed orders, my part of the business was started. I originally made scale models of airplanes, so working in small scales was nothing new. I have traveled extensively with the US Air Force as an Inflight Refueling Technician and have met many artisans around the world who have generously shared tips and hints, ideas and materials.

ARTISAN: THOMAS, MAUREEN

BUSINESS NAME: Maureen Thomas

IDENTIFICATION MARKS:

CATEGORY:

Bears; Clowns; Dolls

AUTOBIOGRAPHY:

I am an Art teacher turned Doll Artist.

ARTISAN: **THOMAS, NOEL & PAT**

BUSINESS NAME: Open House

IDENTIFICATION MARKS:

All marks 1974 to present

Numbered and dated

(Name of House)

CATEGORY:

Accessories; Dollhouses; Furniture; Supplies

HONORS:

IGMA Fellow (Noel & Pat); NAME AOH (Noel & Pat); Exhibit: Toy & Miniature Museum of Kansas City

RECOGNITION:

Nutshell News, Apr. 1980; Aug. 1980; Sept. 1981; Aug. 1982; Oct. 1988; Dec. 1993, pg. 78-82, "Old Friends," Pat Thomas; *Miniature Collector*, No. 2, Jun. 1977; No. 37, Jun. 1983; *Miniature Magazine*, Winter 1978; *9th Century*, Spring 1981; *Americana*, Jul/Aug. 1984; *Westways*, Feb. 1985; *Washington Magazine*, Nov. 1986; *Scale Woodcraft*, Winter 1987; *Elle Decor*, Dec. 1991; *Ripley's Believe it or Not!*, Mar. 15, 1985; *Architectural Digest*, Aug. 1989; *Angelers Magazine*, Nov. 1989; *Masters in Miniature, 12 Artisans At Work, Volume 1*, Anne Day Smith, Kalmbach Publishing, 1987; *Inside the World of Miniatures and Dollhouses*, Rosner & Beckerman, McKay Press, 1976; *American Period Interiors in Miniature*, Kate Doordan Klavan, Scribner's, 1984

AUTOBIOGRAPHY:

What began for Noel and me in 1972, as a dollhouse project for Noel's daughter Robin, became a 1974 move from California to Washington, and career changes for both of us from advertising to making miniatures. Since then we have built over 50 miniature structures, including houses, commercial buildings and roadside stands. Our early work, which was predominantly Victorian, evolved into the later Bungalow style, and on into the eclectic 1920's & 30's Roadside Stand, to Thomas Fantasy Old European. While most of our work resides in private collections, The Toy & Miniature Museum of Kansas City and The Carole & Barry Kaye Museum of Miniatures, Los Angeles, California have a representative selection of our pieces.

Along the way, we began teaching workshops at miniature shows around the country, as well as at the annual IGMA Guild School in Castine, Maine. We have added to our line such things as Famous Thomas Bug Juice, a wood weathering formula, shingles and other building and aging items. Noel's smelly garbage cans have gained a questionable but sizable following, along with the various editions of birdhouses that accompany our teaching projects, and my Mason Lake outdoor chairs and settees. Recently, Noel has added his original miniature watercolors to our offerings.

Noel was born at Christmas time, 1934, in Longview, Washington. He later graduated from Art Center College in Los Angeles and spent 14 years as an advertising art director in New York and Los Angeles. We met in an Los Angeles advertising agency where I (Pat) was a copywriter, and joined forces for the move to Washington. I was born in New York City early in 1946, the first baby boomer. In 1964, I graduated from the Theater Department at Skidmore College, returned to New York where I gave up theater, moved to Los Angeles where I took up writing and Noel.

In 1974, F.A.O. Schwartz took some of our houses on consignment. Through a comedy (in retrospect) of errors, the houses sold, and we got our first commission. The following year we attended our first show, the 1975 NAME National in San Francisco. There, all we were was nervous, and our simple beach house was totally overshadowed (literally and figuratively) by Jim Marcus's first fantastic Russian Embassy. We became friends with Jim but saw our competition, and went home to build a better dollhouse.

Since then we have been honored by both NAME (AOH) and the IGMA (Fellows), as well as by our clients, friends, students and far flung correspondents. It is to those people in particular I have addressed my thirty-two-and-counting articles in *Nutshell News*. In recent years Noel and I have returned part-time to our avocations (Noel is a watercolorist, and I am a poet), though miniatures still occupy our work day week. Because of the time demands of teaching our three to four annual workshops, plus our commissioned houses, we no longer attend shows, but keep up our mail order business.

ARTISAN: **THOMAS, SUE W.**

BUSINESS NAME: Mini Treats and Treasures

IDENTIFICATION MARKS:

CATEGORY:

Accessories: decorative; Beverages; Food

HONORS:

IGMA Artisan 1985

RECOGNITION:

Nutshell News, Feb. 1985, pg. 65, Show Scene; Oct. 1986, Cover; *Miniature Gazette*, Vol. 13, No. 1, Fall 1984, pg. 23, "Good Enough to Eat;" *Miniatures Showcase*, Winter 1982, pg. 31, 38-39; Fall 1987, pg. 24, 32, 34, 49; *The Oak Ridger*, Tennessee, Newspaper, Dec. 1971; Dec. 12, 1973, pg. 18; Dec. 10, 1982, pg. 13; Mar. 22, 1983, "Miniature Hobbyist Makes 'Real Food;" Dec. 10, 1984, pg. 6; *Dollhouse and Miniature News*, May 1976, pg. 7; Oct. 1978, pg. 14; *Knoxville News Sentinel*, Tennessee, Mar. 24, 1983, pg. 1, Feature Section; *Make Your Own Dollhouses and Dollhouse Miniatures*, Marian Maeve O'Brien, Hawthorne Books, Inc., NY, 1975, pg. 230-233; *Make and Furnish Your Own Miniature Rooms*, Marian Maeve O'Brien, Hawthorne Books, Inc., NY, 1978, pg. 51, 54-55

AUTOBIOGRAPHY:

My college work was all in journalism, composing and page make-up. I worked 10 years as a graphic illustrator for Union Carbide Nuclear Company and later served as consultant in that same capacity to UCNC for another 10 years. I have attended many workshops in the miniatures field, but am essentially self-taught.

ARTISAN: **THROOP PAM**

BUSINESS NAME: Pam Throop Historic Homes in Miniature

IDENTIFICATION MARKS:

 with name of house and year completed

CATEGORY:

Dollhouse; Houses: custom; Structures

HONORS:

IGMA Artisan 1983; Fellow 1985

RECOGNITION:

Nutshell News, Jul. 1984, pg. 35-38, "Pam Throop's Climb to the Top," Jane Mitchell; Vol. 18, No. 9, Sept. 1988, Cover, pg. 36; Vol. 20, No. 2, Feb. 1990, pg. 26; Vol. 20, No. 10, Oct. 1990, Cover, pg. 64; *Miniatures Showcase*, Vol. 1, No. 1, Fall 1986, pg. 56-57; Vol. 1, No. 2; Vol. 7, No. 4, Nov. 1992, pg. 52

THROOP, PAM, continued

BIOGRAPHY:

Pam, born in 1939 in Washington, DC, spent much girlhood "Wartime" playing "house" with the elaborate family model railroad. While her mother worked for the Labor Department and her father was a combat correspondent in the Pacific, she and her little brother made believe that the tiny houses her father had made were peopled with lively inhabitants. A postwar move to Chicago, home of the Thorne Rooms, fueled her love of miniature reality. As her newsman father traveled a great deal, he collected miniatures as gifts for her wherever he went. An artist himself, her father encouraged her to make things and to become an assistant architect on the railroad endeavor which grew to include numerous weathered, scratch-built structures. The living warmth of the little railway homes affected Pam's work enormously. When I eventually wanted a dollhouse for my daughter to house my childhood collection, I couldn't find a structure I really liked. To me, they were just boxes with no detail. My daughter and I wanted to shrink ourselves down and move in, but no commercial structure beckoned with living warmth.

Pam had been working part time in local miniature shops, taking classes in furniture construction, wiring, and roomboxes; and decided to build a dollhouse from scratch herself. Her friend, Chris Gancarz, and she rented coop studio space in Dallas, where her family now lived, and went into business as Petite Designs. They wanted to build something "real," so drew on her family love of Americana and a recent visit to Williamsburg, which had seemed to be full of small and interesting buildings. They built a copy of the Dickinson Shop from Pam's measured drawings. She invented a way to cast bricks that looked old, in authentic patterns for the mammoth chimney and foundation and walkways, and made everything: windows, paneling, beaded old siding and cherry floors ripped from stock cherry to authentic widths to look like antique pine. She devised a system of indirect lighting with optional hook-ups for fixtures. The shop and living quarters was very detailed, you could almost walk around inside.

Pam and her family moved to San Francisco where she built a San Francisco "Painted Lady" with a Toy Shoppe on the ground floor for her daughter. Pam, educated at Beloit College in English literature and at Stanford University with a Masters degree and Ph.D. work in history and anthropology, decided to return to history to continue her business. She designed and built a copy of Paul Revere's home in Boston. This and the Williamsburg Shop were shown at a San Anselmo Miniature shop. Both sold to a San Francisco patron and collector of full-scale American art; and both were eventually sent to the Academy of Art in Honolulu. "People had said that she couldn't build and sell furnished houses but she built these, sold them quickly, and was encouraged to continue." Since then Pam has researched and built over 30 structures. She has found "vernacular architecture," the homes that people make to reflect their own time and place with local materials, to be her passion. From a series of New England and Middle Atlantic houses "Pieterhoff, Cranberry Cove and Folly Cove" featured in *Nutshell News*, July 1984, to her recent projects, the cottage home of Sir Edward Fox Talbot (a real house in Lacock, England, with a semi fictitious resident); the Essex, Connecticut, elegant homestead of Captain Josiah Pratt; and the Nantucket diminutive cottage of Captain William Baxter, all have had the roots in historic regional architecture but were homes of lively individuals, recreations of typical homes of an era. Other projects from a tiny antique shop in a Connecticut gardener's cottage to a large English village pub "The Sign of the Angel" or "Load of Mischief" as it was finally called, complete with two bars (for ladies and gents), a tea room, a B and B, family quarters, and a working beer engine have involved absorbing and challenging research and design and invention of new ways to make her own components, like leaded glass windows, from scratch. To include an English cottage, surrounded by a window of tiny blooms, was the featured house in a Macy's Easter flower show.

A request for an authentic English cottage brought about the famous "Morningside Cottage" for Miss Jane Marple. "Pam's need to create a real inhabitant, albeit fictitious, is always a factor in each home she builds, and led to her suggestion of Miss Jane Marple." A series of articles on the joint project appeared over time in *Nutshell News*, and a video walking tour spotlighted the project.

Spending time in research is essential to breathe life into every project. "Pam visited Nantucket Island, photographed, measured and crawled in and out of the whalers' cottages of Sconset to produce her favorite little American cottage, Shanunga, a whalers tiny home and 1890 Summer retreat." The resulting grey shingled gem sold furnished filled with specially commissioned and collected folk art furnishings and accessories from fellow artisans Mark Murphy, Mary O'Brien, George Henglein, Renee Bowen and others; and will eventually go to a museum. While authentic reality is her goal in every piece, it is the warmth, a patina of love, often a little imperfect and worn and embellished with landscaping, which she works to build into her creations.

In addition to commissioned pieces, Pam has built and sold a number of speculative pieces. She averages one thoroughly researched and enjoyed house per year.

ARTISAN: **THURSLUND, IRENE,** (Deceased)
(Submitted by Phyllis Nissen)

BUSINESS NAME: Irene Thurslund

IDENTIFICATION MARKS:
Unmarked

CATEGORY:
Animals: dressed; Beds: dressed; Clothing; Gowns: bridal, night; Lingerie; Millinery

HONORS:
NAME AOH, 1992; Honorary Chairman 1990, "Gas Lights and Red Velvet," Gulf South Miniature & Dollhouse Event, New Orleans, Louisiana

RECOGNITION:
Nutshell News, Vol. 13, No. 2, Feb. 1983, pg. 54, Show Scene; Vol. 14, No. 8, Aug. 1984, pg. 52; Vol. 14, No. 12, Dec. 1984, pg. 71, Show Scene; *Miniature Collector*, No. 39, Oct. 1983, pg. 36, Show Stoppers

BIOGRAPHY:
Irene Thurslund, along with her husband, owned a craft store for many years. About the last five years they owned it, she started carrying a small line of miniatures, and also started collecting miniatures. Her first collector piece was a hundred dollar beautiful handmade signed desk. A man, unknown, brought it into the store to sell, and she fell in love with it but didn't feel she could afford it at that price. Her husband followed the man out of the store and bought it as a surprise. She really loved little things, and that was the beginning of collecting miniatures, her favorite period was Victorian. She sold the store after her husband died and started making miniature hats and beautiful beds and traveling the show circuit.

Irene joined the San Diego Miniature Crafters Club in 1975, and was a member until her death in October 1992. She was past President of the club and the Show Chairman for many years. She was the 1990 Honorary Chairman for the Annual Miniature & Dollhouse Event sponsored by the National Kidney Foundation of Louisiana in New Orleans. She was also a member of NAME and IGMA.

ARTISAN: **THWAITE, SUE ANN**

BUSINESS NAME: Lady Bug

IDENTIFICATION MARKS:

Lady Bug on each scene

CATEGORY:
Containers: scenes; Landscaping: scenes; Treehouses

AUTOBIOGRAPHY:
I started in the world of miniatures as a young working mother, as a way to spend quality time with my twins. My husband and son's hobby was antique cars. My daughter and I would go through the car show flea markets looking for items we could use in her dollhouse. That bolt became a perfect pot belly stove! We saw possibilities where others saw junk. The twins and I spent many Sunday afternoons making Fimo food for the dollhouse kitchen. But kids grow up and the dollhouse was relegated to the attic until we moved years later to the Washington DC area. Then it was unpacked again, reminisced over, put in a corner until my daughter, now in her 20's, saw an advertisement for a local mini show. Heather invited Mom for lunch and the show, for old times sake. We went and that's when I met Jonathan – a tiny porcelain baby, who captured my heart and re-awoke my

interest in miniatures. But this time it was for me! First Johnathan needed furniture, then a family, etc. etc. I was hooked!

When my grandmother passed away I found her old percolator coffee pot. I loved the look of it and it reminded me of my childhood with her. I asked my husband to cut it open and inside I created a scene reminiscent of my grandparents' mountain home. I grew up with the stories my grandfather told me of their beloved mountains. Stories of critters and elves and fairies and their friend the Lady Bug who brought spring on her wings. Now every scene I make has a lady bug to remember the spirit of my grandparents. Creating miniatures is more than just a hobby or business. Through my miniatures I try to recapture the wonderment of childhood. A friend once introduced me saying, "This is Sue – she doesn't think like the rest of us!"

Teaching is a way to share my excitement and inspire the creativity that lies dormant in all of us. I enjoy knowing that at the end of each workshop each person will take away a bit of whimsy and fairy dust.

ARTISAN: **TIDMORE, JIM** (Deceased)

BUSINESS NAME: Tidmore of Pipe Creek

IDENTIFICATION MARKS:

1983 to present

tidmore
of Pipe Creek with date

CATEGORY:

Furniture: custom, period

RECOGNITION:

Nutshell News, Nov. 1987; *Miniatures Showcase; Miniature Gazette*

AUTOBIOGRAPHY:

I am a graduate artist, interior designer, and teacher with minors in architecture and fashion design, and received my last degree in 1953. As an interior designer, I built a couple of ½-inch scale rooms as proposals. The miniature world remained hidden from me, except for the Thorne Rooms, which I frequented as a student in the Art Institute of Chicago.

In 1978, I had three heart operations in a five week period, followed by five heart attacks. The doctors insisted that I retire, and said that I should spend my remaining five years just enjoying the life that I had left. Get a hobby, was the advice. A short time later I saw an X-Acto kit, and remembered the Thorne Rooms. After building, and modifying these and into my third kit, I told my wife, "This is paint by number, and you know how I loathe paint by number!" So I pulled out a book I had compiled as a student, and perused the many sketches that I had done. After buying a table and scroll saw and a few files I began playing. Into my sixth piece, my wife exclaimed that this was too good to hide. So she entered me in the Texas Arts and Crafts Fair. I called her crazy, ruining a good hobby! My first commission came that very day doing many pieces of furniture for a museum. Life just hasn't been the same since.

I am considered by many a master craftsman. Bah, humbug! I'm still a student in my thinking! However, I have pieces across the USA and a few in Europe. But almost always, when one asks how I got started in miniatures, I just tell them, "It fell through the rabbit hole!"

ARTISAN: **TOMBERS, ROSEMARIE G. & PETER W.**

BUSINESS NAME: Rosel's Chandeliers

IDENTIFICATION MARKS:

Unmarked

ROSEL'S
CHANDELIERS
Miniature Lamps For Miniature Homes

Logo

CATEGORY:

Chandeliers; Lamps; Lighting; Sconces

ARTISAN: **TORRE, ROSEMARIE**

BUSINESS NAME: Rosemarie Torre Miniatures

IDENTIFICATION MARKS:

ROSEMARIE TORRE
HANDPAINTED

ROSEMARIE TORRE

ROSEMARIE TORRE
HAND-PAINTED ORIGINAL

brass plaque

CATEGORY:

Designer; Furniture: handpainted, period

HONORS:

IGMA Artisan

RECOGNITION:

Nutshell News, Sept. 1989, pg. 38-42, "Designing Woman," Anne Day Smith; *Miniatures Showcase*, Winter 1990, pg. 37; Winter 1992, pg. 19-20; *Miniature Collector*; *The Long Islander*, Nov. 1977; Nov. 1978; *The New York Times*, Jan. 16, 1983; *Binghamton Paper*, New York, 1985; *Oneonta New York Paper*, 1985; *Catskill Crafts, Artisans of the Catskill Mountains*, Jane Smily, Crown Publishers, NY, 1988

BIOGRAPHY:

Rosemarie M. Torre was born Rosemarie M. Strager in Dresden, Germany. Her schooling was as an artist. She is a third generation artist who came to the US in the fifties and worked as a textile designer. Then she started to do free-lance work, and with some free time built dollhouses for her children. This developed into building her own furniture and then handpainting the miniatures in an Oriental (chinoiserie), French provincial, and Italian styling.

Now a member of IGMA and NAME, she travels the country doing shows and giving workshops in furniture and room settings. At home she maintains her own Dollhouse Museum, which is open to the public, in Roxbury, NY.

ARTISAN: **TRACY, W. FOSTER**

BUSINESS NAME: Dearring – Tracy Ltd.

IDENTIFICATION MARKS:

W. FOSTER TRACY

TRACY, W. FOSTER, continued

CATEGORY:
Musical Instruments

HONORS:
Founder IGMA; Past President, IGMA; Exhibit: The Toy & Miniature Museum, Kansas City

RECOGNITION:
Nutshell News; Miniatures Showcase; Miniature Collector

ARTISAN: **TRAETTINO, BERNARDO**

BUSINESS NAME: Bernardo Traettino Miniatures

IDENTIFICATION MARKS:

CATEGORY:
Dollhouse: custom; Furniture

HONORS:
Honorary membership, British Toymakers Guild

ARTISAN: **TRAILL–HILL, JIM**

IDENTIFICATION MARKS:

C J Traill–Hill with date

CATEGORY:
Furniture; Lamps; Lighting; Silver; Silversmith

RECOGNITION:
Nutshell News, Winter 1977, pg. 36-38; May 1981, pg. 50-52; *Miniature Collector*, No. 19, Jun. 1980, pg. 46, Show Stoppers

ARTISAN: **TRANSUE, JACKI L.**

BUSINESS NAME: Jacki L. Transue

IDENTIFICATION MARKS:

CATEGORY:
Animals: figures; Dolls; Figures

HONORS:
IGMA Artisan

TRANSUE, JACKI L., continued

RECOGNITION:

Nutshell News, Feb. 1993, pg. 74, Show Scene; *Miniatures Showcase*, Fall 1989, pg. 32

BIOGRAPHY:

Jacki Transue lives in upstate New York with her husband, Kevin, and son, Jason. She is a self-taught sculptor who has been sculpting in one-inch scale for the last 15 years (1977). Jacki has been an artisan in the International Guild of Miniature Artisans since 1989. She only does one show a year. She works mainly in porcelain, but also uses resin and oven baked clay as the medium for her sculptures.

ARTISAN: TUCKER, BROOKE

BUSINESS NAME: Brooke Tucker Originals

IDENTIFICATION MARKS:

Rooms identified with brass plate **An Original by Brooke Tucker**

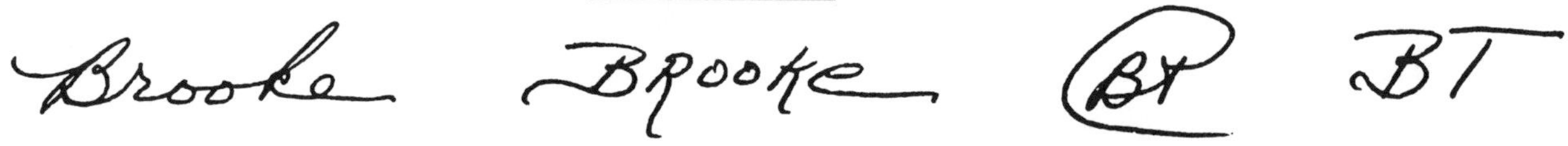

CATEGORY:

Accessories; Roomboxes; Rooms; Room Settings

HONORS:

IGMA Fellow; NAME AOH; Exhibits: Angel's Attic, Santa Monica, California; The Carole & Barry Kaye Museum of Miniatures, Los Angeles, California; Honorary Chairman 1985, "A Show Is Born," Gulf South Miniature & Dollhouse Event, New Orleans, Louisiana

RECOGNITION:

Nutshell News, Vol. 24, No. 10, Oct. 1994, pg. 36-42, "Bed, Breakfast – and Brooke!", Anne Day Smith; Vol. 16, No. 3, Mar. 1986, pg. 34-40, "Brooke Tucker's Yellow Rose of Texas", Anne Day Smith; Vol. 24, No. 12, Dec. 1994, Pg. 56-59, "City Christmas," Anne Day Smith; *Miniature Gazette; Interior Design in Miniature*, Brooke Tucker Originals, Anne Day Smith, Boynton, 1986

BIOGRAPHY:

Brooke Tucker's niche in the world of miniatures is undisputed. She is a Master Miniaturist with a vision for the unique. Her work is widely recognized. Her creativity consistently meets each new challenge to achieve the perfect effect that makes each project more beautiful than the one before.

Her sense of the dramatic and her flair for theatrical design was undoubtedly fostered by her Hollywood background. Brooke grew up in California as the daughter of the well-known actor Forrest Tucker, and her beautiful Earl Carrol showgirl mother. The stage sets were her playground, and their design and construction made a lasting impression on her. Her flair for the extraordinary and distinctive was nurtured in the back lots of those Hollywood sets. Later she entered the entertainment world, touring first with her father in several productions and then striking out on her own on stage and television.

Brooke recalls that miniatures just seemed to appear miraculously in her life. She distinguished herself in this field very early and was one of the first to create contemporary miniature rooms with the unmistakable flair that stamps her work with that special, unsurpassed "Brooke Look." Her rooms capture a moment in time, a prettier, more gracious time, a world into which viewers might escape into their own reveries. What Brooke creates, then is a fantasy in miniature, a world where imagination soars and fantasies come to life.

Brooke is a gifted teacher who has the ability to convey concepts with contagious enthusiasm. In classes conducted all over the country, Brooke teaches her students how to design and build a room, how to avoid costly mistakes, and how to coordinate efforts to achieve a uniform, pleasing design. She unhesitatingly shares her trade secrets and techniques which she has developed over the years. The finished product under her tutelage is not just a miniature project; it is a masterpiece and proudly displayed as a "Brooke Tucker" class project.

Brooke's home in Bremerton, Washington, serves as her studio as well as a Bed and Breakfast for students when she schedules classes there. Her busy schedule includes teaching classes, designing and marketing her original rooms in miniature as well as a line of accessory items. She is a gifted artisan, unsurpassed as a teacher, and, to many of her students, a cherished friend. She reaches for the stars and having attained her goal, shares her accomplishments with all who dare to dream.

ARTISAN: **TUCKER, PHYLLIS S.**

BUSINESS NAME: The Happy Unicorn

IDENTIFICATION MARKS:
Lighting pieces unmarked

Original design concept, individual arms riveted to base, identifies these pieces

Logo on printed material

CATEGORY:
Accessories; Chandeliers; Lighting; Sconces

HONORS:
IGMA Fellow 1981, Crystal Award 1995; NAME AOH, 1986; Exhibit: The Carole & Barry Kaye Museum of Miniatures, Los Angeles, California

RECOGNITION:
Articles written about Phyllis Tucker
Nutshell News, May/Jun. 1979, pg. 43-45; Nov. 1981, pg. 29, "On the Avenue (Fifth Avenue)", Kate Doordan Klavan; Jul. 1982, pg. 55, "Tinier Dwellings;" Feb. 1983, pg. 10; Dec. 1983, pg. 71, Show Scene; Dec. 1984, pg. 70, Show Scene; Mar. 1986, pg. 35, 61, Show Scene; *Miniature Collector*, No. 25, Jun. 1981, pg. 41, Show Stoppers; No. 40, Dec. 1983, pg. 33-35; *Miniature Magazine,* Vol. 8, No. 6, Dec. 1982, Pg. 5; *Miniature Gazette*, Vol. 10, No. 4, Summer 1982, pg. 23; *Cleveland Plain Dealer*, Ohio, Aug. 13, 1983, Saturday Supplement; *Chicago Tribune*, Jan. 26, 1992, pg. 1, Tempo Section; *American Period Interiors in Miniature*, Kate Doordan Klavan, Scribner's, 1984; *Through The Looking Glass*, Boynton and Associates, Inc., Ann Ruble, 1984; *Interior Design in Miniature*, Brooke Tucker Originals, Anne Day Smith, Boynton, 1986; The Carole & Barry Kaye Museum of Miniatures, Los Angeles, California, Videotape, 1993
Articles written by Phyllis Tucker
Nutshell News, Mar. 1981, "Elegant Chandeliers"; Mar. 1985, pg. 34-39, "Lee Taylor's Evolving Collection;" Apr. 1989, pg. 42-47, "The Guild: What It Is and How It Works," pg. 54-59, "The Renaissance Men of Lafayette;" Feb. 1991, pg. 58-62, "Collector, Crafter, Connoisseur;" Aug. 1995, pg. 36-42, "Purveyor of Dreams;" Mar. 1996, pg. 18-20, "A Class Act, Phyllis Tucker;" *Miniature Collector*, Nov/Dec. 1994, "In The Grand European Manner;" *Miniature Gazette*, Spring 1995, pg. 18-20, "The Chrysnbon Tradition," Judy Berman; *NAME National Houseparty Program Book*, Jul. 1995, Judy Berman

AUTOBIOGRAPHY:

When I was a little girl, I got in the most trouble for reading and talking too much. I would climb a big catalpa tree and hide among its large leaves as I read insatiably. As an adult I feel those two sources of difficulty have proved to be among my most valuable assets. I still do both to excess!

My life has been enhanced by wondrous friendships, a sense of history, an avid curiosity, a vivid imagination, a firm belief in the link between all life, and an ever expanding faith in The Supreme Being. These attributes have taken me on many delightful paths that at this time have brought me to the world of miniatures.

I have had most interesting experiences as a professional Santa Claus, a clown, public relation specialist, teller, operetta singer, craft designer and instructor, trade show demonstrator, model maker, writer, journalist, wife to

Richard, and mom to Kathy and Lee. As a miniature artisan I am provided with the opportunity to utilize many of my acquired skills into one area of interest.

Richard's work as a Purchasing Agent in the construction industry has necessitated creating homes in Ohio, Rhode Island, and Illinois. We have two exceptional children. A daughter Kathyrn is a Special Education Coordinator and a son Lee, who has completed work on his Masters degree in Construction Technology.

My first professional brush with miniatures occurred in early 1974. I began making miniature items, animals, toys, foods, fairies, etc. while demonstrating a modeling compound at trade shows. One of the exhibits I built was a complete turn of the century general store. I sculpted and painted all items including a butcher with a dead chicken in his hand! I often wonder what became of that miniature room.

In 1976, I wrote an article for *Profitable Craft Merchandising*, a publication for the craft trades on creating miniatures in Polyform. My work was very primitive and I had no knowledge at that time of the beauty of handcrafted miniatures.

I continued to "dance" around the field of working small as a designer and master model maker in the war game fantasy field. A two headed ogre and a dragon I designed were my favorite creations. I have been trained in the art of lost wax casting and direct metal sculpting.

While living in Rhode Island we visited the mansions of Newport. There I saw the magnificent crystal chandeliers. I perceived them as sculptures, wire armatures with beads, and became intrigued with the artistic and engineering skills needed to create them. Through a series of coincidences, including Rhode Island being the costume jewelry capital of the US, a ready source of supplies, I began making miniature crystal chandeliers.

My specialty has evolved into creating historic reproductions with hand blown glass components supplied by Ferenc Albert. I also do chimeric pieces, others in the manner of existing chandeliers, and crystal accessories such as wall sconce or candelabra.

I was introduced to the miniature show circuit by the Boston Tiny Treasures organization in 1979. A move to Cleveland, Ohio came the very day after that first show!

It has always been a personal objective to assist new artisans whenever possible. I strive to promote the industry as an entity, and to work towards our acceptance as an art form. I sometimes use my aptitude as a writer and speaker to this end.

At times I have performed as a staff consultant and architectural "space" advisor in the creation of miniature museums. I also act as a liaison to bring together a single significant miniature item, or an entire accumulation into a private or museum collection.

As time permits I catalog and video tape collections with voice over descriptions as an estate record or for historical reference. The destiny of these pieces is consequential as important miniatures may be lost or "closeted". It is imperative to respect the privacy of the collector but for the future a provenance of work should be available as it is for full-size art.

I became a Fellow in the International Guild of Miniature Artisans in 1981. I was a Charter member of the Cottage Industry Miniature Trade Association, and was elected to the NAME Academy of Honor in 1987. I was overwhelmed in the Spring of 1995 when the International Guild of Miniature Artisans chose to award me the Crystal Award, their highest honor "in recognition of outstanding contributions throughout the years, to the art of miniatures."

It may be called kismet, destiny, luck, or God's Master Plan. Whatever passageway led me to miniatures I am very grateful. I consider it an honor, a privilege and a great gift to be associated with this fascinating world.

ARTISAN: **TUCKER, ROSEMARY**

BUSINESS NAME: Rosemary Tucker
Rosemary Originals
Originals By Rosemary

IDENTIFICATION MARKS:
1979 to present

CATEGORY:
Costuming; Dolls: porcelain

TUCKER, ROSEMARY, continued

HONORS:

NAME AOH; Honorary Chairman 1988, "A Holiday Shoppers' Festival," Gulf South Miniature & Dollhouse Event, New Orleans, Louisiana

RECOGNITION:

Nutshell News, Apr. 1988, pg. 77; Aug. 1988, pg. 66; *Miniature Showcase*, Spring 1988, pg. 39; *Miniature Gazette*, Spring 1984, Front & Back Covers; Winter 1986; Spring 1987; Summer 1992, pg. 55

BIOGRAPHY:

Rosemary began as a miniaturist around 1982 making bonnets and feathered fashion hats. Soon she was putting the hats on porcelain doll heads. Noting that most dolls were done as caricatures she set out to make miniature dolls with the same elegance as their full-size counterpart and she succeeded.

Rosemary is a doll costumer and hair stylist, she does not make the porcelains. Her interest in the whole field of miniatures led to writing articles and the use of photographs describing the work of other miniaturists, i.e. "The Master File" in the *Nutshell News* and various articles in the *Miniature Gazette*.

Her background includes that of a professional musician and an interior decorator. She was accepted in the National Association of Miniature Enthusiasts Academy of Honor. Rosemary served as the 1988 Honorary Chairman for the Annual Miniature & Dollhouse Event sponsored by the National Kidney Foundation of Louisiana in New Orleans.

ARTISAN: TURCOTTE, TERESA

BUSINESS NAME: Tiny Joys

IDENTIFICATION MARKS:

CATEGORY:

Accessories; Bridal Items; Holiday Items; Millinery

RECOGNITION:

Nutshell News, Oct. 1981, pg. 41, 81

AUTOBIOGRAPHY:

I was born in Washington, DC on November 14, 1940. Actually, I was a late bloomer as far as miniatures go. A year or two after I was married, I met one of my husband's uncles who loved to make all types of wooden rocking chairs. Eventually, each family member received one as a gift. When I got mine, I knew that I was accepted in the family. This led me to my challenge – finding a little table to sit beside the chair; then, a floor lamp for the chair; then something to put on the table, etc. It was difficult to find miniatures in stores at the time, but I succeeded. By then, I was hooked! I always liked tiny things but didn't accept the fact that an adult could love dollhouses until the early 1970's. That's when I was lucky enough to talk to Bernice Kramer and find out about other miniaturists.

My first attempt at making a miniature was a flop. I joined the Minimaniacs Club and one of the members was expecting a baby. We decided to make a shadowbox room for her with items that each of us made. Until then, I was a collector of one to two years and had participated in a couple of simple workshop projects. After my initial panic, I decided that I would make bedroom slippers and a tissue box with tissues that actually popped up as you removed one. I decided to use felt and sew them. The slippers were the first attempt. They came out well on my first try. Then came the tissue box. It also turned out beautifully on the first try – including the tissues that popped up; however, in putting it next to the slippers, I realized it was like accessorizing Dawn and Barbie. Back to the drawing board to scale the tissues down. After that, I had courage to try other things. My first love is Christmas and I enjoy making decorated trees the most. Behind Christmas come the other holidays and special occasion items, then clothing accessories.

ARTISAN: **TURNER, CYRIL B.**

IDENTIFICATION MARKS:

CATEGORY:

Art: fine; Paintings: original

HONORS:

IGMA Artisan, Fellow; 2nd Place, Miniature Painters, Sculptures and Gravers Society of Washington, DC, 1985; Miniature Artist of America, 1988; Australian Societies of Miniature Art, 1990

RECOGNITION:

The Artist & Illustrator's Magazine, Issue 14, Nov. 1987, Painting in Miniature; *Country Life*, Vol. CLXXIX, No. 4623, Mar. 27, 1986, pg. 846, Diary of Events Arts & Antiques; *Painting Miniatures in Acrylics*, Search Press, 1990; *Painting in Acrylics*, Search Press, 1991, English & French Editions, Miniature Section; *Painting Original Fine Art Miniatures*, Cyril B. Turner, 1993, A 21 Pocket Book Informative Series, No. 1 Bases (Lumitex) & No. 2 Bases Various

BIOGRAPHY:

Cyril B. Turner is one of Britain's best known, most prolific and experienced fine art miniaturists, with an international reputation as one of the world's leading master miniaturists. Working exclusively in miniature producing original fine art miniature paintings in most media and categories His greatest asset is being gifted in the fundamental art of miniaturism, which is the act of reducing the image of the subject matter in front of him, and transferring this into a plain base in a very diminutive scale. His works are true miniatures, all originals, created from real life on-sight observations, sketches and notes.

The first non-American to be honored by election to the Miniature Artists of America, he is a member of the Miniature Painters, Sculptures and Gravers Society of Washington, DC, the Miniature Art Society of New Jersey, the Miniature Art Societies of Montana, Georgia, Florida and New Mexico and the Australian Societies of Miniature Art Tasmania, Queensland, New South Wales and Victoria.

His contributions to miniature fine art include the introduction of cold enamel as a medium for miniature painting, 12 of his miniatures painted on this medium have won awards. He has developed a soft pastel technique which enables intricately detailed miniatures to be produced down to a size of half an inch square. BBC-TV has filmed him working on a one-inch diameter miniature in soft pastel from blank ivory to framed miniature. One of his innovations when working in silverpoint, is to work the miniature onto pale colored washes and to paint in the subject matter with light washes, as the base for original silverpoint miniatures.

Due to the endangered species trade embargo on ivory, a popular material used for paintings, he undertook the research and development of Lumitex an acid free ultra-violet proof substitute for ivory. Every essential requirement of a suitable surface for miniature paintings, has been considered and incorporated into this material, coupled with giving it all the characteristics of ivory. Seven of his miniatures painted on Lumitex have won awards.

His work had its first showing on television in 1981 on Anglian TV, and he appeared on BBC-TV in 1991, covering studio working and his one-man exhibition of miniatures at the Assembly House Norwich. He has talked about his one-man exhibitions on Radio Norfolk and Radio Shropshire.

He has won numerous awards worldwide. His works are in many collections throughout the world. They have been exhibited widely from Australia to America, including the Royal Academy London and the Salon des Nations Paris.

ARTISAN: **TURNER, JOE**

BUSINESS NAME: Joe Turner
J. Turner Miniatures, 1989 to 1990

IDENTIFICATION MARKS:

TURNER, JOE, continued

CATEGORY:

Furniture

RECOGNITION:

Nutshell News, Nov. 1992, Cover

AUTOBIOGRAPHY:

I have been building miniatures as a hobby since 1989 when I retired. I had been in construction all my working life, most of it as head of scenic construction for NBC television. I built full-size sets and miniature sets for television. I was commissioned by NBC news to build a model of the FBI Building back in the 1960's, which is the new FBI Building that was built in Washington, DC. Everything that I know today, is self-taught.

ARTISAN: **TYLER, PATRICIA**

BUSINESS NAME: Pat Tyler's "Just Precious" Leather Miniatures

IDENTIFICATION MARKS:

CATEGORY:

Accessories; Furniture: leather; Leather work; Luggage; Trunks

RECOGNITION:

Nutshell News; Miniatures Showcase

U

ARTISAN: **URCIUOLI, MAGGIE**

BUSINESS NAME: Small Ideas

IDENTIFICATION MARKS:

Some unmarked

SMALL IDEAS SI

Handpainted in black or gold ink

SMALL IDEAS

Metal stamp

CATEGORY:

Furniture

HONORS:

IGMA Artisan 1983

RECOGNITION:

Nutshell News; Miniature Collector

AUTOBIOGRAPHY:

I was raised in Connecticut and began painting in oils at 12. I continued as a painter for most of my adult life, majoring in Fine Arts at Boston University and studying painting in Rome for a year after college.

I have worked as a graphic artist and became involved in portraiture for many years. Raising two children, a daughter and a son, made the discipline of painting quite difficult so I decided to store my brushes, anticipating a future with more leisure time.

About this time, my husband built a dollhouse for our daughter and I was given the task of "doing" the inside as well as furnishing it. My good friend, and now partner in *Small Ideas*, Bobbie Schoonmaker, took me to my first miniature show where I was instantly captivated.

From kits to kit "bashing" to furniture from "scratch," I dove in with great enthusiasm. Bobbie's interest in scaling down her beautiful needlepoint occurred about this time so we began an artistic collaboration that has flourished through the years as we keep learning and growing.

We entered this field, professionally, knowing that Queen Anne and Chippendale styles would be our main focus and decided to concentrate on pieces that were difficult to find in miniature. Most of our pieces are a combination of woodworking and needlepoint but we also produce work exclusive of one another. For example, I have recently introduced a line of furniture painted in whimsical patterns while Bobbie enjoys stitching rugs, pillows, etc. to coordinate.

We entered our first show, The IGMA Show in New York City, in 1982 and, in 1983 I was made an Artisan member of the Guild. We currently do two shows a year (as opposed to 10 or 12 when we began) and our pieces are in collections and museums throughout the US, Europe and Australia.

The challenge of learning new techniques and producing new pieces keeps us very busy, stimulated, and even more enthusiastic about the world of miniatures than when we started.

See "Bobbie Schoonmaker"

V

ARTISAN: **VABER, JOAN C.**

BUSINESS NAME: Joan Vaber – Miniature Paintings

IDENTIFICATION MARKS:

J. VABER — Front

Joan Vaber — Back

CATEGORY:
Paintings

HONORS:
IGMA Fellow

RECOGNITION:
Miniature Collector, No. 33, Oct. 1982, pg. 30; *Press Sun Bulletin*, Binghamton, NY, Mar. 29, 1987, Living Sec. C, pg. 1-2

AUTOBIOGRAPHY:
My early interest in painting led directly to my studies at Boston University where I majored in fine arts. After college, raising a family curtailed any extensive professional work in painting, although I kept my hand in with occasional classes under local artists, and producing paintings for friends and family.

In the mid 1970's, a chance request from my mother, who is an avid miniatures collector, to do some paintings for her dollhouse, led to further requests from her friends and other collectors. I attended my first show in 1975, joined IGMA, and have been busy painting miniatures ever since.

ARTISAN: **VALENTINE, BETTY**

BUSINESS NAME: Betty Valentine

IDENTIFICATION MARKS:

BSV

BSV (in heart) — Solid color heart, initials within

CATEGORY:
Furniture

HONORS:
IGMA Artisan; NAME AOH; Exhibits: Summer 1967, Women's Educational and Industrial Union, Boston, MA, Three Centuries of Life in America, Haverhill, MA; Feb. 1970, Gallery 2, Woodstock, Vermont, Future Heirloom; Summer 1972, Vermont Historical Society, The Pavilion, Montpelier, Vermont; Sept/Oct. 1967, Hitchcock Chair Museum, Riverton, CT; Nov/Jan. 1983, G. Fox Department Store, Hartford, CT, Replicas in Miniature

RECOGNITION:
Nutshell News, Summer 1971; Jun. 1985; *Miniatures Showcase*, Fall 1988, pg. 18; *Hobbies Magazine*, Jan. 1971; *Miniature World*, May/Jun. 1979; *House Beautiful Magazine*, Feb. 1978, Crafts dept.; *Amy Vanderbilt's Column*, Jul. 1974; *Hartford Times*, Connecticut, Dec. 21, 1975; *New York Magazine*, 1976; *Dolls' Houses in America*, Flora Gill Jacobs; *The Collector's Guide to Dollhouses*

VALENTINE, BETTY, continued

and Dollhouse Miniatures, Marian Maeve O'Brien, 1974; *This Side of Yesterday in Miniatures*, Catherine B. MacLaren, 1975, pg. 53; *The Complete Book of Making Miniatures*, Thelma Newman and Virginia Merrill, 1975; *The Andrews Collection*, Personal Treasures, Anne Day Smith, 1988, pg. 14, 49, 59, 65, 79, 82

AUTOBIOGRAPHY:

I think I've always loved little things and always enjoyed handcrafts. Paper dolls were big in my childhood with much creative cutting and assembling from the big mail order book. One very important set of characters was Buck Rogers with Wilma and Dr. Huer. I made a small space ship for them out of an oatmeal box, my first real miniature endeavor.

Due to WWII, I went to work early and then married. As a young wife and mother, I sewed out of necessity, and then tried weaving, chair stenciling, rug braiding, chair seating, wood-turning and minor carpentry. For fun, I made a "little" chair to rush-seat, when my sister-in-law told me about Mrs. Thorne's rooms; in miniatures I found the one hobby that took in ALL the others. There were no clubs, no classes, with the only supplies at model train stores, and model ship suppliers. So I'm self-trained and enjoy the challenge of making up my own working drawings. Although I have tried making all kinds of furniture, early on I realized my interest was antique chairs, the most essential item of all. The Boston Museum of Fine Arts, Hartford Athenaeum, and Metropolitan Museum of Art gave me good models to aim for.

I sold my first chair to Joe Gray of Chicago in 1959. He had a column in *Hobbies Magazine*, and was almost the only dealer in miniatures for many years and my only outlet for a long time. In 1970, I met Catherine MacLaren, and when she started *Nutshell News* the following year we all at last began to meet each other, and the rest, the shows, organizations, conventions, new supplies, etc. is history.

The customers are the most wonderful part of all. Their endorsement is the best incentive to keep working. Their ideas and requests keep me trying new things and their sense of fun reassure me that the world can be a good place. I think I continue to improve as my knowledge of furniture and historical context grow, also my "eye" for the line of a piece and knowledge of what I can successfully include and leave out or merely suggest. I hope to make a lot more furniture, several more styles to round out my own collection, and maybe even finish the dollhouse I started in 1967!

ARTISAN: **VAN DER LINDEN, SANDY**

BUSINESS NAME: Linden Swiss Miniatures

IDENTIFICATION MARKS:

Logo

CATEGORY:

Accessories; Kits

RECOGNITION:

Press-Enterprise Newspaper

ARTISAN: **VAN HORN, MITZI**

IDENTIFICATION MARKS:

Few pieces marked

VAN HORN, MITZI, continued

CATEGORY:

Ceramics; Dolls: costumed; Metal; Needlework; Shadow Boxes

HONORS:

Mell Prescott award 1986; NAME AOH; Exhibits: Norfolk Public Library, Norfolk, Virginia; Portsmouth Fine Arts Museum, Portsmouth, Virginia; American Medical Society Womens Auxiliary Headquarters, Chicago, Illinois; Chrysler Museum, Norfolk, Virginia; Hewett Garden Center, Norfolk, Virginia; Williamsburg, Virginia; National Geographic Society, Washington, DC

RECOGNITION:

Nutshell News, Vol. 4, No. 1, Spring 1974, pg. 31; Vol. 4, No. 2, Summer 1974, pg. 24; Vol. 5, No. 4, Winter 1975, pg. 35-38; Fall 1976; Winter 1977; Spring 1987; *Miniature Collector*, No. 8, Aug. 1978, pg. 20-26; *Miniatures Showcase*, 1986; *This Side of Yesterday in Miniatures*, Catherine B. MacLaren, 1975; *Miniatures*, Phillis Miars; *Needlework In Miniature*, Virginia Merrill; *Scale Cabinetmakers Guide*, Vol. I, No. 1; Vol. IV, No. 2; *Old Time Magazine*, Dec. 1986; *Richmond Times*, Virginia, Oct. 1970; *Virginia Pilot*, Dec. 12, 1965; Jun. 1974; Dec. 9, 1977

AUTOBIOGRAPHY:

My interest in miniatures dates to my childhood. In the early 1950's, I met Joe Gray in Chicago and started making small items to trade for treasured Austrian Bronze miniatures he had in his collection. I worked for him for years branching out into many different media's.

My first miniature show was in Williamsburg, Virginia, where I shared a table with Susan Sirkis. It was Susan who encouraged me and talked me into doing more shows. This developed into mail order also and for about ten years I did both. I was a director on the first board of IMA.

In 1979, I went to work for the Douglas Mac Arthur Foundation as Director of the Retail Operation. I soon found I had to discontinue the miniature business. There are so many wonderful artists today, so many beautiful works that I have to laugh at the simple little things I once made.

ARTISAN: **VAN HORN, NANCY A.**

BUSINESS NAME: Nancy's Nostalgia Shoppe

IDENTIFICATION MARKS:

NVH

Needlework

Painting, color corresponding to work
Needlework on furniture, in Gold only

Books

CATEGORY:

Accessories: handpainted; Author; Books: instructional; Landscaping; Needlework; Publications: How-to; Writer

HONORS:

Ribbons awarded at Miniature Shows and Fair Exhibitions

RECOGNITION:

Nutshell News, Aug. 1992, pg. 63; *Miniature Collector*, No. 47, Jan/Feb. 1985, pg. 53; No. 88, Mar/Apr., 1995, pg., 36-41, "The Miniature World of Nancy Van Horn," Marguerite Winter; *Atlanta Journal Constitution,* Gwinette edition, Apr. 5, 1991; *Miniature Dealer*, Mar. 1992, pg. 20-21; *The Andrews Collection*, Personal Treasures, Anne Day Smith, pg. 50

AUTOBIOGRAPHY:

My background includes being raised in Indiana, graduating from Indiana University Business School in 1952. Working for L.S. Ayres department store in Indianapolis in sales, advertising, training dept. and window display. I even wrote an in-house newsletter. From there I became a Travel Agent, a position in Financing in Chicago, the first woman officer in a bank in Greenville, Michigan as an Assistant Trust Officer and a real estate salesman in my husband's real estate firm. As you have surmised, I have lived in several states from New York to Texas.

My miniatures actually go back to when I was a little girl. I still have the dollhouse that I received in 1941, exactly as it was then, including an embroidered table cloth in the kitchen, a construction paper Christmas wreath, and a braided rug. My dollhouse had many scales because furniture was purchased as complete rooms and mine are Tootsie Toy, Schoenhut and Stromberg. In 1939, I was very fortunate to be able to see Colleen Moore's Fairy Castle on display in Indianapolis and Kokomo, Indiana. This created a desire for a large one-inch scale dollhouse.

In 1978, my husband, Louis, had heard me speak of this desire, had given me a dollhouse kit (1,000 pieces) for Christmas. Of course, being a home builder, he thought he could put it together in nothing flat! Eighteen months later, he had almost finished the house. It was actually, completely finished in 1992. At the time, I was having trouble finding the things that I needed for the house and decided other people in the area must have the same problem that I was having. In 1980, when the economic climate became so bad in Michigan, I began thinking about opening a miniature shop in our real estate office which was a Cape Cod house. After several months of research, it seemed feasible to do so. However, I did not have much capital and could not let my husband give me the money so he could say "I told you so!" There was land beside our real estate office that wasn't doing anything, so I decided to divide it into spaces and run a flea market. I sold spaces and also took a space and sold some of my own things. At the end of eight weeks, I had raised $750. Everyone told me I could not start a shop for under $25,000. That sent up red flares as you don't tell me I can't do something. I allowed Louis to give me $250. This gave me $1,000 to start the shop. We went to Boutique Trims and bought $800 worth of miniatures, mostly one of everything. It fit in two boxes in the trunk of the car! I decided I could reorder every week when I sold something. Then we went to The House That Jack Built and bought two dollhouses. He also put four dollhouses on consignment to help me get started. With my own handcrafted items and merchandise from two other craftsmen doing miniatures for me, we were ready to open with half of the inventory handcrafted. This started a trend of high quality miniatures 50% manufactured and 50% handcrafted that lasted through today. I soon had 80 craftsmen making miniatures for me along with my own handpainted items (milkcans), fine needlework including embroidery and knitting, braided rugs, quilts and portable landscaping.

In August 1980, I placed a dollhouse display in a downtown window for the Danish Festival in Greenville, Michigan with a story of how I started and that I planned to open a miniature and dollhouse shop. The newspaper in Greenville was going to print a special edition for Christmas that would come out in October. They asked when I would be opening as they wanted to run a feature article on the shop. I opened Nancy's Nostalgia Shoppe on October 15, 1980, the day the paper came out, in one room of the real estate office using all kinds of unusual items for display pieces, many I had purchased at the flea market. That day I was called for Jury Duty and my friend who was one of my first craftsmen, opened the shop for me. By December, I had sold $12,000 worth of miniatures and was on my way. I then decided to try and help the shop by bringing money in from other states. I started doing miniature shows and covered 6 states including Indiana, Michigan, Ohio, Illinois, Kentucky, and Atlanta, Georgia. I sold my shop in 1989 to the girl who worked for me and it is now Harvey's Miniatures and Dollhouses. I still do shows in the Atlanta area as Nancy's Nostalgia Shoppe with mostly handcrafted items and my books.

To spread the word about miniatures, I started giving miniature talks to organizations in the area on the Wonderful World of Miniatures. During these talks, I traced the history of miniatures as well as scale and all the wonderful possibilities given to the creative mind as miniatures are a whole world to discover not just a toy. Also, we need to remember there are children's miniatures and adult miniatures with one growing into the other without really growing up. At this time, I would have a display of my miniature projects that I had created. I would remind people that none of us started at the top with our craftsmanship, we all had to learn and perfect our crafts as we go along. This also applies to miniatures and emphasizes our NAME motto "Only Through Sharing Can We Really Enjoy Our Treasures." We constantly learn from each other. Desiring to bring my customers and friends together to learn more about miniatures, I started a NAME Miniature Club in the Greenville/Grand Rapids area.

After selling the shop, we moved to Atlanta, Georgia in November 1989 for warmer weather. In May 1990, I went to work for Houseworks, Ltd. in Customer Service. I soon learned that I was the only person in the company who had actually used the products as well as having sold them in my shop for 10 years. In a short time, I was asked to write a book on my porch. The book, *Porches Across America*, became the best seller that year and the basis for the porch contests for two years. Little did I know I was to become an author. At the request of Paul Benamy, I wrote my second book which was an instructional book on finishing a dollhouse or miniature project, *Everything You Wanted To Know About Dollhouses But Didn't Know Who To Ask.* This book has also become very popular and was printed a second time in less than a year. It is wonderful to be able to work in something you love as well as continuing to create and be a member of NAME and two miniature clubs in Atlanta. My whole life now revolves around miniatures. I have a complete room (museum type) in our home of my miniature creations including roomboxes as well as dollhouses, displays and the many ribbons I have won for exhibiting. My dear husband has actually learned to live with miniatures throughout the house, but remember he was responsible for recreating my interest in 1978 after the children were gone.

ARTISAN: **VAN INGEN, PATRICIA**

BUSINESS NAME: Patricia's Miniature Dolls

IDENTIFICATION MARKS:

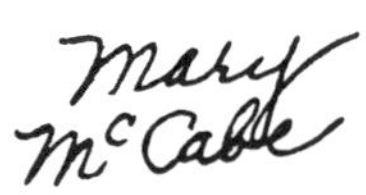

month/year
Used only 6 months

month/year
Inscribed back of head

month/year

Logo

Lynn
Van Ingen
On toys

CATEGORY:
Accessories; Dolls: porcelain

HONORS:
Blue Ribbons: Monroe County Fair; Doll Artisan Guild; Art Shows, Wayland, NY

RECOGNITION:
Nutshell News; Miniatures Showcase; Miniature Dealer

AUTOBIOGRAPHY:

I consider myself a true doll lover. I gave up playing with dolls in my very late teens, only to start making porcelain dolls after raising four "Living Dolls." I had colored photographs and made children's clothes, both of which helped me in my current endeavor, miniature dolls, my avocation.

I was born in Spokane, Washington in 1922 and moved eventually to Rochester, New York. At 59 I learned for the first time of my adoption, in 1924, from my natural brother, who finally made contact after several attempts. I found that I also have a half-brother and other relatives on the West Coast.

Joining CIMTA was a fortunate move for me. If it wasn't for this organization and the friendship of two wonderful members, I probably would have never taken the plunge to come to California. I'm glad I did.

ARTISAN: **VAN KLEECK, RUTH**

BUSINESS NAME: Zenda's Dream Miniatures

IDENTIFICATION MARKS:
Unmarked

CATEGORY:
Accessories; Chandeliers; Lamps; Lighting; Sconces

VAN KLEECK, RUTH, continued

AUTOBIOGRAPHY:

I have been in the miniature business since 1980. I got into it because of the love of dollhouse miniatures and to support my habit of collecting.

ARTISAN: VASI, FERN

BUSINESS NAME: The Willow Tree

IDENTIFICATION MARKS:

All dolls wear a ring
Dolls sold with Certificate of Authenticity

CERTIFICATE OF AUTHENTICITY

IT IS HEREBY CERTIFIED THAT THIS DOLL

NUMBER 12/100

"Briana"

IS AN AUTHENTIC PIECE IN THE LIMITED EDITION

OF

HEIR-BABIES

ATTESTED: Fern Vasi

CATEGORY:

Dolls: porcelain

RECOGNITION:

Nutshell News, Dec. 1991, pg. 74-75; Jul. 1993, pg. 65, Show Scene; *Miniatures Showcase*, Nov. 1992, pg. 14

AUTOBIOGRAPHY:

My miniature background started with a train board I built for my son about 1987. I went to the Mini Bazaar to pick up accessories and I fell in love and started taking classes. I bought a dollhouse kit, made stained glass windows, and so on! I could not find the dolls I wanted, so I jumped in head first. It was very difficult to get the information I needed. One class led to another and I read many books and practiced. The part I love most is "moving" the wet porcelain, turning heads, moving wrists, etc. All my dolls have individually carved fingers and toes. I have been using commercial molds and adding porcelain or carving away, to give them a different look. I have now started making my own molds, but that's another story. I love making miniature dolls and started teaching workshops at Mott's Miniatures.

ARTISAN: VAUGHN, GAIL

BUSINESS NAME: Small Packages

IDENTIFICATION MARKS:

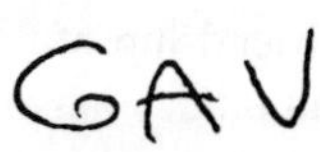

CATEGORY:

Accessories; Dolls: costumed; Furniture; Houses; Scenes: watch case

RECOGNITION:

Miniature Gazette, Spring 1987, pg. 36-37; Winter 1987; *Toybox Magazine*, Vol. 2, No. 2, Fall 1993, pg. 52-55; *Miniature Collector*, No. 85, Sept/Oct. 1994, pg. 54-57

AUTOBIOGRAPHY:

I majored in Art in college and throughout the next 30 years I have worked on many different arts and craft projects. So it was very natural for my late husband and me to build a dollhouse for his granddaughter in 1982, and for me to be bitten by the miniature bug. The first NAME houseparty I went to was in Seattle, Washington in 1985, and I was hopelessly "hooked." In the years since, I have tried to take as many workshops

Washington in 1985, and I was hopelessly "hooked." In the years since, I have tried to take as many workshops from as many artisans as I can fit into my busy schedule. I have always enjoyed learning new techniques and methods and even when I think that I know how to do something, I always learn something new; and I love to teach other miniaturists things that I have learned. I taught my first workshop at a NAME national houseparty in Phoenix, Arizona in 1991 and was fortunate enough to be accepted in Philadelphia for 1992, and Orlando for 1993. Even though I work three "real" jobs (dental receptionist, bookkeeper for a car parts dealer, and sculptured nails and manicures in my home), I spend as many hours as I have left playing minis and trying to create new workshops to teach at the two miniature clubs I belong to; Atlanta Miniature Society, and the Gwinette Area Miniature Enthusiasts.

ARTISAN: **VAUGHN, WALTER**

BUSINESS NAME: Perfect Touch

IDENTIFICATION MARKS:

WLV Walter Vaughn

CATEGORY:

Cabins; Cottages; Dollhouse; Houses; Landscaping; Roomboxes; Rooms

HONORS:

IGMA Artisan; Exhibit, Winthrop Rockefeller Archaeological Museum, Colonial Williamsburg, Virginia

RECOGNITION:

Nutshell News, Oct. 1985, A Micro Mini View of History; Jul. 1988, Walter Vaughn's Miniature Time Machines; *Miniature Gazette*, Spring 1986, pg. 20-22, Building A Bible House; Summer 1986, pg. 8-10, Puzzles From The Past; Summer 1987, pg. 26-27, Looking At Log Cabins; Fall 1987, pg. 15-17, Scenes From Ancient Sumer; *Miniatures Showcase*, Winter 1989, pg. 38, 44; Spring 1991, pg. 47; *Antique Week*, Feb. 13, 1989, Miniature Settings Transport Viewers to Lost Civilization; Jul. 2, 1990, Diorama Depicts Life on 17th Century Plantation; *Slide Presentation*, Preserving History Through Miniatures, NAME Library

BIOGRAPHY:

IGMA Artisan Walter Vaughn has been involved professionally in miniatures since 1981, under the business name, Perfect Touch, both selling to collectors and creating museum displays. His particular area if interest in miniatures is vernacular and historical architecture. Each of his one-of-a-kind, museum quality houses, roomboxes, and dioramas is an extensively researched original design based on archaeological data and historical records. His work is on display at several museums including a 17th century roombox and a large 3' x 3' diorama at the Winthrop Rockefeller Archaeological Museum at Colonial Williamsburg. While he has built houses in all scales ranging from 1 millimeter = 1 foot to 1 inch = 1 foot, he now concentrates mainly on 144th scale houses and landscaping, ¼-inch scale houses, ½-inch scale houses and roomboxes, and some one-inch scale cottages, cabins, and rooms.

ARTISAN: **VENNING, P. M.**

BUSINESS NAME: Pat Venning Porcelain

IDENTIFICATION MARKS:

PV

VENNING, P. M., continued

CATEGORY:
Pottery

RECOGNITION:
Dorset Evening Echo, England, Nov. 1991; Oct. 1992; *Doll House and Miniature Scene*, Issue No. 1, Dec/Jan. 1992, pg. 18; *Doll House World*, Issue No. 15, 1991, pg. 10

AUTOBIOGRAPHY:
I have no formal college training for art, but my occupation for many years concerned the finest detailed technical handbook illustrations, and at the same time my hobby was full-size wheel thrown pottery but "small." Having an eye for detail and determination has led me on to wheel thrown porcelain miniatures.

ARTISAN: VERNON, SID & EILEEN

BUSINESS NAME: Vernon Pottery

IDENTIFICATION MARKS:

VERNON POTTERY

SID & EILEEN VERNON

CATEGORY:
Pottery: reproductions

HONORS:
IGMA Fellow (both)

RECOGNITION:
Miniature Dealer, Vol. 16, No. 5, May 1992, pg. 23; *Country Living Magazine*, Mar. 1992, pg. 102-103; *The Sparkling Star*, Louisville, Kentucky, Mar. 1992, pg. 4

ARTISAN: VICK, PAT

BUSINESS NAME: Genuine Imitations ®

IDENTIFICATION MARKS:
1978 to present

GENUINE IMITATIONS ®
by pat vick
Sticker/Label

Trademark Registered 1979

CATEGORY:
Accessories; Food; Furniture; Kits

AUTOBIOGRAPHY:
My miniatures started with my first dollhouse made by my grandmother in 1940 at Christmas, which was set aside when college came, University of California Los Angeles and Los Angeles State University, followed by

graduate work at Northwestern in Illinois. Many arts and crafts filled the interim when I moved to Colorado in 1977 and finally had a place for my dollhouse in full view, and a miniature shop across the street. I began making food, then wholesaling it to the mini shop, eventually expanding to many mini things and doing shows.

I was a sales engineer working for Johnson Controls, by day until 1995, and worked on miniatures at night and weekends. I also travel to nearby shows and teach workshops in Fimo food, landscaping and other accessory projects, whenever I can. My husband, Bob, and I are active in the Denver Museum of Miniatures, Dolls & Toys.

ARTISAN: **VONDRAK, DEANNA MAYER**

BUSINESS NAME: Deanna Mayer Vondrak
Cantitoe Corners

IDENTIFICATION MARKS:

Cantitoe Corners

CATEGORY:
Kits: needlework, quilts; Needlework; Quilts: American

HONORS:
1st Prize, The Dollhouse Benefit for Autistic Children, April 1979

RECOGNITION:
Nutshell News, May/Jun. 1979, Classic Quilt Designs; *Miniature Collector*, No. 9, Oct. 1978, Deanna Mayer Vondrak and Her World of Miniature Quilts; *House and Gardens*, Vol. 147, No. 8, Miniatures: A Lilliputian Quilt; *Citizen*, Wed. May 9, 1979, Walden Woman Wins in California Contest; *House and Gardens Country Decorating Ideas*, Summer 1981; *Bee Publishing Co.* Newton, CT, Arts & Crafts Sec. Aug. 14, 1981, pg. 13, Miniature Quilts & Historical Needlework in Kit Form; *House Beautiful*, Vol. 124, No. 2, Feb. 1982, Historic Quilt to Sew; *Reproducing Period Furniture and Accessories in Miniature*, Virginia Merrill, Susan Merrill Richardson, Crown, 1981

AUTOBIOGRAPHY:
I was born in New Jersey and studied at Pratt Institute School of Architecture, Parsons School of Design for interior design, Cranbrook Academy of Art for weaving and Hay Stack Mountain School of Crafts, again for weaving. I was a sculptor making delicate metal flowers that move on open root bases. I also make miniature quilts and do historical needlework covering a history of American quilts in miniature, such as the Bird of Paradise, an appliqué quilt in kit form, both full-size and miniature. My work has been on exhibit with Henry Moore for many years. I'm also in the collection of the Washington Toy and Dolls House Museum, Washington, DC.

ARTISAN: **VON FLISS, ROBERT D.**

BUSINESS NAME: High-Button Shoe Miniatures

IDENTIFICATION MARKS:

Robert D. von Fliss

CATEGORY:
Dome Scenes; Roomboxes; Scenes; Store; Vignettes

VON FLISS, ROBERT D., continued

HONORS:

NAME AOH, NAME Mell Prescott Award

RECOGNITION:

Nutshell News, Spring 1978, pg. 18; *Newsweek*, Dec. 9, 1974, pg. 87; *Orange County Illustrated*, Sept. 1980, pg. 46-47; *Orange Coast Magazine*, Aug. 1982, pg. 37-40; *Miniature Gazette*, Vol. 2 No. 1, Fall 1982, pg. 39; Vol. 19, No. 2, Winter 1990, pg. 61; *Small Talk*, Vol. 5, No. 8, pg. Cover, 4-7, 15; *Doll Reader*, May 1983, pg. 91; *Inside The World of Miniatures and Dollhouses*, Rosner & Beckerman, Mc Kay Press, 1976, pg. 193; *Our Miniature World*, NAME, Marie Dettling, pg. 73, 75; *Los Angeles Times*, Dec. 16, 1979, View Section, pg. 29, 41; Aug. 13, 1988, Part 5, pg. 10; *San Francisco Chronicle*, Aug. 3, 1976, pg. 5; *Los Angeles Herald-Examiner*, Oct. 3, 1976, Living Section, pg. 7-8; *Rochester Democrat and Chronicle,* Jul. 29, 1983, pg. 1C; *Orange County Register*, Jul. 21, 1974, pg. 3; Nov. 2, 1980, pg. A12; Jan. 21, 1983, pg. B8; *Fullerton Daily News Tribune*, Mar. 6, 1980, pg. B3; Oct. 27, 1980, pg. E3; Jan. 27, 1983, pg. 3C; Jul. 7, 1988, pg. 1C

AUTOBIOGRAPHY:

My wife and I are two of the original 12 founders of NAME. I spent the next 14 years on the NAME board of directors. I was the originating editor of the *Miniature Gazette* and held that job for 10 years. I was the president of two NAME clubs and the founder of the North Orange County Miniature Guild and served as their chairman for the first few years. In 1982, I served as the hosting chairman of the National Houseparty in Anaheim, California, and have chaired two regional houseparties. I served a term as president of NAME and was their National Houseparty Coordinator for three years. I chaired and presented the Memorial Day Miniature Show at the Grand Hotel in Anaheim for 10 years. From July 22 to September 25, 1988 I was the guest curator at the Fullerton Museum Center in Fullerton, California, and presented a very successful miniature exhibit at that facility. During my years with NAME I have presented many programs, taught a number of workshops and exhibited my collection often at houseparties and local shows. I am honored to be a recipient of the Academy of Honor which was awarded to me for my contribution to the hobby and to the NAME organization.

ARTISAN: **WADE, SUSAN F.**

BUSINESS NAME: Petite Personalities

IDENTIFICATION MARKS:

1993 to present

with date

with date

Signed on left leg or shoe

CATEGORY:

Costuming; Dolls; Figures

HONORS:

IGMA Artisan 1994

AUTOBIOGRAPHY:

I have always held a passion for color and detail, and have been drawn to the arts since childhood. My educational background includes interior design, and is where I learned the basics of design and color theory. When my daughter asked for a dollhouse for Christmas in 1989, I knew I had found my element in the miniature world.

I was in the process of building my own Colonial Williamsburg dollhouse when one day I picked up a miniature doll magazine that featured a doll by Marcia Backstrom, on the cover. I was completely captivated by the character and detail this doll possessed. This was the inspiration that led to my own dollmaking career, and in 1991, I created my first "petite personality."

Since that time, I have concentrated my efforts on refining my dollmaking skills and studying period costume. I am a member of IGMA and in 1994 was elevated to Artisan status in the category of costuming and figures. I consider it a great privilege to be part of the miniature world and the wonderful, talented people associated with it.

ARTISAN: **WAGNER, SYDNIE M.**

BUSINESS NAME: Syd's Shoppe

IDENTIFICATION MARKS:

Small pieces

CATEGORY:

Accessories; Food

RECOGNITION:

Nutshell News, Dec. 1993; Jan. 1994; Feb. 1994; Mar. 1994; Apr. 1994; *Miniatures Showcase*, Nov. 1992; Jan. 1993; Mar. 1993; Jul. 1993; Sept. 1993; Nov. 1993

ARTISAN: **WALDSCHMIDT, SHERRY**

BUSINESS NAME: Miniatures by Sherry

IDENTIFICATION MARKS:

CATEGORY:

Accessories

RECOGNITION:

Nutshell News, Apr. 1990, pg. 69; *Miniatures Showcase*, Spring 1990, pg. 47; Summer 1990, pg. 19, 30, 69; Fall 1991, pg. 30-32

BIOGRAPHY:

Sherry is a member of NAME, IGMA, and three miniature clubs in the Milwaukee, Wisconsin area. She is past president of the Wisconsin Wee World Society. She especially enjoys teaching and has taught classes at NAME National Houseparties as well as local and regional miniature shows.

Sherry's higher education was at the University of Wisconsin-Milwaukee majoring in Art History. Her work has appeared in *Nutshell News* and Miniature Marketplace. In addition to miniatures, Sherry makes and collects porcelain dolls.

ARTISAN: **WALKER, LIZ & GORDON**

BUSINESS NAME: Richard the Twelfth Miniatures

IDENTIFICATION MARKS:

Marks accompanied by reference number, registered and allocated to each piece or set

Dollhouses

Artifacts

CATEGORY:

Chandeliers; Clothing; Dollhouse; Dolls; Figures; Fireplaces; Furniture; Linens; Millinery; Needlework; Roomboxes; Rugs

RECOGNITION:

International Dolls House News, 1991; *Oxford Mail, Time*, 1991; *Oxford Journal*, 1991; *Oxford County Newspaper*, 1992

ARTISAN: **WALKER, MARGARET**

BUSINESS NAME: Miniature Paintings by Margaret Walker

IDENTIFICATION MARKS:

WALKER, MARGARET, continued

CATEGORY:

Paintings

RECOGNITION:

Nutshell News, Feb. 1983, pg. 60, Show Scene; Mar. 1984, pg. 54; Sept. 1986, pg. 73, 82; Sept. 1988, pg. 67; Feb. 1990, pg. 56

AUTOBIOGRAPHY:

My painting career started in 1975 when I was introduced to acrylics. I took classes in landscape painting, and did a seascape workshop. I entered shows in the Dayton-Ormond Beach Florida area, and received a number of awards, including Best of Show.

I was asked to do a dollhouse painting in 1982, and was intrigued with miniature painting. I have been doing them for dollhouse and miniature shows ever since. I have also had paintings accepted for the Miniature Art Society of Florida International Show the past several years.

ARTISAN: **WALL, SANDRA HENRY**

BUSINESS NAME: Inside – Out Miniatures

IDENTIFICATION MARKS:

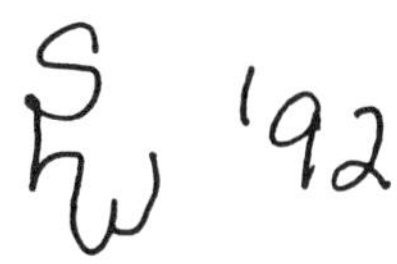

CATEGORY:

Floral Arrangements; Flowers and Plants

HONORS:

IGMA Fellow 1990

AUTOBIOGRAPHY:

I began miniature making in 1983. I have utilized my previous background of interior design and architectural rendering to influence my craft. Since about 1985, I have specialized in miniature silk floral arrangements and plants, using construction techniques I developed. I have a professorship at the Guild School, in Castine, Maine, where I've been teaching for five or more years the various techniques of flower construction, arranging, and landscaping. I also teach these same techniques throughout the United States.

I have been a Guild Fellow since 1990 and the Guild Contact for the state of Illinois, in addition to being a member of NAME.

ARTISAN: **WANNAMAKER, MARJORIE A.**

BUSINESS NAME: Feathers–N–Clay

IDENTIFICATION MARKS:

1982 to 1988

1982 to present

Feathers-N-Clay

Logo

WANNAMAKER, MARJORIE A., continued

CATEGORY:

Animals: critters; Birds

RECOGNITION:

Miniatures Showcase, Nov. 1992, pg. 36-37

AUTOBIOGRAPHY:

I began my miniature hobby in 1981, when I built a dollhouse for myself. I needed a parakeet for a setting and couldn't find any available. Thus, I was forced to make one to meet my needs. Other people saw it and wanted it and the "Bird Lady" sprung wings. Originally I also made crocheted items, foods and numerous other miscellaneous items in one-inch scale. I've made bird cages, needlework stands and bird houses with tole painting on them. I acquired my artistic talents from my grandmother but am essentially self-taught in sculpting and knowledge as it pertains to my work in miniature.

We owned a retail shop called "Our Little Dollhouse," in Chico, California for five years but I now work out of my home under the name of "Feathers-N-Clay" with the main thrust of the line being birds of all types. I work in one-inch, ½-inch and ¼-inch scales.

ARTISAN: **WARD, TOM**

BUSINESS NAME: Grey Wolf Studio

IDENTIFICATION MARKS:

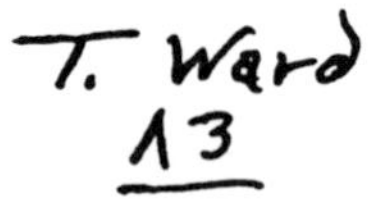

Month and year piece made

Month and year piece made

CATEGORY:

Animals; Dolls; Figures; Taxidermy

ARTISAN: **WARLING, LEILANI & ROGER**

BUSINESS NAME: Warling Miniatures

IDENTIFICATION MARKS:

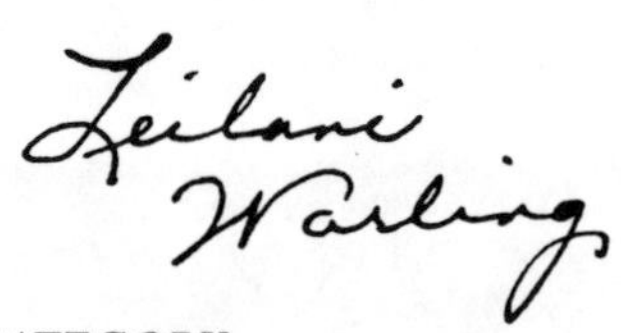

CATEGORY:

Furniture: wicker; Kits: wicker

RECOGNITION:

Nutshell News, Mar. 1986, pg. 36; Sept. 1986, pg. 34; Jan. 1987, pg. 22, 76, Show Scene; May 1987, pg. 31; Aug. 1987, pg. 34; *Miniatures Showcase*, Spring 1987, pg. 31; Summer 1987, pg. 37, 46-47; Spring 1988, pg. 14, 22-23, 31, 40, 41; Nov. 1992, Cover, pg. 32; *Miniature Dealer*, Apr. 1987, pg. 6; Jun. 1987, pg. 21; Feb. 1988, pg. 23; May 1988; Spring 1987, pg. 25; Fall 1987, pg. 71; *Interior Design in Miniature,* Brooke Tucker Originals, Anne Day Smith, Boynton, 1986, pg. 22-23, 48, 86, 87

ARTISAN: **WARNER, BARBARA B.**

BUSINESS NAME: Bright Ideas

IDENTIFICATION MARKS:

Furniture signed either printed or in cursive with date

BWB Logo on heart punch hole glued to bottom of toy or doll

CATEGORY:

Christmas; Dolls: dolls' doll; Furniture: handpainted; Holiday Items; Lamps; Lighting; Toys

RECOGNITION:

Nutshell News, Vol. 14, No. 4, Apr. 1984; Oct. 1984; Jun. 1985, pg. 60; Vol. 16, No. 12, Dec. 1986, pg. 96, 102; Nov. 1990, pg. 79; *Miniatures Catalog*, 6th Edition, pg. 18; *Miniatures Showcase*, Vol. 2, No. 2, Spring 1987, pg. 21; Vol. 4, No. 1, Winter 1989, pg. 24

AUTOBIOGRAPHY:

I have always worked with my hands, doing whatever needed to be done and when help was needed to learn how to make something, I consulted books or on occasion when I could find a teacher, I would take courses. Most was learned in the old school of "Necessity is the mother of invention."

I've been working in the miniature field since 1973. I started out teaching classes in making miniatures at Des Peres Hobby Shop, Des Peres, Missouri. Over the years I've also taught at the Fudge Shop, St. Charles, Missouri, Dream House Miniatures and Village Miniatures, Ballwin, Missouri, and Parkway School District, Adult Education.

By the late 1970's I was making and selling pom-pom animals, storybook dolls, Raggedy Ann and Andy, topsy-turvy dolls, and painting and dressing small plastic dolls as brides, bridesmaids, and Shirley Temple, these were sold wholesale.

In 1981, besides being the Exhibit Room Chairman for the NAME National Houseparty in St. Louis, Missouri, I also made 1200 pom pom teddybears. One appeared in every tote bag given away at the convention.

Since 1982, I have been writing articles for *Nutshell News, Miniatures Showcase,* and the *Miniatures Catalog*. From March 1988 to June 1992, I wrote the Retailers Corner Column in *Miniatures Dealer*. In 1986, Boynton Press published my book, *Dollhouse Lighting.* From 1984 to 1987, I was a partner in the miniatures' shop, Dream House Miniatures, Ballwin, Missouri. During this time and until fall 1990, I painted flower sprays on dollhouse shutters for our customers. These were unsigned. Since 1987, I have sold my miniatures at shows in Kansas City, Belleville, Illinois, and Des Moines, Iowa. In 1991 and 1992, I appeared at shows in Lyndhurst, England and Glasgow, Scotland.

After returning from two years in England, I wrote another book, published by Kalmbach Publications, *The ABC's of Dollhouse Finishing*. I'm also returning to wiring dollhouses and holding lighting demonstrations, and writing "Enhancements," a regular feature in *Nutshell News.*

ARTISAN: **WARNER, THOMAS A. "TOM"** (Deceased)

IDENTIFICATION MARKS:

Thomas A. Warner with year

T. A Warner with year

Brass plate signed in script with vibrating engraver

CATEGORY:

Furniture; Rooms: period

WARNER, THOMAS A., continued

HONORS:

Exhibit: Toy & Miniature Museum of Kansas City

RECOGNITION:

Nutshell News, Vol. 9, No. 1, Jan/Feb. 1979, pg. 85; Vol. 10, No. 1, Jan. 1980, pg. 71; Vol. 11, No. 8, Aug. 1980, pg. 36; Vol. 12, No. 11, Nov. 1982, pg. 51; Vol. 13, No. 10, Oct. 1983, pg. 54-57

ARTISAN: WARREN, B. J. & JAMES "JIM"

BUSINESS NAME: Très Petite Miniatures

IDENTIFICATION MARKS:

 with date

 with date

 with date

CATEGORY:

Furniture: Country; Rocking Horses

HONORS:

IGMA Artisan (B.J.)

RECOGNITION:

Nutshell News, Vol. 21, No. 7, Jul. 1991, Show Scene; *Miniatures Showcase*, Vol. 5, No. 1, Winter 1990, pg. 34-35, 44

AUTOBIOGRAPHY:

B. J. Warren

I majored in fine arts in college, but never really found my medium until my husband gave me a dollhouse for my birthday in 1984. I began making miniature plants and flowers and selling them to miniature shops in exchange for dollhouse items. I may design a piece out of cardboard, then give it to Jim to actually make out of wood. I do the painting and upholstery needed for the pieces Jim makes.

In April of 1989, I did my first miniature show as Très Petite Miniatures and have been doing shows ever since.

Jim Warren

My miniature career began with the purchase of a dollhouse I gave to my wife for a birthday gift. After helping her with the assembly and wiring, the bug hit me to give this hobby a try. B. J. bought me a general store kit. After doing some modifications to the kit and going to many shows to fill the store, I was hooked. I've added to my collection a potting shed, basement bar and gas station. My small basement work bench is now 8 feet long with a separate table for power tools. I do all the wood working.

I'm now making arbors, trellis and country furniture for B. J. to use for selling her flowers at miniature shows, which we have been doing for several years now. We are members of NAME, IGMA, and two miniature clubs.

ARTISAN: **WASSMER, SISTER OLIVIA**

BUSINESS NAME: Sister Olivia's Miniatures

IDENTIFICATION MARKS:

CATEGORY:

Accessories; Figures: creches; Paintings

AUTOBIOGRAPHY:

In the 1970's I completed two 3-year courses with Famous Artist School, one in commercial art and one in fine arts. I have studied under several artists, attending workshops. For the past four years, since 1988, I have studied under a local New Orleans artist, Michael Willmon, MFA.

In 1980, a local miniature dealer saw some of my regular art work and asked me to do miniatures for her, especially my French Quarter scenes. She purchased frames for me, explained what she wanted, and we were in business. From that beginning, I started selling to a few gift shops in the French Quarter. Later, other stores in the area added my paintings to their selections.

For several years I had someone make frames for me. When they moved out of the area, I started making my own frames. Since my first show in 1992, the Gulf South Miniature & Dollhouse Event Memorial Day Weekend in New Orleans, Louisiana, I have gradually added a few other items such as a creches and a carousel to my line.

ARTISAN: **WATERS, ALAN**

BUSINESS NAME: Alan Waters Miniatures

IDENTIFICATION MARKS:

CATEGORY:

Accessories; Animals; Birdcages; Birds; Clcoks; Frames; Furniture: period; Game Table; Kitchen; Metalwork; Mirrors; Musical Instruments; Needlework; Ornaments; Paintings; Sewing; Stationery; Tools; Toys

HONORS:

IGMA Artisan; 1st Prize, Gold Coast Miniature Competition, 1984

RECOGNITION:

Nutshell News, Mar. 1986, pg. 48-50; Dec. 1990, pg. 33, 69; *The Home Miniaturist*, Jul. 1988, pg. 19; *Marlborough Express*, Feb. 1981, pg. 17; *Le Magazine de la Maison de Poupée*, Apr. 1989, pg. 6-7; *The Art of Dollmaking*, Sept. 1994, pg. 31-33; *Decorative Dolls' Houses*, Caroline Hamilton, Ebury Press, London, 1990, pg. 19, 23, 27, 28, 29, 30, 33, 56, 122, 124; *Miniatures d ' art Les Maisons de Poupées d ' aujourd ' hui*, Ingeborg Reisser, Massin, Paris, 1993, pg. 25, 60, 83, 84, 95

AUTOBIOGRAPHY:

I began making miniatures in the United Kingdom in 1974, when there were only a few shops selling miniatures. I have an artistic background and found the change to miniatures both simple and delightful, and I've never stopped!

Having been involved in miniatures for some 20 years, I have exhibited widely around the world and my pieces are in some of the world's most magnificent collections. A personal highlight was when I was told some of my work was once auctioned by Sotheby's in New York.

WATERS, ALAN, continued

At one point I had over 700 different items in my catalogue, and this apparently was by far the largest and most varied selection of miniatures in the world for one person. My work is distinctive in its detail and accuracy and I have received commissions from collectors in no less than 14 countries around the world.

I am very proud to be a miniaturist!

ARTISAN: WATT, JIM

BUSINESS NAME: Tables & Timepieces

IDENTIFICATION MARKS:

Some small pieces unmarked

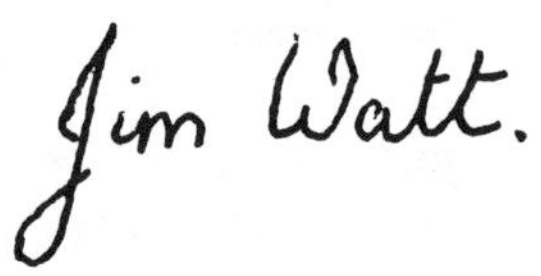

Engraved into wood

CATEGORY:

Clocks; Furniture; Optical; Sports Equipment

HONORS:

Woodworkers Show, Silver Medal, 1986; Gold Metal, 1987; Bronze Medal, 1987, 1988

RECOGNITION:

Nutshell News, Sept. 1991, pg. 29; *Dolls House World*, Issue No. 17, 1992, pg. 30-33; *Home Miniaturist*, Nov. 1989, pg. 5; *Brentwood & Ongar Gazette*, Friday, Jan. 22, 1988, Essex, England, "When Small is a Beautiful Scale," Neville Legge; Thursday, Oct. 1, 1992, pg. 13, "It's a Small World," Keith Brown

ARTISAN: WEAVER, DAWN

BUSINESS NAME: Dawn's Mini's

IDENTIFICATION MARKS:

Some unmarked

CATEGORY:

Flowers and Plants; Jewelry

RECOGNITION:

Nutshell News; Miniatures Showcase; Miniature Gazette; Miniature Collector

AUTOBIOGRAPHY:

I started miniatures in 1978 doing a few shows each year and selling some handcrafted items together with commercial. It was approximately 1980 that I went to all handcrafted items. In 1987, I was early-retired from my secretarial job. Of the 66 early-retirees from the company I was the only one who had a business to fall back on, miniatures!

I now do approximately 36 shows a year, traveling to most in my motorhome, which is also my full-time residence. At the same time I began specializing in smaller scales, but continued to produce my floral "Instant

Gardens" in all scales. As I travel around to various shows I purchase from other dealers, consequently I have a wide variety of ½-inch and ¼-inch scale items representing between 40 and 50 artisans. Some I buy from on a regular basis but many are one-of-a-kind items.

My parents were florists and I worked with them through my teen years until I left Nova Scotia to come to the United States. I was a secretary during my working years. As a young widow most of my energy was used in raising three children. Although always a craft minded person, my current occupation didn't come into being until my family was grown.

ARTISAN: **WEBSTER, TREVOR**

BUSINESS NAME: Vale Dolls' Houses

IDENTIFICATION MARKS:

A VALE HOUSE
TREVOR WEBSTER

CATEGORY:

Dollhouse; Shops

HONORS:

British Toy Makers Guild

RECOGNITION:

Dolls House World; Home Miniaturist, Issue No. 63, pg. 20-25

ARTISAN: **WEGMAN, JOE & PAT**

BUSINESS NAME: The Toy Center
P.J.'s Tole Works

IDENTIFICATION MARKS:

Some unmarked

CATEGORY:

Display Cases; Dollhouse; Houses; Painting: decorative, tole; Roomboxes; Shops

AUTOBIOGRAPHY:

Joseph B. Wegman

For 24 years I owned and operated a primer toy and hobby shop, The Toy Center, Inc., in Richmond, Virginia. I built and decorated miniature roomboxes, shops and houses, some from architectual drawings and photos of full-size houses. With my electrical design background, I enjoy the challenges of electrifying roomboxes and dollhouses. I have incorporated Marklin Z scale trains in the attic of numerous dollhouses as well as garden layouts, combining my love of miniatures and model railroading. I also build full-size furniture which enhances the appearance of a dollhouse or train layout.

In 1985, I started a second business which began with plexiglas display cases with walnut wood bases and has now evolved into custom one-of-a-kind or limited editions of unique items in display cases.

Patricia J. Wegman

In 1982, I began to do Tole and Decorative Painting as a hobby. Having taken many classes from well known artists, my education and skills continue to improve. As well as full-size objects, in 1986 I started tole painting dollhouses. Soon the temptation came and with the encouragement of my husband I began painting miniatures. Using acrylics I paint on canvas, tin, and wood.

ARTISAN: **WEINER, ANN**

BUSINESS NAME: Victorian Vintage

IDENTIFICATION MARKS:

CATEGORY:

Accessories; Furniture: aged; Paintings

AUTOBIOGRAPHY:

Working in the art field since 1970 gave me the opportunity to pursue a career in crafts. I attended various classes and seminars throughout the years but had no formal education in art. I represented the United States in glass art (tinsel painting) at the International Craft Festival at Busch Gardens, Williamsburg, Virginia in 1976 and 1977. I was able to transform my art into miniature scale and started producing items for dollhouses along with my paintings.

In 1980, I organized World of Mini Mania, one of the leading miniature shows on the East Coast, bringing noted artisans to show in this area which has continued to this date. Most recently, a line of miniature aged furniture has been added to the accessories although my work is very limited due to the element of time.

ARTISAN: **WELCH, JEAN**

BUSINESS NAME: The China Closet

IDENTIFICATION MARKS:

All marks 1977 to present

CATEGORY:

Accessories; China: handpainted; Dinnerware; Porcelain

HONORS:

Exhibit: Toy & Miniature Museum of Kansas City

RECOGNITION:

Nutshell News, Jan. 1988, pg. 33; Mar. 1988, pg. 69; Jul. 1988, pg. 63; Sept. 1993, pg. 66; *Miniature Collector*, No. 36, pg. 39-40, "Like Mother, like Daughter: Passing on the Secrets of the Porcelain Trade," Louise A. Fecher; *American Period Interiors in Miniature*, Kate Doordan Klavan, Scribner's, 1984, pg. 61, 81, color plate 4

BIOGRAPHY:

In 1977, Jean Welch started The China Closet. She was joined by her daughter, Teresa. Teresa paints the intricate patterns, and Jean makes the raised floral pieces. Jean studied art at Nebraska University and Kansas City Institute. Teresa learned the trade working with Jean. She is a member of IGMA and NAME.

See "Teresa Welch Stalbaum"

ARTISAN: **WELLS, JAMES R.**

BUSINESS NAME: The Tinkerworks

IDENTIFICATION MARKS:

1991 to present

The TinkerWorks

CATEGORY:

Lanterns; Lighting

RECOGNITION:

Audio Engineering Society Journal (*The Sound Engineering Magazine*)

BIOGRAPHY:

Jim is a musician, music producer, audio engineer and a model railroader. He built and sold his first model railroad at age nine. For the last 15 years, since 1978, he has specialized in the production of music programs, and the design of audio systems for animated displays and theme park attractions and dark rides.

Design and development models are generally one-inch scale, and Jim's model railroading has evolved into this scale as well. This requires a great deal of "scratch building" metal work in copper and brass. A suitable railroad lantern was not available through existing sources, so Jim began fabrication on several prototypes. As each new design is fabricated, a limited number of copies are made and offered to collectors exclusively through Paul's Specialties.

Jim's love for special FX shows in his creative lighting techniques for his lanterns. His love for sound has resulted in the creation of many sounds and systems for his models. "Everything makes noise in my models. I've been collecting sound for years and apply it at every opportunity!"

ARTISAN: **WENK, CAROL**

BUSINESS NAME: Carol Wenk Miniatures

IDENTIFICATION MARKS:

Unmarked

Logo

CATEGORY:

Books: miniature

HONORS:

Founder: Cottage Industry Miniaturists Trade Association

RECOGNITION:

Nutshell News, Jun. 1990

AUTOBIOGRAPHY:

I was a Founder of both the Cleveland Miniature Society, which is the 2nd oldest miniature club, and CIMTA. I have been actively engaged in miniatures for 27 years, since appriximately 1966.

ARTISAN: **WERNER, ARLENE**

BUSINESS NAME: Arlene Werner's Petite Properties

IDENTIFICATION MARKS:

CATEGORY:

Pictures: framed; Photographs; Photography: framed

HONORS:

IGMA Artisan

AUTOBIOGRAPHY:

I have been a collector of miniatures since childhood, but took a serious interest in the artform in 1980 and began an active education to learn everything I could. I have attended the Guild School in Castine, Maine, graduated from Tri-Community School of Photography in Covina, California and have taken numerous miniature classes. My main interests are in the history of the American West and American Indian and Western Art. I am a member of IGMA and NAME.

ARTISAN: **WESSEL, LEE-ANN CHELLIS**

BUSINESS NAME: Demi–Tasse

IDENTIFICATION MARKS:

Impressed with metal stamp, may also be painted

CATEGORY:

Porcelain; Pottery

HONORS:

IGMA Fellow

AUTOBIOGRAPHY:

I have a BFA degree from Moore College of Art, Philadelphia, Pennsylvania 1971, and an MFA degree from the University of Massachusetts, Amherst, 1977.

ARTISAN: **WESTCOTT, PETER F.**

BUSINESS NAME: Peter F. Westcott

IDENTIFICATION MARKS:

CATEGORY:

Roomboxes; Rooms

WESTCOTT, PETER F., continued

RECOGNITION:

Nutshell News, Fall 1977, Thorne Rooms; May 1983; Oct. 1983, The Arizona House; Feb. 1991, Modeling Tips; Oct. 1991, Modeling Tips; Feb. 1992, Modeling Tips; Jun. 1993, Artisan Update; *Miniature Collector*, Jan/Feb. 1987; Summer 1986, The Arizona House; *Miniature Gazette*, Summer 1983, The Arizona House; *The Scale Cabinetmaker*, Vol. 3, No. 2, 3, 4, Vol. 4, No. 1, 1979, The Late Georgian Room; Vol. 5, No. 1, 2 3, 1981, The Williamsburg Interior; Vol. 15, No. 1, 2, 3, 4, 1991, The Bishop's Livingroom; Vol. 16, No. 2, 3, 1992, The Southwestern American Room; Vol. 16, No. 4, 5, 1993, The Southwestern American Room (continued); *Miniature Room Settings*, Helen Ruthberg, 1978; *Contemporary Miniature Room Settings*, Helen Ruthberg, 1980; *Dollhouse and Miniature News*, Marion O'Brian, 1975; *English Country Kitchen*, Dorsett Publications, 1988

AUTOBIOGRAPHY:

After studying architecture at Temple University and Drexel Institute, I spent several years working for various architects as an architectural draftsman. In 1966, I opened my own architectural scale model building firm in the suburbs of Philadelphia. With a five man office, we provided models for clients from New York to the Bahamas. After many years of building commercial models in the area, we decided to move to Phoenix, Arizona in 1971. Upon arriving, I re-opened the model building studio and continued to build architectural scale models for developers and architects in the area. Along with the architectural models, I was asked to be involved with the dollhouse miniatures by teaching roombox classes, and from 1975 through 1977, I maintained the Thorne Rooms Collection at the Phoenix Art Museum, and doing un-furnished roomboxes for various museums and private collectors. I also restored two original Thorne Rooms donated by the family to the Phoenix Art Museum. Along with private commissions, beginning in 1979, I wrote numerous articles for *The Scale Cabinetmaker* publication on how to build architecturally detailed roomboxes in one-inch scale in various styles of architecture.

In 1988, I colaborated with the late Helen Dorsett and wrote on how to build the roombox while Helen wrote on how to build the furniture. Our efforts resulted in the magazine *English Country Kitchen*, Dorsett Publications.

ARTISAN: WESTPHAL, JOAN

BUSINESS NAME: Les Petits Pots

IDENTIFICATION MARKS:

CATEGORY:

Porcelain

HONORS:

IGMA Fellow; Exhibit: Toy & Miniature Museum of Kansas City

RECOGNITION:

Nutshell News, Vol. 14, No. 7, Jul. 1984, pg. 50; Vol. 15, No. 12, Dec. 1985, pg. 64; Vol. 16, No. 7, Jul. 1986, pg. 62; Vol. 17, No. 9, Sept. 1987, pg. 86-89; Vol. 17, No. 10, Oct. 1987, pg. 65, 76, 79; Vol. 17, No. 12, Dec. 1987, pg. 77; Vol. 18, No. 5, May 1988, pg. 40; Vol. 19, No. 5, May 1989, Cover; Vol. 22, No. 2, Feb. 1992, pg. 66; *Miniature Collector*, No. 48, Mar/Apr. 1985, pg. 52

BIOGRAPHY:

Joan Westphal has been a ceramist for more than 30 years, and has studied with Paul Bellardo, Phyllis Hammond, noted ceramists, and at the Craft Student's League in New York City.

ARTISAN: **WHEATLEY, JOAN**

BUSINESS NAME: Hindeloopen Painting
Wee Trees – Original Tree Houses

IDENTIFICATION MARKS:

Logo

CATEGORY:

Accessories; Furniture: handpainted; Tree Houses

HONORS:

IGMA Artisan

RECOGNITION:

Nutshell News, May 1987, pg. 52; *Miniatures Showcase*, Winter 1991, pg. 73

ARTISAN: **WHEELER, JULIE**

BUSINESS NAME: Mini Elegance

IDENTIFICATION MARKS:

Some unmarked

CATEGORY:

Christmas; Holiday Items

RECOGNITION:

Nutshell News, Vol. 16, No. 8, Aug. 1986, pg. 72; Vol. 16, No. 12, Dec. 1986, pg. 52-54; *Miniature Gazette*, Vol. 16, No. 4, Summer 1988, pg. 29; *Florida Today,* Newspaper, Aug. 6, 1988, Sec. E, pg. 1-2

AUTOBIOGRAPHY:

I have been a miniature collector since 1969, and am a Charter Member of NAME. I started my own business in 1983, doing shows nationwide. My work has also been sold in England, France, Japan and Austrailia.

In 1987, I started selling from my home in Florida where my husband and I both worked for NASA at the Kennedy Space Center. We are now retired and have moved to Ohio, and sell only occasionally due to our frequent travel here and abroad.

WHITE, DAVID

BUSINESS NAME: White Mountain Miniatures
White Mountain Woodworking

IDENTIFICATION MARKS: (Submitted by William R. Robertson)

Printed in black ink with year

WHITE, DAVID, , continued

CATEGORY:

Furniture: handpainted

HONORS:

Exhibit: Toy & Miniature Museum of Kansas City

RECOGNITION:

Nutshell News, Feb. 1980, pg. 60; Jul. 1980, pg. 68, 73; Aug. 1980, pg. 32-33, "Colonial Knock-Abouts;" Vol. 13, No. 6, Jun. 1983, pg. 43; Vol. 14, No. 2, Feb. 1984, pg. 53, Show Scene; Vol. 14, No 8, Aug. 1984, pg. 55; Vol. 14, No. 9, Sept. 1984, pg. 72, Show Scene; *Miniature Collector*, No. 36, Apr. 1983, pg. 28-30, "Would You Buy a Piece of Used Furniture From This Man," Reed Ide; No. 39, Oct. 1983, pg. 36, Show Stoppers; No. 44, Jul/Aug. 1984, pg. 52, Show Stoppers; *Miniature Gazette*, Vol. 9, No.4, Summer 1981, pg. 72

ARTISAN: WHITE, HELEN "HOLLIE"

BUSINESS NAME: Little Whittles

IDENTIFICATION MARKS:

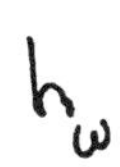

CATEGORY:

Birds: wild; Decoys; Furniture

AUTOBIOGRAPHY:

"A grandmother turned woodcarver." My interest in the miniature world started in 1972 in Benicia, California, when a little man came into my Antique Shop and wanted to know if I would please let him put one of his dollhouses in the shop on consignment. I agreeded and women began taking an interest. I contacted a wholesaler for Concord furniture and accessories, and we were in the miniature business. This all took place from 1972 until 1978. My husband retired and wanted us to move to the Gold Country, Grass Valley, Nevada City. My interests still consumed and with time on my hands while our house was being constructed, Little Whittles was launched. I carved when not sleeping or cooking, sometimes far into the night when all was quiet.

Country furniture and accessories followed, and we did shows for the next four years until we moved to the Pacific Northwest, above Seattle. We are back in California again, and I am still carving! I have been a member of NAME all these years. We had a club in California, and I was President in the 1980's. My decoys are primative or copied from large antique decoys where the heads are separate and can be moved around, with sizes that go all the way down to ¼-inch scale. Shorebirds are all sizes and mounted on stands and the 1990's have brought about fish decoys in all sizes.

ARTISAN: WHITE, MARY GOODNOW

BUSINESS NAME: Pocket People

IDENTIFICATION MARKS:

WHITE, MARY GOODNOW, continued

CATEGORY:

Dolls: porcelain

AUTOBIOGRAPHY:

The many aspects of all original doll making intrigue me and match my abilities. Daughter of a spring manufacture and professional portrait painter, I am both mechanically and artistically drawn to this endeavor. Prior to 1989, I had never seen or heard of scale miniature porcelain dolls. I was an English Literature major and taught English and History in junior high school. I see my dolls as little portraits from history who have somehow magically stepped forward in time so we can examine them and exclaim in disbelief.

Layering and firing permanent china paint on porcelain, I strive for life-like realism in miniature. Expressive, well painted eyes are alluring in a tiny face, and china gloss can rival glass, especially at this scale. I work for good body proportions in soft techniques and properly strung joints in smooth all-bisque. I do two-inch scale as opposed to ½-inch, and I have a collection of molds for reproduction "Candy Store Dolls" from turn-of-the-century. These dolls were originally mass produced and painted hastily with noses and mouths askew. When carefully re-created they are a tribute to the fine sculptors who designed them a century ago. Mine run from 3 to 6 inches in height.

In one-inch scale it is again old reproduction faces I am drawn to. I gave them modern-style wired and soft sculptured bodies. Little girls are my specialty, although I make all ages and both sexes in one-inch scale. I like to sell "en chemise" because of the intricacies of Victorian dress, which I hand stitch and make removable. Many collectors are working miniaturists and want a doll to fit a particular scene. Thus they are left free to do their own style of dress and color match. I have a large selection of Janna Joseph molds, some Doreen Sinnett, also Parker Levi and Seeley.

ARTISAN: **WHITEHEAD, MARY H.**

BUSINESS NAME: Mary H. Whitehead

IDENTIFICATION MARKS:

Animals unmarked

1985 to present: afghans and stuffed bears

CATEGORY:

Crocheting; Toys

RECOGNITION:

Nutshell News, Oct. 1984, pg. 73; Jan. 1987, pg. 72; Jul. 1987, pg. 58; Nov. 1988, pg. 91; Jun. 1989, pg. 63; Jan. 1991, pg. 75; *Miniature Gazette*, Vol. 15, No. 3, Spring 1987, pg. 59; Vol. 20, No. 3, Spring 1992, pg. 37

AUTOBIOGRAPHY:

I have always enjoyed working in various crafts. My grandmother taught me to knit and crochet when I was nine and that is still my favorite work. In 1975, when I discovered miniatures and the delight of crafting tiny items, I knew this was something that would never fail to provide a source of discovery and joy.

ARTISAN: **WHITEHOUSE, S. J.**

BUSINESS NAME: Whitehouse Miniatures

IDENTIFICATION MARKS:

CATEGORY:
Musical Instruments

RECOGNITION:
Dolls and Dolls' Houses, Nov. 1989, pg. 22-25

ARTISAN: **WHITLEDGE, RAY**

BUSINESS NAME: Ray Whitledge Miniatures

IDENTIFICATION MARKS:

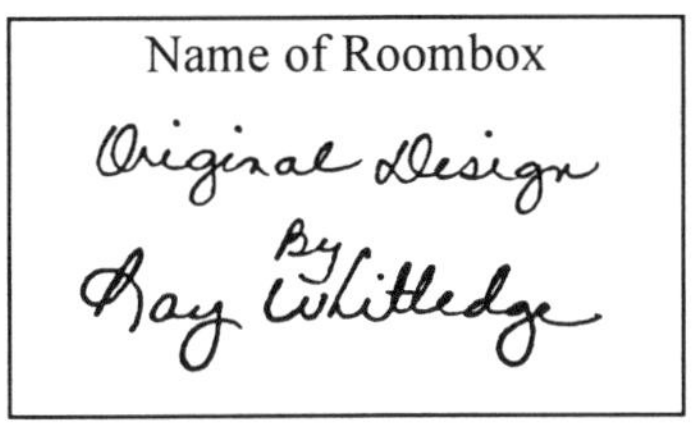

Brass plate attached to front

On individual pieces

Smaller pieces

CATEGORY:
Accessories; Designer: exterior, interior; Dollhouse; Furniture; Houses; Roomboxes: furnished; Rooms; Room Settings

RECOGNITION:
Nutshell News, Jul. 1994, pg. 50-55, 94-97, 108-110

BIOGRAPHY:
Ray Whitledge built model houses as a teen. He studied art and design in high school and at Western Kentucky University. Ray has worked as a design consultant and miniaturist since the 1980's. His work has consisted of roombox and dollhouse commissions as well as custom original design furniture and accessories.

Ray purchased Andrews Miniatures in March of 1995, and since then has sold his creations at shows.

ARTISAN: **WHITTEMORE, FRANCIS**

BUSINESS NAME: Francis Whittemore

IDENTIFICATION MARKS:
Unmarked

CATEGORY:
Glass: handblown; Glassware

HONORS:
NAME AOH; Exhibit: Toy & Miniature Museum of Kansas City

WHITTEMORE, FRANCIS, continued

RECOGNITION:

Nutshell News, Vol. 11, No. 12, Dec. 1981, pg. 63; Vol. 13, No. 10, Oct. 1983, pg. 67; Vol. 14, No. 11, Nov. 1984, pg. 81, 83; *Miniature Collector*, No. 13, Jun. 1979, pg. 24-27, "Glass Artist Francis Whittemore," Reed Ide; No. 29, Feb. 1982, pg. 17

AUTOBIOGRAPHY:

I have made glass since 1938. Collections are in glass and miniature museums. I make replicas of all periods from Egyptian to Art Deco and contemporary.

ARTISAN: WHITWORTH, SHIRLEY

BUSINESS NAME: Expressions In Porcelain

IDENTIFICATION MARKS:

SW with date

CATEGORY:

Dolls: porcelain; Needlework

HONORS:

IGMA Fellow 1993

RECOGNITION:

Nutshell News, Feb. 1992, Show Scene; *Miniatures Showcase*, Summer 1989; Summer, 1991; Winter 1993, Cover, pg. 31, 39; *Dolls In Miniature*, Spring 1992; *The Chronicle*, Willimantic, Connecticut, Oct. 28, 1987; Oct. 10, 1990; May 16, 1992; *Windham Textile and History Museum*, Newsletter, Winter 1989

ARTISAN: WILDFLOWER, TERESA

BUSINESS NAME: Teresa Miniatures

IDENTIFICATION MARKS:

CATEGORY:

Ceramics

AUTOBIOGRAPHY:

I have been producing one-of-a-kind miniature pottery and figurines for more than 20 years, since 1973.

ARTISAN: **WILLIAMS, SELINA**

BUSINESS NAME: Fashions In Miniature

IDENTIFICATION MARKS:
Some unmarked

Smaller pieces
"Cee Cee" nickname

CATEGORY:
Accessories: dolls; Bears; Clothing; Costuming; Dolls

AUTOBIOGRAPHY:
Fashions In Miniature has been in existence since 1992. It all started with a pink and green dress. I wanted a dress on a stand to enhance my miniature lady's boudoir. I looked around, but at that time there weren't many people making period clothing in miniature. All the dresses I found were either white silk or white lace, and I didn't want white. Something in the way of a cotton day dress was more what I had in mind.

I was frustrated at the lack of variety in miniature clothing, and I must have been very vocal about it because Catherine Timberlake, an active miniaturist and also my mother, sent me a book containing instructions on miniature dressmaking and a few basic patterns. Along with the book she sent a piece of fabric, green cotton with pink and green fans all over. Now this was more like it!

I had been making life-sized clothing since the age of 10, but miniature dressmaking employs different techniques, and frankly, I was prepared for this to be another of my failed experiments. The green dress turned out surprisingly well. But the real surprise was how much fun I had making it. I couldn't wait to make another. I soon abandoned that first, simple pattern and began to design more elaborate dresses and bridal gowns drawing on my many years of real-life dressmaking experience. It wasn't long before I had more dresses than I had space to display. Still, I didn't want to stop making them, so I took a table at a local show.

I only intended to do that one show, but I received so much encouragement from my fellow club members at Miniature World of Central Florida and so much support from the members of the Brevard Area Miniatures Association that I decided to go into business. One day I was in Ron's Miniature Shop, and Ron Mummert approached me about making some Halloween costumes to fill a costume shop for a customer. Two weeks later I returned to his shop with 21 different designs. He took 16 and became my first wholesale customer.

At first, all my dresses were built onto the hanger or stand, all my designed stands were flat bottomed and felt covered. I began to offer a line of removable costumes because so many collectors asked for this at shows. It seems that many people buy and assemble kit dolls only to discover that they cannot dress them. My line has expanded from cotton day dresses to bridal gowns, and accessories servents' uniforms, Halloween costumes, feathered and beaded flapper dresses on hangers, little girl's dresses, dressed dolls, dressed and undressed teddy bears and floppy-eared bunnies in crocheted sundresses. The only items in the line that may be ordered in any quantity are the 12 removable costumes. Everything else is available at shows. I like to do one-of-a-kind pieces and plan to keep production work to a minimum. This applies also to Dougybears by Selina, the company name under which I sell my full-sized bears and dolls.

ARTISAN: **WILLIAMS, VIOLA**

BUSINESS NAME: Viola Williams

IDENTIFICATION MARKS:

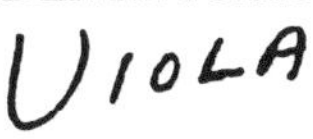

Scored onto lower torso

CATEGORY:
Author; Dolls: porcelain; Publications How-to

WILLIAMS, VIOLA, continued

RECOGNITION:

Nutshell News; Miniatures Showcase; Miniature Gazette; Doll Crafter; Contemporary Doll; Doll Castle News; Dolls in Miniature The Magazine

AUTOBIOGRAPHY:

When I was a little girl my mother had a "rag bag," it resembled a huge pillow case and it was filled with all of the bits and pieces of left-over fabric from the sewing she did for herself and other people. It also contained outgrown clothing that could be recycled to be used for some other purpose. The very nicest thing I remember about the rag bag is that I was allowed to use anything that I found inside it to sew clothes for my dolls.

I can't remember a time when I was not creating things. I discovered some bleached flower sacks, an old pair of my dad's pants, and some blue and white polka dot material. I very quickly combined these discards to create a white blouse with polka dot trim for my sister. One of the legs of my father's old pants became her skirt. Neither my little sister nor I were terribly concerned that I didn't know how to make button holes, or sew in zippers. The clothing pieces we found held together quite well with pins! My sister was young enough to think the outfit was gorgeous and begged to wear it to school the next day. Even after all these years I can still hear my mother softly objecting, "but everyone will think we are so poor." Still, in a show of motherly love, she set aside her own pride and allowed the pride of her daughter to express itself, my sister wore her new outfit to school the next day! However as I grew older I wasn't always so willing to show off my creations. By the time I was a teenager I realized that my work was not always lovely, so I often hid my paintings and other creations. I wanted them to be perfect, and perfection was hard to reach. My parents encouraged me to take art classes and I refused. I was too afraid that one day they would find out that I was not the wonderfully talented daughter that they thought I was. I privately taught myself, having never taken classes, but have taken a few workshops offered by my mini club. When I decided to sculpture original dolls, I knew I could not do so at a class, I would need to be alone, not in a group. I always seem to work best when I am able to "tune out" the world and put every ounce of my concentration on the item I am creating.

I have ventured out from doll making by providing how-to booklets with wardrobe patterns for one-inch scale dolls. I am also co-owner of *Dolls In Miniature The Magazine*, and have occasionally tried my hand at teaching workshops, and continue to make dolls. I have received many words of encouragement and many fine compliments to keep my interest alive. I often wonder if my supporters realize how much their kind words have meant to me. Their encouragement has been a very real part of the creation of my dolls; they are the ones who keep me loyal when I'm tempted to wonder off to try something new and different. Perhaps, I would never have strayed too far. I think there is an elastic string with one end tied to me, and the other to miniature dolls. I suspect I will always bounce back!

ARTISAN: **WILLIAMSON, JUDEÉ**

BUSINESS NAME: Williamson Walton Marble

IDENTIFICATION MARKS:

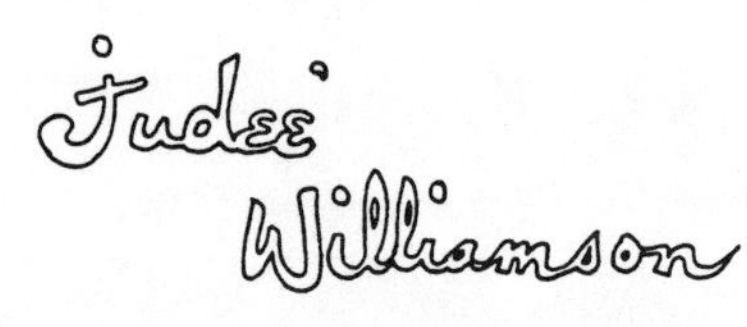

Carved in wood or cut from plastic mirror and mounted on wood, 1974 to 1985

White Gesso banner, black lettering 1975 to 1977

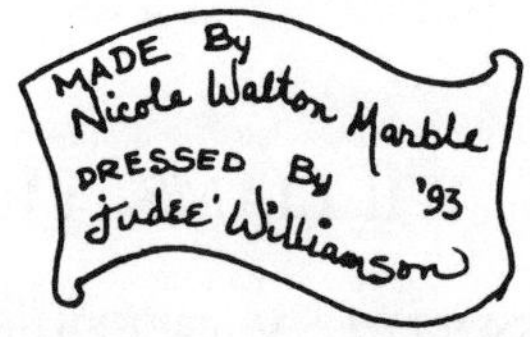

Banner cut from ivory vellum, script in permanent black ink, glued to bottom of furniture 1986 to present

CATEGORY:

Costuming; Designer: interior; Dolls; Furniture; Roomboxes; Rooms; Room Settings

HONORS:

IGMA Artisan

WILLIAMSON, JUDEÉ, continued

RECOGNITION:

Nutshell News, Fall 1976, pg. 59; Winter 1976, pg. 57-60; Spring 1977, pg. 40; Summer 1977, pg. 69; Winter 1977, pg. 73; Spring 1978, pg. 11; Fall 1978, pg. 90; Mar/Apr. 1979, pg. 72-75, Draperies, Barbara Blauman; Summer 1979, Draperies II, Barbara Blauman; Sept/Oct. 1979, pg. 79-80, Draperies III, Barbara Blauman; Nov/Dec. 1979, pg. 80-81, Draperies IV, Barbara Blauman; Mar. 1980, pg. 54; Apr. 1980, pg. 82-83; Jun. 1980, pg. 33, 37, 42-43, 70-72; Nov. 1980, pg. 42; Jan. 1981, pg. 21; Jun. 1981, Cover, pg. 59, 79; Sept. 1982, pg. 28-31; May 1983, Cover; Oct. 1983, pg. 44; Nov. 1983, Cover, pg. 46; Mar. 1984, pg. 59; Dec. 1984, pg. 38; Aug. 1986, pg. 72; Sept. 1986, pg. 44, 57; Oct. 1986, pg. 25, Product Review; Oct. 1987, pg. 78; *Miniature Collector*, Oct. 1978, pg. 11; Feb. 1979, pg. 20-25; Jun. 1979, pg. 30-33, The Shadowbox as Canvas; Oct. 1980, pg. 41-42; Apr. 1982, pg. 35

Williamson Walton Marble "Nicole Walton Marble and Judeé Williamson"

Nutshell News, Oct. 1987; Jan. 1988, pg. 67, 70; Jul. 1988, pg. 32-33; Nov. 1988, pg. 90; Apr. 1989, Cover, pg. 73; Jun. 1989, pg 68; Jul. 1990; May 1991, pg. 65; Sept. 1991, Cover, pg. 69-70; Nov. 1991, pg. 72; Jun. 1992, Show Scene; Jan. 1993, Product Review; Jul. 1993, Show Scene, pg. 66; Nov. 1993, Product Review, pg. 26-27; Jan. 1994, Show Scene; Mar. 1994, pg. 77-78, Build Your Dollhouse, Part 6, Sydnie Wagner; Jun. 1994, pg. 22, 33, 35; Oct. 1994, pg. 63; *Miniatures Showcase*, Spring 1988, pg. 16-17; Winter 1989, pg. 13; Summer 1990, pg. 26-27, 29, 46; Spring 1992, pg. 31; Mar. 1993, More Minis, pg. 52; Sept. 1993, pg. 20, Exciting Decorating Styles; *Contemporary Doll Magazine*, Summer 1991, pg. 62-63; Feb. 1994, pg. 100; *Miniature Collector*, Winter 1993, pg. 33; Spring 1994, pg. 24; Nov/Dec. 1994, pg. 28; *Dallas Life Magazine*, Sept. 5, 1993, pg. 23

BIOGRAPHY:

Judeé Williamson comes to miniatures by way of theater costume design. She has lived most of her life in Michigan with her husband and four (now grown) sons, moving to Arizona in 1987. Discovering miniatures in the early 1970's, she gained fame quickly with her original furniture, room and house designs in one-inch and ½-inch scale. Her sense of style and her realistic techniques with fabrics and dolls have set some high standards for the craft ever since.

Judeé is well known for teaching her creations in classes, originally in Michigan, and now throughout the United States. She is best known for her "Canopy Bed," and has made an estimated 1,000 of them. In 1985, she wrote "Judeé's Beds" and made a video tape on the bed and other classes so others could make her projects. Her unique style has placed her work in museums all over the world. In 1980, she was asked to lecture at the Smithsonian Institution in Washington, DC and made a presentation on a house made for clients from Saudi Arabia – hence it's name, The "Saudi House."

Judeé has designed a number of kits and tools currently on the market. In the late 1970's, she designed a Wing Chair class for which kits are still available; and designed the original Break-Away Roombox now used widely in the craft. About 1974, she did the original design work on making wicker furniture in miniature and taught it to many craftsmen who are still making wicker. Her original techniques in drapery were developed in the late 1970's and are still the standard of realism for the craft. In 1985, Judeé made three video tapes (The Canopy Bed, The Mannequin, and the Dressing Table and Chaise Lounge) for MiniGraphics and designed the kits that go with them. About the same time, she also designed "Judeé's Bowmaker." In 1986, MiniGraphics used Judeé's "Sunken Living Room" on the cover of their advertising booklet, with the plans and instructions for it as an insert. In 1992, she designed "Judeé's TasselMaker."

Judeé formed a partnership with Nicole Walton Marble in 1985 under the business name of Williamson Walton Marble. Since then, they have traveled the US and the Caribbean on the Nutshell News MiniCruise, doing shows and teaching the classes they have designed.

Judeé is an Artisan in the International Guild of Miniature Artisans, and has been a member of the National Association of Miniature Enthusiasts for many years. She is honored by having a slide presentation of her work from the early 1970's through 1985 in the archives of NAME, which is available to all NAME clubs.

See "Nicole Walton Marble"

ARTISAN: **WILLIES, JOAN CORNISH, R.M.S.**

BUSINESS NAME: Joan Willies Miniature Painting Etc.

IDENTIFICATION MARKS:

Joan Willies   WJ R.M.S.

CATEGORY:

Painting

HONORS:

IGMA Fellow; Prestigious Golden Rose Bowl Award, R.M.S., London, England; Hunting Group Award, London, England; Royal Society Miniature Painters, Sculpters and Gravers, London, England; Honorary Member, Miniature Art Society of Florida

RECOGNITION:

Who's Who in Art, pg. 479, 545; *Art Trade Press,* Artists Magazine, 1988, pg. 42-44; *Artists Workbook in Miniatures Painting*, 1988, 1990, 1993; *Miniature Gazette; Federation of British Artists Magazine; Tribute to the Arts,* 1984; *Who's Who of British Artists; International Who's Who of Professional and Business Women*

ARTISAN: **WILMOTH, BETTIE**

BUSINESS NAME: Bettie's Handpainted Porcelain

IDENTIFICATION MARKS:

BW

Logo used on printed material

CATEGORY:

Dishes: porcelain; Dolls: porcelain

RECOGNITION:

Nutshell News, Jun. 1989, pg. 58-59, 60; Jun. 1991, pg. 69; Dec. 1991, pg. 67; *Miniatures Showcase*, Spring 1990, pg. 32; Summer 1991, pg. 20; Winter 1992, pg. 27; Jan. 1993, pg. 34-35

ARTISAN: **WILSON, CAROLYN K.**

BUSINESS NAME: C J's Miniatures

IDENTIFICATION MARKS:

CJ'S
1992

CATEGORY:

Furniture

WILSON, CAROLYN K., continued

RECOGNITION:

Miniatures Showcase, Fall 1986, pg. 36; Winter 1989, pg. 28-29; Jan. 1993, pg. 45; *Miniature Collector*, Jan. 1993

AUTOBIOGRAPHY:

Until 1980, Joan Byer and I thought that our expertise lie in homemaking, husbands, and child rearing. When our nests became empty the same year, we looked at one another and said "What do we do now?" Our first adventure was a search to find Joan's childhood dollhouse. Her mother, unable to locate it found a builder of dollhouses, so we traveled to Joan's native state, New York and returned home to Indiana with two dollhouses. It was a wonderful learning experience as we completed our houses and found other hobbyists as smitten. We enjoyed traveling distances to miniature shops and shows discovering the wonders of handcrafted miniatures.

A friend with an antique business invited us to share space, if we were interested in making the selling of miniatures a business venture. After trying two locations in an area of Indiana without enough population to support such a specialty, we were on the verge of giving up. A Board Member of a living history museum at Fort Wayne, Indiana, an 1816 Fort recreation, asked if we would be interested in creating the simple authentic furnishings of the Fort, in miniature, to be sold in the museum gift shop. Armed with a camera and tape measure, we miniaturized beds, tables and cupboards to one-inch scale reproductions. We left shop keeping and became makers of miniature antiques, evolving and changing as our techniques improved. And so CJ's in it's present form came to be.

Always willing to listen, try, and learn it was suggested that we join CIMTA to see if the shop keepers appreciated our efforts. With that acceptance in 1983 we became full-time handcrafters. Our workshop is located in Carolyn's home in Columbia City, working five days a week, from designing to marketing. Our line of furniture may be found in retail shops and at miniature shows throughout the US. It includes one-inch and ½-inch scale early American and Victorian country pieces. We specialize in the "aged" look, finishing the chairs, cupboards, and pie safes in appropriate colors and walnut, so they appear to be time worn. We are members of CIMTA, NAME and Metro Minis of Fort Wayne, Indiana.

ARTISAN: WINGLER, CAT

BUSINESS NAME: Cat Wingler

IDENTIFICATION MARKS:

CATEGORY:

Dolls: charactor

HONORS:

IGMA Artisan 1994; NAME AOH 1995

RECOGNITION:

Nutshell News, Aug. 1986, pg. 78-81, "Cat Wingler's Fanciful Friends," Sheila DeTurk; *Miniatures Showcase; Miniature Gazette*

AUTOBIOGRAPHY:

I was born in 1947 and raised in Flint, Michigan. My husband, Steve, and I were married in 1965, and have two sons, Steve Jr. and James. We have lived in Wilkesboro, Pennsylvania since 1970. Our children are now married and have families of their own.

I am a doll artist, who specializes in a particular type of doll, I call character dolls or art dolls. I work primarily in one-inch scale although my work has varied from life-size to 1½-inch scale. All my dolls are one-of-a-kind. They are hand sculpted in a polymer modeling compound and assembled on a wire armature. They are then permanently costumed and wigged. I spend a great deal of time researching period costumes, hair styles and fashions. I generally dress each doll in authentic period costuming although I sometimes take artistic license to achieve a specific effect. I do mostly male characters, which is highly unusual for a doll artist. I also do dressed animal characters on a frequent basis, which is also unusual, putting a great emphasis on humor and whimsy. Once in a while I do a serious historical portrait.

My work has been shown often since 1982 in several miniature magazines, including *Nutshell News, Miniatures Showcase,* and the *Miniature Gazette.* The dolls were the subject of feature articles.

I show and sell my dolls at miniature shows all over the United States and have sold them to customers from Canada, Mexico, England, Germany, Japan, Australia, France, and Scotland. I teach classes and seminars on beginning sculpting and basic costuming, and have been teaching at a national level across the US from 1987.

ARTISAN: **WISWELL, WILLADEAN "WILLIE"**

IDENTIFICATION MARKS:

CATEGORY:

Accessories; Furniture

RECOGNITION:

Nutshell News, Vol. 6, No. 4, Winter 1976, pg. 81; Dec. 1991, pg. 70-71; *Miniature Gazette*, Vol. 5, No. 2, Dec. 1976, pg. 5; Vol. 18, No. 3, Spring 1990, pg. 45; Vol. 19, No. 2, Winter 1990, pg. 22-23

AUTOBIOGRAPHY:

My background in miniatures began in 1963. The interest was always their, I'm sure because I had a dollhouse and furniture as a child into my teens. After marriage and my first child, I thought it was time for me to renew my interest. Until 1970, I thought I was alone in this love. I also made everything from balsa wood not knowing other materials were available. I was thrilled when I discovered my first miniature store. I died and went to heaven! I have a huge collection, half of which I made, and half I purchased. I was in Real Estate for 18 years. I have taken classes for miniatures from all the best.

ARTISAN: **WITTMAN, HELEN**

BUSINESS NAME: Wittman Studios
Le Petite Babes

IDENTIFICATION MARKS:

1974 to present

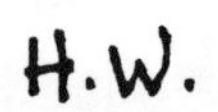

Most dolls numbered
Number with slash indicates Limited Edition, -0-, one of a kind

Bears

CATEGORY:

Bears: porcelain; Dolls; Trunks

HONORS:

IGMA Artisan

RECOGNITION:

Nutshell News, Nov. 1983, Cover

WITTMAN, HELEN, continued

AUTOBIOGRAPHY:

I was born in 1945 in Texas. I graduated from the University of Texas, Austin, with a BFA, and a minor in art. Although my degree was in Stage Design, I had become very interested in costume. I worked in the professional theatre for several years, but quit when my son was born. Eventually I joined an antique doll club and then discovered miniatures. I was fascinated with little things as a child, but didn't discover dollhouses until my late 20's.

The first antique doll I bought was a dollhouse girl. I decided to make some, since everyone liked her. I had never done any ceramics and at the time, there were no classes or books on doll making. I taught myself, with my background in art helping considerably. I kept getting smaller and now do only original two-inch and smaller dolls. My real specialty is china dolls on leather or wood bodies.

I have taken a two year break from work, and am now working on my first big doll and a book on costuming for the doll maker. I am an IGMA Artisan.

ARTISAN: WOLCOTT – MARTINO, MELISSA

BUSINESS NAME: Melissa's Miniatures

IDENTIFICATION MARKS:

1981 to present

Small pieces

CATEGORY:

Art: fine; Frames; Paintings: old masters

HONORS:

IGMA Fellow; Tiffany Window Display, Atlanta, 1987; Exhibit: Safety Harbor Museum, Safety Harbor, Florida, 1981

RECOGNITION:

Nutshell News; Miniature Collector; Miniatures Showcase; The Robb Report, Vol. 10, No. 9, Sept. 1986, pg. 10; *Miniature Gazette*, Vol. 16, No. 1, Fall 1987, pg. 56; *TV Segment*, Live at Five, Miniature Painting Exhibit, 1981, Safety Harbor Museum, Safety Harbor, Florida

AUTOBIOGRAPHY:

I am a graduate of the School of Visual Arts in New York City, where I studied fine art and illustration. I won several awards and my work went on a world tour, becoming part of a permanent collection. Upon graduation, I worked as an art director for a film company in New York before another love, music, came calling. I sang and played bass in two all-female groups, "The Enchanted Forest," and "The maiden Voyage." They took me across the country, to Canada, and the Islands, and on to all the major TV shows, Ed Sullivan, Johnny Carson, Marv Griffin, etc. A skiing accident curtailed my musical career for several months and it was during this time that I was first introduced to the world of miniatures. I was commissioned by a collector to miniaturize some of the original paintings found in an historical mansion. The paintings were so favorably received and I enjoyed doing them so much, I decided to specialize in miniature art and have been so ever since. I am an IGMA Fellow and a member of MASF and NAME.

ARTISAN: WOLFORD, KEITH

IDENTIFICATION MARKS:

KEITH WOLFORD **KW**

Carved in block letters with number

WOLFORD, KEITH, continued

CATEGORY:
Furniture

HONORS:
Exhibit: Toy & Miniature Museum of Kansas City

RECOGNITION:
Miniature Collector, No. 32, Aug. 1982, pg. 34-35, "Obsessed With the Beauty of Bentwood," Curtis P. Middleton

ARTISAN: **WONNACOTT, GEOFFREY P.**

BUSINESS NAME: Geoffrey P. Wonnacott

IDENTIFICATION MARKS:

CATEGORY:
Furniture

HONORS:
IGMA Artisan

RECOGNITION:
Nutshell News, Jul. 1989, pg. 50-52; *Miniature Collector*, Spring 1990, pg. 32-33; *International Dolls House News*, Vol. 17, No. 1, Spring 1988, pg. 21; *Modelling & Miniature Crafts*, Issue No. 6, 1988, pg. 78-79; *The Crafts Ring Journal*, Vol. 1, No. 2, Winter 1988, pg. 22; *Dolls & Dolls Houses*, Issue No. 2, May 1989, pg. 43-44; *Traditional Homes*, Vol. 5, No. 11, Aug. 1989, pg. 61-63; *Dolls House World*, Issue No. 8, 1990, pg. 22-24

ARTISAN: **WOOD, ASPEN Ní**
DOAN, ASPEN

BUSINESS NAME: Native Dancer Miniatures

IDENTIFICATION MARKS:
1992 to present

CATEGORY:
Accessories: Southwest; Landscaping

RECOGNITION:
The Scale Cabinetmaker, Vol. 16, No. 2, Summer 1992, Cover

WOOD, ASPEN NÍ
DOAN, ASPEN, continued

BIOGRAPHY:

Aspen Doan, also known as Aspen Ní Wood, has been creating in the miniature world since 1985 as a part-time artist in California. The first showing of her work was the 2nd annual show by Miniatures West in Culver City, California. In 1985, Aspen was accepted as a dealer in the Top Artisans Miniature Show in Anaheim, California. Since moving to New Mexico in 1991, Aspen continues as a full-time artist, doing miniature shows out of state and introducing her miniatures at local art shows.

ARTISAN: WOODYARD, DOUGLAS

BUSINESS NAME: Doug Woodyard Miniatures

IDENTIFICATION MARKS:

D-W 19--

CATEGORY:

Carts: hand, push; Furniture: period; Vehicles: hand-drawn, horse-drawn

RECOGNITION:

Home Miniaturist, Sept. 1990, pg. 5; *Dolls House World*, Issue No. 6, 1990, pg. 27; *International Dolls House News*, Vol. 19, No. 2, 1990, Cover; Sunday *Times Magazine*, April 12, 1992, pg. 51; *Decorative Dolls' Houses*, Caroline Hamilton, Ebury Press, London, 1990, pg. 52-53

ARTISAN: WYATT, GINGER

BUSINESS NAME: Porcelain by Ginger

IDENTIFICATION MARKS:

1978 to present

Ginger

with date

CATEGORY:

Lamps; Lighting; Porcelain

RECOGNITION:

Miniatures Showcase, Spring 1987, pg. 24

AUTOBIOGRAPHY:

My educational background is Geology, Earth Sciences teaching. I broke my ankle in 1978 while working with lace draped dolls and full-sized sculpture. I had to sit for long periods of time and the sofa was crowded with large pieces, so I began making them smaller and smaller. During this time I obtained a book that mentioned Jackie Andrew's name, and when I recovered I took some of the smaller pieces for her to see. My business was literally born on her kitchen table. I left with an order from Jackie and the names of several shops in this business. I have almost no training as an artist. In 1987, I was involved in an auto accident and since then, because traveling has been difficult, I have done mostly wholesale shows. In the near future I hope to begin retail again.

As far as business goes, I do all my own work, and love nothing more than to surround myself with books or photographs full of porcelain and decide what my next conquest will be and how to make it happen. I make my own molds, clean, fire, and glaze as well as advertise my own work, and I love it!

ARTISAN: **WYATT, MELISSA J.**

BUSINESS NAME: Melissa Wyatt Dolls
Pride & Precious Originals

IDENTIFICATION MARKS:
1988 to present

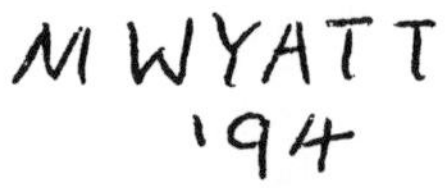

Impressed on bottom of foot

CATEGORY:
Dolls; Figures: historical

HONORS:
IGMA Artisan

RECOGNITION:
Nutshell News, Jan. 1989; Mar. 1991; *Miniatures Showcase*, Summer 1991; Spring 1992; *Contemporary Doll Collector*, Oct/Nov. 1994; *Doll Reader*, May 1992

AUTOBIOGRAPHY:
I started making miniatures in 1987, selling my work so that I could afford to buy the work of others. My early pieces included miniature figurines under one-inch tall and copies of master paintings. In 1988, I began concentrating on historically accurate dolls. My miniature dolls are one-of-a-kind, hand-sculpted from Super Sculpey, costumed in natural fabrics and antique fabrics when available. I have attended many shows on the East Coast, but since the birth of my son in 1991, I have concentrated on building up my mail-order business. Lately, I have been been concentrating on larger one-of-a-kind art dolls.

Y

ARTISAN: **YINGER, JAN**

BUSINESS NAME: Minuette
Wright Guide To Miniatures (1978-1988)

IDENTIFICATION MARKS:
Some unmarked

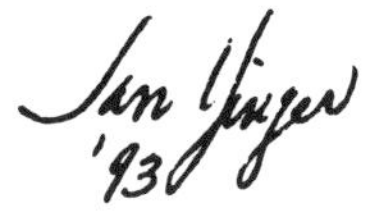

Jan Yinger
Stamp for sculpted cats

CATEGORY:
Accessories: general store; Animals: cats, farm; Food; Holiday Items; Medical; Shops

HONORS:
IGMA Fellow

RECOGNITION:
Nutshell News, Apr. 1981, Cover; *Miniatures Showcase; Miniature Dealer; Edwardsburg Argus*, Feb. 3, 1983; *South Bend Tribune*, Indiana, Mar. 3, 1977; *Hillsdale Daily News*, Sept. 9, 1972

AUTOBIOGRAPHY:

I began miniature work seriously in 1970 after years of interest in tiny things. Dating back to childhood when we played with little plastic horses on rugged dirt paths, day after day, wearing their legs away after long hours on the trail. In 1947, mother built a dollhouse and made furniture for us, unknowingly, the beginnings of new dreams.

In 1968, I built a dollhouse for my children, made all the furniture, foods and accessories. People saw this work and wanted my creations to resell. I was in business! I sold wholesale until 1974 and as orders increased I knew miniatures were becoming more popular. I was anxious to find out what was going on in the miniature world, so I booked my first show under the name of "Mini-Meals." I was hooked! As I progressed, I encouraged family members to make miniatures also.

In 1978, we started a mail-order catalog called "Wright Guide To Miniatures." The catalog ran for 10 years. I discontinued it eventually because it restricted creativity of new items because of continually updating the catalog. Shows gave much more freedom of expression and teaching classes was a great feeling of accomplishment!

In 1989, we became proud owners of a life-sized historical Victorian mansion. My secret dreams at last have a chance of fulfillment making miniatures, teaching classes and offer Bed and Breakfast accommodations in a Victorian Dollhouse! My sister, Mary Ann Ledyard, and husband Grover carried on the Wright Guide tradition while we chose a more Victorian name for our new endeavor, "Minuette." At the beginning of our fourth year, it's a dream come true!

ARTISAN: **YINGLING, JEAN E.**

BUSINESS NAME: Wee Treasures

IDENTIFICATION MARKS:

CATEGORY:
China; Porcelain

YINGLING, JEAN E., continued

HONORS:

IGMA Fellow; Exhibits: National Geographic, Oct. 1987; Toy & Miniature Museum of Kansas City; Allentown Art Museum, Allentown, Pennsylvania, Nov. 1981

RECOGNITION:

Nutshell News, Dec. 1983, Cover; *The Miniature Magazine*, Spring 1980, pg. 13; *Miniature Collector*, No. 19, Jun. 1980, pg. 30-35; *Decorating & Craft Ideas*, pg. 78, 80; *Penn Starter Magazine*, Nov/Dec. 1983; *A Mansion in Miniature*, Bets O'Meara, O'Meara Publications, 1979

AUTOBIOGRAPHY:

Not wanting me to be exposed to the Bohemian lifestyles that an art school would present, my parents insisted I attend a university and learn something "worthwhile." I received a BS from Penn State University in 1959. Six years later, I was studying art with local and visiting artists working in three mediums, oil, watercolors, and clay. It was not until 1975 that I abandoned the easel for the potters wheel and became a miniature ceramist.

My lifelong passion for little things made it possible for me to combine my artistic talents and my "secret hobby" into a full-time business. After taking classes to learn the art of throwing full-size pots, I taught myself how to throw miniature pots. Mold making became another challenge that had to be learned by trial and error. But in the end it all came together and I produced egg shell thin china and porcelain dishes, accessories and figurines. I choose antique designs from 12th Century Chinese to 19th Century European and English manufactures, for my patterns.

ARTISAN: **YOUNG, CAROL**

BUSINESS NAME: Carol Young Miniatures

IDENTIFICATION MARKS:

CATEGORY:

Furniture: bedroom

RECOGNITION:

Miniatures Showcase, Vol. 8, No. 3, May 1993, pg. 30

AUTOBIOGRAPHY:

I started in business on a small scale in 1987, selling my bedroom furniture to a shop in Sarasota. After which, I attended a CIMTA show in 1991 and had a small space at the order table. In 1992, I took a table and brought lots of inventory. The CIMTA show was such a success for me that I am now working full-time in miniature furniture. All of my furniture is for bedrooms, French Provincial and Southwestern, and I design all my pieces.

ARTISAN: **YOUNG, LINDA**

BUSINESS NAME: Lady Jane

IDENTIFICATION MARKS:

Roomboxes

Rugs

YOUNG, LINDA, continued

CATEGORY:
Glass: stained; Roomboxes: stained glass; Rugs: braided

HONORS:
IGMA Artisan

Z

ARTISAN: **ZENNER, JIM**

BUSINESS NAME: Mr. Infinity Scale Objects Co.

IDENTIFICATION MARKS:

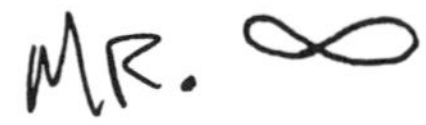

CATEGORY:

Accessories; Household Accessories

RECOGNITION:

Nutshell News; *Miniature Dealer*; *The Observer*, Dec. 18, 1980, Sec. 2, pg. 1, "Big Success From Small Models," Rick Bodamer

BIOGRAPHY:

Jim Zenner is a uniquely gifted artist. His artistic integrity and excellence of original design has earned him an "enviable international reputation." Mr. Zenner's years of scale model making and creation of special effects for the film industry gave him a unique expertise with processes and materials previously not employed in the making of miniatures, under the name "Mr. Infinity Scale Objects Co." At his Long Island studio they produce over 500 intricately detailed miniature accessories from household utensils and shop tools to spider webs, and even a funny pair of "Groucho" glasses complete with pink nose!

ARTISAN: **ZERKEL, DAN**

BUSINESS NAME: Zerkel's Miniatures

IDENTIFICATION MARKS:

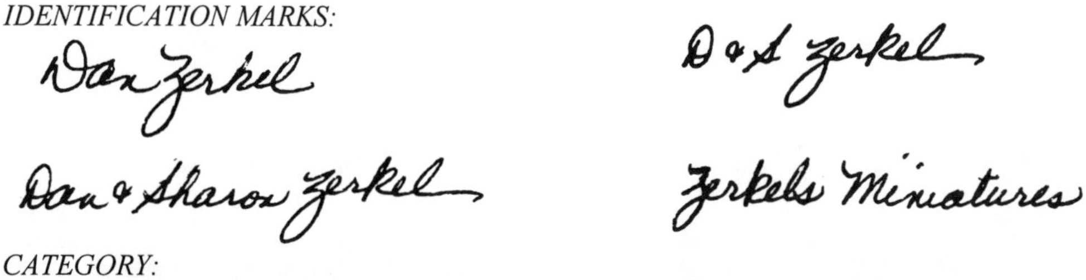

CATEGORY:

Accessories; Buildings; Caning; Furniture: country, Shaker; Toys

HONORS:

NAME AOH

RECOGNITION:

Nutshell News, Vol. 16, No. 8, Aug. 1986, pg. 50-55, "Dan and Sharon Zerkel – Artisans and Collectors," Anne Day Smith

AUTOBIOGRAPHY:

I was born in Dayton, Ohio and have lived in Ohio all my life. I graduated from the University of Cincinnati with a BS in Education and a BA in Art Education. I retired from teaching elementary art with the Cincinnati Board of Education in 1993, after 29 years of teaching.

Sharon and I became interested in miniatures in 1976. With the help of Jean Ellsworth I began making miniatures to sell and teaching classes locally. I first taught a caning class, nationally, at the NAME National

Houseparty in St. Louis, Missouri, in 1981. I have been teaching and selling my miniatures nationally since then. Our most challenging project has been to make 325 Shaker washstands for the NAME Region A-3 Houseparty as souvenirs in 1992.

I have done research on Shaker life and furniture for many years. Toys have always been fascinating to me. I collect some large ones and enjoy making small ones.

Recently, the small scale bug has bitten and I now belong to four NAME clubs: Drawn and Quartered and Mini Mail Club are smaller scale. Former A-3 Representation Team and Married With Minis are the other two clubs.

ARTISAN: **ZERKEL, SHARON**

BUSINESS NAME: Zerkel's Miniatures

IDENTIFICATION MARKS:

Baskets unsigned
1/144 pieces signed and dated

S. Zerkel

Quilts Typed cloth label attached to back

CATEGORY:

Baskets; Caning; Furniture; Quilts

HONORS:

NAME AOH

RECOGNITION:

Nutshell News, Vol. 16, No. 8, Aug. 1986, pg. 50-55, "Dan and Sharon Zerkel – Artisans and Collectors," Anne Day Smith

AUTOBIOGRAPHY:

I was born in Elyria, Ohio and have lived in Ohio all my life. I majored in Art in high school and attended the University of Cincinnati where I studied Interior Design.

Dan and I became interested in dollhouses in 1976 when we built a house for our daughter. We have been interested in miniatures ever since. By 1981, I was making quilts, baskets and toys to sell, and I helped Dan teach our first chair caning class in St. Louis at the NAME National Houseparty. We have been teaching together and separately since then. We have also sold our miniatures nationally since 1981. Quilts and baskets are my major interests.

I belong to three miniature clubs: Married with Minis, Former Region A-3 Team, and Drawn and Quartered.

ARTISAN: **ZINN, ALICE**

BUSINESS NAME: Alice Zinn

IDENTIFICATION MARKS:

ZINN, ALICE, continued

CATEGORY:

Animals

RECOGNITION:

Nutshell News; Miniatures Showcase; Miniature Collector; Long Island Cablevision, New York, 1973

ARTISAN: **ZORICH, KAREN**

BUSINESS NAME: Karen Zorich

IDENTIFICATION MARKS:

CATEGORY:

Accessories; Dishes: porcelain; Dolls; Scenes: fantasy

HONORS:

IGMA Fellow

ARTISAN: **ZORN, BETSY**

BUSINESS NAME: The Ginger Jar

IDENTIFICATION MARKS:

1972 to 1976 Paper labels

1977 to 1990

CATEGORY:

Caning; Furniture

HONORS:

Exhibit: Toy and Miniature Museum of Kansas City

RECOGNITION:

Nutshell News, Winter 1972; Oct. 1988; Dec. 1988, pg. 71-73; Oct. 1989, pg. 78; *Miniatures Showcase*, Summer 1990, pg. 21-22, 69; *Miniatures Calendar*, Nutshell News, 1985; *Engagement Calendar for Miniature Collectors*, Apr/May 1980; *Sphere*, Magazine, Apr. 1976, Mary Jane Graham; *Inside the World of Miniatures & Dollhouses*, Rosner and Beckerman, McKay Press, 1976; *Make and Furnish Your Own Miniature Rooms*, Marion Maeve O'Brien, Hawthorne Books, Inc., NY, 1978; *Make your Own Dollhouses and Dollhouse Miniatures*, Marian Maeve O'Brien, Hawthorne Books, Inc., NY, 1975; *Through the Looking Glass*, Boynton and Associates, Inc., Ann Ruble, 1984; *This Side of Yesterday in Miniature*, Catherine B. MacLaren, 1975; *American Period Interiors in Miniature*, Kate Doordan Klavan , Scribner's, 1984; *The Collectors Guide to Dollhouses and Dollhouse Miniatures*, Marian Maeve O'Brien, 1974

ZORN, BETSY, continued

BIOGRAPHY:

In 1972, Betsy Zorn and Jean Kirkwood combined knowledge, crafting skills, and talents to form "The Ginger Jar." Each had done full-size upholstery, caning, and furniture refinishing, and had an interest in miniatures. Applying these skills to one-inch scale was both challenging and rewarding. The Ginger Jar accepted mail orders, custom requests, and traveled to occasional shows until 1976.

When each family was relocated, Betsy continued doing shows and began teaching miniature making in hopes of finding an apprentice to help with the increasing demand for her miniatures. A little known fact: Jean Welch of "The China Closet" painted her first porcelain miniature in Betsy's kitchen while waiting for her son, Ty, to finish a miniature-making lesson.

In 1978, Betsy's family moved to Wisconsin and she returned to work as a registered nurse. Mail order was stopped, but Betsy did accept custom work and managed to do the first Miniature Marketplace show in Milwaukee in 1987. There she met Natasha Beshenkovsky and Mary Grady O'Brien and the staff of Petite Maison of Lake Forest, Illinois. Betsy crafted selective pieces for each of these artisans until 1990.

As a result of carpal tunnel syndrome surgery, Betsy is no longer able to do the fine handcraft required to make collectable miniatures. But she still corresponds with the many fine friends her hobby/business brought to her, and nurtures those friendships.

Authors and Editors

AARDEMA, BARBARA J.

AUTOBIOGRAPHY:

I was graduated magna cum laude from Western Michigan University in 1972 with an English major. I have been writing for a number of newsletters, newspapers and magazines since 1976. My longest tenure was with *The Muskegon Chronicle*, where I worked as a reporter for eight years. *Muskegon Magazine* published several of my articles on subjects of general interest. I became editor of *Miniature Collector* magazine in October, 1994 and will be writing stories periodically for that publication.

ARMSTRONG, RUTH

also see listing on page 15

CREDITS:

Feature Articles:

Nutshell News, The Scale Cabinetmaker, Miniature Gazette, Creative Crafts and Miniatures, Crafts 'n Things, Michigan Natural Resources, Workbench, Decorating Crafts & Ideas

Series (Feature or How-to):

Women's Household (Tower Press, then White Birches) 1963-1988, How-to hobbies

Books:

Roadside Sundries, Kalmbach Publishing Co.

RECOGNITION:

Citizen Patriot, Jackson, Michigan, Dec. 18, 1983; *Independent*, Jonesville, Michigan, Dec. 22, 1993

AUTOBIOGRAPHY:

I was writing, just for the fun of it, for about fifteen years before I started playing with miniatures and writing mostly about how to make them. If I wrote a letter to an editor, it got printed. If I sent in a sharing of something I knew how-to-do, either they printed it or a kill fee bought it. I guess I just aimed my arrows where they had a target.

Somewhere in the late 1970's, I became a hobbyist who wrote, instead of a writer with hobbies. I used to write about how-to-do something with "nothing," about inexpensive home decor, about nature, household hints, just what was in my world as a housewife of the old home-model. I wrote about sewing. I wrote a booklet early on about cooking with a microwave. I wrote a series about birds. When I began making miniatures for market, back when there weren't many to be found, there wasn't time to write about much more than those, and so my path narrowed.

I'm trying to "retire" and travel, but every once in a while someone writes "I just can't find. . . ." And then I do one more, and share it.

BAHAR, ANN

CREDITS:

Feature Articles:

Nutshell News, Miniature Collector, Little Things Digest, Creative Crafts and Miniatures, Hobbies, Doll Reader, Dolls, Teddy Bear & Friends, Antique Doll World, International Dolls' House News (UK), *Magazine de la Maison de Poupée* (France), *NAME Miniature Gazette, Miniature Book Society Newsletter, Collector Editions*

BAHAR, ANN, continued

Series (Feature or How-to):
Miniature Collector, Jul/Aug. 1984 (Cigar Box Toy Shop); Fall 1988 (Antique Christmas Crèche); *Little Things Digest,* Apr. 1983 (One-inch scale antique butcher shop replica)

Regular Columns:
1982-1990 Editor, Miniature Department, *Hobbies* magazine (monthly feature); 1983 Contributing Editor, *Miniature Collector*

Books:
Miniature Books:
The Russian Icon (Tamazunchale Press, 1988); *The Eiffel Tower*, 1889-1989 (Tabula Rasa Press, 1989); *Queen Mary's Dolls' House Library* (Gleniffer Press, 1991); *Auguste Edouart, Adventure in Shadow* (Tabula Rasa Press, 1992); *Titania's Palace* (Tabula Rasa Press, 1994); *Antique Reproduction Paper Doll Books* (with one-inch scale dolls); *Joan of Arc*, A Paper Doll Book (Hobby House Press, 1990); *Historic French Costumes Paper Doll Book* (Hobby House Press, 1991)
Collector Books:
Santa Dolls, Historical to Contemporary (Hobby House Press, 1992); *Contemporary Artist Dolls from Germany* (Hobby House Press) Fall 1994 publication, co-authored with Ingeborg Riesser

HONORS:
Miniature Book Society Service Award 1992

RECOGNITION:
Reviews of books published:
Miniature Collector; International Dolls' House News; Le Magazine de la Maison de Poupée

Article:
"Qui est Ann Bahar" ("Who is Ann Bahar") in Le Magazine de la Maison de Poupée Winter 1990/1991, Ingeborg Riesser; Featured Researcher of The Month/"Newsletter", Historical Society of Pennsylvania, by Richard Romaniecki, Fall 1992

BIOGRAPHY:
Ann Bahar graduated from Columbia University (1959) with a degree in British Literature and minors in Art History and French. She has loved the arts all her life and empathizes with artists interviewed over the years since, like them, she is happiest when expressing herself through her hands. Interest in the miniature arts, always strong, developed into collecting and writing in the late 1970's. Since her first article appeared in the Nov/Dec. 1979 *Nutshell News*, she has published close to 300 articles in leading miniature and other collector magazines. Subjects range from antique to contemporary dollhouses, crafts, how-to features, historic and contemporary dolls and more than 100 artist profiles for magazine features, close to double the number if you include interviews for her collector books!

In addition to the above, she has researched, designed and written four private-press miniature-format books that include *Queen Mary's Dolls' House Library*, a boxed presentation copy of which was accepted for the personal collection of Her Majesty Queen Elizabeth II. Ann edited and designed two antique-repro French paper doll books (Hobby House Press) that include elegant dolls scaled for the dollhouse, and a major art doll book, *Santa Dolls, Historical to Contemporary* (Hobby House Press, Fall 1992), the first book to deal exclusively with old and new dolls that depict Father Christmas. A chapter on Santa Claus in the dollhouse is included. A second collector doll book, co-authored with Ingeborg Riesser, was scheduled for publication in the Fall of 1994. And a new (her fifth!) miniature book, titled *Titania's Palace*, about the fabulous 1920's dollhouse now at Legoland®Park in Denmark, was published late in 1994 or early in 1995.

BENNETT, BONNIE

also see listing on page 32

CREDITS:

Series (Feature or How-to):

Nutshell News

Regular Columns:

Product reviews, *Nutshell News*

Books:

Early Americana (Furniture how-to), Boynton & Associates, Inc.; *Circus Bedroom* (Furniture how-to), Boynton & Associates, Inc.

BENSON, RON (Deceased)

also see listing on page 34

CREDITS:

Series (Feature or How-to):

Nutshell News, "Kit Renderings"

RECOGNITION:

Nutshell News, Aug. 1994, pg. 44-47; *Richmond Times Dispatch*, Richmond, Virginia, Aug. 10, 1986

AUTOBIOGRAPHY:

I was on the staff of my high school newspaper where I drew awful cartoons and wrote idealistic editorials. I wrote articles for about every other issue of the old *Miniature Showcase.* These were mainly on historical design. I wrote three articles for *Miniature Dealer* on display techniques. I had a number of editorials published in the local newspapers expressing my opinion over something or other.

BITLER, DOUGLESS STRICKLAND

CREDITS:

Feature Articles:

Miniature Collector

Regular Columns:

Nutshell News, "Postscript;" *Miniatures Showcase, Miniature Collector*, "Ask Dougless," "World According to Dougless;" *Miniature Gazette*, "From Dougless • • • With Love;" *IGMA Cube*: Co-editor, "The Guilded Bookworm"

Books:

Ask Dougless, Vol. I, II, III, IV, V

Pamphlets:

The Dougless Guides, I Oriental; II Tudor and The Twenties; III Early Colonial; IV Late Colonial; V Federal; VI Empire; VII Mid-Victorian; VIII Late Victorian; IX Appraisal

RECOGNITION:

Nutshell News, Sept. 1982; *Cleveland Plain Dealer*, Aug. 1982; TV Appearances: Philadelphia, New Orleans, Cleveland

BITLER, DOUGLESS STRICKLAND, continued

BIOGRAPHY:

She received a Bachelor and Master of Arts in English and History at Ohio University and did partial work on her Ph.D. at Kent State University in History. She has done field research in numerous well-known US and European museums. She has authored the *Dougless Guides* which are nine period outlines with over 10,000 facts. Also "Ask Dougless," a series of books Volumes I through V, which are questions and answers on period authenticity and miniaturia. She is a columnist and editor for *Miniature Collector* since 1982, *Miniature Gazette* since 1980 and was a contributing writer for *Miniatures Showcase* and *Nutshell News*. She has held workshops on Origins and Historical background of Period Houses and Furnishings (1600-1930), over 100 lectures in all, across the United States. She has been doing business as Dougless Ltd. since 1976.

COOK, MADELYN W.

also see listing on page 91

CREDITS:

Series (Features or How-to):

Nutshell News, The Scale Cabinetmaker

Booklets:

Nutshell News Plan Service, No. 105 *Wicker Wizardry*, 1981, No. 123 *An Accent on Wicker*, 1983

DELGADO, JEANNE

CREDITS:

Feature Articles:

Nutshell News; Miniatures Showcase; Miniature Dealer; The Miniatures Catalog; Discovering Miniatures; Miniature Gazette; *Beaver Falls* (Pennsylvania) *News-Tribune; The Valley Tribune*

Regular Columns:

Associate Editor *Nutshell News*: since 1987, writer several regular columns; "Days Gone By," *The Valley Tribune*, 1979-1980

Books:

Treasures in Miniature, (co-author), Kalmbach Publishing Co.

Other:

Feature Editor, *Miniatures Catalog 11th, 12th, 13th edition;* contributor, *16th, 17th edition;* Editor/feature writer *News-Tribune Bridal Edition*

AUTOBIOGRAPHY:

I've been writing as long as I can remember. I never had a writing or journalism course, but I learned to read by studying editorial cartoons in *The Chicago Tribune,* and I guess the printer's ink rubbed off. I never had a dollhouse either, but I've loved miniatures, too, almost as long. I still have a tiny pink table and chairs set I got when I was seven.

I began my newspaper writing in ninth grade when my very first letter to the editor was published. Heady stuff! My education at the University of Chicago was one of the greatest gifts of my life. An experimental program that admitted students after two years of high school, the curriculum was prescribed — strictly Liberal Arts. But since the final grade in each subject was based solely on a six-hour written comprehensive exam, we *did* learn to write! I wrote my first feature newspaper articles there too, for *The College Bulletin*, an unsanctioned — and soon squelched — college paper. I also met my future husband, a fellow student. Bob was an embryonic engineer, later specializing in nuclear instrumentation.

After our two daughters were born, I was a stay-at-home mom with all the usual volunteer activities. Somehow I always ended up writing the groups' newsletters. I'd won a few "100 words or less" contests, too, but had never really considered writing as a career. Our lives changed radically when Bob decided to "work for the Chief Engineer" and entered seminary in his mid-30's. After he was ordained an Episcopal priest, I was a full-time clergy wife in a busy parish and again, always writing — press releases, Christmas pageants, church school curriculum, even parishioners' job resumes — and of course, the parish newspaper. (I was both pleased and chagrined when a national magazine featured a series of amusing newspaper ads I had written for our church—and gave my husband the credit!)

Life really did begin at 40 — at least in miniatures and in professional writing. After our girls were in college, I started work for our town's daily newspaper as proof reader and copy editor, and later wrote ad copy and feature articles. And with my first real paychecks in years, I ordered my first miniatures — from the Shackman catalog, and I thought they were just wonderful. When that newspaper was sold six years later, I joined a newly formed weekly as assistant editor, feature writer and columnist, and learned to write on a computer. (Pre-MacIntosh, even pre-PC!) Shortly after, my career ended abruptly when Bob transferred from Western Pennsylvania to a church in Racine, Wisconsin. There I wrote catalog copy for a fledgling small book press and was general assistant to the publisher.

My miniatures meanwhile had crept completely out of the closet. Now I was close enough to Chicago to attend real miniature shows! I avidly read every miniatures magazine I could find. and one day saw an ad in *Nutshell News*: "Free lance writer wanted." I applied, and soon had my first assignment. For several years I was "the Wisconsin connection" for *Nutshell News* (which was still located in Virginia), and free-lanced too for *Miniature Dealer* and later, *Miniatures Showcase*. Shortly before they moved to Kalmbach Publishing Co. in Wisconsin, *Nutshell News's* new editor Sybil Harp called to ask if I'd be interested in applying for an opening on staff. Of course, she had to twist my arm a bit...

DORSETT, JAMES H. & B. HELEN

see listing on page 118

DUKEMAN, CHRIS

CREDITS:

Series (Feature or How-to):

"Make It Country," *Nutshell News*

BUSINESS NAME: Calico Cat Country Miniatures

IDENTIFICATION MARKS:

C. Dukeman '95

CATEGORY:

Accessories: country; Furniture: country, handpainted

RECOGNITION:

Miniature Collector; Battle Creek Enquirer; TV Segment, "On the Michigan Road with Dick Evans," Mar. 1986

AUTOBIOGRAPHY:

I started writing for *Nutshell News* in 1986 after I had entered the calendar contest and didn't win. I wrote articles for a year when Bonnie Shroeder was the editor. I started selling country-style miniatures at a local shop the same year. Also that year my husband contacted our paper and I was interviewed by a lady who wrote a local interest column. That article led to a segment on a local program called "On the Michigan Road with Dick Evens." He used to travel around Michigan and film interesting stories and people. In 1989, I started writing for

Nutshell News again and have written articles ever since. In 1984, I finally got my mail order business off the ground. I do mainly country pieces and primitives with the 18th century my main area of interest.

FIELDS, MARY DURLAND

CREDITS:

Series (Feature or How-to):

Contributing Writer, *Nutshell News* starting in 1992; Contributing Editor, *Miniature Collector* 1980's; *Collector's Showcase, Miniature Quilts, Toybox Victorian Sampler, Dolls, Collector Editions*

Books:

Co-Author, *Treasures In Miniature*, Kalmbach Publishing Co. 1993

Booklet:

NAME Regional Houseparty, Greensboro, NC 1989

HONORS:

Marquis *Who's Who in the South & Southwest*

AUTOBIOGRAPHY:

My favorite toy ever was my eighth birthday present, a handsome dollhouse. My grandmother gave me wonderful English furniture for it and I made curtains from colored tissue paper packed around my mother's new dresses. As I grew up in North Carolina, my interests turned to horses, boys, music, boys, etc. I went to New Orleans to school, graduated from Newcomb College of Tulane University, Phi Beta Kappa, with a degree in English. I married and before too many years, realized I was bringing my three daughters miniature furniture, but I was the one playing. I discovered that the dollhouse I had made for them in Tokyo where we lived while their dad practiced dentistry for Uncle Sam at Camp Drake was really for me. I began seriously collecting in the late 1960s and bought all the books I could find on the subject.

I wrote my first magazine article in the field in 1980 on an old office typewriter. Now I sit in front of a 486SX33 with a CD Rom drive and still love every facet of writing. And all those books are important research sources for me. My work has been published in *Nutshell News, Miniature Collector, Victorian Homes, Antiques & Collecting/Hobbies, Dolls, Victorian Sampler*, *The State* (NC), *Pace* (Piedmont Airlines inflight), the *FRIDAY* magazine of the *Chicago Tribune*, *The Christian Science Monitor, Collector Editions, Toybox, Miniature Quilts*, and more.

FORDER, ESTHER & NICK

CREDITS:

Publication:

International Dolls' House News, Editors

Books: (Nick)

Dollhouse Decorating, Quintet Publishing, Ltd. 1994, Courage Books (US)

Logo:

IDHN

HARP, SYBIL

CREDITS:

Series (Feature or How-to):

New York Times leisure section, *Creative Crafts, The Miniature Magazine, Nutshell News, Grolier's World Book of Knowledge*

Regular Columns:

Sybil's Scratchboard *Creative Crafts*, Sybil's Scribbles *Miniature Magazine*, Between Friends *Nutshell News*

Books:

Miniatures-Consumer Guide

HONORS:

Who's Who of American Women & Who's Who in America 1970's

RECOGNITION:

New York Times; New York Times Magazine; Chicago Tribune; Los Angeles Times

AUTOBIOGRAPHY:

I was graduated Summa Cum Laude from Wilson College, Chambersburg, Pennsylvania with a double major in English Literature and Philosophy. Following graduation I studied Philosophy under a Fulbright grant at the Free University of Amsterdam, where I assisted in translation of the writings of a Dutch theologian.

I married soon after returning from Europe and when my youngest child started school in 1967, I went to work for Carstens Publications in New Jersey as the founding editor of *Creative Crafts* magazine. That was the beginning of my involvement with miniatures. In the early 1970's, I observed the emergence of a "new" hobby. It seemed to be related to crafts but it also had some very distinctive qualities. I decided that the world needed a how-to magazine especially for this hobby, and persuaded my publisher to start *The Miniature Magazine* (1976). In 1979 I joined Boynton and Associates in Clifton, Virginia as Associate Publisher of *Nutshell News.* I appreciated and shared Doug Boynton's vision and enthusiasm for the miniatures hobby. When Kalmbach Publishing Co. acquired *Nutshell News* in 1987, I donned my editor's hat once more and relocated to Wisconsin.

I have devoted most of my working life to promoting miniatures, and it has been a great joy to see it grow into a rewarding hobby and an accepted art form. But most significant to me is the fact that my life has been enriched beyond measure by the creative, talented, and generous people who make up our wonderful world of miniatures.

KALISKI, MARY

CREDITS:

Feature Articles:

Nutshell News, Miniature Collector

Series (Feature or How-to):

Miniature Collector, Fimo How-to make vegetables

AUTOBIOGRAPHY:

My adventure into miniatures has been through the back door. As a child psychologist I have always used toys and play in therapy because play is such a wonderful medium for self expression. In my practice the children's favorite toy has been a large sturdy dollhouse they named the "Bunny House." I'm not certain why they called it the Bunny House, as the house is inhabited by a rag taggle assortment of bears and dolls and of course a few bunnies too. One day after everyone had gone home and I tucked in the last little bear, put back all the tiny cups and saucers, I had a tremendous urge to have a dollhouse of my own, one that I didn't share with the children, one in which everything remained exactly as I had left it. Something about that predictability intrigued me. A small house where the wine glasses were always full, the beds forever made and the dog never dirtied. Little did I know what was ahead of me. The bunnies, being simple creatures never thought of scale or period or style, something I've had to learn along the way. It has been a noteworthy education, one that has given me immense pleasure. At present I have a wonderful collection that is beginning to take some shape. It is hard to limit myself to one style as I love all small things well made, especially china, painted furniture and silver.

But the best part of this hobby by far, has been my involvement with both *Nutshell News* and *Miniature Collector*. As a writer for both of these magazines I not only get to meet the most interesting and creative people but to write about them. And writing is my second love. I have written about collections, collectors and of course artisans. I've gotten to watch Natasha paint her fine furniture, Patricia Paul carve her intricately minute animals and visit with Bill Brinley an 80-year old gentleman who has been carving circus animals since he was six years old. *Nutshell News* and *Miniature Collector* continued support of my work is a treat that is the icing on a wonderfully delicious cake.

KAROBLIS, EVE

see listing on page 213

KEESSEN, RUTH M.

BUSINESS NAME: *Miniature Collector*
Scott Advertising & Publishing Co.

HISTORY OF MINIATURE COLLECTOR:

Miniature Collector Magazine debuted on the miniatures scene in April 1977, published by Robert Rowe of Acquire Publishing Company, Inc. The magazine's editorial credo was stated as "a fascination with all things miniature," and its goal was the production of a magazine of information and beauty serving all interests in miniatures.

Throughout the years *Miniature Collector* has seen many changes as it strived to feature the finest the miniature world had to offer. In 1984, it came under the ownership of Collector Communications and grew from a half-size to full-size magazine. Scott Advertising & Publishing acquired the magazine in 1992 and again *Miniature Collector* underwent a complete facelift and redesign giving it the upscale, quality look and content its readers enjoy today.

Today *Miniature Collector* Magazine is an international bimonthly publication devoted exclusively to the serious collector, craftsman and artist of contemporary and antique scale miniatures. Every issue is illustrated with the highest quality color photography and editorial presentation. Features include the finest miniature artists, manufacturers, retailers and collectors. Regular columns focus on new products, current shows, auctions, how-to projects and historical information.

While change has been part of *Miniature Collector* history, one constant throughout the years has been the Alice In Wonderland logo. Alice, whose fantasy imagination gives her the ability to grow smaller or larger, was incorporated into the masthead from the first issue. She is now seen at the bottom corner of the cover where she demurely gives the "curiouser and curiouser" reader a peek at the Wonderland inside.

MacLAREN, CATHERINE (Deceased)

CREDITS:

Founding Editor and Publisher:
Nutshell News 1971

Books:
This Side of Yesterday in Miniatures 1975, published by *Nutshell News*; NAME National Yearbooks; UFDC Yearbook; *Fashions 1900-70's*, Mosiac Press

HONORS:

IGMA's first Crystal Award

MacLAREN, CATHERINE, continued

RECOGNITION:

Doll's Houses In America, Flora Gill Jacobs, Charles Scribner's Sons, 1974

AUTOBIOGRAPHY:

During Prohibition we were living in New York City and one day my grandmother ordered her chauffeur to take us downtown to F.A.O. Schartz' Toy Store. The floor-walker, carnation in his lapel, bowed and asked us our wants. I reputedly blurted, "A cocktail shaker and glasses for my dollhouse to use on Sundays."

I had, aside from an elegant dollhouse, a metal one which I decided to redecorate a la Dorothy Draper with red enamel paint bought with Sunday School funds and used the top of the crystal set radio in the parlor so I could hear Burns and Allen as I created. Paint that spilled was the same red as my spanked derriere.

I attended the University of Tennessee, wrote for *Mademoiselle's* "College Board." After graduation I became assistant society editor for the *Knoxville Journal*. Then we moved to the New York suburbs, bought a dollhouse for my three daughters, but I was the one who really played with it. Many years later after I had $15.00 left after Christmas bills I had a sudden impulse to call an antique dealer friend and asked if she had any old dollhouses, she happened to have one. I wondered if I was the only one and discovered others near and far besides the need of communication. In 1972, we moved to California along with 14 dollhouses and a publication, *Nutshell News.*

OBOJSKI, ROBERT

CREDITS:

Columns:

Auction Report, *Miniature Collector*

Features:

Miniature Collector

AUTOBIOGRAPHY:

I earned an AB degree in 1951, an AM degree in 1952, and a Ph.D. in 1955 in American Studies from Case Western Reserve University in Cleveland, Ohio. I have spent most of my long writing career writing on hobbies and leisure time activities. I have been Auction editor for *Dolls Magazine,* starting with the first issue published in 1982, and a contributing editor to *Collector Editions* magazine since the first issue published in 1973. *Miniature Collector* was developed from *Collector Editions.*

ROGERS, FAITH B.

also see listing on page 372

CREDITS:

Columns:

"Small Talk" appeared in *Creative Crafts, The Miniature Magazine, Creative Crafts & Miniatures*

Features:

Nutshell News, Miniature Dealer, Miniature Gazette, Dollhouse & Miniature News, The Home Miniaturist

Books:

How to Make a Miniature Christmas Tree & To Light & Decorate It, Fieldwood Co., Inc.

RECOGNITION:

Nutshell News, Artisan Profile

ROGERS, FAITH B., continued

BIOGRAPHY:

Faith and Tom Rogers have always been interested in crafts, the arts and the how-to processes in developing them, although their scholastic emphases were more on the worldly, practical side. Faith studied psychology, participated in campus leadership and earned honors at Occidental College in Los Angeles, where two of her interests were in the school newspaper and yearbook. She was also editor of the *Mortar Board* magazine. Tom graduated from the University of Vermont in chemistry and did additional work at Columbia and the University of Virginia. They met when they both returned to their native New Jersey after Faith had returned from a college-sponsored music and art tour of Europe. They founded the Fieldwood Co., the name a composite of their two towns' suffixes, designing and producing "Chinamic"™ ceramic jewelry, developing their own techniques and designing and building their machinery and kilns. This business continued as a sideline after their marriage and as she continued in the financial world and he in specialty chemicals.

When Faith retired from corporate life to raise their family, she reported for an area newspaper, was extremely active in the restoration of "The Hermitage," a National Historic Site, as well as in the local and state federated women's clubs. From l968 to l985 she wrote free lance and also was on the staff, as editorial assistant and Miniatures Editor of the following: *Creative Crafts, Creative Crafts Christmas Annual, The Miniature Magazine* and *Creative Crafts and Miniatures* magazine. Starting in general full-size crafts, such as; candle making bobbin lace, Christmas decorations, etc., she was soon struck by the potential emergence of a miniatures market and the high in-the-closet interest in mini crafts. Responding to many readers who were looking for sources for dolls, hinges, furniture, dollhouses, etc., she published a source directory in the magazine and updated it continually. Anticipating an interest and reflecting her own in landscaping, she published how-to articles on landscaping the dollhouse, growing real plants in tiny settings and gave workshops on the subject. Her column, "Small Talk" covered houseparties, shows, featured and introduced many crafts people and now-prominent miniature artists and their work and put forth her ideas on trends in the tiny, but expanding world of miniaturia. A series on "Dollhouse Builders across America" is still retained in many homes, she is told, and the two miniature homes she designed, built and published plans for have been replicated in several countries. As members of the Miniature Makers Society, Faith and Tom participated in organizing 16 handcrafted-only shows and wrote all publicity articles for the shows, and for the participating dealers to have published in their local papers.

Seeing the developing interest in handcrafted miniatures, in 1956 they published their first "Precious Little Things" mail order catalog, with Tom's limited edition working wine press on page one. They have participated in countless quality retail and trade shows across the US and in England, selling their miniature creations, as well as those of a few select US artists and teaching classes and workshops. They were featured in an "Artisan Profile" in *Nutshell News*. They've participated in designing and building four miniature rooms for Kips Bay to auction at Christie's, New York. Professionally, Tom traveled extensively abroad, providing technical assistance to international chemical plants and has extended his how-to knowledge from developing chemical processes to developing new miniature products and the procedures for their manufacture. In 1987 he took an early retirement, they moved the miniatures to a hilltop home they designed in rural Vermont from which they operate the mail order and give Open Houses and classes, while Christmas trees grow in their pastures and maple trees give forth sap for their syrup operation.

RUTHBERG, HELEN KARP

CREDITS:

Series (Feature or How-to):

How-to-do projects & rooms *Creative Crafts, The Miniature Magazine, Contemporary Living, Nutshell News Plans* Service

Books:

The Book of Miniatures - Furniture and Accessories, Chilton Book Co. 1977; *Miniature Room Settings*, Chilton Book Co. 1978; *Contemporary Miniature Room Settings*, Chilton Book Co. 1980; *Miniatures*, Black Cat Press 1982

RECOGNITION:

Miniatures, pg. 30, 59-60, By Editors of Consumer Guide, Beekman House 1979; *Middletown Record,* May 1, 1977; *Schenectady Daily Gazette*, Oct. 14, 1993

RUTHBERG, HELEN KARP, continued

AUTOBIOGRAPHY:

No, I did not have a dollhouse as a child but all things small seemed to fascinate me. Drawing was always an integral part of my life and a Bachelor of Fine Arts degree from Syracuse University set me up for many things that were to happen.

Married to a physician, I worked during the early years in advertising art and learned many more facets of the art world. After 12 years I stayed home to raise our only child and for the next 20 years my life was consumed with community projects. I did take the time to master the technique of watercolor painting. I also became a contributing author to *Creative Crafts* magazine and *The Miniature Magazine.*

Finally, inspired by the Faith Bradford dollhouse at The Smithsonian Institution, I dropped out of everything and gave undivided attention to one goal — to write a how-to-craft book about miniatures. Happy to say my first book, published in 1977, is considered a classic. Two more books followed in rapid succession and all are published by Chilton Book Company.

As a fine artist I created many miniature paintings of original design or copies of the masters. These were sold at miniatures shows in which I participated. But my greatest satisfaction comes from knowing that many individuals from young to elderly have enjoyed and benefited from my books.

SALISBURY, SARAH

CREDITS:

Series (Feature or How-to):

Nutshell News, Miniature Gazette

REGULAR COLUMN:

The Private Eye

IDENTIFICATION MARKS:

by Sarah Salisbury **S.S.** show reports and book reviews

HONORS:

IGMA Crystal Award; NAME AOH

RECOGNITION:

Nutshell News, Fall 1978, pg. 28-34; Mar/Apr. 1979, pg. 54-57; May/Jun. 1979, pg. 38-40; Sept/Oct. 1979, pg. 75-77; Jan. 1980, pg. 66-67; Mar. 1980, pg. 50-53, 66-67; Apr. 1980, pg. 32-35; May 1980, pg. 34-36, 66-67; Jun. 1980, pg. 84; Jul. 1980, pg. 68-72; Aug. 1980, pg. 18, 38-43; Dec. 1980, pg. 28-30; Feb. 1981, pg. 46-48, 50-54, 70-72; Mar. 1981, pg. 42-46; Apr. 1981, pg. 38-40, 42-44, 62-64; May 1981, pg. 72-73; Jun. 1981, pg. 58-63; Jul. 1981, pg. 66-70; Sept. 1981, pg. 62-68; Nov. 1981, pg. 40-41; Mar. 1982, pg. 47, 54, 61; Sept. 1982, pg. 61-63; Oct. 1982, pg. 52-54; Nov. 1982, pg. 46-48, 50-53; Apr. 1983, pg. 48-53, 55; Jun. 1983, pg. 53; Aug. 1984. pg. 36-39; Oct. 1984, pg. 18, book review; Nov. 1985, pg. 54-57; Private Eye columns, Mar. 1980 to July 1992

AUTOBIOGRAPHY:

Leaving college to get married in 1940, I was kept busy raising three children until my youngest son was about 7. Then, I went to work as a secretary and "Gal Friday" for a group of psychologists. Along with bookkeeping, typing letters, etc., I also scored psychological tests, helped create new tests, rewrote speeches and articles for my bosses, and did research for their books and papers. I guess you could say it was a valuable learning experience!

I discovered miniatures in 1975, attended my first NAME National Houseparty in San Francisco in 1976, and have been traveling extensively in search of miniatures ever since. I have been to a New Zealand (NZAME) Houseparty, and I go to England for one or two of their shows every year. I have attended the IGMA School in Castine, Maine ever since it began and have been to every Guild Show since its inception. My travels have taken me to Germany, Scotland and, more recently, Japan because of my hobby. Also, I manage to be at shows in many parts of this country, looking for new miniaturists or new items from established crafts people. Whenever possible, I visit historic houses, castles and museums on my travel routes, looking for miniatures or the full-size pieces that inspire them. I am a member of Friends of Miniatures, Denver Museum of Miniatures, Toy & Miniature Museum of Kansas City, and Society of American Miniaturists.

SMITH, ANNE DAY

CREDITS:

Series (Feature or How-to):

Nutshell News, Miniature Dealer, Miniatures Showcase, Creative Crafts & Miniatures, Women's Circle, Cleveland Plain Dealer, Saturday Magazine, Canton (Mass.) *Register, Maine Life, Sunday Woman* (syndicated)

Regular Columns:

RSVP, *Nutshell News*

Books:

The Andrews Collection, Personal Treasures, 1988, Dee's Delights, 105 pages, illustrated; *Masters in Miniature, 12 Artisans At Work, Volume 1*, 1987, Kalmbach Publishing Co., 150 pages, illustrated; *Interior Design in Miniature,* Brooke Tucker Originals, 1986, Boynton, 96 pages, illustrated; *Treasures in Miniature*, 1993, Kalmbach Publishing Co., 105 pages, illustrated, (Contributed three of six chapters on private collections; *Discovering Miniatures*, Your Guide to a Fascinating Hobby, first edition, Kalmbach Publishing Co., (Contributed article, "The Pleasures of Collecting," two of my photos in the second edition)

BIOGRAPHY:

Anne began her journalistic career, as it relates to miniatures, in the mid 1970's when she was a member of the Cleveland Miniaturia Society. She edited and produced a five to 10 page monthly newsletter for the membership. She joined *Nutshell News* as a regular contributor at the suggestion of Catherine B. MacLaren, founding editor, shortly thereafter.

Anne has written over 180 magazine and newspaper articles about miniatures, and has written three books and contributed to a fourth. She has covered shows, written feature and how-to articles about collectors and craftsmen, and has usually taken the photographs to illustrate her articles. She is currently writing a column called RSVP for *Nutshell News* as well.

SMITH, HARRY W.

also see listing on page 412

CREDITS:

Series (Feature or How-to):

Miniature Collector

Books:

The Art of Making Furniture in Miniature, printed by E.P. Dutton, reprinted by Kalmbach Publishing Co. 1993

SNYDER, DEE (Deceased)

CREDITS:

Series (Feature or How-to):

"Nutcracking," later renamed "Collectables" *Nutshell News*

AUTOBIOGRAPHY:

At the age of four I became enthralled with miniatures. My father built me a small dollhouse with four rooms and a green roof. I still have the first piece of furniture, a white china chair decorated with roses. Other items were an iron G.E. refrigerator bank, Betty Boop's wicker set, a Tootsie Toy phone, and a china bath set. In 1941 I got a large Southern mansion with columns, a metal balcony and stairs. It was furnished in Strombecker, Tynie Toy, and dime store metal kitchen furniture.

At that time accessories were not easy to come by – the war had stopped the flow of German and Japanese trinkets and Grandmother Stover had not yet appeared. Little girls leaned heavily on advertising items and found objects. I remember the little hams, the Pet Milk cans, wooden Scotties (Fala?), and the copper dime store charms in the shape of toasters and radios. Window shade pulls provided the wooden tea pots and parrots in the celluloid cages, Cracker Jack prizes helped and we borrowed the flatirons from our Monopoly sets. Older ladies would present us with an occasional Oriental rug that had been a cigarette premium years before. War or no, during the 1940s there always seemed to be an ample supply of brass lamps, andirons, and candlesticks at the dime store. The lamp was reproduced a few years back and now all these items can be seen at antique shows.

A few years later I came under the influence of Mrs. Thorne's rooms and wanted no more dollhouse play. The house was given away and I began to create settings in papered apple crates and bookcases. At this point it became a solitary activity for I felt too old to be playing with dolls. I seriously studied period furniture and started to collect Tynie Toy, old German pieces, Colombian mahogany, and the work of craftsmen. My parents got involved, too. My mother made finely hooked rugs and quilted tiny coverlets that seem to improve with age. My father created an early American fireplace with carved bricks, hewn wood, wrought iron oven door and utensils. Later he made a walnut canopy bed on a jewelers lathe. Edgewood Hall was built by a carpenter to house my collection. The large cupboard contains nine rooms done in Federal style.

Next came college, marriage and babies, and the house stayed with my parents. For many years my mother was caretaker – dusting, mothproofing the rugs, and adding the occasional items. She, too, loved the house and we shared many happy hours in its creation.

During the summer of 1968 I returned to miniaturing with gusto. Three things happened. I saw Faith Bradford's house (at the Smithsonian Institution) and was delighted to note that I had some of the same things. I then discovered the second edition of Flora Jacob's book *Dolls' Houses in America.* Where had I been? I had not seen the first edition. Lastly, I had to retrieve Edgewood Hall and its contents because my father was selling his home.

While waiting for the house to come by van, I discovered that my hobby had become very popular. Numerous books on history and how-to had been published, magazines other than *Hobbies* were taking notice, doll clubs were interested in dollhouses, new lines of furniture had emerged, dealers were getting fine prices for things I had given away, and there was a whole new crop of craftsmen and dealers as well as some familiar names still in business. The word "mini" was in and lovers of little things never had it so good.

As I started refurbishing my old house and expanding my collection, I realized the wealth of new art and craft products that help miniaturists. The products weren't new to me, as I paint, but their application to dollhouse decorating was a revelation! How did I get along without acrylic paint, and trims, gold leaf sprays, and spray adhesive, decoupage papers, and all the rest? I used to use paints that never seemed to dry, pastes that lumped, thumb tacks, and clear nail polish.

Since that summer I have collected and constructed avidly. A partial list of my collection would include three Victorian houses, a Depression house, Casa Tootsie, a Petite Princess model house, a school house, a country store, a Chinatown shop, a toy store, a hat shop, a clock shop, a curio shop, a Pennsylvania Dutch house and barn, a 1960's ranch house, kitchen settings, and Sherlock Holmes' sitting room.

While I enjoy the making and assembling of rooms, I like the research and the hunting even more. Recreating a domestic era authentically takes some study. The hunt for furniture and the viewing of other collections have brought me some fine adventures and friends. It is such an all-encompassing hobby, from power saw to embroidery hoop. I am glad that I rediscovered the small world and all the interesting people in it.

(*Nutshell News*, Sept. 1992, pg. 36-37, by Sybil Harp, Authorized reprint)

STEPHENSON, FRED

also see listing on page 426

CREDITS:

Regular Column

"The Architects Angle," *Nutshell News*

Books:

The Dollhouse Builder's Handbook, Design Tecnics Miniatures

SWANSON, JOANN

CREDITS:

Series (Feature or How-to):

"Small Talk," *Nutshell News*, Dec. 1981; "Joann's Do-It-Yourself," *Nutshell News*, since Jun. 1982

Books:

Granny's Kitchen, Boynton & Associates; *Joann's Do-It-Yourself,* Boynton & Associates; *Bathroom Accessories,* Boynton & Associates

Other:

Collaborative project permanently displayed in Burke Museum, Seattle, WA: historical replica of early Seattle residence.

HONORS:

Judge for 1994 Northwest Flower & Garden Show/Miniature Exhibits

RECOGNITION:

Nutshell News, Vol. 22, No. 8, Aug. 1992, pg. 56-58, "A Visit With Joann," Sybil Harp

AUTOBIOGRAPHY:

Raised in a creative atmosphere, I learned early to make a silk purse from a sow's ear. Over the years I have acquired a wide knowledge in the fields of arts and crafts. Through the art of miniatures I am able to use all of my acquired skills which come together to form a cohesive whole. I continue to research old crafts for my projects which I update or revise with contemporary materials.

Although I have been involved in all aspects of miniatures (over the last quarter century), I have found my niche in showing and encouraging others how to create. As a monthly feature writer for *Nutshell News*, I am able to touch a large audience around the world.

Presently, the creative demands of the column leaves little time for other miniature work, but I continue to do lectures, seminars, and demonstrations when time allows. In my private time I research historical photos and descriptions to use for miniature settings.

THOMAS, NOEL & PAT

also see listing on page 441

CREDITS:

Series:

Nutshell News, Six part series, Sept. 1981 – Aug. 1982; "Creative Notebook," 1988 – present

TUCKER, PHYLLIS S.

also see listing on page 449

CREDITS:

Features:

Nutshell News, Aug. 1995, pg. 36-42, "Judy Berman, Purveyor of Dreams;" *Miniature Gazette*, Spring 1995, pg. 18-20, "The Chrysnbon Tradition," Judy Berman; *NAME National Houseparty Program Book*, Jul. 1995, Judy Berman

Video:

Tee Ridder Miniatures Museum of Nassau County Museum of Art, New York

WAGNER, SYDNIE M.

also see listing on page 465

CREDITS:

Series (Feature or How-to):

Dollhouse series, Sept. 1993, Nov. 1993; *Nutshell News*, Jan. 1994, Feb. 1994, Mar. 1994, Apr. 1994, May 1994; *Miniatures Showcase*, Nov. 1992, Jan. 1993, Mar. 1993, Jul. 1993, Sept. 1993, Nov. 1993

Column:

"Simply Put," *Nutshell News*

Books:

Petite Eats & Mini Treats, Dee's Delights, Inc.

BIOGRAPHY:

Sydnie is a member of IGMA, NAME, and Mini Exchange. She was president for three years of the Milwaukee Miniature Club and is a member of two other clubs. As the NAME State Representative for Wisconsin she helps promote miniatures and was Chairman of the 1995 NAME National Houseparty in Chicago.

Syd's Shoppe is her miniature business and she has sold at several shows and at NAME conventions. She enjoys teaching classes and has taught at "Back to College" in Ashland, Virginia, Miniature Weekend Retreat in Wisconsin, and many local and regional miniature shows. She also made a souvenir for the El Paso, Texas NAME Regional.

Presently she is the Product Review Coordinator for *Nutshell News* and is still doing articles.

WARNER, BARBARA B.

also see listing on page 469

CREDITS:

Series:

"Enhancements," *Nutshell News*

Features:

Nutshell News, Miniatures Showcase, Miniature Catalogue

Columns:

"The Retailer's Corner," *Miniature Dealer*

Books:

Dollhouse Lighting, Boynton & Associates; *The ABC's of Dollhouse Finishing*, From Kit to Masterpiece, Kalmbach Publishing Co.

WESTCOTT, PETER F.

see listing on page 476

INDEX

A

B

C

D

E

F

G

H

I

J

K

L

M

N

O

P

Q

R

S

U

V

W

Y

Z

Allie and Lee Frank
P. O. Box 16023
Minneapolis, MN 55416-0023 USA

* ARTISAN'S SIGNATURE MARKS *

For "*A REFERENCE GUIDE TO MINIATURE MAKERS MARKS*"

PLEASE READ CAREFULLY

Please note that addresses & telephone numbers will not be published. This information is for our use only should it become necessary to contact you for additional information or clarification. Be brief, but as concise as possible. We reserve the right to edit as necessary to retain compatibility and control of format and length. This is an application only and does not necessarily constitute a guarantee of publication. Please TYPE or PRINT all information exactly as you wish it to appear in the book.

YOUR NAME: ______________________________

HOME ADDRESS: ______________________________

CITY: ______________ STATE: ______ ZIP CODE: __________ COUNTRY: ______________

HOME TELEPHONE NO: ______________ BUSINESS TELEPHONE NO: ______________

BUSINESS NAME[S]: ______________________________

BUSINESS ADDRESS: ______________________________

CITY: ______________ STATE: ______ ZIP CODE: __________ COUNTRY: ______________

MARK/LOGO: Please indicate your mark or logo **on a separate sheet of unlined white paper** using **BLACK INK** in the same manner as you sign your pieces. If you do not sign your work, write UNMARKED. If you have more than one business and/or mark/logo, use additional sheets of unlined white paper for each identification mark. Please include particulars plus the beginning and ending years for the use of each. We are going to Xerox your mark/logo from the page for the book, be sure it is precise and clear.

HOW ARE YOUR MINIATURES SOLD? Mail Order____ Retail____ Wholesale____ Locally____

Regionally____ Nationally____ Internationally____ Shows____ Gift Shops____ Other______________

CATEGORY UNDER WHICH YOU WISH TO BE LISTED, RELATING TO THE PIECES YOU MAKE: (More than one category may be used, if applicable)

____

HONORS RECEIVED: Any honor such as IGMA Artisan or Fellow; NAME AOH, etc. ______________

____

RECOGNITION: If your work has been featured in any publication as an article, photo presentation, etc. give name of publication, Volume and Issue number, year and page numbers. You may include newspaper articles or TV coverage if they are an appropriate source of reference. Do not include commercial and/or paid advertising.

____

____

BIOGRAPHY: On a separate sheet of paper, WRITE a brief biography as it relates to your miniature background, it may include college, specialized education or occupation. Please DO NOT send magazine or newspaper articles written by someone else, unless a letter of permission for use accompanies it.